ISBN 978-0-331-75604-3
PIBN 10535424

WESLEY'S HYMNS

AND

THE METHODIST

SUNDAY-SCHOOL HYMN-BOOK.

LONDON:
WESLEYAN METHODIST BOOK-ROOM,
2, CASTLE STREET, CITY ROAD, E.C.
AND 66, PATERNOSTER ROW, E.C.
WESLEYAN METHODIST SUNDAY-SCHOOL UNION,
2, LUDGATE CIRCUS BUILDINGS, E.C.

N. Combined, Pearl 24mo.

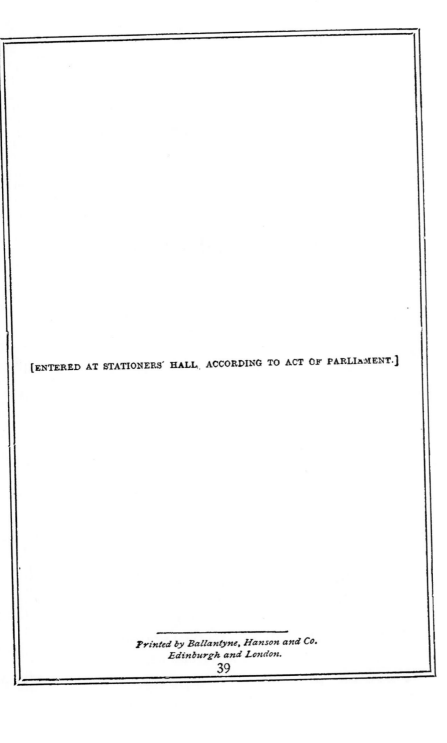

Printed by Ballantyne, Hanson and Co.
Edinburgh and London.

PREFACE.

1. For many years I have been importuned to publish such a hymn-book as might be generally used in all our congregations throughout Great Britain and Ireland. I have hitherto withstood the importunity, as I believed such a publication was needless, considering the various hymn-books which my brother and I have published within these forty years last past; so that it may be doubted whether any religious community in the world has a greater variety of them.

2. But it has been answered, "Such a publication is highly needful upon this very account: for the greater part of the people, being poor, are not able to purchase so many books; and those that have purchased them are, as it were, bewildered in the immense variety. A proper Collection of Hymns for general use, carefully made out of all these books, is therefore still wanting; and one comprised in so moderate a compass, as to be neither cumbersome nor expensive."

3. It has been replied, "You have such a Collection already, (entitled 'Hymns and Spiritual Songs') which I extracted several years ago from a variety of hymn-books." But it is objected, "This is in the other extreme: it is far too small. It does not, it cannot, in so narrow a compass, contain variety enough; not so much as we want, among whom *singing* makes so considerable a part of the public service. What we want is, a Collection not too large, that it may be cheap and portable; nor too small, that it may contain a sufficient variety for all ordinary occasions."

4. Such a Hymn-Book you have now before you. It is not so large as to be either cumbersome or expensive; and it is large enough to contain such a variety of hymns as will not soon be worn threadbare. It is large enough to contain all the important truths of our most holy religion, whether speculative or practical; yea, to illustrate them all, and to prove them both by Scripture and reason; and this is done in a regular order. The hymns are not carelessly jumbled together, but carefully ranged under proper heads, according to the experience of real Christians. So that this book is, in effect, a little body of experimental and practical divinity.

5. As but a small part of these hymns is of my own composing, I do not think it inconsistent with modesty to declare, that I am persuaded no such hymn-book as this has yet been published in the English language. In what other publication of the kind have you so distinct and full an account of Scriptural Christianity? such a declaration of the heights and depths of religion, speculative and practical? so strong cautions against the most plausible errors; particularly those that are now most prevalent? and so clear directions for making your calling and election sure; for perfecting holiness in the fear of God?

6. May I be permitted to add a few words with regard to the *poetry?* Then I will speak to those who are judges thereof, with all freedom and unreserve. To these I may say, without offence, 1. In these hymns there is no doggerel; no botches; nothing put in to patch up the rhyme; no feeble expletives. 2. Here is nothing turgid or bombast, on the one hand, or low and creeping, on the other. 3. Here are no *cant* expressions; no words without meaning. Those who impute this to us know not what they say. We talk common sense, both in prose and verse, and use no word but in a fixed and determinate sense. 4. Here are, allow me to say, both the purity, the strength, and the elegance of the English language; and, at the same time, the utmost simplicity and plainness, suited to every capacity. Lastly, I desire men of taste to judge (these are the only competent judges) whether there be not in some of the following hymns the true spirit of poetry, such as cannot be acquired by art and labour, but must be the gift of nature. By labour a man may become a tolerable imitator of Spenser, Shakspeare, or Milton; and may heap together pretty compound epithets, as "pale-eyed," "meek-eyed," and the like; but unless he be *born* a poet, he will never attain the genuine spirit of poetry.

7. And here I beg leave to mention a thought which has been long upon my mind, and which I should long ago have inserted in the public papers, had I not been unwilling to stir up a nest of hornets. Many gentlemen have done my brother and me (though without naming us) the honour to reprint many of our hymns. Now, they are perfectly welcome so to do, provided they print them just as they are. But I desire they would not attempt to mend them; for they really are not able. None of them is able to mend either the sense or the verse. Therefore, I must beg of them one of these two favours; either to let them stand just as they are, to take them for better for worse; or to add the true reading in the margin, or at the bottom of the page; that we may no longer be accountable either for the nonsense or for the doggerel of other men.

8. But to return. That which is of infinitely more moment than the spirit of poetry, is the spirit of piety. And I trust, all persons of real judgment will find *this* breathing through the whole Collection. It is in this view chiefly, that I would recommend it to every truly pious reader, as a means of raising or quickening the spirit of devotion; of confirming his faith; of enlivening his hope; and of kindling and increasing his love to God and man. When Poetry thus keeps its place, as the hand-maid of Piety, it shall attain, not a poor perishable wreath, but a crown that fadeth not away.

                                                                JOHN WESLEY.
LONDON, *Oct.* 20, 1779.

N.B.—The Hymns distinguished by the prefix of an asterisk were not in the editions published during the life of Mr. Wesley.

The New Supplement to "A Collection of Hymns for the use of the People called Methodists," originally published by John Wesley in 1780, has been compiled under the direction of a Committee appointed by the Conference in 1874.

The "Collection" of 1780 has been circulated by millions, and has been recognised as a priceless treasure, not only by Methodists, but by many other disciples of the One Master. As a testimony to Scripture doctrine and Christian experience, as a monument of piety, a manual of devotion, and a bond of fellowship, it can never cease to be precious to all who cherish the spirit of its authors, and wish well to that revival of religion of which they were the instruments; while, in instances almost innumerable, personal associations have invested portions of its contents with tender, and even sacred interest.

The Conference therefore determined that it should be retained in use, and, while generally revised, should undergo no alteration which would affect its substance or impair its identity. But as altered circumstances, often resulting from the growth of the Connexion, and occasions repeatedly arising in public, social, and domestic life have rendered additional hymns necessary, an attempt has been made to meet the want which has been long felt, and which was by no means adequately provided for by the valuable Supplement published about forty-five years since.

In this compilation the necessities of public worship have been first considered; and it is hoped that an ample supply of composition suitable for mixed congregations is here furnished. In addition to hymns of adoration and thanksgiving, there will be found seventy versions of Psalms, or parts of Psalms (besides those contained in the former Supplement), by means of which that portion of Holy Scripture, which has supplied so large a share of the devotional exercises of Christians generally, will become more fully available for the use of Methodists than it has been for a long time past. Many poems of Charles Wesley also, which up to a late period only existed in manuscript, are now for the first time presented for congregational use; and by the force and sublimity of thought, the depth and tenderness of feeling, and the spirit of fervent piety displayed in them, will fully vindicate the judgment of John Wesley respecting his brother's poetical remains. Well does it become all the lovers of Scriptural Christianity, but especially the Methodists, to be thankful to the Author of every good gift for the endowments and labours of Charles Wesley, which were so long and faithfully consecrated to the promotion of vital and experimental religion, and by which that "power of godliness," which it is the mission of Methodism to spread, has been alike exemplified and vindicated. The full extent to which these labours have been rendered serviceable to the cause of Christ can only be known in the day when all secret things shall be revealed.

The Spirit of its living Head having never departed from the Church, it follows that those in all ages who by the Holy Ghost have called Jesus Lord should have been occupied with attempts to set forth his praise. As in the old time, they still "prophesy and do not cease," so that our age is richer in good hymns than any that have gone before it. The Committee have been glad to avail themselves of the labours of both contemporaries and predecessors, and accordingly the present volume is enriched by a selection from the works of modern hymnologists as well as from the accumulated treasures of the past. The names of authors, as presented in the "Index of First Lines," will help to exemplify the substantial unity existing between all believers in Christ, notwithstanding the many causes which at present hinder its full manifestation to the world.

It may be proper to add that the Committee, while mainly desirous to provide by this Supplement for the wants of congregations, have not restricted themselves to that object. "The People called Methodists" were supposed by their Founder to have many uses for good hymns besides singing them in public assemblies; and he selected for them accordingly. Here also will be found some adapted to personal and private,

rather than to collective worship, or to praising the Lord "secretly among the faithful," rather than "in the congregation;" but none, it is hoped, which will not minister
"to exhortation, edification, or comfort:" and for these objects they humbly invoke
the blessing of God upon their work.

The Committee offer respectful thanks to the authors and publishers concerned,
for permission courteously given to use hymns in which they have a copyright. A list
of these, as far as known, is given below. If they have in any instance failed to seek
for permission where they ought to have done so, such omission has been entirely un-
intentional, and they trust this apology for it will be accepted.

The Right Rev. the Lord Bishop of Lincoln; the Very Rev. the Dean of West-
minster the Right Hon. and Rev. the Earl Nelson; the Rev. Sir H. W. Baker, Bart.;
the Rev. Sir G. Prevost, Bart.; the Rev. W. J. Hall. M.A., and the Rev. W. Josiah
Irons, D.D., Prebendaries of St. Paul's; the Rev. B. H. Kennedy, D.D., Canon of Ely;
the Rev. Horatius Bonar, D.D.; the (late) Rev. J. S. Monsell, LL.D.; the Rev. W. M.
Punshon, LL.D.; the Rev. Messrs. J. Ellerton, M.A., J. M. Fuller, M.A., Arthur Tozer-
Russell, M.A., the Rev. S. J. Stone, M.A., the Rev. H. Twells, M.A., the Rev. Ed. Cas-
wall, and the Rev. E. E. Jenkins, M.A.; Sir Charles Reed; Richard Massie, Esq.; Gran-
ville R. Ryder, Esq; Thomas Montgomery Foster, Esq.; T. Stamford Raffles, Esq.;
George Rawson, Esq.; Miss C. Winkworth; Mrs. Lynch; and H. L. L., the Authors or
representatives of the Authors of hymns; and Messrs. Murray, Longm ; Nisbet,
Rivingtons, Masters, Hayes, Novello, Daldy, Isbister & Co., and the Committee of the
Society for Promoting Christian Knowledge, and the Committee of the Religious Tract
Society, the Publishers of the several volumes from which hymns have been selected.

CONTENTS.

A COLLECTION OF HYMNS.

PART I.

CONTAINING INTRODUCTORY HYMNS.

SECTION I.

EXHORTING SINNERS TO RETURN TO GOD.

1
           C. M.

1 O FOR a thousand tongues to sing
    My great Redeemer's praise,
The glories of my God and King,
    The triumphs of his grace !

2 My gracious Master and my God,
    Assist me to proclaim,
To spread through all the earth abroad
    The honours of thy name.

3 Jesus ! the name that charms our fears,
    That bids our sorrows cease ;
'Tis music in the sinner's ears,
    'Tis life, and health, and peace.

4 He breaks the power of cancelled sin,
    He sets the prisoner free ;
His blood can make the foulest clean,
    His blood availed for me.

5 He speaks, and, listening to his voice,
    New life the dead receive,
The mournful, broken hearts rejoice,
    The humble poor believe.

6 Hear him, ye deaf ; his praise, ye dumb,
    Your loosened tongues employ ;
Ye blind, behold your Saviour come,
    And leap, ye lame, for joy.

7 Look unto him, ye nations, own
    Your God, ye fallen race ;
Look, and be saved through faith alone,
    Be justified by grace.

8 See all your sins on Jesus laid:
    The Lamb of God was slain,
His soul was once an offering made
    For every soul of man.

9 Awake from guilty nature's sleep,
    And Christ shall give you light,
Cast all your sins into the deep,
    And wash the Æthiop white.

10 With me, your chief, ye then shall know,
    Shall feel your sins forgiven ;
Anticipate your heaven below,
    And own that love is heaven.

2
    Luke xiv. 16—24.   L. M.

1 COME, sinners, to the gospel feast,
    Let every soul be Jesu's guest ;
Ye need not one be left behind,
For God hath bidden all mankind.

2 Sent by my Lord, on you I call,
    The invitation is to ALL :
Come, all the world ; come, sinner, thou,
    All things in Christ are ready now.

3 Come, all ye souls by sin opprest,
    Ye restless wanderers after rest,
Ye poor, and maimed, and halt, and blind,
    In Christ a hearty welcome find.

4 Come and partake the gospel feast ;
    Be saved from sin ; in Jesus rest ;
O taste the goodness of your God,
    And eat his flesh, and drink his blood !

5 Ye vagrant souls, on you I call ;
    (O that my voice could reach you all !)
Ye all may now be justified,
    Ye all may live, for Christ hath died.

6 My message as from God receive,
    Ye all may come to Christ, and live !
O let his love your hearts constrain,
    Nor suffer him to die in vain !

7 His love is mighty to compel ;
    His conquering love consent to feel,
Yield to his love's resistless power,
    And fight against your God no more.

8 See him set forth before your eyes,
    That precious, bleeding sacrifice !
His offered benefits embrace,
    And freely now be saved by grace.

9 This is the time; no more delay !
    This is the acceptable day,
Come in, this moment, at his call,
    And live for him who died for all.

3
10 s. & 11 s.   John vii. 37—39.

1 O ALL that pass by, To Jesus draw near,
    He utters a cry, Ye sinners, give ear !
From hell to retrieve you, He spreads out
    his hands ;   [stands.
Now, now to receive you, He graciously

2 If any man thirst, And happy would be,
The vilest and worst May come unto me,
May drink of my Spirit, Excepted is none,
Lay claim to my merit, And take for his
    own.

3 Whoever receives The life-giving word,
In Jesus believes, His God and his Lord,
In him a pure river Of life shall arise,
Shall in the believer Spring up to the skies.

1

4 My God and my Lord! Thy call I obey,
My soul on thy word Of promise I stay,
Thy kind invitation I gladly embrace,
Athirst for salvation, Salvation by grace.

5 O hasten the hour! Send down from above
The Spirit of power, Of health, and of love,
Of filial fear, Of knowledge and grace,
Of wisdom and prayer, Of joy and of praise;

6 The Spirit of faith, Of faith in thy blood,
Which saves us from wrath, And brings us
to God, [sin,
Removes the huge mountain Of indwelling
And opens a fountain That washes us clean.

4   Isaiah lv. 1—3.   L. M.

1 HO! every one that thirsts, draw nigh!
('Tis God invites the fallen race)
Mercy and free salvation buy;
Buy wine, and milk, and gospel grace.

2 Come to the living waters, come!
Sinners, obey your Maker's call:
Return, ye weary wanderers, home,
And find my grace is free for all.

3 See from the Rock a fountain rise!
For you in healing streams it rolls;
Money ye need not bring, nor price,
Ye labouring, burdened, sin-sick souls.

4 Nothing ye in exchange shall give,
Leave all you have and are behind,
Frankly the gift of God receive,
Pardon and peace in Jesus find.

5 Why seek ye that which is not bread,
Nor can your hungry souls sustain?
On ashes, husks, and air ye feed;
Ye spend your little all in vain.

6 In search of empty joys below,
Ye toil with unavailing strife;
Whither, ah! whither would ye go?
I have the words of endless life.

7 Hearken to me with earnest care,
And freely eat substantial food,
The sweetness of my mercy share,
And taste that I alone am good.

8 I bid you all my goodness prove,
My promises for all are free,
Come, taste the manna of my love,
And let your souls delight in me.

9 Your willing ear and heart incline,
My words believingly receive;
Quickened your souls by faith divine
An everlasting life shall live.

5   10 s & 11 s.

1 THY faithfulness, Lord, Each moment
we find,
So true to thy word, So loving and kind!
Thy mercy so tender To all the lost race,
The vilest offender May turn and find
grace.

2 The mercy I feel To others I show,
I set to my seal That Jesus is true: [call,
Ye all may find favour Who come at his
O come to my Saviour, His grace is for all!

3 To save what was lost, From heaven he
came;
Come, sinners, and trust In Jesus's name,

2

He offers you pardon; He bids you be free;
"If sin be your burden, O come unto me!"

4 O let me commend My Saviour to you,
The publican's friend And Advocate too,
For you he is pleading His merits and
death,
With God interceding For sinners beneath.

5 Then let us submit His grace to receive,
Fall down at his feet And gladly believe:
We all are forgiven For Jesus's sake:
Our title to heaven His merits we take.

"Why will ye die, O house of Israel?" **6**
8-7 s.   Ezekiel xviii. 31.

1 SINNERS, turn, why will ye die?
God, your Maker, asks you why?
God, who did your being give,
Made you with himself to live;
He the fatal cause demands,
Asks the work of his own hands,
Why, ye thankless creatures, why
Will ye cross his love, and die?

2 Sinners, turn, why will ye die?
God, your Saviour, asks you why?
God, who did your souls retrieve,
Died himself, that ye might live;
Will you let him die in vain?
Crucify your Lord again?
Why, ye ransomed sinners, why
Will you slight his grace, and die?

3 Sinners, turn, why will ye die?
God, the Spirit, asks you why?
He who all your lives hath strove,
Wooed you to embrace his love:
Will you not his grace receive?
Will you still refuse to live?
Why, ye long-sought sinners, why
Will you grieve your God, and die?

4 Dead, already dead within,
Spiritually dead in sin,
Dead to God while here you breathe,
Pant ye after second death?
Will you still in sin remain,
Greedy of eternal pain?
O ye dying sinners, why,
Why will you for ever die?

7
8-7 s.   The same subject.

1 LET the beasts their breath resign,
Strangers to the life divine;
Who their God can never know,
Let their spirit downward go.
You for higher ends were born,
You may all to God return,
Dwell with him above the sky:
Why will you for ever die?

2 You, on whom he favours showers,
You, possest of nobler powers,
You, of reason's powers possest,
You, with will and memory blest,
You, with finer sense endued,
Creatures capable of God;
Noblest of his creatures, why,
Why will you for ever die?

3 You, whom he ordained to be
Transcripts of the Deity;
You, whom he in life doth hold;
You, for whom himself was sold;

You, on whom he still doth wait,
Whom he would again create ;
Made by him, and purchased, why,
Why will you for ever die ?

4 You, who own his record true,
You, his chosen people, you.
You, who call the Saviour Lord,
You, who read his written word,
You, who see the gospel-light,
Claim a crown in Jesu's right ;
Why will you, ye Christians, why
Will the house of Israel die ?

8

The same subject. 8 - 7 s.

1 WHAT could your Redeemer do
More than he hath done for you ?
To procure your peace with God,
Could he more than shed his blood ?
After all his waste of love,
All his drawings from above,
Why will you your Lord deny ?
Why will you resolve to die ?

2 Turn, he cries, ye sinners, turn ;
By his life your God hath sworn,
He would have you turn and live,
He would all the world receive.
If your death were his delight,
Would he you to life invite ?
Would he ask, obtest, and cry,
Why will you resolve to die ?

3 Sinners, turn, while God is near :
Dare not think him insincere :
Now, even now, your Saviour stands,
All day long he spreads his hands,
Cries, Ye will not happy be !
No, ye will not come to me !
Me, who life to none deny :
Why will you resolve to die ?

4 Can you doubt if God is love ?
If to all his bowels move ?
Will you not his word receive ?
Will you not his OATH believe ?
See ! the suffering God appears !
Jesus weeps ! believe his tears !
Mingled with his blood, they cry,
Why will you resolve to die ?

9

L. M.

1 SINNERS. obey the gospel-word !
Haste to the supper of my Lord !
Be wise to know your gracious day ;
All things are ready, come away !

2 Ready the Father is to own
And kiss his late-returning son ;
Ready your loving Saviour stands,
And spreads for you his bleeding hands.

3 Ready the Spirit of his love
Just now the stony to remove,
To apply, and witness with the blood,
And wash and seal the sons of God.

4 Ready for you the angels wait,
To triumph in your blest estate ;
Tuning their harps, they long to praise
The wonders of redeeming grace.

5 The Father, Son, and Holy Ghost
Is ready, with their shining host :

A 2

All heaven is ready to resound,
" The dead's alive ! the lost is found ! "

6 Come then, ye sinners, to your Lord,
In Christ to paradise restored ;
His proffered benefits embrace,
The plenitude of gospel grace :

7 A pardon written with his blood,
The favour and the peace of God ;
The seeing eye, the feeling sense,
The mystic joys of penitence ;

8 The godly grief, the pleasing smart,
The meltings of a broken heart,
The tears that tell your sins forgiven,
The sighs that waft your souls to heaven:

9 The guiltless shame, the sweet distress,
The unutterable tenderness,
The genuine, meek humility,
The wonder, " Why such love to me ? "

10 The o'erwhelming power of saving grace,
The sight that veils the seraph's face ;
The speechless awe that dares not move,
And all the silent heaven of love.

10

10 s & 11 s. John vii. 37—39.

1 YE thirsty for God, To Jesus give ear.
And take, through his blood, A power
to draw near ;
His kind invitation Ye sinners embrace,
Accepting salvation, Salvation by grace.

2 Sent down from above, Who governs the
skies,
In vehement love To sinners he cries,
Drink into my Spirit, Who happy would
be,
And all things inherit By coming to me.

3 O Saviour of all, Thy word we believe !
And come at thy call, Thy grace to receive;
The blessing is given Wherever thou art,
The earnest of heaven Is love in the heart.

4 To us at thy feet The Comforter give,
Who gasp to admit Thy Spirit, and live ;
The weakest believers Acknowledge for
thine,
And fill us with rivers Of water divine.

11

L. M. 2 Corinthians v. 20.

1 GOD, the offended God most high,
Ambassadors to rebels sends ;
His messengers his place supply,
And Jesus begs us to be friends.

2 Us, in the stead of Christ, they pray,
Us, in the stead of God, intreat,
To cast our arms. our sins. away,
And find forgiveness at his feet.

3 Our God in Christ ! thine embassy,
And proffered mercy, we embrace ;
And gladly reconciled to thee,
Thy condescending goodness praise.

4 Poor debtors, by our Lord's request
A full acquittance we receive !
And criminals, with pardon blest,
We, at our Judge's instance, live !

3

SECTION II.

(1.) DESCRIBING THE PLEASANTNESS OF RELIGION.

12 S. M.

1 COME, ye that love the Lord,
   And let your joys be known ;
Join in a song with sweet accord,
   While ye surround his throne
   Let those refuse to sing
   Who never knew our God :
But servants of the heavenly King
   May speak their joys abroad.

2 The God that rules on high,
   That all the earth surveys,
That rides upon the stormy sky,
   And calms the roaring seas ;
   This awful God is ours,
   Our Father and our love ;
He will send down his heavenly powers,
   To carry us above.

3 There we shall see his face,
   And never, never sin ;
There, from the rivers of his grace,
   Drink endless pleasures in :
   Yea, and before we rise
   To that immortal state,
The thoughts of such amazing bliss
   Should constant joys create.

4 The men of grace have found
   Glory begun below ;
Celestial fruit on earthly ground
   From faith and hope may grow :
   Then let our songs abound,
   And every tear be dry ;
We are marching through Immanuel's
   To fairer worlds on high.   [ground.

13 8 - 7 s.

1 HAPPY soul that free from harms
   Rests within his Shepherd's arms !
Who his quiet shall molest?
Who shall violate his rest?
Jesus doth his spirit bear,
Jesus takes his every care ;
He who found the wandering sheep,
Jesus still delights to keep.

2 O that I might so believe,
Steadfastly to Jesus cleave,
On his only love rely,
Smile at the destroyer nigh ;
Free from sin and servile fear,
Have my Jesus ever near,
All his care rejoice to prove,
All his paradise of love !

3 Jesus, seek thy wandering sheep,
Bring me back, and lead, and keep ;
Take on thee my every care,
Bear me, on thy bosom bear :
Let me know my Shepherd's voice,
More and more in thee rejoice,
More and more of thee receive,
Ever in thy Spirit live :

4 Live, till all thy life I know,
Perfect through my Lord below,

Gladly then from earth remove,
Gathered to the fold above.
O that I at last may stand
With the sheep at thy right hand,
Take the crown so freely given,
Enter in by thee to heaven !

14

L. M.   Proverbs iii. 13—18.

1 HAPPY the man that finds the grace,
   The blessing of God's chosen race,
The wisdom coming from above,
The faith that sweetly works by love.

2 Happy beyond description he
Who knows, the Saviour died for me,
The gift unspeakable obtains,
And heavenly understanding gains.

3 Wisdom divine ! Who tells the price
Of wisdom's costly merchandise?
Wisdom to silver we prefer,
And gold is dross compared to her.

4 Her hands are filled with length of days,
True riches, and immortal praise,
Riches of Christ, on all bestowed,
And honour that descends from God.

5 To purest joys she all invites,
Chaste, holy, spiritual delights ;
Her ways are ways of pleasantness,
And all her flowery paths are peace.

6 Happy the man who wisdom gains,
Thrice happy who his guest retains !
He owns, and shall for ever own,
Wisdom, and Christ, and heaven are one.

15

C. M.

1 HAPPY the souls to Jesus joined,
   And saved by grace alone,
Walking in all his ways they find
   Their heaven on earth begun.

2 The church triumphant in thy love,
   Their mighty joys we know ;
They sing the Lamb in hymns above,
   And we in hymns below.

3 Thee in thy glorious realm they praise,
   And bow before thy throne,
We in the kingdom of thy grace :
   The kingdoms are but one.

4 The holy to the holiest leads,
   From thence our spirits rise,
And he that in thy statutes treads
   Shall meet thee in the skies.

16

L. M.   Primitive Christianity.

1 HAPPY the souls that first believed,
   To Jesus and each other cleaved,
Joined by the unction from above
In mystic fellowship of love.

2 Meek, simple followers of the Lamb,
They lived, and spake, and thought the
They joyfully conspired to raise   [same ;
Their ceaseless sacrifice of praise.

3 With grace abundantly endued,
A pure, believing multitude,
They all were of one heart and soul,
And only love inspired the whole.

4 O what an age of golden days !
O what a choice, peculiar race !

Washed in the Lamb's all-cleansing blood,
Anointed kings and priests to God!

5 Ye different sects, who all declare,
"Lo, here is Christ!" or, "Christ is there!"
Your stronger proofs divinely give,
And show me where the Christians live.

6 The gates of hell cannot prevail;
The church on earth can never fail;
Ah, join me to thy secret ones!
Ah, gather all thy living stones!

7 Scattered o'er all the earth they lie,
Till thou collect them with thine eye,
Draw by the music of thy name,
And charm into a beauteous frame.

8 For this the pleading Spirit groans,
And cries in all thy banished ones;
Greatest of gifts, thy love impart,
And make us of one mind and heart.

9 Join every soul that looks to thee
In bonds of perfect charity:
Now, Lord, the glorious fulness give,
And all in all for ever live!

17   SECOND PART.   L. M.

1 JESUS, from whom all blessings flow,
Great builder of thy church below,
If now thy Spirit moves my breast,
Hear, and fulfil thine own request!

2 The few that truly call thee Lord,
And wait thy sanctifying word,
And thee their utmost Saviour own,
Unite, and perfect them in one.

3 O let them all thy mind express,
Stand forth thy chosen witnesses,
Thy power unto salvation show,
And perfect holiness below!

4 In them let all mankind behold
How Christians lived in days of old,
Mighty their envious foes to move,
A proverb of reproach—and love.

5 From every sinful wrinkle free,
Redeemed from all iniquity,
The fellowship of saints make known;
And, O my God, might I be one!

6 O might my lot be cast with these,
The least of Jesu's witnesses!
O that my Lord would count me meet
To wash his dear disciples' feet!

7 This only thing do I require:
Thou knowest 'tis all my heart's desire
Freely what I receive to give,
The servant of thy church to live;

8 After my lowly Lord to go,
And wait upon thy saints below;
Enjoy the grace to angels given,
And serve the royal heirs of heaven.

9 Lord, if I now thy drawings feel,
And ask according to thy will,
Confirm the prayer, the seal impart,
And speak the answer to my heart.

18   7 s & 6 s.

1 MAKER, Saviour of mankind,
Who hast on me bestowed
An immortal soul, designed
To be the house of God;

Come, and now reside in me,
Never, never to remove;
Make me just and good, like thee,
And full of power and love.

2 Bid me in thy image rise,
A saint, a creature new,
True, and merciful, and wise,
And pure, and happy too.
This thy primitive design,
That I should in thee be blest,
Should within the arms divine
For ever, ever rest.

3 Let thy will on me be done;
Fulfil my heart's desire,
Thee to know and love alone,
And rise in raptures higher;
Thee, descending on a cloud,
When with ravished eyes I see,
Then I shall be filled with God
To all eternity!

10 s & 11 s.   **19**

1 REJOICE ever more With angels above,
In Jesus's power, In Jesus's love:
With glad exultation Your triumph proclaim,
Ascribing salvation To God and the Lamb.

2 Thou, Lord, our relief In trouble hast been;
Hast saved us from grief, Hast saved us free
from sin;
The power of thy Spirit Hath set our hearts
And now we inherit All fulness in thee.

3 All fulness of peace, All fulness of joy,
And spiritual bliss That never shall cloy:
To us it is given In Jesus to know
A kingdom of heaven, A heaven below.

4 No longer we join While sinners invite,
Nor envy the swine Their brutish delight:
Their joy is all sadness, Their mirth is all
vain, is pain.
Their laughter is madness, Their pleasure

5 O might they at last With sorrow return,
The pleasures to taste For which they were
Our Jesus receiving, Our happiness prove,
The joy of believing, The heaven of love!

6 - 7 s.   **20**

1 WEARY souls, that wander wide,
From the central point of bliss,
Turn to Jesus crucified,
Fly to those dear wounds of his:
Sink into the purple flood;
Rise into the life of God!

2 Find in Christ the way of peace,
Peace unspeakable, unknown;
By his pain he gives you ease,
Life by his expiring groan;
Rise, exalted by his fall,
Find in Christ your all in all.

3 O believe the record true,
God to you his Son hath given!
Ye may now be happy too,
Find on earth the life of heaven,
Live the life of heaven above,
All the life of glorious love.

4 This the universal bliss,
 Bliss for every soul designed,
God's original promise this,
 God's great gift to all mankind?
Blest in Christ this moment be!
Blest to all eternity!

21

S. M.

1 YE simple souls that stray
 Far from the path of peace,
That lonely, unfrequented way
 To life and happiness,
 Why will ye folly love,
 And throng the downward road.
And hate the wisdom from above,
 And mock the sons of God?

2 Madness and misery
 Ye count our life beneath;
And nothing great or good can see,
 Or glorious, in our death:
 As only born to grieve,
 Beneath your feet we lie;
And utterly contemned we live,
 And unlamented die.

3 So wretched and obscure,
 The men whom ye despise,
So foolish, impotent, and poor,
 Above your scorn we rise:
 We, through the Holy Ghost,
 Can witness better things;
For He whose blood is all our boast
 Hath made us priests and kings.

4 Riches unsearchable
 In Jesu's love we know;
And pleasures, springing from the well
 Of life, our souls o'erflow;
 The Spirit we receive
 Of wisdom, grace, and power:
And always sorrowful we live,
 Rejoicing evermore.

5 Angels our servants are,
 And keep in all our ways,
And in their watchful hands they bear
 The sacred sons of grace:
 Unto that heavenly bliss
 They all our steps attend;
And God himself our Father is,
 And Jesus is our friend.

6 With him we walk in white,
 We in his image shine,
Our robes are robes of glorious light,
 Our righteousness divine;
 On all the kings of earth
 With pity we look down,
And claim, in virtue of our birth,
 A never-fading crown.

(2.) DESCRIBING THE GOODNESS OF GOD.

22

C. M.

1 BEHOLD the Saviour of mankind
 Nailed to the shameful tree!
How vast the love that him inclined
 To bleed and die for thee!

2 Hark, how he groans! while nature shakes,
 And earth's strong pillars bend;

6

The temple's veil in sunder breaks,
 The solid marbles rend.

3 'Tis done! the precious ransom's paid,
 "Receive my soul," he cries!
See where he bows his sacred head!
 He bows his head, and dies!

4 But soon he'll break death's envious chain,
 And in full glory shine:
O Lamb of God! was ever pain,
 Was ever love, like thine?

23

L. M.

1 EXTENDED on a cursed tree,
 Besmeared with dust, and sweat, and blood
See there, the King of glory see! [blood
 Sinks and expires the Son of God.

2 Who, who, my Saviour, this hath done?
 Who could thy sacred body wound?
No guilt thy spotless heart hath known,
 No guile hath in thy lips been found.

3 I, I alone, have done the deed!
 'Tis I thy sacred flesh have torn;
My sins have caused thee, Lord, to bleed,
 Pointed the nail, and fixed the thorn.

4 The burden, for me to sustain
 Too great, on thee, my Lord, was laid;
To heal me, thou hast borne my pain;
 To bless me, thou a curse wast made

5 In the devouring lion's teeth,
 Torn, and forsook of all, I lay;
Thou sprang'st into the jaws of death,
 From death to save the helpless prey

6 My Saviour how shall I proclaim?
 How pay the mighty debt I owe?
Let all I have, and all I am,
 Ceaseless to all thy glory show.

7 Too much to thee I cannot give;
 Too much I cannot do for thee;
Let all thy love, and all thy grief,
 Graven on my heart for ever be!

8 The meek, the still, the lowly mind,
 O may I learn from thee, my God,
And love, with softest pity joined,
 For those that trample on thy blood!

9 Still let thy tears, thy groans, thy sighs,
 O'erflow my eyes, and heave my breast
Till loose from flesh and earth I rise,
 And ever in thy bosom rest.

24

8-7 s.

1 SAVIOUR, if thy precious love
 Could be merited by mine,
Faith these mountains would remove;
 Faith would make me ever thine;
But when all my care and pains
 Worth can ne'er create in me,
Nought by me thy fulness gains;
 Vain the hope to purchase thee.

2 Cease, O man, thy worth to weigh,
 Give the needless contest o'er;
Mine thou art! while thus I say,
 Yield thee up, and ask no more;
What thy estimate may be,
 Only can by him be told
Who, to ransom wretched thee,
 Thee to gain, himself was sold.

8 But when all in me is sin,
   How can I thy grace obtain?
How presume thyself to win?
   God of love, the doubt explain?
Or if thou the means supply,
   Lo to thee I all resign!
Make me, Lord—I ask not why;
   How I ask not,—ever thine.

25*   Matthew xi. 28.   8 s & 6 s.

1 STUPENDOUS love of God most high!
   He comes to meet us from the sky
     In mildest majesty;
Full of unutterable grace,
He calls the weary burdened race,
   "Come all for help to me."

2 Tired with the greatness of my way,
From him I would no longer stray;
     But rest in Jesus have;
Weary of sin, from sin would cease,
Weary of mine own righteousness,
   And stoop, myself to save.

3 Weary of passions unsubdued,
Weary of vows in vain renewed,
     Of forms without the power,
Of prayers, and hopes, complaints, and
My fainting soul in silence owns [groans,
   I can hold out no more.

4 Beneath this mountain load of grief,
Of guilt and desperate unbelief,
     Jesus, thy creature see:
With all my nature's weight oppressed,
I sink, I die for want of rest,
   Yet cannot come to thee.

5 Mine utter helplessness I feel;
But thou, who gav'st the feeble will,
     The effectual grace supply;
Be thou my strength, my light, my way,
And bid my soul the call obey,
   And to thy bosom fly.

6 Fulfil thine own intense desire,
And now into my heart inspire
     The power of faith and love;
Then, Saviour, then to thee I come,
And find on earth the life, the home,
   The rest of saints above.

26   L. M.

1 I THIRST, thou wounded Lamb of God,
To wash me in thy cleansing blood,
To dwell within thy wounds; then pain
Is sweet, and life or death is gain.

2 Take my poor heart, and let it be
For ever closed to all but thee!
Seal thou my breast, and let me wear
That pledge of love for ever there!

3 How blest are they who still abide
Close sheltered in thy bleeding side.
Who life and strength from thence derive,
And by thee move, and in thee live.

4 What are our works but sin and death,
Till thou thy quickening Spirit breathe!
Thou giv'st the power thy grace to move;
O wondrous grace! O boundless love!

5 How can it be, thou heavenly King,
That thou shouldst us to glory bring?

Make slaves the partners of thy throne,
Decked with a never-fading crown?

6 Hence our hearts melt, our eyes o'erflow,
Our words are lost; nor will we know.
Nor will we think of aught beside,
"My Lord, my Love is crucified."

7 Ah, Lord! enlarge our scanty thought,
To know the wonders thou hast wrought;
Unloose our stammering tongues, to tell
Thy love immense, unsearchable.

8 First-born of many brethren thou!
To thee, lo! all our souls we bow:
To thee our hearts and hands we give:
Thine may we die, thine may we live!

27   2 - 6 s & 4 - 7 s.

1 SAVIOUR, the world's and mine,
   Was ever grief like thine!
Thou my pain, my curse hast took,
   All my sins were laid on thee;
Help me, Lord; to thee I look,
   Draw me, Saviour, after thee.

2 'Tis done! my God hath died!
   My Love is crucified!
Break, this stony heart of mine;
   Pour, mine eyes, a ceaseless flood;
Feel, my soul, the pangs divine;
   Catch, my heart, the issuing blood!

3 When, O my God, shall I
   For thee submit to die?
How the mighty debt repay?
   Rival of thy passion prove?
Lead me in thyself, the Way;
   Melt my hardness into love.

4 To love is all my wish,
   I only live for this;
Grant me, Lord, my heart's desire,
   There by faith for ever dwell;
This I always will require,
   Thee, and only thee, to feel.

5 Thy power I pant to prove,
   Rooted and fixed in love;
Strengthened by thy Spirit's might,
   Wise to fathom things divine.
What the length, and breadth, and height,
   What the depth of love like thine.

6 Ah! give me this to know,
   With all thy saints below;
Swells my soul to compass thee,
   Gasps in thee to live and move:
Filled with all the Deity,
   All immersed and lost in love!

28   6 - 8 s.

1 O LOVE divine! what hast thou done!
   The immortal God hath died for me!
The Father's co-eternal Son
   Bore all my sins upon the tree;
The immortal God for me hath died!
My Lord, my Love is crucified.

2 Behold him, all ye that pass by,
   The bleeding Prince of life and peace!
Come, see, ye worms, your Maker die,
   And say, was ever grief like his?
Come, feel with me his blood applied:
My Lord, my Love is crucified.

7

3 Is crucified for me and you,
    To bring us rebels back to God:
Believe, believe the record true,
    Ye all are bought with Jesu's blood,
Pardon for all flows from his side;
My Lord, my Love is crucified. ιι

4 Then let us sit beneath his cross,
    And gladly catch the healing stream,
All things for him account but loss,
    And give up all our hearts to him;
Of nothing think or speak beside,
" My Lord, my Love is crucified."

29   Matthew xi. 28.   8 - 7 s.

1 COME, ye weary sinners, come,
    All who groan beneath your load,
Jesus calls his wanderers home,
    Hasten to your pardoning God!
Come, ye guilty spirits oppressed,
    Answer to the Saviour's call,
" Come, and I will give you rest,
    Come, and I will save you all."

2 Jesus, full of truth and love,
    We thy kindest word obey:
Faithful let thy mercies prove,
    Take our load of guilt away;
Fain we would on thee rely,
    Cast on thee our every care,
To thine arms of mercy fly,
    Find our lasting quiet there.

3 Burdened with a world of grief,
    Burdened with our sinful load,
Burdened with this unbelief,
    Burdened with the wrath of God;
Lo! we come to thee for ease,
    True and gracious as thou art,
Now our groaning souls release,
    Write forgiveness on our heart.

30   6 - 8 s.

1 WHERE shall my wondering soul begin?
    How shall I all to heaven aspire?
A slave redeemed from death and sin,
    A brand plucked from eternal fire,
How shall I equal triumphs raise,
Or sing my great Deliverer's praise?

2 O how shall I the goodness tell,
    Father, which thou to me hast showed?
That I, a child of wrath and hell,
    I should be called a child of God,
Should know, should feel my sins forgiven,
Blest with this antepast of heaven!

3 And shall I slight my Father's love?
    Or basely fear his gifts to own?
Unmindful of his favours prove?
    Shall I, the hallowed cross to shun,
Refuse his righteousness to impart,
By hiding it within my heart?

4 No! though the ancient dragon rage,
    And call forth all his host to war,
Though earth's self-righteous sons engage,
    Them and their god alike I dare;
Jesus, the sinner's friend, proclaim;
Jesus, to sinners still the same.

5 Outcasts of men, to you I call,
    Harlots, and publicans, and thieves!
He spreads his arms to embrace you all;
    Sinners alone his grace receives;
8

No need of him the righteous have;
He came the lost to seek and save.

6 Come, O my guilty brethren, come,
    Groaning beneath your load of sin,
His bleeding heart shall make you room,
    His open side shall take you in;
He calls you now, invites you home;
Come, O my guilty brethren, come!

7 For you the purple current flowed
    In pardons from his wounded side,
Languished for you the eternal God,
    For you the Prince of glory died:
Believe, and all your sin's forgiven;
Only believe, and yours is heaven!

31   6 - 8 s.

1 SEE, sinners, in the gospel glass,
    The friend and Saviour of mankind!
Not one of all the apostate race
    But may in him salvation find!
His thoughts, and words, and actions prove,
His life and death,—that God is love!

2 Behold the Lamb of God, who bears
    The sins of all the world away!
A servant's form he meekly wears,
    He sojourns in a house of clay,
His glory is no longer seen,
But God with God is man with men.

3 See where the God incarnate stands,
    And calls his wandering creatures home,
He all day long spreads out his hands,
    " Come, weary souls, to Jesus come!
Ye all may hide you in my breast,
Believe, and I will give you rest.

4 " Ah! do not of my goodness doubt;
    My saving grace for all is free;
I will in no wise cast him out
    That comes a sinner unto me:
I can to none myself deny,
Why, sinners, will ye perish, why?"

32   6 - 8 s.

1 SINNERS, believe the gospel word,
    Jesus is come your souls to save!
Jesus is come, your common Lord;
    Pardon for all through him may have,
May now be saved, whoever will;
This man receiveth sinners still.

2 See where the lame, the halt, the blind,
    The deaf, the dumb, the sick, the poor,
Flock to the friend of human kind,
    And freely all accept their cure;
To whom did he his help deny?
Whom in his days of flesh pass by?

3 Did not his word the fiends expel,
    The lepers cleanse, and raise the dead?
Did he not all their sickness heal,
    And satisfy their every need?
Did he reject his helpless clay,
Or send them sorrowful away?

4 Nay, but his bowels yearned to see
    The people hungry, scattered, faint;
Nay, but he uttered over thee,
    Jerusalem, a true complaint;
Jerusalem, who shedd'st his blood,
That, with his tears, for thee hath flowed.

33
6 - 8 s.

1 WOULD Jesus have the sinner die?
Why hangs he then on yonder tree?
What means that strange expiring cry?
(Sinners, he prays for you and me)
"Forgive them, Father, O forgive,
They know not that by me they live!"

2 Adam descended from above,
Our loss of Eden to retrieve,
Great God of universal love,
If all the world through thee may live,
In us a quickening spirit be,
And witness thou hast died for me!

3 Thou loving, all-atoning Lamb,
Thee—by thy painful agony,
Thy bloody sweat, thy grief and shame,
Thy cross and passion on the tree,
Thy precious death and life—I pray,
Take all, take all my sins away!

4 O let me kiss thy bleeding feet,
And bathe and wash them with my tears!
The story of thy love repeat
In every drooping sinner's ears,
That all may hear the quickening sound,
Since I, even I, have mercy found.

5 O let thy love my heart constrain!
Thy love for every sinner free,
That every fallen soul of man
May taste the grace that found out me;
That all mankind with me may prove
Thy sovereign everlasting love.

34
4 - 6 s & 2 - 8 s.

1 LET earth and heaven agree,
Angels and men be joined,
To celebrate with me
The Saviour of mankind;
To adore the all-atoning Lamb,
And bless the sound of Jesu's name.

2 Jesus, transporting sound!
The joy of earth and heaven;
No other help is found,
No other name is given,
By which we can salvation have;
But Jesus came the world to save.

3 Jesus, harmonious name!
It charms the hosts above;
They evermore proclaim
And wonder at his love;
'Tis all their happiness to gaze,
'Tis heaven to see our Jesu's face.

4 His name the sinner hears,
And is from sin set free;
'Tis music in his ears,
'Tis life and victory;
New songs do now his lips employ,
And dances his glad heart for joy.

5 Stung by the scorpion sin,
My poor expiring soul
The balmy sound drinks in,
And is at once made whole:
See there my Lord upon the tree!
I hear, I feel, he died for me.

6 O unexampled love!
O all-redeeming grace!
How swiftly didst thou move
To save a fallen race!

What shall I do to make it known
What thou for all mankind hast done?

7 O for a trumpet voice,
On all the world to call!
To bid their hearts rejoice
In him who died for all;
For all my Lord was crucified,
For all, for all my Saviour died!

C. M. ## 35

1 JESUS, thou all-redeeming Lord,
Thy blessing we implore,
Open the door to preach thy word,
The great effectual door.

2 Gather the outcasts in, and save
From sin and Satan's power;
And let them now acceptance have,
And know their gracious hour.

3 Lover of souls! thou know'st to prize
What thou hast bought so dear;
Come then, and in thy people's eyes
With all thy wounds appear.

4 Appear, as when of old confest
The suffering Son of God;
And let them see thee in thy vest
But newly dipt in blood.

5 The hardness from their hearts remove,
Thou who for all hast died;
Show them the tokens of thy love,
Thy feet, thy hands, thy side.

6 Thy feet were nailed to yonder tree,
To trample down their sin;
Thy hands stretched out they all may see,
To take thy murderers in.

7 Thy side an open fountain is,
Where all may freely go,
And drink the living streams of bliss,
And wash them white as snow.

8 Ready thou art the blood to apply,
And prove the record true;
And all thy wounds to sinners cry,
" I suffered this for you!"

C. M. ## 36

1 LOVERS of pleasure more than God,
For you he suffered pain;
Swearers, for you he spilt his blood;
And shall he bleed in vain?

2 Misers, for you his life he paid,
Your basest crimes he bore:
Drunkards, your sins on him were laid,
That you might sin no more.

3 The God of love, to earth he came,
That you might come to heaven;
Believe, believe in Jesu's name,
And all your sin's forgiven.

4 Believe in him that died for thee,
And, sure as he hath died,
Thy debt is paid, thy soul is free,
And thou art justified.

C. M. ## 37

1 E US! the name high over all,
In hell, or earth, or sky,
Angels and men before it fall,
And devils fear and fly.

2 Jesus ! the name to sinners dear,
 The name to sinners given ;
It scatters all their guilty fear,
 It turns their hell to heaven.

3 Jesus ! the prisoner's fetters breaks,
 And bruises Satan's head ;
Power into strengthless souls it speaks,
 And life into the dead.

4 O that the world might taste and see
 The riches of his grace !
The arms of love that compass me
 Would all mankind embrace.

5 His only righteousness I show,
 His saving truth proclaim,
'Tis all my business here below
 To cry, " Behold the Lamb l "

6 Happy, if with my latest breath
 I may but gasp his name ;
Preach him to all, and cry in death,
 " Behold, behold the Lamb l "

38*
    6 - 8 s.   Second Metre.

1 O GOD, of good the unfathomed sea !
 Who would not give his heart to thee?
Who would not love thee with his might ?
O Jesu, lover of mankind,
Who would not his whole soul and mind,
 With all thy strength, to thee unite?

2 Thou shin'st with everlasting rays ;
Before the insufferable blaze
 Angels with both wings veil their eyes ;
Yet free as air thy bounty streams
On all thy werks ; thy mercy's beams
 Diffusive as thy sun's arise.

3 Astonished at thy frowning brow,
Earth, hell, and heaven's strong pillars
 Terrible majesty is thine ! [bow ;
Who then can that vast love express
Which bows thee down to me, who less
 Than nothing am, till thou art mine ?

4 High throned on heaven's eternal hill,
In number, weight, and measure still
 Thou sweetly orderest all that is :
And yet thou deign'st to come to me,
And guide my steps, that I, with thee
 Enthroned, may reign in endless bliss.

5 Fountain of good l all blessing flows
From thee ; no want thy fulness knows ;
 What but thyself canst thou desire?
Yes ; self-sufficient as thou art,
Thou dost desire my worthless heart ;
 This, only this, dost thou require.

6 Primeval Beauty ! in thy sight
The first-born, fairest sons of light
 See all their brightest glories fade :
What then to me thine eyes could turn,
In sin conceived, of woman born,
 A worm, a leaf, a blast, a shade ?

7 Hell's armies tremble at thy nod, ·
And trembling own the Almighty God,
 Sovereign of earth, hell, air, and sky :
But who is this that comes from far,
Whose garments rolled in blood appear ?
 'Tis God made man, for man to die !

8 O God, of good the unfathomed sea !
Who would not give his heart to thee ?
Who would not love thee with his might ?
 10

O Jesu, lover of mankind,
Who would not his whole soul and mind,
 With all his strength, to thee unite ?

*39
L. M.

1 FATHER, whose everlasting love
 Thy only Son for sinners gave,
Whose grace to all did freely move,
 And sent him down the world to save ;

2 Help us thy mercy to extol,
 Immense, unfathomed, unconfined ;
To praise the Lamb who died for all,
 The general Saviour of mankind.

3 Thy undistinguishing regard
 Was cast on Adam's fallen race ;
For all thou hast in Christ prepared
 Sufficient, sovereign, saving grace.

4 The world he suffered to redeem ;
 For all he hath the atonement made ;
For those that will not come to him
 The ransom of his life was paid.

5 Why then, thou universal Love,
 Should any of thy grace despair ?
To all, to all, thy bowels move,
 But straitened in our own we are.

6 Arise, O God, maintain thy cause l
 The fulness of the Gentiles call ;
Lift up the standard of thy cross,
 And all shall own thou diedst for all.

40
10 s & 11 s.

1 YE neighbours, and friends Of Jesus,
 draw near :
His love condescends By titles so dear
To call and invite you His triumph to
 prove,
And freely delight you In Jesus's love.

2 The Shepherd who died His sheep to re-
 deem,
On every side Are gathered to him [race ;
The weary and burdened, The reprobate
And wait to be pardoned Through Jesus's
 grace.

3 The blind are restored Through Jesus's
 name,   [Lamb :
They see their dear Lord, And follow the
The halt they are walking, And running
 their race :
The dumb they are talking Of Jesus's grace.

4 The deaf hear his voice And comforting
 word,
It bids them rejoice In Jesus their Lord,
" Thy sins are forgiven, Accepted thou
 art ; "   [their heart.
They listen, and heaven Springs up in

5 The lepers from all Their spots are made
 clean,   [sin :
The dead by his call Are raised from their
In Jesu's compassion The sick find a cure,
And gospel salvation Is preached to the
 poor.

6 To us and to them Is published the word :
Then let us proclaim Our life-giving Lord,
Who now is reviving His work in our days,
And mightily striving To save us by grace.

7 O Jesus! ride on Till all are subdued,
  Thy mercy make known, And sprinkle thy
    blood;   [song
  Display thy salvation, And teach the new
  To every nation, And people, and tongue.

(3.) DESCRIBING DEATH.

41

Psalm xc. 1—5.   C. M.

1 O GOD! our help in ages past,
    Our hope for years to come,
  Our shelter from the stormy blast,
    And our eternal home:

2 Under the shadow of thy throne:
    Still may we dwell secure;
  Sufficient is thine arm alone,
    And our defence is sure.

3 Before the hills in order stood,
    Or earth received her frame,
  From everlasting thou art God.
    To endless years the same.

4 A thousand ages in thy sight
    Are like an evening gone,
  Short as the watch that ends the night
    Before the rising sun.

5 The busy tribes of flesh and blood,
    With all their cares and fears,
  Are carried downward by the flood,
    And lost in following years.

6 Time, like an ever-rolling stream,
    Bears all its sons away;
  They fly forgotten, as a dream
    Dies at the opening day.

7 O God! our help in ages past,
    Our hope for years to come,
  Be thou our guard while life shall last,
    And our perpetual home.

42

                              C. M.

1 THEE we adore, eternal name!
    And humbly own to thee,
  How feeble is our mortal frame,
    What dying worms we be!

2 Our wasting lives grow shorter still,
    As days and months increase;
  And every beating pulse we tell
    Leaves but the number less.

3 The year rolls round, and steals away
    The breath that first it gave;
  Whate'er we do, where'er we be,
    We are travelling to the grave.

4 Dangers stand thick through all the
    To push us to the tomb;   [ground,
  And fierce diseases wait around,
    To hurry mortals home.

5 Great God! on what a slender thread
    Hang everlasting things;
  The eternal states of all the dead
    Upon life's feeble strings!

6 Infinite joy, or endless woe,
    Depends on every breath;
  And yet how unconcerned we go
    Upon the brink of death!

7 Waken, O Lord, our drowsy sense,
    To walk this dangerous road!
  And if our souls be hurried hence,
    May they be found with God!

43

S. M.

1 AND am I born to die?
    To lay this body down?
  And must my trembling spirit fly
    Into a world unknown—
  A land of deepest shade,
    Unpierced by human thought,
  The dreary regions of the dead,
    Where all things are forgot?

2 Soon as from earth I go,
    What will become of me?
  Eternal happiness or woe
    Must then my portion be;
  Waked by the trumpet's sound.
    I from my grave shall rise,
  And see the Judge with glory crowned.
    And see the flaming skies.

3 How shall I leave my tomb?
    With triumph or regret?
  A fearful or a joyful doom,
    A curse or blessing meet?
  Will angel-bands convey
    Their brother to the bar?
  Or devils drag my soul away,
    To meet its sentence there?

4 Who can resolve the doubt
    That tears my anxious breast?
  Shall I be with the damned cast out,
    Or numbered with the blest?
  I must from God be driven,
    Or with my Saviour dwell;
  Must come at his command to heaven
    Or else—depart to hell.

5 O thou that wouldst not have
    One wretched sinner die,
  Who diedst thyself. my soul to save
    From endless misery!
  Show me the way to shun
    Thy dreadful wrath severe,
  That when thou comest on thy throne,
    I may with joy appear.

6 Thou art thyself the Way;
    Thyself in me reveal;
  So shall I spend my life's short day
    Obedient to thy will;
  So shall I love my God,
    Because he first loved me,
  And praise thee in thy bright abode.
    To all eternity.

44

8 s & 6 s.

1 AND am I only born to die?
    And must I suddenly comply
  With nature's stern decree?
  What after death for me remains?
  Celestial joys, or hellish pains,
    To all eternity?

2 How then ought I on earth to live,
  While God prolongs the kind reprieve,
    And props the house of clay?
  My sole concern, my single care,
  To watch, and tremble, and prepare
    Against the fatal day.

3 No room for mirth or trifling here,
  For worldly hope, or worldly fear,
    If life so soon is gone;

11

If now the Judge is at the door,
And all mankind must stand before
    The inexorable throne!
4 No matter which my thoughts employ,
    A moment's misery, or joy;
        But O! when both shall end,
    Where shall I find my destined place?
    Shall I my everlasting days
        With fiends or angels spend?
5 Nothing is worth a thought beneath
    But how I may escape the death
        That never, never dies;
    How make mine own election sure,
    And, when I fail on earth, secure
        A mansion in the skies.
6 Jesus, vouchsafe a pitying ray,
    Be thou my guide, be thou my way
        To glorious happiness;
    Ah, write the pardon on my heart,
    And whensoe'er I hence depart,
        Let me depart in peace.

45   L. M.

1 SHRINKING from the cold hand of death,
    I too shall gather up my feet,
Shall soon resign this fleeting breath,
    And die, my fathers' God to meet.
2 Numbered among thy people, I
    Expect with joy thy face to see;
Because thou didst for sinners die,
    Jesus, in death remember me!
3 O that without a lingering groan
    I may the welcome word receive!
My body with my charge lay down,
    And cease at once to work and live.

46   Isaiah xl. 6—8.   L. M.

1 THE morning flowers display their
        sweets,
    And gay their silken leaves unfold,
As careless of the noontide heats,
    As fearless of the evening cold.
2 Nipt by the wind's unkindly blast,
    Parched by the sun's directer ray,
The momentary glories waste,
    The short-lived beauties die away.
3 So blooms the human face divine,
    When youth its pride of beauty shows;
Fairer than spring the colours shine,
    And sweeter than the virgin rose.
4 Or worn by slowly-rolling years,
    Or broke by sickness in a day,
The fading glory disappears,
    The short-lived beauties die away.
5 Yet these, new rising from the tomb,
    With lustre brighter far shall shine;
Revive with ever-during bloom,
    Safe from diseases and decline.
6 Let sickness blast, let death devour,
    If heaven must recompense our pains:
Perish the grass, and fade the flower,
    If firm the word of God remains.

47   5 5 5 11.

1 COME, let us anew
    Our journey pursue,
12

Roll round with the year,
And never stand still till the Master appear,
2 His adorable will
    Let us gladly fulfil,
    And our talents improve,   [love.
By the patience of hope, and the labour of
3 Our life is a dream;
    Our time as a stream
    Glides swiftly away,
And the fugitive moment refuses to stay.
4 The arrow is flown,
    The moment is gone;
    The millennial year
Rushes on to our view, and eternity's here.
5 O that each in the day
    Of his coming may say,
    "I have fought my way through,
I have finished the work thou didst give me
        to do!"
6 O that each from his Lord
    May receive the glad word,
    "Well and faithfully done! [throne."
Enter into my joy, and sit down on my

48

L. M.

1 PASS a few swiftly-fleeting years,
    And all that now in bodies live
Shall quit, like me, the vale of tears,
    Their righteous sentence to receive.
2 But all, before they hence remove,
    May mansions for themselves prepare
In that eternal house above;
    And, O my God, shall I be there?

49

8 s.

1 REJOICE for a brother deceased,
    Our loss is his infinite gain;
A soul out of prison released,
    And freed from its bodily chain;
With songs let us follow his flight,
    And mount with his spirit above,
Escaped to the mansions of light,
    And lodged in the Eden of love.
2 Our brother the haven hath gained,
    Out-flying the tempest and wind,
His rest he hath sooner obtained,
    And left his companions behind,
Still tossed on a sea of distress,
    Hard toiling to make the blest shore,
Where all is assurance and peace,
    And sorrow and sin are no more.
3 There all the ship's company meet
    Who sailed with the Saviour beneath,
With shouting each other they greet,
    And triumph o'er trouble and death:
The voyage of life's at an end,
    The mortal affliction is past;
The age that in heaven they spend,
    For ever and ever shall last.

50

8 - 7 s.

1 BLESSING, honour, thanks, and praise,
    Pay we, gracious God, to thee;
Thou, in thine abundant grace,
    Givest us the victory;
True and faithful to thy word,
    Thou hast glorified thy Son.

Jesus Christ, our dying Lord,
 He for us the fight hath won.

2 Lo! the prisoner is released,
 Lightened of his fleshly load;
Where the weary are at rest,
 He is gathered into God;
Lo! the pain of life is past,
 All his warfare now is o'er,
Death and hell behind are cast,
 Grief and suffering are no more.

3 Yes, the Christian's course is run,
 Ended is the glorious strife;
Fought the fight, the work is done,
 Death is swallowed up of life!
Borne by angels on their wings,
 Far from earth the spirit flies,
Finds his God, and sits and sings,
 Triumphing in Paradise.

4 Join we then, with one accord,
 In the new, the joyful song;
Absent from our loving Lord
 We shall not continue long;
We shall quit the house of clay,
 We a better lot shall share,
We shall see the realms of day,
 Meet our happy brother there.

5 Let the world bewail their dead,
 Fondly of their loss complain,
Brother, friend, by Jesus freed,
 Death to thee, to us, is gain;
Thou art entered into joy:
 Let the unbelievers mourn;
We in songs our lives employ,
 Till we all to God return.

51

8 - 7 s.

1 HARK! a voice divides the sky,
 Happy are the faithful dead!
In the Lord who sweetly die,
 They from all their toils are freed;
Them the Spirit hath declared
 Blest, unutterably blest,
Jesus is their great reward,
 Jesus is their endless rest.

2 Followed by their works, they go
 Where their Head hath gone before;
Reconciled by grace below,
 Grace hath opened mercy's door;
Justified through faith alone,
 Here they knew their sins forgiven,
Here they laid their burden down,
 Hallowed, and made meet for Heaven.

3 Who can now lament the lot
 Of a saint in Christ deceased?
Let the world, who know us not,
 Call us hopeless and unblest:
When from flesh the spirit freed
 Hastens homeward to return,
Mortals cry, "A man is dead!"
 Angels sing, "A child is born!"

4 Born into the world above,
 They our happy brother greet,
Bear him to the throne of love,
 Place him at the Saviour's feet;
Jesus smiles, and says, "Well done,
 Good and faithful servant thou;
Enter, and receive thy crown,
 Reign with me triumphant now"

5 Angels catch the approving sound,
 Bow, and bless the just award;
Hail the heir with glory crowned,
 Now rejoicing with his Lord:
Fuller joys ordained to know,
 Waiting for the general doom,
When the archangel's trump shall blow,
 "Rise, ye dead, to judgment come!"

2 - 6 s & 4 - 7 s.

52

1 AGAIN we lift our voice,
 And shout our solemn joys;
Cause of highest raptures this,
 Raptures that shall never fail,
See a soul escaped to bliss,
 Keep the Christian festival!

2 Our friend has gone before
 To that celestial shore;
He hath left his mates behind,
 He hath all the storms outrode;
Found the rest we toil to find,
 Landed in the arms of God.

3 And shall we mourn to see
 Our fellow-prisoner free?
Free from doubts, and griefs, and fears,
 In the haven of the skies!
Can we weep to see the tears
 Wiped for ever from his eyes?

4 No, dear companion, no!
 We gladly let thee go,
From a suffering church beneath,
 To a reigning church above:
Thou hast more than conquered death;
 Thou art crowned with life and love.

5 Thou, in thy youthful prime,
 Hast leaped the bounds of time,
Suddenly from earth released;
 Lo! we now rejoice for thee,
Taken to an early rest,
 Caught into eternity.

6 Thither may we repair,
 That glorious bliss to share!
We shall see the welcome day,
 We shall to the summons bow;
Come, Redeemer, come away,
 Now prepare, and take us now.

8 - 7 s. *A Funeral Hymn.* ***53**

1 GLORY be to God on high,
 God in whom we live and die,
God, who guides us by his love,
 Takes us to his throne above!
Angels that surround his throne
 Sing the wonders he hath done,
Shout, while we on earth reply,
 Glory be to God on high!

2 God of everlasting grace,
 Worthy thou of endless praise,
Thou hast all thy blessings shed
 On the living and the dead;
Thou wast here their sure defence,
 Thou hast borne their spirits hence,
Worthy thou of endless praise,
 God of everlasting grace.

3 Thanks be all ascribed to thee,
 Blessing, power, and majesty,
Thee, by whose almighty name
 They their latest foe o'ercame;

13

Thou the victory hast won,
Saved them by thy grace alone,
Caught them up thy face to see,
Thanks be all ascribed to thee!

4 Happy in thy glorious love,
We shall from the vale remove,
Glad partakers of our hope,
We shall soon be taken up;
Meet again our heavenly friends,
Blest with bliss that never ends,
Joined to all thy hosts above,
Happy in thy glorious love!

---

54 (4.) DESCRIBING JUDGMENT.
7 s & 6 s.

1 HEARKEN to the solemn voice,
The awful midnight cry;
Waiting souls, rejoice, rejoice,
And see the Bridegroom nigh;
Lo! he comes to keep his word,
Light and joy his looks impart;
Go ye forth to meet your Lord,
And meet him in your heart.

2 Ye who faint beneath the load
Of sin, your heads lift up;
See your great redeeming God,
He comes, and bids you hope:
In the midnight of your grief,
Jesus doth his mourners cheer,
Lo! he brings you sure relief;
Believe, and feel him here.

3 Ye whose loins are girt, stand forth!
Whose lamps are burning bright,
Worthy, in your Saviour's worth,
To walk with him in white:
Jesus bids your hearts be clean,
Bids you all his promise prove;
· Jesus comes to cast out sin,
And perfect you in love.

4 Wait we all in patient hope,
Till Christ, the Judge, shall come;
We shall soon be all caught up
To meet the general doom:
In an hour to us unknown,
As a thief in deepest night,
Christ shall suddenly come down,
With all his saints in light.

5 Happy he whom Christ shall find
Watching to see him come;
Him the Judge of all mankind
Shall bear triumphant home:
Who can answer to his word?
Which of you dares meet his day?
"Rise, and come to judgment!"—Lord,
We rise, and come away.

55 S. M.

1 THOU Judge of quick and dead,
Before whose bar severe,
With holy joy, or guilty dread,
We all shall soon appear;
Our cautioned souls prepare
For that tremendous day,
And fill us now with watchful care,
And stir us up to pray:

2 To pray, and wait the hour,
That awful hour unknown,
14

When, robed in majesty and power,
Thou shalt from heaven come down,
The immortal Son of man,
To judge the human race,
With all thy Father's dazzling train,
With all thy glorious grace.

3 To damp our earthly joys,
To increase our gracious fears,
For ever let the archangel's voice
Be sounding in our ears;
The solemn midnight cry,
"Ye dead, the Judge is come,
Arise, and meet him in the sky,
And meet your instant doom!"

4 O may we thus be found
Obedient to his word,
Attentive to the trumpet's sound,
And looking for our Lord!
O may we thus ensure
A lot among the blest:
And watch a moment to secure
An everlasting rest!

L. M. **56**

1 HE comes! he comes! the Judge severe
The seventh trumpet speaks him near,
His lightnings flash, his thunders roll,
How welcome to the faithful soul!

2 From heaven angelic voices sound,
See the almighty Jesus crowned,
Girt with omnipotence and grace!
And glory decks the Saviour's face.

3 Descending on his azure throne,
He claims the kingdoms for his own;
The kingdoms all obey his word,
And hail him their triumphant Lord.

4 Shout, all the people of the sky,
And all the saints of the most High!
Our Lord, who now his right obtains,
For ever and for ever reigns.

L. M. **57**

1 THE great archangel's trump shall sound
(While twice ten thousand thunders
roar,)
Tear up the graves, and cleave the ground,
And make the greedy sea restore.

2 The greedy sea shall yield her dead,
The earth no more her slain conceal;
Sinners shall lift their guilty head,
And shrink to see a yawning hell.

3 But we, who now our Lord confess,
And faithful to the end endure,
Shall stand in Jesu's righteousness,
Stand, as the Rock of ages, sure.

4 We, while the stars from heaven shall fall
And mountains are on mountains hurled,
Shall stand unmoved amidst them all,
And smile to see a burning world.

5 The earth, and all the works therein,
Dissolve by raging flames destroyed,
While we survey the awful scene,
And mount above the fiery void.

6 By faith we now transcend the skies,
And on that ruined world look down;
By love above all height we rise,
And share the everlasting throne.

58
7 s & 6 s.

1 JESUS, faithful to his word,
Shall with a shout descend;
All heaven's host their glorious Lord
Shall pompously attend:
Christ shall come with dreadful noise,
Lightnings swift, and thunders loud;
With the great archangel's voice,
And with the trump of God.

2 First the dead in Christ shall rise;
Then we that yet remain
Shall be caught up to the skies,
And see our Lord again:
We shall meet him in the air,
All rapt up to heaven shall be,
Find, and love, and praise him there,
To all eternity.

3 Who can tell the happiness
This glorious hope affords?
Joy unuttered we possess
In these reviving words:
Happy while on earth we breathe,
Mightier bliss ordained to know,
Trampling down sin, hell, and death,
To the third heaven we go.

59
8 s & 6 s.

1 THOU God of glorious majesty,
To thee, against myself, to thee,
A worm of earth, I cry;
A half-awakened child of man;
An heir of endless bliss or pain;
A sinner born to die!

2 Lo! on a narrow neck of land,
'Twixt two unbounded seas I stand,
Secure, insensible;
A point of time, a moment's space,
Removes me to that heavenly place,
Or shuts me up in hell.

3 O God, mine inmost soul convert!
And deeply on my thoughtful heart
Eternal things impress:
Give me to feel their solemn weight,
And tremble on the brink of fate,
And wake to righteousness.

4 Before me place, in dread array,
The pomp of that tremendous day,
When thou with clouds shalt come,
To judge the nations at thy bar;
And tell me, Lord, shall I be there
To meet a joyful doom?

5 Be this my one great business here,
With serious industry and fear
Eternal bliss to ensure;
Thine utmost counsel to fulfil,
And suffer all thy righteous will,
And to the end endure.

6 Then, Saviour, then my soul receive,
Transported from this vale to live
And reign with thee above,
Where faith is sweetly lost in sight,
And hope in full supreme delight,
And everlasting love.

60
8 s & 7 s.

1 RIGHTEOUS God! whose vengeful phials
All our fears and thoughts exceed,

Big with woes and fiery trials,
Hanging, bursting o'er our head;
While thou visitest the nations,
Thy selected people spare:
Arm our cautioned souls with patience,
Fill our humbled hearts with prayer.

2 If thy dreadful controversy
With all flesh is now begun,
In thy wrath remember mercy,
Mercy first and last be shown:
Plead thy cause with sword and fire,
Shake us till the curse remove,
Till thou com'st, the world's desire,
Conquering all with sovereign love.

3 Every fresh alarming token
More confirms the faithful word;
Nature (for its Lord hath spoken)
Must be suddenly restored:
From this national confusion,
From this ruined earth and skies,
See the times of restitution,
See the new creation rise!

4 Vanish, then, this world of shadows,
Pass the former things away;
Lord, appear! appear to glad us
With the dawn of endless day!
O conclude this mortal story,
Throw this universe aside!
Come, eternal King of glory,
Now descend, and take thy bride!

61
7 s & 6 s †.

1 STAND the omnipotent decree!
Jehovah's will be done!
Nature's end we wait to see,
And hear her final groan:
Let this earth dissolve, and blend
In death the wicked and the just,
Let those ponderous orbs descend,
And grind us into dust.

2 Rests secure the righteous man!
At his Redeemer's beck,
Sure to emerge, and rise again,
And mount above the wreck;
Lo! the heavenly spirit towers,
Like flame, o'er nature's funeral pyre,
Triumphs in immortal powers,
And claps his wings of fire!

3 Nothing hath the just to lose
By worlds on worlds destroyed;
Far beneath his feet he views,
With smiles, the flaming void;
Sees the universe renewed,
The grand millennial reign begun,
Shouts, with all the sons of God,
Around the eternal throne.

4 Resting in this glorious hope
To be at last restored,
Yield we now our bodies up
To earthquake, plague, or sword;
Listening for the call divine,
The latest trumpet of the seven,
Soon our soul and dust shall join,
And both fly up to heaven.

62
8 s & 6 s.

1 HOW happy are the little flock, [Rock,
Who, safe beneath their guardian

15

In all commotions rest !
When war's and tumult's waves run high,
  Unmoved above the storm they lie,
    They lodge in Jesu's breast.

2 Such happiness, O Lord, have we,
  By mercy gathered unto thee,
    Before the floods descend :
And while the bursting clouds come down,
We mark the vengeful day begun,
    And calmly wait the end.

3 The plague, and dearth, and din of war,
Our Saviour's swift approach declare,
    And bid our hearts arise ;
Earth's basis shook confirms our hope ;
Its cities' fall but lifts us up,
    To meet thee in the skies.

4 Thy tokens we with joy confess ?
The war proclaims the Prince of peace,
    The earthquake speaks thy power.
The famine all thy fulness brings,
The plague presents thy healing wings,
    And nature's final hour.

5 Whatever ills the world befall,
A pledge of endless good we call,
    A sign of Jesus near :
His chariot will not long delay,
We hear the rumbling wheels, and pray,
    Triumphant Lord, appear !

6 Appear with clouds on Zion's hill,
Thy word and mystery to fulfil,
    Thy confessors to approve.
Thy members on thy throne to place,
And stamp thy name on every face,
    In glorious, heavenly love !

63   C. M.

1 WOE to the men on earth who dwell,
  Nor dread the Almighty's frown,
When God doth all his wrath reveal,
  And shower his judgments down !

2 Sinners, expect those heaviest showers,
  To meet your God prepare ;
For, lo ! the seventh angel pours
  His phial in the air.

3 Lo ! from their seats the mountains leap,
  The mountains are not found ;
Transported far into the deep,
  And in the ocean drowned.

4 Who then shall live, and face the throne,
  And face the Judge severe?
When heaven and earth are fled and gone,
  O where shall I appear?

5 Now, only now, against that hour
  We may a place provide ;
Beyond the grave, beyond the power
  Of hell, our spirits hide :

6 Firm in the all-destroying shock,
  May view the final scene ;
For, lo ! the everlasting Rock
  Is cleft to take us in.

64   SECOND PART.   C. M.

1 BY faith we find the place above,
  The Rock that rent in twain ;
Beneath the shade of dying love,
  And in the clefts remain.
16

2 Jesus, to thy dear wounds we flee,
  We sink into thy side ;
Assured that all who trust in thee
  Shall evermore abide.

3 Then let the thundering trumpet sound,
  The latest lightning glare,
The mountains melt, the solid ground
  Dissolve as liquid air ;

4 The huge celestial bodies roll,
  Amidst that general fire,
And shrivel as a parchment-scroll,
  And all in smoke expire !

5 Yet still the Lord, the Saviour reigns,
  When nature is destroyed,
And no created thing remains
  Throughout the flaming void.

6 Sublime upon his azure throne,
  He speaks the almighty word ;
His *fiat* is obeyed ! 'tis done ;
  And Paradise restored.

7 So be it ! let this system end,
  This ruinous earth and skies,
The new Jerusalem descend,
  The new creation rise !

8 Thy power omnipotent assume,
  Thy brightest majesty !
And when thou dost in glory come,
  My Lord, remember me !

65   4-6 s & 2-8 s.

1 YE virgin souls, arise,
  With all the dead awake !
Unto salvation wise,
  Oil in your vessels take ;
Upstarting at the midnight cry,
"Behold the heavenly Bridegroom nigh !"

2 He comes, he comes to call
  The nations to his bar,
And raise to glory all
  Who fit for glory are ;
Made ready for your full reward,
Go forth with joy to meet your Lord.

3 Go, meet him in the sky,
  Your everlasting Friend ;
Your Head to glorify,
  With all his saints ascend :
Ye pure in heart, obtain the grace
To see, without a veil, his face !

4 Ye that have here received
  The unction from above,
And in his Spirit lived,
  Obedient to his love,
Jesus shall claim you for his bride :
Rejoice with all the sanctified !

5 The everlasting doors
  Shall soon the saints receive,
Above yon angel powers
  In glorious joy to live ;
Far from a world of grief and sin,
With God eternally shut in.

6 Then let us wait to hear
  The trumpet's welcome sound ;
To see our Lord appear,
  Watching let us be found :
When Jesus doth the heavens bow,
Be found—as, Lord, thou find'st us now !

66*

8 7 8, 7 4 7.

1 LO ! He comes with clouds descending,
Once for favoured sinners slain ;
Thousand thousand saints attending,
Swell the triumph of his train :
Hallelujah !
God appears on earth to reign.

2 Every eye shall now behold him
Robed in dreadful majesty ;
Those who set at nought and sold him,
Pierced and nailed him to the tree,
Deeply wailing,
Shall the true Messiah see.

3 The dear tokens of his passion
Still his dazzling body bears ;
Cause of endless exultation
To his ransomed worshippers ;
With what rapture
Gaze we on those glorious scars !

4 Yea, Amen ! let all adore thee,
High on thy eternal throne ;
Saviour, take the power and glory,
Claim the kingdom for thine own ;
Jah, Jehovah,
Everlasting God, come down !

67

(5.) DESCRIBING HEAVEN.

2 - 6 s & 4 - 7 s.

1 HOW weak the thoughts, and vain,
Of self-deluding men !
Men who, fixed to earth alone,
Think their houses shall endure,
Fondly call their lands their own,
To their distant heirs secure.

2 How happy then are we,
Who build, O Lord, on thee !
What can our foundation shock ?
Though the shattered earth remove,
Stands our city on a rock,
On the Rock of heavenly love.

3 A house we call our own
Which cannot be o'erthrown ;
In the general ruin sure,
Storms and earthquakes it defies ;
Built immovably secure,
Built eternal in the skies.

4 High on Immanuel's land
We see the fabric stand :
From a tottering world remove
To our steadfast mansion there ;
Our inheritance above
Cannot pass from heir to heir.

5 Those amaranthine bowers
(Unalienably ours)
Bloom, our infinite reward,
Rise, our permanent abode :
From the founded world prepared ;
Purchased by the blood of God.

6 O might we quickly find
The place for us designed ;
See the long-expected day
Of our full redemption here ;
Let the shadows flee away,
Let the new-made world appear !

---

7 High on thy great white throne,
O King of saints come down !
In the new Jerusalem
Now triumphantly descend ;
Let the final trump proclaim
Joys begun which ne'er shall end !

68

8 s & 6 s.

1 HOW happy is the pilgrim's lot !
How free from every anxious thought,
From worldly hope and fear !
Confined to neither court nor cell,
His soul disdains on earth to dwell,
He only sojourns here.

2 This happiness in part is mine,
Already saved from self-design,
From every creature-love ;
Blest with the scorn of finite good,
My soul is lightened of its load,
And seeks the things above.

3 The things eternal I pursue,
A happiness beyond the view
Of those that basely pant
For things by nature felt and seen ;
Their honours, wealth, and pleasures mean
I neither have nor want.

4 I have no babes to hold me here ;
But children more securely dear
For mine I humbly claim,
Better than daughters or than sons,
Temples divine of living stones,
Inscribed with Jesu's name.

5 No foot of land do I possess,
No cottage in this wilderness,
A poor wayfaring man,
I lodge awhile in tents below ;
Or gladly wander to and fro,
Till I my Canaan gain.

6 Nothing on earth I call my own ;
A stranger, to the world unknown,
I all their goods despise ;
I trample on their whole delight,
And seek a country out of sight,
A country in the skies.

7 There is my house and portion fair,
My treasure and my heart are there,
And my abiding home ;
For me my elder brethren stay,
And angels beckon me away,
And Jesus bids me come.

8 I come, thy servant, Lord, replies,
I come to meet thee in the skies,
And claim my heavenly rest ;
Now let the pilgrim's journey end,
Now, O my Saviour, Brother, Friend,
Receive me to thy breast !

69

6 - 8 s.

1 THOU, Lord, on whom I still depend,
Shalt keep me faithful to the end ;
I trust thy truth, and love, and power
Shall save me till my latest hour ;
And when I lay this body down,
Reward with an immortal crown.

2 Jesus, in thy great name I go
To conquer death, my final foe ;

17

And when I quit this cumbrous clay,
And soar on angels' wings away,
My soul the second death defies,
And reigns eternal in the skies.

3 Eye hath not seen, nor ear hath heard,
What Christ hath for his saints prepared,
Who conquer through their Saviour's might,
Who sink into perfection's height,
And trample death beneath their feet,
And gladly die their Lord to meet.

4 Dost thou desire to know and see
What thy mysterious name shall be?
Contending for thy heavenly home,
Thy latest foe in death o'ercome ;
Till then, thou searchest out in vain
What only conquest can explain.

70   8 s.

1 I LONG to behold Him arrayed
With glory and light from above,
The King in his beauty displayed,
His beauty of holiest love :
I languish and sigh to be there,
Where Jesus hath fixed his abode ;
O when shall we meet in the air,
And fly to the mountain of God !

2 With him I on Zion shall stand,
(For Jesus hath spoken the word)
The breadth of Immanuel's land
Survey by the light of my Lord ;
But when, on thy bosom reclined,
Thy face I am strengthened to see,
My fulness of rapture I find,
My heaven of heavens in thee.

3 How happy the people that dwell
Secure in the city above !
No pain the inhabitants feel,
No sickness or sorrow shall prove !
Physician of souls, unto me
Forgiveness and holiness give ;
And then from the body set free,
And then to the city receive.

71   6 - 8 s.

1 LEADER of faithful souls, and guide
Of all that travel to the sky,
Come and with us, even us, abide,
Who would on thee alone rely,
On thee alone our spirits stay,
While held in life's uneven way.

2 Strangers and pilgrims here below,
This earth, we know, is not our place,
And hasten through the vale of woe ;
And, restless to behold thy face,
Swift to our heavenly country move,
Our everlasting home above.

3 We have no abiding city here,
But seek a city out of sight ;
Thither our steady course we steer,
Aspiring to the plains of light,
Jerusalem, the saints' abode,
Whose founder is the living God.

4 Patient the appointed race to run,
This weary world we cast behind ;
From strength to strength we travel on,
The new Jerusalem to find ;
18

Our labour this, our only aim,
To find the new Jerusalem.

5 Through thee, who all our sins hast borne,
Freely and graciously forgiven,
With songs to Zion we return,
Contending for our native heaven ;
That palace of our glorious King,
We find it nearer while we sing.

6 Raised by the breath of love divine,
We urge our way with strength renewed,
The church of the first-born to join,
We travel to the mount of God,
With joy upon our heads arise,
And meet our Captain in the skies.

72   6 - 8 s.

1 SAVIOUR, on me the grace bestow
To trample on my mortal foe ;
Conqueror of death with thee to rise,
And claim my station in the skies,
Fixed as the throne which ne'er can move,
A pillar in thy church above.

2 As beautiful as useful there,
May I that weight of glory bear,
With all who finally o'ercome,
Supporters of the heavenly dome ;
Of perfect holiness possessed,
For ever in thy presence blessed.

3 Write upon me the name divine,
And let thy Father's nature shine,
His image visibly exprest,
His glory pouring from my breast,
O'er all my bright humanity,
For ever like the God I see !

4 Inscribing with the city's name,
The heavenly new Jerusalem,
To me the victor's title give,
Among thy glorious saints to live,
And all their happiness to know,
A citizen of heaven below.

5 When thou hadst all thy foes o'ercome,
Returning to thy glorious home,
Thou didst receive the full reward,
That I might share it with my Lord ;
And thus thy own new name obtain,
And one with thee for ever reign.

73   8 s.

1 AWAY with our sorrow and fear !
We soon shall recover our home,
The city of saints shall appear,
The day of eternity come :
From earth we shall quickly remove,
And mount to our native abode,
The house of our Father above,
The palace of angels and God.

2 Our mourning is all at an end,
When, raised by the life-giving word,
We see the new city descend,
Adorned as a bride for her Lord ;
The city so holy and clean,
No sorrow can breathe in the air ;
No gloom of affliction or sin,
No shadow of evil is there.

3 By faith we already behold
That lovely Jerusalem here ;

Her walls are of jasper and gold,
  As crystal her buildings are clear ;
Immovably founded in grace,
  She stands as she ever hath stood;
And brightly her builder displays,
  And flames with the glory of God.

4 No need of the sun in that day,
  Which never is followed by night,
Where Jesus's beauties display
  A pure and a permanent light :
The Lamb is their light and their sun,
  And lo ! by reflection they shine,
With Jesus ineffably one,
  And bright in effulgence divine !

5 The saints in his presence receive
  Their great and eternal reward :
In Jesus, in heaven they live,
  They reign in the smile of their Lord :
The flame of angelical love
  Is kindled at Jesus's face ;
And all the enjoyment above
  Consists in the rapturous gaze.

74
S. M.

1 WE know, by faith we know,
  If this vile house of clay,
This tabernacle, sink below
  In ruinous decay,
We have a house above,
  Not made with mortal hands ;
And firm, as our Redeemer's love,
That heavenly fabric stands.

2 It stands securely high,
  Indissolubly sure ;
Our glorious mansion in the sky
  Shall evermore endure :
O were we entered there,
  To perfect heaven restored !
O were we all caught up to share
  The triumph of our Lord !

3 For this in faith we call,
  For this we weep and pray ;
O might the tabernacle fall !
  O might we 'scape away !
Full of immortal hope,
  We urge the restless strife,
And hasten to be swallowed up
  Of everlasting life.

4 Absent, alas ! from God,
  We in the body mourn,
And pine to quit this mean abode,
  And languish to return.
Jesus, regard our vows,
  And change our faith to sight ;
And clothe us with our nobler house,
  Of empyrean light !

5 O let us put on thee
  In perfect holiness,
And rise prepared thy face to see,
  Thy bright, unclouded face !
Thy grace with glory crown,
  Who hast the earnest given,
And now triumphantly come down,
  And take our souls to heaven !

75
8- 7 s.

1 LIFT your eyes of faith, and see
  Saints and angels joined in one ;

What a countless company
  Stand before yon dazzling throne !
Each before his Saviour stands,
  All in milk-white robes arrayed,
Palms they carry in their hands,
  Crowns of glory on their head.

2 Saints begin the endless song,
  Cry aloud in heavenly lays,
Glory doth to God belong,
  God, the glorious Saviour, praise :
All salvation from him came,
  Him, who reigns enthroned on high :
Glory to the bleeding Lamb,
  Let the morning stars reply.

3 Angel-powers the throne surround,
  Next the saints in glory they ;
Lulled with the transporting sound,
  They their silent homage pay,
Prostrate on their face before
  God and his Messiah fall ;
Then in hymns of praise adore,
  Shout the Lamb that died for all.

4 Be it so, they all reply,
  Him let all our orders praise ;
Him that did for sinners die,
  Saviour of the favoured race !
Render we our God his right,
  Glory, wisdom, thanks, and power,
Honour, majesty, and might ;
  Praise him, praise him evermore !

76
8 - 7 s.

1 WHAT are these arrayed in white,
  Brighter than the noonday sun ?
Foremost of the sons of light,
  Nearest the eternal throne ?
These are they that bore the cross,
  Nobly for their Master stood ;
Sufferers in his righteous cause,
  Followers of the dying God.

2 Out of great distress they came,
  Washed their robes by faith below,
In the blood of yonder Lamb,
  Blood that washes white as snow :
Therefore are they next the throne,
  Serve their Maker day and night ;
God resides among his own,
  God doth in his saints delight.

3 More than conquerors at last,
  Here they find their trials o'er ;
They have all their sufferings past,
  Hunger now and thirst no more :
No excessive heat they feel
  From the sun's directer ray,
In a milder clime they dwell,
  Region of eternal day.

4 He that on the throne doth reign,
  Them the Lamb shall always feed,
With the tree of life sustain,
  To the living fountains lead ;
He shall all their sorrows chase,
  All their wants at once remove,
Wipe the tears from every face,
  Fill up every soul with love.

77
8 s.

1 THE Church in her militant state
  Is weary, and cannot forbear ;

The saints in an agony wait
  To see him again in the air;
The Spirit invites, in the bride.
  Her heavenly Lord to descend,
And place her, enthroned at his side,
  In glory that never shall end.

2 The news of his coming I hear,
  And join in the catholic cry,
O Jesus, in triumph appear,
  Appear in the clouds of the sky!
Whom only I languish to love,
  In fulness of majesty come,
And give me a mansion above,
  And take to my heavenly home.

78　　　　　　　　8 s.

1 THE thirsty are called to their Lord,
    His glorious appearing to see;
And, drawn by the power of his word,
  The promise I know is for me:
I thirst for the streams of thy grace,
  I gasp for the Spirit of love;
I long for a glimpse of thy face,
  And then to behold it above.

2 Thy call I exult to obey,
  And come, in the spirit of prayer,
Thy joy in that happiest day,
  Thy kingdom of glory, to share:
To drink the pure river of bliss,
  With life everlasting o'erflowed,
Implunged in the crystal abyss,
  And lost in the ocean of God.

79　　　　　　　　8 s.

1 A FOUNTAIN of life and of grace
    In Christ, our Redeemer, we see:
For us, who his offers embrace,
  · For all, it is open and free.
Jehovah himself doth invite
  To drink of his pleasures unknown,
The streams of immortal delight,
  That flow from his heavenly throne.

2 As soon as in him we believe,
  By faith of his Spirit we take;
And, freely forgiven, receive
  The mercy for Jesus's sake;
We gain a pure drop of his love,
  The life of eternity know,
Angelical happiness prove,
  Aud witness a heaven below.

(6.) DESCRIBING HELL.

80　　　　　　　　C. M.

1 TERRIBLE thought! shall I alone,
    Who may be saved—shall I—
Of all, alas! whom I have known,
  Through sin for ever die?

2 While all my old companions dear,
  With whom I once did live,
Joyful at God's right hand appear,
  A blessing to receive;

3 Shall I—amidst a ghastly band,
    Dragged to the judgment-seat—
Far on the left with horror stand,
  My fearful doom to meet?
20

4 Ah, no! I still may turn and live,
  For still his wrath delays;
He now vouchsafes a kind reprieve,
  And offers me his grace.

5 I will accept his offers now,
  From every sin depart,
Perform my oft-repeated vow,
  And render him my heart.

6 I will improve what I receive,
  The grace through Jesus given;
Sure, if with God on earth I live,
  To live with him in heaven.

SECTION III.

PRAYING FOR A BLESSING.

81

6 - 8 s.

1 FATHER of omnipresent grace!
    We seem agreed to seek thy face;
But every soul assembled here
Doth naked in thy sight appear:
Thou know'st who only bows the knee,
And who in heart approaches thee.

2 Thy Spirit hath the difference made
Betwixt the living and the dead;
Thou now dost into some inspire
The pure, benevolent desire:
O that even now thy powerful call
May quicken and convert us all!

3 The sinners suddenly convince,
O'erwhelmed beneath their load of sins;
To-day, while it is called to-day,
Awake, and stir them up to pray,
Their dire captivity to own,
And from the iron furnace groan.

4 Then, then acknowledge, and set free
The people bought, O Lord, by thee!
The sheep for whom their Shepherd bled,
For whom we in thy Spirit plead:
Let all in thee redemption find,
And not a soul be left behind.

82

L. M.

1 SHEPHERD of souls, with pitying eye,
    The thousands of our Israel see:
To thee in their behalf we cry,
  Ourselves but newly found in thee.

2 See where o'er desert wastes they err,
  And neither food nor feeder have,
Nor fold, nor place of refuge near,
  For no man cares their souls to save.

3 Wild as the untaught Indian's brood
  The Christian savages remain;
Strangers, yea, enemies to God,
  They make thee spill thy blood in vain.

4 Thy people, Lord, are sold for nought,
  Nor know they their Redeemer nigh;
They perish, whom thyself hast bought,
  Their souls for lack of knowledge die.

5 The pit its mouth hath opened wide,
  To swallow up its careless prey:
Why should *they* die, when *thou* hast died,
  Hast died to bear their sins away?

6 Why should the foe thy purchase seize?
   Remember, Lord, thy dying groans:
The meed of all thy sufferings these,
   O claim them for thy ransomed ones!

7 Extend to these thy pardoning grace,
   To these be thy salvation showed:
O add them to thy chosen race!
   O sprinkle all their hearts with blood!

8 Still let the publicans draw near:
   Open the door of faith and heaven,
And grant their hearts thy word to hear,
   And witness all their sins forgiven.

83
C. M

1 THOU Son of God, whose flaming eyes
   Our inmost thoughts perceive,
Accept the evening sacrifice
   Which now to thee we give.

2 We bow before thy gracious throne,
   And think ourselves sincere;
But show us, Lord, is every one
   Thy real worshipper?

3 Is here a soul that knows thee not,
   Nor feels his want of thee?
A stranger to the blood which bought
   His pardon on the tree?

4 Convince him now of unbelief,
   His desperate state explain;
And fill his heart with sacred grief,
   And penitential pain.

5 Speak with that voice which wakes the
   And bid the sleeper rise!   [dead,
And bid his guilty conscience dread
   The death that never dies.

6 Extort the cry, "What must be done
   To save a wretch like me?
How shall a trembling sinner shun
   That endless misery?

7 "I must this instant now begin
   Out of my sleep to awake;
And turn to God, and every sin
   Continually forsake:

8 "I must for faith incessant cry,
   And wrestle, Lord, with thee:
I must be born again, or die
   To all eternity."

84
C. M.

1 COME, O thou all-victorious Lord!
   Thy power to us make known;
Strike with the hammer of thy word,
   And break these hearts of stone.

2 O that we all might now begin
   Our foolishness to mourn;
And turn at once from every sin,
   And to our Saviour turn!

3 Give us ourselves and thee to know,
   In this our gracious day;
Repentance unto life bestow,
   And take our sins away.

4 Conclude us first in unbelief,
   And freely then release;
Fill every soul with sacred grief,
   And then with sacred peace.

5 Impoverish, Lord, and then relieve,
   And then enrich the poor;

The knowledge of our sickness give,
   The knowledge of our cure.

6 That blessed sense of guilt impart,
   And then remove the load;
Trouble, and wash the troubled heart
   In the atoning blood.

7 Our desperate state through sin declare,
   And speak our sins forgiven;
By perfect holiness prepare,
   And take us up to heaven.

S. M.
85

1 SPIRIT of faith, come down,
   Reveal the things of God;
And make to us the Godhead known,
   And witness with the blood:
'Tis thine the blood to apply,
   And give us eyes to see,
Who did for every sinner die,
   Hath surely died for me.

2 No man can truly say
   That Jesus is the Lord,
Unless thou take the veil away,
   And breathe the living word;
Then, only then, we feel
   Our interest in his blood,
And cry, with joy unspeakable,
   "Thou art my Lord, my God!"

3 O that the world might know
   The all-atoning Lamb!
Spirit of faith, descend, and show
   The virtue of his name;
The grace which all may find,
   The saving power impart;
And testify to all mankind,
   And speak in every heart.

4 Inspire the living faith,
   Which whosoe'er receives,
The witness in himself he hath,
   And consciously believes;
The faith that conquers all,
   And doth the mountain move,
And saves whoe'er on Jesus call,
   And perfects them in love.

2-6s & 4-7s.
86

1 SINNERS, your hearts lift up,
   Partakers of your hope!
This, the day of Pentecost;
   Ask, and ye shall all receive,
Surely now the Holy Ghost
   God to all that ask shall give.

2 Ye all may freely take
   The grace for Jesu's sake;
He for every man hath died,
He for all hath risen again;
Jesus now is glorified,
   Gifts he hath received for men.

3 He sends them from the skies
   On all his enemies;
By his cross he now hath led
Captive our captivity;
We shall all be free indeed,
Christ, the Son, shall make us free.

4 Blessings on all he pours,
   In never-ceasing showers,

21

All he waters from above;
  Offers all his joy and peace,
Settled comfort, perfect love,
  Everlasting righteousness.

5 All may from him receive
  A power to turn and live;
Grace for every soul is free,
  All may hear the effectual call;
All the light of life may see,
  All may feel he died for all.

6 Drop down in showers of love,
  Ye heavens, from above!
Righteousness, ye skies, pour down!
  Open, earth, and take it in!
Claim the Spirit for your own,
  Sinners, and be saved from sin!

7 Father, behold, we claim
  The gift in Jesu's name!
Him, the promised Comforter,
  Into all our spirits pour;
Let him fix his mansion here,
  Come, and never leave us more.

87   *Before Reading the Scriptures.*   C. M.

1 COME, Holy Ghost, our hearts inspire,
  Let us thine influence prove,
Source of the old prophetic fire,
  Fountain of light and love.

2 Come, Holy Ghost, (for moved by thee
  The prophets wrote and spoke)
Unlock the truth, thyself the key,
  Unseal the sacred book.

3 Expand thy wings, celestial Dove,
  Brood o'er our nature's night;
On our disordered spirits move,
  And let there now be light.

4 God, through himself, we then shall know,
  If thou within us shine,
And sound, with all thy saints below,
  The depths of love divine.

88   *The same subject.*   C. M.

1 FATHER of all, in whom alone
  We live, and move, and breathe,
One bright celestial ray dart down,
  And cheer thy sons beneath.

2 While in thy word we search for thee,
  (We search with trembling awe!)
Open our eyes, and let us see
  The wonders of thy law.

3 Now let our darkness comprehend
  The light that shines so clear;
Now the revealing Spirit send,
  And give us ears to hear.

4 Before us make thy goodness pass,
  Which here by faith we know;
Let us in Jesus see thy face,
  And die to all below.

89   2 Timothy iii. 16, 17.   6-8 s.

1 INSPIRER of the ancient seers,
  Who wrote from thee the sacred page,
The same through all succeeding years,
  To us, in our degenerate age,
The spirit of thy word impart,
And breathe the life into our heart.

22

2 While now thine oracles we read,
  With earnest prayer and strong desire,
O let thy Spirit from thee proceed,
  Our souls to awaken and inspire,
Our weakness help, our darkness chase,
And guide us by the light of grace!

3 Whene'er in error's paths we rove,
  The living God through sin forsake,
Our conscience by thy word reprove,
  Convince and bring the wanderers back,
Deep wounded by thy Spirit's sword,
And then by Gilead's balm restored.

4 The sacred lessons of thy grace,
  Transmitted through thy word, repeat,
And train us up in all thy ways,
  To make us in thy will complete;
Fulfil thy love's redeeming plan,
And bring us to a perfect man.

5 Furnished out of thy treasury,
  O may we always ready stand
To help the souls redeemed by thee,
  In what their various states demand;
To teach, convince, correct, reprove,
And build them up in holiest love!

6-8 s.   Luke xxiv. 45.   *90

1 COME, O thou Prophet of the Lord,
  Thou great Interpreter divine,
Explain thine own transmitted word,
  To teach and to inspire is thine;
Thou only canst thyself reveal,
Open the book, and loose the seal.

2 Whate'er the ancient prophets spoke
  Concerning thee, O Christ, make known;
Chief subject of the sacred book,
  Thou fillest all, and thou alone;
Yet there our Lord we cannot see,
Unless thy Spirit lend the key.

3 Now, Jesus, now the veil remove,
  The folly of our darkened heart;
Unfold the wonders of thy love,
  The knowledge of thyself impart;
Our ear, our inmost soul, we bow,
Speak, Lord, thy servants hearken now.

PART II. CONVINCING.

SECTION I.

DESCRIBING FORMAL RELIGION.

C. M.   **91**

1 LONG have I seemed to serve thee, Lord,
  With unavailing pain;
Fasted, and prayed, and read thy word,
  And heard it preached in vain.

2 Oft did I with the assembly join,
  And near thine altar drew;
A form of godliness was mine,
  The power I never knew.

3 I rested in the outward law,
  Nor knew its deep design;
The length and breadth I never saw,
  And height, of love divine.

4 To please thee thus, at length I see,
   Vainly I hoped and strove;
For what are outward things to thee,
   Unless they spring from love?

5 I see the perfect law requires
   Truth in the inward parts,
Our full consent, our whole desires,
   Our undivided hearts.

6 But I of means have made my boast,
   Of means an idol made;
The spirit in the letter lost,
   The substance in the shade.

7 Where am I now, or what my hope?
   What can my weakness do?
Jesus, to thee my soul looks up,
   'Tis thou must make it new.

92
C. M.

1 STILL for thy loving-kindness, Lord,
   I in thy temple wait;
I look to find thee in thy word,
   Or at thy table meet.

2 Here, in thine own appointed ways,
   I wait to learn thy will;
Silent I stand before thy face,
   And hear thee say, "Be still!"

3 "Be still! and know that I am God!"—
   'Tis all I live to know;
To feel the virtue of thy blood,
   And spread its praise below.

4 I wait my vigour to renew,
   Thine image to retrieve,
The veil of outward things pass through,
   And gasp in thee to live.

5 I work, and own the labour vain,
   And thus from works I cease;
I strive, and see my fruitless pain,
   Till God create my peace.

6 Fruitless, till thou thyself impart,
   Must all my efforts prove;
They cannot change a sinful heart;
   They cannot purchase love.

7 I do the thing thy laws enjoin,
   And then the strife give o'er;
To thee I then the whole resign,
   I trust in means no more.

8 I trust in him who stands between
   The Father's wrath and me;
Jesu, thou great eternal Mean,
   I look for all from thee.

93
S. M.

1 MY gracious, loving Lord,
   To thee what shall I say?
Well may I tremble at thy word,
   And scarce presume to pray!
Ten thousand wants have I;
   Alas! I all things want;
And thou hast bid me always cry,
   And never, never faint.

2 Yet, Lord, well might I fear,
   Fear even to ask thy grace;
So oft have I, alas! drawn near,
   And mocked thee to thy face:

With all pollutions stained,
   Thy hallowed courts I trod,
Thy name and temple I profaned,
   And dared to call thee God!

3 Nigh with my lips I drew,
   My lips were all unclean;
Thee with my heart I never knew,
   My heart was full of sin;
Far from the living Lord,
   As far as hell from heaven,
Thy purity I still abhorred,
   Nor looked to be forgiven.

4 My nature I obeyed,
   My own desires pursued;
And still a den of thieves I made
   The hallowed house of God.
The worship he approves
   To him I would not pay;
My selfish ends and creature-loves
   Had stole my heart away.

5 A goodly, formal saint
   I long appeared in sight,
By self and Satan taught to paint
   My tomb, my nature, white.
The Pharisee within
   Still undisturbed remained,
The strong man, armed with guilt of sin,
   Safe in his palace reigned.

6 But O! the jealous God
   In my behalf came down;
Jesus himself the stronger showed,
   And claimed me for his own:
My spirit he alarmed,
   And brought into distress;
He shook and bound the strong man armed
   In his self-righteousness.

7 Faded my virtuous show,
   My form without the power;
The sin-convincing Spirit blew,
   And blasted every flower:
My mouth was stopped, and shame
   Covered my guilty face;
I fell on the atoning Lamb,
   And I was saved by grace.

C. M.   Jeremiah vii. 4.   ## 94

1 THE men who slight thy faithful word,
   In their own lies confide,
These are the temple of the Lord,
   And heathens all beside!

2 The temple of the Lord are these,
   The only church and true,
Who live in pomp, and wealth, and ease,
   And Jesus never knew.

3 The temple of the Lord—they pull
   Thy living temples down,
And cast out every gracious soul
   That trembles at thy frown:

4 O wouldst thou, Lord, reveal their sins,
   And turn their joy to grief,
The world, the Christian world, convince
   Of damning unbelief!

5 The formalists confound, convert,
   And to thy people join;
And break, and fill the broken heart
   With confidence divine!

SECTION II.

DESCRIBING INWARD RELIGION.

95   L. M.

1 AUTHOR of faith, eternal Word,
    Whose Spirit breathes the active
Faith, like its Finisher and Lord, [flame;
    To-day as yesterday the same;

2 To thee our humble hearts aspire,
    And ask the gift unspeakable;
Increase in us the kindled fire,
    In us the work of faith fulfil.

3 By faith we know thee strong to save;
    (Save us, a present Saviour thou l)
Whate'er we hope, by faith we have,
    Future and past subsisting now.

4 To him that in thy name believes
    Eternal life with thee is given;
Into himself he all receives,
    Pardon, and holiness, and heaven.

5 The things unknown to feeble sense,
    Unseen by reason's glimmering ray,
With strong, commanding evidence,
    Their heavenly origin display.

6 Faith lends its realizing light,
    The clouds disperse, the shadows fly;
The Invisible appears in sight,
    And God is seen by mortal eye.

96   S. M.

1 HOW can a sinner know
    His sins on earth forgiven?
How can my gracious Saviour show
    My name inscribed in heaven?
What we have felt and seen,
    With confidence we tell;
And publish to the sons of men
    The signs infallible.

2 We who in Christ believe
    That he for us hath died;
We all his unknown peace receive,
    And feel his blood applied;
Exults our rising soul,
    Disburdened of her load,
And swells unutterably full
    Of glory and of God.

3 His love, surpassing far
    The love of all beneath,
We find within our hearts, and dare
    The pointless darts of death:
Stronger than death and hell
    The mystic power we prove;
And conquerors of the world, we dwell
    In heaven, who dwell in love.

4 We by his Spirit prove
    And know the things of God,
The things which freely of his love
    He hath on us bestowed;
His Spirit to us he gave,
    And dwells in us, we know;
The witness in ourselves we have,
    And all its fruits we show.

5 The meek and lowly heart
    That in our Saviour was,
To us his Spirit doth impart,
    And signs us with his cross:
24

Our nature's turned, our mind
    Transformed in all its powers;
And both the witnesses are joined,
    The Spirit of God with ours.

6 Whate'er our pardoning Lord
    Commands, we gladly do;
And guided by his sacred word,
    We all his steps pursue: ,
His glory our design,
    We live our God to please;
And rise with filial fear divine,
    To perfect holiness.

*97

8 s & 6 s.

1 THOU great mysterious God unknown,
    Whose love hath gently led me on,
      Even from my infant days.
Mine inmost soul expose to view,
And tell me, if I ever knew
      Thy justifying grace.

2 If I have only known thy fear,
    And followed with a heart sincere
      Thy drawings from above,
Now, now the further grace bestow,
And let my sprinkled conscience know
      Thy sweet forgiving love.

3 Short of thy love I would not stop,
    A stranger to the gospel hope,
      The sense of sin forgiven;
I would not, Lord, my soul deceive,
Without the inward witness live,
      That antepast of heaven.

4 If now the witness were in me,
    Would he not testify of thee
      In Jesus reconciled?
And should I not with faith draw nigh,
And boldly Abba, Father, cry,
      And know myself thy child?

5 Whate'er obstructs thy pardoning love,
    Or sin, or righteousness remove,
      Thy glory to display;
Mine heart of unbelief convince,
And now absolve me from my sins,
      And take them all away.

6 Father, in me reveal thy Son,
    And to my inmost soul make known
      How merciful thou art:
The secret of thy love reveal,
And by thine hallowing Spirit dwell
      For ever in my heart!

98

7 s & 6 s †.

1 UPRIGHT, both in heart and will,
    We by our God were made;
But we turned from good to ill,
    And o'er the creature strayed;
Multiplied our wandering thought,
Which first was fixed on God alone,
    In ten thousand objects sought
    The bliss we lost in one.

2 From our own inventions vain
    Of fancied happiness,
Draw us to thyself again,
    And bid our wanderings cease;
Jesus, speak our souls restored
    By love's divine simplicity,
Re-united to our Lord,
    And wholly lost in thee!

PART III.

SECTION I.

PRAYING FOR REPENTANCE.

99   6 - 8 s.

1 FATHER of lights, from whom proceeds
    Whate'er thy every creature needs,
Whose goodness, providently nigh,
Feeds the young ravens when they cry,
To thee I look ; my heart prepare,
Suggest, and hearken to my prayer.

2 Since by thy light myself I see
Naked, and poor, and void of thee,
Thy eyes must all my thoughts survey,
Preventing what my lips would say ;
Thou seest my wants, for help they call,
And ere I speak thou know'st them all.

3 Thou know'st the baseness of my mind,
Wayward, and impotent, and blind ;
Thou know'st how unsubdued my will,
Averse from good and prone to ill ;
Thou know'st how wide my passions rove,
Nor checked by fear, nor charmed by love!

4 Fain would I know, as known by thee,
And feel the indigence I see ;
Fain would I all my vileness own,
And deep beneath the burden groan ;
Abhor the pride that lurks within,
Detest and loathe myself and sin.

5 Ah! give me, Lord, myself to feel,
My total misery reveal ;
Ah! give me, Lord, (I still would say)
A heart to mourn, a heart to pray ;
My business this, my only care,
My life, my every breath, be prayer.

100   L. M.

1 JESU, my Advocate above,
    My friend before the throne of love,
If now for me prevails thy prayer,
If now I find thee pleading there,
If thou the secret wish convey,
And sweetly prompt my heart to pray ;
Hear, and my weak petitions join,
Almighty Advocate, to thine.

2 Fain would I know my utmost ill,
And groan my nature's weight to feel,
To feel the clouds that round me roll,
The night that hangs upon my soul,
The darkness of my carnal mind,
My will perverse, my passions blind,
Scattered o'er all the earth abroad,
Immeasurably far from God.

3 Jesu, my heart's desire obtain!
My earnest suit present, and gain ;
My fulness of corruption show,
The knowledge of myself bestow ;
A deeper displacence at sin,
A sharper sense of hell within,
A stronger struggling to get free,
A keener appetite for thee.

4 O sovereign Love, to thee I cry,
Give me thyself, or else I die!

Save me from death, from hell set free,
Death, hell, are but the want of thee,
Quickened by thy imparted flame,
Saved, when possessed of thee, I am ;
My life, my only heaven thou art,
O might I feel thee in my heart!

6 - 7 s.   **101**

1 SAVIOUR, Prince of Israel's race,
    See me from thy lofty throne ;
Give the sweet relenting grace,
    Soften this obdurate stone!
Stone to flesh, O God, convert ;
Cast a look, and break my heart!

2 By thy Spirit, Lord, reprove,
    All my inmost sins reveal,
Sins against thy light and love
    Let me see, and let me feel ;
Sins that crucified my God,
Spilt again thy precious blood.

3 Jesu, seek thy wandering sheep,
    Make me restless to return ;
Bid me look on thee, and weep,
    Bitterly as Peter mourn,
Till I say, by grace restored,
" Now thou know'st I love thee, Lord!"

4 Might I in thy sight appear,
    As the publican distrest,
Stand, not daring to draw near,
    Smite on my unworthy breast,
Groan the sinner's only plea,
" God, be merciful to me I"

5 O remember me for good,
    Passing through the mortal vale!
Show me the atoning blood,
    When my strength and spirit fail ;
Give my gasping soul to see
Jesus crucified for me!

S. M.   **102**

1 O THAT I could repent!
    With all my idols part,
And to thy gracious eye present
    A humble, contrite heart ;
A heart with grief opprest
    For having grieved my God,
A troubled heart that cannot rest,
    Till sprinkled with thy blood.

2 Jesus, on me bestow
    The penitent desire ;
With true sincerity of woe
    My aching breast inspire ;
With softening pity look,
    And melt my hardness down,
Strike with thy love's resistless stroke,
    And break this heart of stone!

S. M.   **103**

1 O THAT I could revere
    My much-offended God!
O that I could but stand in fear
    Of thy afflicting rod!
If mercy cannot draw,
    Thou by thy threatenings move,
And keep an abject soul in awe,
    That will not yield to love.

2 Show me the naked sword
    Impending o'er my head ;

25

O let me tremble at thy word,
  And to my ways take heed!
  With sacred horror fly
  From every sinful snare;
Nor ever, in my Judge's eye,
  My Judge's anger dare.

3 Thou great tremendous God,
  The conscious awe impart:
The grace be now on me bestowed,
  The tender, fleshly heart;
  For Jesu's sake alone
  The stony heart remove,
And melt at last, O melt me down
  Into the mould of love!

104
2 Kings xxii. 19, 20.   C. M

1 O FOR that tenderness of heart
    Which bows before the Lord,
Acknowledging how just thou art,
  And trembles at thy word!
O for those humble, contrite tears
  Which from repentance flow,
That consciousness of guilt which fears
  The long-suspended blow!

2 Saviour, to me in pity give
  The sensible distress,
The pledge thou wilt at last receive,
  And bid me die in peace;
Wilt from the dreadful day remove,
  Before the evil come;
My spirit hide with saints above,
  My body in the tomb.

105
S. M.

1 O THAT I could repent!
    O that I could believe!
Thou by thy voice the marble rent,
  The rock in sunder cleave!
  Thou, by thy two-edged sword,
  My soul and spirit part,
Strike with the hammer of thy word,
  And break my stubborn heart!

2 Saviour, and Prince of peace,
  The double grace bestow;
Unloose the bands of wickedness,
  And let the captive go:
  Grant me my sins to feel,
  And then the load remove;
Wound, and pour in, my wounds to heal,
  The balm of pardoning love.

3 For thy own mercy's sake,
  The cursed thing remove;
And into thy protection take
  The prisoner of thy love:
  In every trying hour
  Stand by my feeble soul;
And screen me from my nature's power,
  Till thou hast made me whole.

4 This is thy will, I know,
  That I should holy be,
Should let my sin this moment go,
  This moment turn to thee:
  O might I now embrace
  Thy all-sufficient power;
And never more to sin give place,
  And never grieve thee more!
26

106
7 s & 6 s †.

1 JESU, let thy pitying eye
    Call back a wandering sheep!
False to thee, like Peter, I
  Would fain, like Peter, weep:
Let me be by grace restored,
On me be all long-suffering shown;
  Turn, and look upon me, Lord,
  And break my heart of stone.

2 Saviour, Prince, enthroned above,
  Repentance to impart,
Give me, through thy dying love,
  The humble, contrite heart:
Give what I have long implored,
A portion of thy grief unknown;
  Turn, and look upon me, Lord,
  And break my heart of stone.

3 See me, Saviour, from above,
  Nor suffer me to die:
Life, and happiness, and love,
  Drop from thy gracious eye:
Speak the reconciling word,
And let thy mercy melt me down;
  Turn, and look upon me, Lord,
  And break my heart of stone.

4 Look, as when thine eye pursued
  The first apostate man,
Saw him weltering in his blood,
  And bade him rise again;
Speak my paradise restored,
Redeem me by thy grace alone;
  Turn, and look upon me, Lord,
  And break my heart of stone.

5 Look, as when thy pity saw
  Thine own in a strange land,
Forced to obey the tyrant's law,
  And feel his heavy hand:
Speak the soul-redeeming word,
And out of Egypt call thy son;
  Turn, and look upon me, Lord,
  And break my heart of stone.

6 Look, as when thy grace beheld
  The harlot in distress,
Dried her tears, her pardon sealed,
  And bade her go in peace:
Vile, like her, and self-abhorred
I at thy feet for mercy groan;
  Turn, and look upon me, Lord,
  And break my heart of stone.

7 Look, as when thy languid eye
  Was closed, that we might live;
"Father," (at the point to die
  My Saviour gasped) "forgive!"
Surely, with that dying word,
He turns, and looks, and cries, "'Tis
O my bleeding, loving Lord, [done!"
  Thou break'st my heart of stone!

*107
L. M.   Isaiah lxi. 1—3.

1 THE Spirit of the Lord our God,
    (Spirit of power, and health, and love)
The Father hath on Christ bestowed,
  And sent him from his throne above;

2 Prophet, and Priest, and King of peace,
  Anointed to declare his will,
To minister his pardoning grace,
  And every sin-sick soul to heal.

3 Sinners, obey the heavenly call;
　　Your prison-doors stand open wide;
　Go forth, for he hath ransomed all,
　　For every soul of man hath died.

4 'Tis his the drooping soul to raise,
　　To rescue all by sin opprest,
　To clothe them with the robes of praise,
　　And give their weary spirits rest;

5 To help their grovelling unbelief,
　　Beauty for ashes to confer,
　The oil of joy for abject grief,
　　Triumphant joy for sad despair;

6 To make them trees of righteousness,
　　The planting of the Lord below,
　To spread the honour of his grace,
　　And on to full perfection grow.

SECTION II.

FOR MOURNERS CONVINCED OF SIN.

108
　　　　　　　　　　　　　　　　　　C. M.

1 ENSLAVED to sense, to pleasure prone,
　　Fond of created good,
　Father, our helplessness we own,
　　And trembling taste our food.

2 Trembling we taste; for, ah! no more
　　To thee the creatures lead;
　Changed, they exert a baneful power,
　　And poison while they feed.

3 Cursed for the sake of wretched man,
　　They now engross him whole;
　With pleasing force on earth detain,
　　And sensualize his soul.

4 Grovelling on earth we still must lie,
　　Till Christ the curse repeal;
　Till Christ, descending from on high,
　　Infected nature heal.

5 Come then, our heavenly Adam, come,
　　Thy healing influence lend,
　Hallow our food, reverse our doom,
　　And bid us eat and live!

6 The bondage of corruption break,
　　For this our spirits groan;
　Thy only will we fain would seek,
　　O save us from our own!

7 Turn the full stream of nature's tide;
　　Let all our actions tend
　To thee their source; thy love the guide,
　　Thy glory be the end.

8 Earth then a scale to heaven shall be,
　　Sense shall point out the road,
　The creatures all shall lead to thee,
　　And all we taste be God.

109
　　　Revelation iii. 17.　　7 s & 6 s t.

1 WRETCHED, helpless, and distrest,
　　Ah! whither shall I fly?
　Ever gasping after rest,
　　I cannot find it nigh:
　Naked, sick, and poor, and blind,
　Fast bound in sin and misery,
　　Friend of sinners, let me find
　B　　My help, my all, in thee!

2 I am all unclean, unclean,
　　Thy purity I want;
　My whole heart is sick of sin,
　　And my whole head is faint;
　Full of putrefying sores,
　Of bruises, and of wounds, my soul
　Looks to Jesus, help implores,
　　And gasps to be made whole.

3 In the wilderness I stray,
　　My foolish heart is blind,
　Nothing do I know; the way
　　Of peace I cannot find:
　Jesu, Lord, restore my sight,
　And take, O take, the veil away!
　Turn my darkness into light,
　　My midnight into day.

4 Naked of thine image, Lord,
　　Forsaken, and alone,
　Unrenewed, and unrestored,
　　I have not thee put on;
　Over me thy mantle spread,
　Send down thy likeness from above,
　Let thy goodness be displayed,
　　And wrap me in thy love.

5 Poor, alas! thou know'st I am,
　　And would be poorer still,
　See my nakedness and shame,
　　And all my vileness feel;
　No good thing in me resides,
　My soul is all an aching void
　Till thy Spirit here abides,
　　And I am filled with God.

6 Jesus, full of truth and grace,
　　In thee is all I want;
　Be the wanderer's resting-place,
　　A cordial to the faint;
　Make me rich, for I am poor;
　In thee may I my Eden find;
　To the dying health restore,
　　And eyesight to the blind.

7 Clothe me with thy holiness,
　　Thy meek humility;
　Put on me my glorious dress,
　　Endue my soul with thee;
　Let thine image be restored,
　Thy name and nature let me prove,
　With thy fulness fill me, Lord,
　　And perfect me in love.

110
7 s & 6 s t.

1 JESU, friend of sinners, hear,
　　Yet once again I pray;
　From my debt of sin set clear,
　　For I have nought to pay;
　Speak, O speak, the kind release,
　A poor backsliding soul restore!
　Love me freely, seal my peace,
　　And bid me sin no more.

2 For my selfishness and pride
　　Thou hast withdrawn thy grace,
　Left me long to wander wide,
　　An outcast from thy face;
　But I now my sins confess,
　And mercy, mercy, I implore;
　Love me freely, seal my peace,
　　And bid me sin no more.

3 Though my sins as mountains rise,
　　And swell and reach to heaven,

Mercy is above the skies,
  I may be still forgiven;
Infinite my sin's increase,
But greater is thy mercy's store;
  Love me freely, seal my peace,
  And bid me sin no more.

4 Sin's deceitfulness hath spread
  A hardness o'er my heart;
But if thou thy Spirit shed,
  This hardness shall depart;
Shed thy love, thy tenderness,
And let me feel thy softening power;
  Love me freely, seal my peace,
  And bid me sin no more.

5 From the oppressive power of sin
  My struggling spirit free;
Perfect righteousness bring in,
  Unspotted purity;
Speak, and all this war shall cease,
And sin shall give its raging o'er;
  Love me freely, seal my peace,
  Aud bid me sin no more.

6 For this only thing I pray,
  And this will I require,
Take the power of sin away,
  Fill me with pure desire;
Perfect me in holiness,
Thine image to my soul restore;
  Love me freely, seal my peace,
  And bid me sin no more.

111*
Isaiah li. 1—4. L. M.

1 THUS saith the Lord i Who seek the
    Lamb,
Who follow after righteousness,
Look to the rock from whence ye came,
The father of the faithful race.

2 Children of faithful Abraham these
  Who dare expect salvation here,
The Lord shall give them gospel peace,
And all his hopeless mourners cheer;

3 Shall soon his fallen Zion raise,
  Her waste and desolate places build;
Pour out the Spirit of his grace,
And make her wilds a fruitful field.

4 The barren souls shall be restored,
  The desert all renewed shall rise,
Bloom as the garden of the Lord,
A fair terrestrial paradise.

5 Gladness and joy shall there be found,
  Thanksgiving and the voice of praise;
The voice of melody shall sound,
And every heart be filled with grace.

6 A law shall soon from him proceed,
  A living, life-infusing word,
The truth that makes you free indeed,
The eternal Spirit of your Lord.

7 His mercy he will cause to rest
  Where all may see their sins forgiven;
May rise, no more by guilt opprest,
And bless the light that leads to heaven.

112
The Good Samaritan.
Luke x. 30. 7 s & 6 s †.

1 WOE is me! what tongue can tell
    My sad afflicted state,
Who my anguish can reveal,
  Or all my woes relate?
28

Fallen among thieves I am,
And they have robbed me of my God,
Turned my glory into shame,
And left me in my blood.

2 O thou good Samaritan ! ' ~
  In thee is all my hope;
Only thou canst succour man,
  And raise the fallen up:
Hearken to my dying cry:
My wounds compassionately see;
Me, a sinner, pass not by,
Who gasp for help from thee.

3 Still thou journeyest where I am,
  Still thy compassions move;
Pity is with thee the same,
  And all thy heart is love:
Stoop to a poor sinner, stoop,
And let thy healing grace abound,
Heal my bruises, and bind up
My spirit's every wound.

4 Saviour of my soul, draw nigh,
  In mercy haste to me,
At the point of death I lie,
  And cannot come to thee;
Now thy kind relief afford,
The wine and oil of grace pour in;
Good Physician, speak the word,
And heal my soul of sin.

5 Pity to my dying cries
  Hath drawn thee from above,
Hovering over me, with eyes
  Of reverence and love.
Now, even now, I see thy face;
The balm of Gilead I receive;
Thou hast saved me by thy grace,
And bade the sinner live.

6 Surely now the bitterness
  Of second death is past;
O my Life, my Righteousness,
  On thee my soul is cast!
Thou hast brought me to thine inn.
And I am of thy promise sure;
Thou shalt cleanse me from all sin,
And all my sickness cure.

7 Perfect then the work begun,
  And make the sinner whole;
All thy will on me be done,
  My body, spirit, soul:
Still preserve me safe from harms,
And kindly for thy patient care,
Take me, Jesus, to thine arms,
And keep me ever there.

6 - 8 s. 113

1 O THOU whom fain my soul would love!
    Whom I would gladly die to know;
This veil of unbelief remove,
  And show me, all thy goodness show;
Jesus, thyself in me reveal,
Tell me thy name, thy nature tell.

2 Hast thou been with me, Lord, so long,
  Yet thee, my Lord, have I not known!
I claim thee with a faltering tongue,
  I pray thee, in a feeble groan,
Tell me, O tell me, who thou art,
And speak thy name into my heart!

3 If now thou talkest by the way
  With such an abject worm as me,

Thy mystery of grace display ;
Open mine eyes that I may see,
That I may understand thy word,
And now cry out—"It is the Lord !"

114
6 - 8 s.

1 JESU, in whom the weary find
Their late, but permanent repose,
Physician of the sin-sick mind,
Relieve my wants, assuage my woes ;
And let my soul on thee be cast,
Till life's fierce tyranny be past.

2 Loosed from my God, and far removed,
Long have I wandered to and fro,
O'er earth in endless circles roved,
Nor found whereon to rest below :
Back to my God at last I fly,
For O, the waters still are high !

3 Selfish pursuits, and nature's maze,
The things of earth, for thee I leave ;
Put forth thy hand, thy hand of grace,
Into the ark of love receive,
Take this poor fluttering soul to rest,
And lodge it, Saviour, in thy breast.

4 Fill with inviolable peace,
'Stablish and keep my settled heart ;
In thee may all my wanderings cease,
From thee no more may I depart :
Thy utmost goodness called to prove,
Loved with an everlasting love !

115
7 s & 6 s t.

1 LET the world their virtue boast,
Their works of righteousness ;
I, a wretch undone and lost,
Am freely saved by grace ;
Other title I disclaim ;
This, only this, is all my plea,
I the chief of sinners am,
But Jesus died for me.

2 Happy they whose joys abound
Like Jordan's swelling stream,
Who their heaven in Christ have found,
And give the praise to him :
Meanest follower of the Lamb,
His steps I at a distance see ;
I the chief of sinners am,
But Jesus died for me.

3 I, like Gideon's fleece, am found
Unwatered still, and dry,
While the dew on all around
Falls plenteous from the sky ;
Yet my Lord I cannot blame,
The Saviour's grace for all is free ;
I the chief of sinners am,
But Jesus died for me.

4 Surely he will lift me up,
For I of him have need,
I cannot give up my hope,
Though I am cold and dead :
To bring fire on earth he came,
O that it might kindled be !
I the chief of sinners am,
But Jesus died for me.

5 Jesus, thou for me hast died,
And thou in me shalt live,

I shall feel thy death applied,
I shall thy life receive ;
Yet, when melted in the flame
Of love, this shall be all my plea,
I the chief of sinners am,
But Jesus died for me.

116
6 - 7 s.

1 SAVIOUR, cast a pitying eye,
Bid my sins and sorrows end ;
Whither should a sinner fly ?
Art not thou the sinner's friend ?
Rest in thee I gasp to find,
Wretched I, and poor, and blind.

2 Haste, O haste, to my relief !
From the iron furnace take ;
Rid me of my sin and grief,
For thy love and mercy's sake ;
Set my heart at liberty,
Show forth all thy power in me.

3 Me, the vilest of the race,
Most unholy, most unclean ;
Me, the farthest from thy face,
Full of misery and sin :
Me with arms of love receive,
Me, of sinners chief, forgive !

4 Jesus, on thine only name
For salvation I depend,
In thy gracious hands I am,
Save me, save me to the end ;
Let the utmost grace be given,
Save me quite from hell to heaven.

117
C. M.

1 GOD is in this and every place ;
But O how dark and void
To me ! 'tis one great wilderness,
This earth without my God.

2 Empty of him who all things fills,
Till he his light impart,
Till he his glorious self reveals,
The veil is on my heart.

3 O thou who seest and know'st my grief,
Thyself unseen, unknown !
Pity my helpless unbelief,
And take away the stone.

4 Regard me with a gracious eye,
The long-sought blessing give ;
And bid me, at the point to die,
Behold thy face and live.

5 Now, Jesus, now, the Father's love
Shed in my heart abroad :
The middle wall of sin remove,
And let me into God.

118
8 s & 6 s.

1 AUTHOR of faith, to thee I cry,
To thee, who wouldst not have me [die,
But know the truth and live ;
Open mine eyes to see thy face,
Work in my heart the saving grace,
The life eternal give.

2 Shut up in unbelief I groan,
And blindly serve a God unknown,

29

Till thou the veil remove;
The gift unspeakable impart,
And write thy name upon my heart,
  And manifest thy love.

I know the work is only thine,
The gift of faith is all divine;
  But, if on thee we call,
Thou wilt the benefit bestow,
And give us hearts to feel and know
  That thou hast died for all.

4 Thou bidd'st us knock and enter in,
Come unto thee, and rest from sin,
  The blessing seek and find;
Thou bidd'st us ask thy grace, and have:
Thou canst, thou wouldst, this moment
  Both me and all mankind.   [save

5 Be it according to thy word!
Now let me find my pardoning Lord,
  Let what I ask be given;
The bar of unbelief remove,
Open the door of faith and love,
  And take me into heaven.

119*   *Before Private Prayer.*   C. M.

1 FATHER of Jesus Christ, my Lord,
    I humbly seek thy face,
Encouraged by the Saviour's word
  To ask thy pardoning grace.

2 Entering into my closet, I
    The busy world exclude,
In secret prayer for mercy cry,
  And groan to be renewed.

3 Far from the paths of men, to thee
    I solemnly retire;
See, thou who dost in secret see,
  And grant my heart's desire.

4 Thy grace I languish to receive,
  · The Spirit of love and power,
Blameless before thy face to live,
  To live and sin no more.

5 Fain would I all thy goodness feel,
    And know my sins forgiven,
And do on earth thy perfect will
  As angels do in heaven.

6 O Father, glorify thy Son,
    And grant what I require;
For Jesu's sake the gift send down,
  And answer me by fire!

7 Kindle the flame of love within,
    Which may to heaven ascend,
And now the work of grace begin,
  Which shall in glory end.

120*   6 - 8 s.

1 COMFORT, ye ministers of grace,
    Comfort my people, saith your God!
Ye soon shall see his smiling face,
  His golden sceptre, not his rod,
And own, when now the cloud's removed,
He only chastened whom he loved.

2 Who sow in tears, in joy shall reap;
    The Lord shall comfort all that mourn;
Who now go on their way and weep,
  With joy they doubtless shall return,
And bring their sheaves with vast increase,
And have their fruit to holiness.
30

121

6 - 8 s.

1 EXPAND thy wings, celestial Dove,
    And, brooding o'er my nature's night
Call forth the ray of heavenly love;
  Let there in my dark soul be light;
And fill the illustrated abyss
With glorious beams of endless bliss.

2 Let there be light, again command,
  And light there in our hearts shall be,
We then through faith shall understand
  Thy great mysterious majesty;
And, by the shining of thy grace,
Behold in Christ thy glorious face.

3 Father of everlasting grace,
  Be mindful of thy changeless word;
We worship toward that holy place
  In which thou dost thy name record,
Dost make thy gracious nature known,
That living temple of thy Son.

4 Thou dost with sweet complacence see
  The temple filled with light divine;
And art thou not well pleased with me,
  Who, turning to that heavenly shrine,
Through Jesus to thy throne apply,
Through Jesus for acceptance cry?

5 With all who for redemption groan,
  Father, in Jesu's name I pray,
And still we cry and wrestle on,
  Till mercy take our sins away:
Hear from thy dwelling-place in heaven,
And now pronounce our sins forgiven.

122

8 s & 6 s.

1 O THOU who hast our sorrows borne,
    Help us to look on thee and mourn,
      On thee whom we have slain,
Have pierced a thousand thousand times,
And by reiterated crimes
      Renewed thy mortal pain.

2 Vouchsafe us eyes of faith to see
  The Man transfixed on Calvary,
      To know thee, who thou art,
The one eternal God and true;
And let the sight affect, subdue,
      And break my stubborn heart.

3 Lover of souls, to rescue mine,
Reveal the charity divine,
      That suffered in my stead;
That made thy soul a sacrifice,
And quenched in death those flaming eyes,
      And bowed that sacred head.

4 The veil of unbelief remove,
  And by thy manifested love,
      And by thy sprinkled blood,
Destroy the love of sin in me,
  And get thyself the victory,
      And bring me back to God.

5 Now let thy dying love constrain
  My soul to love its God again,
      Its God to glorify;
And lo! I come thy cross to share,
  Echo thy sacrificial prayer,
      And with my Saviour die.

123
C. M.

1 LET the redeemed give thanks and praise
  To a forgiving God !
My feeble voice I cannot raise
Till washed in Jesu's blood :

2 Till, at thy coming from above,
  My mountain-sins depart,
And fear gives place to filial love,
And peace o'erflows my heart.

3 Prisoner of hope. I still attend
  The appearing of my Lord.
These endless doubts and fears to end,
And speak my soul restored ;

4 Restored by reconciling grace,
  With present pardon blest,
And fitted by true holiness
For my eternal rest.

5 The peace which man can ne'er conceive,
  The love and joy unknown,
Now, Father, to thy servant give,
And claim me for thine own.

6 My God, in Jesus pacified,
  My God, thyself declare,
And draw me to his open side,
And plunge the sinner there.

124
8 s & 6 s.

1 O THAT I, first of love possessed,
  With my Redeemer's presence blessed,
  Might his salvation see !
Before thou dost my soul require,
Allow me, Lord, my heart's desire,
  And show thyself to me.

2 Appear my sanctuary from sin,
  Open thine arms and take me in,
  By thine own presence hide ;
Hide in the place where Moses stood,
And show me now the face of God,
  My Father pacified.

3 What but thy manifested grace
  Can guilt, and fear, and sorrow chase,
  The cause of grief destroy ?
Thy mercy makes salvation sure,
Makes all my heart and nature pure,
  And fills with hallowed joy.

4 Come quickly, Lord, the veil remove,
  Pass as a God of pardoning love
  Before my ravished eyes ;
And when I in thy person see
Jehovah's glorious majesty, .
  I find my paradise.

125
C. M.

1 O THAT I could my Lord receive,
  Who did the world redeem,
Who gave his life, that I might live
A life concealed in him !

2 O that I could the blessing prove,
  My heart's extreme desire,
Live happy in my Saviour's love,
And in his arms expire !

3 Mercy I ask to seal my peace,
  That, kept by mercy's power,
I may from every evil cease.
And never grieve thee more !

4 Now if thy gracious will it be,
  Even now, my sins remove,
And set my soul at liberty
By thy victorious love.

5 In answer to ten thousand prayers,
  Thou pardoning God, descend :
Number me with salvation's heirs,
My sins and troubles end.

6 Nothing I ask or want beside,
  Of all in earth or heaven,
But let me feel thy blood applied,
And live and die forgiven.

126
L M.

1 TOO strong I was to conquer sin,
  When 'gainst it first I turned my face ;
Nor knew my want of power within,
Nor knew the omnipotence of grace.

2 In nature's strength I sought in vain
  For what my God refused to give ;
I could not then the mastery gain,
Or lord of all my passions live.

3 But, for the glory of thy name,
  Vouchsafe me now the victory ;
Weakness itself thou know'st I am,
And cannot share the praise with thee.

4 Because I now can nothing do,
  Jesus, do all the work alone ;
And bring my soul triumphant through,
To wave its palm before thy throne.

5 Great God ! unknown, invisible,
  Appear, my confidence to abase,
To make me all my vileness feel,
And blush at my own righteousness.

6 Thy glorious face in Christ display,
  That, silenced by thy mercy's power,
My mouth I in the dust may lay,
And never boast or murmur more.

127
L. M.

1 WHEREWITH, O God, shall I draw
    near,
  And bow myself before thy face ?
How in thy purer eyes appear ?
What shall I bring to gain thy grace ?

2 Will gifts delight the Lord most high ?
  Will multiplied oblations please ?
Thousands of rams his favour buy,
Or slaughtered hecatombs appease ?

3 Can these avert the wrath of God ?
  Can these wash out my guilty stain ?
Rivers of oil, and seas of blood,
Alas ! they all must flow in vain.

4 Whoe'er to thee themselves approve,
  Must take the path thy word hath
Justi e pursue, and mercy love, [showed:
And humbly walk by faith with God.

5 But though my life henceforth be thine,
  Present for past can ne'er atone ;
Though I to thee the whole resign,
I only give thee back thine own.

6 What have I then wherein to trust ?
  I nothing have, I nothing am ;
Excluded is my every boast,
My glory swallowed up in shame.

7 Guilty I stand before thy face,
  On me I feel thy wrath abide;
'Tis just the sentence should take place;
  'Tis just;—but O thy Son hath died!

8 Jesus, the Lamb of God hath bled,
  He bore our sins upon the tree;
Beneath our curse he bowed his head;
  'Tis finished! he hath died for me!

9 See where before the throne he stands,
  And pours the all-prevailing prayer;
Points to his side, and lifts his hands,
  And shows that I am graven there.

10 He ever lives for me to pray;
  He prays that I with him may reign:
Amen to what my Lord doth say:
  Jesus, thou canst not pray in vain.

128   C. M.

1 WITH glorious clouds encompassed
    Whom angels dimly see,   [round,
Will the Unsearchable be found,
  Or God appear to me?

2 Will he forsake his throne above,
  Himself to worms impart?
Answer, thou Man of grief and love,
  And speak it to my heart!

3 In manifested love explain
  Thy wonderful design:
What meant the suffering Son of man,
  The streaming blood divine?

4 Didst thou not in our flesh appear,
  And live and die below,
That I may now perceive thee near,
  And my Redeemer know?

5 Come then, and to my soul reveal
  The heights and depths of grace,
The wounds which all my sorrows heal,
  That dear disfigured face.

6 Before my eyes of faith confest,
  Stand forth a slaughtered Lamb;
And wrap me in thy crimson vest,
  And tell me all thy name.

7 Jehovah in thy person show,
  Jehovah crucified!
And then the pardoning God I know,
  And feel the blood applied:

8 I view the Lamb in his own light,
  Whom angels dimly see,
And gaze, transported at the sight,
  Through all eternity.

129   L. M.

1 ADAM descended from above,
    Federal Head of all mankind,
The covenant of redeeming love
  In thee let every sinner find.

2 Its Surety, thou alone hast paid
  The debt we to thy Father owed;
For the whole world atonement made,
  And sealed the pardon with thy blood.

3 Thee, the paternal grace divine
  A universal blessing gave,
A light in every heart to shine,
  A Saviour every soul to save.

4 Light of the Gentile world, appear!
  Command the blind thy rays to see;

Our darkness chase, our sorrows cheer,
  And set thy plaintive prisoners free.

5 Me, me, who still in darkness sit,
  Shut up in sin and unbelief,
Bring forth out of this hellish pit,
  This dungeon of despairing grief.

6 Open mine eyes the Lamb to know,
  Who bears the general sin away;
And to my ransomed spirit show
  The glories of eternal day.

130

6 - 8 s.

1 THOU God unsearchable, unknown,
    Who still conceal'st thyself from me,
Hear an apostate spirit groan,
  Broke off, and banished far from thee;
But conscious of my fall I mourn,
  And fain I would to thee return.

2 Send forth one ray of heavenly light,
  Of gospel hope, of humble fear,
To guide me through the gulf of night,
  My poor desponding soul to cheer,
Till thou my unbelief remove,
  And show me all thy glorious love.

3 A hidden God indeed thou art!
  Thy absence I this moment feel;
Yet must I own it from my heart,
  Concealed, thou art a Saviour still;
And though thy face I cannot see,
  I know thine eye is fixed on me.

4 My Saviour thou, not yet revealed,
  Yet will I thee my Saviour call;
Adore thy hand, from sin withheld;
  Thy hand shall save me from my fall:
Now, Lord, throughout my darkness shine,
  And show thyself for ever mine.

131

L. M.

1 LORD, I despair myself to heal:
    I see my sin, but cannot feel:
I cannot till thy Spirit blow,
  And bid the obedient waters flow.

2 'Tis thine a heart of flesh to give,
  Thy gifts I only can receive;
Here then to thee I all resign;
  To draw, redeem, and seal, is thine.

3 With simple faith on thee I call,
  My Light, my Life, my Lord, my all:
I wait the moving of the pool,
  I wait the word that speaks me whole.

4 Speak, gracious Lord, my sickness cure,
  Make my infected nature pure,
Peace, righteousness, and joy impart,
  And pour thyself into my heart.

132

L. M.

1 JESU, the sinner's friend, to thee,
    Lost and undone, for aid I flee,
Weary of earth, myself, and sin,
  Open thine arms and take me in.

2 Pity, and heal my sin-sick soul;
  'Tis thou alone canst make me whole;
Fallen, till in me thine image shine,
  And cursed I am, till thou art mine.

3 Awake, the woman's conquering Seed,
  Awake, and bruise the serpent's head;

Tread down thy foes, with power control
The beast and devil in my soul.

4 The mansion for thyself prepare,
Dispose my heart by entering there ;
'Tis this alone can make me clean,
'Tis this alone can cast out sin.

5 At last I own it cannot be
That I should fit myself for thee ;
Here then to thee I all resign,
Thine is the work, and only thine.

6 What shall I say thy grace to move?
Lord, I am sin, but thou art love :
I give up every plea beside,
"Lord, I am damned, but thou hast died."

133
L. M.

1 JESU, whose glory's streaming rays,
Though duteous to thy high command,
Not seraphs view with open face,
But veiled before thy presence stand ;

2 How shall weak eyes of flesh, weighed
down
With sin, and dim with error's night,
Dare to behold thy awful throne,
Or view thy unapproached light?

3 Restore my sight ! let thy free grace
An entrance to the holiest give ;
Open mine eyes of faith ! thy face
So shall I see ; yet seeing live.

4 Thy golden sceptre from above
Reach forth : see, my whole heart I bow :
Say to my soul, "Thou art my love,
My chosen 'midst ten thousand, thou !"

5 O Jesus, full of grace ! the sighs
Of a sick heart with pity view ;
Hark, how my silence speaks, and cries,
"Mercy, thou God of mercy, show !"

6 I know thou canst not but be good ;
How shouldst thou, Lord, thy grace re-
strain?
Thou, Lord, whose blood so freely flowed,
To save me from all guilt and pain.

134
6-8 s.

1 JESU, if still the same thou art,
If all thy promises are sure,
Set up thy kingdom in my heart,
And make me rich, for I am poor :
To me be all thy treasures given,
The kingdom of an inward heaven.

2 Thou hast pronounced the mourners blest ;
And lo ! for thee I ever mourn :
I cannot, no, I will not rest,
Till thou, my only rest, return ;
Till thou, the Prince of peace, appear,
And I receive the Comforter.

3 Where is the blessedness bestowed
On all that hunger after thee?
I hunger now, I thirst for God ;
See the poor fainting sinner, see,
And satisfy with endless peace,
And fill me with thy righteousness.

4 Ah, Lord ! if thou art in that sigh,
Then hear thyself within me pray ;
Hear in my heart thy Spirit's cry,
Mark what my labouring soul would say;

Answer the deep unuttered groan,
And show that thou and I are one.

5 Shine on thy work, disperse the gloom,
Light in thy light I then shall see,
Say to my soul, "Thy light is come,
Glory divine is risen on thee,
Thy warfare's past, thy mourning's o'er ;
Look up, for thou shalt weep no more."

6 Lord, I believe the promise sure,
And trust thou wilt not long delay :
Hungry, and sorrowful, and poor,
Upon thy word myself I stay ;
Into thine hands my all resign,
And wait till all thou art is mine.

135
C. M.

1 JESU, if still thou art to-day
As yesterday the same,
Present to heal, in me display
The virtue of thy name.

2 If still thou goest about to do
Thy needy creatures good,
On me, that I thy praise may show,
Be all thy wonders showed.

3 Now, Lord, to whom for help I call,
Thy miracles repeat ;
With pitying eyes behold me fall
A leper at thy feet.

4 Loathsome, and vile, and self-abhorred,
I sink beneath my sin ;
But, if thou wilt, a gracious word
Of thine can make me clean.

5 Thou seest me deaf to thy command,
Open, O Lord, my ear ;
Bid me stretch out my withered hand,
And lift it up in prayer.

6 Silent, (alas ! thou know'st how long)
My voice I cannot raise ;
But O ! when thou shalt loose my tongue,
The dumb shall sing thy praise.

7 Lame at the pool I still am found :
Give, and my strength employ ;
Light as a hart I then shall bound,
The lame shall leap for joy.

8 Blind from my birth to guilt and thee,
And dark I am within ;
The love of God I cannot see,
The sinfulness of sin.

9 But thou, they say, art passing by ;
O let me find thee near !
Jesu, in mercy hear my cry,
Thou Son of David, hear !

10 Behold me waiting in the way
For thee, the heavenly light ;
Command me to be brought, and say,
"Sinner, receive thy sight !"

136
C. M.   SECOND PART.

1 WHILE dead in trespasses I lie,
Thy quickening Spirit give ;
Call me, thou Son of God, that I
May hear thy voice and live.

2 While, full of anguish and disease,
My weak distempered soul
Thy love compassionately sees,
O let it make me whole !

33

3 Cast out thy foes, and let them still
To Jesu's name submit;
Clothe with thy righteousness, and heal,
And place me at thy feet.

4 To Jesu's name if all things now
A trembling homage pay,
O let my stubborn spirit bow,
My stiff-necked will obey!

5 Impotent, dumb, and deaf, and blind,
And sick, and poor I am,
But sure a remedy to find
For all in Jesu's name.

6 I know in thee all fulness dwells,
And all for wretched man;
Fill every want my spirit feels,
And break off every chain.

7 If thou impart thyself to me,
No other good I need;
If thou, the Son, shalt make me free,
I shall be free indeed.

8 I cannot rest till in thy blood
I full redemption have;
But thou, through whom I come to God,
Canst to the utmost save.

9 From sin, the guilt, the power, the pain,
Thou wilt redeem my soul;
Lord, I believe, and not in vain,
My faith shall make me whole.

10 I too with thee shall walk in white,
With all thy saints shall prove
What is the length, and breadth, and
And depth of perfect love.   [height,

137   S. M.

1 WHEN shall thy love constrain,
And force me to thy breast?
When shall my soul return again,
To her eternal rest?

2 Ah! what avails my strife,
My wandering to and fro?
Thou hast the words of endless life:
Ah! whither should I go?

3 Thy condescending grace
To me did freely move;
It calls me still to seek thy face,
And stoops to ask my love.

4 Lord, at thy feet I fall!
I groan to be set free;
I fain would now obey the call,
And give up all for thee.

5 To rescue me from woe,
Thou didst with all things part;
Didst lead a suffering life below,
To gain my worthless heart.

6 My worthless heart to gain,
The God of all that breathe
Was found in fashion as a man,
And died a cursed death.

7 And can I yet delay
My little all to give?
To tear my soul from earth away,
For Jesus to receive?

8 Nay, but I yield, I yield!
I can hold out no more,
I sink, by dying love compelled,
And own thee conqueror.

9 Though late, I all forsake,
My friends, my all resign;
Gracious Redeemer, take, O take,
And seal me ever thine!

10 Come and possess me whole,
Nor hence again remove;
Settle and fix my wavering soul
With all thy weight of love.

11 My one desire be this,
Thy only love to know;
To seek and taste no other bliss,
No other good below.

12 My Life, my Portion thou,
Thou all-sufficient art;
My Hope, my heavenly treasure, now
Enter, and keep my heart.

138   C. M.

1 O THAT thou wouldst the heavens rend
In majesty come down;
Stretch out thine arm omnipotent,
And seize me for thine own!

2 Descend, and let thy lightning burn
The stubble of thy foe;
My sins o'erturn, o'erturn, o'erturn,
And make the mountains flow.

3 Thou my impetuous spirit guide,
And curb my headstrong will;
Thou only canst drive back the tide,
And bid the sun stand still.

4 What though I cannot break my chain,
Or e'er throw off my load?
The things impossible to men
Are possible to God.

5 Is there a thing too hard for thee,
Almighty Lord of all,
Whose threatening looks dry up the sea,
And make the mountains fall?

6 Who, who shall in thy presence stand,
And match Omnipotence,
Ungrasp the hold of thy right hand,
Or pluck the sinner thence?

7 Sworn to destroy, let earth assail;
Nearer to save thou art,
Stronger than all the powers of hell,
And greater than my heart.

8 Lo! to the hills I lift mine eye,
Thy promised aid I claim;
Father of mercies, glorify
Thy favourite Jesu's name.

9 Salvation in that name is found,
Balm of my grief and care;
A medicine for my every wound,
All, all I want is there!

139   C. M.   SECOND PART.

1 JESU! Redeemer, Saviour, Lord,
The weary sinner's friend,
Come to my help, pronounce the word,
And bid my troubles end.

2 Deliverance to my soul proclaim,
And life, and liberty;
Shed forth the virtue of thy name,
And Jesus prove to me!

3 Faith to be healed thou know'st I have,
For thou that faith hast given;

44

Thou canst, thou wilt the sinner save,
And make me meet for heaven.

4 Thou canst o'ercome this heart of mine,
Thou wilt victorious prove,
For everlasting strength is thine,
And everlasting love.

5 Thy powerful Spirit shall subdue
Unconquerable sin,
Cleanse this foul heart, and make it new,
And write thy law within.

6 Bound down with twice ten thousand ties,
Yet let me hear thy call,
My soul in confidence shall rise,
Shall rise and break through all.

7 Speak, and the deaf shall hear thy voice,
The blind his sight receive,
The dumb in songs of praise rejoice,
The heart of stone believe.

8 The Æthiop then shall change his skin,
The dead shall feel thy power,
The loathsome leper shall be clean,
And I shall sin no more.

140 *Wrestling Jacob.*
Genesis xxxii. 24—31.   6 - 8 s.

1 COME, O thou Traveller unknown,
Whom still I hold, but cannot see!
My company before is gone,
And I am left alone with thee;
With thee all night I mean to stay,
And wrestle till the break of day.

2 I need not tell thee who I am,
My misery and sin declare;
Thyself hast called me by my name,
Look on thy hands, and read it there;
But who, I ask thee, who art Thou?
Tell me Thy name, and tell me now.

3 In vain thou strugglest to get free,
I never will unloose my hold!
Art thou the Man that died for me?
The secret of thy love unfold;
Wrestling, I will not let thee go,
Till I thy name, thy nature know.

4 Wilt thou not yet to me reveal
Thy new, unutterable name?
Tell me, I still beseech thee, tell;
To know it now resolved I am;
Wrestling, I will not let thee go,
Till I thy name, thy nature know.

5 What though my shrinking flesh complain,
And murmur to contend so long?
I rise superior to my pain,
When I am weak, then I am strong;
And when my all of strength shall fail,
I shall with the God-man prevail.

141 SECOND PART.   6 - 8 s.

1 YIELD to me now, for I am weak,
But confident in self-despair;
Speak to my heart, in blessings speak,
Be conquered by my instant prayer;
Speak, or thou never hence shalt move,
And tell me if thy name is Love.

2 'Tis Love! 'tis Love! thou diedst for me!
I hear thy whisper in my heart;
The morning breaks, the shadows flee,
Pure, universal love thou art;
B 2

To me, to all, thy bowels move;
Thy nature and thy name is Love.

3 My prayer hath power with God; the grace
Unspeakable I now receive;
Through faith I see thee face to face,
I see thee face to face, and live!
In vain I have not wept and strove;
Thy nature and thy name is Love.

4 I know thee, Saviour, who thou art,
Jesus, the feeble sinner's friend;
Nor wilt thou with the night depart,
But stay and love me to the end;
Thy mercies never shall remove;
Thy nature and thy name is Love.

5 The Sun of righteousness on me
Hath rose with healing in his wings,
Withered my nature's strength; from thee
My soul its life and succour brings;
My help is all laid up above;
Thy nature and thy name is Love.

6 Contented now upon my thigh
I halt, till life's short journey end;
All helplessness, all weakness, I
On thee alone for strength depend,
Nor have I power from thee to move;
Thy nature and thy name is Love.

7 Lame as I am, I take the prey,
Hell, earth, and sin, with ease o'ercome;
I leap for joy, pursue my way,
And as a bounding hart fly home,
Through all eternity to prove
Thy nature and thy name is Love.

8 - 7 s.   **142**

1 DROOPING soul, shake off thy fears,
Fearful soul, be strong, be bold;
Tarry till the Lord appears,
Never, never quit thy hold!
Murmur not at his delay,
Dare not set thy God a time,
Calmly for his coming stay,
Leave it, leave it all to him.

2 Fainting soul, be bold, be strong;
Wait the leisure of thy Lord;
Though it seem to tarry long,
True and faithful is his word;
On his word my soul I cast,
(He cannot himself deny)
Surely it shall speak at last;
It shall speak, and shall not lie.

3 Every one that seeks shall find,
Every one that asks shall have,
Christ, the Saviour of mankind,
Willing, able, all to save;
I shall his salvation see,
I in faith on Jesus call,
I from sin shall be set free,
Perfectly set free from all.

4 Lord, my time is in thine hand,
Weak and helpless as I am,
Surely thou canst make me stand;
I believe in Jesu's name:
Saviour in temptation thou;
Thou hast saved me heretofore;
Thou from sin dost save me now,
Thou shalt save me evermore.

143*
8 - 7 s.

1 JESU, Lover of my soul,
Let me to thy bosom fly,
While the nearer waters roll,
While the tempest still is high :
Hide me, O my Saviour, hide,
Till the storm of life be past !
Safe into the haven guide,
O receive my soul at last!

2 Other refuge have I none,
Hangs my helpless soul on thee :
Leave, ah l leave me not alone,
Still support and comfort me :
All my trust on thee is stayed.
All my help from thee I bring ;
Cover my defenceless head
With the shadow of thy wing.

3 Thou, O Christ, art all I want,
More than all in thee I find I
Raise the fallen, cheer the faint,
Heal the sick, and lead the blind ;
Just and holy is thy name,
I am all unrighteousness ;
False and full of sin I am,
Thou art full of truth and grace.

4 Plenteous grace with thee is found,
Grace to cover all my sin,
Let the healing streams abound ;
Make and keep me pure within :
Thou of life the fountain art,
Freely let me take of thee,
Spring thou up within my heart,
Rise to all eternity.

144
8 s & 6 s.

1 THEE, Jesu, thee, the sinner's friend,
I follow on to apprehend,
Renew the glorious strife ;
Divinely confident and bold,
With faith's strong arm on thee lay hold,
Thee my eternal life.

2 Thy heart, I know, thy tender heart
Doth in my sorrows feel its part,
And at my tears relent ,
My powerful sighs thou canst not bear,
Nor stand the violence of my prayer,
My prayer omnipotent.

3 Give me the grace, the love I claim ;
Thy Spirit now demands thy name ;
Thou know'st the Spirit's will ;
He helps my soul's infirmity,
And strongly intercedes for me
With groans unspeakable.

4 Prisoner of hope, to thee I turn,
And, calmly confident, I mourn,
And pray, and weep for thee :
Tell me thy love, thy secret tell,
Thy mystic name in me reveal,
Reveal thyself in me.

5 Descend, pass by me, and proclaim,
O Lord of hosts, thy glorious name,
The Lord, the gracious Lord,
Long-suffering, merciful, and kind ;
The God who always bears in mind
His everlasting word.
36

6 Plenteous he is in truth and grace ;
He wills that all the fallen race
Should turn, repent, and live :
His pardoning grace for all is free ;
Transgression, sin, iniquity,
He freely doth forgive.

7 Mercy he doth for thousands keep ;
He goes and seeks the one lost sheep,
And brings his wanderer home ;
And every soul that sheep might be :
Come then, my Lord, and gather me,
My Jesus, quickly come !

145
8 s & 6 s.

1 O JESUS, let me bless thy name !
All sin, alas ! thou know'st I am,
But thou all pity art :
Turn into flesh my heart of stone ;
Such power belongs to thee alone :
Turn into flesh my heart.

2 A poor, unloving wretch, to thee
For help against myself I flee ;
Thou only canst remove
The hindrances out of the way,
And soften my unyielding clay,
And mould it into love.

3 O let thy Spirit shed abroad
The love, the perfect love of God,
In this cold heart of mine !
O might he now descend, and rest,
And dwell for ever in my breast,
And make it all divine !

4 What shall I do my suit to gain ?
O Lamb of God for sinners slain.
I plead what thou hast done !
Didst thou not die the death for me ?
Jesu, remember Calvary,
And break my heart of stone.

5 Take the dear purchase of thy blood,
My Friend and Advocate with God,
My Ransom and my Peace ;
Surety, who all my debt hast paid,
For all my sins atonement made,
The Lord my Righteousness.

146
8 s & 6 s.

1 STILL, Lord, I languish for thy grace,
Reveal the beauties of thy face,
The middle wall remove ;
Appear, and banish my complaint ;
Come, and supply my only want,
Fill all my soul with love.

2 O conquer this rebellious will !
Willing thou art and ready still,
Thy help is always nigh ;
The hardness from my heart remove,
And give me, Lord, O give me love,
Or at thy feet I die !

3 To thee I lift my mournful eye :
Why am I thus ?—O tell me why
I cannot love my God !
The hindrance must be all in me ;
It cannot in my Saviour be.
Witness that streaming blood !

4 It cost thy blood my heart to win,
To buy me from the power of sin,

And make me love again;
Come then, my Lord, thy right assert,
Take to thyself my ransomed heart,
Nor bleed, nor die in vain.

147   8 s & 6 s.

1 O LOVE divine, how sweet thou art !
    When shall I find my willing heart
All taken up by thee?
I thirst, I faint, I die to prove
The greatness of redeeming love,
    The love of Christ to me !

2 Stronger his love than death or hell ;
Its riches are unsearchable ;
    The first-born sons of light
Desire in vain its depths to see,
They cannot reach the mystery,
    The length, and breadth, and height.

3 God only knows the love of God ;
O that it now were shed abroad
    In this poor stony heart !
For love I sigh, for love I pine :
This only portion, Lord, be mine,
    Be mine this better part !

4 O that I could for ever sit
With Mary at the Master's feet !
    Be this my happy choice :
My only care, delight, and bliss,
My joy, my heaven on earth, be this,
    To hear the Bridegroom's voice !

5 O that with humbled Peter I
Could weep, believe, and thrice reply
    My faithfulness to prove,
" Thou know'st, (for all to thee is known)
Thou know'st, O Lord, and thou alone,
    Thou know'st that thee I love ! "

6 O that I could with favoured John
Recline my weary head upon
    The great Redeemer's breast !
From care, and sin, and sorrow free,
Give me, O Lord, to find in thee
    My everlasting rest.

148   6 - 8 s.

1 FATHER of Jesus Christ the Just,
    My Friend and Advocate with thee,
Pity a soul that fain would trust
In him who lived and died for me :
But only thou canst make him known,
And in my heart reveal thy Son.

2 If, drawn by thine alluring grace,
    My want of living faith I feel,
Show me in Christ thy smiling face ;
What flesh and blood can ne'er reveal,
Thy co-eternal Son, display,
And call my darkness into day

3 The gift unspeakable impart ;
    Command the light of faith to shine,
To shine in my dark, drooping heart,
    And fill me with the life divine :
Now bid the new creation be !
O God, let there be faith in me !

4 Thee, without faith I cannot please,
    · Faith without thee I cannot have ;
But thou hast sent the Prince of peace
    To seek my wandering soul, and save ;

O Father, glorify thy Son,
And save me for his sake alone !

5 Save me through faith in Jesu's blood,
    That blood which he for all did shed ;
For me, for me, thou know'st it flowed,
    For me, for me, thou hear'st it plead ;
Assure me now my soul is thine,
And all thou art in Christ is mine !

6 - 7 s.   " O ! when wilt thou come
            unto me ? "—Psalm ci. 2.   **149**

1 WHY not now, my God, my God !
    Ready if thou always art,
Make in me thy mean abode,
    Take possession of my heart?
If thou canst so greatly bow,
Friend of sinners, why not now?

2 God of love, in this my day
    For thyself to thee I cry ;
Dying, if thou still delay
    Must I not for ever die ?
Enter now thy poorest home,
Now, my utmost Saviour, come !

C. M.   **150**

1 THOU hidden God, for whom I groan,
    Till thou thyself declare,
God inaccessible, unknown,
    Regard a sinner's prayer !
A sinner weltering in his blood,
    Unpurged and unforgiven ;
Far distant from the living God,
    As far as hell from heaven.

2 An unregenerate child of man,
    To thee for faith I call ;
Pity thy fallen creature's pain,
    And raise me from my fall.
The darkness which through thee I feel
    Thou only canst remove ;
Thy own eternal power reveal,
    Thy Deity of love.

3 Thou hast in unbelief shut up,
    That grace may let me go ;
In hope believing against hope,
    I wait the truth to know :
Thou wilt in me reveal thy name,
    Thou wilt thy light afford ;
Bound and oppressed, yet thine I am,
    The prisoner of the Lord.

4 I would not to thy foe submit,
    I hate the tyrant's chain ;
Send forth the prisoner from the pit,
    Nor let me cry in vain !
Show me the blood that bought my peace,
    The covenant blood apply,
And all my griefs at once shall cease,
    And all my sins shall die.

5 Now, Lord, if thou art power, descend,
    The mountain sin remove ;
My unbelief and troubles end,
    If thou art truth and love :
Speak, Jesu, speak into my heart
    What thou for me hast done ;
One grain of living faith impart,
    And God is all my own !

2 - 6 s & 4 - 7 s.   **151**

1 OUT of the deep I cry,
    Just at the point to die ;

37

Hastening to infernal pain,
Jesus, Lord, I cry to thee ;
Help a feeble child of man,
Show forth all thy power in me.

2 On thee I ever call,
Saviour and friend of all ;
Well thou know'st my desperate case ;
Thou my curse and sin remove,
Save me by thy richest grace.
Save me by thy pardoning love.

3 How shall a sinner find
The Saviour of mankind ?
Canst thou not accept my prayer ?
Not bestow the grace I claim ?
Where are thy old mercies ? where
All the powers of Jesu's name ?

4 I will not let thee go,
Till I thy mercy know :
Let me hear the welcome sound,
Speak, if still thou canst forgive ;
Speak, and let the lost be found ;
Speak, and let the dying live.

5 Thy love is all my plea,
Thy passion speaks for me ;
By thy pangs and bloody sweat,
By thy depth of grief unknown,
Save me, gasping at thy feet,
Save, O save, thy ransomed one !

6 What hast thou done for me !
O think on Calvary !
By thy mortal groans and sighs,
By thy precious death I pray,
Hear my dying spirit's cries,
Take, O take, my sins away !

152 S. M.

1 AH ! whither should I go,
Burdened, and sick, and faint ?
To whom should I my troubles show,
And pour out my complaint ?
My Saviour bids me come,
Ah ! why do I delay ?
He calls the weary sinner home,
And yet from him I stay !

2 What is it keeps me back,
From which I cannot part,
Which will not let my Saviour take
Possession of my heart ?
Some cursed thing unknown
Must surely lurk within,
Some idol, which I will not own,
Some secret bosom-sin.

3 Jesu, the hindrance show,
Which I have feared to see ;
Yet let me now consent to know
What keeps me out of thee :
Searcher of hearts, in mine
Thy trying power display ;
Into its darkest corners shine,
And take the veil away.

4 I now believe in thee
Compassion reigns alone ;
According to my faith to me
O let it, Lord, be done !
In me is all the bar,
Which thou wouldst fain remove ;
Remove it, and I shall declare
That God is only love.
38

*153 C. M.   Philippians ii. 13.

1 I SEEM desirous to repent,
But cannot without thee
Soften this hard heart, or lament
My own obduracy ;
Gladly I would thy word believe,
My dear Redeemer know,
But neither can rejoice, nor grieve,
Till thou the power bestow.

2 I would, more sensibly distressed,
Throughout this evil day
Struggle to utter my request,
But cannot, cannot pray, ;
Until the Spirit from on high
His needful aid impart,
And raise a supplicating cry
Within my broken heart.

3 My want of thankfulness, and love,
And every grace, I own,
Nor will the mountains e'er remove
Till thou, my God, come down ;
Till thou thine own desires fulfil,
Thyself to sinners join,
And kindly work in me to will
And do the will divine.

154 6-8s.

1 FAIN would I leave the world below,
Of pain and sin the dark abode,
Where shadowy joy or solid woe
Allures or tears me from my God ;
Doubtful and insecure of bliss,
Since faith alone confirms me his.

2 Till then, to sorrow born, I sigh,
And gasp and languish after home ;
Upward I send my streaming eye,
Expecting till the Bridegroom come :
Come quickly, Lord ! thy own receive ;
Now let me see thy face, and live.

3 Absent from thee, my exiled soul
Deep in a fleshly dungeon groans ;
Around me clouds of darkness roll,
And labouring silence speaks my moans:
Come quickly, Lord ! thy face display,
And look my darkness into day.

4 Sorrow, and sin, and death are o'er,
If thou reverse the creature's doom ;
Sad Rachel weeps her loss no more,
If thou, the God, the Saviour come ;
Of thee possessed, in thee we prove
The light, the life, the heaven of love.

155 L. M.

1 GOD of my life, what just return
Can sinful dust and ashes give ?
I only live my sin to mourn ;
To love my God I only live.

2 To thee, benign and saving Power,
I consecrate my lengthened days
While, marked with blessings, every hour
Shall speak thy co-extended praise.

3 Be all my added life employed
Thine image in my soul to see ;
Fill with thyself the mighty void,
Enlarge my heart to compass thee.

4 O give me, Saviour, give me more !
Thy mercies to my soul reveal :

Alas! I see their endless store,
  But O, I cannot, cannot feel!
5 The blessing of thy love bestow,
  For this my cries shall never fail;
Wrestling, I will not let thee go,
  I will not, till thy suit prevail.

6 I'll weary thee with my complaint.
  Here at thy feet for ever lie,
With longing sick, with groaning faint;
  O give me love or else I die!

7 Come then, my Hope, my Life, my Lord,
  And fix in me thy lasting home;
Be mindful of thy gracious word,
  Thou with thy promised Father come!

8 Prepare, and then possess my heart,
  O take me, seize me, from above!
Thee may I love, for God thou art!
  Thee may I feel, for God is love!

156*

6 - 7 s.

1 O DISCLOSE thy lovely face!
  Quicken all my drooping powers;
Gasps my fainting soul for grace,
  As a thirsty land for showers;
Haste, my Lord, no more delay,
Come, my Saviour, come away!

2 Well thou know'st I cannot rest
  Till I fully rest in thee,
Till I am of thee possessed,
  Till, from every sin set free,
All the life of faith I prove,
All the joy and heaven of love.

3 With me O continue, Lord!
  Keep me, or from thee I fly;
Strength and comfort from thy word
  Imperceptibly supply,
Hold me till I apprehend,
Make me faithful to the end.

157

L. M.

1 MY sufferings all to thee are known,
  Tempted in every point like me;
Regard my grief, regard thy own,
  Jesus, remember Calvary!

2 O call to mind thy earnest prayers,
  Thy agony, and sweat of blood,
Thy strong and bitter cries and tears,
  Thy mortal groan, "My God! my God!"

3 For whom didst thou the cross endure?
  Who nailed thy body to the tree?
Did not thy death my life procure?
  O let thy pity answer me!

4 Art thou not touched with human woe?
  Hath pity left the Son of man?
Dost thou not all my sorrows know,
  And claim a share in all my pain?

5 Have I not heard, have I not known,
  That thou, the everlasting Lord,
Whom heaven and earth their Maker own,
  Art always faithful to thy word?

6 Thou wilt not break a bruised reed,
  Or quench the smallest spark of grace,
Till through the soul thy power is spread,
  Thy all-victorious righteousness.

7 The day of small and feeble things
  I know thou never wilt despise;

I know, with healing in his wings
  The Sun of righteousness shall rise.

8 With labour faint thou wilt not fall,
  Or wearied give the sinner o'er,
Till in this earth thy judgments dwell,
  And, born of God, I sin no more.

8 - 7 s.

158

1 O MY God, what must I do?
  Thou alone the way canst show;
Thou canst save me in this hour,
I have neither will nor power:
God if over all thou art,
Greater than my sinful heart,
All thy power on me be shown,
Take away the heart of stone.

2 Take away my darling sin;
Make me willing to be clean;
Make me willing to receive
All thy goodness waits to give:
Force me, Lord, with all to part,
Tear these idols from my heart;
Now thy love almighty show,
Make even me a creature new.

3 Jesus, mighty to renew,
Work in me to will and do?
Turn my nature's rapid tide,
Stem the torrent of my pride,
Stop the whirlwind of my will,
Speak, and bid the sun stand still;
Now thy love almighty show,
Make even me a creature new.

4 Arm of God, thy strength put on,
Bow the heavens, and come down;
All my unbelief o'erthrow,
Lay the aspiring mountain low;
Conquer thy worst foe in me,
Get thyself the victory;
Save the vilest of the race,
Force me to be saved by grace.

6 - 8 s.

159

1 LAY to thy hand, O God of grace!
  O God, the work is worthy thee!
See at thy feet of all the race
  The chief, the vilest sinner see;
And let me all thy mercy prove,
Thine utmost miracle of love.

2 Speak, and a holy thing and clean
  Shall strangely be brought out of me,
My Æthiop-soul shall change her skin,
  Redeemed from all iniquity;
I, even I, shall then proclaim
The wonders wrought by Jesu's name.

3 Thee I shall then for ever praise,
  In spirit and in truth adore;
While all I am declares thy grace,
  And, born of God, I sin no more,
Thy pure and heavenly nature share,
And fruit unto perfection bear.

5 5 11, 5 5 11.

160

1 O JESUS my Hope,
  For me offered up,
Who with clamour pursued thee to Cal-
The blood thou hast shed, [vary's top.
For me let it plead, [derer's stead.
And declare thou hast died in thy mur-

2 Come then from above,
    Its hardness remove,
And vanquish my heart with the sense of
    Thy love on the tree   [thy love;
    Display unto me,
And the servant of sin in a moment is free.

3 Neither passion nor pride
    Thy cross can abide,
But melt in the fountain that streams from
    Let thy life-giving blood [thy side ;
    Remove all my load,   [me to God.
And purge my foul conscience, and bring

4 Now, now let me know
    Its virtue below,
Let it wash me, and I shall be whiter than
    Let it hallow my heart,   [snow;
    And thoroughly convert,   [art.
And make me, O Lord, in the world as thou

5 Each moment applied
    My weakness to hide,
Thy blood be upon me, and always abide,
    My Advocate prove
    With the Father above,   [love.
And speak me at last to the throne of thy

161   L. M.

1 STAY, thou insulted Spirit, stay,
    Though I have done thee such despite,
Nor cast the sinner quite away,
Nor take thine everlasting flight.

2 Though I have steeled my stubborn heart,
    And still shook off my guilty fears,
And vexed, and urged thee to depart,
    For many long rebellious years ;

3 Though I have most unfaithful been
    Of all who e'er thy grace received,
Ten thousand times thy goodness seen,
    Ten thousand times thy goodness
    grieved;

4 Yet O ! the chief of sinners spare,
    In honour of my great High-priest,
Nor in thy righteous anger swear
To exclude me from thy people's rest.

5 This only woe I deprecate,
    This only plague I pray remove;
Nor leave me in my lost estate,
Nor curse me with this want of love.

6 Now, Lord, my weary soul release,
    Up-raise me with thy gracious hand,
And guide into thy perfect peace,
    And bring me to the promised land.

162*   S. M.

1 O MY offended God,
    If now at last I see
That I have trampled on thy blood,
    And done despite to thee,
If I begin to wake
Out of my deadly sleep,
Into thy arms of mercy take,
    And there for ever keep.

2 No other right have I
    Than what the world may claim;
All, all may to their God draw nigh
    Through faith in Jesu's name;
Thou all the debt hast paid;
This is my only plea,
40

The covenant God in thee hath made
    With all mankind and me.
3 Thou hast obtained the grace
    That all may turn and live ;
And lo ! thy offer I embrace,
    Thy mercy I receive:
Whene'er the wicked man
Turns from his sin to thee,
His late repentance is not vain,
    He shall accepted be.

4 Thy death hath bought the power
    For every sinful soul,
That all may know their gracious hour,
    And be by faith made whole :
Thou hast for sinners died,
    That all might come to God :
The covenant thou hast ratified,
    And sealed it with thy blood.

5 He that believes in thee,
    And doth till death endure,
He shall be saved eternally ;
    The covenant is sure:
The mountains shall give place,
    Thy covenant cannot move,
The covenant of thy general grace,
    Thy all-redeeming love.

L. M.   163

1 WHEN, gracious Lord, when shall it be,
    That I shall find my all in thee,
The fulness of thy promise prove,
The seal of thine eternal love ?

2 A poor blind child I wander here,
If haply I may feel thee near :
O dark ! dark ! dark ! I still must say,
Amid the blaze of gospel day.

3 Thee, only thee, I fain would find,
And cast the world and flesh behind ;
Thou, only thou, to me be given,
Of all thou hast in earth or heaven.

4 Whom man forsakes thou wilt not leave,
Ready the outcasts to receive,
Though all my simpleness I own,
And all my faults to thee are known.

5 Ah, wherefore did I ever doubt !
Thou wilt in no wise cast me out,
A helpless soul that comes to thee,
With only sin and misery.

6 Lord, I am sick, my sickness cure ;
I want, do thou enrich the poor :
Under thy mighty hand I stoop,
O lift the abject sinner up !

7 Lord, I am blind, be thou my sight ;
Lord, I am weak, be thou my might ;
A helper of the helpless be,
And let me find my all in thee !

7s & 6s †.   *The Woman of Canaan.*   164
              Matthew xv. 22—28.

1 LORD, regard my earnest cry,
    A potsherd of the earth ;
A poor guilty worm am I,
    A Canaanite by birth :
Save me from this tyranny,
From all the power of Satan save ;
Mercy, mercy upon me,
    Thou Son of David, have !

2 To the sheep of Israel's fold
   Thou in thy flesh wast sent;
Yet the Gentiles now behold
   In thee their covenant:
See me then, with pity see,
A sinner whom thou cam'st to save,
   Mercy, mercy upon me,
   Thou Son of David, have!

3 Still I cannot part with thee,
   I will not let thee go:
Mercy, mercy upon me,
   Thou Son of David, show!
Vilest of the sinful race,
On thee, importunate, I call,
   Help me, Jesus, show thy grace;
   Thy grace is free for all.

4 Nothing am I in thy sight,
   Nothing have I to plead;
Unto dogs it is not right
   To cast the children's bread:
Yet the dogs the crumbs may eat
That from the master's table fall;
   Let the fragments be my meat;
   Thy grace is free for all.

5 Give me, Lord, the victory,
   My heart's desire fulfil,
Let it now be done to me
   According to my will!
Give me living bread to eat,
And say, in answer to my call,
   "Canaanite, thy faith is great!
   My grace is free for all."

6 If thy grace for all is free,
   Thy call now let me hear;
Show this token upon me,
   And bring salvation near!
Now the gracious word repeat,
The word of healing to my soul,
   "Canaanite, thy faith is great!
   Thy faith hath made thee whole."

165
8 s.

1 COME holy celestial Dove,
   To visit a sorrowful breast,
My burden of guilt to remove,
   And bring me assurance and rest!
Thou only hast power to relieve
   A sinner o'erwhelmed with his load,
The sense of acceptance to give,
   And sprinkle his heart with the blood.

2 With me if of old thou hast strove,
   And strangely withheld from my sin,
And tried, by the lure of thy love,
   My worthless affections to win;
The work of thy mercy revive,
   Thy uttermost mercy exert,
And kindly continue to strive,
   And hold, till I yield thee my heart.

3 Thy call if I ever have known,
   And sighed from myself to get free,
And groaned the unspeakable groan,
   And longed to be happy in thee;
Fulfil the imperfect desire,
   Thy peace to my conscience reveal,
The sense of thy favour inspire,
   And give me my pardon to feel.

4 If when I had put thee to grief,
   And madly to folly returned,

Thy pity hath been my relief,
   And lifted me up as I mourned;
Most pitiful Spirit of grace,
   Relieve me again, and restore,
My Spirit in holiness raise,
   To fall and to suffer no more.

5 If now I lament after God,
   And gasp for a drop of thy love,
If Jesus hath bought thee with blood,
   For me to receive from above;
Come, heavenly Comforter, come,
   True witness of mercy divine,
And make me thy permanent home,
   And seal me eternally thine!

7 s & 6 s †. *The Pool of Bethesda.* **166**
John v. 2—9.

1 JESU, take my sins away,
   And make me know thy name!
Thou art now, as yesterday
   And evermore, the same;
Thou my true Bethesda be;
I know within thine arms is room,
   All the world may unto thee,
   Their House of Mercy, come.

2 Mercy then there is for me,
   (Away my doubts and fears!)
Plagued with an infirmity
   For many tedious years.
Jesu, cast a pitying eye!
Thou long hast known my desperate case;
   Poor and helpless here I lie,
   And wait the healing grace.

3 Long hath thy good Spirit strove
   With my distempered soul,
But I still refused thy love,
   And would not be made whole;
Hardly now at last I yield,
I yield with all my sins to part;
   Let my soul be fully healed,
   And throughly cleansed my heart.

4 Pain, and sickness, at thy word,
   And sin, and sorrow flies:
Speak to me, Almighty Lord,
   And bid my spirit rise!
Bid me bear the hallowed cross,
Which thou, my Lord, hast borne before;
   Walk in all thy righteous laws,
   And go and sin no more.

7 s & 6 s † **167**

1 LAMB of God, for sinners slain,
   To thee I feebly pray;
Heal me of my grief and pain,
   O take my sins away!
From this bondage, Lord, release,
No longer let me be opprest;
   Jesus, Master, seal my peace,
   And take me to thy breast!

2 Wilt thou cast a sinner out
   Who humbly comes to thee?
No, my God, I cannot doubt
   Thy mercy is for me;
Let me then obtain the grace,
And be of paradise possest;
   Jesus, Master, seal my peace,
   And take me to thy breast!

3 Worldly good I do not want,
   Be that to others given;

41

Only for thy love I pant,
  My all in earth and heaven;
This the crown I fain would seize,
The good wherewith I would be blest;
  Jesus, Master, seal my peace,
  And take me to thy breast!

4 This delight I fain would prove,
  And then resign my breath;
Join the happy few whose love
  Was mightier than death.
Let it not my Lord displease
That I would die to be thy guest;
  Jesus, Master, seal my peace,
  And take me to thy breast!

SECTION III.

FOR PERSONS CONVINCED OF BACKSLIDING.

168   8 - 7 s.

1 DEPTH of mercy! can there be
    Mercy still reserved for me?
Can my God his wrath forbear?,
Me, the chief of sinners, spare?
I have long withstood his grace,
Long provoked him to his face,
Would not hearken to his calls,
Grieved him by a thousand falls.

2 I have spilt his precious blood,
Trampled on the Son of God,
Filled with pangs unspeakable,
I, who yet am not in hell!
Whence to me this waste of love?
Ask my Advocate above!
See the cause in Jesu's face,
Now before the throne of grace.

3 Lo! I cumber still the ground:
Lo! an Advocate is found:
" Hasten not to cut him down,
Let this barren soul alone."
Jesus speaks, and pleads his blood!
He disarms the wrath of God;
Now my Father's bowels move,
Justice lingers into love.

4 Kindled his relentings are,
Me he now delights to spare,
Cries, " How shall I give thee up?"
Lets the lifted thunder drop.
There for me the Saviour stands;
Shows his wounds, and spreads his
God is love! I know, I feel;   [hands!
Jesus weeps, and loves me still.

5 Jesus, answer from above,
Is not all thy nature love?
Wilt thou not the wrong forget,
Suffer me to kiss thy feet?
If I rightly read thy heart,
If thou all compassion art,
Bow thine ear, in mercy bow,
Pardon and accept me now.

6 Pity from thine eye let fall,
By a look my soul recall;
Now the stone to flesh convert,
Cast a look, and break my heart:
42

Now incline me to repent,
Let me now my fall lament,
Now my foul revolt deplore,
Weep, believe, and sin no more.

            *169
C. M.

1 JESUS, the all-restoring Word,
  My fallen spirit's hope,
After thy lovely likeness, Lord,
  Ah, when shall I wake up?

2 Thou, O my God, thou only art
  The Life, the Truth, the Way;
Quicken my soul, instruct my heart,
  My sinking footsteps stay.

3 Of all thou hast in earth below,
  In heaven above, to give,
Give me thy only love to know,
  In thee to walk and live.

4 Fill me with all the life of love;
  In mystic union join
Me to thyself, and let me prove
  The fellowship divine.

5 Open the intercourse between
  My longing soul and thee,
Never to be broke off again
  To all eternity.

            170
6 - 8 s.

1 O 'TIS enough, my God, my God!
  Here let me give my wanderings o'er,
No longer trample on thy blood,
  And grieve thy gentleness no more;
No more thy lingering anger move,
Or sin against thy light and love.

2 O Lord, if mercy is with thee,
  Now let it all on me be shown;
On me, the chief of sinners, me,
  Who humbly for thy mercy groan,
Me to thy Father's grace restore,
Nor let me ever grieve thee more!

3 Fountain of unexhausted love,
  Of infinite compassions, hear;
My Saviour and my Prince above,
  Once more in my behalf appear;
Repentance, faith, and pardon give,
O let me turn again and live!

            171
6 - 8 s.

1 O GOD, if thou art love indeed,
  Let it once more be proved in me,
That I thy mercy's praise may spread,
  For every child of Adam free;
O let me now the gift embrace!
O let me now be saved by grace!

2 If all long-suffering thou hast shown
  On me, that others may believe,
Now make thy loving-kindness known,
  Now the all-conquering Spirit give,
Spirit of victory and power,
That I may never grieve thee more.

3 Grant my importunate request!
  It is not my desire, but thine;
Since thou wouldst have the sinner blest,
  Now let me in thine image shine,
Nor ever from thy footsteps move,
But more than conquer through thy love

4 Be it according to thy will!
  Set my imprisoned spirit free;
The counsel of thy grace fulfil;
  Into thy glorious liberty
My spirit, soul, and flesh restore,
And I shall never grieve thee more.

172 S. M.

1 O UNEXHAUSTED grace!
    O love unsearchable!
I am not gone to my own place,
  I am not yet in hell!
Earth doth not open yet,
  My soul to swallow up!
And, hanging o'er the burning pit,
  I still am forced to hope.

2 I hope at last to find
    The kingdom from above.
The settled peace, the constant mind,
  The everlasting love;
The sanctifying grace
  That makes me meet for home;
I hope to see thy glorious face,
  Where sin can never come.

3 What shall I do to keep
    The blessed hope I feel?
Still let me pray, and watch, and weep,
  And serve thy pleasure still;
O may I never grieve
  My kind, long-suffering Lord!
But steadfastly to Jesus cleave,
  And answer all his word.

4 Lord, if thou hast bestowed
    On me this gracious fear,
This horror of offending God,
  O keep it always here!
And that I never more
  May from thy ways depart,
Enter with all thy mercy's power,
  And dwell within my heart.

173 6 - 7 s.

1 JESUS, I believe thee near,
    Now my fallen soul restore!
Now my guilty conscience clear,
  Give me back my peace and power,
Stone to flesh again convert,
Write forgiveness on my heart.

2 I believe thy pardoning grace,
    As at the beginning, free;
Open are thy arms to embrace
  Me, the worst of rebels, me;
In me all the hindrance lies;
Called, I still refuse to rise.

3 Yet, for thy own mercy's sake,
    Patience with thy rebel have;
Me thy mercy's witness make,
  Witness of thy power to save;
Make me willing to be free,
Restless to be saved by thee.

4 Now the gracious work begin,
    Now for good some token give;
Give me now to feel my sin,
  Give me now my sin to leave;
Bid me look on thee and mourn;
Bid me to thy arms return.

5 Take this heart of stone away,
    Melt me into gracious tears;

Grant me power to watch and pray,
  Till thy lovely face appears,
Till thy favour I retrieve,
Till by faith again I live.

174 8 s.

1 HOW shall a lost sinner in pain
    Recover his forfeited peace?
When brought into bondage again,
  What hope of a second release?
Will mercy itself be so kind
  To spare such a rebel as me?
And O! can I possibly find
  Such plenteous redemption in thee?

2 O Jesus! of thee I inquire,
    If still thou art able to save?
The brand to pluck out of the fire,
  And ransom my soul from the grave?
The help of thy Spirit restore,
  And show me the life-giving blood,
And pardon a sinner once more,
  And bring me again unto God.

3 O Jesus! in pity draw near,
    Come quickly to help a lost soul;
To comfort a mourner appear,
  And make a poor Lazarus whole!
The balm of thy mercy apply,
  (Thou seest the sore anguish I feel)
Save, Lord, or I perish, I die,
  O save, or I sink into hell!

4 I sink, if thou longer delay
    Thy pardoning mercy to show;
Come quickly, and kindly display
  The power of thy passion below!
By all thou hast done for my sake,
  One drop of thy blood I implore,
Now, now let it touch me, and make
  The sinner a sinner no more!

175 7 s & 6 s †.

1 GOD of my salvation, hear,
    And help me to believe!
Simply do I now draw near,
  Thy blessing to receive:
Full of sin, alas! I am,
  But to thy wounds for refuge flee;
Friend of sinners, spotless Lamb,
  Thy blood was shed for me.

2 Standing now as newly slain,
    To thee I lift mine eye!
Balm of all my grief and pain,
  Thy grace is always nigh:
Now, as yesterday, the same
  Thou art, and wilt for ever be;
Friend of sinners, spotless Lamb,
  Thy blood was shed for me.

3 Nothing have I, Lord, to pay,
    Nor can thy grace procure,
Empty send me not away,
  For I, thou know'st, am poor:
Dust and ashes is my name,
  My all is sin and misery;
Friend of sinners, spotless Lamb,
  Thy blood was shed for me.

4 No good word, or work, or thought,
    Bring I to gain thy grace;
Pardon I accept unbought,
  Thy proffer I embrace,

Coming, as at first I came,
To take, and not bestow on thee;
Friend of sinners, spotless Lamb,
Thy blood was shed for me.

5 Saviour, from thy wounded side
I never will depart;
Here will I my spirit hide
When I am pure in heart:
Till my place above I claim,
This only shall be all my plea,
Friend of sinners, spotless Lamb,
Thy blood was shed for me.

176
6 - 8 s.

1 O GOD, thy righteousness we own,
Judgment is at thy house begun !
With humble awe thy rod we hear,
And guilty in thy sight appear,
We cannot in thy judgment stand,
But sink beneath thy mighty hand.

2 Our mouth as in the dust we lay,
And still for mercy, mercy, pray;
Unworthy to behold thy face,
Unfaithful stewards of thy grace,
Our sin and wickedness we own,
And deeply for acceptance groan.

3 We have not, Lord, thy gifts improved,
But basely from thy statutes roved,
And done thy loving Spirit despite,
And sinned against the clearest light ;
Brought back thy agonizing pain,
And nailed thee to thy cross again.

4 Yet do not drive us from thy face,
A stiff-necked and hard-hearted race ;
But O ! in tender mercy break
The iron sinew in our neck;
The softening power of love impart,
And melt the marble of our heart.

177
6 - 8 s.

1 JESUS, thou know'st my sinfulness,
My faults are not concealed from thee ;
A sinner in my last distress,
To thy dear wounds I fain would flee,
And never, never thence depart,
Close sheltered in thy loving heart.

2 How shall I find the living way,
Lost, and confused, and dark, and blind?
Ah, Lord, my soul is gone astray !
Ah, Shepherd, seek my soul, and find,
And in thy arms of mercy take,
And bring the weary wanderer back.

3 Weary and sick of sin I am ;
I hate it, Lord, and yet I love :
When wilt thou rid me of my shame ?
When wilt thou all my load remove ?
Destroy the fiend that lurks within,
And speak the word of power, " Be clean ! "

4 O Lord, if I at last discern
That I am sin, and thou art love,
If now o'er me thy bowels yearn,
Give me a token from above ;
And conquer my rebellious will,
And bid my murmuring heart be still.

5 Sin only let me not commit,
(Sin never can advance thy praise)
44

And lo ! I lay me at thy feet,
And wait unwearied all my days,
Till my appointed time shall come,
And thou shalt call thine exile home.

178
6 - 8 s. *" Wilt thou not from this time cry unto me, My father ? "*
Jeremiah iii. 4.

1 YES, from this instant now, I will
To my offended Father cry ;
My base ingratitude I feel,
Vilest of all thy children, I,
Not worthy to be called thy son ;
Yet will I thee my Father own.

2 Guide of my life hast thou not been,
And rescued me from passion's power ?
Ten thousand times preserved from sin,
Nor let the greedy grave devour ?
And wilt thou now thy wrath retain,
Nor ever love thy child again ?

3 Ah, canst thou find it in thy heart
To give me up, so long pursued?
Ah, canst thou finally depart,
And leave thy creature in his blood ?
Leave me, out of thy presence cast,
To perish in my sins at last ?

4 If thou hast willed me to return,
If weeping at thy feet I fall,
The prodigal thou wilt not spurn,
But pity, and forgive me all,
In answer to my Friend above,
In honour of his bleeding love !

179
7 s & 6 s †.

1 FATHER, if thou must reprove
For all that I have done,
Not in anger, but in love
Chastise thine humbled son ;
Use the rod, and not the sword,
Correct with kind severity ;
Bring me not to nothing, Lord !
But bring me home to thee.

2 True and faithful as thou art,
To all thy Church and me,
Give a new, believing heart,
That knows and cleaves to thee ;
Freely our backslidings heal,
And, by thy precious blood restored,
Grant that every soul may feel,
" Thou art my pardoning Lord ! "

3 Might we now with pure desire
Thine only love request ;
Now, with willing heart entire,
Return to Christ our rest !
When we our whole hearts resign,
O Jesus, to be filled with thee,
Thou art ours, and we are thine,
Through all eternity.

180
L. M.   Isaiah lvii. 18, 19.

1 SAVIOUR, I now with shame confess
My thirst for creature happiness ;
By base desires I wronged thy love,
And forced thy mercy to remove.

2 Yet would I not regard thy stroke ;
But when thou didst thy grace revoke,
And when thou didst thy face conceal,
Thy absence I refused to feel.

3 I knew not that the Lord was gone,
In my own froward will went on,
And lived to the desires of men;
And thou hast all my wanderings seen.

4 Yet, O the riches of thy grace!
Thou, who hast seen my evil ways,
Wilt freely my backslidings heal,
And pardon on my conscience seal.

5 For this I at thy footstool wait,
Till thou my peace again create;
Fruit of thy gracious lips, restore
My peace, and bid me sin no more!

6 Far off, yet at thy feet, I lie,
Till thou again thy blood apply;
Till thou repeat my sins forgiven,
As far from God as hell from heaven.

7 But, for thy truth and mercy's sake,
My comfort thou wilt give me back,
And lead me on from grace to grace,
In all the paths of righteousness;

8 Till, throughly saved, my new-born soul,
And perfectly by faith made whole,
Doth bright in thy full image rise,
To share thy glory in the skies.

181
Hebrews v. 7, 8.   L. M.

1 THOU Man of griefs, remember me,
Who never canst thyself forget!
Thy last mysterious agony,
Thy fainting pangs, and bloody sweat!

2 When, wrestling in the strength of prayer,
Thy spirit sunk beneath its load,
Thy feeble flesh abhorred to bear
The wrath of an almighty God.

3 Father, if I may call thee so,
Regard my fearful heart's desire,
Remove this load of guilty woe,
Nor let me in my sins expire!

4 I tremble lest the wrath divine,
Which bruises now my sinful soul,
Should bruise this wretched soul of mine
Long as eternal ages roll.

5 To thee my last distress I bring,
The heightened fear of death I find;
The tyrant, brandishing his sting,
Appears, and hell is close behind.

6 I deprecate that death alone,
That endless banishment from thee;
O save, and give me to thy Son,
Who trembled, wept, and bled for me!

SECTION IV.
FOR BACKSLIDERS RECOVERED.

182
7s & 6s.

1 I WILL hearken what the Lord
Will say concerning me:
Hast thou not a gracious word
For one who waits on thee?
Speak it to my soul, that I
May in thee have peace and power.
Never from my Saviour fly,
And never grieve thee more.

2 How have I thy Spirit grieved
Since first with me he strove,

Obstinately disbelieved,
And trampled on thy love I
I have sinned against the light;
I have broke from thy embrace;
No, I would not, when I might,
Be freely saved by grace.

3 After all that I have done
To drive thee from my heart,
Still thou wilt not leave thine own,
Thou wilt not yet depart;
Wilt not give the sinner o'er;
Ready art thou now to save,
Bidd'st me come, as heretofore,
That I thy life may have.

4 O thou meek and gentle Lamb!
Fury is not in thee;
Thou continuest still the same,
And still thy grace is free;
Still thine arms are open wide,
Wretched sinners to receive;
Thou hast once for sinners died,
That all may turn and live.

5 Lo! I take thee at thy word,
My foolishness I mourn;
Unto thee, my bleeding Lord,
However late, I turn!
Yes, I yield, I yield at last,
Listen to thy speaking blood;
Me, with all my sins, I cast
On my atoning God!

183
6 - 7 s.

1 JESU, Shepherd of the sheep,
Pity my unsettled soul!
Guide, and nourish me, and keep,
Till thy love shall make me whole;
Give me perfect soundness, give,
Make me steadfastly believe.

2 I am never at one stay,
Changing every hour I am;
But thou art, as yesterday,
Now and evermore the same;
Constancy to me impart,
Stablish with thy grace my heart.

3 Give me faith to hold me up,
Walking over life's rough sea,
Holy, purifying hope
Still my soul's sure anchor be;
That I may be always thine,
Perfect me in love divine.

184
C. M.

1 God, my God, to thee I cry,
Thee only would I know;
My purifying blood apply,
And wash me white as snow.

2 Touch me, and make the leper clean,
Purge my iniquity;
Unless thou wash my soul from sin,
I have no part in thee.

3 But art thou not already mine?
Answer, if mine thou art!
Whisper within, thou Love divine,
And cheer my drooping heart.

4 Tell me again my peace is made,
And bid the sinner live;
The debt's discharged, the ransom's paid,
My Father must forgive.

5 Behold, for me the victim bleeds,
  His wounds are opened wide;
For me the blood of sprinkling pleads,
  And speaks me justified.

6 O why did I my Saviour leave?
  So soon unfaithful prove!
How could I thy good Spirit grieve,
  And sin against thy love?

7 I forced thee first to disappear,
  I turned thy face aside;
Ah, Lord! if thou hadst still been here,
  Thy servant had not died.

8 But O, how soon thy wrath is o'er,
  And pardoning love takes place!
Assist me, Saviour, to adore
  The riches of thy grace.

9 O could I lose myself in thee,
  Thy depth of mercy prove,
Thou vast, unfathomable sea
  Of unexhausted love!

10 My humbled soul, when thou art near,
  In dust and ashes lies;
How shall a sinful worm appear,
  Or meet thy purer eyes?

11 I loathe myself when God I see,
  And into nothing fall;
Content if thou exalted be,
  And Christ be all in all.

185   8 - 7 s.

1 AFTER all that I have done,
  Saviour, art thou pacified?
Whither shall my vileness run?
  Hide me, earth, the sinner hide!
Let me sink into the dust,
  Full of holy shame, adore!
Jesus Christ, the good, the just,
  Bids me go, and sin no more.

2 O confirm the gracious word,
  Jesus, Son of God and man!
Let me never grieve thee, Lord,
  Never turn to sin again:
Till my all in all thou art,
  Till thou bring thy nature in,
Keep this feeble, trembling heart,
  Save me, save me, Lord, from sin!

186   6 - 8 s.

1 WEARY of wandering from my God,
  And now made willing to return,
I hear, and bow me to the rod;
  For thee, not without hope, I mourn;
I have an Advocate above,
  A Friend before the throne of Love.

2 O Jesus, full of truth and grace,
  More full of grace than I of sin,
Yet once again I seek thy face;
  Open thine arms, and take me in,
And freely my backslidings heal,
  And love the faithless sinner still.

3 Thou know'st the way to bring me back,
  My fallen spirit to restore;
O! for thy truth and mercy's sake,
  Forgive and bid me sin no more;
The ruins of my soul repair,
  And make my heart a house of prayer.

46

4 The stone to flesh again convert,
  The veil of sin again remove;
Sprinkle thy blood upon my heart,
  And melt it by thy dying love;
This rebel heart by love subdue,
  And make it soft, and make it new.

5 Give to mine eyes refreshing tears,
  And kindle my relentings now;
Fill my whole soul with filial fears,
  To thy sweet yoke my spirit bow;
Bend by thy grace, O bend or break,
  The iron sinew in my neck!

6 Ah! give me, Lord, the tender heart
  That trembles at the approach of sin;
A godly fear of sin impart,
  Implant, and root it deep within,
That I may dread thy gracious power,
  And never dare to offend thee more.

187   7 s & 6 s †.

1 SON of God, if thy free grace
  Again hath raised me up,
Called me still to seek thy face,
  And given me back my hope;
Still thy timely help afford,
And all thy loving-kindness show:
  Keep me, keep me, gracious Lord,
  And never let me go!

2 By me, O my Saviour, stand,
  In sore temptation's hour;
Save me with thine outstretched hand,
  And show forth all thy power;
O be mindful of thy word,
Thy all-sufficient grace bestow:
  Keep me, keep me, gracious Lord,
  And never let me go!

3 Give me, Lord, a holy fear,
  And fix it in my heart,
That I may from evil near
  With timely care depart;
Sin be more than hell abhorred;
Till thou destroy the tyrant foe,
  Keep me, keep me, gracious Lord,
  And never let me go!

4 Never let me leave thy breast,
  From thee, my Saviour, stray;
Thou art my support and rest,
  My true and living Way;
My exceeding great Reward,
In heaven above, and earth below:
  Keep me, keep me, gracious Lord,
  And never let me go!

188   7 s & 6 s †.

1 LORD, and is thine anger gone?
  And art thou pacified?
After all that I have done,
  Dost thou no longer chide?
Infinite thy mercies are,
Beneath the weight I cannot move;
  O! 'tis more than I can bear,
  The sense of pardoning love.

2 Let it still my heart constrain,
  And all my passions sway;
Keep me, lest I turn again
  Out of the narrow way;
Force my violence to be still,
  And captivate my every thought;

Charm, and melt, and change my will,
And bring me down to nought.

3 If I have begun once more
Thy sweet return to feel,
If even now I find thy power
Present my soul to heal,
Still and quiet may I lie,
Nor struggle out of thine embrace;
Never more resist, or fly
From thy pursuing grace.

4 To the cross, thine altar, bind
Me with the cords of love;
Freedom let me never find
From thee, my Lord, to move;
That I never, never more
May with my much-loved Master part,
To the posts of mercy's door
O nail my willing heart!

5 See my utter helplessness,
And leave me not alone;
O preserve in perfect peace,
And seal me for thine own;
More and more thyself reveal,
Thy presence let me always find;
Comfort, and confirm, and heal
My feeble, sin-sick mind.

6 As the apple of an eye
Thy weakest servant keep;
Help me at thy feet to lie,
And there for ever weep;
Tears of joy mine eyes o'erflow,
That I have any hope of heaven;
Much of love I ought to know,
For I have much forgiven.

PART IV. FOR BELIEVERS.

SECTION I.
REJOICING.

189   6 - 8 s.

1 NOW I have found the ground wherein
Sure my soul's anchor may remain,
The wounds of Jesus, for my sin
Before the world's foundation slain;
Whose mercy shall unshaken stay,
When heaven and earth are fled away.

2 Father, thine everlasting grace
Our scanty thought surpasses far,
Thy heart still melts with tenderness,
Thy arms of love still open are,
Returning sinners to receive,
That mercy they may taste and live.

3 O Love, thou bottomless abyss,
My sins are swallowed up in thee!
Covered is my unrighteousness,
Nor spot of guilt remains on me,
While Jesu's blood, through earth and skies,
Mercy, free, boundless mercy, cries.

4 With faith I plunge me in this sea,
Here is my hope, my joy, my rest;
Hither, when hell assails, I flee,
I look into my Saviour's breast:
Away, sad doubt, and anxious fear!
Mercy is all that's written there.

5 Though waves and storms go o'er my head,
Though strength, and health, and friends be gone,
Though joys be withered all and dead,
Though every comfort be withdrawn,
On this my steadfast soul relies,
Father, thy mercy never dies.

6 Fixed on this ground will I remain,
Though my heart fail, and flesh decay;
This anchor shall my soul sustain,
When earth's foundations melt away;
Mercy's full power I then shall prove,
Loved with an everlasting love.

L. M.   **190**

1 JESU, thy blood and righteousness
My beauty are, my glorious dress;
Midst flaming worlds in these arrayed,
With joy shall I lift up my head.

2 Bold shall I stand in thy great day,
For who aught to my charge shall lay?
Fully absolved through these I am,
From sin and fear, from guilt and shame.

3 The holy, meek, unspotted Lamb,
Who from the Father's bosom came,
Who died for me, even me, to atone,
Now for my Lord and God I own.

4 Lord, I believe thy precious blood,
Which at the mercy-seat of God
For ever doth for sinners plead,
For me, even for my soul, was shed.

5 Lord, I believe, were sinners more
Than sands upon the ocean shore,
Thou hast for all a ransom paid,
For all a full atonement made.

6 When from the dust of death I rise,
To claim my mansion in the skies,
Even then this shall be all my plea,
Jesus hath lived, hath died, for me.

7 Thus Abraham, the friend of God,
Thus all heaven's armies bought with [blood,
Saviour of sinners thee proclaim;
Sinners, of whom the chief I am.

8 Jesu, be endless praise to thee,
Whose boundless mercy hath for me,
For me and all thy hands have made,
An everlasting ransom paid.

9 Ah! give to all thy servants, Lord,
With power to speak thy gracious word,
That all who to thy wounds will flee,
May find eternal life in thee.

10 Thou God of power, thou God of love,
Let the whole world thy mercy prove!
Now let thy word o'er all prevail;
Now take the spoils of death and hell.

11 O let the dead now hear thy voice,
Now bid thy banished ones rejoice,
Their beauty this, their glorious dress,
Jesu, thy blood and righteousness!

2 - 6 s & 4 - 7 s.   Luke xv. 20—24.   **191**

1 THEE, O my God and King,
My Father, thee I sing!
Hear, well-pleased, the joyous sound,
Praise from earth and heaven receive;
Lost, I now in Christ am found,
Dead, by faith in Christ I live.

2 Father, behold thy son,
In Christ I am thy own ;
Stranger loug to thee, and rest,
See the prodigal is come :
Open wide thine arms and breast,
Take the weary wanderer home.

3 Thine eye observed from far,
Thy pity looked me near ;
Me thy bowels yearned to see,
Me thy mercy ran to find,
Empty, poor, and void of thee,
Hungry, sick, and faint, and blind.

4 Thou on my neck didst fall,
Thy kiss forgave me all :
Still thy gracious words I hear,
Words that made the Saviour mine,
" Haste, for him the robe prepare,
His be righteousness divine ! "

192   Romans x. 6—9.   7 s & 6 s.

1 OFT I in my heart have said,
Who shall ascend on high,
Mount to Christ, my glorious Head,
And bring him from the sky?
Borne on contemplation's wing,
Surely I shall find him there,
Where the angels praise their King,
And gain the morning-star.

2 Oft I in my heart have said,
Who to the deep shall stoop,
Sink with Christ among the dead,
From thence to bring him up?
Could I but my heart prepare,
By unfeigned humility,
Christ would quickly enter there,
And ever dwell with me.

3 But the righteousness of faith
Hath taught me better things :
" Inward turn thine eyes," it saith,
(While Christ to me it brings)
" Christ is ready to impart
Life to all, for life who sigh :
In thy mouth, and in thy heart,
The word is ever nigh."

193   2 - 6 s & 4 - 7 s.

1 O FILIAL Deity,
Accept my new-born cry !
See the travail of thy soul,
Saviour, and be satisfied ;
Take me now, possess me whole,
Who for me, for me, hast died !

2 Of life thou art the tree,
My immortality !
Feed this tender branch of thine,
Ceaseless influence derive ;
Thou the true, the heavenly Vine ;
Grafted into thee I live.

3 Of life the fountain thou,
I know—I feel it now !
Faint and dead no more I droop ;
Thou art in me ; thy supplies,
Every moment springing up,
Into life eternal rise.

4 Thou the good Shepherd art,
From thee I ne'er shall part ;
Thou my keeper and my guide,
Make me still thy tender care ;
48

Gently lead me by thy side,
Sweetly in thy bosom bear.

5 Thou art my daily Bread ;
O Christ, thou art my Head !
Motion, virtue, strength, to me,
Me thy living member, flow ;
Nourished I, and fed by thee,
Up to thee in all things grow.

6 Prophet, to me reveal
Thy Father's perfect will ;
Never mortal spake like thee,
Human prophet like divine :
Loud and strong their voices be,
Small, and still, and inward thine.

7 On thee, my Priest, I call,
Thy blood atoned for all ;
Still the Lamb as slain appears,
Still thou stand'st before the throne,
Ever offering up my prayers,
These presenting with thine own.

8 Jesu, thou art my King,
From thee my strength I bring ;
Shadowed by thy mighty hand,
Saviour, who shall pluck me thence ?
Faith supports ; by faith I stand,
Strong in thy omnipotence.

194

2 - 6 s & 4 - 7 s.

1 ARISE, my soul, arise,
Thy Saviour's sacrifice !
All the names that love could find,
All the forms that love could take,
Jesus in himself hath joined,
Thee, my soul, his own to make.

2 Equal with God most high,
He laid his glory by ;
He, the eternal God, was born,
Man with men he deigned to appear ;
Object of his creatures' scorn,
Pleased a servant's form to wear.

3 Hail ! everlasting Lord,
Divine, incarnate Word !
Thee let all my powers confess,
Thee my latest breath proclaim ;
Help, ye angel-choirs, to bless,
Shout the loved Immanuel's name !

4 Fruit of a virgin's womb,
The promised blessing's come ;
Christ, the fathers' hope of old,
Christ, the woman's conquering Seed,
Christ, the Saviour long foretold,
Born to bruise the serpent's head.

5 Jesus, to thee I bow,
The Almighty's Fellow thou !
Thou, the Father's only Son !
Pleased he ever is in thee ;
Just and holy thou alone,
Full of grace and truth for me.

195

2 - 6 s & 4 - 7 s.   SECOND PART.

1 HIGH above every name,
Jesus, the great I AM !
Bows to Jesus every knee,
Things in heaven, and earth, and hell ;
Saints adore him, demons flee,
Fiends, and men, and angels feel !

2 He left his throne above,
   Emptied of all but love:
Whom the heavens cannot contain,
   God vouchsafed a worm to appear,
Lord of glory, Son of man,
   Poor, and vile, and abject here.

3 His own on earth he sought,
   His own received him not,
Him a sign by all blasphemed,
   Outcast and despised of men,
Him they all a madman deemed,
   Bold to scoff the Nazarene.

4 Hail, Galilean King!
   Thy humble state I sing,
Never shall my triumphs end ;
   Hail, derided Majesty !
Jesus, hail ! the sinner's friend,
   Friend of publicans,—and me.

196   L. M.

1 INTO thy gracious hands I fall,
   And with the arms of faith embrace ;
O King of glory, hear my call,
   O raise me, heal me, by thy grace !
Now righteous through thy wounds I am ;
   No condemnation now I dread :
I taste salvation in thy name,
   Alive in thee, my living Head.

2 Still let thy wisdom be my guide,
   Nor take thy light from me away,
Still with me let thy grace abide,
   That I from thee may never stray :
Let thy word richly in me dwell ;
   Thy peace and love my portion be ;
My joy to endure and do thy will,
   Till perfect I am found in thee.

3 Arm me with thy whole armour, Lord !
   Support my weakness with thy might,
Gird on my thigh thy conquering sword,
   And shield me in the threatening fight :
From faith to faith, from grace to grace,
   So in thy strength shall I go on,
Till heaven and earth flee from thy face,
   And glory end what grace begun.

197   Isaiah xii.   8 - 7 s.

1 HAPPY soul who sees the day,
   The glad day of gospel grace !
Thee, my Lord, (thou then wilt say)
   Thee will I for ever praise ;
Though thy wrath against me burned,
   Thou dost comfort me again ;
All thy wrath aside is turned,
   Thou hast blotted out my sin.

2 Me, behold ! thy mercy spares,
   Jesus my salvation is:
Hence my doubts, away my fears !
   Jesus is become my peace :
JAH, JEHOVAH, is my Lord,
   Ever merciful and just ;
I will lean upon his word,
   I will on his promise trust.

3 Strong I am, for he is strong,
   Just in righteousness divine :
He is my triumphal song ;
   All he has, and is, is mine :
Mine, and yours, whoe'er believe ;
   On his name whoe'er shall call

Freely shall his grace receive ;
   He is full of grace for all.

4 Therefore shall ye draw with joy
   Water from salvation's well ;
Praise shall your glad tongues employ,
   While his streaming grace ye feel ;
Each to each ye then shall say,
   " Sinners, call upon his name ;
O rejoice to see his day,
   See it, and his praise proclaim !"

5 Glory to his name belongs,
   Great, and marvellous, and high ;
Sing unto the Lord your songs,
   Cry to every nation, cry !
Wondrous things the Lord hath done,
   Excellent his name we find ;
This to all mankind is known ;
   Be it known to all mankind ! :

6 Zion, shout thy Lord and King,
   Israel's HOLY ONE is he !
Give him thanks, rejoice, and sing ;
   Great he is, and dwells in thee.
O the grace unsearchable !
   While eternal ages roll,
God delights in man to dwell,
   Soul of each believing soul.

10 s & 11 s.   198

1 O WHAT shall I do My Saviour to praise,
   So faithful and true, So plenteous in grace,
So strong to deliver, So good to redeem
   The weakest believer That hangs upon him !

2 How happy the man Whose heart is set free,
   The people that can Be joyful in thee !
Their joy is to walk in The light of thy face,
   And still they are talking Of Jesus's grace.

3 Their daily delight Shall be in thy name ;
   They shall as their right Thy righteousness claim ;
Thy righteousness wearing, And cleansed by thy blood,
   Bold shall they appear in The presence of [God.

4 For thou art their boast, Their glory and power ;
   And I also trust To see the glad hour,
My soul's new creation, A life from the dead,
   The day of salvation, That lifts up my [head.

5 For Jesus, my Lord, Is now my defence ;
   I trust in his word, None plucks me from thence ; [will do ;
Since I have found favour, He all things
   My King and my Saviour Shall make me anew.

6 Yes, Lord, I shall see The bliss of thine own,
   Thy secret to me Shall soon be made known ;
For sorrow and sadness I joy shall receive,
   And   in the gladness Of all that believe.

10 s & 11 s.   199

1 O HEAVENLY King, Look down from above !
   Assist us to sing Thy mercy and love :

So sweetly o'erflowing, So plenteous the store. [more.
Thou still art bestowing, And giving us

2 O God of our life, We hallow thy name!
Our business and str.fe Is thee to proclaim;
Accept our thanksgiving For creating grace; [praise.
The living, the living Shall show forth thy

3 Our Father and Lord, Almighty art thou;
Preserved by thy word, We worship thee now;
The bountiful donor Of all we enjoy,
Our tongues to thine honour, And lives we employ.

4 But O! above all, Thy kindness we praise,
From sin and from thrall Which saves the lost race; [deem.
Thy Son thou hast given The world to re-
And bring us to heaven Whose trust is in him.

5 Wherefore of thy love We sing and rejoice,
With angels above We lift up our voice:
Thy love each believer Shall gladly adore,
For ever and ever, When time is no more.

200
10 s & 11 s.

1 Father, my God, I long for thy love,
MY O shed it abroad; Send Christ from above!
My heart ever fainting He only can cheer,
And all things are wanting, Till Jesus is here.

2 O when shall my tongue Be filled with thy praise!
While all the day long I publish thy grace,
Thy honour and glory To sinners forth show, [true.
Till sinners adore thee, And own thou art

3 Thy strength and thy power I now can pro-
claim, [name;
Preserved every hour Through Jesus's
For thou art still by me, And holdest my hand; [stand.
No ill can come nigh me, By faith while I

4 My God is my guide: Thy mercies abound,
On every side They compass me round;
Thou sav'st me from sickness, From sin dost retrieve, [believe.
And strengthen my weakness, And bid me

5 Thou holdest my soul In spiritual life,
My foes dost control, And quiet their strife;
Thou rulest my passion, My pride and self-will, ["Stand still!"
To see thy salvation, Thou bidd'st me

6 I stand, and admire Thine outstretched arm, [harm;
I walk through the fire, And suffer no
Assaulted by evil, I scorn to submit,
The world and the devil Fall under my feet.

7 I wrestle not now, But trample on sin,
For with me art thou, And shalt be with-
in; [power.
While stronger and stronger In Jesus's
I go on to conquer, Till sin is no more.

201
6-8 s.

1 AND can it be, that I should gain
An interest in the Saviour's blood?

50

Died he for me, who caused his pain?
For me, who him to death pursued?
Amazing love! how can it be
That thou, my God, shouldst die for me?

2 'Tis mystery all! The Immortal dies!
Who can explore his strange design?
In vain the first-born seraph tries
To sound the depths of love divine!
'Tis mercy all! let earth adore,
Let angel-minds inquire no more.

3 He left his Father's throne above,
(So free, so infinite his grace!)
Emptied himself of all but love,
And bled for Adam's helpless race:
'Tis mercy all, immense and free,
For, O my God, it found out me!

4 Long my imprisoned spirit lay
Fast bound in sin and nature's night;
Thine eye diffused a quickening ray,
I woke, the dungeon flamed with light
My chains fell off, my heart was free,
I rose, went forth, and followed thee.

5 No condemnation now I dread,
Jesus, and all in him, is mine!
Alive in him, my living Head,
And clothed in righteousness divine,
Bold I approach the eternal throne. [own.
And claim the crown, through Christ my

202
4 - 6 s & 2 - 8 s.

1 ARISE, my soul, arise,
Shake off thy guilty fears;
The bleeding sacrifice
In my behalf appears;
Before the throne my Surety stands;
My name is written on his hands.

2 He ever lives above,
For me to intercede,
His all-redeeming love,
His precious blood, to plead;
His blood atoned for all our race,
And sprinkles now the throne of grace.

3 Five bleeding wounds he bears,
Received on Calvary;
They pour effectual prayers,
They strongly speak for me:
"Forgive him, O forgive," they cry,
"Nor let that ransomed sinner die!"

4 The Father hears him pray,
His dear Anointed One;
He cannot turn away
The presence of his Son:
His Spirit answers to the blood,
And tells me I am born of God.

5 My God is reconciled,
His pardoning voice I hear,
He owns me for his child,
I can no longer fear,
With confidence I now draw nigh,
And, Father, Abba, Father, cry!

203
L. M.

1 GLORY to God, whose sovereign grace
Hath animated senseless stones;
Called us to stand before his face,
And raised us into Abraham's sons!

2 The people that in darkness lay,
In sin and error's deadly shade,
Have seen a glorious gospel day,
In Jesu's lovely face displayed.

3 Thou only, Lord, the work hast done,
  And bared thine arm in all our sight;
Hast made the reprobates thine own,
  And claimed the outcasts as thy right.

4 Thy single arm, almighty Lord,
  To us the great salvation brought,
Thy Word, thy all-creating Word,
  That spake at first the world from nought.

5 For this the saints lift up their voice,
  And ceaseless praise to thee is given;
For this the hosts above rejoice,
  We raise the happiness of heaven.

6 For this. no longer sons of night,
  To thee our thankful hearts we give;
To thee, who call'dst us into light,
  To thee we die, to thee we live.

7 Suffice that for the season past
  Hell's horrid language filled our tongues,
We all thy words behind us cast,
  And lewdly sang the drunkard's songs.

8 But, O the power of grace divine!
  In hymns we now our voices raise,
Loudly in strange hosannas join,
  And blasphemies are turned to praise!

204 *"I will sing with the Spirit,"*
&c.—1 Cor. xiv. 15. 8 s & 6 s.

1 JESUS, thou soul of all our joys,
  For whom we now lift up our voice,
    And all our strength exert;
Vouchsafe the grace we humbly claim,
Compose into a thankful frame,
    And tune thy people's heart.

2 While in the heavenly work we join,
Thy glory be our whole design,
    Thy glory, not our own:
Still let us keep our end in view,
And still the pleasing task pursue,
    To please our God alone.

3 The secret pride, the subtle sin,
O let it never more steal in,
    To offend thy glorious eyes,
To desecrate our hallowed strain,
And make our solemn service vain,
    And mar our sacrifice!

4 To magnify thy awful name,
To spread the honours of the Lamb,
    Let us our voices raise;
Our souls' and bodies' powers unite,
Regardless of our own delight,
    And dead to human praise.

5 Still let us on our guard be found,
And watch against the power of sound
    With sacred jealousy;
Lest haply sense should damp our zeal,
And music's charms bewitch and steal
    Our hearts away from thee.

6 That hurrying strife far off remove,
That noisy burst of selfish love,
    Which swells the formal song;
The joy from out our hearts arise,
And speak and sparkle in our eyes,
    And vibrate on our tongue.

7 Thee let us praise, our common Lord,
And sweetly join with one accord
    Thy goodness to proclaim,
Jesus, thyself in us reveal,
And all our faculties shall feel
    Thy harmonizing name

8 With calmly-reverential joy,
O let us all our lives employ
    In setting forth thy love;
And raise in death our triumph higher,
And sing with all the heavenly choir,
    That endless song above!

5 5 12. **205**

1 MY God, I am thine,
    What a comfort divine, [mine!
What a blessing to know that my Jesus is

2 In the heavenly Lamb
    Thrice happy I am, [his name.
And my heart it doth dance at the sound of

3 True pleasures abound
    In the rapturous sound; [found:
And whoever hath found it hath paradise

4 My Jesus to know,
    And feel his blood flow,
'Tis life everlasting, 'tis heaven below.

5 Yet onward I haste
    To the heavenly feast: [taste!
That, that is the fulness; but this is the

6 And this I shall prove,
    Till with joy I remove
To the heaven of heavens in Jesus's love.

6 - 8 s. **206**

1 WHAT am I, O thou glorious God!
    And what my father's house to thee
That thou such mercies hast bestowed
  On me, the chief of sinners, me!
I take the blessing from above,
And wonder at thy boundless love.

2 Me in my blood thy love passed by,
    And stopped, my ruin to retrieve;
Wept o'er my soul thy pitying eye,
    Thy bowels yearned, and sounded
      "Live!"
Dying, I heard the welcome sound,
And pardon in thy mercy found.

3 Honour, and might, and thanks, and praise
    I render to my pardoning God,
And spread thy saving name abroad,
    the riches of thy grace,
That only name to sinners 'iven,
Which lifts poor dying worms to heaven

4 Jesus, I bless thy gracious power,
    And all within me shouts thy name;
Thy name let every soul adore,
    Thy power let every tongue proclaim:
Thy grace let every sinner know,
And find with me their heaven below.

8 - 7 s. **207**

1 JESUS is our common Lord,
    He our loving Saviour is;
By his death to life restored.
    Misery we exchange for bliss;
Bliss to carnal minds unknown,
O 'tis more than tongue can tell!
Only to believers shown,
Glorious and unspeakable.

2 Christ, our Brother and our Friend,
    Shows us his eternal love;
Never shall our triumphs end,
    Till we take our seats above.

Let us walk with him in white,
For our bridal day prepare,
For our partnership in light,
For our glorious meeting there.

208
Revelation iii. 20.　　C. M.

1 COME, let us, who in Christ believe,
Our common Saviour praise,
To him with joyful voices give
The glory of his grace.

2 He now stands knocking at the door
Of every sinner's heart;
The worst need keep him out no more,
Or force him to depart.

3 Through grace we hearken to thy voice,
Yield to be saved from sin;
In sure and certain hope rejoice,
That thou wilt enter in.

4 Come quickly in, thou heavenly guest,
Nor ever hence remove;
But sup with us, and let the feast
Be everlasting love.

209
6 - 8 s.

1 THOU hidden source of calm repose,
Thou all-sufficient Love Divine,
My help and refuge from my foes,
Secure I am, if thou art mine;
And lo! from sin, and grief, and shame,
I hide me, Jesus, in thy name.

2 Thy mighty name salvation is,
And keeps my happy soul above;
Comfort it brings, and power, and peace,
And joy, and everlasting love;
To me, with thy dear name, are given
Pardon, and holiness, and heaven.

3 Jesu, my all in all thou art;
My rest in toil, my ease in pain,
The medicine of my broken heart,
In war my peace, in loss my gain,
My smile beneath the tyrant's frown,
In shame my glory and my crown:

4 In want my plentiful supply,
In weakness my almighty power,
In bonds my perfect liberty,
My light in Satan's darkest hour,
In grief my joy unspeakable,
My life in death, my heaven in hell.

210
6 - 8 s.

1 THEE will I love, my strength, my tower,
Thee will I love, my joy, my crown,
Thee will I love with all my power,
In all thy works, and thee alone;
Thee will I love, till the pure fire
Fill my whole soul with chaste desire.

2 Ah, why did I so late thee know,
Thee, lovelier than the sons of men!
Ah, why did I no sooner go
To thee, the only ease in pain!
Ashamed, I sigh, and inly mourn,
That I so late to thee did turn.

3 In darkness willingly I strayed,
I sought thee, yet from thee I roved;
Far wide my wandering thoughts were
spread,
Thy creatures more than thee I loved;
52

And now if more at length I see, [thee.
'Tis through thy light and comes from

4 I thank thee, uncreated Sun, [shined;
That thy bright beams on me have
I thank thee, who hast overthrown
My foes, and healed my wounded mind;
I thank thee, whose enlivening voice
Bids my freed heart in thee rejoice.

5 Uphold me in the doubtful race,
Nor suffer me again to stray;
Strengthen my feet with steady pace
Still to press forward in thy way;
My soul and flesh, O Lord of might,
Fill, satiate, with thy heavenly light.

6 Give to mine eyes refreshing tears,
Give to my heart chaste, hallowed fires,
Give to my soul, with filial fears,
The love that all heaven's host inspires;
That all my powers, with all their might,
In thy sole glory may unite.

7 Thee will I love, my joy, my crown,
Thee will I love, my Lord, my God;
Thee will I love, beneath thy frown,
Or smile, thy sceptre, or thy rod;
What though my flesh and heart decay?
Thee shall I love in endless day!

211
10 s & 11 s.

1 LET all men rejoice, By Jesus restored!
We lift up our voice, And call him
our Lord; [thrall,
His joy is to bless us, And free us from
From all that oppress us He rescues us all.

2 Him Prophet, and King, And Priest we
proclaim,
We triumph and sing Of Jesus's name;
Poor idiots he teaches To show forth his
praise,
And tell of the riches Of Jesus's grace.

3 No matter how dull The scholar whom he
Takes into his school, And gives him to see;
A wonderful fashion Of teaching he hath,
And wise to salvation He makes us through
faith.

4 The wayfaring men, Though fools, shall
not stray,
His method so plain, So easy his way;
The simplest believer His promise may
prove,
And drink of the river Of Jesus's love.

5 Poor outcasts of men, Whose souls were
despised,
And left with disdain, By Jesus are prized;
His gracious creation In us he makes
known, [own.
And brings us salvation, And calls us his

212
10 s & 11 s.

1 MY brethren beloved, Your calling ye see;
In Jesus approved, No goodness have
we,
No riches or merit, No wisdom or might,
But all things inherit Through Jesus's right.

2 Yet not many wise His summons obey,
And great ones despise So vulgar a way,
And strong ones will never Their helpless-
ness own, [alone.
Or stoop to find favour Through mercy

3 And therefore our God The outcasts hath
    chose,   [us;
  His righteousness showed To heathens like
  When wise ones rejected His offers of grace,
  His goodness elected The foolish and base.
4 To baffle the wise, And noble, and strong,
  He bade us arise, An impotent throng;
  Poor ignorant wretches, We gladly embrace
  A Prophet who teaches Salvation by grace.
5 The things that were not, His mercy bids
    live;
  His mercy unbought We freely receive;
  His gracious compassion We thankfully
    prove,
  And all our salvation Ascribe to his love.

213*
C. M.

1 MY God, the spring of all my joys,
    The life of my delights,
  The glory of my brightest days,
    And comfort of my nights!
2 In darkest shades, if thou appear,
    My dawning is begun;
  Thou art my soul's bright morning star,
    And thou my rising sun.
3 The opening heavens around me shine
    With beams of sacred bliss,
  If Jesus shows his mercy mine,
    And whispers I am his.
4 My soul would leave this heavy clay
    At that transporting word;
  Run up with joy the shining way,
    To see and praise my Lord.
5 Fearless of hell and ghastly death,
    I'd break through every foe,
  The wings of love, and arms of faith,
    Would bear me conqueror through.

214
C. M.

1 TALK with us, Lord, thyself reveal,
    While here o'er earth we rove;
  Speak to our hearts, and let us feel
    The kindling of thy love.
2 With thee conversing, we forget
    All time, and toil, and care;
  Labour is rest, and pain is sweet,
    If thou, my God, art here.
3 Here then, my God, vouchsafe to stay,
    And bid my heart rejoice;
  My bounding heart shall own thy sway,
    And echo to thy voice.
4 Thou callest me to seek thy face;
    'Tis all I wish to seek;
  To attend the whispers of thy grace,
    And hear thee inly speak.
5 Let this my every hour employ,
    Till I thy glory see;
  Enter into my Master's joy,
    And find my heaven in thee.

215
7 s & 6 s.

1 GLORIOUS Saviour of my soul,
    I lift it up to thee;
  Thou hast made the sinner whole,
    Hast set the captive free;
  Thou my debt of death hast paid,
    Thou hast raised me from my fall,

Thou hast full atonement made:
    My Saviour died for all.
2 What could my Redeemer move
    To leave his Father's breast?
  Pity drew him from above,
    And would not let him rest;
  Swift to succour sinking man,
    Sinking into endless woe,
  Jesus to our rescue ran,
    And God appeared below.
3 God, in this dark vale of tears,
    A man of griefs was seen;
  Here for three and thirty years
    He dwelt with sinful men.
  Did they know the Deity?
    Did they own him, who he was?
  See the friend of sinners, see!
    He hangs on yonder cross!
4 Yet thy wrath I cannot fear,
    Thou gentle, bleeding Lamb!
  By thy judgment I am clear,
    Healed by thy stripes I am:
  Thou for me a curse wast made,
    That I might in thee be blest;
  Thou hast my full ransom paid,
    And in thy wounds I rest.

C. M.
216

1 INFINITE, unexhausted Love!
    Jesus and love are one!
  If still to me thy bowels move,
    They are restrained to none.
2 What shall I do my God to love?
    My loving God to praise?
  The length, and breadth, and height to
    And depth of sovereign grace? [prove,
3 Thy sovereign grace to all extends,
    Immense and unconfined;
  From age to age it never ends;
    It reaches all mankind.
4 Throughout the world its breadth is
    Wide as infinity;   [known,
  So wide, it never passed by one,
    Or it had passed by me.
5 My trespass was grown up to heaven;
    But far above the skies,
  In Christ abundantly forgiven,
    I see thy mercies rise.
6 The depth of all-redeeming love
    What angel-tongue can tell?
  O may I to the utmost prove
    The gift unspeakable!
7 Deeper than hell, it plucked me thence;
    Deeper than inbred sin,
  Jesus's love my heart shall cleanse
    When Jesus enters in.
8 Come quickly, gracious Lord, and take
    Possession of thine own;
  My longing heart vouchsafe to make
    Thine everlasting throne!
9 Assert thy claim, maintain thy right,
    Come quickly from above;
  And sink me to perfection's height,
    The depth of humble love.

C. M.
217

1 JESUS, to thee I now can fly,
    On whom my help is laid:
53

Oppressed by sins, I lift my eye,
  And see the shadows fade.
2 Believing on my Lord, I find
  A sure and present aid:
On thee alone my constant mind
  Is every moment stayed.
3 Whate'er in me seems wise, or good,
  Or strong, I here disclaim:
I wash my garments in the blood
  Of the atoning Lamb.
4 Jesus, my Strength, my Life, my Rest,
  On thee will I depend,
Till summoned to the marriage-feast,
  When faith in sight shall end.

218
8 - 7 s.

1 SEE how great a flame aspires,
  Kindled by a spark of grace!
Jesu's love the nations fires,
  Sets the kingdoms on a blaze;
To bring fire on earth he came,
  Kindled in some hearts it is,
O that all might catch the flame,
  All partake the glorious bliss!
2 When he first the work begun,
  Small and feeble was his day;
Now the word doth swiftly run,
  Now it wins its widening way;
More and more it spreads and grows,
  Ever mighty to prevail,
Sin's strongholds it now o'erthrows,
  Shakes the trembling gates of hell.
3 Sons of God, your Saviour praise!
  He the door hath opened wide;
He hath given the word of grace,
  Jesu's word is glorified;
Jesus, mighty to redeem,
  He alone the work hath wrought;
Worthy is the work of him,
  Him who spake a world from nought.
4 Saw ye not the cloud arise,
  Little as a human hand?
Now it spreads along the skies,
  Hangs o'er all the thirsty land;
Lo! the promise of a shower
  Drops already from above;
But the Lord will shortly pour
  All the Spirit of his love!

219
5 5 5 11, 5 5 5 11.

1 ALL thanks be to God,
  Who scatters abroad,
Throughout every place,
By the least of his servants, his savour of
  Who the victory gave,   [grace!
  The praise let him have,
For the work he hath done:
All honour and glory to Jesus alone!
  2 Our conquering Lord
    Hath prospered his word,
    Hath made it prevail,
And mightily shaken the kingdom of hell,
    His arm he hath bared,
    And a people prepared
    His glory to show,
And witness the power of his passion below,
  3 He hath opened a door
    To the penitent poor,

54

And rescued from sin,
And admitted the harlots and publicans in;
    They have heard the glad sound,
    They have liberty found
    Through the blood of the Lamb,
And plentiful pardon in Jesus's name.
  4 And shall we not sing
    Our Saviour and King?
    Thy witnesses, we
With rapture ascribe our salvation to thee.
    Thou, Jesus, hast blessed,
    And believers increased,
    Who thankfully own
We are freely forgiven through mercy alone.
  5 His Spirit revives
    His work in our lives,
    His wonders of grace,
So mightily wrought in the primitive days.
    O that all men might know
    His tokens below,
    Our Saviour confess,   [peace!
And embrace the glad tidings of pardon and
  6 Thou Saviour of all,
    Effectually call
    The sinners that stray;
And O let a nation be born in a day!
    Thy sign let them see,
    And flow unto thee
    For the oil and the wine,
For the blissful assurance of favour divine.
  7 Our heathenish land
    Beneath thy command
    In mercy receive,
And make us a pattern to all that believe:
    Then, then let it spread,
    Thy knowledge and dread,
    Till the earth is o'erflowed,   [God.
And the universe filled with the glory of

8 s.

220

1 ALL glory to God in the sky,
  And peace upon earth be restored!
O Jesus, exalted on high,
  Appear our omnipotent Lord!
Who, meanly in Bethlehem born,
  Didst stoop to redeem a lost race,
Once more to thy creatures return,
  And reign in thy kingdom of grace.
2 When thou in our flesh didst appear,
  All nature acknowledged thy birth;
Arose the acceptable year,
  And heaven was opened on earth:
Receiving its Lord from above,
  The world was united to bless
The giver of concord and love,
  The Prince and the author of peace.
3 O wouldst thou again be made known!
  Again in thy Spirit descend,
And set up in each of thine own
  A kingdom that never shall end.
Thou only art able to bless,
  And make the glad nations obey,
And bid the dire enmity cease,
  And bow the whole world to thy sway.
4 Come then to thy servants again,
  Who long thy appearing to know,
Thy quiet and peaceable reign
  In mercy establish below;

All sorrow before thee shall fly,
  And anger and hatred be o'er,
And envy and malice shall die,
  And discord afflict us no more.
5 No horrid alarum of war
    Shall break our eternal repose,
No sound of the trumpet is there,
  Where Jesus's Spirit o'erflows ;
Appeased by the charms of thy grace,
  We all shall in amity join,
And kindly each other embrace,
  And love with a passion like thine.

221
7 s & 6 s.

1 MEET and right it is to sing,
    In every time and place,
Glory to our heavenly King,
  The God of truth and grace ;
Join we then with sweet accord,
  All in one thanksgiving join,
Holy, holy, holy Lord,
  Eternal praise be thine !

2 Thee the first-born sons of light,
  In choral symphonies,
Praise by day, day without night,
  And never, never cease ;
Angels and archangels all
  Praise the mystic Three in One,
Sing, and stop, and gaze, and fall
  O'erwhelmed before thy throne.

3 Vying with that happy choir,
  Who chant thy praise above,
We on eagles' wings aspire,
  The wings of faith and love ;
Thee they sing with glory crowned,
  We extol the slaughtered Lamb ;
Lower if our voices sound,
  Our subject is the same.

4 Father, God, thy love we praise,
  Which gave thy Son to die ;
Jesus, full of truth and grace,
  Alike we glorify ;
Spirit. Comforter divine,
  Praise by all to thee be given ;
Till we in full chorus join,
  And earth is turned to heaven.

222
8 s & 6 s.

1 HOW happy, gracious Lord ! are we,
  Divinely drawn to follow thee,
Whose hours divided are
Betwixt the mount and multitude ;
Our day is spent in doing good,
Our night in praise and prayer.

2 With us no melancholy void,
No period lingers unemployed,
  Or unimproved, below ; ·
Our weariness of life is gone,
Who live to serve our God alone,
  And only thee to know.

3 The winter's night and summer's day
Glide imperceptibly away,
  Too short to sing thy praise ;
Too few we find the happy hours,
And haste to join those heavenly powers,
  In everlasting lays.

4 With all who chant thy name on high,
And, " Holy, holy, holy," cry,
  A bright harmonious throng,

We long thy praises to repeat,
And, restless, sing around thy seat
    The new, eternal song.

6 - 8 s.   Psalm cxiv.   ## 223

1 WHEN Israel out of Egypt came,
    And left the proud oppressor's land,
Supported by the great I AM,
Safe in the hollow of his hand,
The Lord in Israel reigned alone,
And Judah was his favourite throne.

2 The sea beheld his power, and fled,
  Disparted by the wondrous rod ;
Jordan ran backward to its head,
  And Sinai felt the incumbent God ;
The mountains skipped like frighted rams,
The hills leaped after them as lambs !

3 What ailed thee, O thou trembling sea?
  What horror turned the river back?
Was nature's God displeased with thee?
  And why should hills or mountains
    shake?   [rams !
Ye mountains huge, that skipped like
Ye hills, that leaped as frighted lambs !

4 Earth ! tremble on, with all thy sons,
  In presence of thy awful Lord,
Whose power inverted nature owns,
  Her only law his sovereign word :
He shakes the centre with his nod,
And heaven bows down to Jacob's God.

5 Creation, varied by his hand,
  The omnipotent Jehovah knows ;
The sea is turned to solid land,
  The rock into a fountain flows :
And all things, as they change, proclaim
The Lord eternally the same.

6 - 8 s.
Second Metre.   Psalm cxlvi.   ## 224

1 I'LL praise my Maker while I've breath,
  And when my voice is lost in death,
  Praise shall employ my nobler powers ;
My days of praise shall ne'er be past,
While life, and thought, and being last,
  Or immortality endures.

2 Happy the man whose hopes rely
  On Israel's God : he made the sky,
  And earth, and seas, with all their train ;
His truth for ever stands secure,
He saves the opprest, he feeds the poor,
  And none shall find his promise vain.

3 The Lord pours eyesight on the blind ;
  The Lord supports the fainting mind ;
  He sends the labouring conscience peace;
He helps the stranger in distress,
The widow, and the fatherless,
  And grants the prisoner sweet release.

4 I'll praise him while he lends me breath,
  And when my voice is lost in death,
  Praise shall employ my nobler powers ;
My days of praise shall ne'er be past,
While life, and thought, and being last,
  Or immortality endures.

L. M.   Psalm cxlvii.   ## 225

1 PRAISE ye the Lord ! 'tis good to raise
    Your hearts and voices in his praise ;
His nature and his works invite
To make this duty our delight.

2 He formed the stars, those heavenly
  flames,   [names,
 He counts their numbers, calls their
 His wisdom's vast, and knows no bound,
 A deep where all our thoughts are
  drowned.

3 Sing to the Lord ; exalt him high,
 Who spreads his clouds along the sky,
 There he prepares the fruitful rain,
 Nor lets the drops descend in vain.

4 He makes the grass the hills adorn,
 And clothes the smiling fields with corn ;
 The beasts with food his hands supply,
 And the young ravens when they cry.

5 What is the creature's skill or force ?
 The sprightly man, or warlike horse ?
 The piercing wit, the active limb ?
 All are too mean delights for him.

6 But saints are lovely in his sight,
 He views his children with delight ;
 He sees their hope, he knows their fear,
 And looks and loves his image there.

226
          C. M.

1 ETERNAL Wisdom ! Thee we praise,
  Thee the creation sings,
 With thy loved name, rocks, hills, and
 And heaven's high palace rings. [seas,

2 Thy hand, how wide it spreads the sky !
  How glorious to behold !
 Tinged with a blue of heavenly dye,
 And starred with sparkling gold.

3 There thou hast bid the globes of light
  Their endless circles run :
 There the pale planet rules the night,
 The day obeys the sun.

4 If down I turn my wondering eyes
  On clouds and storms below,
 Those under-regions of the skies
 Thy numerous glories show.

5 The noisy winds stand ready there
  Thy orders to obey ;
 With sounding wings they sweep the air,
 To make thy chariot way.

6 There, like a trumpet loud and strong,
  Thy thunder shakes our coast,
 While the red lightnings wave along,
 The banners of thy host.

7 On the thin air, without a prop,
  Hang fruitful showers around ;
 At thy command they sink, and drop
 Their fatness on the ground.

8 Lo ! here thy wondrous skill arrays
  The earth in cheerful green :
 A thousand herbs thy art displays,
 A thousand flowers between.

9 There, the rough mountains of the deep
  Obey thy strong command,
 Thy breath can raise the billows steep,
 Or sink them to the sand.

10 Thy glories blaze all nature round,
  And strike the wondering sight,
 Through skies, and seas, and solid ground,
 With terror and delight.

11 Infinite strength and equal skill
  Shine through thy works abroad,
56

Our souls with vast amazement fill,
 And speak the builder God.

12 But the mild glories of thy grace
 Our softer passions move ;
 Pity divine in Jesu's face
 We see, adore, and love.

L. M.   *An Evening Hymn.*   **227**

1 HOW do thy mercies close me round !
  For ever be thy name adored !
 I blush in all things to abound ;
 The servant is above his Lord !

2 Inured to poverty and pain,
  A suffering life my Master led ;
 The Son of God, the Son of man,
 He had not where to lay his head.

3 But lo ! a place he hath prepared
  For me, whom watchful angels keep ;
 Yea, he himself becomes my guard,
 He smooths my bed, and gives me sleep.

4 Jesus protects ; my fears, be gone !
  What can the Rock of ages move ?
 Safe in thy arms I lay me down,
 Thy everlasting arms of love.

5 While thou art intimately nigh,
  Who, who shall violate my rest ?
 Sin, earth, and hell I now defy ;
 I lean upon my Saviour's breast.

6 I rest beneath the Almighty's shade,
  My griefs expire, my troubles cease :
 Thou, Lord, on whom my soul is stayed,
 Wilt keep me still in perfect peace.

7 Me for thine own thou lov'st to take,
  In time and in eternity ;
 Thou never, never wilt forsake
 A helpless worm that trusts in thee.

8 s.   *Canticles i. 7.*   ***228**

1 THOU Shepherd of Israel, and mine,
  The joy and desire of my heart,
 For closer communion I pine,
  I long to reside where thou art :
 The pasture I languish to find
  Where all, who their Shepherd obey,
 Are fed, on thy bosom reclined,
  And screened from the heat of the day.

2 Ah ! show me that happiest place,
  The place of thy people's abode,
 Where saints in an ecstasy gaze,
  And hang on a crucified God ;
 Thy love for a sinner declare,
  Thy passion and death on the tree :
 My spirit to Calvary bear,
  To suffer and triumph with thee.

3 'Tis there, with the lambs of thy flock,
  There only, I covet to rest,
 To lie at the foot of the rock,
  Or rise to be hid in thy breast ;
 'Tis there I would always abide,
  And never a moment depart,
 Concealed in the cleft of thy side,
  Eternally held in thy heart.

4 - 6 s &
2 - 8 s.   *A Birthday Hymn.*   **229**

1 GOD of my life, to thee
  My cheerful soul I raise !

Thy goodness bade me be,
  And still prolongs my days;
I see my natal hour return,
And bless the day that I was born.

2 A clod of living earth,
  I glorify thy name,
From whom alone my birth,
  And all my blessings, came;
Creating and preserving grace
Let all that is within me praise.

3 Long as I live beneath,
  To thee O let me live!
To thee my every breath
  In thanks and praises give!
Whate'er I have, whate'er I am,
Shall magnify my Maker's name.

4 My soul and all its powers
  Thine, wholly thine, shall be;
All, all my happy hours
  I consecrate to thee;
Me to thine image now restore,
And I shall praise thee evermore.

5 I wait thy will to do,
  As angels do in heaven;
In Christ a creature new,
  Most graciously forgiven,
I wait thy perfect will to prove,
All sanctified by spotless love.

6 Then, when the work is done,
  The work of faith with power,
Receive thy favoured son,
  In death's triumphant hour;
Like Moses to thyself convey,
And kiss my raptured soul away.

230   *A Birthday Hymn.*   6 - 8 s.

1 FOUNTAIN of life and all my joy,
  Jesus, thy mercies I embrace;
The breath thou giv'st, for thee employ,
  And wait to taste thy perfect grace;
No more forsaken and forlorn,
I bless the day that I was born.

2 Preserved through faith by power divine,
  A miracle of grace I stand!
I prove the strength of Jesus mine!
  Jesus, upheld by thy right hand,
Though in my flesh I feel the thorn,
I bless the day that I was born.

3 Weary of life, through inbred sin,
  I was, but now defy its power;
When as a flood the foe comes in,
  My soul is more than conqueror;
I tread him down with holy scorn,
And bless the day that I was born.

4 Come, Lord, and make me pure within,
  And let me now be filled with God!
Live to declare I'm saved from sin:
  And if I seal the truth with blood,
My soul, from out the body torn,
Shall bless the day that I was born.

231   *A Birthday Hymn.*   5 5 9, 5 5 9.

1 AWAY with our fears!
  The glad morning appears
When an heir of salvation was born!
  From Jehovah I came,
  For his glory I am,
And to him I with singing return.

2 Thee, Jesus, alone,
  The fountain I own
Of my life and felicity here;
  And cheerfully sing
  My Redeemer and King,
Till his sign in the heavens appear.

3 With thanks I rejoice
  In thy fatherly choice
Of my state and condition below;
  If of parents I came
  Who honoured thy name,
'Twas thy wisdom appointed it so.

4 I sing of thy grace,
  From my earliest days
Ever near to allure and defend;
  Hitherto thou hast been
  My preserver from sin,
And I trust thou wilt save to the end.

5 O the infinite cares,
  And temptations, and snares,
Thy hand hath conducted me through!
  O the blessings bestowed
  By a bountiful God,
And the mercies eternally new!

6 What a mercy is this,
  What a heaven of bliss,
How unspeakably happy am I!
  Gathered into the fold,
  With thy people enrolled,
With thy people to live and to die!

7 O the goodness of God,
  Employing a clod
His tribute of glory to raise!
  His standard to bear,
  And with triumph declare
His unspeakable riches of grace.

8 O the fathomless love,
  That has deigned to approve
And prosper the work of my hands!
  With my pastoral crook,
  I went over the brook,
And, behold, I am spread into bands!

9 Who, I ask in amaze,
  Hath begotten me these?
And inquire from what quarter they came?
  My full heart it replies,
  They are born from the skies,
And gives glory to God and the Lamb.

10 All honour and praise
  To the Father of grace,
To the Spirit, and Son, I return!
  The business pursue
  He hath made me to do,
And rejoice that I ever was born.

11 In a rapture of joy
  My life I employ,
The God of my life to proclaim;
  'Tis worth living for this,
  To administer bliss
And salvation in Jesus's name.

12 My remnant of days
  I spend in his praise,
Who died the whole world to redeem;
  Be they many or few,
  My days are his due,
And they all are devoted to him.

232
4·6 s & 2·8 s.

1 YOUNG men and maidens, raise
    Your tuneful voices high;
Old men and children, praise
    The Lord of earth and sky;
Him Three in One, and One in Three,
Extol to all eternity.

2 The universal King
    Let all the world proclaim;
Let every creature sing
    His attributes and name!
Him Three in One, and One in Three,
Extol to all eternity.

3 In his great name alone
    All excellences meet,
Who sits upon the throne,
    And shall for ever sit:
Him Three in One, and One in Three,
Extol to all eternity.

4 Glory to God belongs,
    Glory to God be given,
Above the noblest songs
    Of all in earth or heaven!
Him Three in One, and One in Three,
Extol to all eternity.

233
8·7 s.

1 HAPPY man whom God doth aid!
    God our souls and bodies made;
God on us, in gracious showers,
Blessings every moment pours;
Compasses with angel-bands,
Bids them bear us in their hands;
Parents, friends, 'twas God bestowed,
Life, and all, descend from God.

2 He this flowery carpet spread,
Made the earth on which we tread;
God refreshes in the air,
Covers with the clothes we wear,
Feeds us with the food we eat,
Cheers us by his light and heat,
Makes his sun on us to shine;
All our blessings are divine!

3 Give him then, and ever give,
Thanks for all that we receive!
Man we for his kindness love,
How much more our God above?
Worthy thou, our heavenly Lord,
To be honoured and adored;
God of all-creating grace,
Take the everlasting praise!

234
L. M.

1 LET all that breathe Jehovah praise,
    Almighty, all-creating Lord!
Let earth and heaven his power confess,
Brought out of nothing by his word.

2 He spake the word, and it was done,
The universe his word obeyed;
His Word is his eternal Son,
And Christ the whole creation made.

3 Jesus, the Lord and God most high,
Maker of all mankind and me,
Me thou hast made to glorify,
To know, and love, and live to thee.
58

4 Wherefore to thee my heart I give,
    (But thou must first bestow the power),
And if for thee on earth I live,
    Thee I shall soon in heaven adore.

L. M.   *The Lord's Prayer.* ## 235

1 FATHER of all! whose powerful voice
    Called forth this universal frame;
Whose mercies over all rejoice,
    Through endless ages still the same;
Thou by thy word upholdest all;
    Thy bounteous love to all is showed,
Thou hear'st thy every creature's call,
    And fillest every mouth with good.

2 In heaven thou reign'st enthroned in
        light,
Nature's expanse beneath thee spread,
Earth, air, and sea, before thy sight,
    And hell's deep gloom, are open laid;
Wisdom, and might, and love are thine;
Prostrate before thy face we fall,
Confess thine attributes divine,
    And hail the sovereign Lord of all.

3 Thee, sovereign Lord, let all confess
    That moves in earth, or air, or sky,
Revere thy power, thy goodness bless,
    Tremble before thy piercing eye;
All ye who owe to him your birth,
    In praise your every hour employ:
Jehovah reigns! be glad, O earth!
    And shout, ye morning stars, for joy!

L. M.   SECOND PART. ## 236

1 SON of thy Sire's eternal love,
    Take to thyself thy mighty power,
Let all earth's sons thy mercy prove.
Let all thy bleeding grace adore;
The triumphs of thy love display,
    In every heart reign thou alone,
Till all thy foes confess thy sway,
    And glory ends what grace begun.

2 Spirit of grace, and health, and power,
    Fountain of light and love below,
Abroad thy healing influence shower,
    O'er all the nations let it flow;
Inflame our hearts with perfect love,
    In us the work of faith fulfil;
So not heaven's host shall swifter move
Than we on earth, to do thy will.

3 Father, 'tis thine each day to yield
    Thy children's wants a fresh supply,
Thou cloth'st the lilies of the field,
    And hearest the young ravens cry:
On thee we cast our care; we live
    Through thee, who know'st our every
O feed us with thy grace, and give [need;
    Our souls this day the living bread!

L. M.   THIRD PART. ## 237

1 ETERNAL, spotless Lamb of God,
    Before the world's foundation slain,
Sprinkle us ever with thy blood,
    O cleanse, and keep us ever clean!
To every soul (all praise to thee!)
    Our bowels of compassion move;
And all mankind by this may see
    God is in us; for God is love.

2 Giver and Lord of life, whose power
  And guardian care for all are free,
To thee, in fierce temptation's hour,
  From sin and Satan let us flee ;
Thine, Lord, we are, and ours thou art,
  In us be all thy goodness showed ;
Renew, enlarge, and fill our heart [God.
  With peace, and joy, and heaven, and

3 Blessing and honour, praise and love,
  Co-equal, co-eternal Three,
In earth below, and heaven above,
  By all thy works be paid to thee !
Thrice Holy ! thine the kingdom is,
  The power omnipotent is thine,
And when created nature dies,
  Thy never-ceasing glories shine.

238

                            8 - 7 s.

1 MEET and right it is to praise
    God, the giver of all grace,
God, whose mercies are bestowed
On the evil and the good ;
He prevents his creatures' call,
Kind and merciful to all ;
Makes his sun on sinners rise,
Showers his blessings from the skies.

2 Least of all thy creatures, we
Daily thy salvation see ;
As by heavenly manna fed,
Through a world of dangers led ;
Through a wilderness of cares ;
Through ten thousand thousand snares,
More than now our hearts conceive,
More than we could know, and live !

3 Here, as in the lion's den,
Undevoured we still remain ;
Pass secure the watery flood,
Hanging on the arm of God ;
Here we raise our voices higher,
Shout in the refiner's fire,
Clap our hands amidst the flame,
Glory give to Jesu's name. ƒ

4 Jesu's name in Satan's hour
Stands our adamantine tower ;
Jesus doth his own defend,
Love, and save us to the end.
Love shall make us persevere
Till our conquering Lord appear,
Bear us to our thrones above,
Crown us with his heavenly love.

239

                            C. M.

1 HAIL! Father, Son, and Holy Ghost,
  One God, in Persons Three !
Of thee we make our joyful boast,
  Our songs we make of thee.

2 Thou neither canst be felt nor seen,
  Thou art a Spirit pure ;
Thou from eternity hast been,
  And always shalt endure.

3 Present alike in every place,
  Thy Godhead we adore ;
Beyond the bounds of time and space,
  Thou dwell'st for evermore.

4 In wisdom infinite thou art,
  Thine eye doth all things see ;
And every thought of every heart
  Is f l known to thee.
    Cu ly

5 Whate'er thou wilt, in earth below
  Thou dost, in heaven above :
But chiefly we rejoice to know
  The almighty God of love.

6 Thou lov'st whate'er thy hands have made,
  Thy goodness we rehearse,
In shining characters displayed
  Throughout our universe.

7 Mercy, with love and endless grace,
  O'er all thy works doth reign ;
But mostly thou delight'st to bless
  Thy favourite creature, man.

8 Wherefore, let every creature give
  To thee the praise designed,
But, chiefly, Lord, the thanks receive,
  The hearts of all mankind.

240

L. M.   *The Attributes of God.*

1 O GOD, thou bottomless abyss !
  Thee to perfection who can know ?
O height immense ! What words suffice
  Thy countless attributes to show ?
Unfathomable depths thou art ;
  O plunge me in thy mercy's sea !
Void of true wisdom is my heart ;
  With love embrace and cover me :
While thee, all-infinite, I set
  By faith before my ravished eye,
My weakness bends beneath the weight ;
  O'erpowered I sink, I faint, I die.

2 Eternity thy fountain was,
  Which, like thee, no beginning knew ;
Thou wast ere time began his race,
  Ere glowed with stars the ethereal blue.
Greatness unspeakable is thine,
  Greatness, whose undiminished ray,
When short-lived worlds are lost, shall
    shine,
When earth and heaven are fled away.
Unchangeable, all-perfect Lord,
  Essential life's unbounded sea,
What lives and moves, lives by thy word ;
  It lives, and moves, and is from thee.

3 Thy parent-hand, thy forming skill,
  Firm fixed this universal chain ;
Else empty, barren darkness still
  Had held his unmolested reign.
Whate'er in earth, or sea, or sky,
  Or shuns or meets the wandering
    thought,
Escapes or strikes the searching eye,
  By thee was to perfection brought ;
High is thy power above all height,
  Whate'er thy will decrees is done ;
Thy wisdom, equal to thy might,
  Only to thee, O God, is known !

4 Heaven's glory is thy awful throne,
  Yet earth partakes thy gracious sway :
Vain man ! thy wisdom folly own,
  Lost is thy reason's feeble ray.
What our dim eye could never see,
  Is plain and naked to thy sight ;
What thickest darkness veils, to thee
  Shines clearly as the morning light.
In light thou dwell'st ; light that no shade,
  No variation, ever knew ;
Heaven, earth, and hell, stand all dis-
  And open to thy piercing view. [played,

241 SECOND PART. L. M.

1 THOU, true and only God, lead'st forth
    The immortal armies of the sky;
Thou laugh'st to scorn the gods of earth,
    Thou thunderest, and amazed they fly.
With downcast eye the angelic choir
    Appear before thy awful face;
Trembling they strike the golden lyre,
    And through heaven's vault resound thy
        praise.
In earth, in heaven, in all thou art;
    The conscious creature feels thy nod,
Whose forming hand on every part
    Impressed the image of its God.

2 Thine, Lord, is wisdom, thine alone;
    Justice and truth before thee stand;
Yet, nearer to thy sacred throne,
    Mercy withholds thy lifted hand.
Each evening shows thy tender love,
    Each rising morn thy plenteous grace;
Thy wakened wrath doth slowly move,
    Thy willing mercy flies apace.
To thy benign indulgent care,
    Father, this light, this breath we owe;
And all we have, and all we are,
    From thee, great Source of being, flow.

3 Parent of good, thy bounteous hand
    Incessant blessings down distils,
And all in air, or sea, or land,
    With plenteous food and gladness fills.
All things in thee live, move, and are,
    Thy power infused doth all sustain;
Even those thy daily favours share
    Who thankless spurn thy easy reign.
Thy sun thou bidd'st his genial ray
    Alike on all impartial pour;
To all, who hate or bless thy sway,
    Thou bidd'st descend the fruitful shower.

4 Yet, while at length who scorned thy might
    Shall feel thee a consuming fire,
How sweet the joys, the crown how bright,
    Of those who to thy love aspire!
All creatures, praise the eternal name!
    Ye hosts that to his court belong,
Cherubic choirs, seraphic flames,
    Awake the everlasting song!
Thrice Holy! thine the kingdom is,
    The power omnipotent is thine,
And when created nature dies,
    Thy never-ceasing glories shine.

242 The same subject. 7 s & 6 s.

1 GLORIOUS God, accept a heart
    That pants to sing thy praise:
Thou without beginning art,
    And without end of days;
Thou, a Spirit invisible,
    Dost to none thy fulness show;
None thy majesty can tell,
    Or all thy Godhead know.

2 All thine attributes we own,
    Thy wisdom, power, and might;
Happy in thyself alone,
    In goodness infinite.
Thou thy goodness hast displayed,
    On thine every work imprest;
Lov'st whate'er thy hands have made,
    But man thou lov'st the best.
60

3 Willing thou that all should know
    Thy saving truth, and live,
Dost to each or bliss or woe
    With strictest justice give;
Thou with perfect righteousness
    Renderest every man his due,
Faithful in thy promises,
    And in thy threatenings too.

4 Thou art merciful to all
    Who truly turn to thee,
Hear me then for pardon call,
    And show thy grace to me;
Me, through mercy reconciled,
    Me, for Jesus's sake forgiven,
Me receive, thy favoured child,
    To sing thy praise in heaven.

7 s & 6 s. The same subject. 243

1 THOU, my God, art good and wise,
    And infinite in power,
Thee let all in earth and skies
    Continually adore!
Give me thy converting grace,
    That I may obedient prove,
Serve my Maker all my days,
    And my Redeemer love.

2 For my life, and clothes, and food,
    And every comfort here,
Thee, my most indulgent God,
    I thank with heart sincere;
For the blessings numberless
    Which thou hast already given,
For my smallest spark of grace,
    And for my hope of heaven.

3 Gracious God, my sins forgive,
    And thy good Spirit impart;
Then I shall in thee believe
    With all my loving heart;
Always unto Jesus look,
    Him in heavenly glory see,
Who my cause hath undertook,
    And ever prays for me.

4 Grace, in answer to his prayer,
    And every grace bestow,
That I may with zealous care
    Perform thy will below;
Rooted in humility,
    Still in every state resigned,
Plant, almighty Lord, in me
    A meek and lowly mind.

5 Poor and vile in my own eyes,
    With self-abasing shame
Still I would myself despise,
    And magnify thy name;
Thee let every creature bless,
    Praise to God alone be given,
God alone deserves the praise
    Of all in earth and heaven.

7 s & 6 s †. The same subject. 244

1 THOU, the great, eternal Lord,
    Art high above our thought!
Worthy to be feared, adored,
    By all thy hands have wrought;
None can with thyself compare;
    Thy glory fills both earth and sky;
We, and all thy creatures, are
    As nothing in thine eye.

2 Of thy great unbounded power
   To thee the praise we give,
Infinitely great, and more
   Than heart can e'er conceive ;
When thou wilt to work proceed,
   Thy purpose firm none can withstand,
Frustrate the determined deed,
   Or stay the almighty hand.

3 Thou, O God, art wise alone !
   Thy counsel doth excel ;
Wonderful thy works we own,
   Thy ways unsearchable ;
Who can sound the mystery,
   Thy judgments' deep abyss explain ?
Thine, whose eyes in darkness see,
   And search the heart of man.

245

The same subject.   7 s & 6 s †.

1 GOOD thou art, and good thou dost,
   Thy mercies reach to all,
Chiefly those who on thee trust,
   And for thy mercy call ;
New they every morning are ;
   As fathers when their children cry,
Us thou dost in pity spare,
   And all our wants supply.

2 Mercy o'er thy works presides ;
   Thy providence displayed
Still preserves, and still provides
   For all thy hands have made ;
Keeps with most distinguished care
   The man who on thy love depends ;
Watches every numbered hair,
   And all his steps attends.

3 Who can sound the depths unknown
   Of thy redeeming grace ?
Grace that gave thine only Son
   To save a ruined race !
Millions of transgressors poor
   Thou hast for Jesu's sake forgiven,
Made them of thy favour sure,
   And snatched from hell to heaven.

4 Millions more thou ready art
   To save, and to forgive ;
Every soul and every heart
   Of man thou wouldst receive :
Father, now accept of mine,
   Which now, through Christ, I offer thee ;
Tell me now, in love divine,
   That thou hast pardoned me !

246

Psalm cxvi. 8.   L. M.

1 MY soul, through my Redeemer's care,
   Saved from the second death I feel,
My eyes from tears of dark despair,
   My feet from falling into hell.

2 Wherefore to him my feet shall run,
   My eyes on his perfections gaze,
My soul shall live for God alone,
   And all within me shout his praise.

247

1 Samuel ii. 2.   L. M.

1 HOLY as thou, O Lord, is none !
   Thy holiness is all thy own ;
A drop of that unbounded sea
   Is ours, a drop derived from thee.

2 And when thy purity we share,
   Thy only glory we declare ;
And humbled into nothing own,
   Holy and pure is God alone.

3 Sole, self-existing God and Lord,
   By all thy heavenly hosts adored,
Let all on earth bow down to thee,
   And own thy peerless majesty ;

4 Thy power unparalleled confess,
   Established on the rock of peace ;
The rock that never shall remove,
   The rock of pure, almighty love.

C. M.   1 Chronicles xxix. 10—13.   ### 248

1 BLEST be our everlasting Lord,
   Our Father, God, and King !
Thy sovereign goodness we record,
   Thy glorious power we sing.

2 By thee the victory is given ;
   The majesty divine,
And strength, and might, and earth, and
   And all therein, are thine.   [heaven.

3 The kingdom, Lord, is thine alone,
   Who dost thy right maintain,
And, high on thine eternal throne,
   O'er men and angels reign.

4 Riches, as seemeth good to thee,
   Thou dost, and honour, give ;
And kings their power and dignity
   Out of thy hand receive.

5 Thou hast on us the grace bestowed
   Thy greatness to proclaim ;
And therefore now we thank our God,
   And praise thy glorious name.

6 Thy glorious name and nature's powers
   Thou dost to us make known ;
And all the Deity is ours,
   Through thy incarnate Son.

C M.   Exodus xxxiv. 5, 6.   ### 249

1 GREAT God ! to me the sight afford
   To him of old allowed ;
And let my faith behold its Lord
   Descending in a cloud.

2 In that revealing Spirit come down,
   Thine attributes proclaim,
And to my inmost soul make known
   The glories of thy name.

3 Jehovah, Christ, I thee adore,
   Who gav'st my soul to be !
Fountain of being, and of power,
   And great in majesty.

4 The Lord, the mighty God, thou art ;
   But let me rather prove
That name in-spoken to my heart,
   That favourite name of Love.

5 Merciful God, thyself proclaim
   In this polluted breast ;
Mercy is thy distinguished name,
   Which suits a sinner best.

6 Our misery doth for pity call,
   Our sin implores thy grace ;
And thou art merciful to all
   Our lost, apostate race.

250

SECOND PART.   C. M

1 THY ceaseless, unexhausted love,
    Unmerited and free,
Delights our evil to remove,
    And helps our misery.

2 Thou waitest to be gracious still;
    Thou dost with sinners bear,
That, saved, we may thy goodness feel,
    And all thy grace declare.

3 Thy goodness and thy truth to me,
    To every soul, abound,
A vast, unfathomable sea,
    Where all our thoughts are drowned.

4 Its streams the whole creation reach,
    So plenteous is the store,
Enough for all, enough for each,
    Enough for evermore.

5 Faithful, O Lord, thy mercies are,
    A rock that cannot move!
A thousand promises declare
    Thy constancy of love.

6 Throughout the universe it reigns,
    Unalterably sure;
And while the truth of God remains,
    The goodness must endure.

251

Luke xi. 2.   C. M.

1 FATHER of me, and all mankind,
    And all the hosts above,
Let every understanding mind
    Unite to praise thy love;

2 To know thy nature, and thy name,
    One God in Persons Three;
And glorify the great I AM,
    Through all eternity.

3 Thy kingdom come, with power and grace,
    To every heart of man;
Thy peace, and joy, and righteousness
    In all our bosoms reign.

4 The righteousness that never ends,
    But makes an end of sin;
The joy that human thought transcends,
    Into our souls bring in;

5 The kingdom of established peace,
    Which can no more remove;
The perfect power of godliness,
    The omnipotence of love.

252

Numbers vi. 24—26.   C. M.

1 COME, Father, Son, and Holy Ghost,
    One God in Persons Three,
Bring back the heavenly blessing, lost
    By all mankind and me.

2 Thy favour, and thy nature too,
    To me, to all restore;
Forgive, and after God renew,
    And keep us evermore.

3 Eternal Sun of righteousness,
    Display thy beams divine,
And cause the glories of thy face
    Upon my heart to shine.

4 Light in thy light O may I see,
    Thy grace and mercy prove,
Revived, and cheered, and blessed by thee,
    The God of pardoning love!
    c2

5 Lift up thy countenance serene,
    And let thy happy child
Behold, without a cloud between,
    The Godhead reconciled.

6 That all-comprising peace bestow
    On me, through grace forgiven,
The joys of holiness below,
    And then the joys of heaven.

S. M.   *253

1 FATHER, in whom we live,
    In whom we are, and move,
The glory, power, and praise receive
    Of thy creating love.
Let all the angel-throng
    Give thanks to God on high;
While earth repeats the joyful song,
    And echoes to the sky.

2 Incarnate Deity,
    Let all the ransomed race
Render in thanks their lives to thee
    For thy redeeming grace.
The grace to sinners showed
    Ye heavenly choirs proclaim,
And cry, "Salvation to our God,
    Salvation to the Lamb!"

3 Spirit of Holiness,
    Let all thy saints adore
Thy sacred energy, and bless
    Thine heart-renewing power.
Not angel-tongues can tell
    Thy love's ecstatic height,
The glorious joy unspeakable,
    The beatific sight.

4 Eternal, Triune Lord!
    Let all the hosts above,
Let all the sons of men, record
    And dwell upon thy love.
When heaven and earth are fled
    Before thy glorious face,
Sing all the saints thy love hath made
    Thine everlasting praise!

Philippians i. 10;   254
2 Peter iii. 12.

L. M.

1 THE day of Christ, the day of God,
    We humbly hope with joy to see,
Washed in the sanctifying blood
    Of an expiring Deity,
Who did for us his life resign;
    There is no other God but one;
For all the plenitude divine
    Resides in the eternal Son.

2 Spotless, sincere, without offence,
    O may we to his day remain,
Who trust the blood of God to cleanse
    Our souls from every sinful stain.
Lord, we believe the promise sure;
    The purchased Comforter impart,
Apply thy blood to make us pure,
    To keep us pure in life and heart.

3 Then let us see that day supreme,
    When none thy Godhead shall deny,
Thy sovereign Majesty blaspheme,
    Or count thee less than the most High:
When all who on their God believe,
    Who here thy last appearing love,
Shall thy consummate joy receive,
    And see thy glorious face above.

255

6 - 8 s.

1 SPIRIT of truth, essential God,
Who didst thy ancient saints inspire,
Shed in their hearts thy love abroad,
And touch their hallowed lips with fire ;
Our God from all eternity,
World without end we worship thee !

2 Still we believe, almighty Lord,
Whose presence fills both earth and
The meaning of the written word [heaven,
Is by thy inspiration given ;
Thou only dost thyself explain
The secret mind of God to man.

3 Come, then, divine Interpreter,
The scriptures to our hearts apply ;
And, taught by thee, we God revere,
Him in Three Persons magnify ;
In each the Triune God adore,
Who was, and is for evermore.

256

C. M.

1 HAIL ! Father, Son, and Spirit great,
Before the birth of time
Enthroned in everlasting state,
JEHOVAH, ELOHIM !

2 A mystical plurality
We in the Godhead own,
Adoring One in Persons Three,
And Three in nature One.

3 From thee our being we receive,
The creatures of thy grace ;
And, raised out of the earth, we live
To sing our Maker's praise.

4 Thy powerful, wise, and loving mind
Did our creation plan ;
And all the glorious Persons joined
To form thy favourite, man.

5 Again thou didst, in council met,
Thy ruined work restore,
Established in our first estate,
To forfeit it no more.

6 And when we rise in love renewed,
Our souls resemble thee,
An image of the Triune God,
To all eternity.

257* *"Glory be to God on high,"* &c.
(Communion Service.)   7 s.

1 GLORY be to God on high,
God whose glory fills the sky ;
Peace on earth to man forgiven,
Man, the well-beloved of heaven.

2 Sovereign Father, heavenly King,
Thee we now presume to sing ;
Glad, thine attributes confess,
Glorious all, and numberless.

3 Hail, by all thy works adored !
Hail, the everlasting Lord !
Thee with thankful hearts we prove
God of power, and God of love.

4 Christ our Lord and God we own,
Christ, the Father's only Son,
Lamb of God for sinners slain,
Saviour of offending man.

5 Bow thine ear, in mercy bow,
Hear, the world's atonement, thou !

Jesus, in thy name we pray,
Take, O take our sins away !

6 Powerful advocate with God,
Justify us by thy blood ;
Bow thine ear, in mercy bow,
Hear, the world's atonement, thou !

7 Hear, for thou, O Christ, alone
Art with God the Father one,
One the Holy Ghost with thee,
One supreme, eternal THREE.

258
C. M.   Numbers vi. 24—26.

1 JEHOVAH, God the Father, bless,
And thy own work defend !
With mercy's outstretched arms embrace,
And keep us to the end !
Preserve the creatures of thy love,
By providential care
Conducted to the realms above,
To sing thy goodness there.

2 Jehovah, God the Son, reveal
The brightness of thy face ;
And all thy pardoned people fill
With plenitude of grace !
Shine forth with all the Deity,
Which dwells in thee alone ;
And lift us up thy face to see
On thy eternal throne.

3 Jehovah, God the Spirit, shine,
Father and Son to show !
With bliss ineffable, divine,
Our ravished hearts o'erflow.
Sure earnest of that happiness
Which human hope transcends,
Be thou our everlasting peace,
When grace in glory ends !

259
C. M.

1 HAIL ! holy, holy, holy Lord !
Whom One in Three we know :
By all thy heavenly host adored,
By all thy church below.

2 One undivided Trinity
With triumph we proclaim ;
Thy universe is full of thee,
And speaks thy glorious name.

3 Thee, Holy Father, we confess,
Thee, Holy Son, adore,
Thee, Spirit of truth and holiness,
We worship evermore.

4 The incommunicable right,
Almighty God ! receive,
Which angel-choirs, and saints in light,
And saints embodied give.

5 Three Persons equally divine
We magnify and love ;
And both the choirs ere long shall join,
To sing thy praise above.

6 Hail ! holy, holy, holy Lord,
(Our heavenly song shall be)
Supreme, essential One, adored
In co-eternal Three !

260
8 - 7 s.

1 HOLY, holy, holy Lord,
God the Father, and the Word,

63

God the Comforter, receive
Blessings more than we can give !
Mixed with those beyond the sky,
Chanters to the Lord most high,
We our hearts and voices raise,
Echoing thy eternal praise.

2 One, inexplicably Three,
Three, in simplest Unity,
God, incline thy gracious ear,
Us, thy lisping creatures, hear !
Thee while man, the earth-born, sings,
Angels shrink within their wings,
Prostrate seraphim above
Breathe unutterable love.

3 Happy they who never rest,
With thy heavenly presence blest !
They the heights of glory see,
Sound the depths of Deity !
Fain with them our souls would vie,
Sink as low, and mount as high ;
Fall o'erwhelmed with love, or soar,
Shout, or silently adore !

261

6 - 8 s.

1 COME, Father, Son, and Holy Ghost,
Whom one all-perfect God we own,
Restorer of thine image lost,
Thy various offices make known ;
Display, our fallen souls to raise,
Thy whole economy of grace.

2 Jehovah in Three Persons, come,
And draw, and sprinkle us, and seal,
Poor, guilty, dying worms, in whom
Thou dost eternal life reveal ;
The knowledge of thyself bestow,
And all thy glorious goodness show.

3 Soon as our pardoned hearts believe
That thou art pure, essential love,
The proof we in ourselves receive
Of the three witnesses above ;
Sure, as the saints around thy throne,
That Father, Word, and Spirit, are One.

4 O that we now, in love renewed,
Might blameless in thy sight appear :
Wake we in thy similitude,
Stamped with the Triune character ;
Flesh, spirit, soul, to thee resign,
And live and die entirely thine !

262

C. M.

1 A thousand oracles divine
Their common beams unite,
That sinners may with angels join
To worship God aright ;
To praise a Trinity adored
By all the hosts above,
And one thrice-holy God and Lord
Through endless ages love.

2 Triumphant host ! they never cease
To laud and magnify
The Triune God of holiness,
Whose glory fills the sky ;
Whose glory to this earth extends,
When God himself imparts,
And the whole Trinity descends
Into our faithful hearts.

3 By faith the upper choir we meet,
And challenge them to sing
64

Jehovah on his shining seat,
Our Maker and our King.
But God made flesh is wholly ours,
And asks our nobler strain ;
The Father of celestial powers,
The friend of earth-born man !

4 Ye seraphs nearest to the throne,
With rapturous amaze
On us, poor ransomed worms, look down
For heaven's superior praise ;
The King, whose glorious face ye see,
For us his crown resigned ;
That fulness of the Deity,
He died for all mankind !

*263

C. M.

1 FATHER, how wide thy glory shines !
How high thy wonders rise !
Known through the earth by thousand
By thousands through the skies. [signs,

2 Those mighty orbs proclaim thy power,
Their motions speak thy skill ;
And on the wings of every hour
We read thy patience still.

3 Part of thy name divinely stands
On all thy creatures writ ;
They show the labour of thy hands,
Or impress of thy feet.

4 But when we view thy strange design
To save rebellious worms,
Where vengeance and compassion join
In their divinest forms ;

5 Here the whole Deity is known,
Nor dares a creature guess
Which of the glories brightest shone,
The justice, or the grace.

6 Now the full glories of the Lamb
Adorn the heavenly plains !
Bright seraphs learn Immanuel's name,
And try their choicest strains.

7 O may I bear some humble part
In that immortal song !
Wonder and joy shall tune my heart,
And love command my tongue.

264

S. M.

1 O ALL-CREATING God !
At whose supreme decree
Our body rose, a breathing clod,
Our souls sprang forth from thee ;

2 For this thou hast designed,
And formed us man for this,
To know and love thyself, and find
In thee our endless bliss.

SECTION II.

FOR BELIEVERS FIGHTING.

265

S. M.

1 O MAY thy powerful word
Inspire a feeble worm
To rush into thy kingdom, Lord,
And take it as by storm !

2 O may we all improve
  The grace already given,
To seize the crown of perfect love,
  And scale the mount of heaven !

266   S. M.

1 SOLDIERS of Christ, arise,
  And put your armour on,
Strong in the strength which God supplies
  Through his eternal Son ;
  Strong in the Lord of hosts,
  And in his mighty power,
Who in the strength of Jesus trusts
  Is more than conqueror.

2 Stand then in his great might,
  With all his strength endued ;
But take, to arm you for the fight,
  The panoply of God ;
  That, having all things done,
  And all your conflicts passed,
Ye may o'ercome through Christ alone,
  And stand entire at last.

3 Stand then against your foes
  In close and firm array ;
Legions of wily fiends oppose
  Throughout the evil day ;
  But meet the sons of night,
  But mock their vain design,
Armed in the arms of heavenly light
  Of righteousness divine.

4 Leave no unguarded place,
  No weakness of the soul,
Take every virtue, every grace,
  And fortify the whole ;
  Indissolubly joined,
  To battle all proceed ;
But arm yourselves with all the mind
  That was in Christ, your Head.

267   SECOND PART.   S. M.

1 BUT, above all, lay hold
  On faith's victorious shield ;
Armed with that adamant and gold,
  Be sure to win the field ;
  If faith surround your heart,
  Satan shall be subdued,
Repelled his every fiery dart,
  And quenched with Jesu's blood.

2 Jesus hath died for you !
  What can his love withstand ?
Believe, hold fast your shield, and who
  Shall pluck you from his hand ?
  Believe that Jesus reigns,
  All power to him is given ;
Believe, till freed from sin's remains,
  Believe yourselves to heaven !

3 To keep your armour bright,
  Attend with constant care,
Still walking in your Captain's sight,
  And watching unto prayer.
  Ready for all alarms,
  Steadfastly set your face,
And always exercise your arms,
  And use your every grace.

4 Pray, without ceasing pray,
  Your Captain gives the word ;
His summons cheerfully obey,
  And call upon the Lord ;

To God your every want
  In instant prayer display ;
Pray always ; pray, and never faint ;
  Pray, without ceasing pray.

S. M.   THIRD PART.   268

1 IN fellowship, alone,
  To God with faith draw near,
Approach his courts, besiege his throne
  With all the powers of prayer :
  Go to his temple, go,
  Nor from his altar move ;
Let every house his worship know,
  And every heart his love.

2 To God your spirits dart,
  Your souls in words declare,
Or groan, to him who reads the heart,
  The unutterable prayer :
  His mercy now implore,
  And now show forth his praise,
In shouts, or silent awe, adore
  His miracles of grace.

3 Pour out your souls to God,
  And bow them with your knees,
And spread your hearts and hands abroad,
  And pray for Zion's peace ;
  Your guides and brethren bear
  For ever on your mind ;
Extend the arms of mighty prayer,
  In grasping all mankind.

4 From strength to strength go on,
  Wrestle, and fight, and pray,
Tread all the powers of darkness down,
  And win the well-fought day ;
  Still let the Spirit cry
  In all his soldiers, " Come,"
Till Christ the Lord descend from high,
  And take the conquerors home.

6 - 8 s.   269

1 SURROUNDED by a host of foes,
  Stormed by a host of foes within,
Nor swift to flee, nor strong to oppose,
  Single, against hell, earth, and sin,
Single, yet undismayed, I am ;
I dare believe in Jesu's name.

2 What though a thousand hosts engage,
  A thousand worlds, my soul to shake ?
I have a shield shall quell their rage,
  And drive the alien armies back ;
Portrayed it bears a bleeding Lamb ;
I dare believe in Jesu's name.

3 Me to retrieve from Satan's hands,
  Me from this evil world to free,
To purge my sins, and loose my bands,
  And save from all iniquity,
My Lord and God from heaven he came ;
I dare believe in Jesu's name.

4 Salvation in his name there is,
  Salvation from sin, death, and hell,
Salvation into glorious bliss,
  How great salvation, who can tell !
But all he hath for mine I claim ;
I dare believe in Jesu's name.

S. M.   270

1 EQUIP me for the war,
  And teach my hands to fight,

My simple, upright heart prepare,
  And guide my words aright;
  Control my every thought,
  My whole of sin remove;
Let all my works in thee be wrought,
  Let all be wrought in love.

2 O arm me with the mind,
  Meek Lamb! which was in thee,
And let my knowing zeal be joined
  With perfect charity;
  With calm and tempered zeal
Let me enforce thy call,
And vindicate thy gracious will
  Which offers life to all.

3 O do not let me trust
  In any arm but thine!
Humble, O humble to the dust
  This stubborn soul of mine!
  A feeble thing of nought,
With lowly shame I own,
The help which upon earth is wrought,
  Thou dost it all alone.

4 O may I love like thee!
  In all thy footsteps tread,
Thou hatest all iniquity,
  But nothing thou hast made.
  O may I learn the art
With meekness to reprove;
To hate the sin with all my heart,
  But still the sinner love.

271   7 s & 6 s.

1 O ALMIGHTY God of love,
    Thy holy arm display!
Send me succour from above
  In this my evil day;
  Arm my weakness with thy power,
Woman's Seed appear within!
  Be my safeguard and my tower
  Against the face of sin.

2 Could I of thy strength take hold,
  And always feel thee near,
Confident, divinely bold,
  My soul would scorn to fear:
Nothing should my firmness shock;
  Though the gates of hell assail,
Were I built upon the rock,
  They never could prevail.

3 Rock of my salvation, haste,
  Extend thy ample shade,
  Let it over me be cast,
  And screen my naked head;
Save me from the trying hour,
  Thou my sure protection be;
Shelter me from Satan's power,
  Till I am fixed on thee.

4 Set upon thyself my feet,
  And make me surely stand:
From temptation's rage and heat
  Cover me with thy hand;
Let me in the cleft be placed,
  Ne'er from my defence remove,
In thine arms of love embraced,
  Of everlasting love.

272   Isaiah xliii. I, 2.   6 - 8 s.

1 PEACE, doubting heart! my God's I am;
  Who formed me man, forbids my fear;
66

The Lord hath called me by my name;
  The Lord protects, for ever near;
His blood for me did once atone,
And still he loves and guards his own.

2 When, passing through the watery deep,
  I ask in faith his promised aid,
The waves an awful distance keep,
  And shrink from my devoted head;
Fearless their violence I dare;
They cannot harm, for God is there!

3 To him mine eye of faith I turn,
  And through the fire pursue my way;
The fire forgets its power to burn,
  The lambent flames around me play;
I own his power, accept the sign,
And shout to prove the Saviour mine.

4 Still nigh me, O my Saviour, stand!
  And guard in fierce temptation's hour;
Hide in the hollow of thy hand,
  Show forth in me thy saving power,
Still be thy arms my sure defence,
Nor earth nor hell shall pluck me thence.

5 Since thou hast bid me come to thee,
  (Good as thou art, and strong to save)
I'll walk o'er life's tempestuous sea,
  Upborne by the unyielding wave,
Dauntless, though rocks of pride be near,
And yawning whirlpools of despair.

6 When darkness intercepts the skies,
  And sorrow's waves around me roll,
When high the storms of passion rise,
  And half o'erwhelm my sinking soul,
My soul a sudden calm shall feel,
And hear a whisper, " Peace; be still!"

7 Though in affliction's furnace tried,
  Unhurt on snares and death I'll tread;
Though sin assail, and hell, thrown wide,
  Pour all its flames upon my head,
Like Moses' bush, I'll mount the higher,
And flourish unconsumed in fire.

273

10 s & 11 s.

1 O MNIPOTENT Lord, My Saviour and
    King.   [bring;
Thy succour afford, Thy righteousness
Thy promises bind thee Compassion to
  have,   [save.
Now, now let me find thee Almighty to

2 Rejoicing in hope, And patient in grief,
To thee I look up For certain relief;
I fear no denial, No danger I fear, [near.
Nor start from the trial, While Jesus is

3 I every hour In jeopardy stand; [hand;
But thou art my power, And holdest my
While yet I am calling, Thy succour I feel,
It saves me from falling, Or plucks me
  from hell.

4 O who can explain This struggle for life!
This travail and pain, This trembling and
  strife!   [mult, and war,
Plague, earthquake, and famine, And tu-
The wonderful coming Of Jesus declare.

5 For every fight Is dreadful and loud,
The warrior's delight Is slaughter and
  blood,
His foes overturning, Till all shall expire;
But this is with burning And fuel of fire.

6 Yet God is above Men, devils, and sin,
  My Jesus's love The battle shall win,
  So terribly glorious His coming shall be,
  His love all-victorious Shall conquer for me.

7 He all shall break through; His truth and
    his grace
  Shall bring me into The plentiful place,
  Through much tribulation, Through water
    and fire,   [of desire.
  Through floods of temptation, And flames

8 On Jesus, my power, Till then I rely,
  All evil before His presence shall fly;
  When I have my Saviour, My sin shall
    depart,
  And Jesus for ever Shall reign in my heart.

274
7s & 6s.

1 O MY old, my bosom foe,
    Rejoice not over me!
  Ofttimes thou hast laid me low,
    And wounded mortally;
  Yet thy prey thou couldst not keep;
  Jesus, when I lowest fell,
  Heard me cry out of the deep,
  And brought me up from hell.

2 Foolish world, thy shouts forbear,
    Till thou hast won the day;
  Could thy wisdom keep me there,
    When in thy hands I lay?
  If my heart to thee incline,
    Christ again shall set it free:
  I am his, and he is mine
    To all eternity.

3 Satan, cease thy empty boast,
    And give thy triumphs o'er;
  Still thou seest I am not lost,
    While Jesus can restore:
  Though through thy deceit I fall,
    Surely I shall rise again,
  Christ my King is over all,
    And I with him shall reign.

4 O my threefold enemy,
    To whom I long did bow,
  See your lawful captive, see,
    No more your captive now!
  Now before my face ye fly;
    More than conqueror now I am;
  Sin, the world, and hell defy,
    In Jesu's powerful name.

275
Psalm cx. 1.   C. M.

1 THE Lord unto my Lord hath said,
    "Sit thou, in glory sit,
  Till I thine enemies have made
    To bow beneath thy feet."

2 Jesu, my Lord, mighty to save,
    What can my hopes withstand,
  While thee my Advocate I have,
    Enthroned at God's right hand?

3 Nature is subject to thy word,
    All power to thee is given,
  The uncontrolled, almighty Lord
    Of hell, and earth, and heaven.

4 And shall my sins thy will oppose?
    Master, thy right maintain!
  O let not thy usurping foes
    In me thy servant reign:
    C 2

5 Come then, and claim me for thine own,
    Saviour, thy right assert!
  Come, gracious Lord, set up thy throne,
    And reign within my heart!

6 So shall I bless thy pleasing sway;
    And, sitting at thy feet,
  Thy laws with all my heart obey,
    With all my soul submit.

7 So shall I do thy will below,
    As angels do above;
  The virtue of thy passion show,
    The triumphs of thy love.

8 Thy love the conquest more than gains;
    To all I shall proclaim,
  Jesus the King, the conqueror reigns,
    Bow down to Jesu's name!

9 To thee shall earth and hell submit,
    And every foe shall fall,
  Till death expires beneath thy feet,
    And God is all in all.

*276
77, 447, 77, 447.

1 WORSHIP, and thanks, and blessing,
    And strength ascribe to Jesus!
      Jesus alone
      Defends his own,
  When earth and hell oppress us.
  Jesus with joy we witness
  Almighty to deliver;
      Our seals set to,
      That God is true,
  And reigns a King for ever.

2 Omnipotent Redeemer,
  Our ransomed souls adore thee:
      Our Saviour thou,
      We find it now,
  And give thee all the glory.
  We sing thine arm unshortened,
  Brought through our sore temptation;
      With heart and voice
      In thee rejoice,
  The God of our salvation.

3 Thine arm hath safely brought us
  A way no more expected,
      Than when thy sheep
      Passed through the deep,
  By crystal walls protected.
  Thy glory was our rearward,
  Thine hand our lives did cover,
      And we, even we,
      Have passed the sea,
  And marched triumphant over.

4 The world, and Satan's malice
  Thou, Jesus, hast confounded;
      And, by thy grace,
      With songs of praise
  Our happy souls resounded.
  Accepting our deliverance,
  We triumph in thy favour,
      And for the love
      Which now we prove,
  Shall praise thy name for ever.

277
S. M.

1 JESUS, the conqueror, reigns,
    In glorious strength arrayed,
  His kingdom over all maintains,
  And bids the earth be glad.

Ye sons of men, rejoice
In Jesu's mighty love,
Lift up your heart, lift up your voice,
To him who rules above.

2 Extol his kingly power,
Kiss the exalted Son,
Who died, and lives, to die no more,
High on his Father's throne ;
Our Advocate with God,
He undertakes our cause,
And spreads through all the earth abroad
The victory of his cross.

3 That bloody banner see,
And in your Captain's sight,
Fight the good fight of faith with me,
My fellow-soldiers, fight !
In mighty phalanx joined,
To battle all proceed ;
Armed with the unconquerable mind
Which was in Christ your Head.

4 Urge on your rapid course,
Ye blood-besprinkled bands ;
The heavenly kingdom suffers force,
'Tis seized by violent hands ;
See there the starry crown
That glitters through the skies l
Satan, the world, and sin, tread down,
And take the glorious prize.

5 Through much distress and pain,
Through many a conflict won,
Through blood, ye must the entrance gain ;
Yet, O disdain to fear !
Courage ! your Captain cries,
Who all your toil foreknew ;
Toil ye shall have ; yet all despise,
I have o'ercome for you.

6 The world cannot withstand
Its ancient conqueror,
The world must sink beneath the hand
Which arms us for the war ;
This is the victory !
Before our faith they fall ;
Jesus hath died for you and me ;
Believe, and conquer all !

278   *David and Goliath.*   **7 s & 6 s.**
                   1 Samuel xvii.

1 WHO is this gigantic foe
That proudly stalks along,
Overlooks the crowd below,
In brazen armour strong?
Loudly of his strength he boasts,
On his sword and spear relies;
Meets the God of Israel's hosts,
And all their force defies.

2 Tallest of the earth-born race,
They tremble at his power,
Flee before the monster's face,
And own him conqueror.
Who this mighty champion is,
Nature answers from within;
He is my own wickedness,
My own besetting sin.

3 In the strength of Jesu's name,
I with the monster fight ;
Feeble and unarmed I am,
But Jesus is my might ;
Mindful of his mercies past,
Still I trust the same to prove ;
68

Still my helpless soul I cast
On his redeeming love.

4 With my sling and stone I go
To fight the Philistine ;
God hath said it shall be so,
And I shall conquer sin ;
On his promise I rely,
Trust in an almighty Lord,
Sure to win the victory,
For he hath spoke the word.

5 In the strength of God I rise,
I run to meet my foe ;
Faith the word of power applies,
And lays the giant low ;
Faith in Jesu's conquering name
Slings the sin-destroying stone ;
Points the word's unerring aim,
And brings the monster down.

6 Rise, ye men of Israel, rise,
Your routed foe pursue ;
Shout his praises to the skies
Who conquers sin for you ;
Jesus doth for you appear,
He his conquering grace affords,
Saves you, not with sword and spear,
The battle is the Lord's.

7 Every day the Lord of hosts
His mighty power displays :
Stills the proud Philis'ine's boast,
The threatening Gittite slays ;
Israel's God let all below
Conqueror over sin proclaim ;
O that all the earth might know
The power of Jesu's name !

L. M.   **279**

1 SHALL I, for fear of feeble man,
The Spirit's course in me restrain?
Or, undismayed, in deed and word,
Be a true witness for my Lord?

2 Awed by a mortal's frown, shall I
Conceal the word of God most high?
How then before thee shall I dare
To stand, or how thine anger bear?

3 Shall I, to soothe the unholy throng,
Soften thy truths, and smooth my tongue,
To gain earth's gilded toys, or flee
The cross, endured, my God, by thee?

4 What then is he whose scorn I dread,
Whose wrath or hate makes me afraid?
A man ! an heir of death ! a slave
To sin ! a bubble on the wave !

5 Yea, let men rage, since thou wilt spread
Thy shadowing wings around my head ;
Since in all pain thy tender love
Will still my sure refreshment prove.

6 Saviour of men, thy searching eye
Doth all my inmost thoughts descry ;
Doth aught on earth my wishes raise,
Or the world's pleasures, or its praise?

7 The love of Christ doth me constrain
To seek the wandering souls of men ;
With cries, entreaties, tears, to save,
To snatch them from the gaping grave.

8 For this let men revile my name,
No cross I shun, I fear no shame,
All hail, reproach, and welcome, pain !
Only thy terrors, Lord, restrain.

9 My life, my blood, I here present,
  If for thy truth they may be spent,
  Fulfil thy sovereign counsel, Lord!
  Thy will be done, thy name adored!

10 Give me thy strength, O God of power;
  Then let winds blow, or thunders roar,
  Thy faithful witness will I be:
  'Tis fixed; I can do all through thee!

280
L. M.

1 THE Lord is King, and earth submits,
    Howe'er impatient, to his sway,
  Between the cherubim he sits,
  And makes his restless foes obey.

2 All power is to our Jesus given,
    O'er earth's rebellious sons he reigns;
  He mildly rules the hosts of heaven,
  And holds the powers of hell in chains.

3 In vain doth Satan rage his hour,
  Beyond his chain he cannot go;
  Our Jesus shall stir up his power,
  And soon avenge us of our foe.

4 Jesus shall his great arm reveal;
    Jesus, the woman's conquering Seed,
  (Though now the serpent bruise his heel)
  Jesus shall bruise the serpent's head.

5 The enemy his tares hath sown,
  But Christ shall shortly root them up,
  Shall cast the dire accuser down,
  And disappoint his children's hope;

6 Shall still the proud Philistine's noise,
  Baffle the sons of unbelief,
  Nor long permit them to rejoice,
  But turn their triumph into grief.

7 Come, glorious Lord, the rebels spurn,
    Scatter thy foes, victorious King!
  And Gath and Askelon shall mourn,
  And all the sons of God shall sing;

8 Shall magnify the sovereign grace
  Of him that sits upon the throne;
  And earth and heaven conspire to praise
  Jehovah, and his conquering Son.

281
8 s & 6 s.

1 ARE there not in the labourer's day
    Twelve hours, in which he safely may
  His calling's work pursue?
  Though sin and Satan still are near,
  Nor sin nor Satan can I fear,
  With Jesus in my view.

2 Not all the powers of hell can fright
  A soul that walks with Christ in light,
  He walks and cannot fall;
  Clearly he sees, and wins his way,
  Shining unto the perfect day,
  And more than conquers all.

3 Light of the world, thy beams I bless;
  On thee, bright Sun of righteousness,
  My faith hath fixed its eye;
  Guided by thee, through all I go,
  Nor fear the ruin spread below,
  For thou art always nigh.

4 Ten thousand snares my path beset;
  Yet will I, Lord, the work complete
  Which thou to me hast given;

Regardless of the pains I feel,
Close by the gates of death and hell,
  I urge my way to heaven.

5 Still will I strive, and labour still,
  With humble zeal to do thy will,
    And trust in thy defence:
  My soul into thy hands I give;
  And, if he can obtain thy leave,
    Let Satan pluck me thence I

282
8 s & 6 s.

1 BUT can it be, that I should prove
    For ever faithful to thy love,
  From sin for ever cease?
  I thank thee for the blessed hope;
  It lifts my drooping spirits up,
  It gives me back my peace.

2 In thee, O Lord, I put my trust,
  Mighty, and merciful, and just;
    Thy sacred word is passed;
  And I, who dare thy word receive,
  Without committing sin shall live,
    Shall live to God at last.

3 I rest in thine almighty power;
  The name of Jesus is a tower,
    That hides my life above:
  Thou canst, thou wilt my helper be;
  My confidence is all in thee,
    The faithful God of love.

4 While still to thee for help I call,
  Thou wilt not suffer me to fall,
    Thou canst not let me sin;
  And thou shalt give me power to pray,
  Till all my sins are purged away,
    And all thy mind brought in.

5 Wherefore, in never-ceasing prayer,
  My soul to thy continual care
    I faithfully commend;
  Assured that thou through life shalt save,
  And show thyself beyond the grave
    My everlasting Friend.

283
6 - 8 s.   Exodus xxxiii. 18—23.

1 O GOD, my hope, my heavenly rest,
    My all of happiness below,
  Grant my importunate request.
  To me, to me, thy goodness show;
  Thy beatific face display,
  The brightness of eternal day.

2 Before my faith's enlightened eyes
  Make all thy gracious goodness pass;
  Thy goodness is the sight I prize,
  O might I see thy smiling face!
  Thy nature in my soul proclaim,
  Reveal thy love, thy glorious name!

3 There, in the place beside thy throne,
    Where all that find acceptance stand,
  Receive me up into thy Son;
  Cover me with thy mighty hand;
  Set me upon the rock, and hide
  My soul in Jesu's wounded side.

4 O put me in the cleft; empower
  My soul the glorious sight to bear!
  Descend in this accepted hour,
  Pass by me, and thy name declare;
  Thy wrath withdraw, thy hand remove,
  And show thyself the God of love.

284 SECOND PART. 6 - 8 s.

1 TO thee, great God of love ! I bow,
And prostrate in thy sight adore ;
By faith I see thee passing now ;
I have, but still I ask for more,
A glimpse of love cannot suffice,
My soul for all thy presence cries.

2 I cannot see thy face, and live,
Then let me see thy face, and die !
Now, Lord, my gasping spirit receive,
Give me on eagles' wings to fly,
With eagles' eyes on thee to gaze,
And plunge into the glorious blaze.

3 The fulness of my vast reward
A blest eternity shall be ;
But hast thou not on earth prepared
Some better thing than this for me ?
What, but one drop ! one transient sight !
I want a sun, a sea of light.

4 Moses thy backward parts might view,
But not a perfect sight obtain ;
The Gospel doth thy fulness show
To us, by the commandment slain ;
The dead to sin shall find the grace,
The pure in heart shall see thy face.

5 More favoured than the saints of old,
Who now by faith approach to thee
Shall all with open face behold
In Christ the glorious Deity ;
Shall see, and put the Godhead on,
The nature of thy sinless Son.

6 This, this is our high calling's prize !
Thine image in thy Son I claim ;
And still to higher glories rise,
Till all transformed I know thy name,
And glide to all my heaven above,
My highest heaven in Jesu's love.

285 L. M.

1 COME, Saviour, Jesus, from above !
Assist me with thy heavenly grace ;
Empty my heart of earthly love,
And for thyself prepare the place.

2 O let thy sacred presence fill,
And set my longing spirit free !
Which pants to have no other will,
But day and night to feast on thee.

3 While in this region here below,
No other good will I pursue ;
I'll bid this world of noise and show,
With all its glittering snares, adieu !

4 That path with humble speed I'll seek,
In which my Saviour's footsteps shine ;
Nor will I hear, nor will I speak,
Of any other love but thine.

5 Henceforth may no profane delight
Divide this consecrated soul ;
Possess it thou, who hast the right,
As Lord and Master of the whole.

6 Wealth, honour, pleasure, and what else
This short-enduring world can give,
Tempt as ye will, my soul repels,
To Christ alone resolved to live.

7 Thee I can love, and thee alone,
With pure delight and inward bliss :

70

To know thou tak'st me for thine own,
O what a happiness is this !

8 Nothing on earth do I desire,
But thy pure love within my breast ;
This, only this, will I require,
And freely give up all the rest.

286

L. M.

1 ABRAHAM, when severely tried,
His faith by his obedience showed,
He with the harsh command complied,
And gave his Isaac back to God.

2 His son the father offered up,
Son of his age, his only son,
Object of all his joy and hope,
And less beloved than God alone.

3 O for a faith like his, that we
The bright example may pursue !
May gladly give up all to thee,
To whom our more than all is due.

4 Now, Lord, to thee our all we leave,
Our willing soul thy call obeys ;
Pleasure, and wealth, and fame we give,
Freedom, and life to win thy grace.

5 Is there a thing than life more dear ?
A thing from which we cannot part ?
We can ; we now rejoice to tear
The idol from our bleeding heart.

6 Jesus, accept our sacrifice ;
All things for thee we count but loss ;
Lo ! at thy word our Isaac dies,
Dies on the altar of thy cross.

7 For what to thee, O Lord, we give,
A hundred-fold we here obtain ;
And soon with thee shall all receive,
And loss shall be eternal gain.

287

8 - 7 s. *An Evening Hymn.*

1 OMNIPRESENT God ! whose aid
No one ever asked in vain,
Be this night about my bed,
Every evil thought restrain ;
Lay thy hand upon my soul,
God of my unguarded hours !
All my enemies control,
Hell, and earth, and nature's powers.

2 O thou jealous God ! come down,
God of spotless purity,
Claim, and seize me for thy own,
Consecrate my heart to thee ;
Under thy protection take,
Songs in the night season give ;
Let me sleep to thee, and wake,
Let me die to thee, and live.

3 Only tell me I am thine,
And thou wilt not quit thy right ;
Answer me in dreams divine,
Dreams and visions of the night :
Bid me even in sleep go on,
Restlessly my God desire,
Mourn for God in every groan,
God in every thought require.

4 Loose me from the chains of sense,
Set me from the body free,
Draw with stronger influence
My unfettered soul to thee ;

In me, Lord, thyself reveal,
   Fill me with a sweet surprise;
Let me thee when waking feel,
   Let me in thy image rise.
5 Let me of thy life partake,
   Thy own holiness impart,
O that I might sweetly wake
   With my Saviour in my heart!
O that I might know thee mine!
   O that I might thee receive!
Only live the life divine,
   Only to thy glory live!

6 Or if thou my soul require
   Ere I see the morning light,
Grant me, Lord, my heart's desire,
   Perfect me in love to-night;
Finish thy great work of love,
   Cut it short in righteousness,
Fit me for the realms above,
   Change, and bid me die in peace.

288
8 s & 6 s.

1 O GOD, thy faithfulness I plead!
   My present help in time of need,
   My great Deliverer thou!
Haste to my aid, thine ear incline,
And rescue this poor soul of mine,
   I claim the promise now!

2 Where is the way? Ah, show me where,
That I thy mercy may declare,
   The power that sets me free:
How can I my destruction shun?
How can I from my nature run?
   Answer, O God, for me!

3 One only way the erring mind
Of man, short-sighted man, can find,
   From inbred sin to fly:
Stronger than love, I fondly thought,
Death, only death can cut the knot,
   Which love cannot untie.

4 But thou, O Lord, art full of grace;
Thy love can find a thousand ways
   To foolish man unknown;
My soul upon thy love I cast,
I rest me, till the storm is past,
   Upon thy love alone.

5 Thy faithful, wise, and mighty love
Shall every stumbling-block remove,
   And make an open way;
Thy love shall burst the shades of death,
And bear me from the gulf beneath,
   To everlasting day.

289
L. M.

1 GOD of my life, whose gracious power
   Through varied deaths my soul hath led,
Or turned aside the fatal hour,
   Or lifted up my sinking head;

2 In all my ways thy hand I own,
   Thy ruling Providence I see:
Assist me still my course to run,
   And still direct my paths to thee.

3 Oft hath the sea confessed thy power,
   And given me back at thy command;
It could not, Lord, my life devour,
   Safe in the hollow of thine hand.

4 Oft from the margin of the grave
   Thou, Lord, hast lifted up my head,
Sudden, I found thee near to save;
   The fever owned thy touch, and fled.

5 Whither, O whither should I fly,
   But to my loving Saviour's breast?
Secure within thine arms to lie,
   And safe beneath thy wings to rest.

6 I have no skill the snare to shun,
   But thou, O Christ, my wisdom art!
I ever into ruin run,
   But thou art greater than my heart.

7 Foolish, and impotent, and blind,
   Lead me a way I have not known;
Bring me, where I my heaven may find,
   The heaven of loving thee alone.

8 Enlarge my heart to make thee room;
   Enter, and in me ever stay,
The crooked then shall straight become,
   The darkness shall be lost in day.

L. M.
290

1 MY God, if I may call thee mine, [far,
   From heaven and thee removed so
Draw nigh; thy pitying ear incline,
   And cast not out my languid prayer.

2 Gently the weak thou lov'st to lead,
   Thou lov'st to prop the feeble knee;
O break not then a bruised reed,
   Nor quench the smoking flax in me!

3 Buried in sin, thy voice I hear,
   And burst the barriers of my tomb,
In all the marks of death appear,
   Forth at thy call, though bound, I come

4 Give me, O give me fully, Lord,
   Thy resurrection's power to know;
Free me indeed, repeat the word,
   And loose my bands, and let me go.

5 Fain would I go to thee, my God,
   Thy mercies and my wants to tell:
To feel my pardon sealed in blood,
   Saviour, thy love I wait to feel.

6 Freed from the power of cancelled sin,
   When shall my soul triumphant prove?
Why breaks not out the fire within
   In flames of joy, and praise, and love?

7 Jesus, to thee my soul aspires;
   Jesus, to thee I plight my vows;
Keep me from earthly, base desires,
   My God, my Saviour, and my Spouse.

8 Fountain of all-sufficient bliss,
   Thou art the good I seek below,
Fulness of joy in thee there is,
   Without,—'tis misery all, and woe.

L. M.
291

1 FONDLY my foolish heart essays
   To augment the source of perfect bliss,
Love's all-sufficient sea to raise
   With drops of creature happiness.

2 O Love, thy sovereign aid impart,
   And guard the gift thyself hast given:
My portion thou, my treasure art,
   And life, and happiness, and heaven.

3 Would aught on earth my wishes share,
   Though dear as life the idol be,

The idol from my breast I'd tear,
Resolved to seek my all in thee.

4 Whate'er I fondly counted mine,
  To thee, my Lord, I here restore:
Gladly I all for thee resign;
  Give me thyself, I ask no more.

292   Isaiah xxxii. 2.   7s & 6s †.

1 TO the haven of thy breast,
    O Son of man, I fly !
Be my refuge and my rest,
  For O the storm is high !
Save me from the furious blast,
A covert from the tempest be !
Hide me, Jesus, till o'erpast
  The storm of sin I see.

2 Welcome as the water-spring
  To a dry, barren place,
O descend on me, and bring
  Thy sweet refreshing grace ;
O'er a parched and weary land
As a great rock extends its shade,
Hide me, Saviour, with thine hand,
  And screen my naked head.

3 In the time of my distress
  Thou hast my succour been,
In my utter helplessness
  Restraining me from sin ;
O how swiftly didst thou move
To save me in the trying hour !
Still protect me with thy love,
  And shield me with thy power.

4 First and last in me perform
  The work thou hast begun ;
Be my shelter from the storm,
  My shadow from the sun ;
Weary, parched with thirst, and faint,
Till thou the abiding Spirit breathe,
Every moment, Lord, I want
  The merit of thy death.

5 Never shall I want it less,
  When thou the gift hast given,
Filled me with thy righteousness,
  And sealed the heir of heaven ;
I shall hang upon my God,
Till I thy perfect glory see ;
  Till the sprinkling of thy blood
  Shall speak me up to thee.

293   L. M.

1 JESUS, my King, to thee I bow,
    Enlisted under thy command ;
Captain of my salvation, thou
  Shalt lead me to the promised land.

2 Thou hast a great deliverance wrought,
  The staff from off my shoulder broke,
Out of the house of bondage brought,
  And freed me from the Egyptian yoke.

3 O'er the vast howling wilderness,
  To Canaan's bounds thou hast me led ;
Thou bidd'st me now the land possess,
  And on thy milk and honey feed.

4 I see an open door of hope,
  Legions of sin in vain oppose ;
Bold I with thee, my Head, march up,
  And triumph o'er a world of foes.

72

5 Gigantic lusts come forth to fight,
  I mark, disdain, and all break through,
I tread them down in Jesu's might,
  Through Jesus I can all things do,

6 Lo ! the tall sons of Anak rise !
  Who can the sons of Anak meet ?
Captain, to thee I lift mine eyes,
  And lo ! they fall beneath my feet.

7 Passion, and appetite, and pride,
  (Pride, my old, dreadful, tyrant-foe)
I see cast down on every side,
  And conquering, I to conquer go.

8 My Lord in my behalf appears ;
  Captain, thy strength-inspiring eye
Scatters my doubts, dispels my fears,
  And makes the host of aliens fly.

9 Who can before my Captain stand ?
  Who is so great a King as mine ?
High over all is thy right hand,
  And might and majesty are thine !

SECTION III.

FOR BELIEVERS PRAYING.

294

6 - 8 s.

1 JESU, thou sovereign Lord of all,
    The same through one eternal day,
Attend thy feeblest followers' call,
  And O instruct us how to pray !
Pour out the supplicating grace,
And stir us up to seek thy face.

2 We cannot think a gracious thought,
  We cannot feel a good desire,
Till thou, who call'dst a world from nought,
  The power into our hearts inspire ;
And then we in thy Spirit groan,
And then we give thee back thine own.

3 Jesus, regard the joint complaint
  Of all thy tempted followers here,
And now supply the common want,
  And send us down the Comforter ;
The spirit of ceaseless prayer impart,
And fix thy Agent in our heart.

4 To help our soul's infirmity,
  To heal thy sin-sick people's care,
To urge our God-commanding plea,
  And make our hearts a house of prayer,
The promised Intercessor give,
And let us now thyself receive.

5 Come in thy pleading Spirit down
  To us who for thy coming stay ;
Of all thy gifts we ask but one,
  We ask the constant power to pray ;
Indulge us, Lord, in this request,
Thou canst not then deny the rest.

295

7 s & 6 s †.   Luke xviii. 1.

1 COME, ye followers of the Lord,
    In Jesu's service join,
Jesus gives the sacred word,
  The ordinance divine ;
Let us his command obey,
And ask and have whate'er we want ;
Pray we, every moment pray,
  And never, never faint.

2 Place no longer let us give
   To the old tempter's will;
Never more our duty leave,
   While Satan cries, "Be still;"
Stand we in the ancient way,
And here with God ourselves acquaint;
   Pray we, every moment pray,
   And never, never faint.

3 Be it weariness and pain
   To slothful flesh and blood,
Yet we will the cross sustain,
   And bless the welcome load;
All our griefs to God display,
And humbly pour out our complaint:
   Pray we, every moment pray,
   And never, never faint.

4 Let us patiently endure,
   And still our wants declare;
All the promises are sure
   To persevering prayer;
Till we see the perfect day,
And each wakes up a sinless saint,
   Pray we, every moment pray,
   And never, never faint.

5 Pray we on when all renewed
   And perfected in love,
Till we see the Saviour-God
   Descending from above;
All his heavenly charms survey,
Beyond what angel minds can paint;
   Pray we, every moment pray,
   And never, never faint.

296   *In a hurry of business.*   S. M.

1 HELP, Lord! the busy foe
   Is as a flood come in!
Lift up a standard, and o'erthrow
   The soul-distracting sin:
This sudden tide of care
   Roll back, O God, from me,
Nor let the rapid current bear
   My soul away from thee.

2 The praying Spirit breathe,
   The watching power impart,
From all entanglements beneath
   Call off my anxious heart;
My feeble mind sustain,
   By worldly thoughts opprest;
Appear, and bid me turn again
   To my eternal rest.

3 Swift to my rescue come,
   Thy own this moment seize;
Gather my wandering spirit home,
   And keep in perfect peace;
Suffered no more to rove
   O'er all the earth abroad,
Arrest the prisoner of thy love,
   And shut me up in God.

297   C. M.

1 SHEPHERD Divine, our wants relieve
   In this our evil day,
To all thy tempted followers give
   The power to watch and pray.

2 Long as our fiery trials last,
   Long as the cross we bear,
O let our souls on thee be cast
   In never-ceasing prayer!

3 The Spirit of interceding grace
   Give us in faith to claim;
To wrestle till we see thy face,
   And know thy hidden name.

4 Till thou thy perfect love impart,
   Till thou thyself bestow,
Be this the cry of every heart,
   "I will not let thee go:

5 "I will not let thee go, unless
   Thou tell thy name to me,
With all thy great salvation bless,
   And make me all like thee:

6 "Then let me on the mountain-top
   Behold thy open face,
Where faith in sight is swallowed up,
   And prayer in endless praise."

6-8 s.   *Exodus xxxii. 10.*   **298**

1 O WONDROUS power of faithful prayer!
   What tongue can tell the almighty
God's hands or bound or open are; [grace?
   As Moses or Elijah prays:
Let Moses in the Spirit groan,
And God cries out, "Let me alone!

2 "Let me alone, that all my wrath
   May rise the wicked to consume!"
While justice hears thy praying faith,
   It cannot seal the sinner's doom:
My Son is in my servant's prayer,
And Jesus forces me to spare."

3 O blessed word of gospel grace!
   Which now we for our Israel plead,
A faithless and backsliding race,
   Whom thou hast out of Egypt freed.
O do not then in wrath chastise,
Nor let thy whole displeasure rise!

4 Father, we ask in Jesu's name,
   In Jesu's power and spirit pray;
Divert thy vengeful thunder's aim,
   O turn thy threatening wrath away!
Our guilt and punishment remove,
And magnify thy pardoning love.

5 Father, regard thy pleading Son!
   Accept his all-availing prayer,
And send a peaceful answer down,
   In honour of our Spokesman there;
Whose blood proclaims our sins forgiven,
And speaks thy rebels up to heaven.

7 s & 6 s †.   *Luke xviii. 1—8.*   **299**

1 JESUS, thou hast bid us pray,
   Pray always, and not faint;
With the word a power convey
   To utter our complaint;
Quiet shalt thou never know,
Till we from sin are fully freed;
   O avenge us of our foe,
   And bruise the serpent's head!

2 We have now begun to cry,
   And we will never end,
Till we find salvation nigh,
   And grasp the sinner's friend;
Day and night we'll speak our woe,
With thee importunately plead;
   O avenge us of our foe,
   And bruise the serpent's head!

73

3 Speak the word, and we shall be
  From all our bands released,
  Only thou canst set us free,
  By Satan long oppressed ;
Now thy power almighty show,
Arise, the woman's conquering Seed !
  O avenge us of our foe,
  And bruise the serpent's head !

4 To destroy his work of sin,
  Thyself in us reveal ;
  Manifest thyself within
  Our flesh, and fully dwell
With us, in us, here below ;
Enter, and make us free indeed ;
  O avenge us of our foe,
  And bruise the serpent's head !

5 Stronger than the strong man, thou
  His fury canst control :
  Cast him out, by entering now,
  And keep our ransomed soul ;
Satan's kingdom overthrow,
On all the powers of darkness tread ;
  O avenge us of our foe,
  And bruise the serpent's head !

6 To the never-ceasing cries
  Of thine elect attend ;
  Send deliverance from the skies,
  The mighty Spirit send :
Though to man thou seemest slow,
Our cries thou seemest not to heed,
  O avenge us of our foe,
  And bruise the serpent's head !

7 Come, O come, all-glorious Lord !
  No longer now delay ;
  With thy Spirit's two-edged sword
  The crooked serpent slay !
Bare thine arm, and give the blow,
Root out and kill the hellish seed,
  O avenge us of our foe,
  And bruise the serpent's head !

8 Jesus, hear thy Spirit's call,
  Thy bride, who bids thee come ;
  Come, thou righteous Judge of all,
  Pronounce the tempter's doom ;
Doom him to infernal woe,
For him and for his angels made ;
  Now avenge us of our foe,
  For ever bruise his head !

300   Revelation iii. 19.   S. M.

1 JESUS, I fain would find
    Thy zeal for God in me,
Thy yearning pity for mankind,
  Thy burning charity.

2 In me thy Spirit dwell !
    In me thy bowels move !
So shall the fervour of my zeal
  Be the pure flame of love.

301   S. M.

1 JESUS, my strength, my hope,
    On thee I cast my care,
With humble confidence look up,
  And know thou hear'st my prayer.
Give me on thee to wait,
  Till I can all things do,
On thee, almighty to create,
  Almighty to renew.

2 I want a sober mind,
  A self-renouncing will,
That tramples down and casts behind
  The baits of pleasing ill ;
A soul inured to pain,
  To hardship, grief, and loss,
Bold to take up, firm to sustain
  The consecrated cross.

3 I want a godly fear,
  A quick-discerning eye,
That looks to thee when sin is near,
  And sees the tempter fly ;
A spirit still prepared,
  And armed with jealous care,
For ever standing on its guard,
  And watching unto prayer.

4 I want a heart to pray,
  To pray and never cease,
Never to murmur at thy stay,
  Or wish my sufferings less.
This blessing, above all,
  Always to pray, I want,
Out of the deep on thee to call,
  And never, never faint.

5 I want a true regard,
  A single, steady aim,
(Unmoved by threatening or reward)
  To thee and thy great name ;
A jealous, just concern
  For thine immortal praise ;
A pure desire that all may learn,
  And glorify thy grace.

6 I rest upon thy word ;
  The promise is for me ;
My succour and salvation, Lord,
  Shall surely come from thee :
But let me still abide,
  Nor from my hope remove,
Till thou my patient spirit guide
  Into thy perfect love.

7 s.   Isaiah xxviii. 9.   **302**

1 LORD, that I may learn of thee,
    Give me true simplicity ;
Wean my soul, and keep it low,
  Willing thee alone to know.

2 Let me cast my reeds aside,
  All that feeds my knowing pride,
Not to man, but God submit,
  Lay my reasonings at thy feet ;

3 Of my boasted wisdom spoiled,
  Docile, helpless, as a child,
Only seeing in thy light,
  Only walking in thy might.

4 Then infuse the teaching grace,
  Spirit of truth and righteousness ;
Knowledge, love divine, impart,
  Life eternal, to my heart.

S. M.   **303**

1 AH, when shall I awake
    From sin's soft-soothing power,
The slumber from my spirit shake,
  And rise to fall no more !
Awake, no more to sleep,
  But stand with constant care,
Looking for God my soul to keep,
  And watching unto prayer !

2 O could I always pray,
    And never, never faint,
But simply to my God display
    My every care and want i
    I know that thou wouldst give
    More than I can request ;
Thou still art ready to receive
    My soul to perfect rest.

3 I feel thee willing, Lord,
    A sinful world to save,
All may obey thy gracious word,
    May peace and pardon have ,
    Not one of all the race
    But may return to thee,
But at the throne of sovereign grace
    May fall and weep, like me.

4 Here will I ever lie,
    And tell thee all my care,
And, Father, Abba, Father, cry,
    And pour a ceaseless prayer ;
    Till thou my sins subdue,
    Till thou my sins destroy,
My spirit after God renew,
    And fill with peace and joy.

5 Messiah, Prince of peace,
    Into my soul bring in
Thy everlasting righteousness,
    And make an end of sin.
    Into all those that seek
    Redemption through thy blood
The sanctifying Spirit speak,
    The plenitude of God.

6 Let us in patience wait
    Till faith shall make us whole ;
Till thou shalt all things new create
    In each believing soul ;
    Who can resist thy will !
    Speak, and it shall be done !
Thou shalt the work of faith fulfil,
    And perfect us in one,

304 *The Beatitudes.*
    Matthew v. 1—12.   8 s & 6 s.

1 SAVIOUR, on me the want bestow,
    Which all that feel shall surely know
        Their sins on earth forgiven ;
Give me to prove the kingdom mine,
And taste, in holiness divine,
        The happiness of heaven.

2 Meeken my soul, thou heavenly Lamb,
    That I in the new earth may claim
        My hundred-fold reward ;
My rich inheritance possess,
Co-heir with the great Prince of peace,
        Co-partner with my Lord.

3 Me with that restless thirst inspire,
    That sacred, infinite desire,
        And feast my hungry heart ;
Less than thyself cannot suffice ;
My soul for all thy fulness cries,
        For all thou hast, and art.

4 Mercy who show shall mercy find ;
    Thy pitiful and tender mind
        Be, Lord, on me bestowed ;
So shall I still the blessing gain,
And to eternal life retain
        The mercy of my God.

5 Jesus, the crowning grace impart ;
    Bless me with purity of heart,
        That, now beholding thee,
I soon may view thy open face,
On all thy glorious beauties gaze,
        And God for ever see !

6 Not for my fault or folly's sake,
    The name, or mode, or form, I take,
        But for true holiness,
Let me be wronged, reviled, abhorred ;
And thee, my sanctifying Lord,
        In life and death confess.

7 Called to sustain the hallowed cross,
    And suffer for thy righteous cause,
        Pronounce me doubly blest ;
And let thy glorious Spirit, Lord,
Assure me of my great reward,
        In heaven's eternal rest.

SECTION IV.

FOR BELIEVERS WATCHING.

S. M.   **305**

1 GRACIOUS Redeemer, shake
    This slumber from my soul !
Say to me now, " Awake, awake ! "
    And Christ shall make thee whole,"
    Lay to thy mighty hand !
    Alarm me in this hour,
And make me fully understand
    The thunder of thy power.

2 Give me on thee to call,
    Always to watch and pray,
Lest I into temptation fall,
    And cast my shield away ;
    For each assault prepared
    And ready may I be,
For ever standing on my guard,
    And looking up to thee.

3 O do thou always warn
    My soul of evil near !
When to the right or left I turn,
    Thy voice still let me hear ;
    " Come back ! this is the way,
    Come back, and walk herein ! "
O may I hearken and obey,
    And shun the paths of sin !

4 Thou seest my feebleness ;
    Jesus, be thou my power,
My help and refuge in distress,
    My fortress and my tower
    Give me to trust in thee,
    Be thou my sure abode,
My horn, and rock, and buckler be,
    My Saviour, and my God.

5 Myself I cannot save,
    Myself I cannot keep.
But strength in thee I surely have,
    Whose eyelids never sleep ;
    My soul to thee alone
    Now therefore I commend ;
Thou, Jesus, love me as thy own,
    And love me to the end.

F

306
6 - 8 s.

1 FATHER, to thee I lift mine eyes,
  My longing eyes, and restless heart;
Before the morning watch I rise,
  And wait to taste how good thou art,
To obtain the grace I humbly claim,
The saving power of Jesu's name.

2 This slumber from my soul O shake!
  Warn by thy Spirit's inward call;
Let me to righteousness awake,
  And pray that I no more may fall,
Or give to sin or Satan place,
But walk in all thy righteous ways.

3 O wouldst thou, Lord, thy servant guard,
  'Gainst every known or secret foe!
A mind for all assaults prepared,
  A sober, vigilant mind bestow,
Ever apprized of danger nigh,
And when to fight, and when to fly.

4 O never suffer me to sleep
  Secure within the verge of hell!
But still my watchful spirit keep
  In lowly awe and loving zeal;
And bless me with a godly fear,
And plant that guardian-angel here.

5 Attended by the sacred dread,
  And wise from evil to depart,
Let me from strength to strength proceed,
  And rise to purity of heart;
Through all the paths of duty move,
From humble faith to perfect love.

307
C. M.

1 GOD of all grace and majesty,
  Supremely great and good!
If I have mercy found with thee,
  Through the atoning blood,
The guard of all thy mercies give,
  And to my pardon join
A fear lest I should ever grieve
  The gracious Spirit divine.

2 If mercy is indeed with thee,
  May I obedient prove,
Nor e'er abuse my liberty,
  Or sin against thy love:
This choicest fruit of faith bestow
  On a poor sojourner;
And let me pass my days below
  In humbleness and fear.

3 Rather I would in darkness mourn
  The absence of thy peace,
Than e'er by light irreverence turn
  Thy grace to wantonness:
Rather I would in painful awe
  Beneath thine anger move,
Than sin against the gospel law
  Of liberty and love.

4 But O! thou wouldst not have me live
  In bondage, grief, or pain,
Thou dost not take delight to grieve
  The helpless sons of men;
Thy will is my salvation, Lord;
  And let it now take place,
And let me tremble at the word
  Of reconciling grace.

5 Still may I walk as in thy sight,
  My strict observer see;
76

And thou by reverent love unite
  My child-like heart to thee;
Still let me, till my days are past,
  At Jesu's feet abide,
So shall he lift me up at last,
  And seat me by his side.

308
C. M.

1 I WANT a principle within
  Of jealous, godly fear,
A sensibility of sin,
  A pain to feel it near;
I want the first approach to feel
  Of pride, or fond desire,
To catch the wandering of my will,
  And quench the kindling fire.

2 That I from thee no more may part,
  No more thy goodness grieve,
The filial awe, the fleshly heart,
  The tender conscience, give.
Quick as the apple of an eye,
  O God, my conscience make!
Awake my soul, when sin is nigh,
  And keep it still awake.

3 If to the right or left I stray,
  That moment, Lord, reprove;
And let me weep my life away,
  For having grieved thy love:
O may the least omission pain
  My well-instructed soul,
And drive me to the blood again
  Which makes the wounded whole!

309
8 s & 6 s.

1 HELP, Lord, to whom for help I fly,
  And still my tempted soul stand by
    Throughout the evil day;
The sacred watchfulness impart,
And keep the issues of my heart,
  And stir me up to pray.

2 My soul with thy whole armour arm;
  In each approach of sin alarm,
    And show the danger near;
Surround, sustain, and strengthen me,
And fill with godly jealousy,
  And sanctifying fear.

3 Whene'er my careless hands hang down,
  O let me see thy gathering frown,
    And feel thy warning eye;
And starting cry from ruin's brink
Save, Jesus, or I yield, I sink,
  O save me, or I die!

4 If near the pit I rashly stray,
  Before I wholly fall away,
    The keen conviction dart!
Recall me by that pitying look,
That kind, upbraiding glance, which broke
  Unfaithful Peter's heart.

5 In me thine utmost mercy show,
  And make me like thyself below,
    Unblamable in grace;
Ready prepared, and fitted here,
By perfect holiness, to appear
  Before thy glorious face.

310
C. M.

1 JESUS, my Master and my Lord,
  I would thy will obey,

Humbly receive thy warning word,
And always watch and pray.
My constant need of watchful prayer
I daily see and feel,
To keep me safe from every snare
Of sin, and earth, and hell.

2 Into a world of ruffians sent,
I walk on hostile ground,
Wild human bears on slaughter bent,
And ravening wolves, surround:
The lion seeks my soul to slay
In some unguarded hour,
And waits to tear his sleeping prey,
And watches to devour.

3 But worse than all my foes I find
The enemy within,
The evil heart, the carnal mind,
My own insidious sin:
My nature every moment waits
To render me secure,
And all my paths with ease besets,
To make my ruin sure.

4 But thou hast given a loud alarm;
And thou shalt still prepare
My soul for all assaults, and arm
With never-ceasing prayer:
O do not suffer me to sleep,
Who on thy love depend;
But still thy faithful servant keep,
And save me to the end!

311

S. M.

1 BID me of men beware,
And to my ways take heed,
Discern their every secret snare,
And circumspectly tread ;
O may I calmly wait
Thy succours from above ;
And stand against their open hate,
And well-dissembled love !

2 My spirit, Lord, alarm,
When men and devils join ;
'Gainst all the powers of Satan arm
In panoply divine ;
O may I set my face
His onsets to repel ;
Quench all his fiery darts, and chase
The fiend to his own hell:

3 But, above all, afraid
Of my own bosom-foe,
Still let me seek to thee for aid,
To thee my weakness show ;
Hang on thy arm alone,
With self-distrusting care,
And deeply in the spirit groan
The never-ceasing prayer.

4 Give me a sober mind,
A quick-discerning eye,
The first approach of sin to find,
And all occasions fly.
Still may I cleave to thee,
And never more depart,
But watch with godly jealousy
Over my evil heart.

5 Thus may I pass my days
Of sojourning beneath,
And languish to conclude my race,
And render up my breath;

In humble love and fear,
Thine image to regain,
And see thee in the clouds appear,
And rise with thee to reign !

L. M. ## 312

1 JESU, my Saviour, Brother, Friend,
On whom I cast my every care,
On whom for all things I depend,
Inspire, and then accept, my prayer.

2 If I have tasted of thy grace,
The grace that sure salvation brings,
If with me now thy Spirit stays,
And hovering hides me in his wings,

3 Still let him with my weakness stay,
Nor for a moment's space depart,
Evil and danger turn away,
And keep till he renews my heart.

4 When to the right or left I stray,
His voice behind me may I hear,
" Return, and walk in Christ thy Way ;
Fly back to Christ, for sin is near."

5 His sacred unction from above
Be still my comforter and guide ;
Till all the hardness he remove,
And in my loving heart reside.

6 Jesus, I fain would walk in thee,
From nature's every path retreat ;
Thou art my Way, my leader be,
And set upon the rock my feet.

7 Uphold me, Saviour, or I fall,
O reach me out thy gracious hand !
Only on thee for help I call,
Only by faith in thee I stand.

L. M. ## 313

1 PIERCE, fill me with an humble fear ;
My utter helplessness reveal !
Satan and sin are always near,
Thee may I always nearer feel.

2 O that to thee my constant mind
Might with an even flame aspire,
Pride in its earliest motions find,
And mark the risings of desire !

3 O that my tender soul might fly
The first abhorred approach of ill,
Quick as the apple of an eye,
The slightest touch of sin to feel !

4 Till thou anew my soul create,
Still may I strive, and watch, and pray,
Humbly and confidently wait,
And long to see the perfect day.

S. M. ## 314

1 HARK, how the watchmen cry,
Attend the trumpet's sound !
Stand to your arms, the foe is nigh,
The powers of hell surround :
Who bow to Christ's command,
Your arms and hearts prepare !
The day of battle is at hand !
Go forth to glorious war !

2 See on the mountain-top
The standard of your God !
In Jesus' name I lift it up,
All stained with hallowed blood.

His standard-bearer, I
To all the nations call,
Let all to Jesu's cross draw nigh!
He bore the cross for all.

3 Go up with Christ your Head,
Your Captain's footsteps see;
Follow your Captain, and be led
To certain victory.
All power to him is given,
He ever reigns the same;
Salvation, happiness, and heaven
Are all in Jesu's name.

4 Only have faith in God;
In faith your foes assail,
Not wrestling against flesh and blood,
But all the powers of hell;
From thrones of glory driven,
By flaming vengeance hurled,
They throng the air, and darken heaven,
And rule the lower world.

315   SECOND PART.   S. M.

1 ANGELS your march oppose,
   Who still in strength excel,
Your secret, sworn, eternal foes,
Countless, invisible.
With rage that never ends
Their hellish arts they try;
Legions of dire malicious fiends,
And spirits enthroned on high.

2 On earth the usurpers reign,
Exert their baneful power,
O'er the poor fallen sons of men
They tyrannize their hour:
But shall believers fear?
But shall believers fly?
Or see the bloody cross appear,
And all their power defy?

3 Jesu's tremendous name
Puts all our foes to flight:
Jesus, the meek, the angry Lamb,
A Lion is in fight.
By all hell's host withstood,
We all hell's host o'erthrow;
And conquering them, through Jesu's blood,
We still to conquer go.

4 Our Captain leads us on;
He beckons from the skies,
And reaches out a starry crown,
And bids us take the prize:
"Be faithful unto death;
Partake my victory;
And thou shalt wear this glorious wreath,
And thou shalt reign with me."

316   L. M.

1 ETERNAL Power, whose high abode
   Becomes the grandeur of a God,
Infinite lengths beyond the bounds
Where stars revolve their little rounds!

2 Thee while the first archangel sings,
He hides his face behind his wings,
And ranks of shining thrones around
Fall worshipping, and spread the ground

3 Lord, what shall earth and ashes do?
We would adore our Maker too!
From sin and dust to thee we cry,
The Great, the Holy, and the High.

4 Earth from afar hath heard thy fame,
And worms have learned to lisp thy name:
But O! the glories of thy mind
Leave all our soaring thoughts behind!

5 God is in heaven, and men below:
Be short our tunes, our words be few!
A solemn reverence checks our songs,
And praise sits silent on our tongues.

317   L. M.   Matthew v. 13.

1 Lord, with trembling I confess,
A HA gracious soul may fall from grace;
The salt may lose its seasoning power,
And never, never, find it more.

2 Lest that my fearful case should be,
Each moment knit my soul to thee;
And lead me to the mount above,
Through the low vale of humble love.

318   S. M.   Leviticus viii. 35.

1 A CHARGE to keep I have,
   A God to glorify,
A never-dying soul to save,
And fit it for the sky;
To serve the present age,
My calling to fulfil:
O may it all my powers engage
To do my Master's will!

2 Arm me with jealous care,
As in thy sight to live;
And O thy servant, Lord, prepare
A strict account to give!
Help me to watch and pray,
And on thyself rely.
Assured, if I my trust betray,
I shall for ever die.

319   6-8 s.   Nehemiah v. 9.

1 WATCHED by the world's malignant
   eye,
Who load us with reproach and shame,
As servants of the Lord most High,
As zealous for his glorious name,
We ought in all his paths to move,
With holy fear and humble love.

2 That wisdom, Lord, on us bestow,
From every evil to depart;
To stop the mouth of every foe,
While, upright both in life and heart,
The proofs of godly fear we give,
And show them how the Christians live.

320   8 s & 6 s.   Job xxviii. 28.

1 BE it my only wisdom here
   To serve the Lord with filial fear,
With loving gratitude;
Superior sense may I display,
By shunning every evil way,
And walking in the good.

2 O may I still from sin depart!
A wise and understanding heart,
Jesus, to me be given;
And let me through thy Spirit know
To glorify my God below,
And find my way to heaven.

SECTION V.
FOR BELIEVERS WORKING.

321
C. M.

1 SUMMONED my labour to renew,
  And glad to act my part,
Lord, in thy name my work I do,
  And with a single heart.

2 End of my every action thou,
  In all things thee I see:
Accept my hallowed labour now,
  I do it unto thee.

3 Whate'er the Father views as thine,
  He views with gracious eyes;
Jesus, this mean oblation join
  To thy great sacrifice.

4 Stamped with an infinite desert,
  My work he then shall own;
Well pleased with me, when mine thou art,
And I his favoured son.

322
C. M.

1 SERVANT of all, to toil for man
  Thou didst not, Lord, refuse;
Thy majesty did not disdain
  To be employed for us!

2 Thy bright example I pursue,
  To thee in all things rise;
And all I think, or speak, or do,
  Is one great sacrifice.

3 Careless through outward cares I go,
  From all distraction free;
My hands are but engaged below,
  My heart is still with thee.

323
S. M.

1 GOD of almighty love,
  By whose sufficient grace
I lift my heart to things above,
  And humbly seek thy face;
Through Jesus Christ the Just,
  My faint desires receive;
And let me in thy goodness trust,
  And to thy glory live.

2 Whate'er I say or do,
  Thy glory be my aim;
My offerings all be offered through
  The ever-blessed name!
Jesu, my single eye
  Be fixed on thee alone:
Thy name be praised on earth, on high;
  Thy will by all be done!

3 Spirit of faith, inspire
  My consecrated heart;
Fill me with pure, celestial fire,
  With all thou hast, and art;
My feeble mind transform,
  And, perfectly renewed,
Into a saint exalt a worm,
  A worm exalt to God!

324
L. M.

1 FORTH in thy name, O Lord, I go,
  My daily labour to pursue,
Thee, only thee, resolved to know,
  In all I think, or speak, or do.

2 The task thy wisdom hath assigned
  O let me cheerfully fulfil,
In all my works thy presence find,
  And prove thy acceptable will!

3 Thee may I set at my right hand,
  Whose eyes my inmost substance see;
And labour on at thy command,
  And offer all my works to thee.

4 Give me to bear thy easy yoke,
  And every moment watch and pray,
And still to things eternal look,
  And hasten to thy glorious day.

5 For thee delightfully employ
  Whate'er thy bounteous grace hath given;
And run my course with even joy,
  And closely walk with thee to heaven.

325
7 s & 6 s †.

1 LO! I come with joy to do
  The Master's blessed will;
Him in outward works pursue,
  And serve his pleasure still;
Faithful to my Lord's commands,
I still would choose the better part,
Serve with careful Martha's hands,
  And loving Mary's heart.

2 Careful without care I am,
  Nor feel my happy toil,
Kept in peace by Jesu's name,
  Supported by his smile;
Joyful thus my faith to show,
I find his service my reward;
Every work I do below,
  I do it to the Lord.

3 Thou, O Lord, in tender love
  Dost all my burdens bear.
Lift my heart to things above,
  And fix it ever there!
Calm on tumult's wheel I sit,
Midst busy multitudes alone,
Sweetly waiting at thy feet,
  Till all thy will be done.

4 Thou, O Lord, my portion art,
  Before I hence remove!
Now my treasure and my heart
  Are all laid up above;
Far above all earthly things,
While yet my hands are here employed,
Sees my soul the King of kings,
  And freely talks with God.

5 O that all the art might know
  Of living thus to thee!
Find their heaven begun below,
  And here thy glory see!
Walk in all the works prepared
By thee, to exercise their grace,
Till they gain their full reward,
  And see thy glorious face!

326
6 - 8 s.   Exodus xiii. 21.

1 CAPTAIN of Israel's host, and guide
  Of all who seek the land above,
Beneath thy shadow we abide,
  The cloud of thy protecting love:
Our strength, thy grace; our rule, thy word;
Our end, the glory of the Lord.

2 By thine unerring Spirit led,
  We shall not in the desert stray;

We shall not full direction need,
Nor miss our providential way;
As far from danger as from fear,
While love, almighty love, is near.

327   Leviticus vi. 13.   L. M.

1 O THOU who camest from above
   The pure celestial fire to impart,
Kindle a flame of sacred love
   On the mean altar of my heart!

2 There let it for thy glory burn
   With inextinguishable blaze;
And trembling to its source return,
   In humble prayer and fervent praise.

3 Jesus, confirm my heart's desire
   To work, and speak, and think for thee;
Still let me guard the holy fire,
   And still stir up thy gift in me;

4 Ready for all thy perfect will,
   My acts of faith and love repeat,
Till death thy endless mercies seal,
   And make the sacrifice complete.

328   Deuteronomy vi. 7.   6-8 s.

1 WHEN quiet in my house I sit,
   Thy book be my companion still,
My joy thy sayings to repeat,
   Talk o'er the records of thy will,
And search the oracles divine,
Till every heartfelt word be mine.

2 O may the gracious words divine
   Subject of all my converse be!
So will the Lord his follower join,
   And walk and talk himself with me;
So shall my heart his presence prove,
And burn with everlasting love.

3 Oft as I lay me down to rest,
   O may the reconciling word
Sweetly compose my weary breast!
   While, on the bosom of my Lord,
I sink in blissful dreams away,
And visions of eternal day.

4 Rising to sing my Saviour's praise,
   Thee may I publish all day long;
And let thy precious word of grace
   Flow from my heart, and fill my tongue;
Fill all my life with purest love,
And join me to the church above.

SECTION VI.
FOR BELIEVERS SUFFERING.

329   C. M.

1 THEE, Jesus, full of truth and grace,
   Thee, Saviour, we adore,
Thee in affliction's furnace praise,
   And magnify thy power.

2 Thy power, in human weakness shown,
   Shall make us all entire;
We now thy guardian presence own,
   And walk unburned in fire.

3 Thee, Son of man, by faith we see,
    And glory in our guide;
Surrounded and upheld by thee,
   T   fiery test abide.

80oo

4 The fire our graces shall refine,
   Till, moulded from above,
We bear the character divine,
   The stamp of perfect love.

330

6-8 s.

1 SAVIOUR of all, what hast thou done,
   What hast thou suffered on the tree?
Why didst thou groan thy mortal groan,
   Obedient unto death for me?
The mystery of thy passion show,
The end of all thy griefs below.

2 Thy soul, for sin an offering made,
   Hath cleared this guilty soul of mine:
Thou hast for me a ransom paid,
   To change my human to divine,
To cleanse from all iniquity,
And make the sinner all like thee.

3 Pardon, and grace, and heaven to buy,
   My bleeding Sacrifice expired;
But didst thou not my Pattern die,
   That, by thy glorious Spirit fired,
Faithful to death I might endure,
And make the crown by suffering sure?

4 Thou didst the meek example leave,
   That I might in thy footsteps tread,
Might like the Man of sorrows grieve,
   And groan, and bow with thee my head,
Thy dying in my body bear,
And all thy state of suffering share.

5 Thy every perfect servant, Lord,
   Shall as his patient Master be;
To all thy inward life restored,
   And outwardly conformed to thee,
Out of thy grave the saint shall rise,
And grasp, through death, the glorious
   prize.

6 This is the strait and royal way,
   That leads us to the courts above;
Here let me ever, ever stay,
   Till, on the wings of perfect love,
I take my last triumphant flight
From Calvary's to Zion's height.

*331

6-8 s.   Hebrews xii. 11.

1 AFFLICTED by a gracious God,
   The stroke I patiently sustain,
Grievous to feeble flesh and blood;
   Unable to rejoice in pain,
Beneath my Father's hand I bow,
And groan to feel his chastening now.

2 But when he hath my patience proved,
   And sees me to his will resigned,
His heavy hand and rod removed,
   Shall leave the blest effect behind,
The sure, inviolable peace,
The ripened fruit of righteousness.

3 This pain, this consecrated pain,
   With which my soul and flesh are filled,
His instrument if he ordain,
   The pure and perfect love shall yield;
But by whatever means 'tis done,
The work and praise are all his own.

6-8 s.   Luke ix. 23.   **332**

1 MASTER, I own thy lawful claim,
   Thine, wholly thine, I long to be!

Thou seest, at last, I willing am
  Where'er thou go'st to follow thee ;
Myself in all things to deny,
Thine, wholly thine, to live and die

2 Whate'er my sinful flesh requires
  For thee I cheerfully forego,
My covetous and vain desires,
  My hopes of happiness below,
My senses' and my passions' food,
And all my thirst for creature-good.

3 Pleasure, and wealth, and praise no more
  Shall lead my captive soul astray,
My fond pursuits I all give o'er,
  Thee, only thee, resolved to obey ;
My own in all things to resign,
And know no other will but thine.

4 All power is thine in earth and heaven,
  All fulness dwells in thee alone ;
Whate'er I have was freely given,
  Nothing but sin I call my own,
Other propriety disclaim ;
Thou only art the great I AM.

5 Wherefore to thee I all resign ;
  Being thou art, and love, and power ;
Thy only will be done, not mine !
  Thee, Lord, let heaven and earth adore !
Flow back the rivers to the sea,
And let our all be lost in thee !

333
8 s & 6 s.

1 COME on, my partners in distress,
  My comrades through the wilderness,
  Who still your bodies feel ;
Awhile forget your griefs and fears,
And look beyond this vale of tears,
  To that celestial hill.

2 Beyond the bounds of time and space,
Look forward to that heavenly place,
  The saints' secure abode :
On faith's strong eagle-pinions rise,
And force your passage to the skies,
  And scale the mount of God.

3 Who suffer with our Master here,
We shall before his face appear,
  And by his side sit down ;
To patient faith the prize is sure,
And all that to the end endure
  The cross, shall wear the crown

4 Thrice blessed, bliss-inspiring hope !
It lifts the fainting spirits up,
  It brings to life the dead ;
Our conflicts here shall soon be past,
And you and I ascend at last,
  Triumphant with our Head.

5 That great mysterious Deity
We soon with open face shall see ;
  The beatific sight
Shall fill heaven's sounding courts with
And wide diffuse the golden blaze [praise,
  Of everlasting light.

6 The Father shining on his throne,
The glorious co-eternal Son,
  The Spirit, one and seven,
Conspire our rapture to complete ;
And lo ! we fall before his feet,
  And silence heightens heaven.

7 In hope of that ecstatic pause,
Jesus, we now sustain the cross,
  And at thy footstool fall ;
Till thou our hidden life reveal,
Till thou our ravished spirits fill,
  And God is all in all !

334
8 s & 6 s.   2 Samuel xvi. 10.

LORD, I adore thy gracious will ;
  Through every instrument of ill
  My Father's goodness see ;
Accept the complicated wrong
Of Shimei's hand and Shimei's tongue,
  As kind rebukes from thee !

335
7 s & 6 s †.

1 CAST on the fidelity
  Of my redeeming Lord,
I shall his salvation see,
  According to his word :
Credence to his word I give ;
My Saviour in distresses past
Will not now his servant leave,
  But bring me through at last.

2 Better than my boding fears
  To me thou oft hast proved,
Oft observed my silent tears,
  And challenged thy beloved ;
Mercy to my rescue flew,
And death ungrasped his fainting prey,
Pain before thy face withdrew,
  And sorrow fled away.

3 Now as yesterday the same,
  In all my troubles nigh,
Jesus, on thy word and name
  I steadfastly rely ;
Sure as now the grief I feel,
The promised joy I soon shall have ;
Saved again, to sinners tell
  Thy power and will to save.

4 To thy blessed will resigned,
  And stayed on that alone,
I thy perfect strength shall find,
  Thy faithful mercies own ;
Compassed round with songs of praise,
My all to my Redeemer give,
Spread thy miracles of grace,
  And to thy glory live.

336
7 s & 6 s.

1 FATHER, in the name I pray
  Of thy incarnate Love,
Humbly ask, that as my day
  My suffering strength may prove ;
When my sorrows most increase,
  Let thy strongest joys be given ;
Jesu, come with my distress,
  And agony is heaven !

2 Father, Son, and Holy Ghost,
  For good remember me !
Me, whom thou hast caused to trust
  For more than life on thee ;
With me in the fire remain,
  Till like burnished gold I shine,
Meet, through consecrated pain,
  To see the face divine.

337
L. M.

1 ETERNAL Beam of light divine,
   Fountain of unexhausted love,
In whom the Father's glories shine [above ;
   Through earth beneath, and heaven

2 Jesu, the weary wanderer's rest,
   Give me thy easy yoke to bear,
With steadfast patience arm my breast,
   With spotless love, and lowly fear.

3 Thankful I take the cup from thee,
   Prepared and mingled by thy skill,
Though bitter to the taste it be,
   Powerful the wounded soul to heal.

4 Be thou, O Rock of ages, nigh !   [gone,
   So shall each murmuring thought be
And grief, and fear, and care shall fly,
   As clouds before the mid-day sun.

5 Speak to my warring passions, " Peace ! "
   Say to my trembling heart, " Be still ! "
Thy power my strength and fortress is,
   For all things serve thy sovereign will.

6 O death ! where is thy sting? Where now
   Thy boasted victory, O grave ?
Who shall contend with God? or who
   Can hurt whom God delights to save ?

338
L. M.

1 THOU Lamb of God, thou Prince of peace,
   For thee my thirsty soul doth pine,
My longing heart implores thy grace ;
   O make me in thy likeness shine !

2 With fraudless, even, humble mind,
   Thy will in all things may I see ;
In love be every wish resigned,
   And hallowed my whole heart to thee.

3 When pain o'er my weak flesh prevails,
   With lamb-like patience arm my breast ;
When grief my wounded soul assails,
   In lowly meekness may I rest.

4 Close by thy side still may I keep,
   Howe'er life's various currents flow,
With steadfast eye mark every step,
   And follow thee where'er thou go.

5 Thou, Lord, the dreadful fight hast won,
   Alone thou hast the winepress trod ;
In me thy strengthening grace be shown,
   O may I conquer through thy blood !

6 So when on Zion thou shalt stand,
   And all heaven's host adore their King,
Shall I be found at thy right hand,
   And free from pain thy glories sing.

339
L. M.

1 O THOU to whose all-searching sight
   The darkness shineth as the light,
Search, prove my heart ; it pants for thee ;
   O burst these bonds, and set it free !

2 Wash out its stains, refine its dross,
   Nail my affections to the cross ;
Hallow each thought ; let all within
   Be clean, as thou, my Lord, art clean !

3 If in this darksome wild I stray,
   Be thou my light, be thou my way ;
No foes, no violence I fear,
   No fraud, while thou, my God, art near.

82

4 When rising floods my soul o'erflow,
   When sinks my heart in waves of woe,
Jesu, thy timely aid impart,
   And raise my head, and cheer my heart.

5 Saviour, where'er thy steps I see,
   Dauntless, untired, I follow thee !
O let thy hand support me still,
   And lead me to thy holy hill !

6 If rough and thorny be the way,
   My strength proportion to my day ;
Till toil, and grief, and pain shall cease,
   Where all is calm, and joy, and peace.

SECTION VII.
SEEKING FOR FULL REDEMPTION.

S. M.

340

1 THE thing my God doth hate
   That I no more may do,
Thy creature, Lord, again create,
   And all my soul renew ;
My soul shall then, like thine,
   Abhor the thing unclean,
And, sanctified by love divine,
   For ever cease from sin.

2 That blessed law of thine,
   Jesus, to me impart ;
The Spirit's law of life divine,
   O write it in my heart !
Implant it deep within,
   Whence it may ne'er remove,
The law of liberty from sin,
   The perfect law of love.

3 Thy nature be my law,
   Thy spotless sanctity,
And sweetly every moment draw
   My happy soul to thee.
Soul of my soul remain !
   Who didst for all fulfil,
In me, O Lord, fulfil again
   Thy heavenly Father's will !

L. M.

341

1 O JESUS, let thy dying cry
   Pierce to the bottom of my heart,
Its evils cure, its wants supply,
   And bid my unbelief depart.

2 Slay the dire root and seed of sin ;
   Prepare for thee the holiest place ;
Then, O essential Love, come in !
   And fill thy house with endless praise.

3 Let me, according to thy word,
   A tender, contrite heart receive,
Which grieves at having grieved its Lord,
   And never can itself forgive ;

4 A heart thy joys and griefs to feel,
   A heart that cannot faithless prove,
A heart where Christ alone may dwell,
   All praise, all meekness, and all love.

C. M.

342

1 GOD of eternal truth and grace,
   Thy faithful promise seal !
Thy word, thy oath, to Abraham's race,
   In us, even us, fulfil.

2 Let us, to perfect love restored,
   Thy image here retrieve,
And in the presence of our Lord
   The life of angels live.

3 That mighty faith on me bestow
   Which cannot ask in vain,
Which holds, and will not let thee go,
   Till I my suit obtain ;

4 Till thou into my soul inspire
   The perfect love unknown,
And tell my infinite desire,
   " Whate'er thou wilt, be done."

5 But is it possible that I
   Should live and sin no more ?
Lord, if on thee I dare rely,
   The faith shall bring the power.

6 On me that faith divine bestow
   Which doth the mountain move ;
And all my spotless life shall show
   The omnipotence of love.

343
Psalm ll. 10.   C. M.

1 O FOR a heart to praise my God,
   A heart from sin set free !
A heart that always feels thy blood
   So freely spilt for me !

2 A heart resigned, submissive, meek,
   My great Redeemer's throne,
Where only Christ is heard to speak,
   Where Jesus reigns alone ;

3 An humble, lowly, contrite heart,
   Believing, true, and clean ;
Which neither life nor death can part
   From him that dwells within ;

4 A heart in every thought renewed,
   And full of love divine ;
Perfect, and right, and pure, and good,
   A copy, Lord, of thine !

5 Thy tender heart is still the same,
   And melts at human woe :
Jesus, for thee the distressed I am,
   I want thy love to know.

6 My heart, thou know'st, can never rest,
   Till thou create my peace ;
Till, of my Eden re-possessed,
   From every sin I cease.

7 Fruit of thy gracious lips, on me
   Bestow that peace unknown,
The hidden manna, and the tree
   Of life, and the white stone.

8 Thy nature, gracious Lord, impart !
   Come quickly from above,
Write thy new name upon my heart,
   Thy new, best name of love.

344
6- 8 s.

1 THOU hidden love of God, whose height,
   Whose depth unfathomed no man
     knows,
I see from far thy beauteous light,
   Inly I sigh for thy repose ;
My heart is pained, nor can it be
At rest, till it finds rest in thee.

2 Thy secret voice invites me still
   The sweetness of thy yoke to prove ;

And fain I would ; but though my will
   Seems fixed, yet wide my passions rove ;
Yet hindrances strew all the way ;
I aim at thee, yet from thee stray.

3 'Tis mercy all, that thou hast brought
   My mind to seek her peace in thee ;
Yet, while I seek but find thee not,
   No peace my wandering soul shall see ;
O when shall all my wanderings end,
And all my steps to thee-ward tend !

4 Is there a thing beneath the sun
   That strives with thee my heart to share ?
Ah, tear it thence, and reign alone,
   The Lord of every motion there !
Then shall my heart from earth be free,
When it hath found repose in thee.

5 O hide this self from me, that I
   No more, but Christ in me, may live !
My vile affections crucify,
   Nor let one darling lust survive !
In all things nothing may I see,
Nothing desire or seek, but thee !

6 O Love, thy sovereign aid impart,
   To save me from low-thoughted care :
Chase this self-will through all my heart,
   Through all its latent mazes there,
Make me thy duteous child, that I
Ceaseless may, "Abba, Father," cry !

7 Ah no ! ne'er will I backward turn ;
   Thine wholly, thine alone, I am :
Thrice happy he who views with scorn
   Earth's toys, for thee his constant flame !
O help, that I may never move
From the blest footsteps of thy love !

8 Each moment draw from earth away
   My heart, that lowly waits thy call ;
Speak to my inmost soul, and say,
   " I am thy love, thy God, thy all !"
To feel thy power, to hear thy voice,
To taste thy love, be all my choice.

4 - 6 s & 2 - 8 s.   ## 345

1 YE ransomed sinners, hear,
   The prisoners of the Lord,
And wait till Christ appear,
   According to his word :
Rejoice in hope, rejoice with me,
We shall from all our sins be free.

2 Let others hug their chains,
   For sin and Satan plead,
And say, from sin's remains
   They never can be freed :
Rejoice in hope, rejoice with me,
We shall from all our sins be free.

3 In God we put our trust ;
   If we our sins confess,
Faithful he is, and just,
   From all unrighteousness
To cleanse us all, both you and me ;
We shall from all our sins be free.

4 Surely in us the hope
   Of glory shall appear ;
Sinners, your heads lift up,
   And see redemption near :
Again I say, Rejoice with me,
We shall from all our sins be free.

5 Who Jesu's sufferings share,
  My fellow-prisoners now,
Ye soon the wreath shall wear
  On your triumphant brow :
Rejoice in hope, rejoice with me,
We shall from all our sins be free.

6 The word of God is sure,
  And never can remove,
We shall in heart be pure,
  And perfected in love :
Rejoice in hope, rejoice with me,
We shall from all our sins be free.

7 Then let us gladly bring
  Our sacrifice of praise,
Let us give thanks, and sing,
  And glory in his grace:
Rejoice in hope, rejoice with me,
We shall from all our sins be free.

346   C. M.

1 FOR ever here my rest shall be,
  Close to thy bleeding side;
This all my hope, and all my plea,
For me the Saviour died!

2 My dying Saviour, and my God,
  Fountain for guilt and sin,
Sprinkle me ever with thy blood,
And cleanse, and keep me clean.

3 Wash me, and make me thus thine own,
  Wash me, and mine thou art,
Wash me, but not my feet alone,
My hands, my head, my heart.

4 The atonement of thy blood apply,
  Till faith to sight improve,
Till hope in full fruition die,
And all my soul be love.

347   C. M.

1 JESUS, my Life! thyself apply,
  Thy Holy Spirit breathe;
My vile affections crucify,
Conform me to thy death.

2 Conqueror of hell, and earth, and sin,
  Still with thy rebel strive ;
Enter my soul, and work within,
And kill, and make alive!

3 More of thy life, and more, I have,
  As the old Adam dies :
Bury me, Saviour, in thy grave,
That I with thee may rise.

4 Reign in me, Lord, thy foes control,
  Who would not own thy sway ;
Diffuse thine image through my soul,
Shine to the perfect day.

5 Scatter the last remains of sin,
  And seal me thine abode:
O make me glorious all within,
A temple built by God!

348   Isaiah xxxv.   8-7 s.

1 HEAVENLY Father, sovereign Lord,
  Ever faithful to thy word,
Humbly we our seal set to,
Testify that thou art true.
Lo! for us the wilds are glad,
All in cheerful green arrayed,

84

Opening sweets they all disclose,
Bud and blossom as the rose.

2 Hark ! the wastes have found a voice,
  Lonely deserts now rejoice,
Gladsome hallelujahs sing,
All around with praises ring.
Lo! abundantly they bloom,
Lebanon is hither come,
Carmel's stores the heavens dispense,
Sharon's fertile excellence.

3 See, these barren souls of ours
  Bloom, and put forth fruits and flowers,
Flowers of Eden, fruits of grace,
Peace, and joy, and righteousness.
We behold (the abjects we !)
Christ, the incarnate Deity,
Christ, in whom thy glories shine,
Excellence of strength divine.

4 Ye that tremble at his frown,
  He shall lift your hands cast down ;
Christ, who all your weakness sees,
He shall prop your feeble knees.
Ye of fearful hearts, be strong;
Jesus will not tarry long ;
Fear not lest his truth should fail,
Jesus is unchangeable.

5 God, your God, shall surely come,
  Quell your foes, and seal their doom,
He shall come and save you too ;
We, O Lord, have found thee true!
Blind we were, but now we see,
Deaf, we hearken now to thee,
Dumb, for thee our tongues employ,
Lame, and lo! we leap for joy.

6 Faint we were, and parched with drought,
  Water at thy word gushed out,
Streams of grace our thirst repress,
Starting from the wilderness ;
Still we gasp thy grace to know,
Here for ever let it flow,
Make the thirsty land a pool ;
Fix the Spirit in our soul.

8-7 s.   SECOND PART.   349

1 WHERE the ancient dragon lay,
  Open for thyself a way !
There let holy tempers rise,
All the fruits of Paradise.
Lead us in the way of peace,
In the path of righteousness,
Never by the sinner trod,
Till he feels the cleansing blood.

2 There the simple cannot stray,
  Babes, though blind, may find the way,
Find, nor ever thence depart,
Safe in lowliness of heart ;
Far from fear, from danger far,
No devouring beast is there,
There the humble walk secure;
God hath made their footsteps sure.

3 Jesus, mighty to redeem,
  Let our lot be cast with them ;
Far from earth our souls remove,
Ransomed by thy dying love.
Leave us not below to mourn ;
Fain we would to thee return,
Crowned with righteousness, arise
Far above these nether skies.

4 Come, and all our sorrows chase,
Wipe the tears from every face;
Gladness let us now obtain,
Partners of thine endless reign.
Death, the latest foe, destroy,
Sorrow then shall yield to joy,
Gloomy grief shall flee away,
Swallowed up in endless day.

350

7 s

1 HOLY Lamb, who thee receive,
Who in thee begin to live,
Day and night they cry to thee,
As thou art, so let us be!

2 Jesu, see my panting breast!
See I pant in thee to rest!
Gladly would I now be clean,
Cleanse me now from every sin.

3 Fix, O fix my wavering mind!
To thy cross my spirit bind;
Earthly passions far remove,
Swallow up my soul in love.

4 Dust and ashes though we be,
Full of sin and misery,
Thine we are, thou Son of God!
Take the purchase of thy blood!

5 Who in heart on thee believes,
He the atonement now receives,
He with joy beholds thy face,
Triumphs in thy pardoning grace.

6 See, ye sinners, see the flame,
Rising from the slaughtered Lamb,
Marks the new, the living way,
Leading to eternal day!

7 Jesus, when this light we see,
All our soul's athirst for thee;
When thy quickening power we prove,
All our heart dissolves in love.

8 Boundless wisdom, power divine,
Love unspeakable are thine:
Praise by all to thee be given,
Sons of earth, and hosts of heaven!

351

6-8 s. Second Metre.

1 COME, Holy Ghost, all quickening fire!
Come, and my hallowed heart inspire,
Sprinkled with the atoning blood;
Now to my soul thyself reveal,
Thy mighty working let me feel,
And know that I am born of God.

2 Thy witness with my spirit bear,
That God, my God, inhabits there:
Thou, with the Father, and the Son,
Eternal light's co-eval beam;
Be Christ in me, and I in him,
Till perfect we are made in one.

3 When wilt thou my whole heart subdue?
Come, Lord, and form my soul anew.
Emptied of pride, and wrath, and hell:
Less than the least of all thy store
Of mercies, I myself abhor;
All, all my vileness may I feel.

4 Humble, and teachable, and mild,
O may I, as a little child,
My lowly Master's steps pursue!

Be anger to my soul unknown,
Hate, envy, jealousy, be gone;
In love create thou all things new.

5 Let earth no more my heart divide,
With Christ may I be crucified,
To thee with my whole soul aspire;
Dead to the world and all its toys,
Its idle pomp, and fading joys,
Be thou alone my one desire!

6 Be thou my joy, be thou my dread;
In battle cover thou my head,
Nor earth nor hell I then shall fear;
I then shall turn my steady face,
Want, pain defy, enjoy disgrace,
Glory in dissolution near.

7 My will be swallowed up in thee;
Light in thy light still may I see,
Beholding thee with open face;
Called the full power of faith to prove,
Let all my hallowed heart be love,
And all my spotless life be praise.

8 Come, Holy Ghost, all quickening fire!
My consecrated heart inspire,
Sprinkled with the atoning blood;
Still to my soul thyself reveal,
Thy mighty working may I feel,
And know that I am one with God.

2-6 s & 4-7 s.

352

1 JESUS, thou art our King!
To me thy succour bring;
Christ, the mighty One, art thou,
Help for all on thee is laid;
This the word; I claim it now,
Send me now the promised aid.

2 High on thy Father's throne,
O look with pity down!
Help, O help, attend my call,
Captive lead captivity:
King of glory, Lord of all,
Christ, be Lord, be King to me!

3 I pant to feel thy sway,
And only thee to obey,
Thee my spirit gasps to meet;
This my one, my ceaseless prayer,
Make, O make my heart thy seat,
O set up thy kingdom there!

4 Triumph and reign in me,
And spread thy victory;
Hell, and death, and sin control,
Pride, and wrath, and every foe,
All subdue; through all my soul
Conquering, and to conquer go.

6-8 s. Second Metre.

353

1 O JESU, source of calm repose,
Thy like nor man nor angel knows,
Fairest among ten thousand fair!
Even those whom death's sad fetters bound,
Whom thickest darkness compassed round,
Find light and life, if thou appear.

2 Effulgence of the light divine,
Ere rolling planets knew to shine,
Ere time its ceaseless course began,
Thou, when the appointed hour was come,
Didst not abhor the virgin's womb,
But, God with God, wast man with man.

3 The world, sin, death, oppose in vain;
Thou, by thy dying, death hast slain,
  My great Deliverer, and my God;
In vain does the old dragon rage,
In vain all hell its powers engage, [blood.
  None can withstand thy conquering

4 Lord over all, sent to fulfil
Thy gracious Father's sovereign will,
  To thy dread sceptre will I bow:
With duteous reverence at thy feet,
Like humble Mary, lo! I sit;
  Speak, Lord, thy servant heareth now.

5 Renew thine image, Lord, in me,
Lowly and gentle may I be;
  No charms but these to thee are dear:
No anger may'st thou ever find,
No pride, in my unruffled mind, [there!
  But faith, and heaven-born peace, be

6 A patient, a victorious mind,
That life and all things casts behind,
  Springs forth obedient to thy call,
A heart that no desire can move,
But still to adore, believe, and love,
  Give me, my Lord, my life, my all!

354
                                 7 s & 6 s †.

1 EVER fainting with desire,
  For thee, O Christ, I call;
Thee I restlessly require,
  I want my God, my all!
Jesu, dear redeeming Lord,
I wait thy coming from above;
  Help me, Saviour, speak the word,
  And perfect me in love.

2 Wilt thou suffer me to go
  Lamenting all my days?
Shall I never, never know
  Thy sanctifying grace?
Wilt thou not the light afford,
The darkness from my soul remove?
  Help me, Saviour, speak the word,
  And perfect me in love.

3 Lord, if I on thee believe,
  The second gift impart;
With the indwelling Spirit give
  A new, a contrite heart;
If with love thy heart is stored,
If now o'er me thy mercies move,
  Help me, Saviour, speak the word,
  And perfect me in love.

4 Let me gain my calling's hope,
  O make the sinner clean!
Dry corruption's fountain up,
  Cut off the entail of sin;
Take me into thee, my Lord,
And I shall then no longer rove:
  Help me, Saviour, speak the word,
  And perfect me in love.

5 Thou, my Life, my treasure be,
  My Portion here below;
Nothing would I seek but thee,
  Thee only would I know,
My exceeding great Reward,
My heaven on earth, my heaven above!
  Help me, Saviour, speak the word,
  And perfect me in love.

6 Grant me now the bliss to feel
  Of those that are in thee;
86

Son of God, thyself reveal,
  Engrave thy name on me;
As in heaven be here adored,
And let me now the promise prove;
  Help me, Saviour, speak the word,
  And perfect me in love.

7 s.   Philippians ii. 5.   ## 355

1 JESU, shall I never be
  Firmly grounded upon thee?
Never by thy work abide,
Never in thy wounds reside?

2 O how wavering is my mind,
Tossed about with every wind!
O how quickly doth my heart
From the living God depart!

3 Jesu, let my nature feel,
Thou art God unchangeable:
JAH, JEHOVAH, great I AM,
Speak into my soul thy name.

4 Grant that every moment I
May believe, and feel thee nigh;
Steadfastly behold thy face,
Stablished with abiding grace.

5 Plant, and root, and fix in me
All the mind that was in thee;
Settled peace I then shall find;
Jesu's is a *quiet* mind.

6 Anger I no more shall feel,
Always even, always still,
Meekly on my God reclined;
Jesu's is a *gentle* mind.

7 I shall suffer and fulfil
All my Father's gracious will,
Be in all alike resigned;
Jesu's is a *patient* mind.

8 When 'tis deeply rooted here,
Perfect love shall cast out fear;
Fear doth servile spirits bind;
Jesu's is a *noble* mind.

9 When I feel it fixed within,
I shall have no power to sin;
How shall sin an entrance find?
Jesu's is a *spotless* mind.

10 I shall nothing know beside
Jesus, and him crucified;
Perfectly to him be joined;
Jesu's is a *loving* mind.

11 I shall triumph evermore,
Gratefully my God adore,
God so good, so true, so kind;
Jesu's is a *thankful* mind.

12 Lowly, loving, meek, and pure,
I shall to the end endure,
Be no more to sin inclined;
Jesu's is a *constant* mind.

13 I shall fully be restored
To the image of my Lord,
Witnessing to all mankind,
Jesu's is a *perfect* mind.

C. M.   ## 356

1 LORD, I believe thy every word,
  Thy every promise, true;
And lo! I wait on thee, my Lord,
  Till I my strength renew.

2 If in this feeble flesh I may
  Awhile show forth thy praise,
Jesu, support the tottering clay,
  And lengthen out my days.

3 If such a worm as I can spread,
  The common Saviour's name,
Let him who raised thee from the dead
  Quicken my mortal frame.

4 Still let me live thy blood to show
  Which purges every stain;
And gladly linger out below
  A few more years in pain.

5 Spare me till I my strength of soul,
  Till I thy love retrieve,
Till faith shall make my spirit whole,
  And perfect soundness give.

6 Faith to be healed thou know'st I have,
  From sin to be made clean;
Able thou art from sin to save,
  From all indwelling sin.

7 Surely thou canst, I do not doubt,
  Thou wilt, thyself impart;
The bond-woman's base son cast out,
  And take up all my heart.

8 I shall my ancient strength renew:
  The excellence divine
(If thou art good, if thou art true)
  Throughout my soul shall shine.

9 I shall, a weak and helpless worm,
  Through Jesus strengthening me,
Impossibilities perform,
  And live from sinning free.

10 For this in steadfast hope I wait;
  Now, Lord, my soul restore;
Now the new heavens and earth create,
  And I shall sin no more.

357
Matthew vi. 10.   C. M.

1 JESU, the Life, the Truth, the Way,
  In whom I now believe,
As taught by thee, in faith I pray,
  Expecting to receive.

2 Thy will by me on earth be done,
  As by the choirs above,
Who always see thee on thy throne,
  And glory in thy love.

3 I ask in confidence the grace,
  That I may do thy will,
As angels, who behold thy face,
  And all thy words fulfil.

4 Surely I shall, the sinner I
  Shall serve thee without fear;
My heart no longer gives the lie
  To my deceitful prayer.

5 When thou the work of faith hast
  I shall be pure within.   [wrought,
Nor sin in deed, or word, or thought;
  For angels never sin.

6 From thee no more shall I depart,
  No more unfaithful prove,
But love thee with a constant heart;
  For angels always love.

7 I all thy holy will shall prove:
  I, a weak, sinful worm,
When thee with all my heart I love,
  Shall all thy law perform.

8 The graces of my second birth
  To me shall all be given;
And I shall do thy will on earth,
  As angels do in heaven.

358
7 s & 6 s.

1 OPEN, Lord, my inward ear,
  And bid my heart rejoice;
Bid my quiet spirit hear
  Thy comfortable voice;
Never in the whirlwind found,
  Or where earthquakes rock the place,
Still and silent is the sound,
  The whisper of thy grace.

2 From the world of sin, and noise,
  And hurry, I withdraw;
For the small and inward voice
  I wait with humble awe;
Silent am I now and still,
  Dare not in thy presence move;
To my waiting soul reveal
  The secret of thy love.

3 Thou didst undertake for me,
  For me to death wast sold;
Wisdom in a mystery
  Of bleeding love unfold;
Teach the lesson of thy cross,
  Let me die with thee to reign;
All things let me count but loss,
  So I may thee regain.

4 Show me, as my soul can bear,
  The depth of inbred sin!
All the unbelief declare,
  The pride that lurks within;
Take me, whom thyself hast bought,
  Bring into captivity
Every high aspiring thought,
  That would not stoop to thee.

5 Lord, my time is in thy hand,
  My soul to thee convert;
Thou canst make me understand,
  Though I am slow of heart;
Thine in whom I live and move,
  Thine the work, the praise is thine;
Thou art wisdom, power, and love,
  And all thou art is mine.

359
7 s & 6 s.   Daniel iii.

1 GOD of Israel's faithful three,
  Who braved a tyrant's ire,
Nobly scorned to bow the knee,
  And walked unhurt in fire;
Breathe their faith into my breast,
  Arm me in this fiery hour;
Stand, O Son of man, confest
  In all thy saving power!

2 Lo! on dangers, deaths, and snares
  I every moment tread,
Hell without a veil appears,
  And flames around my head;
Sin increases more and more,
  Sin in all its strength returns,
Seven times hotter than before
  The fiery furnace burns.

3 But while thou, my Lord, art nigh,
  My soul disdains to fear;
Sin and Satan I defy,
  Still impotently near,

Earth and hell their wars may wage;
Calm I mark their vain design,
Smile to see them idly rage
Against a child of thine.

360   Romans iv. 13, &c.   C. M.

1 FATHER of Jesus Christ, my Lord,
My Saviour, and my Head,
I trust in thee, whose powerful word
Hath raised him from the dead.

2 Thou know'st for my offence he died,
And rose again for me,
Fully and freely justified,
That I might live to thee.

3 Eternal life to all mankind
Thou hast in Jesus given;
And all who seek, in him shall find
The happiness of heaven.

4 O God! thy record I believe,
In Abraham's footsteps tread;
And wait, expecting to receive,
The Christ, the promised seed.

5 Faith in thy power thou seest I have,
For thou this faith hast wrought;
Dead souls thou callest from their grave,
And speakest worlds from nought.

6 Things that are not, as though they were,
Thou callest by their name;
Present with thee the future are,
With thee, the great I AM.

7 In hope, against all human hope,
Self-desperate, I believe;
Thy quickening word shall raise me up,
Thou shalt thy Spirit give.

8 The thing surpasses all my thought,
But faithful is my Lord;
Through unbelief I stagger not,
For God hath spoke the word.

9 Faith, mighty faith, the promise sees,
And looks to that alone;
Laughs at impossibilities,
And cries, It shall be done!

10 To thee the glory of thy power
And faithfulness I give;
I shall in Christ, in that glad hour,
And Christ in me shall live.

11 Obedient faith, that waits on thee,
Thou never wilt reprove;
But thou wilt form thy Son in me,
And perfect me in love.

361   C. M

1 MY God! I know, I feel thee mine,
And will not quit my claim,
Till all I have is lost in thine,
And all renewed I am.

2 I hold thee with a trembling hand,
But will not let thee go,
Till steadfastly by faith I stand,
And all thy goodness know.

3 When shall I see the welcome hour,
That plants my God in me!
Spirit of health, and life, and power,
And perfect liberty!

4 Jesus, thine all-victorious love
Shed in my heart abroad;

Then shall my feet no longer rove,
Rooted and fixed in God.

5 Love only can the conquest win,
The strength of sin subdue,
(My own unconquerable sin)
And form my soul anew.

6 Love can bow down the stubborn neck,
The stone to flesh convert,
Soften, and melt, and pierce, and break
An adamantine heart.

7 O that in me the sacred fire
Might now begin to glow,
Burn up the dross of base desire,
And make the mountains flow!

8 O that it now from heaven might fall,
And all my sins consume!
Come, Holy Ghost, for thee I call,
Spirit of burning, come!

9 Refining fire, go through my heart,
Illuminate my soul;
Scatter thy life through every part,
And sanctify the whole.

10 No longer then my heart shall mourn,
While, purified by grace,
I only for his glory burn,
And always see his face.

11 My steadfast soul, from falling free,
Shall then no longer move;
But Christ be all the world to me,
And all my heart be love.

C. M.   Matthew x. 39.   362

1 BE it according to thy word;
This moment let it be!
O that I now, my gracious Lord,
Might lose my life for thee!

2 Now, Jesus, let thy powerful death
Into my being come;
Slay the old Adam with thy breath;
The man of sin consume.

3 My old affections mortify,
Nail to the cross my will;
Daily and hourly bid me die,
Or altogether kill.

4 Jesus, my Life, appear within,
And bruise the serpent's head;
Enter my soul, extirpate sin,
Cast out the cursed seed.

5 Hast thou not made me willing, Lord?
Would I not die this hour?
Then speak the killing, quickening word!
Slay, raise me, by thy power.

6 Slay me, and I in thee shall trust,
With thy dead men arise,
Awake, and sing out of the dust,
Soon as this nature dies.

7 O let it now make haste to die,
The mortal wound receive!
So shall I live; and yet not I,
But Christ in me shall live.

8 Be it according to thy word;
This moment let it be!
The life I lose for thee, my Lord,
I find again in thee.

363
L. M.

1 WHAT! never speak one evil word,
Or rash, or idle, or unkind!
O how shall I, most gracious Lord,
This mark of true perfection find?

2 Thy sinless mind in me reveal,
Thy Spirit's plenitude impart;
And all my spotless life shall tell
The abundance of a loving heart.

3 Saviour, I long to testify
The fulness of thy saving grace;
O might thy Spirit the blood apply,
Which bought for me the sacred peace!

4 Forgive, and make my nature whole,
My inbred malady remove;
To perfect health restore my soul,
To perfect holiness and love.

364
John iv. 10.　　6 - 8 s.

1 JESUS, the gift divine I know,
The gift divine I ask of thee;
That living water now bestow,
Thy Spirit and thyself, on me:
Thou, Lord, of life the fountain art,
Now let me find thee in my heart.

2 Thee let me drink, and thirst no more
For drops of finite happiness;
Spring up, O well, in heavenly power,
In streams of pure perennial peace,
In joy that none can take away,
In life which shall for ever stay.

3 Father, on me the grace bestow,
Unblamable before thy sight,
Whence all the streams of mercy flow;
Mercy, thy own supreme delight,
To me, for Jesu's sake, impart,
And plant thy nature in my heart.

4 Thy mind throughout my life be shown,
While, listening to the wretch's cry,
The widow's and the orphan's groan,
On mercy's wings I swiftly fly,
The poor and helpless to relieve,
My life, my all, for them to give.

5 Thus may I show the Spirit within,
Which purges me from every stain,
Unspotted from the world and sin,
My faith's integrity maintain;
The truth of my religion prove
By perfect purity and love.

365
6 - 8 s.　　Second Metre.

1 O GOD of my salvation, hear,
And help a sinner to draw near
With boldness to the throne of grace:
Help me thy benefits to sing,
And smile to see me feebly bring
My humble sacrifice of praise.

2 I cannot praise thee as I would;
But thou art merciful and good,
I know thou never wilt despise
The day of small and feeble things,
But bear me, till on eagles' wings
To all the heights of love I rise.

3 I thank thee for that gracious taste,
(Which pride would not permit to last)
That touch of love, that pledge of heaven:

Surely on me my Father smiled,
And once I knew him reconciled,
And once I felt my sins forgiven.

4 My Lord and God I then could see,
My Saviour, who hath died for me,
To bring the rebel near to God;
Thou didst, thou didst thy peace impart;
Pardon was written on my heart,
In largest characters of blood.

5 Vilest of all the sons of men,
When I to folly turned again,
And sinned against thy light and love,
Grace did much more than sin abound;
Amazed, I still forgiveness found,
And thanked my Advocate above.

6 Saviour, for this I thank thee now;
My Saviour to the utmost, thou
Hast snatched me from the gates of hell;
That I to all mankind may prove
Thy free, thine everlasting love,
Which all mankind with me may feel.

7 The boundless love that found out me
For every soul of man is free,
None of thy mercy need despair;
Patient, and pitiful, and kind,
Thee every soul of man may find,
And, freely saved, thy grace declare.

8 A vile, backsliding sinner, I
Ten thousand deaths deserve to die,
Yet still by sovereign grace I live!
Saviour, to thee I still look up;
I see an open door of hope,
And wait thy fulness to receive.

9 How shall I thank thee for the grace,
The trust I have to see thy face,
When sin shall all be purged away I
The night of doubts and fears is past;
The morning star appears at last,
And I shall see the perfect day.

6 - 8 s.
Second Metre.　SECOND PART.　## 366

1 I SOON shall hear thy quickening voice,
Shall always pray, give thanks, rejoice;
(This is thy will and faithful word)
My spirit meek, my will resigned,
Lowly as thine shall be my mind,
The servant shall be as his Lord.

2 Already, Lord, I feel thy power;
Preserved from evil every hour,
My great Preserver I proclaim:
Safety and strength in thee I have;
I find, I find thee strong to save,
And know that Jesus is thy name.

3 By faith I every moment stand,
Strangely upheld by thy right hand,
I my own wickedness eschew:
A sinner, I am kept from sin;
And thou shalt make me pure within,
And thou shalt form my soul anew.

4 Come then, and loose my stammering tongue,
Teach me the new, the joyful song,
And perfect in a babe thy praise:
I want a thousand lives to employ
In publishing the sounds of joy,
The gospel of thy general grace.

89

5 Come, Lord, thy Spirit bids thee come;
  Give me thyself, and take me home;
    Be now the glorious earnest given!
The counsel of thy grace fulfil,
Thy kingdom come, thy perfect will
    Be done on earth, as 'tis in heaven.

367

S. M.

1 O COME, and dwell in me,
    Spirit of power within!
And bring the glorious liberty
    From sorrow, fear, and sin.
The seed of sin's disease,
    Spirit of health, remove,
Spirit of finished holiness,
    Spirit of perfect love.

2 Hasten the joyful day
    Which shall my sins consume,
When old things shall be passed away,
    And all things new become.
The original offence
    Out of my soul erase,
Enter thyself, and drive it hence,
    And take up all the place.

3 I want the witness, Lord,
    That all I do is right,
According to thy will and word,
    Well-pleasing in thy sight:
I ask no higher state;
    Indulge me but in this,
And soon or later then translate
    To my eternal bliss.

368

7s & 6s†.

1 FATHER, see this living clod,
    This spark of heavenly fire,
See my soul, the breath of God,
    Doth after God aspire:
Let it still to heaven ascend,
    Till I my principle rejoin,
Blended with my glorious end,
    And lost in love divine.

2 Lord, if thou from me hast broke
    The power of outward sin,
Burst this Babylonish yoke,
    And make me free within;
Bid my inbred sin depart,
And I thy utmost word shall prove,
Upright both in life and heart,
    And perfected in love.

3 God of all-sufficient grace,
    My God in Christ thou art;
Bid me walk before thy face,
    Till I am pure in heart;
Till, transformed by faith divine,
I gain that perfect love unknown,
Bright in all thine image shine,
    By putting on thy Son.

4 Father, Son, and Holy Ghost,
    In council join again,
To restore thine image lost
    By frail, apostate man;
O might I thy form express,
Through faith begotten from above,
Stamped with real holiness,
    And filled with perfect love!

29

L. M.   Ezekiel xvi. 62, 63.   ## 369

1 O GOD, most merciful and true!
    Thy nature to my soul impart;
Stablish with me the covenant new,
    And write perfection on my heart.

2 To real holiness restored,
    O let me gain my Saviour's mind!
And, in the knowledge of my Lord,
    Fulness of life eternal find.

3 Remember, Lord, my sins no more,
    That them I may no more forget;
But sunk in guiltless shame adore
    With speechless wonder at thy feet.

4 O'erwhelmed with thy stupendous grace,
    I shall not in thy presence move,
But breathe unutterable praise,
    And rapturous awe, and silent love.

5 Then every murmuring thought and vain
    Expires, in sweet confusion lost;
I cannot of my cross complain,
    I cannot of my goodness boast.

6 Pardoned for all that I have done,
    My mouth as in the dust I hide;
And glory give to God alone,
    My God for ever pacified!

C. M.   ## 370

1 DEEPEN the wound thy hands have
    In this weak, helpless soul,   [made
Till mercy, with its balmy aid,
    Descends to make me whole.

2 The sharpness of thy two-edged sword
    Enable me to endure;
Till bold to say, My hallowing Lord
    Hath wrought a perfect cure.

3 I see the exceeding broad command,
    Which all contains in one:
Enlarge my heart to understand
    The mystery unknown.

4 O that with all thy saints I might
    By sweet experience prove,
What is the length, and breadth, and
    And depth, of perfect love!   [height,

8 s.   ## 371

1 WHAT now is my object and aim?
    What now is my hope and desire?
To follow the heavenly Lamb,
    And after his image aspire;
My hope is all centred in thee,
    I trust to recover thy love,
On earth thy salvation to see,
    And then to enjoy it above.

2 I thirst for a life-giving God,
    A God that on Calvary died;
A fountain of water and blood,
    Which gushed from Immanuel's side!
I gasp for the stream of thy love,
    The spirit of rapture unknown,
And then to re-drink it above,
    Eternally fresh from the throne.

7 s & 6 s.   Psalm lxxxi. 10.   ## 372

GIVE me the enlarged desire,
    And open, Lord, my soul,

Thy own fulness to require,
  And comprehend the whole :
Stretch my faith's capacity
  Wider, and yet wider still ;
Then with all that is in thee
  My soul for ever fill !

373
6 - 8 s.

1 JESU, thy boundless love to me
  No thought can reach, no tongue de-
O knit my thankful heart to thee, [clare ;
  And reign without a rival there !
Thine wholly, thine alone, I am,
Be thou alone my constant flame.

2 O grant that nothing in my soul
  May dwell, but thy pure love alone ;
O may thy love possess me whole,
  My joy, my treasure, and my crown !
Strange flames far from my heart remove ;
My every act, word, thought, be love.

3 O Love, how cheering is thy ray !
  All pain before thy presence flies,
Care, anguish, sorrow, melt away,
  Where'er thy healing beams arise ;
O Jesu, nothing may I see,
Nothing desire, or seek, but thee !

4 Unwearied may I this pursue,
  Dauntless to the high prize aspire ;
Hourly within my soul renew
  This holy flame, this heavenly fire ;
And day and night be all my care
To guard the sacred treasure there.

5 My Saviour, thou thy love to me
  In shame, in want, in pain, hast
For me, on the accursed tree, [showed ;
  Thou pouredst forth thy guiltless blood ;
Thy wounds upon my heart impress,
Nor aught shall the loved stamp efface.

6 More hard than marble is my heart,
  And foul with sins of deepest stain ;
But thou the mighty Saviour art,
  Nor flowed thy cleansing blood in vain ;
Ah, soften, melt this rock, and may
Thy blood wash all these stains away !

7 O that I, as a little child,
  May follow thee, and never rest
Till sweetly thou hast breathed thy mild
  And lowly mind into my breast !
Nor ever may we parted be,
Till I become one spirit with thee.

8 Still let thy love point out my way ;
  How wondrous things thy love hath
Still lead me, lest I go astray ; [wrought !
  Direct my word, inspire my thought ;
And if I fall, soon may I hear
Thy voice, and know that love is near.

9 In suffering be thy love my peace,
  In weakness be thy love my power ;
And when the storms of life shall cease,
  Jesus, in that important hour,
In death as life be thou my guide,
And save me, who for me hast died.

374
6 - 8 s

1 COME, Holy Ghost, all quickening fire !
  Come, and in me delight to rest ;

Drawn by the lure of strong desire,
  O come and consecrate my breast !
The temple of my soul prepare,
And fix thy sacred presence there.

2 If now thy influence I feel,
  If now in thee begin to live,
Still to my heart thyself reveal,
  Give me thyself, for ever give :
A point my good, a drop my store,
Eager I ask, I pant for more.

3 Eager for thee I ask and pant,
  So strong the principle divine
Carries me out with sweet constraint,
  Till all my hallowed soul is thine ;
Plunged in the Godhead's deepest sea,
And lost in thine immensity.

4 My peace, my life, my comfort thou,
  My treasure, and my all thou art !
True witness of my sonship, now
  Engraving pardon on my heart,
Seal of my sins in Christ forgiven,
Earnest of love, and pledge of heaven.

5 Come then, my God, mark out thine heir,
  Of heaven a larger earnest give !
With clearer light thy witness bear,
  More sensibly within me live ;
Let all my powers thine entrance feel,
And deeper stamp thyself the seal.

6 - 8 s.
375

1 SAVIOUR from sin, I wait to prove
  That Jesus is thy healing name ;
To lose, when perfected in love,
  Whate'er I have, or can, or am :
I stay me on thy faithful word,
"The servant shall be as his Lord."

2 Answer that gracious end in me
  For which thy precious life was given,
Redeem from all iniquity,
  Restore, and make me meet for heaven ;
Unless thou purge my every stain,
Thy suffering and my faith are vain.

3 Didst thou not in the flesh appear
  Sin to condemn, and man to save ?
That perfect love might cast out fear ?
  That I thy mind in me might have ?
In holiness show forth thy praise,
And serve thee all my spotless days ?

4 Didst thou not die that I might live
  No longer to myself, but thee ?
Might body, soul, and spirit give
  To him who gave himself for me ?
Come then, my Master, and my God,
Take the dear purchase of thy blood.

5 Thy own peculiar servant claim,
  For thy own truth and mercy's sake ;
Hallow in me thy glorious name ;
  Me for thine own this moment take,
And change, and throughly purify ;
Thine only may I live and die.

6 - 8 s.
376

1 I WANT the Spirit of power within,
  Of love, and of a healthful mind ;
Of power, to conquer inbred sin,
  Of love, to thee and all mankind,
Of health, that pain and death defies,
Most vigorous when the body dies

2 When shall I hear the inward voice
   Which only faithful souls can hear?
Pardon, and peace, and heavenly joys
   Attend the promised Comforter;
O come, and righteousness divine,
And Christ, and all with Christ, are mine!

3 O that the Comforter would come!
   Nor visit as a transient guest,
But fix in me his constant home,
   And take possession of my breast,
And fix in me his loved abode,
The temple of indwelling God!

4 Come, Holy Ghost, my heart inspire!
   Attest that I am born again;
Come, and baptize me now with fire,
   Nor let thy former gifts be vain;
I cannot rest in sins forgiven,
Where is the earnest of my heaven?

5 Where the indubitable seal
   That ascertains the kingdom mine?
The powerful stamp I long to feel,
   The signature of love divine;
O shed it in my heart abroad,
Fulness of love, of heaven, of God!

377 6 - 8 s. Second Metre.

1 FATHER of everlasting grace,
   Thy goodness and thy truth we praise,
Thy goodness and thy truth we prove;
   Thou hast, in honour of thy Son,
The gift unspeakable sent down,
The Spirit of life, and power, and love.

2 Send us the Spirit of thy Son,
   To make the depths of Godhead known,
To make us share the life divine;
   Send him the sprinkled blood to apply,
Send him our souls to sanctify,
 ·And show and seal us ever thine.

3 So shall we pray, and never cease,
   So shall we thankfully confess
Thy wisdom, truth, and power, and love;
   With joy unspeakable adore,
And bless and praise thee evermore,
And serve thee as thy hosts above:

4 Till, added to that heavenly choir,
   We raise our songs of triumph higher,
And praise thee in a bolder strain,
   Out-soar the first-born seraph's flight,
And sing, with all our friends in light,
Thy everlasting love to man.

378 6 - 8 s.

1 WHAT shall I do my God to love,
   My Saviour, and the world's, to praise?
Whose bowels of compassion move
   To me, and all the fallen race,
Whose mercy is divinely free
For all the fallen race, and me!

2 I long to know, and to make known,
   The heights and depths of love divine,
The kindness thou to me hast shown,
   Whose every sin was counted thine!
My God for me resigned his breath!
He died to save my soul from death!

3 How shall I thank thee for the grace
   On me and all mankind bestowed!

O that my every breath were praise!
   O that my heart were filled with God!
My heart would then with love o'erflow,
And all my life thy glory show.

4 See me, O Lord, athirst and faint!
   Me, weary of forbearing, see,
And let me feel thy love's constraint,
   And freely give up all for thee;
True in the fiery trial prove,
And pay thee back thy dying love.

379 6 - 8 s.

1 O LOVE, I languish at thy stay!
   I pine for thee with lingering smart;
Weary and faint through long delay,
   When wilt thou come into my heart?
From sin and sorrow set me free,
And swallow up my soul in thee?

2 Come, O thou universal Good!
   Balm of the wounded conscience, come!
The hungry, dying spirit's food,
   The weary, wandering pilgrim's home;
Haven to take the shipwrecked in,
My everlasting rest from sin!

3 Be thou, O Love, whate'er I want;
   Support my feebleness of mind,
Relieve the thirsty soul, the faint
   Revive, illuminate the blind,
The mournful cheer, the drooping lead,
And heal the sick, and raise the dead.

4 Come, O my comfort and delight!
   My strength and health, my shield and
My boast, and confidence, and might, [sun,
   My joy, my glory, and my crown,
My gospel hope, my calling's prize,
My tree of life, my paradise!

5 The secret of the Lord thou art,
   The mystery so long unknown;
Christ in a pure and perfect heart,
   The name inscribed in the white stone,
The Life divine, the little leaven,
My precious pearl, my present heaven.

380 6 - 8 s.

1 PRISONERS of hope, lift up your heads,
   The day of liberty draws near!
Jesus, who on the serpent treads,
   Shall soon in your behalf appear,
The Lord will to his temple come,
Prepare your hearts to make him room.

2 Ye all shall find, whom in his word
   Himself hath caused to put your trust,
The Father of our dying Lord
   Is ever to his promise just;
Faithful, if we our sins confess,
To cleanse from all unrighteousness.

3 Yes, Lord, we must believe thee kind,
   Thou never canst unfaithful prove;
Surely we shall thy mercy find,
   Who ask, shall all receive thy love;
Nor canst thou it to me deny,
I ask, the chief of sinners I!

4 O ye of fearful hearts, be strong!
   Your downcast eyes and hands lift up!
Ye shall not be forgotten long,
   Hope to the end, in Jesus hope!

Tell him ye wait his grace to prove,
And cannot fail, if God is love !

5 Prisoners of hope, be strong, be bold,
Cast off your doubts, disdain to fear !
Dare to believe : on Christ lay hold !
Wrestle with Christ in mighty prayer,
Tell him, " We will not let thee go,
Till we thy name, thy nature know."

6 Hast thou not died to purge our sin,
And risen, thy death for us to plead ?
To write thy law of love within
Our hearts, and make us free indeed ?
That we our Eden might regain,
Thou diedst, and couldst nct die in vain.

7 Lord, we believe, and wait the hour
Which all thy great salvation brings ;
The Spirit of love, and health, and power,
Shall come, and make us priests and
kings ;
Thou wilt perform thy faithful word,
" The servant shall be as his Lord."

8 The promise stands for ever sure,
And we shall in thine image shine,
Partakers of a nature pure,
Holy, angelical, divine ;
In spirit joined to thee the Son,
As thou art with thy Father one.

9 Faithful and True, we now receive
The promise ratified by thee :
To thee the when and how we leave,
In time and in eternity ;
We only hang upon thy word,
" The servant shall be as his Lord."

381

7 s.

1 WHEN, my Saviour, shall I be
Perfectly resigned to thee ?
Poor and vile in my own eyes,
Only in thy wisdom wise !

2 Only thee content to know,
Ignorant of all below,
Only guided by thy light,
Only mighty in thy might !

3 So I may thy Spirit know,
Let him as he listeth blow ;
Let the manner be unknown,
So I may with thee be one.

4 Fully in my life express
All the heights of holiness,
Sweetly let my spirit prove
All the depths of humble love !

382

Zechariah iv. 7.   7 s & 6 s.

1 O GREAT mountain, who art thou,
Immense, immovable ?
High as heaven aspires thy brow,
Thy foot sinks deep as hell !
Thee, alas, I long have known,
Long have felt thee fixed within ;
Still beneath thy weight I groan ;
Thou art Indwelling Sin.

2 Thou art darkness in my mind,
Perverseness in my will,
Love inordinate and blind,
That always cleaves to ill ;
Every passion's wild excess,
Anger, lust, and pride, thou art ;

Thou art sin and sinfulness,
And unbelief of heart.

3 Not by human might or power
Canst thou be moved from hence :
But thou shalt flow down before
Divine omnipotence ;
My Zerubbabel is near ;
I have not believed in vain :
Thou, when Jesus doth appear,
Shalt sink into a plain.

4 Christ the head, the corner-stone,
Shall be brought forth in me ;
Glory be to Christ alone !
His grace shall set me free :
I shall shout my Saviour's name,
Him I evermore shall praise ;
All the work of grace proclaim,
Of sanctifying grace.

5 Christ hath the foundation laid,
And Christ shall build me up ;
Surely I shall soon be made
Partaker of my hope ;
Author of my faith he is,
He its finisher shall be ;
Perfect love shall seal me his
To all eternity.

7 s & 6 s.   SECOND PART.   ## 383

1 WHO hath slighted or contemned
The day of feeble things ?
I shall be by grace redeemed ;
'Tis grace salvation brings :
Ready now my Saviour stands ;
Him I now rejoice to see
With the plummet in his hands,
To build and finish me.

2 I right early shall awake,
And see the perfect day ;
Soon the Lamb of God shall take
My inbred sin away :
When to me my Lord shall come,
Sin for ever shall depart ;
Jesus takes up all the room
In a believing heart.

3 Son of God, arise, arise,
And to thy temple come !
Look, and with thy flaming eyes
The man of sin consume ;
Slay him with thy Spirit, Lord ;
Reign thou in my heart alone ;
Speak the sanctifying word,
And seal me all thine own.

C. M.   ## 384

1 I KNOW that my Redeemer lives,
And ever prays for me ;
A token of his love he gives,
A pledge of liberty.

2 I find him lifting up my head,
He brings salvation near,
His presence makes me free indeed,
And he will soon appear.

3 He wills that I should holy be,
What can withstand his will ?
The counsel of his grace in me
He surely shall fulfil.

4 Jesus, I hang upon thy word;
   I steadfastly believe
Thou wilt return and claim me, Lord,
   And to thyself receive.

5 Joyful in hope, my spirit soars
   To meet thee from above,
Thy goodness thankfully adores;
   And sure I taste thy love.

6 Thy love I soon expect to find,
   In all its depth and height:
To comprehend the Eternal Mind,
   And grasp the Infinite.

7 When God is mine, and I am his,
   Of paradise possest,
I taste unutterable bliss,
   And everlasting rest.

8 The bliss of those that fully dwell,
   Fully in thee believe,
'Tis more than angel-tongues can tell,
   Or angel-minds conceive.

9 Thou only know'st, who didst obtain,
   And die to make it known;
'The great salvation now explain,
   And perfect us in one!

385   8 s & 7 s.

1 LOVE Divine, all loves excelling,
      Joy of heaven, to earth come down!
Fix in us thy humble dwelling,
   All thy faithful mercies crown;
Jesu, thou art all compassion,
   Pure, unbounded love thou art;
Visit us with thy salvation,
   Enter every trembling heart.

2 Come, almighty to deliver,
   Let us all thy grace receive;
.Suddenly return, and never,
   Never more, thy temples leave;
Thee we would be always blessing,
   Serve thee as thy hosts above,
Pray, and praise thee, without ceasing,
   Glory in thy perfect love.

3 Finish then thy new creation,
   Pure and spotless let us be;
Let us see thy great salvation,
   Perfectly restored in thee;
Changed from glory into glory,
   Till in heaven we take our place,
Till we cast our crowns before thee,
   Lost in wonder, love, and praise!

386   Isaiah li. 9.   L. M.

1 ARM of the Lord, awake, awake!
      Thine own immortal strength put on!
With terror clothed, hell's kingdom shake,
   And cast thy foes with fury down!

2 As in the ancient days appear!
   The sacred annals speak thy fame;
Be now omnipotently near,
   To endless ages still the same.

3 Thy arm, Lord, is not shortened now,
   It wants not now the power to save;
Still present with thy people, thou [wave,
   Bear'st them through life's disparted

4 By death and hell pursued in vain,
   To thee the ransomed seed shall come,
94

Shouting their heavenly Zion gain,
   And pass through death triumphant
      home.

5 The pain of life shall there be o'er,
   The anguish and distracting care,
There sighing grief shall weep no more,
   And sin shall never enter there.

6 Where pure, essential joy is found,
   The Lord's redeemed their heads shall
With everlasting gladness crowned, [raise,
   And filled with love, and lost in praise.

S. M.   ## 387

1 PRISONERS of hope, arise,
      And see your Lord appear;
Lo! on the wings of love he flies,
   And brings redemption near;
Redemption in his blood
   He calls you to receive:
"Look unto me, the pardoning God;
   Believe," he cries, "believe!"

2 The reconciling word
   We thankfully embrace;
Rejoice in our redeeming Lord,
   A blood-besprinkled race.
We yield to be set free;
   Thy counsel we approve;
Salvation, praise, ascribe to thee,
   And glory in thy love.

3 Jesus, to thee we look,
   Till saved from sin's remains;
Reject the inbred tyrant's yoke,
   And cast away his chains.
Our nature shall no more
   O'er us dominion have;
By faith we apprehend the power
   Which shall for ever save.

L. M.   Matthew xi. 28.   ## 388

1 O THAT my load of sin were gone!
      O that I could at last submit
At Jesu's feet to lay it down,
   To lay my soul at Jesu's feet!

2 When shall mine eyes behold the Lamb,
   The God of my salvation see?
Weary, O Lord, thou know'st I am,
   Yet still I cannot come to thee.

3 Rest for my soul I long to find:
   Saviour of all, if mine thou art,
Give me thy meek and lowly mind,
   And stamp thine image on my heart.

4 Break off the yoke of inbred sin,
   And fully set my spirit free;
I cannot rest till pure within,
   Till I am wholly lost in thee.

5 Fain would I learn of thee, my God;
   Thy light and easy burden prove,
The cross, all stained with hallowed blood,
   The labour of thy dying love.

6 I would; but thou must give the power,
   My heart from every sin release;
Bring near, bring near, the joyful hour,
   And fill me with thy perfect peace.

7 Come, Lord! the drooping sinner cheer,
   Nor let thy chariot-wheels delay;
Appear, in my poor heart appear!
   My God, my Saviour, come away!

389
C. M.

1 O JESUS, at thy feet we wait,
   Till thou shalt bid us rise,
Restored to our unsinning state,
   To love's sweet paradise.

2 Saviour from sin, we thee receive,
   From all indwelling sin;
Thy blood, we steadfastly believe,
   Shall make us throughly clean.

3 Since thou wouldst have us free from sin,
   And pure as those above,
Make haste to bring thy nature in,
   And perfect us in love.

4 The counsel of thy love fulfil;
   Come quickly, gracious Lord!
Be it according to thy will,
   According to thy word!

5 According to our faith in thee
   Let it to us be done;
O that we all thy face might see,
   And know as we are known!

6 O that the perfect grace were given,
   The love diffused abroad!
O that our hearts were all a heaven,
   For ever filled with God!

390
6 - 7 s.

1 SINCE the Son hath made me free,
   Let me taste my liberty;
Thee behold with open face,
Triumph in thy saving grace,
Thy great will delight to prove,
Glory in thy perfect love.

2 Abba, Father! hear thy child,
Late in Jesus reconciled,
Hear, and all the graces shower,
All the joy, and peace, and power,
All my Saviour asks above,
All the life and heaven of love.

3 Lord, I will not let thee go,
Till the blessing thou bestow;
Hear my Advocate divine!
Lo! to his my suit I join;
Joined to his, it cannot fail;
Bless me; for I will prevail!

4 Heavenly Adam, Life divine,
Change my nature into thine!
Move and spread throughout my soul,
Actuate and fill the whole!
Be it I no longer now
Living in the flesh, but Thou.

5 Holy Ghost, no more delay!
Come, and in thy temple stay!
Now thine inward witness bear,
Strong, and permanent, and clear;
Spring of life, thyself impart,
Rise eternal in my heart!

391
Ezekiel xxxvi. 25, &c.   L. M.

1 GOD of all power, and truth, and grace,
   Which shall from age to age endure,
Whose word, when heaven and earth shall pass,
   Remains and stands for ever sure;

2 That I thy mercy may proclaim,
   That all mankind thy truth may see,

Hallow thy great and glorious name,
   And perfect holiness in me.

3 Thy sanctifying Spirit pour,   [clean;
   To quench my thirst, and make me
Now, Father, let the gracious shower
   Descend, and make me pure from sin.

4 Purge me from every sinful blot,
   My idols all be cast aside;
Cleanse me from every sinful thought,
   From all the filth of self and pride.

5 Give me a new, a perfect heart,
   From doubt, and fear, and sorrow free;
The mind which was in Christ impart,
   And let my spirit cleave to thee.

6 O take this heart of stone away!
   Thy sway it doth not, cannot own;
In me no longer let it stay,
   O take away this heart of stone!

7 O that I now, from sin released,
   Thy word may to the utmost prove,
Enter into the promised rest,
   The Canaan of thy perfect love!

392
L. M.   SECOND PART.

1 FATHER, supply my every need,
   Sustain the life thyself hast given,
Call for the never-failing bread,   [heaven.
   The manna that comes down from

2 The gracious fruits of righteousness,
   Thy blessings' unexhausted store,
In me abundantly increase;
   Nor ever let me hunger more.

3 Let me no more, in deep complaint,
   "My leanness, O my leanness!" cry;
Alone consumed with pining want,
   Of all my Father's children, I.

4 The painful thirst, the fond desire,
   Thy joyous presence shall remove;
But my full soul shall still require
   A whole eternity of love.

393
L. M.   THIRD PART.

1 HOLY, and true, and righteous Lord,
   I wait to prove thy perfect will,
Be mindful of thy gracious word,
   And stamp me with thy Spirit's seal.

2 Open my faith's interior eye,
   Display thy glory from above;
And all I am shall sink and die,
   Lost in astonishment and love.

3 Confound, o'erpower me by thy grace,
   I would be by myself abhorred;
All might, all majesty, all praise,
   All glory, be to Christ my Lord.

4 Now let me gain perfection's height,
   Now let me into nothing fall;
Be less than nothing in thy sight,
   And feel that Christ is all in all!

394
6 - 8 s.

1 O GOD of our forefathers, hear,
   And make thy faithful mercies known!
To thee through Jesus we draw near,
Thy suffering, well-beloved Son,
In whom thy smiling face we see,
In whom thou art well-pleased with me.

95

2 With solemn faith we offer up,
   And spread before thy glorious eyes,
That only ground of all our hope,
   That precious, bleeding sacrifice,
Which brings thy grace on sinners down,
And perfects all our souls in one.

3 Acceptance through his only name,
   Forgiveness in his blood, we have;
But more abundant life we claim
   Through him who died our souls to save,
To sanctify us by his blood,
And fill with all the life of God.

4 Father, behold thy dying Son,
   And hear the blood that speaks above:
On us let all thy grace be shown,
   Peace, righteousness, and joy, and love,
Thy kingdom come to every heart,
And all thou hast, and all thou art.

395
L. M.

1 O GOD, to whom, in flesh revealed,
   The helpless all for succour came,
The sick to be relieved and healed,
   And found salvation in thy name;

2 With publicans and harlots, I,
   In these thy Spirit's gospel-days,
To thee, the sinner's friend, draw nigh,
   And humbly sue for saving grace.

3 Thou seest me helpless and distrest,
   Feeble, and faint, and blind, and poor,
Weary, I come to thee for rest,
   And sick of sin, implore a cure.

4 My sin's incurable disease
   Thou, Jesus, thou alone, canst heal,
Inspire me with thy power and peace,
   And pardon on my conscience seal.

5 A touch, a word, a look from thee,
   Can turn my heart, and make it clean,
Purge the foul, inbred leprosy,
   And save me from my bosom sin.

6 Lord, if thou wilt, I do believe
   Thou canst the saving grace impart,
Thou canst this instant now forgive,
   And stamp thine image on my heart.

7 My heart, which now to thee I raise,
   I know thou canst this moment cleanse,
The deepest stains of sin efface,
   And drive the evil spirit hence.

8 Be it according to thy word,
   Accomplish now thy work in me;
And let my soul, to health restored,
   Devote its little all to thee.

396
L. M.

1 O THOU, whom once they flocked to hear,
   Thy words to hear, thy power to feel;
Suffer the sinners to draw near,
   And graciously receive us still.

2 They that be whole, thyself hast said,
   No need of a physician have;
But I am sick, and want thine aid,
   And want thine utmost power to save.

3 Thy power, and truth, and love divine,
   The same from age to age endure;
A word, a gracious word of thine,
   The most inveterate plague can cure.
96

4 Helpless howe'er my spirit lies,
   And long hath languished at the pool,
A word of thine shall make me rise,
   And speak me in a moment whole.

5 Eighteen, or eight and thirty, years,
   Or thousands, are alike to thee:
Soon as thy saving grace appears,
   My plague is gone, my heart is free.

6 Make this the acceptable hour!
   Come, O my soul's physician, thou!
Display thy sanctifying power,
   And show me thy salvation now.

L. M.
397

1 JESU, thy far-extended fame
   My drooping soul exults to hear;
Thy name, thy all-restoring name,
   Is music in a sinner's ear.

2 Sinners of old thou didst receive,
   With comfortable words and kind,
Their sorrows cheer, their wants relieve,
   Heal the diseased, and cure the blind.

3 And art thou not the Saviour still,
   In every place and age the same?
Hast thou forgot thy gracious skill,
   Or lost the virtue of thy name?

4 Faith in thy changeless name I have;
   The good, the kind physician, thou
Art able now our souls to save,
   Art willing to restore them now.

5 Though eighteen hundred years are past
   Since thou didst in the flesh appear,
Thy tender mercies ever last;
   And still thy healing power is here!

6 Wouldst thou the body's health restore,
   And not regard the sin-sick soul?
The sin-sick soul thou lov'st much more,
   And surely thou shalt make it whole.

7 All my disease, my every sin,
   To thee, O Jesus, I confess;
In pardon, Lord, my cure begin,
   And perfect it in holiness.

8 That token of thine utmost good
   Now, Saviour, now on me bestow;
And purge my conscience with thy blood,
   And wash my nature white as snow.

7 s.
398

1 SAVIOUR of the sin-sick soul,
   Give me faith to make me whole!
Finish thy great work of grace,
Cut it short in righteousness.

2 Speak the second time, "Be clean!"
Take away my inbred sin;
Every stumbling-block remove,
Cast it out by perfect love.

3 Nothing less will I require,
Nothing more can I desire;
None but Christ to me be given,
None but Christ in earth or heaven!

4 O that I might now decrease!
O that all I am might cease!
Let me into nothing fall,
Let my Lord be all in all!

399

8 - 7 s.

1 LIGHT of life, seraphic fire,
    Love divine, thyself impart;
Every fainting soul inspire,
    Shine in every drooping heart:
Every mournful sinner cheer,
    Scatter all our guilty gloom,
Son of God, appear, appear!
    To thy human temples come.

2 Come in this accepted hour,
    Bring thy heavenly kingdom in:
Fill us with the glorious power,
    Rooting out the seeds of sin
Nothing more can we require,
    We will covet nothing less;
Be thou all our heart's desire,
    All our joy, and all our peace!

400

7 s.

1 JESUS comes with all his grace,
    Comes to save a fallen race;
Object of our glorious hope,
Jesus comes to lift us up!

2 Let the living stones cry out!
Let the sons of Abraham shout!
Praise we all our lowly King,
Give him thanks, rejoice, and sing!

3 He hath our salvation wrought,
He our captive souls hath bought;
He hath reconciled to God,
He hath washed us in his blood.

4 We are now his lawful right,
Walk as children of the light;
We shall soon obtain the grace,
Pure in heart, to see his face.

5 We shall gain our calling's prize;
After God we all shall rise,
Filled with joy, and love, and peace,
Perfected in holiness.

6 Let us then rejoice in hope,
Steadily to Christ look up;
Trust to be redeemed from sin,
Wait, till he appear within.

7 Fools and madmen let us be,
Yet is our sure trust in thee:
Faithful is the promised word,
We shall all be as our Lord.

8 Hasten, Lord, the perfect day!
Let thy every servant say,
I have now obtained the power,
Born of God, to sin no more.

401

Mark ix. 23.   6 - 8 s.

1 ALL things are possible to him
    That can in Jesus name believe;
Lord, I no more thy truth blaspheme,
    Thy truth I lovingly receive;
I can, I do believe in thee,
All things are possible to me.

2 The most impossible of all
    Is, that I e'er from sin should cease;
Yet shall it be, I know it shall;
    Jesus, look to thy faithfulness!
If nothing is too hard for thee,
All things are possible to me.

3 Though earth and hell the word gainsay,
    The word of God can never fail;
The Lamb shall take my sins away,
    Tis certain, though impossible;
The thing impossible shall be,
All things are possible to me.

4 When thou the work of faith hast wrought,
    I here shall in thine image shine,
Nor sin in deed, or word, or thought;
    Let men exclaim, and fiends repine,
They cannot break the firm decree;
All things are possible to me.

5 Thy mouth, O Lord, hath spoke, hath sworn
    That I shall serve thee without fear,
Shall find the pearl which others spurn;
    Holy, and pure, and perfect here,
The servant as his Lord shall be,
All things are possible to me.

6 All things are possible to God,
    To Christ, the power of God in man;
To me, when I am all renewed,
    When I in Christ am formed again,
And witness, from all sin set free,
All things are possible to me.

402

7 s & 6 s.

1 O MIGHT I this moment cease
    From every work of mine,
Find the perfect holiness,
    The righteousness divine!
Let me thy salvation see;
    Let me do thy perfect will;
Live in glorious liberty,
    And all thy fulness feel.

2 O cut short the work, and make
    Me now a creature new!
For thy truth and mercy's sake
    The gracious wonder show;
Call me forth thy witness, Lord,
    Let my life declare thy power;
To thy perfect love restored,
    O let me sin no more!

3 Fain would I the truth proclaim
    That makes me free indeed,
Glorify my Saviour's name,
    And all its virtues spread;
Jesus all our wants relieves,
    Jesus, mighty to redeem,
Saves, and to the utmost saves,
    All those that come to him.

403

C. M.

1 LORD, I believe a rest remains
    To all thy people known,
A rest where pure enjoyment reigns,
    And thou art loved alone:

2 A rest, where all our soul's desire
    Is fixed on things above;
Where fear, and sin, and grief expire,
    Cast out by perfect love.

3 O that I now the rest might know,
    Believe, and enter in!
Now, Saviour, now the power bestow,
    And let me cease from sin.

4 Remove this hardness from my heart,
    This unbelief remove;
To me the rest of faith impart,
    The sabbath of thy love.

5 I would be thine, thou know'st I would,
    And have thee all my own;
Thee, O my all-sufficient good!
    I want, and thee alone.

6 Thy name to me, thy nature grant!
    This, only this be given:
Nothing beside my God I want,
    Nothing in earth or heaven.

7 Come, O my Saviour, come away!
    Into my soul descend;
No longer from thy creature stay,
    My author and my end!

8 Come, Father, Son, and Holy Ghost,
    And seal me thine abode!
Let all I am in thee be lost,
    Let all be lost in God.

404   8 s & 6 s.

1 O GLORIOUS hope of perfect love!
    It lifts me up to things above,
    It bears on eagles' wings;
It gives my ravished soul a taste,
And makes me for some moments feast
    With Jesu's priests and kings.

2 Rejoicing now in earnest hope,
I stand, and from the mountain-top
    See all the land below;
Rivers of milk and honey rise,
And all the fruits of paradise
    In endless plenty grow.

3 A land of corn, and wine, and oil,
Favoured with God's peculiar smile,
    With every blessing blest;
There dwells the Lord our Righteousness,
And keeps his own in perfect peace,
    And everlasting rest.

4 O that I might at once go up!
No more on this side Jordan stop,
    But now the land possess;
This moment end my legal years,
Sorrows, and sins, and doubts, and fears,
    A howling wilderness.

5 Now, O my Joshua, bring me in!
Cast out thy foes; the inbred sin,
    The carnal mind, remove;
The purchase of thy death divide!
Give me with all the sanctified
    The heritage of love!

405   C. M.

1 O JOYFUL sound of gospel grace!
    Christ shall in me appear;
I, even I, shall see his face,
    I shall be holy here.

2 This heart shall be his constant home;
    I hear his Spirit's cry,
" Surely," he saith, " I quickly come,"
    He saith, who cannot lie.

3 The glorious crown of righteousness
    To me reached out I view;
Conqueror through him, I soon shall seize,
    And wear it as my due.

4 The promised land, from Pisgah's top,
    I now exult to see;
My hope is full (O glorious hope!)
    Of immortality.

98

5 He visits now the house of clay,
    He shakes his future home;
O wouldst thou, Lord, on this glad day,
    Into thy temple come!

6 With me, I know, I feel, thou art;
    But this cannot suffice,
Unless thou plantest in my heart
    A constant paradise.

7 My earth thou waterest from on high
    But make it all a pool;
Spring up, O well, I ever cry,
    Spring up within my soul!

8 Come, O my God, thyself reveal,
    Fill all this mighty void;
Thou only canst my spirit fill:
    Come, O my God, my God!

9 Fulfil, fulfil my large desires,
    Large as infinity;
Give, give me all my soul requires,
    All, all that is in thee!

406
C. M.

1 WHAT is our calling's glorious hope,
    But inward holiness?
For this to Jesus I look up,
    I calmly wait for this.

2 I wait, till he shall touch me clean,
    Shall life and power impart,
Give me the faith that casts out sin,
    And purifies the heart.

3 This is the dear redeeming grace,
    For every sinner free;
Surely it shall on me take place,
    The chief of sinners, me.

4 From all iniquity, from all,
    He shall my soul redeem;
In Jesus I believe, and shall
    Believe myself to him.

5 When Jesus makes my heart his home,
    My sin shall all depart;
And lo! he saith, I quickly come,
    To fill and rule thy heart.

6 Be it according to thy word!
    Redeem me from all sin;
My heart would now receive thee, Lord,
    Come in, my Lord, come in!

407
Deuteronomy xxxiii.
26—29.
7 s & 6 s.

1 NONE is like Jeshurun's God,
    So great, so strong, so high,
Lo! he spreads his wings abroad,
    He rides upon the sky!
Israel is his first-born son;
    God, the Almighty God, is thine;
See him to thy help come down,
    The excellence divine.

2 Thee the great Jehovah deigns
    To succour and defend;
Thee the eternal God sustains,
    Thy Maker and thy friend:
Israel, what hast thou to dread?
    Safe from all impending harms,
Round thee and beneath are spread
    The everlasting arms.

3 God is thine; disdain to fear
    The enemy within;

God shall in thy flesh appear,
 And make an end of sin;
God the man of sin shall slay,
Fill thee with triumphant joy;
God shall thrust him out, and say,
 "Destroy them all, destroy!"

4 All the struggle then is o'er,
 And wars and fightings cease,
Israel then shall sin no more,
 But dwell in perfect peace;
All his enemies are gone;
 Sin shall have in him no part;
Israel now shall dwell alone,
 With Jesus in his heart.

5 In a land of corn and wine
 His lot shall be below;
Comforts there, and blessings join,
 And milk and honey flow;
Jacob's well is in his soul;
 Gracious dew his heavens distil,
Fill his soul, already full,
 And shall for ever fill.

6 Blest, O Israel, art thou!
 What people is like thee?
Saved from sin, by Jesus, now
 Thou art, and still shalt be;
Jesus is thy seven-fold shield,
 Jesus is thy flaming sword;
Earth, and hell, and sin, shall yield
 To God's almighty Word.

408
L. M.

1 HE wills that I should holy be,
 That holiness I long to feel;
That full divine conformity
 To all my Saviour's righteous will.

2 See, Lord, the travail of thy soul
 Accomplished in the change of mine,
And plunge me, every whit made whole,
 In all the depths of love divine.

3 On thee, O God, my soul is stayed,
 And waits to prove thine utmost will;
The promise, by thy mercy made,
 Thou canst, thou wilt, in me fulfil.

4 No more I stagger at thy power,
 Or doubt thy truth, which cannot move:
Hasten the long-expected hour,
 And bless me with thy perfect love.

5 Jesus, thy loving Spirit alone
 Can lead me forth, and make me free,
Burst every bond through which I groan,
 And set my heart at liberty:

6 Now let thy Spirit bring me in,
 And give thy servant to possess
The land of rest from inbred sin,
 The land of perfect holiness.

7 Lord, I believe thy power the same,
 The same thy truth and grace endure;
And in thy blessed hands I am,
 And trust thee for a perfect cure.

8 Come, Saviour, come, and make me whole!
 Entirely all my sins remove;
To perfect health restore my soul,
 To perfect holiness and love.

409
C. M.

1 JESUS, my Lord, I cry to thee,
 Against the spirit unclean;
D 2

I want a constant liberty,
 A perfect rest from sin.

2 Expel the fiend out of my heart,
 By love's almighty power;
Now, now command him to depart,
 And never enter more.

3 Thy killing and thy quickening power,
 Jesus, in me display;
The life of nature from this hour,
 My pride and passion, slay.

4 Then, then, my utmost Saviour, raise
 My soul with saints above,
To serve thy will, and spread thy praise,
 And sing thy perfect love.

5 This moment I thy truth confess;
 This moment I receive
The heavenly gift, the dew of grace,
 And by thy mercy live.

6 The next, and every moment, Lord,
 On me thy Spirit pour;
And bless me, who believe thy word,
 With that last glorious shower.

S. M.   ## 410

1 FATHER, I dare believe
 Thee merciful and true:
Thou wilt my guilty soul forgive,
 My fallen soul renew.
Come then for Jesu's sake,
 And bid my heart be clean;
An end of all my troubles make,
 An end of all my sin.

2 I will, through grace, I will,
 I do, return to thee;
Take, empty it, O Lord, and fill
 My heart with purity!
For power I feebly pray:
 Thy kingdom now restore,
To-day, while it is called to-day,
 And I shall sin no more.

3 I cannot wash my heart,
 But by believing thee,
And waiting for thy blood to impart
 The spotless purity:
While at thy cross I lie,
 Jesus, the grace bestow,
Now thy all-cleansing blood apply,
 And I am white as snow.

7 s & 6 s †.   I Corinthians vi. 20.   ## 411

1 GOD! who didst so dearly buy
 These wretched souls of ours,
Help us thee to glorify
 With all our ransomed powers:
Ours they are not, Lord, but thine;
O let the vessels of thy grace,
Body, soul, and spirit, join
 In our Redeemer's praise!

2 Father, Son, and Spirit, come,
 And with thine own abide:
Holy Ghost, to make thee room,
 Our hearts we open wide;
Thee, and only thee request,
To every asking sinner given!
Come, our life, and peace, and rest,
 Our all in earth and heaven.

412   1 Kings xviii.   L. M.

1 THOU God that answerest by fire,
   On thee in Jesu's name we call ;
Fulfil our faithful hearts' desire,
   And let on us thy Spirit fall.

2 Bound on the altar of thy cross,
   Our old offending nature lies ;
Now, for the honour of thy cause,
   Come, and consume the sacrifice !

3 Consume our lusts as rotten wood,
   Consume our stony hearts within !
Consume the dust, the serpent's food,
   And dry up all the streams of sin.

4 Its body totally destroy !
   Thyself The Lord, The God, approve !
And fill our hearts with holy joy,
   And fervent zeal, and perfect love.

5 O that the fire from heaven might fall,
   Our sins its ready victims find,
Seize on our sins, and burn up all,
   Nor leave the least remains behind !

6 Then shall our prostrate souls adore ;
   The Lord, He is the God, confess :
He is the God of saving power !
   He is the God of hallowing grace !

413   1 Timothy iii. 16.   7 s & 6 s †.

1 ONCE thou didst on earth appear,
   For all mankind to atone ;
Now be manifested here,
   And bid our sin be gone !
Come, and by thy presence chase
Its nature with its guilt and power ;
Jesus, show thine open face,
   And sin shall be no more.

2 Thou who didst so greatly stoop
   To a poor virgin's womb,
Here thy mean abode take up ;
   To me, my Saviour, come !
Come, and Satan's works destroy,
And let me all thy Godhead prove,
Filled with peace, and heavenly joy,
   And pure eternal love.

3 Then my soul, with strange delight,
   Shall comprehend and feel
What the length, and breadth, and height
   Of love unspeakable :
Then I shall the secret know,
Which angels would search out in vain ;
God was man, and served below,
   That man with God might reign !

414   *" When shall it once be ? "*
       Jeremiah xiii. 27.   7 s & 6 s.

1 NOW, even now, I yield, I yield,
   With all my sins to part ;
Jesus, speak my pardon sealed,
   And purify my heart ;
Purge the love of sin away,
   Then I into nothing fall ;
Then I see the perfect day,
   And Christ is all in all.

2 Jesus, now our hearts inspire
   With that pure love of thine ;
Kindle now the heavenly fire,
   To brighten and refine ;
100

Purify our faith like gold,
   All the dross of sin remove ;
Melt our spirits down, and mould
   Into thy perfect love.

C. M.   **415**

1 JESUS hath died that I might live,
   Might live to God alone ;
In him eternal life receive,
   And be in spirit one.

2 Saviour, I thank thee for the grace,
   The gift unspeakable !
And wait with arms of faith to embrace,
   And all thy love to feel.

3 My soul breaks out in strong desire
   The perfect bliss to prove ;
My longing heart is all on fire
   To be dissolved in love.

4 Give me thyself ; from every boast,
   From every wish set free ;
Let all I am in thee be lost ;
   But give thyself to me.

5 Thy gifts, alas, cannot suffice
   Unless thyself be given ;
Thy presence makes my paradise,
   And where thou art is heaven !

C. M.   **416**

1 I ASK the gift of righteousness,
   The sin-subduing power,
Power to believe, and go in peace,
   And never grieve thee more.

2 I ask the blood-bought pardon sealed,
   The liberty from sin,
The grace infused, the love revealed,
   The kingdom fixed within.

3 Thou hear'st me for salvation pray,
   Thou seest my heart's desire ;
Made ready in thy powerful day,
   Thy fulness I require.

4 My vehement soul cries out opprest,
   Impatient to be freed ;
Nor can I, Lord, nor will I rest,
   Till I am saved indeed.

5 Art thou not able to convert ?
   Art thou not willing too ?
To change this old rebellious heart,
   To conquer and renew ?

6 Thou canst, thou wilt, I dare believe,
   So arm me with thy power,
That I to sin shall never cleave,
   Shall never feel it more.

C. M.   **417**

1 COME, O my God, the promise seal,
   This mountain, sin, remove ;
Now in my gasping soul reveal
   The virtue of thy love.

2 I want thy life, thy purity,
   Thy righteousness, brought in ;
I ask, desire, and trust in thee,
   To be redeemed from sin.

3 For this, as taught by thee, I pray,
   And can no longer doubt ;
Remove from hence ! to sin I say,
   Be cast this moment out !

4 Anger and sloth, desire and pride,
   This moment be subdued !
Be cast into the crimson tide
   Of my Redeemer's blood !

5 Saviour, to thee my soul looks up,
   My present Saviour thou !
In all the confidence of hope,
   I claim the blessing now.

6 'Tis done ! thou dost this moment save,
   With full salvation bless ;
Redemption through thy blood I have,
   And spotless love and peace.

SECTION VIII.
FOR BELIEVERS SAVED.

418
   Revelation i. 4, 5.   7 s & 6 s †.

1 TRUE and faithful Witness, thee,
   O Jesus, we receive ;
Fulness of the Deity,
   In all thy people live !
First begotten from the dead,
Call forth thy living witnesses ;
   King of saints, thine empire spread
   O'er all the ransomed race.

2 Grace, the fountain of all good,
   Ye happy saints receive,
With the streams of peace o'erflowed,
   With all that God can give ;
He who is, and was, in peace,
And grace, and plenitude of power,
   Come your favoured souls to bless,
   And never leave you more !

3 Let the Spirit before his throne,
   Mysterious One and Seven,
In his various gifts sent down,
   Be to the churches given ;
Let the pure seraphic joy
From Jesus Christ, the Just, descend ;
   Holiness without alloy,
   And bliss that ne'er shall end.

419
   2 Timothy i. 7.   L. M.

1 QUICKENED with our immortal Head,
   Who daily, Lord, ascend with thee,
Redeemed from sin, and free indeed,
   We taste our glorious liberty.

2 Saved from the fear of hell and death,
   With joy we seek the things above ;
And all thy saints the spirit breathe
   Of power, sobriety, and love.

3 Power o'er the world, the fiend, and sin,
   We through thy gracious Spirit feel ;
Full power the victory to win,
   And answer all thy righteous will.

4 Pure love to God thy members find,
   Pure love to every soul of man ;
And in thy sober, spotless mind,
   Saviour, our heaven on earth we gain.

420
   Colossians iii. 1—4.   L. M.

1 YE faithful souls, who Jesus know,
   If risen indeed with him ye are,
Superior to the joys below,
   His resurrection's power declare.

2 Your faith by holy tempers prove,
   By actions show your sins forgiven,
And seek the glorious things above,
   And follow Christ, your Head, to heaven

3 There your exalted Saviour see,
   Seated at God's right hand again,
In all his Father's majesty,
   In everlasting pomp to reign.

4 To him continually aspire,
   Contending for your native place ;
And emulate the angel-choir,
   And only live to love and praise.

5 For who by faith your Lord receive,
   Ye nothing seek or want beside ;
Dead to the world and sin ye live,
   Your creature-love is crucified.

6 Your real life, with Christ concealed,
   Deep in the Father's bosom lies ;
And, glorious as your Head revealed,
   Ye soon shall meet him in the skies.

S. M.   2 Timothy iv. 7.   **421**

1 " I THE good fight have fought,"
   O when shall I declare !
The victory by my Saviour got
   I long with Paul to share.
O may I triumph so,
   When all my warfare's past !
And, dying, find my latest foe
   Under my feet at last.

2 This blessed word be mine,
   Just as the port is gained,
" Kept by the power of grace divine,
   I have the faith maintained."
The apostles of my Lord,
   To whom it first was given,
They could not speak a greater word,
   Nor all the saints in heaven.

L. M.   Jeremiah ix. 23, 24.   **422**

1 LET not the wise his wisdom boast,
   The mighty glory in his might,
The rich in flattering riches trust,
   Which take their everlasting flight.
The rush of numerous years bears down
   The most gigantic strength of man ;
And where is all his wisdom gone,
   When dust he turns to dust again ?

2 One only gift can justify
   The boasting soul that knows his God ;
When Jesus doth his blood apply,
   I glory in his sprinkled blood.
The Lord my Righteousness I praise ;
   I triumph in the love divine,
The wisdom, wealth, and strength of grace,
   In Christ to endless ages mine.

7 s & 6 s †.   Revelation i. 5, 6.   **423**

1 WHO can worthily commend
   Thy love unsearchable !
Love that made thee condescend
   Our curse and death to feel ;
Thou, the great eternal God,
   Who didst thyself our ransom pay,
Hast, with thy own precious blood,
   Washed all our sins away.

2 By the Spirit of our Head
　　Anointed priests and kings,
Conquerors of the world, we tread
　　On all created things;
Sit in heavenly places down.
While yet we in the flesh remain;
　　Now, partakers of thy throne,
　　Before thy Father reign.

3 In thy members here beneath
　　The Intercessor prays;
Here we in the Spirit breathe
　　Unutterable praise;
Offer up our all to God;
And God beholds, with gracious eyes.
　　First the purchase of thy blood,
　　And then our sacrifice.

4 Jesus, let thy kingdom come!
　　(Inspired by thee we pray)
Previous to the general doom,
　　The everlasting day:
Take possession of thine own,
And let us then our Saviour see
　　Glorious on thy heavenly throne,
　　To all eternity.

424　　Ezekiel xxxiv. 26.　　7s & 6s †.

1 US, who climb thy holy hill,
　　A general blessing make,
Let the world our influence feel,
　　Our gospel grace partake;
Grace to help in time of need,
Pour out on sinners from above,
　　All thy Spirit's fulness shed,
　　In showers of heavenly love.

2 Make our earthly souls a field
　　Which God delights to bless;
Let us in due season yield
　　The fruits of righteousness:
Make us trees of paradise,
Which more and more thy praise may
Deeper sink, and higher rise,　　[show,
　　And to perfection grow.

425　　1 Kings xix. 13.　　L. M.

1 THE voice that speaks Jehovah near,
　The still small voice, I long to hear;
O might it now my Lord proclaim,
And fill my soul with holy shame!

2 Ashamed I must for ever be,
Afraid the God of love to see,
If saints and prophets hide their face,
And angels tremble while they gaze!

426　　1 Chronicles xxix. 5.　　S. M.

1 LORD, in the strength of grace,
　　With a glad heart and free,
Myself, my residue of days,
　　I consecrate to thee.

2 Thy ransomed servant, I
　　Restore to thee thy own;
And, from this moment, live or die
　　To serve my God alone.

427　　　　　　8 - 7s.

1 GOD of all-redeeming grace,
　By thy pardoning love compelled,
To thee our souls we raise,
Up to thee our bodies yield:
102

Thou our sacrifice receive,
　Acceptable through thy Son,
While to thee alone we live,
　While we die to thee alone.

2 Meet it is, and just, and right,
　　That we should be wholly thine,
In thine only will delight,
　　In thy blessed service join:
O that every work and word
　Might proclaim how good thou art!
" Holiness unto the Lord "
　Still be written on our heart.

428　　C. M.

1 LET Him to whom we now belong
　　His sovereign right assert,
And take up every thankful song,
　　And every loving heart.

2 He justly claims us for his own,
　　Who bought us with a price;
The Christian lives to Christ alone,
　　To Christ alone he dies.

3 Jesus, thine own at last receive!
　　Fulfil our hearts' desire,
And let us to thy glory live,
　　And in thy cause expire.

4 Our souls and bodies we resign;
　　With joy we render thee
Our all, no longer ours, but thine
　　To all eternity.

429　　6 - 8 s.

1 BEHOLD the servant of the Lord!
　I wait thy guiding eye to feel,
To hear and keep thy every word,
　To prove and do thy perfect will,
Joyful from my own works to cease,
Glad to fulfil all righteousness.

2 Me if thy grace vouchsafe to use,
　Meanest of all thy creatures, me,
The deed, the time, the manner choose,
　Let all my fruit be found of thee;
Let all my works in thee be wrought,
By thee to full perfection brought.

3 My every weak, though good design,
　O'errule, or change, as seems thee meet;
Jesus, let all my work be thine!
　Thy work, O Lord, is all complete,
And pleasing in thy Father's sight;
Thou only hast done all things right.

4 Here then to thee thy own I leave;
　Mould as thou wilt thy passive clay;
But let me all thy stamp receive,
　But let me all thy words obey,
Serve with a single heart and eye,
And to thy glory live and die.

430　　6 - 7 s.

1 FATHER, Son, and Holy Ghost,
　One in Three, and Three in One,
As by the celestial host,
　Let thy will on earth be done;
Praise by all to thee be given,
Glorious Lord of earth and heaven!

2 Vilest of the sinful race,
　Lo! I answer to thy call;
Meanest vessel of thy grace,
　Grace divinely free for all.

Lo! I come to do thy will,
All thy counsel to fulfil.

3 If so poor a worm as I
   May to thy great glory live,
All my actions sanctify,
   All my words and thoughts receive;
Claim me for thy service, claim
All I have, and all I am.

4 Take my soul and body's powers;
   Take my memory, mind, and will,
All my goods, and all my hours,
   All I know, and all I feel,
All I think, or speak, or do;
Take my heart;—but make it new!

5 Now, O God, thine own I am,
   Now I give thee back thine own;
Freedom, friends, and health, and fame,
   Consecrate to thee alone:
Thine I live, thrice happy I!
Happier still if thine I die.

6 Father, Son, and Holy Ghost,
   One in Three, and Three in One,
As by the celestial host,
   Let thy will on earth be done;
Praise by all to thee be given,
Glorious Lord of earth and heaven!

431

6-8 s.

1 O GOD, what offering shall I give
   To thee, the Lord of earth and skies?
My spirit, soul, and flesh receive,
   A holy, living sacrifice;
Small as it is, 'tis all my store;
More shouldst thou have, if I had more.

2 Now then, my God, thou hast my soul,
   No longer mine, but thine I am;
Guard thou thine own, possess it whole,
   Cheer it with hope, with love inflame;
Thou hast my spirit, there display
Thy glory to the perfect day.

3 Thou hast my flesh, thy hallowed shrine,
   Devoted solely to thy will;
Here let thy light for ever shine,
   This house still let thy presence fill;
O Source of life, live, dwell, and move
In me, till all my life be love!

4 O never in these veils of shame,
   Sad fruits of sin, my glorying be!
Clothe with salvation, through thy name,
   My soul, and let me put on thee!
Be living faith my costly dress,
And my best robe thy righteousness.

5 Send down thy likeness from above,
   And let this my adorning be;
Clothe me with wisdom, patience, love,
   With lowliness and purity,
Than gold and pearls more precious far,
And brighter than the morning star.

6 Lord, arm me with thy Spirit's might,
   Since I am called by thy great name;
In thee let all my thoughts unite,
   Of all my works be thou the aim;
Thy love attend me all my days,
And my sole business be thy praise!

432

C. M.

1 FATHER, into thy hands alone
   I have my all restored;

My all thy property I own,
   The steward of the Lord.

2 Hereafter none can take away
   My life, or goods, or fame;
Ready at thy demand to lay
   Them down I always am.

3 Confiding in thy only love,
   Through Jesus strengthening me,
I wait thy faithfulness to prove,
   And give back all to thee.

4 Take when thou wilt into thy hands,
   And as thou wilt require;
Resume by the Chaldean bands,
   Or the devouring fire.

5 Determined all thy will to obey,
   Thy blessings I restore;
Give, Lord, or take thy gifts away,
   I praise thee evermore.

433

6-8 s.

1 GIVE me the faith which can remove
   And sink the mountain to a plain;
Give me the child-like praying love,
   Which longs to build thy house again;
Thy love let it my heart o'erpower,
And all my simple soul devour.

2 I want an even strong desire,
   I want a calmly-fervent zeal,
To save poor souls out of the fire,
   To snatch them from the verge of hell,
And turn them to a pardoning God,
And quench the brands in Jesu's blood.

3 I would the precious time redeem,
   And longer live for this alone,
To spend, and to be spent, for them
   Who have not yet my Saviour known;
Fully on these my mission prove,
And only breathe, to breathe thy love.

4 My talents, gifts, and graces, Lord,
   Into thy blessed hands receive;
And let me live to preach thy word,
   And let me to thy glory live;
My every sacred moment spend
In publishing the sinner's friend.

5 Enlarge, inflame, and fill my heart
   With boundless charity divine!
So shall I all my strength exert,
   And love them with a zeal like thine;
And lead them to thy open side,
The sheep for whom their Shepherd died.

434

7 s.

1 JESUS, all-atoning Lamb,
   Thine, and only thine, I am;
Take my body, spirit, soul;
Only thou possess the whole

2 Thou my one thing needful be:
Let me ever cleave to thee;
Let me choose the better part;
Let me give thee all my heart.

3 Fairer than the sons of men,
Do not let me turn again,
Leave the fountain-head of bliss,
Stoop to creature-happiness.

4 Whom have I on earth below?
Thee, and only thee, I know;

Whom have I in heaven but thee?
Thou art all in all to me.

5 All my treasure is above,
All my riches is thy love:
Who the worth of love can tell?
Infinite, unsearchable!

6 Thou, O love, my portion art:
Lord, thou know'st my simple heart!
Other comforts I despise,
Love be all my paradise.

7 Nothing else can I require,
Love fills up my whole desire;
All thy other gifts remove,
Still thou giv'st me all in love!

435   C. M.

1 FATHER, to thee my soul I lift,
    My soul on thee depends,
Convinced that every perfect gift
From thee alone descends.

2 Mercy and grace are thine alone,
And power and wisdom too;
Without the Spirit of thy Son
We nothing good can do.

3 We cannot speak one useful word,
One holy thought conceive,
Unless, in answer to our Lord,
Thyself the blessing give.

4 His blood demands the purchased grace;
His blood's availing plea
Obtained the help for all our race,
And sends it down to me.

5 Thou all our works in us hast wrought;
Our good is all divine;
The praise of every virtuous thought,
And righteous word, is thine.

6 From thee, through Jesus, we receive
The power on thee to call,
In whom we are, and move, and live:
Our God is all in all!

436   S. M.

1 JESU, my Truth, my Way,
    My sure, unerring light,
On thee my feeble steps I stay,
Which thou wilt guide aright.

2 My Wisdom and my guide,
My Counsellor thou art;
O never let me leave thy side,
Or from thy paths depart!

3 I lift my eyes to thee,
Thou gracious, bleeding Lamb,
That I may now enlightened be,
And never put to shame.

4 Never will I remove
Out of thy hands my cause;
But rest in thy redeeming love,
And hang upon thy cross.

5 Teach me the happy art
In all things to depend
On thee; O never, Lord, depart,
But love me to the end!

6 Still stir me up to strive
With thee in strength divine;
And every moment, Lord, revive
This fainting soul of mine.

104

7 Persist to save my soul
Throughout the fiery hour,
Till I am every whit made whole,
And show forth all thy power.

8 Through fire and water bring
Into the wealthy place;
And teach me the new song to sing,
When perfected in grace.

9 O make me all like thee,
Before I hence remove!
Settle, confirm, and stablish me,
And build me up in love.

10 Let me thy witness live,
When sin is all destroyed;
And then my spotless soul receive,
And take me home to God.

L. M.   Psalm lxiii.   437

1 O GOD, my God, my all thou art!
    Ere shines the dawn of rising day,
Thy sovereign light within my heart,
Thy all-enlivening power display.

2 For thee my thirsty soul doth pant,
While in this desert land I live;
And hungry as I am, and faint,
Thy love alone can comfort give.

3 In a dry land, behold, I place
My whole desire on thee, O Lord;
And more I joy to gain thy grace,
Than all earth's treasures can afford.

4 More dear than life itself, thy love
My heart and tongue shall still employ;
And to declare thy praise will prove
My peace, my glory, and my joy.

5 In blessing thee with grateful songs
My happy life shall glide away;
The praise that to thy name belongs
Hourly with lifted hands I'll pay.

6 Abundant sweetness, while I sing
Thy love, my ravished heart o'erflows;
Secure in thee, my God and King,
Of glory that no period knows.

7 Thy name, O God, upon my bed
Dwells on my lips, and fires my thought;
With trembling awe, in midnight shade,
I muse on all thy hands have wrought.

8 In all I do I feel thine aid;
Therefore thy greatness will I sing,
O God, who bidd'st my heart be glad
Beneath the shadow of thy wing!

9 My soul draws nigh and cleaves to thee;
Then let or earth or hell assail,
Thy mighty hand shall set me free;
For whom thou sav'st, he ne'er shall fail.

6 - 8 s.   Second Metre.   Hebrews xiii. 20, 21.   438

1 O GOD of peace and pardoning love,
    Whose bowels of compassion move
To every sinful child of man,
Jesus, our Shepherd great and good,
Who dying bought us with his blood,
Thou hast brought us back to life again!

His blood to all our souls apply;
(His blood alone can sanctify,
Which first did for our sins atone)

The covenant of redemption seal;
The depth of love, of God, reveal,
  And speak us perfected in one.

2 O might our every work and word
Express the tempers of our Lord,
  The nature of our Head above!
His Spirit send into our hearts,
Engraving on our inmost parts
  The living law of holiest love.

Then shall we do, with pure delight,
Whate'er is pleasing in thy sight,
  As vessels of thy richest grace;
And, having thy whole counsel done,
To thee and thy co-equal Son
  Ascribe the everlasting praise.

439
6 - 8 s. Second Metre.

1 THY power and saving truth to show,
  A warfare at thy charge I go,
Strong in the Lord, and thy great might;
Gladly take up the hallowed cross;
And, suffering all things for thy cause,
  Beneath thy bloody banner fight.

A spectacle to fiends and men,
To all their fierce or cool disdain
  With calmest pity I submit;
Determined nought to know, beside
My Jesus and him crucified,
  I tread the world beneath my feet.

2 Superior to their smile or frown,
On all their goods my soul looks down,
  Their pleasures, wealth, and power, and state:
The man that dares their god despise,
The Christian, he alone is wise;
  The Christian, he alone is great.

O God, let all my life declare
How happy all thy servants are,
  How far above these earthly things;
How pure, when washed in Jesu's blood,
How intimately one with God,
  A heaven-born race of priests and kings

3 For this alone I live below,
The power of godliness to show,
  The wonders wrought by Jesu's name:
O that I might but faithful prove;
Witness to all thy pardoning love,
  And point them to the atoning Lamb!
Let me to every creature cry,
The poor and rich, the low and high,
  Believe, and feel thy sins forgiven!
Damned, till by Jesus saved, thou art!
Till Jesu's blood hath washed thy heart,
  Thou canst not find the gate of heaven!

440
6 - 8 s. Second Metre

1 THOU, Jesu, thou my breast inspire,
  And touch my lips with hallowed fire,
  And loose a stammering infant's tongue;
Prepare the vessel of thy grace,
Adorn me with the robes of praise,
  And mercy shall be all my song;
Mercy for all who know not God,
Mercy for all in Jesu's blood,
  Mercy, that earth and heaven transcends;

Love, that o'erwhelms the saints in light,
The length, and breadth, and depth, and height
Of love divine, which never ends!

2 A faithful witness of thy grace,
Well may I fill the allotted space,
  And answer all thy great design;
Walk in the works by thee prepared;
And find annexed the vast reward,
  The crown of righteousness divine:
When I have lived to thee alone,
Pronounce the welcome word, "Well done!"
  And let me take my place above
Enter into my Master's joy,
And all eternity employ
  In praise, and ecstasy, and love.

SECTION IX.
FOR BELIEVERS INTERCEDING.

6 - 8 s.

441

1 LET God, who comforts the distrest
  Let Israel's consolation hear!
Hear, Holy Ghost, our joint request,
  And show thyself the Comforter,
And swell the unutterable groan,
And breathe our wishes to the throne!

2 We weep for those that weep below,
  And burdened, for the afflicted sigh;
The various forms of human woe
  Excite our softest sympathy,
Fill every heart with mournful care,
And draw out all our souls in prayer.

3 We wrestle for the ruined race,
  By sin eternally undone,
Unless thou magnify thy grace,
  And make thy richest mercy known,
And make thy vanquished rebels find
Pardon in Christ for all mankind.

4 Father of everlasting love,
  To every soul thy Son reveal,
Our guilt and sufferings to remove,
  Our deep, original wound to heal;
And bid the fallen race arise,
And turn our earth to paradise.

6 - 8 s.

442

1 OUR earth we now lament to see
  With floods of wickedness o'erflowed,
With violence, wrong, and cruelty,
  One wide-extended field of blood,
Where men like fiends each other tear,
In all the hellish rage of war.

2 As listed on Abaddon's side,
  They mangle their own flesh, and slay:
Tophet is moved, and opens wide
  Its mouth for its enormous prey;
And myriads sink beneath the grave,
And plunge into the flaming wave.

3 O might the universal friend
  This havoc of his creatures see!
Bid our unnatural discord end;
  Declare us reconciled in thee,
Write kindness on our inward parts,
And chase the murderer from our hearts!

105

4 Who now against each other rise,
　The nations of the earth, constrain
To follow after peace, and prize
　The blessings of thy righteous reign,
The joys of unity to prove,
The paradise of perfect love !

443* 6 - 8 s.

1 ARM of the Lord, awake, awake !
　　The terrors of the Lord display ;
Out of their sins the nations shake,
　Tear their vain confidence away ;
Conclude them all in unbelief,
And fill their hearts with sacred grief.

2 Of judgment now the world convince,
　The end of Jesu's coming show ;
To sentence their usurping prince,
　Him and his works destroy below ;
To finish and abolish sin,
And bring the heavenly nature in.

3 Then the whole earth again shall rest,
　And see its paradise restored ;
Then every soul, in Jesus blest,
　Shall bear the image of its Lord,
In finished holiness renewed,
Immeasurably filled with God.

444 *For the Heathen.* 6 - 8 s.

1 LORD over all, if thou hast made,
　　Hast ransomed every soul of man,
Why is the grace so long delayed ?
　Why unfulfilled the saving plan ?
The bliss, for Adam's race designed,
When will it reach to all mankind ?

2 Art thou the God of Jews alone ?
　And not the God of Gentiles too ?
To Gentiles make thy goodness known ;
　· Thy judgments to the nations show ;
Awake them by the gospel call ;
Light of the world, illumine all !

3 The servile progeny of Ham
　Seize as the purchase of thy blood ;
Let all the heathen know thy name ;
　From idols to the living God
Their blinded votaries convert ;
And shine in every pagan heart !

4 As lightning launched from east to west,
　The coming of thy kingdom be ;
To thee, by angel-hosts confest,
　Bow every soul and every knee ;
Thy glory let all flesh behold,
And then fill up thy heavenly fold.

445 Numbers xxiv. 17. 6 - 8 s.

1 O COME, thou radiant morning Star,
　　Again in human darkness shine !
Arise resplendent from afar !
　Assert thy royalty divine !
Thy sway o'er all the earth maintain,
And now begin thy glorious reign.

2 Thy kingdom, Lord, we long to see :
　Thy sceptre o'er the nations shake !
To erect that final monarchy,
　Edom for thy possession take ;
Take (for thou didst their ransom find)
The purchased souls of all mankind.
106

3 Now let thy chosen ones appear,
　And valiantly the truth maintain !
Dispread thy gracious kingdom here,
　Fly on the rebel sons of men,
Seize them with faith divinely bold,
And force the world into thy fold.

C. M. ## 446

1 JESU, the word of mercy give,
　　And let it swiftly run ;
And let the priests themselves believe,
　And put salvation on.

2 Clothed with the spirit of holiness,
　May all thy people prove
The plenitude of gospel grace,
　The joy of perfect love. ,

3 Jesus, let all thy lovers shine
　Illustrious as the sun ;
And, bright with borrowed rays divine,
　Their glorious circuit run :

4 Beyond the reach of mortals, spread
　Their light where'er they go ;
And heavenly influences shed
　On all the world below.

5 As giants may they run their race,
　Exulting in their might ;
As burning luminaries, chase
　The gloom of hellish night :

6 As the bright Sun of righteousness,
　Their healing wings display ;
And let their lustre still increase
　Unto the perfect day.

S. M. ## 447

1 MESSIAH, Prince of peace !
　　Where men each other tear,
Where war is learned, they must confess,
　Thy kingdom is not there.
Who, prompted by thy foe,
　Delight in human blood,
Apollyon is their king, we know,
　And Satan is their god.

2 But shall he still devour
　The souls redeemed by Thee ?
Jesus, stir up thy glorious power
　And end the apostasy !
Come, Saviour, from above,
　O'er all our hearts to reign ;
And plant the kingdom of thy love
　In every heart of man.

3 Then shall we exercise
　The hellish art no more,
While thou our long-lost paradise
　Dost with thyself restore.
Fightings and wars shall cease,
　And, in thy Spirit given,
Pure joy and everlasting peace
　Shall turn our earth to heaven.

6 - 8 s. Isaiah xlv. 22, &c. ## *448

1 ETERNAL Lord of earth and skies,
　　We wait thy Spirit's latest call :
Bid all our fallen race arise,
　Thou who hast purchased life for all ;
Whose only name, to sinners given,
Snatches from hell, and lifts to heaven.

2 The word thy sacred lips has past,
  The sure irrevocable word,
That every soul shall bow at last,
  And yield allegiance to its Lord;
The kingdoms of the earth shall be
For ever subjected to thee.

3 Jesus, for this we still attend,
  Thy kingdom in the isles to prove;
The law of sin and death to end,
  We wait for all the power of love,
The law of perfect liberty,
The law of life which is in thee.

4 O might it now from thee proceed,
  With thee, into the souls of men!
Throughout the world thy gospel spread;
  And let thy glorious Spirit reign,
On all the ransomed race bestowed;
And let the world be filled with God!

449

Isaiah xi. 5, 13.　　7 s & 6 s †.

1 TRUE and faithful Witness, thou
  In righteousness hast sworn,
Every knee to thee shall bow,
  And every heart shall turn;
Girt with equity and might,
Arise to administer thy grace,
Claim the kingdoms in thy right,
  And govern all our race.

2 Visit us, bright morning Star,
  And bring the perfect day!
Urged by faith's incessant prayer.
  No longer, Lord, delay:
Now destroy the envious root;
The ground of nature's feuds remove;
Fill the earth with golden fruit,
  With ripe, millennial love.

450

For the Jews.　　S. M.

1 MESSIAH, full of grace,
  Redeemed by thee, we plead
The promise made to Abraham's race,
  To souls for ages dead.

2 Their bones, as quite dried up,
  Throughout the vale appear:
Cut off and lost their last faint hope
  To see thy kingdom here.

3 Open their graves, and bring
  The outcasts forth, to own
Thou art their Lord, their God and King,
  Their true Anointed One.

4 To save the race forlorn,
  Thy glorious arm display!
And show the world a nation born,
  A nation in a day!

451

Romans xi. 15—27.　　6 - 8 s.

1 FATHER of faithful Abraham, hear
  Our earnest suit for Abraham's seed!
Justly they claim the softest prayer
  From us, adopted in their stead,
Who mercy through their fall obtain,
And Christ by their rejection gain.

2 But hast thou finally forsook,
  For ever cast thy own away?
Wilt thou not bid the outcasts look
  On him they pierced, and weep, and
    pray?

Yes, gracious Lord, thy word is passed;
All Israel shall be saved at last.

3 Come then, thou great Deliverer, come!
  The veil from Jacob's heart remove;
Receive thy ancient people home!
  That, quickened by thy dying love,
The world may their reception find
Life from the dead for all mankind.

452

S. M.　　Isaiah lxvi. 19, 20.

1 ALMIGHTY God of love,
  Set up the attracting sign,
And summon whom thou dost approve
  For messengers divine!
From favoured Abraham's seed
  The new apostles choose,
In isles and continents to spread
  The dead-reviving news.

2 Them, snatched out of the flame,
  Through every nation send,
The true Messiah to proclaim,
  The universal friend;
That all the God unknown
  May learn of Jews to adore,
And see thy glory in thy Son,
  Till time shall be no more.

3 O that the chosen band
  Might now their brethren bring,
And gathered out of every land,
  Present to Zion's King!
Of all the ancient race
  Not one be left behind,
But each, impelled by secret grace,
  His way to Canaan find.

4 We know it must be done,
  For God hath spoke the word:
All Israel shall the Saviour own,
  To their first state restored;
Rebuilt by his command,
  Jerusalem shall rise;
Her temple on Moriah stand
  Again, and touch the skies.

5 Send then thy servants forth,
  To call the Hebrews home;
From East, and West, and South, and North,
  Let all the wanderers come;
Where'er in lands unknown
  The fugitives remain,
Bid every creature help them on,
  Thy holy mount to gain.

6 An offering to their God,
  There let them all be seen,
Sprinkled with water and with blood,
  In soul and body clean;
With Israel's myriads sealed,
  Let all the nations meet,
And show the mystery fulfilled,
  Thy family complete!

*453

S. M. *For England.* Acts xix. 20.

1 JESUS, the word bestow,
  The true immortal seed;
Thy gospel then shall greatly grow,
  And all our land o'erspread:
Through earth extended wide
  Shall mightily prevail,
Destroy the works of self and pride,
  And shake the gates of hell

2 Its energy exert
In the believing soul ;
Diffuse thy grace through every part,
And sanctify the whole ;
Its utmost virtue show
In pure consummate love,
And fill with all thy life below,
And give us thrones above.

454   Revelation iii. 14—19.   L. M.

1 GOD of unspotted purity,
Us and our works canst thou behold!
Justly we are abhorred by thee,
For we are neither hot nor cold.

2 We call thee Lord, thy faith profess,
But do not from our hearts obey ;
In soft Laodicean ease
We sleep our useless lives away.

3 We live in pleasure, and are dead,
In search of fame and wealth we live:
Commanded in thy steps to tread,
We seek sometimes, but never strive.

4 A lifeless form we still retain ;
Of this we make our empty boast,
Nor know the name we take in vain ;
The power of godliness is lost!

5 How long, great God, have we appeared
Abominable in thy sight!
Better that we had never heard
Thy word, or seen the gospel light.

6 Better that we had never known
The way to heaven through saving grace,
Than basely in our lives disown,
And slight and mock thee to thy face.

7 Thou rather wouldst that we were cold,
Than seem to serve thee without zeal ;
Less guilty if, with those of old,
We worshipped Thor and Woden still.

8 Less grievous will the judgment-day
To Sodom and Gomorrah prove,
Than us, who cast our faith away,
And trample on thy richer love.

455   SECOND PART.   L. M.

1 O LET us our own works forsake,
Ourselves, and all we have deny :
Thy condescending counsel take,
And come to thee pure gold to buy!

2 O might we, through thy grace, attain
The faith thou never wilt reprove,
The faith that purges every stain,
The faith that always works by love!

3 O might we see, in this our day,
The things belonging to our peace,
And timely meet thee in thy way
Of judgments, and our sins confess!

4 Thy fatherly chastisements own,
With filial awe revere thy rod ;
And turn, with zealous haste, and run
Into the outstretched arms of God.

456   Acts ii. 39.   L. M.

1 FATHER, if justly still we claim
To us and ours the promise made,
To us be graciously the same,
And crown with living fire our head.
108

2 Our claim admit, and from above
Of holiness the Spirit shower,
Of wise discernment, humble love,
And zeal, and unity, and power. ~

3 The Spirit of convincing speech,
Of power demonstrative, impart,
Such as may every conscience reach,
And sound the unbelieving heart ;

4 The Spirit of refining fire,
Searching the inmost of the mind,
To purge all fierce and foul desire,
And kindle life more pure and kind ;

5 The Spirit of faith, in this thy day,
To break the power of cancelled sin,
Tread down its strength, o'erturn its sway,
And still the conquest more than win.

6 The Spirit breathe of inward life,
Which in our hearts thy laws may write;
Then grief expires, and pain, and strife,
'Tis nature all, and all delight.

457

L. M.   SECOND PART.

1 ON all the earth thy Spirit shower ;
The earth in righteousness renew ;
Thy kingdom come, and hell's o'erpower,
And to thy sceptre all subdue.

2 Like mighty winds, or torrents fierce,
Let it opposers all o'errun ;
And every law of sin reverse,
That faith and love may make all one.

3 Yea, let thy Spirit in every place
Its richer energy declare ;
While lovely tempers, fruits of grace,
The kingdom of thy Christ prepare.

4 Grant this, O holy God and true!
The ancient seers thou didst inspire ;
To us perform the promise due ;
Descend, and crown us now with fire!

458

L. M.

1 AUTHOR of faith, we seek thy face
For all who feel thy work begun ;
Confirm and strengthen them in grace,
And bring thy feeblest children on.

2 Thou seest their wants, thou know'st their
names,
Be mindful of thy youngest care ;
Be tender of thy new-born lambs,
And gently in thy bosom bear.

3 The lion roaring for his prey,
And ravening wolves on every side,
Watch over them to tear and slay,
If found one moment from their guide.

4 Satan his thousand arts essays,
His agents all their powers employ,
To blast the blooming work of grace,
The heavenly offspring to destroy.

5 Baffle the crooked serpent's skill,
And turn his sharpest dart aside ;
Hide from their eyes the devilish ill,
O save them from the demon, pride!

6 In safety lead thy little flock,
From hell, the world, and sin secure ;
And set their feet upon the rock,
And make in thee their goings sure.

459

S. M.

1 SHEPHERD of Israel hear
    Our supplicating cry;
And gather in the souls sincere
    That from their brethren fly.
Scattered through devious ways,
    Collect thy feeble flock;
And join by thine atoning grace,
    And hide them in the rock.

2 O wouldst thou end the storm,
    That keeps us still apart!
The thing impossible perform,
    And make us of one heart,
One spirit and one mind,
    The same that was in thee:
O might we all again be joined
    In perfect harmony!

3 The soul-transforming word
    In us, even us, fulfil;
Join to thyself, our common Lord,
    And all thy servants seal.
Confer the grace unknown,
    The mystic charity;
As thou art with the Father one,
    Unite us all in thee.

4 So shall the world believe
    Our record, Lord, and thine;
And all with thankful hearts receive
    The Messenger divine,
Sent from his throne above,
    To Adam's offspring given,
To join and perfect us in love,
    And take us up to heaven.

460*

Isaiah lxvi. 18.   S. M.

1 FATHER of boundless grace,
    Thou hast in part fulfilled
Thy promise made to Adam's race,
    In God incarnate sealed.
A few from every land
    At first to Salem came,
And saw the wonders of thy hand,
    And saw the tongues of flame.

2 Yet still we wait the end,
    The coming of our Lord;
The full accomplishment attend
    Of thy prophetic word.
Thy promise deeper lies
    In unexhausted grace,
And new-discovered worlds arise
    To sing their Saviour's praise.

3 Beloved for Jesu's sake,
    By him redeemed of old,
All nations must come in, and make
    One undivided fold:
While gathered in by thee,
    And perfected in one,
They all at once thy glory see
    In thine eternal Son.

461

6 - 8 s.

1 SAVIOUR, to thee we humbly cry!
    The brethren we have lost restore;
Recall them by thy pitying eye, [power,
    Retrieve them from the Tempter's
By thy victorious blood cast down,
    Nor suffer him to take their crown.

2 Beguiled alas! by Satan's art,
    We see them now far off removed,
The burden of our bleeding heart,
    The souls whom once in thee we loved.
Whom still we love with grief and pain,
    And weep for their return in vain.

3 In vain, till thou the power bestow,
    The double power of quickening grace,
And make the happy sinners know
    Their Tempter, with his angel-face,
Who leads them captive at his will,
    Captive—but happy sinners still!

4 O wouldst thou break the fatal snare
    Of carnal self-security;
And let them feel the wrath they bear,
    And let them groan their want of thee,
Robbed of their false, pernicious peace,
    Stripped of their fancied righteousness!

5 The men of careless lives, who deem
    Thy righteousness accounted theirs,
Awake out of the soothing dream,
    Alarm their souls with humble fears:
Thou jealous God, stir up thy power,
    And let them sleep in sin no more!

6 Long as the guilt of sin shall last,
    Them in its misery detain;
Hold their licentious spirits fast,
    Bind them with their own nature's chain,
Nor ever let the wanderers rest,
    Till lodged again in Jesu's breast.

L. M.   ## 462

1 O LET the prisoners' mournful cries
    As incense in thy sight appear!
Their humble wailings pierce the skies,
    If haply they may feel thee near.

2 The captive exiles make their moans,
    From sin impatient to be free:
Call home, call home thy banished ones!
    Lead captive their captivity!

3 Show them the blood that bought their peace,
    The anchor of their steadfast hope;
And bid their guilty terrors cease,
    And bring the ransomed prisoners up.

4 Out of the deep regard their cries,
    The fallen raise, the mourners cheer;
O Sun of righteousness, arise,
    And scatter all their doubt and fear!

5 Pity the day of feeble things;
    O gather every halting soul!
And drop salvation from thy wings,
    And make the contrite sinner whole.

6 Stand by them in the fiery hour,
    Their feebleness of mind defend;
And in their weakness show thy power,
    And make them patient to the end.

7 O satisfy their soul in drought!
    Give them thy saving health to see;
And let thy mercy find them out;
    And let thy mercy reach to me.

6 - 7 s.   *For the Nation.*   ## 463

1 LAMB of God, who hear'st away
    All the sins of all mankind,
Bow a nation to thy sway;
    While we may acceptance find,

Let us thankfully embrace
The last offers of thy grace.

2 Thou thy messengers hast sent,
Joyful tidings to proclaim,
Willing we should all repent,
Know salvation in thy name,
Feel our sins by grace forgiven,
Find in thee the way to heaven.

3 Jesus, roll away the stone!
Good Physician, show thy art!
Make thy healing virtue known,
Break the unbelieving heart,
By thy bloody cross subdue;
Tell them, "I have died for you!"

4 Let thy dying love constrain
Those who disregard thy frown;
Sink the mountain to a plain;
Bring the pride of sinners down;
Soften the obdurate crowd;
Melt the rebels with thy blood!

464
Isaiah xxxiii. 5, 6.　　7 s & 6 s †.

1 JESUS, from thy heavenly place,
Thy dwelling in the sky,
Fill our church with righteousness,
Our want of faith supply;
Faith our strong protection be,
And godliness, with all its power,
Stablish our posterity,
Till time shall be no more.

2 Let the Spirit of grace o'erflow
Our re-converted land:
Let the least and greatest know
And bow to thy command:
Wisdom, pure religious fear,
Our King's peculiar treasure prove,
Blest with piety sincere,
Inspired with humble love.

465
For the King.　　C. M.

1 SOVEREIGN of all! whose will ordains
The powers on earth that be,
By whom our rightful Monarch reigns,
Subject to none but thee:

2 Stir up thy power, appear, appear,
And for thy servant fight;
Support thy great vicegerent here,
And vindicate *his* right.

3 Lo! in the arms of faith and prayer
We bear *him* to thy throne;
Receive thy own peculiar care,
The Lord's anointed one.

4 With favour look upon *his* face;
Thy love's pavilion spread,
And watchful troops of angels place
Around *his* sacred head.

5 Guard *him* from all who dare oppose
Thy delegate and thee;
From open and from secret foes,
From force and perfidy!

6 Confound whoe'er *his* ruin seek,
Or into friends convert:
Give *him his* adversaries' neck;
Give *him his* people's heart.

7 Let us, for conscience' sake, revere
The man of thy right hand;
119

Honour and love thine image here,
And bless *his* mild command.

8 Thou only didst the blessing give;
The glory, Lord, be thine:
Let all with thankful joy receive
The benefit divine.

9 To those who thee in *him* obey,
The Spirit of grace impart:
His dear, *his* sacred burden lay
On every loyal heart.

10 Still let us pray, and never cease,
"Defend *him*, Lord, defend:
Stablish *his* throne in glorious peace,
And save *him* to the end!"

466
8 s & 6 s.　　Job xxxiv. 29.

1 A NATION God delights to bless,
Can all our raging foes distress,
Or hurt whom they surround?
Hid from the general scourge we are,
Nor see the bloody waste of war,
Nor hear the trumpet's sound.

2 O might we, Lord! the grace improve,
By labouring for the rest of love,
The soul-composing power;
Bless us with that internal peace,
And all the fruits of righteousness,
Till time shall be no more.

467
L. M.　　For Parents.

1 FATHER of all, by whom we are,
For whom was made whatever is;
Who hast entrusted to our care
A candidate for glorious bliss:

2 Poor worms of earth, for help we cry,
For grace to guide what grace has given;
We ask for wisdom from on high,
To train our infant up for heaven.

3 We tremble at the danger near,
And crowds of wretched parents see,
Who, blindly fond, their children rear
In tempers far as hell from thee:

4 Themselves the slaves of sense and praise,
Their babes who pamper and admire,
And make the helpless infants pass
To murderer-Moloch through the fire.

5 Rather this hour resume his breath,
From selfishness and pride to save;
By death prevent the second death,
And hide him in the silent grave!

6 Or, if thou grant a longer date,
With resolute wisdom us endue,
To point him out his lost estate,
His dire apostasy to show:

7 To time our every smile or frown,
To mark the bounds of good and ill;
And beat the pride of nature down,
And subjugate his rising will.

8 Him let us tend, severely kind,
As guardians of his giddy youth;
As set to form his tender mind,
By principles of virtuous truth:

9 To fit his soul for heavenly grace,
Discharge the Christian parents' part,
And keep him, till thy love takes place,
And Jesus rises in his heart.

468

For Parents. C. M.

1 GOD only wise, almighty, good,
   Send forth thy truth and light,
To point us out the narrow road,
   And guide our steps aright:

2 To steer our dangerous course between
   The rocks on either hand;
And fix us in the golden mean,
   And bring our charge to land.

3 Made apt, by thy sufficient grace,
   To teach as taught by thee,
We come to train in all thy ways
   Our rising progeny:

4 Their selfish will in time subdue,
   And mortify their pride;
And lend their youth a sacred clew
   To find the Crucified.

5 We would in every step look up,
   By thy example taught
To alarm their fear, excite their hope,
   And rectify their thought.

6 We would persuade their hearts to obey,
   With mildest zeal proceed;
And never take the harsher way,
   When love will do the deed.

7 For this we ask, in faith sincere,
   The wisdom from above,
To touch their hearts with filial fear,
   And pure, ingenuous love:

8 To watch their will, to sense inclined;
   Withhold the hurtful food;
And gently bend their tender mind,
   And draw their souls to God.

469

For Parents. C. M.

1 FATHER of lights! thy needful aid
   To us that ask impart;
Mistrustful of ourselves, afraid
   Of our own treacherous heart.

2 O'erwhelmed with justest fear, again
   To thee for help we call:
Where many mightier have been slain,
   By thee unsaved, we fall.

3 Unless restrained by grace we are,
   In vain the snare we see;
We see, and rush into the snare
   Of blind idolatry.

4 Ah! what avails superior light,
   Without superior love?
We see the truth, we judge aright,
   And wisdom's ways approve:

5 We mark the idolising throng,
   Their cruel fondness blame;
Their children's souls we know they
     wrong;
   And we shall do the same.

6 In spite of our resolves, we fear
   Our own infirmity;
And tremble at the trial near,
   And cry, O God, to thee!

7 We soon shall do what we condemn,
   And, down the current borne,
With shame confess our nature's stream
   Too strong for us to turn.

8 Our only help in danger's hour,
   Our only strength, thou art!
Above the world, and Satan's power,
   And greater than our heart!

9 Us from ourselves thou canst secure,
   In nature's slippery ways;
And make our feeble footsteps sure
   By thy sufficient grace.

10 If on thy promised grace alone
   We faithfully depend,
Thou surely wilt preserve thy own,
   And keep them to the end:

11 Wilt keep us tenderly discreet
   To guard what thou hast given;
And bring our child with us to meet
   At thy right hand in heaven.

L. M. *For the Head of a Household.* **470**

1 MASTER supreme, I look to thee
   For grace and wisdom from above;
Vested with thy authority,
   Endue me with thy patient love:

2 That, taught according to thy will
   To rule my family aright,
I may the appointed charge fulfil,
   With all my heart, and all my might.

3 Inferiors as a sacred trust
   I from the sovereign Lord receive,
That what is suitable and just
   Impartial I to all may give:

4 O'erlook them with a guardian eye;
   From vice and wickedness restrain;
Mistakes and lesser faults pass by,
   And govern with a looser rein.

5 The servant faithfully discreet,
   Gentle to him, and good, and mild,
Him would I tenderly entreat,
   And scarce distinguish from a child.

6 Yet let me not my place forsake,
   The occasion of his stumbling prove,
The servant to my bosom take,
   Or mar him by familiar love.

7 Order if some invert, confound,
   Their Lord's authority betray,
I hearken to the gospel sound,
   And trace the providential way.

8 As far from abjectness as pride,
   With condescending dignity,
Jesus, I make thy word my guide,
   And keep the post assigned by thee.

9 O could I emulate the zeal
   Thou dost to thy poor servants bear!
The troubles, griefs, and burdens feel
   Of souls entrusted to my care:

10 In daily prayer to God commend
   The souls whom Jesus died to save;
And think how soon my sway may end,
   And all be equal in the grave!

8 s & 6 s. *For the same.* **471**

1 HOW shall I walk my God to please,
   And spread content and happiness
     O'er all beneath my care?
A pattern to my household give,
And as a guardian angel live,
     As Jesu's messenger?

111

2 The opposite extremes I see,
  Remissness and severity,
    And know not how to shun
The precipice on either hand,
While in the narrow path I stand,
    And dread to venture on.

3 Shall I, through indolence supine,
Neglect, betray, my charge divine,
    My delegated power?
The souls I from my Lord receive,
Of each I an account must give,
    At that tremendous hour!

4 Lord over all, and God most high!
Jesus, to thee for help I fly,
    For constant power and grace:
That, taught by thy good Spirit and led,
I may with confidence proceed,
    And all thy footsteps trace.

5 O teach me my first lesson now!
And, while to thy sweet yoke I bow,
    Thy easy service prove,
Lowly and meek in heart, I see
The art of governing like thee
    Is governing by love.

472   *For the same.*   8 s & 6 s.

I AND my house will serve the Lord:
  But first obedient to his word
    I must myself appear;
By actions, words, and tempers show,
That I my heavenly Master know,
    And serve with heart sincere.

2 I must the fair example set;
From those that on my pleasure wait
    The stumbling-block remove;
Their duty by my life explain;
And still in all my works maintain
    The dignity of love.

3 Easy to be entreated, mild,
Quickly appeased and reconciled,
    A follower of my God,
A saint indeed, I long to be,
And lead my faithful family
    In the celestial road.

4 Lord, if thou didst the wish infuse,
A vessel fitted for thy use
    Into thy hands receive!
Work in me both to will and do;
And show them how believers true
    And real Christians live.

5 With all-sufficient grace supply;
And lo! I come to testify
    The wonders of thy name,
Which saves from sin, the world, and hell;
Whose virtue every heart may feel,
    And every tongue proclaim.

6 A sinner, saved myself from sin,
I come my family to win,
    To preach their sins forgiven;
Children, and wife, and servants seize,
And through the paths of pleasantness
    Conduct them all to heaven.

473 *A Prayer for Children.* 6 - 8 s.

1 COME, Father, Son, and Holy Ghost,
  To whom we for our children cry;
The good desired and wanted most
  Out of thy richest grace supply;

The sacred discipline be given,
To train and bring them up for heaven.

2 Answer on them the end of all
  Our cares, and pains, and studies here;
On them, recovered from their fall,
  Stamped with the humble character,
Raised by the nurture of the Lord,
To all their paradise restored.

3 Error and ignorance remove,
  Their blindness both of heart and mind;
Give them the wisdom from above,
  Spotless, and peaceable, and kind
In knowledge pure their minds renew,
And store with thoughts divinely true.

4 Learning's redundant part and vain
  Be all cut off, and cast aside,
But let them, Lord, the substance gain,
  In every solid truth abide;
Swiftly acquire, and ne'er forego,
The knowledge fit for man to know.

5 Unite the pair so long disjoined,
  Knowledge and vital piety:
Learning and holiness combined,
  And truth and love, let all men see
In those whom up to thee we give,
Thine, wholly thine, to die and live.

6 Father, accept them through thy Son,
  And ever by thy Spirit guide!
Thy wisdom in their lives be shown,
  Thy name confessed and glorified;
Thy power and love diffused abroad,
Till all the earth is filled with God.

6 - 8 s.   *The same subject.*   **474**

1 CAPTAIN of our salvation, take
  The souls we here present to thee,
And fit for thy great service make
  These heirs of immortality;
And let them in thine image rise,
And then transplant to Paradise.

2 Unspotted from the world and pure,
  Preserve them for thy glorious cause.
Accustomed daily to endure
  The welcome burden of thy cross;
Inured to toil and patient pain,
Till all thy perfect mind they gain.

3 Our sons henceforth be wholly thine,
  And serve and love thee all their days;
Infuse the principle divine
  In all who here expect thy grace;
Let each improve the grace bestowed;
Rise every child a man of God!

4 Train up thy hardy soldiers, Lord,
  In all their Captain's steps to tread!
Or send them to proclaim the word,
  Thy gospel through the world to spread,
Freely as they receive to give,
And preach the death by which we live.

6 - 8 s.   *The same subject.*   **475**

1 BUT who sufficient is to lead
  And execute the vast design!
How can our arduous toil succeed,
  When earth and hell their forces join
The meanest instruments to o'erthrow
Which thou hast ever used below?

2 Mountains, alas! on mountains rise,
　To make our utmost efforts vain;
The work our feeble strength defies,
　And all the helps and hopes of man;
Our utter impotence we see;
　But nothing is too hard for thee.

3 The things impossible to men
　Thou canst for thine own people do:
Thy strength be in our weakness seen:
　Thy wisdom in our folly show!
Prevent, accompany, and bless,
　And crown the whole with full success.

4 Unless the power of heavenly grace,
　The wisdom of the Deity,
Direct and govern all our ways,
　And all our works be wrought in thee,
Our blighted works we know shall fail,
　And earth and hell at last prevail.

5 But, O almighty God of love,
　Into thy hands the matter take !
The mountain-obstacles remove,
　For thy own truth and mercy's sake;
Fulfil in ours thy own design,
　And prove the work entirely thine.

476 *At the Baptism of Adults.* L. M.

1 COME, Father, Son, and Holy Ghost,
　Honour the means ordained by thee!
Make good our apostolic boast,
　And own thy glorious ministry.

2 We now thy promised presence claim,
　Sent to disciple all mankind,
Sent to baptize into thy name ;
　We now thy promised presence find.

3 Father! in these reveal thy Son :
　In these, for whom we seek thy face,
The hidden mystery make known,
　The inward, pure, baptizing grace.

4 Jesus! with us thou always art:
　Effectuate now the sacred sign,
The gift unspeakable impart,
　And bless the ordinance divine.

5 Eternal Spirit! descend from high,
　Baptizer of our spirits thou !
The sacramental seal apply,
　And witness with the water now !

6 O that the souls baptized therein
　May now thy truth and mercy feel ;
May rise and wash away their sin !
　Come, Holy Ghost, their pardon seal !

477 *For the same occasion.* 7 s & 6 s

1 FATHER, Son, and Holy Ghost,
　In solemn power come down !
Present with thy heavenly host,
　Thine ordinance to crown :
See a sinful worm of earth !
　Bless to *him* the cleansing flood,
Plunge *him*, by a second birth,
　Into the depths of God.

2 Let the promised inward grace
　Accompany the sign ;
On *his* new-born soul impress
　The character divine;

Father, all thy name reveal !
Jesus, all thy name impart !
Holy Ghost, renew, and dwell
For ever in *his* heart !

PART V.

SECTION I.

FOR THE SOCIETY ON MEETING.

S. M.

478

1 AND are we yet alive,
　And see each other's face ?
Glory and praise to Jesus give
For his redeeming grace !
Preserved by power divine
To full salvation here,
Again in Jesu's praise we join,
　And in his sight appear.

2 What troubles have we seen,
　What conflicts have we past,
Fightings without, and fears within,
Since we assembled last !
But out of all the Lord
Hath brought us by his love ;
And still he doth his help afford,
　And hides our life above.

3 Then let us make our boast
　Of his redeeming power,
Which saves us to the uttermost,
Till we can sin no more :
Let us take up the cross,
Till we the crown obtain :
And gladly reckon all things loss,
　So we may Jesus gain.

8 - 7 s.

479

1 PEACE be on this house bestowed,
　Peace on all that here reside !
Let the unknown peace of God
With the man of peace abide.
Let the Spirit now come down ;
Let the blessing now take place !
Son of peace, receive thy crown,
Fulness of the gospel grace.

2 Christ, my Master and my Lord,
Let me thy forerunner be ;
O be mindful of thy word ;
Visit them, and visit me !
To this house, and all herein,
Now let thy salvation come !
Save our souls from inbred sin,
Make us thy eternal home.

3 Let us never, never rest,
Till the promise is fulfilled ;
Till we are of thee possessed,
Pardoned, sanctified, and sealed ;
Till we all, in love renewed,
Find the pearl that Adam lost,
Temples of the living God,
Father, Son, and Holy Ghost !

8 - 7 s.

480

1 GLORY be to God above,
　God from whom all blessings flow ;

113

Make we mention of his love,
  Publish we his praise below ;
Called together by his grace,
  We are met in Jesu's name ;
See with joy each other's face.
  Followers of the bleeding Lamb.

2 Let us then sweet counsel take,
  How to make our calling sure,
Our election how to make
  Past the reach of hell secure ;
Build we each the other up ;
  Pray we for our faith's increase.
Solid comfort, settled hope,
  Constant joy, and lasting peace.

3 More and more let love abound ;
  Let us never, never rest,
Till we are in Jesus found,
  Of our paradise possest ;
He removes the flaming sword,
  Calls us back, from Eden driven ;
To his image here restored,
  Soon he takes us up to heaven.

481
10 s & 11 s.

1 ALL thanks to the Lamb, Who gives us to meet !
His love we proclaim, His praises repeat ;
We own him our Jesus, Continually near
To pardon and bless us, And perfect us here.

2 In him we have peace, In him we have power.
Preserved by his grace Throughout the dark hour,
In all our temptation He keeps us to prove
His utmost salvation, His fulness of love.

3 Through pride and desire Unhurt we have gone,
Through water and fire In him we went on ;
The world and the devil Through him we o'ercame,
Our Saviour from evil, For ever the same.

4 When we would have spurned His mercy and grace,
To Egypt returned, And fled from his face,
He hindered our flying, (His goodness to show,)
And st____ us by crying, "Will ye also go ?" opped

5 O what shall we do Our Saviour to love ?
To make us anew, Come, Lo__, from above !
The fruit of thy passion, Thy holiness give,
Give us the salvation Of all that believe.

6 Come, Jesus, and loose the stammerer's tongue,
And teach even us The spiritual song ;
Let us without ceasing Give thanks for thy grace,
And glory, and blessing, And honour, and praise.

482
S. M.

1 SAVIOUR of sinful men,
  Thy goodness we proclaim,
Which brings us here to meet again,
  And triumph in thy name ;
Thy mighty name hath been
  Our safeguard and our tower ;

Hath saved us from the world, and sin,
  And all the accuser's power.

2 Jesus, take all the praise,
  That still on earth we live,
Unspotted in so foul a place,
  And innocently grieve !
We shall from Sodom flee,
  When perfected in love ;
And haste to better company,
  Who wait for us above.

3 Awhile in flesh disjoined,
  Our friends that went before
We soon in paradise shall find,
  And meet to part no more.
In yon thrice-happy seat,
  Waiting for us they are ;
And thou shalt there a husband meet !
  And I a parent there !

4 O ! what a mighty change
  Shall Jesu's sufferers know,
While o'er the happy plains they range,
  Incapable of woe !
No ill-requited love
  Shall there our spirits wound ;
No base ingratitude above,
  No sin in heaven is found.

5 There all our griefs are spent !
  There all our sorrows end !
We cannot there the fall lament
  Of a departed friend !
A brother dead to God,
  By sin, alas ! undone :
No father there, in passion loud,
  Cries, "O my son, my son !"

6 Nor slightest touch of pain,
  Nor sorrow's least alloy,
Can violate our rest, or stain
  Our purity of joy :
In that eternal day
  No clouds nor tempests rise,
These gushing tears are wiped away
  For ever from our eyes.

483
6 - 8 s.

1 JESU, to thee our hearts we lift,
  (May all our hearts with love o erflow !)
With thanks for thy continued gift,
  That still thy precious name we know,
Retain our sense of sin forgiven,
And wait for all our inward heaven.

2 What mighty troubles hast thou shown
  Thy feeble, tempted followers here !
We have through fire and water gone,
  But saw thee on the floods appear,
But felt thee present in the flame,
And shouted our Deliverer's name.

3 When stronger souls their faith forsook,
  And, lulled in worldly, hellish peace,
Leaped desperate from their guardian Rock,
  And headlong plunged in sin's abyss,
Thy strength was in our weakness shown
And still it guards and keeps thine own

4 All are not lost or wandered back ;
  All have not left thy church and thee ;
There are who suffer for thy sake,
  Enjoy thy glorious infamy,

114

Esteem the scandal of the cross,
And only seek divine applause.
5 Thou who hast kept us to this hour,
O keep us faithful to the end !
When, robed with majesty and power,
Our Jesus shall from heaven descend,
His friends and confessors to own,
And seat us on his glorious throne.

484

10 s & 11 s.

1 APPOINTED by thee, We meet in thy
name,
And meekly agree To follow the Lamb,
To trace thy example, The world to disdain,
And constantly trample On pleasure and
pain.
2 Rejoicing in hope, We humbly go on,
And daily take up The pledge of our crown;
In doing and bearing The will of our Lord.
We still are preparing To meet our reward.
O Jesus appear ! No longer delay
To sanctify here, And bear us away,
The end of our meeting On earth let us see,
Triumphantly sitting In glory with thee !

485

S. M.

1 JESU, we look to thee,
Thy promised presence claim !
Thou in the midst of us shalt be,
Assembled in thy name :
Thy name salvation is,
Which here we come to prove ;
Thy name is life, and health, and peace,
And everlasting love.
2 Not in the name of pride
Or selfishness we meet ;
From nature's paths we turn aside,
And worldly thoughts forget.
We meet, the grace to take
Which thou hast freely given ;
We meet on earth for thy dear sake,
That we may meet in heaven.
3 Present we know thou art,
But O thyself reveal !
Now, Lord, let every bounding heart
The mighty comfort feel.
O may thy quickening voice
The death of sin remove ;
And bid our inmost souls rejoice
In hope of perfect love !

486

C. M.

1 SEE, Jesu, thy disciples see,
The promised blessing give !
Met in thy name, we look to thee,
Expecting to receive.
2 Thee we expect, our faithful Lord,
Who in thy name are joined ;
We wait, according to thy word.
Thee in the midst to find.
3 With us thou art assembled here,
But O thyself reveal !
Son of the living God, appear !
Let us thy presence feel.
4 Breathe on us, Lord, in this our day,
And these dry bones shall live ;
Speak peace into our hearts, and say,
"The Holy Ghost receive !"

5 Whom now we seek, O may we meet !
Jesus, the crucified,
Show us thy bleeding hands and feet,
Thou who for us hast died.
6 Cause us the record to receive,
Speak, and the tokens show ;
"O be not faithless, but believe
In me, who died for you !"

487

7 s & 6 s.   Ecclesiastes iv. 9—12.

1 TWO are better far than one
For counsel or for fight ;
How can one be warm alone,
Or serve his God aright ?
Join we then our hearts and hands,
Each to love provoke his friend ;
Run the way of his commands,
And keep it to the end.
2 Woe to him whose spirits droop,
To him who falls alone !
He has none to lift him up,
To help his weakness on :
Happier we each other keep,
We each other's burdens bear ;
Never need our footsteps slip,
Upheld by mutual prayer.
3 Who of twain hath made us one,
Maintains our unity,
Jesus is the corner-stone,
In whom we all agree ;
Servants of one common Lord,
Sweetly of one heart and mind,
Who can break a threefold cord,
Or part whom God hath joined ?
4 O that all with us might prove
The fellowship of saints !
Find supplied, in Jesu's love,
What every member wants :
Grasp we our high calling's prize,
Feel our sins on earth forgiven,
Rise, in his whole image rise,
And meet our Head in heaven !

SECTION II.

FOR THE SOCIETY GIVING THANKS.

488

5 5 9, 5 5 9.

1 HOW happy are we
Who in Jesus agree
To expect his return from above ?
We sit under our Vine,
And delightfully join
In the praise of his excellent love.
2 How pleasant and sweet,
In his name when we meet,
Is his fruit to our spiritual taste.
We are banqueting here
On angelical cheer,
And the joys that eternally last.
3 Invited by him,
We drink of the stream
Ever flowing in bliss from the throne ?
Who in Jesus believe,
We the Spirit receive
That proceeds from the Father and Son.

4 The unspeakable grace
  He obtained for our race,
And the Spirit of faith he imparts;
  Then, then we conceive
  How in heaven they live,
By the kingdom of God in our hearts.

5 True believers have seen
  The Saviour of men,
As his head he on Calvary bowed;
  We shall see him again,
  When, with all his bright train,
He descends on the luminous cloud.

6 We remember the word
  Of our crucified Lord,
When he went to prepare us a place;
  "I will come in that day,
  And transport you away,
And admit to a sight of my face."

7 With earnest desire
  After thee we aspire,
And long thy appearing to see,
  Till our souls thou receive
  In thy presence to live,
And be perfectly happy in thee.

8 Come, Lord, from the skies,
  And command us to rise,
Ready made for the mansions above;
  With our Head to ascend,
  And eternity spend
In a rapture of heavenly love.

489
6 - 8 s.   Second Metre.

1 HOW good and pleasant 'tis to see,
  When brethren cordially agree,
  And kindly think and speak the same!
A family of faith and love,
Combined to seek the things above,
  And spread the common Saviour's fame.

The God of grace, who all invites,
Who in our unity delights,
  Vouchsafes our intercourse to bless;
Revives us with refreshing showers,
The fulness of his blessing pours,
  And keeps our minds in perfect peace.

2 Jesus, thou precious corner-stone,
Preserve inseparably one
  Whom thou didst by thy Spirit join:
Still let us in thy Spirit live,
And to thy church the pattern give
  Of unanimity divine.

Still let us to each other cleave,
And from thy plenitude receive
  Constant supplies of hallowing grace;
Till to a perfect man we rise,
O'ertake our kindred in the skies,
  And find prepared our heavenly place.

490*
Christian Fellowship.   'L. M.

1 BRETHREN in Christ, and well-beloved,
  To Jesus and his servants dear,
Enter and show yourselves approved;
  Enter, and find that God is here.

2 Welcome from earth: lo, the right hand
  Of fellowship to you we give!

With open hearts and hands we stand,
  And you in Jesu's name receive.

3 Say, are your hearts resolved as ours?
  Then let them burn with sacred love;
Then let them taste the heavenly powers,
  Partakers of the joys above.

4 Jesu, attend, thyself reveal!
  Are we not met in thy great name?
Thee in the midst we wait to feel,
  We wait to catch the spreading flame.

5 Thou God that answerest by fire,
  The Spirit of burning now impart;
And let the flames of pure desire
  Rise from the altar of our heart.

6 Truly our fellowship below
  With thee and with the Father.is;
In thee eternal life we know,
  And heaven's unutterable bliss.

7 In part we only know thee here,
  But wait thy coming from above;
And we shall then behold thee near,
  And we shall all be lost in love.

491
559, 559.

1 COME away to the skies,
  My beloved, arise,
And rejoice in the day thou wast born;
  On this festival day,
  Come exulting away,
And with singing to Zion return.

2 We have laid up our love
  And treasure above,
Though our bodies continue below;
  The redeemed of the Lord,
  We remember his word,
And with singing to Paradise go.

3 With singing we praise
  The original grace,
By our heavenly Father bestowed:
  Our being receive
  From his bounty, and live
To the honour and glory of God.

4 For thy glory we are,
  Created to share
Both the nature and kingdom divine;
  Created again,
  That our souls may remain
In time and eternity thine.

5 With thanks we approve
  The design of thy love,
Which hath joined us in Jesus's name;
  So united in heart,
  That we never can part,
Till we meet at the feast of the Lamb.

6 There, there at his feet
  We shall suddenly meet,
And be parted in body no more!
  We shall sing to our lyres,
  With the heavenly choirs,
And our Saviour in glory adore.

7 Hallelujah, we sing,
  To our Father and King,
And his rapturous praises repeat;
  To the Lamb that was slain,
  Hallelujah again,
Sing all heaven, and fall at his feet!

8 In assurance of hope,
  We to Jesus look up,
Till his banner unfurled in the air
  From our graves we shall see,
  And cry out, "It is he!"
And fly up to acknowledge him there

492
L. M.

1 WHAT shall we offer our good Lord,
    Poor nothings! for his boundless
        grace?
Fain would we his great name record,
  And worthily set forth his praise.

2 Great object of our growing love,
  To whom our more than all we owe,
Open the fountain from above,
  And let it our full souls o'erflow.

3 So shall our lives thy power proclaim,
  Thy grace for every sinner free;
Till all mankind shall learn thy name,
  Shall all stretch out their hands to thee.

4 Open a door which earth and hell
  May strive to shut, but strive in vain;
Let thy word richly in us dwell,
  And let our gracious fruit remain.

5 O multiply the sower's seed!
  And fruit we every hour shall bear,
Throughout the world thy gospel spread,
  Thy everlasting truth declare.

6 We all, in perfect love renewed,
  Shall know the greatness of thy power;
Stand in the temple of our God
  As pillars, and go out no more.

493
Isaiah ix. 2—5.   —   6 - 8 s.

1 THE people that in darkness lay,
    The confines of eternal night,
We, we have seen a gospel day,
  The glorious beams of heavenly light;
His Spirit in our hearts hath shone,
And showed the Father in the Son.

2 Father of everlasting grace,
  Thou hast in us thy arm revealed,
Hast multiplied the faithful race,
  Who, conscious of their pardon sealed,
Of joy unspeakable possest,
Anticipate their heavenly rest.

3 In tears who sowed, in joy we reap,
  And praise thy goodness all day long:
Him in our eye of faith we keep,
  Who gave us our triumphal song,
And doth his spoils to all divide,
A lot among the sanctified.

4 Thou hast our bonds in sunder broke,
  Took all our load of guilt away;
From sin, the world, and Satan's yoke,
  (Like Israel saved in Midian's day)
Redeemed us by our conquering Lord,
Our Gideon, and his Spirit's sword.

5 Not like the warring sons of men,
  With shouts, and garments rolled in
        blood,
Our Captain doth the fight maintain;
  But, lo! the burning Spirit of God
Kindles in each a secret fire;
And all our sins as smoke expire.

494
6 - 8 s.   Genesis xxviii. 16, 17.

1 LO! God is here! let us adore,
    And own how dreadful is this place!
Let all within us feel his power,
  And silent bow before his face:
Who know his power, his grace who prove,
Serve him with awe, with reverence love.

2 Lo! God is here! him day and night
  The united choirs of angels sing;
To him, enthroned above all height,
  Heaven's host their noblest praises bring;
Disdain not, Lord, our meaner song,
Who praise thee with a stammering tongue.

3 Gladly the toys of earth we leave,
  Wealth, pleasure, fame, for thee alone;
To thee our will, soul, flesh, we give,
  O take, O seal them for thine own!
Thou art the God, thou art the Lord;
Be thou by all thy works adored.

4 Being of beings! may our praise
  Thy courts with grateful fragrance fill;
Still may we stand before thy face,
  Still hear and do thy sovereign will;
To thee may all our thoughts arise,
Ceaseless, accepted sacrifice.

5 In thee we move: all things of thee
  Are full, thou source and life of all;
Thou vast unfathomable sea!
  (Fall prostrate, lost in wonder fall,
Ye sons of men, for God is man!)
All may we lose, so thee we gain.

6 As flowers their opening leaves display,
  And glad drink in the solar fire,
So may we catch thy every ray,
  So may thy influence us inspire;
Thou beam of the eternal beam,
Thou purging fire, thou quickening flame.

495
5 5 5 11, 5 5 5 11.

1 COME, let us arise,
    And press to the skies;
    The summons obey,
My friends, my beloved, and hasten away.
    The Master of all
    For our service doth call,
    And deigns to approve,   [love.
With smiles of acceptance, our labour of

2 His burden who bear,
    We alone can declare
    How easy his yoke,
While to love and good works we each other
    By word and by deed,   [provoke;
    The bodies in need,
    The souls to relieve,
And freely as Jesus hath given to give.

3 Then let us attend
    Our heavenly Friend,
    In his members distrest,
By want, or affliction, or sickness opprest:
    The prisoner relieve,
    The stranger receive,
    Supply all their wants,   [saints.
And spend and be spent in assisting his

4 Thus while we bestow
    Our moments below,

117

Ourselves we forsake,
And refuge in Jesus's righteousness take:
  His passion alone
  The foundation we own;
  And pardon we claim,
And eternal redemption, in Jesus's name.

496
      Matthew vi. 33.   10 s & 11 s.

1 THE   r   is the Lord's, And all it contains:
  The truth of his words For ever remains;
  The saints have a mountain Of blessings
   in him;
His grace is the fountain, His peace is the
   stream.

2 To him our request We now have made
   known,
  Who sees what is best For each of his own :
  Our heathenish care, We cast it aside;
  He heareth the prayer, And he will pro-
   vide.

3 The modest and meek The earth shall pos-
   sess :
  Th kingdom who seek Of Jesus's grace
  The power of his Spirit Shall joyfully own,
  And all things inherit In virtue of one.

497
            4 - 6 s & 2 - 8 s.

1 COME, all whoe'er have set
   Your faces Zion-ward,
  In Jesus let us meet,
   And praise our common Lord;
  In Jesus let us still go on,
  Till all appear before his throne

2 Nearer, and nearer still,
   We to our country come,
  To that celestial hill,
   The weary pilgrim's home,
  The new Jerusalem above,
  The seat of everlasting love.

3 The ransomed sons of God,
   All earthly things we scorn,
  And to our high abode
   With songs of praise return :
  From strength to strength we still proceed,
  With crowns of joy upon our head.

4 The peace and joy of faith
   Each moment may we feel ;
  Redeemed from sin and wrath,
   From earth, and death, and hell,
  We to our Father's house repair,
  To meet our elder Brother there.

5 Our Brother, Saviour, Head,
   Our all in all, is he ;
  And in his steps who tread,
   We soon his face shall see;
  Shall see him with our glorious friends,
  And then in heaven our journey ends.

498
         55511, 55511.

1 COME, let us anew
   Our journey pursue,
  With vigour arise,
And press to our permanent place in the
  Of heavenly birth,   [skies.
  Though wandering on earth,

118

   This is not our place ;   [less
But strangers and pilgrims ourselves we con-

2 At Jesus's call
  We gave up our all ;
  And still we forego
For Jesus's sake our enjoyments below.
  No longing we find
  For the country behind ;
  But onward we move,
And still we are seeking a country above :

3 A country of joy,
  Without any alloy,
  We thither repair :
Our hearts and our treasure already are
  We march hand in hand   [there
  To Immanuel's land :
  No matter what cheer
We meet with on earth ; for eternity's near.

4 The rougher our way,
  The shorter our stay ;
  The tempests that rise
Shall gloriously hurry our souls to the skies.
  The fiercer the blast,
  The sooner 'tis past ;
  The troubles that come,   [home.
Shall come to our rescue, and hasten us

559, 559.   ## 499

1 COME, let us ascend,
   My companion and friend,
To a taste of the banquet above ;
  If thy heart be as mine,
  If for Jesus it pine,
Come up into the chariot of love.

2 Who in Jesus confide,
  We are bold to outride
The storms of affliction beneath ;
  With the prophet we soar
  To the heavenly shore,
And outfly all the arrows of death.

3 By faith we are come
  To our permanent home :
By hope we the rapture improve ;
  By love we still rise,
  And look down on the skies,
For the heaven of heavens is love.

4 Who on earth can conceive
  How happy we live,
In the palace of God, the great King ?
  What a concert of praise,
  When our Jesus's grace
The whole heavenly company sing !

5 What a rapturous song,
  When the glorified throng
In the spirit of harmony join :
  Join all the glad choirs,
  Hearts, voices, and lyres,
And the burden is, " Mercy divine ! "

6 Hallelujah, they cry,
  To the King of the sky,
To the great everlasting I AM ;
  To the Lamb that was slain,
  And liveth again,
Hallelujah to God and the Lamb !

7 The Lamb on the throne,
  Lo ! he dwells with his own,
And to rivers of pleasure he leads ;

With his mercy's full blaze,
With the sight of his face,
Our beatified spirits he feeds.

8 Our foreheads proclaim
His ineffable name;
Our bodies his glory display;
A day without night
We feast in his sight,
And eternity seems as a day!

500*

C. M.

1 ALL praise to our redeeming Lord,
Who joins us by his grace,
And bids us, each to each restored,
Together seek his face.

2 He bids us build each other up;
And, gathered into one,
To our high calling's glorious hope
We hand in hand go on.

3 The gift which he on one bestows,
We all delight to prove;
The grace through every vessel flows,
In purest streams of love.

4 Even now we think and speak the same,
And cordially agree;
Concentred all, through Jesu's name,
In perfect harmony.

5 We all partake the joy of one,
The common peace we feel,
A peace to sensual minds unknown,
A joy unspeakable.

6 And if our fellowship below
In Jesus be so sweet,
What heights of rapture shall we know,
When round his throne we meet!

SECTION III.

FOR THE SOCIETY PRAYING.

501

C. M.

1 JESUS, great Shepherd of the sheep,
To thee for help we fly:
Thy little flock in safety keep;
For O! the wolf is nigh.

2 He comes, of hellish malice full,
To scatter, tear, and slay;
He seizes every straggling soul,
As his own lawful prey.

3 Us into thy protection take,
And gather with thy arm;
Unless the fold we first forsake,
The wolf can never harm.

4 We laugh to scorn his cruel power,
While by our Shepherd's side;
The sheep he never can devour,
Unless he first divide.

5 O do not suffer him to part
The souls that here agree;
But make us of one mind and heart,
And keep us one in thee!

6 Together let us sweetly live,
Together let us die;
And each a starry crown receive,
And reign above the sky.

502

C. M.

1 COME, thou omniscient Son of man,
Display thy sifting power;
Come with thy Spirit's winnowing fan,
And throughly purge thy floor.

2 The chaff of sin, the accursed thing,
Far from our souls be driven!
The wheat into thy garner bring,
And lay us up for heaven.

3 Look through us with thy eyes of flame,
The clouds and darkness chase;
And tell me what by sin I am,
And what I am by grace.

4 Whate'er offends thy glorious eyes,
Far from our hearts remove;
As dust before the whirlwind flies,
Disperse it by thy love.

5 Then let us all thy fulness know,
From every sin set free;
Saved, to the utmost saved below,
And perfectly like thee.

503

C. M.

1 TRY us, O God, and search the ground
Of every sinful heart,
Whate'er of sin in us is found,
O bid it all depart!

2 When to the right or left we stray,
Leave us not comfortless;
But guide our feet into the way
Of everlasting peace.

3 Help us to help each other, Lord,
Each other's cross to bear,
Let each his friendly aid afford,
And feel his brother's care.

4 Help us to build each other up,
Our little stock improve;
Increase our faith, confirm our hope,
And perfect us in love.

5 Up into thee, our living Head,
Let us in all things grow,
Till thou hast made us free indeed,
And spotless here below.

6 Then, when the mighty work is wrought,
Receive thy ready bride:
Give us in heaven a happy lot
With all the sanctified.

504

C. M.

1 JESUS, united by thy grace,
And each to each endeared,
With confidence we seek thy face,
And know our prayer is heard.

2 Still let us own our common Lord,
And bear thine easy yoke,
A band of love, a threefold cord,
Which never can be broke.

3 Make us into one spirit drink;
Baptize into thy name;
And let us always kindly think,
And sweetly speak, the same.

4 Touched by the loadstone of thy love,
Let all our hearts agree,
And ever towards each other move,
And ever move towards thee.

5 To thee, inseparably joined,
 Let all our spirits cleave ;
O may we all the loving mind
 That was in thee receive !

6 This is the bond of perfectness,
 Thy spotless charity ;
O let us (still we pray) possess
 The mind that was in thee !

7 Grant this, and then from all below
 Insensibly remove :
Our souls their change shall scarcely
 Made perfect first in love ! [know,

8 With ease our souls through death shall
 Into their paradise,   [glide
And thence, on wings of angels, ride
 Triumphant through the skies.

9 Yet, when the fullest joy is given,
 The same delight we prove,
In earth, in paradise, in heaven,
 Our all in all is love.

505   John xvii. 20, &c.   L. M.

1 UNCHANGEABLE, almighty Lord,
 Our souls upon thy truth we stay ;
Accomplish now thy faithful word,
 And give, O give us all one way !

2 O let us all join hand in hand
 Who seek redemption in thy blood,
Fast in one mind and spirit stand,
 And build the temple of our God !

3 Thou only canst our wills control,
 Our wild unruly passions bind,
Tame the old Adam in our soul,
 And make us of one heart and mind.

4 Speak but the reconciling word, [side,
 The winds shall cease, the waves sub-
We all shall praise our common Lord,
 Our Jesus, and him crucified.

5 Giver of peace and unity,
 Send down thy mild, pacific Dove ;
We all shall then in one agree,
 And breathe the spirit of thy love.

6 We all shall think and speak the same,
 Delightful lesson of thy grace !
One undivided Christ proclaim,
 And jointly glory in thy praise.

7 O let us take a softer mould,
 Blended and gathered into thee :
Under one Shepherd make one fold,
 Where all is love and harmony !

8 Regard thine own eternal prayer,
 And send a peaceful answer down ;
To us thy Father's name declare ;
 Unite and perfect us in one !

9 So shall the world believe and know
 That God hath sent thee from above,
When thou art seen in us below,
 And every soul displays thy love.

506   John xiv. 16, 17.   7 s & 6 s.

- 1 FATHER of our dying Lord,
 Remember us for good ;
 O fulfil his faithful word,
  And hear his speaking blood !
120

Give us that for which he prays ;
 Father, glorify thy Son !
Show his truth, and power, and grace,
 And send the Promise down.

2 True and faithful Witness, thou,
 O Christ, thy Spirit give !
Hast thou not received him now,
 That we might now receive ?
Art thou not our living Head ?
 Life to all thy limbs impart ;
Shed thy love, thy Spirit shed
 In every waiting heart.

3 Holy Ghost, the Comforter,
 The gift of Jesus, come ;
Glows our heart to find thee near,
 And swells to make thee room ;
Present with us thee we feel,
 Come, O come, and in us be !
With us, in us, live and dwell,
 To all eternity.

L. M.   Revelation iii. 20.   507

1 SAVIOUR of all, to thee we bow,
 And own thee faithful to thy word ;
We hear thy voice, and open now
 Our hearts to entertain our Lord.

2 Come in, come in, thou heavenly guest,
 Delight in what thyself hast given ;
On thy own gifts and graces feast,
 And make the contrite heart thy heaven.

3 Smell the sweet odour of our prayers,
 Our sacrifice of praise approve,
And treasure up our gracious tears,
 And rest in thy redeeming love.

4 Beneath thy shadow let us sit,
 Call us thy friends, and love, and bride,
And bid us freely drink and eat
 Thy dainties, and be satisfied.

5 O let us on thy fulness feed,
 And eat thy flesh, and drink thy blood !
Jesu, thy blood is drink indeed,
 Jesu, thy flesh is angels' food.

6 The heavenly manna faith imparts,
 Faith makes thy fulness all our own ;
We feed upon thee in our hearts,
 And find that heaven and thou art one.

7 s.   508

1 GOD of love, that hear'st the prayer,
 Kindly for thy people care,
Who on thee alone depend :
Love us, save us to the end.

2 Save us, in the prosperous hour,
From the flattering tempter's power,
From his unsuspected wiles,
From the world's pernicious smiles.

3 Cut off our dependence vain
On the help of feeble man,
Every arm of flesh remove ;
Stay us on thy only love !

4 Men of worldly, low design,
Let not these thy people join,
Poison our simplicity,
Drag us from our trust in thee.

5 Save us from the great and wise,
Till they sink in their own eyes,

Tamely to thy yoke submit,
Lay their honours at thy feet.

6 Never let the world break in ;
Fix a mighty gulf between :
Keep us little and unknown,
Prized and loved by God alone.

7 Let us still to thee look up,
Thee, thy Israel's Strength and Hope ;
Nothing know, or seek, beside
Jesus, and him crucified.

8 Far above all earthly things,
Look we down on earthly kings ;
Taste our glorious liberty,
Find our happy all in thee !

509

7 s.

1 JESUS, Lord, we look to thee,
Let us in thy name agree ;
Show thyself the Prince of peace ;
Bid our jars for ever cease.

2 By thy reconciling love
Every stumbling-block remove ;
Each to each unite, endear,
Come, and spread thy banner here!

3 Make us of one heart and mind,
Courteous, pitiful, and kind,
Lowly, meek, in thought and word,
Altogether like our Lord.

4 Let us for each other care,
Each the other's burden bear,
To thy church the pattern give,
Show how true believers live.

5 Free from anger and from pride,
Let us thus in God abide ;
All the depths of love express,
All the heights of holiness !

6 Let us then with joy remove
To the family above ;
On the wings of angels fly,
Show how true believers die.

510

4 - 6 s & 2 - 8 s.

1 THOU God of truth and love,
We seek thy perfect way,
Ready thy choice to approve,
Thy providence to obey :
Enter into thy wise design,
And sweetly lose our will in thine.

2 Why hast thou cast our lot
In the same age and place ?
And why together brought
To see each other's face ?
To join with softest sympathy,
And mix our friendly souls in thee !

3 Didst thou not make us one,
That we might one remain,
Together travel on,
And bear each other's pain ;
Till all thy utmost goodness prove,
And rise renewed in perfect love ?

4 Surely thou didst unite
Our kindred spirits here,
That all hereafter might
Before thy throne appear ;
Meet at the marriage of the Lamb,
And all thy glorious love proclaim.

5 Then let us ever bear
The blessed end in view,
And join, with mutual care,
To fight our passage through ;
And kindly help each other on,
Till all receive the starry crown.

6 O may thy Spirit seal
Our souls unto that day,
With all thy fulness fill,
And then transport away !
Away to our eternal rest,
Away to our Redeemer's breast !

6 - 8 s.   Exodus xxxiv. 9, 10.   **511**

1 FORGIVE us, for thy mercy's sake,
Our multitude of sins forgive !
And for thy own possession take,
And bid us to thy glory live :
Live in thy sight, and gladly prove
Our faith by our obedient love.

2 The covenant of forgiveness seal,
And all thy mighty wonders show !
Our inbred enemies expel ;
And conquering them to conquer go,
Till all of pride and wrath be slain,
And not one evil thought remain !

3 O put it in our inward parts,
The living law of perfect love !
Write the new precept in our hearts :
We shall not then from thee remove,
Who in thy glorious image shine,
Thy people, and for ever thine.

6 - 7 s.   **512**

1 CENTRE of our hopes thou art,
End of our enlarged desires ;
Stamp thine image on our heart,
Fill us now with heavenly fires ;
Cemented by love divine,
Seal our souls for ever thine.

2 All our works in thee be wrought,
Levelled at one common aim ;
Every word, and every thought,
Purge in the refining flame :
Lead us through the paths of peace,
On to perfect holiness.

3 Let us altogether rise,
To thy glorious life restored,
Here regain our paradise,
Here prepare to meet our Lord ;
Here enjoy the earnest given,
Travel hand in hand to heaven !

6 - 8 s.   **513**

1 JESUS, with kindest pity see
The souls that would be one in thee :
If now, accepted in thy sight,
Thou dost our upright hearts unite,
Allow us even on earth to prove
The noblest joys of heavenly love.

2 Before thy glorious eyes we spread
The wish which doth from thee proceed :
Our love from earthly dross refine ;
Holy, angelical, divine,
Thee its great Author let it show,
And back to the pure fountain flow.

3 A drop of that unbounded sea,
O Lord, resorb it into thee!
While all our souls, with restless strife,
Spring up into eternal life,
And, lost in endless raptures, prove
Thy whole immensity of love.

4 A spark of that ethereal fire,
Still let it to its source aspire,
To thee in every wish return,
Intensely for thy glory burn;
While all our souls fly up to thee,
And blaze through all eternity.

514   7 s.

1 FATHER, at thy footstool see
Those who now are one in thee;
Draw us by thy grace alone,
Give, O give us to thy Son!

2 Jesus, friend of human kind,
Let us in thy name be joined;
Each to each unite, and bless;
Keep us still in perfect peace.

3 Heavenly, all-alluring Dove,
Shed thy over-shadowing love,
Love, the sealing grace, impart;
Dwell within our single heart.

4 Father, Son, and Holy Ghost,
Be to us what Adam lost,
Let us in thine image rise;
Give us back our paradise.

515   *The Communion of Saints.*   8 - 7 s.

1 FATHER, Son, and Spirit, hear
Faith's effectual fervent prayer;
Hear, and our petitions seal,
Let us now the answer feel.
Still our fellowship increase,
Knit us in the bond of peace;
Join our new-born spirits, join
Each to each, and all to thine.

2 Build us in one body up,
Called in one high calling's hope:
One the Spirit whom we claim,
One the pure baptismal flame,
One the faith, and common Lord,
One the Father lives adored,
Over, through, and in us all,
God incomprehensible.

3 One with God, the source of bliss,
Ground of our communion this:
Life of all that live below,
Let thine emanations flow!
Rise eternal in our heart;
Thou our long-sought Eden art;
Father, Son, and Holy Ghost,
Be to us what Adam lost.

516   SECOND PART.   8 - 7 s.

1 OTHER ground can no man lay,
Jesus takes our sins away;
Jesus the foundation is,
This shall stand, and only this:
Fitly framed in him we are,
All the building rises fair;
Let it to a temple rise,
Worthy him who fills the skies

122

2 Husband of thy church below,
Christ, if thee our Lord we know,
Unto thee, betrothed in love,
Always let us faithful prove;
Never rob thee of our heart,
Never give the creature part;
Only thou possess the whole;
Take our body, spirit, soul.

3 Steadfast let us cleave to thee;
Love the mystic union be,
Union to the world unknown,
Joined to God, in spirit one:
Wait we till the Spouse shall come,
Till the Lamb shall take us home,
For his heaven the bride prepare,
Solemnize our nuptials there.

517

7 s.   THIRD PART.

1 CHRIST, our Head, gone up on high,
Be thou in thy Spirit nigh:
Advocate with God, give ear ·
To thine own effectual prayer!

2 One the Father is with thee;
Knit us in like unity;
Make us, O uniting Son,
One, as Thou and He are one!

3 Still, O Lord, (for thine we are)
Still to us his name declare:
Thy revealing Spirit give,
Whom the world cannot receive.

4 Fill us with the Father's love;
Never from our souls remove;
Dwell in us, and we shall be
Thine through all eternity.

518

7 s.   FOURTH PART.

1 CHRIST, from whom all blessings
flow,
Perfecting the saints below,
Hear us, who thy nature share,
Who thy mystic body are.

2 Join us, in one spirit join,
Let us still receive of thine;
Still for more on thee we call;
Thou who fillest all in all.

3 Closer knit to thee, our Head;
Nourish us, O Christ, and feed!
Let us daily growth receive,
More and more in Jesus live.

4 Jesus, we thy members are,
Cherish us with kindest care,
Of thy flesh and of thy bone,
Love, for ever love thine own!

5 Move, and actuate, and guide:
Divers gifts to each divide;
Placed according to thy will,
Let us all our work fulfil;

6 Never from our office move,
Needful to each other prove;
Use the grace on each bestowed,
Tempered by the art of God.

7 Sweetly may we all agree,
Touched with softest sympathy;
Kindly for each other care;
Every member feel its share

8 Wounded by the grief of one,
Now let all the members groan ;
Honoured if one member is,
All partake the common bliss.

9 Many are we now and one,
We who Jesus have put on ;
There is neither bond nor free,
Male nor female, Lord, in thee !

10 Love, like death, hath all destroyed,
Rendered all distinctions void ;
Names, and sects, and parties fall :
Thou, O Christ, art all in all !

519

The Love-Feast. 8 - 7 s.

1 COME, and let us sweetly join
Christ to praise in hymns divine !
Give we all, with one accord,
Glory to our common Lord ;
Hands, and hearts, and voices raise ;
Sing as in the ancient days ;
Antedate the joys above,
Celebrate the feast of love.

2 Strive we, in affection strive ;
Let the purer flame revive,
Such as in the martyrs glowed,
Dying champions for their God :
We, like them, may live and love ;
Called we are their joys to prove,
Saved with them from future wrath.
Partners of like precious faith.

3 Sing we then in Jesu's name,
Now as yesterday the same ;
One in every time and place,
Full for all of truth and grace :
We for Christ, our Master, stand,
Lights in a benighted land :
We our dying Lord confess ;
We are Jesu's witnesses.

4 Witnesses that Christ hath died,
We with him are crucified ;
Christ hath burst the bands of death,
We his quickening Spirit breathe ;
Christ is now gone up on high,
Thither all our wishes fly ;
Sits at God's right hand above ;
There with him we reign in love !

520

SECOND PART. 8 - 7 s.

1 COME, thou high and lofty Lord !
Lowly, meek, incarnate Word !
Humbly stoop to earth again,
Come and visit abject men !
Jesus, dear expected guest,
Thou art bidden to the feast,
For thyself our hearts prepare,
Come, and sit, and banquet there !

2 Jesus, we thy promise claim,
We are met in thy great name ;
In the midst do thou appear,
Manifest thy presence here !
Sanctify us, Lord, and bless,
Breathe thy Spirit, give thy peace,
Thou thyself within us move,
Make our feast a feast of love.

3 Let the fruits of grace abound ;
Let in us thy bowels sound ;
E

Faith, and love, and joy increase,
Temperance and gentleness ;
Plant in us thy humble mind ;
Patient, pitiful, and kind,
Meek and lowly let us be,
Full of goodness, full of thee.

4 Make us all in thee complete,
Make us all for glory meet,
Meet to appear before thy sight,
Partners with the saints in light.
Call, O call us each by name,
To the marriage of the Lamb ;
Let us lean upon thy breast,
Love be there our endless feast !

521

8 - 7 s. THIRD PART.

1 LET us join, ('tis God commands)
Let us join our hearts and hands ;
Help to gain our calling's hope,
Build we each the other up :
God his blessings shall dispense,
God shall crown his ordinance ;
Meet in his appointed ways :
Nourish us with social ce.

2 Let us then as brethren love,
Faithfully his gifts improve,
Carry on the earnest strife,
Walk in holiness of life ;
Still forget the things behind,
Follow Christ in heart and mind,
Toward the mark unwearied press,
Seize the crown of righteousness.

3 Plead we thus for faith alone,
Faith which by our works is shown :
God it is who justifies ;
Only faith the grace applies ;
Active faith that lives within,
Conquers earth, and hell, and sin,
Sanctifies, and makes us whole,
Forms the Saviour in the soul.

4 Let us for this faith contend,
Sure salvation is its end :
Heaven already is begun,
Everlasting life is won.
Only let us persevere,
Till we see our Lord appear,
Never from the rock remove,
Saved by faith, which works by love.

522

8 - 7 s. FOURTH PART.

1 PARTNERS of a glorious hope,
Lift your hearts and voices up,
Jointly let us rise, and sing
Christ our Prophet, Priest, and King !
Monuments of Jesu's grace,
Speak we by our lives his praise ;
Walk in him we have received,
Show we not in vain believed.

2 While we walk with God in light,
God our hearts doth still unite ;
Dearest fellowship we prove,
Fellowship in Jesu's love :
Sweetly each, with each combined,
In the bonds of duty joined,
Feels the cleansing blood applied,
Daily feels that Christ hath died.

3 Still, O Lord, our faith increase,
Cleanse from all unrighteousness.

Thee the unholy cannot see:
Make, O make us meet for thee!
Every vile affection kill,
Root out every seed of ill,
Utterly abolish sin,
Write thy law of love within.

4 Hence may all our actions flow,
Love the proof that Christ we know;
Mutual love the token be,
Lord, that we belong to.thee:
Love, thine image, love impart!
Stamp it on our face and heart!
Only love to us be given!
Lord, we ask no other heaven.

523   L. M.

1 O THOU, our Husband, Brother, Friend,
    Behold a cloud of incense rise!
The prayers of saints to heaven ascend,
    Grateful, accepted sacrifice.

2 Regard our prayers for Zion's peace;
    Shed in our hearts thy love abroad;
Thy gifts abundantly increase:
    Enlarge, and fill us all with God.

3 Before thy sheep, great Shepherd, go,
    And guide into thy perfect will;
Cause us thy hallowed name to know,
    The work of faith in us fulfil.

4 Help us to make our calling sure;
    O let us all be saints indeed,
And pure as thou thyself art pure,
    Conformed in all things to our Head!

5 Take the dear purchase of thy blood:
    Thy blood shall wash us white as snow;
Present us sanctified to God,
    And perfected in love below.

6 That blood which cleanses from all sin,
    That efficacious blood apply,
And wash, and make us wholly clean,
    And change, and thoroughly sanctify.

7 From all iniquity redeem,
    Cleanse by the water and the word,
And free from every spot of blame,
    And make the servant as his Lord!

524   6 - 8 s.   Second Metre.

1 OUR friendship sanctify and guide:
    Unmixed with selfishness and pride,
Thy glory be our single aim!
In all our intercourse below,
Still let us in thy footsteps go,
 . And never meet but in thy name.
Fix on thyself our single eye:
Still let us on thyself rely,
    For all the help that each conveys,
The help as from thy hand receive,
And still to thee all glory give,
    All thanks, all might, all love, all praise.

2 Whate'er thou dost on one bestow,
Let each the double blessing know;
    Let each the common burden bear;
In comforts and in griefs agree;
And wrestle for his friends with thee,
    In all the omnipotence of prayer.
  124

Our mutual prayer accept and seal;
In all thy glorious self reveal:
    All with the fire of love baptize:
Thy kingdom in our souls restore;
And keep till we can sin no more,
    Till all in thy whole image rise.

3 Witnesses of the all-cleansing blood,
Long may we work the works of God,
    And do thy will like those above;
Together spread the gospel sound,
And scatter peace on all around,
    And joy, and happiness, and love.
True yoke-fellows, by love compelled
To labour in the gospel field,
    Our all let us delight to spend
In gathering thy lambs and sheep;
Assured that thou our souls wilt keep,
    Wilt keep us faithful to the end.

525   6 - 8 s.   Revelation xxii. 21.

1 JESU, thou great redeeming Lord,
    The kingdom of thy peace restored
Let all thy followers perceive,
And happy in thy Spirit live;
Retain the grace through thee bestowed,
The favour and the power of God.

2 Give all thy saints to find in thee
The fulness of the Deity;
His nature, life, and mind to prove,
In perfect holiness and love:
Fountain of grace, thyself make known
With God and man for ever one.

3 Still with and in thy people dwell;
Thy gracious plenitude reveal;
Till coming with thy heavenly train
We eye to eye behold the Man,
And share thy majesty divine,
And mount our thrones encircling thine.

526   8 s & 6 s.

1 EXCEPT the Lord conduct the plan,
    The best concerted schemes are vain,
    And never can succeed;   [nought;
We spend our wretched strength for
But if our works in thee be wrought,
    They shall be blest indeed.

2 Lord, if thou didst thyself inspire
Our souls with this intense desire
Thy goodness to proclaim,
Thy glory if we now intend,
O let our deed begin and end
    Complete in Jesu's name!

3 In Jesu's name, behold, we meet,
Far from an evil world retreat,
    And all its frantic ways;
One only thing resolved to know,
And square our useful lives below
    By reason and by grace.

4 Not in the tombs we pine to dwell,
Not in the dark monastic cell,
    By vows and grates confined;
Freely to all ourselves we give,
Constrained by Jesu's love to live
    The servants of mankind.

5 Now, Jesus, now thy love impart,
To govern each devoted heart,
    And fit us for thy will:

Deep founded in the truth of grace,
Build up thy rising church, and place
The city on the hill.

6 O let our faith and love abound!
O let our lives to all around
With purest lustre shine!
That all around our works may see,
And give the glory, Lord, to thee,
The heavenly light divine.

527
8 s & 6 s.

1 COME, wisdom, power, and grace
divine,
Come, Jesus, in thy name to join
A happy chosen band;
Who fain would prove thine utmost will,
And all thy righteous laws fulfil,
In love's benign command.

2 If pure essential love thou art,
Thy nature into every heart,
Thy loving self, inspire;
Bid all our simple souls be one,
United in a bond unknown,
Baptized with heavenly fire.

3 Still may we to our centre tend,
To spread thy praise our common end,
To help each other on;
Companions through the wilderness,
To share a moment's pain, and seize
An everlasting crown.

4 Jesus, our tendered souls prepare!
Infuse the softest social care,
The warmest charity,
The pity of the bleeding Lamb,
The virtues of thy wondrous name,
The heart that was in thee.

5 Supply what every member wants;
To found the fellowship of saints,
Thy Spirit, Lord, supply;
So shall we all thy love receive,
Together to thy glory live,
And to thy glory die.

528
8 s & 6 s.

1 O SAVIOUR, cast a gracious smile!
Our gloomy guilt, and selfish guile,
And shy distrust remove;
The true simplicity impart,
To fashion every passive heart,
And mould it into love.

2 Our naked hearts to thee we raise;
Whate'er obstructs thy work of grace,
For ever drive it hence;
Exert thy all-subduing power,
And each regenerate soul restore
To child-like innocence.

3 Soon as in thee we gain a part,
Our spirit purged from nature's art
Appears, by grace forgiven;
We then pursue our sole design,
To lose our melting will in thine,
And want no other heaven.

4 O that we now the power might feel
To do on earth thy blessed will,
As angels do above!

In thee, the Life, the Truth, the Way,
To walk, and perfectly to obey
Thy sweet constraining love!

5 Jesus, fulfil our one desire,
And spread the spark of living fire
Through every hallowed breast;
Bless with divine conformity,
And give us now to find in thee
Our everlasting rest.

529
3 - 7 s.

1 HOLY Lamb, who thee confess,
Followers of thy holiness,
Thee they ever keep in view,
Ever ask, "What shall we do?"
Governed by thy only will,
All thy words we would fulfil,
Would in all thy footsteps go,
Walk as Jesus walked below.

2 While thou didst on earth appear,
Servant to thy servants here,
Mindful of thy place above,
All thy life was prayer and love.
Such our whole employment be,
Works of faith and charity;
Works of love on man bestowed,
Secret intercourse with God.

3 Early in the temple met,
Let us still our Saviour greet;
Nightly to the mount repair,
Join our praying pattern there.
There by wrestling faith obtain
Power to work for God again,
Power his image to retrieve,
Power, like thee, our Lord, to live.

4 Vessels, instruments of grace,
Pass we thus our happy days
'Twixt the mount and multitude,
Doing or receiving good;
Glad to pray and labour on,
Till our earthly course is run,
Till we, on the sacred tree,
Bow the head and die like thee.

530
8 s & 7 s.

1 COME, thou all-inspiring Spirit,
Into every longing heart!
Bought for us by Jesu's merit,
Now thy blissful self impart;
Sign our uncontested pardon,
Wash us in the atoning blood!
Make our hearts a watered garden;
Fill our spotless souls with God.

2 If thou gav'st the enlarged desire,
Which for thee we ever feel,
Now our panting souls inspire,
Now our cancelled sin reveal;
Claim us for thy habitation;
Dwell within our hallowed breast;
Seal us heirs of full salvation,
Fitted for our heavenly rest.

3 Give us quietly to tarry,
Till for all thy glory meet,
Waiting, like attentive Mary,
Happy at the Saviour's feet;

125

Keep us from the world unspotted,
From all earthly passions free,
Wholly to thyself devoted,
Fixed to live and die for thee.

4 Wrestling on in mighty prayer,
Lord, we will not let thee go,
Till thou all thy mind declare,
All thy grace on us bestow;
Peace, the seal of sin forgiven,
Joy, and perfect love impart,
Present, everlasting heaven,
All thou hast, and all thou art!

531　　Ezekiel xxxiv. 29, 30.　7 s & 6 s t

1 CHRIST, whose glory fills the skies,
That famous Plant thou art:
Tree of Life eternal, rise
In every longing heart!
Bid us find the food in thee
For which our deathless spirits pine,
Fed with immortality,
And filled with love divine.

2 Long we have our burden borne,
Our own unfaithfulness,
Object of the heathen's scorn,
Who mocked our scanty grace;
Jesus, our reproach remove;
Let sin no more thy people shame!
Show us rooted in thy love,
In life and death the same.

3 In thy spotless people show
Thy power and constancy;
Give us thus to feel and know
Our fellowship with thee:
Give us all thy mind to express,
And blameless in our Lord to abide,
Transcripts of thy holiness,
Thy fair, unspotted bride.

532　　Jeremiah l. 5.　C. M.

1 COME, let us use the grace divine,
And all, with one accord,
In a perpetual covenant join
Ourselves to CHRIST the LORD:

2 Give up ourselves, through Jesu's power,
His name to glorify;
And promise, in this sacred hour,
For GOD to live and die.

3 The covenant we this moment make
Be ever kept in mind:
We will no more our God forsake,
Or cast his words behind.

4 We never will throw off his fear
Who hears our solemn vow:
And if thou art well-pleased to hear,
Come down, and meet us now!

5 Thee, Father, Son, and Holy Ghost,
Let all our hearts receive;
Present with the celestial host,
The peaceful answer give!

6 To each the covenant blood apply,
Which takes our sins away;
And register our names on high,
And keep us to that day!
136

SECTION IV.

FOR THE SOCIETY AT PARTING.

533
4-6 s & 2-8 s.

1 LORD, we thy will obey,
And in thy pleasure rest;
We, only we, can say,
"Whatever is, is best;"
Joyful to meet, willing to part,
Convinced we still are one in heart.

2 Hereby we sweetly know
Our love proceeds from thee,
We let each other go,
From every creature free:
And cry, in answer to thy call,
"Thou art, O Christ, our all in all!"

3 Our Husband, Brother, Friend,
Our Counsellor divine!
Thy chosen ones depend
On no support but thine:
Our everlasting Comforter!
We cannot want, if thou art here.

4 Still let us, gracious Lord,
Sit loose to all below;
And to thy love restored,
No other portion know;
Stand fast in glorious liberty,
And live and die wrapped up in thee!

534
C. M.

1 BLEST be the dear uniting love,
That will not let us part!
Our bodies may far off remove,
We still are one in heart.

2 Joined in one spirit to our Head,
Where he appoints we go;
And still in Jesu's footsteps tread,
And show his praise below.

3 O may we ever walk in him,
And nothing know beside;
Nothing desire, nothing esteem,
But Jesus crucified.

4 Closer and closer let us cleave
To his beloved embrace:
Expect his fulness to receive
And grace to answer grace.

5 Partakers of the Saviour's grace,
The same in mind and heart,
Nor joy, nor grief, nor time, nor place,
Nor life, nor death can part.

6 But let us hasten to the day
Which shall our flesh restore,
When death shall all be done away,
And bodies part no more!

535
S. M.

1 AND let our bodies part,
To different climes repair!
Inseparably joined in heart
The friends of Jesus are!
Jesus, the corner-stone,
Did first our hearts unite,
And still he keeps our spirits one,
Who walk with him in white.

2 O let us still proceed
  In Jesu's work below ;
And, following our triumphant Head,
  To farther conquests go !
The vineyard of their Lord
  Before his labourers lies ;
And, lo ! we see the vast reward
  Which waits us in the skies.

3 O let our heart and mind
  Continually ascend,
That haven of repose to find
  Where all our labours end ;
  Where all our toils are o'er,
  Our suffering and our pain !
Who meet on that eternal shore
  Shall never part again.

4 O happy, happy place,
  Where saints and angels meet !
There we shall see each other's face,
  And all our brethren greet :
  The church of the first-born,
  We shall with them be blest,
And, crowned with endless joy, return
  To our eternal rest.

5 With joy we shall behold,
  In yonder blest abode,
The patriarchs and prophets old,
  And all the saints of God.
  Abraham and Isaac there,
  And Jacob, shall receive
The followers of their faith and prayer,
  Who now in bodies live.

6 We shall our time beneath
  Live out in cheerful hope,
And fearless pass the vale of death,
  And gain the mountain-top.
  To gather home his own
  God shall his angels send,
And bid our bliss, on earth begun,
  In deathless triumph end.

536

4 · 6 s & 2 - 8 s.

1 JESUS, accept the praise
    That to thy name belongs ;
Matter of all our lays,
    Subject of all our songs :
Through thee we now together came,
And part exulting in thy name.

2 In flesh we part awhile,
    But still in spirit joined,
To embrace the happy toil
    Thou hast to each assigned ;
And while we do thy blessed will,
We bear our heaven about us still.

3 O let us thus go on
    In all thy pleasant ways,
And, armed with patience, run
    With joy the appointed race !
Keep us, and every seeking soul,
Till all attain the heavenly goal.

4 There we shall meet again,
    When all our toils are o'er,
And death, and grief, and pain,
    And parting are no more ;
We shall with all our brethren rise,
And grasp thee in the flaming skies.

5 O happy, happy day,
  That calls thy exiles home !
The heavens shall pass away,
  The earth receive its doom ;
Earth we shall view, and heaven destroyed,
And shout above the fiery void.

6 These eyes shall see them fall,
  Mountains, and stars, and skies !
These eyes shall see them all
  Out of their ashes rise !
These lips his praises shall rehearse,
Whose nod restores the universe.

7 According to his word,
  His oath to sinners given,
We look to see restored
  The ruined earth and heaven !
In a new world his truth to prove,
A world of righteousness and love.

8 Then let us wait the sound
  That shall our souls release ;
And labour to be found
  Of him in spotless peace,
In perfect holiness renewed,
Adorned with Christ, and meet for God.

C. M.   ## 537

1 GOD of all consolation, take
    The glory of thy grace !
Thy gifts to thee we render back
    In ceaseless songs of praise.

2 Through thee we now together came,
    In singleness of heart :
We met, O Jesus, in thy name,
    And in thy name we part.

3 We part in body, not in mind,
    Our minds continue one ;
And, each to each in Jesus joined,
    We hand in hand go on.

4 Subsists as in us all one soul,
    No power can make us twain ;
And mountains rise and oceans roll
    To sever us, in vain.

5 Present we still in spirit are,
    And intimately nigh,
While on the wings of faith and prayer
    We each to other fly.

6 Our life is hid with Christ in God ;
    Our Life shall soon appear,
And shed his glory all abroad
    In all his members here.

7 The heavenly treasure now we have
    In a vile house of clay ;
But he shall to the utmost save,
    And keep it to that day.

8 Our souls are in his mighty hand,
    And he shall keep them still ;
And you and I shall surely stand
    With him on Zion's hill !

9 Him eye to eye we there shall see,
    Our face like his shall shine :
O what a glorious company,
    When saints and angels join !

10 O what a joyful meeting there !
    In robes of white arrayed,
Palms in our hands we all shall bear
    And crowns upon our head.!

27

11 Then let us lawfully contend,
    And fight our passage through ;
Bear in our faithful minds the end,
    And keep the prize in view.

12 Then let us hasten to the day
    When all shall be brought home ;
Come, O Redeemer, come away,
    O Jesus, quickly come !

538

8 - 7 s.

1 JESUS, soft, harmonious name,
    Every faithful heart's desire ;
See thy followers, O Lamb !
    All at once to thee aspire :
Drawn by thy uniting grace,
    After thee we swiftly run,
Hand in hand we seek thy face :
    Come, and perfect us in one.

2 Mollify our harsher will ;
    Each to each our tempers suit,
By thy modulating skill,
    Heart to heart, as lute to lute :
Sweetly on our spirits move,
    Gently touch the trembling strings ;
Make the harmony of love,
    Music for the King of kings.

3 See the souls that hang on thee !
    Severed though in flesh we are,
Joined in spirit all agree ;
    All thy only love declare ;
Spread thy love to all around :
    Hark ! we now our voices raise !
Joyful consentaneous sound,
    Sweetest symphony of praise.

4 Jesu's praise be all our song ;
    While we Jesu's praise repeat,
Glide our happy hours along,
    Glide with down upon their feet !
Far from sorrow, sin, and fear,
    Till we take our seats above,
Live we all as angels here,
    Only sing, and praise, and love.

128

C. M.

539

1 LIFT up your hearts to things above,
    Ye followers of the Lamb,
And join with us to praise his love,
    And glorify his name.

2 To Jesus's name give thanks and sing,
    Whose mercies never end :
Rejoice ! rejoice ! the Lord is king ;
    The King is now our friend !

3 We, for his sake, count all things loss ;
    On earthly good look down ;
And joyfully sustain the cross,
    Till we receive the crown.

4 O let us stir each other up,
    Our faith by works to approve,
By holy, purifying hope,
    And the sweet task of love !

5 Love us, though far in flesh disjoined,
    Ye lovers of the Lamb ;
And ever bear us on your mind,
    Who think and speak the same :

6 You on our minds we ever bear,
    Whoe'er to Jesus bow ;
Stretch out the arms of faith and prayer,
    And lo ! we reach you now.

7 Surely we now your souls embrace,
    With you we now appear
Present before the throne of grace,
    And you, and Christ, are here.

8 The blessings all on you be shed,
    Which God in Christ imparts ;
We pray the Spirit of our Head
    Into your faithful hearts.

9 Mercy and peace your portion be,
    To carnal minds unknown,
The hidden manna, and the tree
    Of life, and the white stone.

10 Live till the Lord in glory come,
    And wait his heaven to share :
Our Saviour now prepares our home :
    Go on ;—we'll meet you there.

S^{UPP}LEME^{NT}.

SECTION I.

SELECT PSALMS.

540

Psalm i.   C. M.

1 HOW blest is he who ne'er consents
     By ill advice to walk;
Nor stands in sinners' ways, nor sits
     Where men profanely talk.

2 But makes the perfect law of God
     His study and delight;
Devoutly reads therein by day,
     And meditates by night.

3 Like some fair tree which, fed by streams,
     With timely fruit doth bend,
He still shall flourish, and success
     All his designs attend.

4 Ungodly men and their attempts
     No lasting root shall find,
Untimely withered, and dispersed
     Like chaff before the wind.

5 Their guilt shall strike the wicked dumb
     Before their Judge's face;
No formal hypocrite shall then
     Among the saints have place.

6 For God approves the just man's ways,
     To happiness they tend;
But sinners and the paths they tread
     Shall both in ruin end.

541

Psalm ii.   6 - 8 s.

1 HOW are the Gentiles all on fire!
     Why rage they with vain menacing?
'Gainst God, and his Anointed King,
Earth's haughty potentates conspire;
Break we (say they) their servile bands,
And cast their cords from our free hands.

2 But God from his celestial throne
Shall laugh, and their attempts deride;
Then high incensed thus check their pride,
(His wrath in their confusion shown)
Lo! I my King have crowned, and will
Enthrone, on Zion's sacred hill.

3 That great decree I shall declare;
For thus I heard Jehovah say,
"Thou art my Son, begot this day;
Request, and I will grant thy prayer,
Subject all nations to thy throne,
And make the sea-bound earth thine own.

4 "Thou shalt an iron sceptre sway,
As earthen vessels, break their bones;"
Be wise then, ye who sit on thrones,
And judges grave, advice obey;
With joyful fear O serve the Lord!
With trembling joy embrace his Word.

5 In reverent homage kiss the Son,
     Lest he his wrathful looks display,
And so ye perish in the way,
His anger newly but begun;
Then blessed only are the just,
Who on the Anointed fix their trust.

6 - 7 s.   **Psalm iii.**   **542**

1 THOU, Lord, art a shield for me,
     Succour still I find in thee;
Now thou liftest up my head,
Now I glory in thine aid,
Confident in thy defence,
Strong in thine omnipotence.

2 To the Lord I cried; the cry
Brought my helper from the sky;
By my kind protector kept,
Safe I laid me down and slept,
Slept within his arms, and rose;
Blest him for the sweet repose.

3 Thine it is, O Lord, to save;
Strength in thee thy people have;
Safe from sin in thee they rest,
With the gospel-blessing blest,
Wait to see the perfect grace,
Heaven on earth in Jesu's face.

C. M.   **Psalm v.**   **543**

1 ON thee, O God of purity,
     I wait for hallowing grace;
None without holiness shall see
     The glories of thy face:

2 In souls unholy and unclean
     Thou never canst delight;
Nor shall they, while unsaved from sin,
     Appear before thy sight.

3 Thou hatest all that evil do,
     Or speak iniquity,
The heart unkind, the heart untrue,
     Are both abhorred by thee.

4 But as for me, with humble fear
     I will approach thy gate,
Though most unworthy to draw near,
     Or in thy courts to wait;

5 I trust in thy unbounded grace,
     To all so freely given,
And worship toward thy holy place,
     And lift my soul to heaven.

6 Lead me in all thy righteous ways,
     Nor suffer me to slide,
Point out the path before my face;
     My God, be thou my guide!

7 All those that put their trust in thee,
   Thy mercy shall proclaim,
And sing with cheerful melody
   Their great Redeemer's name.

8 Protected by thy guardian grace,
   They shall extol thy power,
Rejoice, give thanks, and shout thy praise,
   And triumph evermore.

544   Psalm viii.   C. M.

1 O LORD, how good, how great art thou,
   In heaven and earth the same 1
There angels at thy footstool bow,
   Here babes thy grace proclaim.

2 When glorious in the nightly sky
   Thy moon and stars I see,
O what is man 1 I wondering cry,
   To be so loved by thee 1

3 To him thou hourly deign'st to give
   New mercies from on high ;
Didst quit thy throne with him to live,
   For him in pain to die.

4 Close to thine own bright seraphim
   His favoured path is trod ;
And all beside are serving him,
   That he may serve his God.

O Lord, how good, how great art thou,
   In heaven and earth the same 1
There angels at thy footstool bow,
   Here babes thy grace proclaim.

545   Psalm ix.   6 - 8 s.   Second Metre.

1 THEE will I praise with all my heart,
   And tell mankind how good thou art,
How marvellous thy works of grace ;
Thy name I will in songs record,
And joy and glory in my Lord,
 · Extolled above all thanks and praise.

2 The Lord will save his people here ;
   In times of need their Help is near,
To all by sin and hell oppressed :
And they that know thy name will trust
In thee, who to thy promise just
   Hast never left a soul distressed.

3 The Lord is by his judgments known ;
   He helps his poor afflicted one,
His sorrows all he bears in mind ;
The mourner shall not always weep,
Who sows in tears in joy shall reap,
   With grief who seeks with joy shall find.

4 A helpless soul that looks to thee
   Is sure at last thy face to see,
And all thy goodness to partake ;
The sinner who for thee doth grieve,
And longs, and labours to believe,
   Thou never, never wilt forsake.

546   Psalm x.   C. M.

1 O GOD, the help of all thy saints,
   Our hope in time of ill :
We trust thee, though thy face be hid,
   And seek thy presence still.

2 Why should the men of pride and sin
   Thy truth and power defy ;

130

And boast, as if their evil way
   Were hidden from thine eye ?

3 Lord, thou hast seen ; arise and save ;
   To thee our cause we bring ;
Reign thou in righteousness and power,
   For thou alone art King.

4 All our desires to thee are known ;
   Thy help is ever near ;
O first prepare our hearts to pray,
   And then accept our prayer 1

547   L. M.   Psalm xiii.

1 HOW long wilt thou forget me, Lord?
   Wilt thou for ever hide thy face ?
Leave me unchanged, and unrestored,
   An alien from the life of grace ?

2 How long shall I inquire within,
   And seek thee in my heart, in vain,
Vexed with the dire remains of sin,
   Galled with the tyrant's iron chain ?

3 How long shall Satan's rage prevail ?
   (I ask thee with a faltering tongue)
See at thy feet my spirit fail,
   And hear me feebly groan, "How long?"

4 Ah 1 suffer not my foe to boast
   His victory o'er a child of thine ;
Nor let the proud Philistines' host,
   In Satan's hellish triumph join.

5 Will they not charge my fall on thee ?
   Will they not dare my God to blame ?
My God, forbid the blasphemy,
   Be jealous for thy glorious name 1

6 My trust is in thy gracious power,
   I glory in salvation near ;
Rejoice in hope of that glad hour
   When perfect love shall cast out fear.

7 I sing the goodness of the Lord,
   The goodness I experience now ;
And still I hang upon thy word,
   My Saviour to the utmost thou 1

548   8 s & 6 s.   Psalm xvi.

1 O LORD, thy faithful servant save,
   Faith in thy name thou know'st I have;
My soul hath called thee mine :
My good cannot to thee extend,
My good did first from thee descend,
   And all I have is thine.

2 The Lord himself my portion is ;
   Thou reachest out my cup of bliss,
   And wilt no more remove ;
My fair inheritance thou art ;
The needful thing, the better part,
   I find in perfect love.

3 The Lord I will for ever bless ;
   The Counsellor and Prince of peace,
   He teaches me his will ;
He doth with nightly pains chastise,
And makes me to salvation wise
   By every scourge I feel.

4 Him have I set before my face,
   The pardoning God of boundless grace,
   Of everlasting love ;
By faith I always see him stand,
And with him placed on my right hand
   I never shall remove.

5 Wherefore my heart doth now rejoice ;
  I wait to hear thy quickening voice ;
  My flesh exults in hope ;
  Thou wilt not leave me in the grave ;
  Sure confidence in thee I have
  That thou wilt raise me up.

6 Thou wilt the path of life display,
  And lead me in thyself the way,
  Till all thy grace is given :
  Fulness of joy with thee there is ;
  Thy presence makes the perfect bliss,
  And where thou art is heaven.

549
Another.   C. M.

1 SAVE me, O God ; for thou alone
  My tower of refuge art ;
  Thou art my Lord, my only good ;
  I bless thee from my heart.

2 The Lord alone shall be my cup,
  And mine inheritance :
  And thou art he that guards my lot
  From every evil chance.

3 The fields wherein my lot is cast
  In loveliness excel,
  And in her pleasant heritage
  My soul delights to dwell.

4 I thank the Lord who teacheth me
  To read his will aright ;
  Yea, by his blessing do my reins
  Correct me every night.

5 I set the Lord before my face,
  And trust in him alone ;
  At my right hand the Lord doth stand ;
  I shall not be o'erthrown.

6 Therefore my heart is very glad ;
  My spirit shall rejoice ;
  My flesh in tranquil hope shall rest,
  For thou wilt crown thy choice.

7 The path of life thou wilt display,
  And keep for me in store
  The fulness of thy joy, and peace
  With thee for evermore.

550
Psalm xvi. 8.   8 s & 6 s.

1 O THAT I could, in every place,
  By faith behold Jehovah's face,
  My strict observer see ;
  Present my heart and reins to try,
  And feel the influence of his eye
  For ever fixed on me !

2 Discerning thee, my Saviour, stand
  My Advocate at God's right hand,
  I never shall remove ;
  I cannot fall, upheld by thee,
  Or sin against the majesty
  Of omnipresent love.

3 Now, Saviour, now appear, appear !
  And let me always see thee near,
  And know as I am known :
  My spirit to thyself unite,
  And bear me through a sea of light
  To that eternal throne.

551
Psalm xviii.   C. M.

1 O GOD, my strength and fortitude,
  In truth I will love thee ;
  E 2

Thou art my castle and defence
  In my necessity.

2 When I, beset with pain and grief
  Prayed to my God for grace ;
  Forthwith my God heard my complaint,
  Out of his holy place.

3 The Lord descended from above,
  And bowed the heavens high,
  And underneath his feet he cast
  The darkness of the sky.

4 On cherub and on cherubim
  Full royally he rode ;
  And on the wings of all the winds
  Came flying all abroad.

5 He brought me forth in open place,
  That so I might be free ;
  And kept me safe, because he had
  A favour unto me.

6 Unspotted are the ways of God,
  His word is truly tried ;
  He is a sure defence to such
  As in his ways abide.

552
L. M.   Psalm xix.

1 THE spacious firmament on high,
  With all the blue ethereal sky,
  And spangled heavens, a shining frame,
  Their great original proclaim.

2 The unwearied sun, from day to day,
  Does his Creator's power display ;
  And publishes to every land
  The work of an almighty hand.

3 Soon as the evening shades prevail,
  The moon takes up the wondrous tale,
  And nightly to the listening earth
  Repeats the story of her birth :

4 Whilst all the stars that round her burn,
  And all the planets in their turn,
  Confirm the tidings as they roll,
  And spread the truth from pole to pole.

5 What though in solemn silence all
  Move round this dark terrestrial ball ;
  What though no real voice or sound
  Amidst their radiant orbs be found ;

6 In reason's ear they all rejoice,
  And utter forth a glorious voice,
  For ever singing as they shine,
  " The hand that made us is divine."

553
L. M.   Another.

1 THE heavens declare thy glory, Lord,
  In every star thy wisdom shines ;
  But when our eyes behold thy word,
  We read thy name in fairer lines.

2 The rolling sun, the changing light,
  And night and day, thy power confess ;
  But the blest volume thou hast writ
  Reveals thy justice and thy grace.

3 Sun, moon, and stars convey thy praise
  Round the whole earth, and never stand ;
  So when thy truth began its race,
  It touched and glanced on every land.

4 Nor shall thy spreading gospel rest
  Till through the world thy truth has run ;
  Till Christ has all the nations blest
  That see the light or feel the sun.

5 Great Sun of righteousness, arise,
Bless the dark world with heavenly light:
Thy gospel makes the simple wise;
Thy laws are pure, thy judgments right.

554   Psalm xxiii.   6 - 7 s.

1 JESUS the good Shepherd is;
    Jesus died the sheep to save;
He is mine, and I am his;
    All I want in him I have,
Life, and health, and rest, and food,
All the plenitude of God.

2 Jesus loves and guards his own;
    Me in verdant pastures feeds;
Makes me quietly lie down,
    By the streams of comfort leads:
Following him where'er he goes,
Silent joy my heart o'erflows.

3 He in sickness makes me whole,
    Guides into the paths of peace;
He revives my fainting soul,
    Stablishes in righteousness;
Who for me vouchsafed to die,
Loves me still,—I know not why!

4 Unappalled by guilty fear,
    Through the mortal vale I go;
My eternal Life is near;
    Thee, my Life, in death I know;
Bless thy chastening, cheering rod,
Die into the arms of God!

5 Till that welcome hour I see,
    Thou before my foes dost feed;
Bidd'st me sit and feast with thee,
    Pour'st thy oil upon my head;
Giv'st me all I ask, and more,
Mak'st my cup of joy run o'er.

6 Love divine shall still embrace,
    Love shall keep me to the end;
Surely all my happy days
    I shall in thy temple spend,
Till I to thy house remove,
Thy eternal house above!

555   *Another.*   C. M.

1   Shepherd will supply my need,
MY JEHOVAH is his name;
In pastures fresh he makes me feed,
    Beside the living stream.

2 He brings my wandering spirit back,
    When I forsake his ways;
And leads me, for his mercy's sake,
    In paths of truth and grace.

3 When I walk through the shades of death,
    Thy presence is my stay:
A word of thy supporting breath
    Drives all my fears away.

4 Thy hand, in sight of all my foes,
    Doth now my table spread:
My cup with blessings overflows,
    Thine oil anoints my head.

5 The sure provisions of my God
    Attend me all my days:
O may thine house be mine abode,
    And all my work be praise!

132

C. M.   *Another.*   556

1 THE Lord's my shepherd, I'll not want,
    He makes me down to lie
In pastures green; he leadeth me
    The quiet waters by.

2 My soul he doth restore again,
    And me to walk doth make
Within the paths of righteousness,
    Even for his own name's sake.

3 Yea, though I walk in death's dark vale,
    Yet will I fear no ill:
For thou art with me, and thy rod
    And staff me comfort still.

4 My table thou hast furnished
    In presence of my foes;
My head thou dost with oil anoint,
    And my cup overflows.

5 Goodness and mercy all my life
    Shall surely follow me,
And in God's house for evermore
    My dwelling-place shall be.

L. M.   Psalm xxiv.   557

1 THE earth with all her fulness owns
    Jehovah for her sovereign Lord;
The countless myriads of her sons
    Rose into being at his word.

2 His word did out of nothing call
    The world, and founded all that is;
Launched on the floods this solid ball,
    And fixed it in the floating seas.

3 But who shall quit this low abode,
    Who shall ascend the heavenly place,
And stand upon the mount of God,
    And see his Maker face to face?

4 The man whose hands and heart are clean
    That blessed portion shall receive;
Whoe'er by grace is saved from sin,
    Hereafter shall in glory live.

5 He shall obtain the starry crown;
    And, numbered with the saints above,
The God of his salvation own,
    The God of his salvation love.

L. M.   SECOND PART.

6 OUR Lord is risen from the dead!
    Our Jesus is gone up on high!
The powers of hell are captive led,
    Dragged to the portals of the sky;

7 There his triumphal chariot waits,
    And angels chant the solemn lay:
Lift up your heads, ye heavenly gates;
    Ye everlasting doors, give way!

8 Loose all your bars of massy light,
    And wide unfold the ethereal scene;
He claims these mansions as his right;
    Receive the King of glory in!

9 Who is this King of glory? Who?
    The Lord that all our foes o'ercame;
The world, sin, death, and hell o'erthrew;
    And Jesus is the Conqueror's name.

10 Lo! his triumphal chariot waits,
    And angels chant the solemn lay:
Lift up your heads, ye heavenly gates;
    Ye everlasting doors, give way!

11 Who is this King of glory? Who?
　The Lord, of glorious power possessed;
　The King of saints, and angels too,
　　God over all, for ever blessed!

558

Psalm xxvii.　　　C. M.

1 ONE thing with all my soul's desire
　　I sought, and will pursue;
What thine own Spirit doth inspire,
　Lord, for thy servant do.,

2 Grant me within thy courts a place,
　　Among thy saints a seat,
For ever to behold thy face,
　And worship at thy feet.

3 "Seek ye my face;"—without delay,
　　When thus I heard thee speak,
My heart would leap for joy, and say,
　"Thy face, Lord, will I seek."

4 Then leave me not when griefs assail,
　　And earthly comforts flee;
When father, mother, kindred fail,
　My God will think on me.

5 Oft had I fainted, and resigned
　　Of every hope my hold,
But mine afflictions brought to mind
　Thy benefits of old.

6 Wait on the Lord, with courage wait,
　　My soul, disdain to fear;
The righteous Judge is at the gate,
　And thy redemption near.

559

Psalm xxx.　　　L. M.

1 I PRAISE thee, Lord, who o'er my foes
　　Hast raised my head in triumph high,
Not slow to mark my secret woes,
　Not deaf to my desponding cry.
I praise thee, Lord; my heart was faint,
　My feet were sinking to the grave,
But thou wast nigh to hear my plaint,
　To hear, to heal me, and to save.

2 A moment, and thine anger dies;
　　Thy grace is life for evermore:
The sun may set on weeping eyes,
　But joy returns when night is o'er.
In song before the Lord rejoice,
　His praise let all his saints proclaim,
And still, with thankful heart and voice,
　Give glory to his holy name.

3 In prosperous times I dared to say
　　"My mountain stands for ever sure;"
But thou didst turn thy face away;—
　O grief too heavy to endure!
And then I raised my voice in prayer:
　"Lord, to my humble suit attend;
In pity yet thy servant spare,
　And be my helper, and my friend.

4 "What profit in my blood is found?
　　What voices from the tomb are heard?
Can dust to distant years resound
　The mercies of thy faithful word?"
Gladness for mourning thou hast given,
　That I may thank thee all my days,
And every saint in earth and heaven
　· Swell the loud anthem of thy praise.

S. M.　　　Psalm xxxi.　　**560**

1 MY spirit on thy care,
　　Blest Saviour, I recline;
.Thou wilt not leave me in despair,
　For thou art Love divine.

2 In thee I place my trust,
　　On thee I calmly rest;
I know thee good, I know thee just,
　And count thy choice the best.

3 Whate'er events betide,
　　Thy will they all perform;
Safe in thy breast my head I hide,
　Nor fear the coming storm.

4 Let good or ill befall,
　　It must be good for me;
Secure of having thee in all,
　Of having all in thee.

L. M.　　　Psalm xxxii.　　**561**

1 BLEST is the man, supremely blest,
　　Whose wickedness is all forgiven,
Who finds in Jesu's wounds his rest,
　And sees the smiling face of heaven.·

2 Blest is the man, to whom his Lord
　No more imputes iniquity,
Whose spirit is by grace restored,
　From all the guile of Satan free.

3 But while through pride I held my tongue,
　Nor owned my helpless unbelief,
My bones were wasted all day long,
　My strength consumed with pining grief

4 Resolved at last, "To God," I cried,
　"My sins I will at large confess;
My shame I will no longer hide,
　My depth of desperate wickedness.

5 "All will I own unto my Lord,
　Without reserve, or cloaking art:"
I said; and felt the pardoning word,
　Thy mercy spoke it to my heart.

6 For this shall every child of God
　Thy power and faithful love declare,
And claim the grace on all bestowed
　Who make to thee their timely prayer.

L. M.　　　SECOND PART.

7 THOU art my hiding-place: in thee
　　I rest secure from sin and hell;
Safe in the love that ransomed me,
　And sheltered in thy wounds, I dwell.

8 Still shall thy grace to me abound;
　The countless wonders of thy grace
I still shall tell to all around,
　And sing my great Deliverer's praise.

9 "I will instruct thy child-like heart,"
　(My Teacher saith, for ever nigh)
"Nor let thee from my paths depart,
　But guide thee with my gracious eye:

10 "Only my gracious look obey,
　And yield my perfect will to approve,
Nor cast my easy yoke away,
　Nor stop thine ears against my love."

11 Ye faithful souls, rejoice in him
　Whose arms are still your sure defence
Your Lord is mighty to redeem:
　Believe, and who shall pluck you thence

562   Psalm xxxiv.   C. M.

1 THROUGH all the changing scenes of life,
    In trouble and in joy,
The praises of my God shall still
    My heart and tongue employ.

2 Of his deliverance I will boast,
    Till all that are distressed
From my example comfort take,
    And charm their griefs to rest.

3 O magnify the Lord with me,
    With me exalt his name !
When in distress to him I called,
    He to my rescue came.

4 The hosts of God encamp around
    The dwellings of the just :
Deliverance he affords to all
    Who on his succour trust.

5 O make but trial of his love ;
    Experience will decide
How blessed they are, and only they,
    Who in his truth confide.

6 Fear him, ye saints, and you will then
    Have nothing else to fear ;
Make you his service your delight,
    He'll make your wants his care.

563   Psalm xxxvi.   L. M.

1 HIGH in the heavens, eternal God,
    Thy goodness in full glory shines ;
Thy truth shall break through every cloud
    That veils and darkens thy designs.

2 For ever firm thy justice stands,
    As mountains their foundations keep ;
Wise are the wonders of thy hands ;
    Thy judgments are a mighty deep.

3 Thy providence is kind and large,
    Both man and beast thy bounty share ;
The whole creation is thy charge,
    But saints are thy peculiar care.

4 My God, how excellent thy grace,
    Whence all our hope and comfort springs!
The sons of Adam in distress
    Fly to the shadow of thy wings.

5 Life, like a fountain rich and free,
    Springs from the presence of the Lord ;
And in thy light our souls shall see
    The glories promised in thy word.

564   Psalm xxxix.   L. M.

1 ALMIGHTY Maker of my frame,
    Teach me the measure of my days,
Teach me to know how frail I am,
    And spend the remnant to thy praise.

2 My days are shorter than a span ;
    A little point my life appears :
How frail, at best, is dying man !
    How vain are all his hopes and fears !

3 Vain his ambition, noise, and show ;
    Vain are the cares which rack his mind :
He heaps up treasures, mixed with woe,
    And dies, and leaves them all behind.

4 O be a nobler portion mine !
    My God, I bow before thy throne :
Earth's fleeting treasures I resign,
    And fix my hope on thee alone.

134

S. M.   *Another.*   **565**

1 LORD, let me know mine end,
    My days, how brief their date,
That I may timely comprehend
    How frail my best estate.

2 My life is but a span,
    Mine age as nought with thee ;
Man, in his highest honour, man
    Is dust and vanity.

3 A shadow even in health,
    Disquieted with pride,
Or racked with care, he heaps up wealth
    Which unknown heirs divide.

4 What seek I now, O Lord ?
    My hope is in thy Name ;
Blot out my sins from thy record,
    Nor give me up to shame.

5 Dumb at thy feet I lie,
    For thou hast brought me low ;
Remove thy judgments, lest I die,
    I faint beneath thy blow.

6 At thy rebuke the bloom
    Of man's vain beauty flies ;
And grief shall, like a moth, consume
    All that delights our eyes.

7 Have pity on my fears,
    Hearken to my request,
Turn not in silence from my tears,
    But give the mourner rest.

8 A stranger, Lord, with thee
    I walk in pilgrimage,
Where all my fathers once, like me,
    Sojourned from age to age.

9 O spare me yet, I pray ;
    Awhile my strength restore,
Ere I am summoned hence away,
    And seen on earth no more.

C. M.   Psalm xl.   **566**

1 DAY after day I sought the Lord,
    And waited patiently ;
Until he bent down from his throne,
    And hearkened to my cry.

2 He drew me from the fearful pit,
    And from the miry clay :
He placed my feet upon a rock,
    And led me in his way.

3 He taught my soul a new-made song,
    A song of holy praise,
All they who see these things, with fear
    Their hopes to God shall raise.

4 Most blessed is the man whose hope
    Upon the Lord relies ;
Who follows not the proud, nor those
    That turn aside to lies.

5 O Lord, what wonders hast thou wrought,
    All number far above !
Thy thoughts to us-ward overflow
    With mercy, grace, and love.

C. M.   SECOND PART.

6 SHOW forth thy mercy, gracious Lord ;
    O take it not away !
Thy loving-kindness and thy truth,
    Let them be still my stay.

7 For countless sorrows hem me round;
    And my iniquities
So hold me fast, and drag me down,
    I cannot raise my eyes:

8 My hairs in number they surpass;
    Hence is my heart dismayed;
Vouchsafe, O Lord, to rescue me!
    O hasten to my aid.

9 Let those who seek thee faithfully
    In peace and joy abide;
Let those who love thy grace still say,
    " The Lord be magnified."

10 Poor am I, and in need; yet God
    Care of my soul doth take.
Thou art my help; my Saviour thou;
    Lord, no long tarrying make.

567
Psalm xlii.   C. M.

1 AS pants the hart for cooling streams,
    When heated in the chase,
So longs my soul, O God, for thee,
    And thy refreshing grace.

2 For thee, my God, the living God,
    My thirsty soul doth pine;
O when shall I behold thy face,
    Thou Majesty divine!

3 God of my strength, how long shall I,
    Like one forgotten, mourn?
Forlorn, forsaken, and exposed
    To my oppressor's scorn.

4 Why restless, why cast down, my soul?
    Hope still, and thou shalt sing
The praise of him who is thy God,
    Thy health's eternal spring.

568
Psalm xlv.   6 - 8 s.

1 MY heart is full of Christ, and longs
    Its glorious matter to declare!
Of him I make my loftier songs,
    I cannot from his praise forbear;
My ready tongue makes haste to sing
The glories of my heavenly King.

2 Fairer than all the earth-born race,
    Perfect in comeliness thou art;
Replenished are thy lips with grace,
    And full of love thy tender heart:
God ever blest! we bow the knee,
And own all fulness dwells in thee.

3 Gird on thy thigh the Spirit's sword,
    And take to thee thy power divine;
Stir up thy strength, almighty Lord,
    All power and majesty are thine;
Assert thy worship and renown;
O all-redeeming God, come down!

4 Come, and maintain thy righteous cause,
    And let thy glorious toil succeed;
Dispread the victory of thy cross,
    Ride on, and prosper in thy deed;
Through earth triumphantly ride on,
And reign in every heart alone.

569
Psalm xlvi.   L. M

1 GOD is the refuge of his saints,
    When storms of sharp distress invade,
Ere we can offer our complaints.
    Behold him present with his aid!

2 Let mountains from their seats be hurled
    Down to the deep, and buried there,
Convulsions shake the solid world,
    Our faith shall never yield to fear.

3 Loud may the troubled ocean roar;
    In sacred peace our souls abide;
While every nation, every shore,
    Trembles, and dreads the swelling tide

4 There is a stream, whose gentle flow
    Supplies the city of our God,
Life, love, and joy still gliding through,
    And watering our divine abode.

5 Zion enjoys her monarch's love,
    Secure against the threatening hour;
Nor can her firm foundation move,
    Built on his faithfulness and power.

SECOND PART.   L. M.

6 LET Zion in her King rejoice,
    Though Satan rage, and kingdoms
He utters his almighty voice,   [rise:
    The nations melt, the tumult dies.

7 The Lord of old for Jacob fought;
    And Jacob's God is still our aid:
Behold the works his hand hath wrought!
    What desolations he hath made!

8 From sea to sea, through all their shores,
    He makes the noise of battle cease;
When from on high his thunder roars,
    He awes the trembling world to peace.

9 He breaks the bow, he cuts the spear;
    Chariots he burns with heavenly flame:
Keep silence, all the earth, and hear
    The sound and glory of his name:

10 " Be still, and learn that I am God,
    Exalted over all the lands;
I will be known and feared abroad:
    For still my throne in Zion stands."

11 O Lord of hosts, almighty King!
    While we so near thy presence dwell,
Our faith shall rest secure, and sing
    Defiance to the gates of hell.

570
8 7, 8 7, 4 7.   Another.

1 GOD, our hope and strength abiding,
    Soothes our dread, exceeding nigh:
Fear we not the world subsiding,
    Roots of mountains heaving high,
        Darkly heaving
    Where in ocean's heart they lie.

2 Let them roar, his awful surges,
    Let them boil—each dark-browed hill
Tremble, where the proud wave urges;
    Here is yet one quiet rill:
        Her calm waters,
    Zion's joy, flow clear and still.

3 Joy of God's abode, the station
    Where the Eternal fixed his tent:—
God is there, a strong salvation,
    On her place she towers unbent.
        God will aid her
    Ere the stars of morn be spent.

4 Heathens rage, dominions tremble,
    God spake out, earth melts away:
God is where our hosts assemble,
    Jacob's God, our rock, and stay.
        Come, behold him
    O'er the wide earth wars allay.

5 Come, behold God's work of wonder,
　Scaring, wasting earth below;
　How he knapped the spear in sunder,
　　How he brake the warrior's bow.
　　　Wild war chariots
　　Burn before him, quenched as tow.
6 " Silence—for the Almighty know me;
　O'er the heathen throned am I,
　Throned where earth must crouch below
　　me "—
　　　Lord of hosts, we know Thee nigh:
　　　　God of Jacob,
　　Thou art still our rock on high.

571 Psalm xlvii. 7 s.

1 CLAP your hands, ye people all,
　　Praise the God on whom ye call;
　Lift your voice, and shout his praise,
　Triumph in his sovereign grace !

2 Glorious is the Lord most High,
　Terrible in majesty;
　He his sovereign sway maintains,
　King o'er all the earth he reigns.

3 Jesus is gone up on high,
　Takes his seat above the sky:
　Shout the angel-choirs aloud,
　Echoing to the trump of God.

4 Sons of earth, the triumph join,
　Praise him with the host divine;
　Emulate the heavenly powers,
　Their victorious Lord is ours.

5 Shout the God enthroned above,
　Trumpet forth his conquering love;
　Praises to our Jesus sing,
　Praises to our glorious King !

6 Power is all to Jesus given,
　Power o'er hell, and earth, and heaven !
　Power he now to us imparts;
　Praise him with believing hearts.

7 Wonderful in saving power,
　Him let all our hearts adore;
　Earth and heaven repeat the cry,—
　" Glory be to God most High ! "

572 Psalm xlviii. 7 s & 6 s.

1 GREAT is our redeeming Lord,
　　In power, and truth, and grace;
　Him, by highest heaven adored,
　　His church on earth doth praise :
　In the city of our God,
　　In his holy mount below,
　Publish, spread his name abroad,
　　And all his greatness show.

2 For thy loving-kindness, Lord,
　　We in thy temple stay;
　Here thy faithful love record,
　　Thy saving power display :
　With thy name thy praise is known,
　　Glorious thy perfections shine;
　Earth's remotest bounds shall own
　　Thy works are all divine.

3 See the gospel church secure,
　　And founded on a rock;
　All her promises are sure;
　　Her bulwarks who can shock?
136

Count her every precious shrine;
　Tell, to after-ages tell,
Fortified by power divine,
　The church can never fail.

4 Zion's God is all our own,
　Who on his love rely;
We his pardoning love have known,
　And live to Christ, and die :
To the new Jerusalem
　He our faithful guide shall be :
Him we claim, and rest in him,
　Through all eternity.

S. M. Another. 573

1 GREAT is the Lord our God,
　　And let his praise be great;
He makes his churches his abode,
　His most delightful seat.

2 These temples of his grace,
　How beautiful they stand !
The honours of our native place,
　And bulwarks of our land.

3 In Zion God is known
　A refuge in distress;
How bright has his salvation shone
　Through all her palaces.

4 In every new distress
　We'll to his house repair;
We'll think upon his wondrous grace,
　And seek deliverance there.

L. M. Psalm li. 574

1 SHOW pity, Lord; O Lord, forgive;
　　Let a repenting rebel live;
Are not thy mercies large and free?
May not a sinner trust in thee?

2 My lips with shame my sins confess
Against thy law, against thy grace !
Lord, should thy judgment be severe,
I am condemned, but thou art clear.

3 Lord, I am vile, conceived in sin,
And born unholy and unclean;
Sprung from the man whose guilty fall
Corrupts the race and taints us all.

4 Behold, I fall before thy face;
My only refuge is thy grace;
No outward form can make me clean,
The leprosy lies deep within.

5 Yet save a trembling sinner, Lord,
Whose hope, still hovering round thy word,
Would light on some sweet promise there,
Some sure support against despair.

6 A broken heart, my God, my King,
Is all the sacrifice I bring;
The God of grace will ne'er despise
A broken heart for sacrifice.

L. M. SECOND PART.

7 O THOU that hear'st when sinners cry,
　　Though all my crimes before thee lie,
Behold me not with angry look,
But blot their memory from thy book !

8 Create my nature pure within,
And form my soul averse from sin;
Let thy good Spirit ne'er depart,
Nor hide thy presence from my heart.

9 I cannot live without thy light,
Cast out and banished from thy sight:
Thy saving strength, O Lord, restore,
And guard me that I fall no more.

10 Though I have grieved thy Spirit, Lord,
His help and comfort still afford;
And let a wretch come near thy throne,
To plead the merits of thy Son.

11 My soul lies humbled in the dust,
And owns thy dreadful sentence just:
Look down, O Lord, with pitying eye,
And save the soul condemned to die.

12 Then will I teach the world thy ways;
Sinners shall learn thy sovereign grace;
I'll lead them to my Saviour's blood,
And they shall praise a pardoning God.

13 O may thy love inspire my tongue!
Salvation shall be all my song,
And all my powers shall join to bless
The Lord my strength and righteousness.

575
Psalm lvi.   8 s & 6 s.

1 THROUGH God I will his word proclaim,
And bless the mighty Jesu's name,
In whom I still confide:
Jesus is good, and strong, and true;
I will not fear what men can do,
When God is on my side.

I now beneath their fury groan,
But thou hast all my wanderings known,
The hasty flights I took;
Thou treasurest up my counted tears;
And all my sighs, and griefs, and fears
Are noted in thy book.

3 Whenever on the Lord I cry,
My foes, I know, shall fear and fly,
For God is on my side;
Through thee I will thy word proclaim,
And bless the mighty Jesu's name,
And still in him confide.

4 In God I trust, the good, the true;
I will not fear what flesh can do,
For Jesus takes my part:
I bless thee, Saviour, for thy grace,
Offer my sacrifice of praise,
And yield thee all my heart.

576
Psalm lvii.   6 - 8 s.

1 MY heart is fixed, O God, my heart
Is fixed to triumph in thy grace:
(Awake, my lute, and bear a part)
My glory is to sing thy praise,
Till all thy nature I partake,
And bright in all thine image wake.

2 Thee will I praise among thine own;
Thee will I to the world extol,
And make thy truth and goodness known:
Thy goodness, Lord, is over all;
Thy truth and grace the heavens transcend;
Thy faithful mercies never end.

3 Be thou exalted, Lord, above
The highest name in earth or heaven;
Let angels sing thy glorious love,
And bless the name to sinners given;
All earth and heaven their King proclaim!
Bow every knee to Jesu's name!

L. M.   Psalm lxiii.   **577**

1 GREAT God, indulge my humble claim,
Be thou my hope, my joy, my rest:
The glories that compose thy name
Stand all engaged to make me blessed.

2 Thou great and good, thou just and wise,
Thou art my Father and my God;
And I am thine, by sacred ties,
Thy son, thy servant bought with blood.

3 With fainting heart, and lifted hands,
For thee I long, to thee I look,
As travellers in thirsty lands
Pant for the cooling water-brook.

4 Should I from thee, my God, remove,
Life could no lasting bliss afford;
My joy, the sense of pardoning love,
My guard, the presence of my Lord.

5 I'll lift my hands, I'll raise my voice,
While I have breath to pray or praise;
This work shall make my heart rejoice,
And fill the circle of my days.

(*See also Hymn* 437.)

7 s & 6 s.   Psalm lxv.   **578**
A Harvest Thanksgiving.

1 FULL of providential love,
Thou dost thy sons sustain,
Send thy blessings from above
In earth-enriching rain;
From thy river in the skies
Streams through airy channels flow,
Bid the springing corn arise,
And cheer the world below.

2 Kindly do the showers distil
Taught by the art of God,
All the settled furrows fill,
And soften every clod;
Thou the acceptable year
Dost with smiling plenty crown:
Clouds the treasured fatness bear,
And drop in blessings down.

3 Springs the watered wilderness
Into a fruitful field;
Earth her hundredfold increase
Doth at thy bidding yield;
Hills and vales with praises ring,
Joy ascends to heaven above;
Laugh the harvesters, and sing
The bounteous God of love.

8 - 7 s.   *Another.*   **579**

1 O THOU God who hearest prayer,
All shall come to thee that live:
Sins too great for us to bear
Thou wilt pity and forgive.
Great, O God, thy saving grace,
Wonderful thy truth is found:
Hope of earth's extremest race,
Hope of ocean's utmost bound.

2 God of goodness, from thy store
Earth receives the wealthy rain;
Thy full channels gushing o'er
Raise for man the springing grain.
Earth, by thy soft dews prepared,
Fills her furrows, smooths her soil;

And her crops with rich reward
  Bless the labourer's happy toil.
3 With thy gifts the year is crowned;
  Clouds, thy chariots, from on high
Scatter o'er the desert ground
  Drops of fatness, as they fly.
Gladness girds the mountain height,
  Fleecy meads with gladness ring:
Vales, with gleaming harvest white,
  Shout for gladness, shout and sing.

580   Psalm lxvi.   8 s & 7 s.

1 EARTH, with all thy thousand voices,
  Praise in songs the eternal King;
Praise his name, whose praise rejoices
  Ears that hear, and tongues that sing.
Lord, from each far-peopled dwelling
  Earth shall raise the glad acclaim;
All shall kneel, thy greatness telling,
  Sing thy praise and bless thy name.

2 Come and hear the wondrous story,
  How our mighty God of old,;
In the terrors of his glory,
  Back the flowing billows rolled:
Walled within the threatening waters,
  Free we passed the upright wave;
Then was joy to Israel's daughters,
  Loud they sang his power to save.

3 Bless the Lord, who ever liveth;
  Sound his praise through every land.
Who our dying souls reviveth,
  By whose arm upheld we stand.
Now upon this cheerful morrow
  We thine altars will adorn,
And the gifts we vowed in sorrow
  Pay on joy's returning morn.

4 Come, each faithful soul, who fearest
  Him who fills the eternal throne:
Hear, rejoicing while thou hearest,
  What our God for us hath done:
When we made our supplication,
  When our voice in prayer was strong,
Straight we found his glad salvation;
  And his mercy fills our tongue.

581   Psalm lxvii.   S. M.

1 TO bless thy chosen race,
  In mercy, Lord, incline,
And cause the brightness of thy face
  On all thy saints to shine;

2 That so thy wondrous way
  May through the world be known;
While distant lands their tribute pay,
  And thy salvation own.

3 Let all the nations join
  To celebrate thy fame;
Yea, let the world, O Lord, combine
  To praise thy glorious name!

4 O let them shout and sing
  With joy and pious mirth!
For thou, the righteous Judge and King,
  Shalt govern all the earth.

582   Another.   6 - 7 s.

1 GOD of mercy, God of grace,
  Show the brightness of thy face,
138

Shine upon us, Saviour, shine,
Fill thy church with light divine;
And thy saving health extend
Unto earth's remotest end.

2 Let the people praise thee, Lord,
Be by all that live adored;
Let the nations shout and sing
Glory to their Saviour King;
At thy feet their tribute pay,
And thy holy will obey.

3 Let the people praise thee, Lord;
Earth shall then her fruits afford;
God to man his blessing give,
Man to God devoted live;
All below and all above
One in joy and light and love.

583   S. M.   Psalm lxviii. 18.

1 JESUS, Jehovah, God,
  Thou art gone up on high,
Amidst the angelic multitude,
  Thy chariots through the sky;
In majesty supreme,
  Absolute God confessed,
Captive thyself hast taken them
  Who all mankind oppressed.

2 Thou hast in triumph led
  Our enemies and thine,
And, more than conqueror, displayed
  The omnipotence divine:
We see them all before
  Thy bleeding cross subdued,
And prostrate at thy feet adore
  The one eternal God.

584   C. M.   Psalm lxxi.

The aged Christian's Prayer and Song.

1 GOD of my childhood and my youth,
  The guide of all my days,
I have declared thy heavenly truth,
  And told thy wondrous ways.

2 Wilt thou forsake my hoary hairs,
  And leave my fainting heart?
Who shall sustain my sinking years
  If God my strength depart?

3 Let me thy power and truth proclaim
  To the surviving race;
And leave a savour of thy name
  When I shall quit my place.

4 Oft have I heard thy threatenings roar,
  And oft endured the grief;
But when thy hand has pressed me sore,
  Thy grace was my relief.

5 By long experience have I known
  Thy sovereign power to save;
At thy command I venture down
  Securely to the grave.

6 When I lie buried deep in dust,
  My flesh shall be thy care;
These withering limbs with thee I trust,
  To raise them strong and fair.

585   L. M.   Psalm lxxii.

1 GREAT God, whose universal sway
  The known and unknown worlds obey,

Now give the kingdom to thy Son,
Extend his power, exalt his throne.

2 The sceptre well becomes his hands;
All heaven submits to his commands;
His justice shall avenge the poor,
And pride and rage prevail no more.

3 With power he vindicates the just,
And treads the oppressor in the dust:
His worship and his fear shall last
Till the full course of time be past.

4 As rain on meadows newly mown,
So shall he send his influence down:
His grace on fainting souls distils,
Like heavenly dew on thirsty hills.

5 The heathen lands, that lie beneath
The shades of overspreading death,
Revive at his first dawning light;
And deserts blossom at the sight.

6 The saints shall flourish in his days,
Decked in the robes of joy and praise;
Peace, like a river, from his throne
Shall flow to nations yet unknown.

SECOND PART.   L. M.

7 JESUS shall reign where'er the sun
   Doth his successive journeys run;
His kingdom stretch from shore to shore,
Till suns shall rise and set no more.

8 For him shall endless prayer be made,
And praises throng to crown his head;
His name like sweet perfume shall rise
With every morning sacrifice.

9 People and realms of every tongue
Dwell on his love with sweetest song;
And infant voices shall proclaim
Their young Hosannas to his name.

10 Blessings abound where'er he reigns;
The prisoner leaps to lose his chains;
The weary find eternal rest;
And all the sons of want are blest.

11 Where he displays his healing power,
Death and the curse are known no more:
In him the tribes of Adam boast
More blessings than their father lost.

12 Let every creature rise, and bring
Its grateful honours to our King;
Angels descend with songs again,
And earth prolong the joyful strain.

586

Another.   7 6, 7 6, 7 6, 7 6.

1 HAIL to the Lord's Anointed;
   Great David's greater son!
Hail, in the time appointed,
   His reign on earth begun!
He comes to break oppression,
   To set the captive free,
To take away transgression,
   And rule in equity.

2 He comes, with succour speedy,
   To those who suffer wrong;
To help the poor and needy,
   And bid the weak be strong;
To give them songs for sighing,
   Their darkness turn to light,
Whose souls, condemned and dying,
   Were precious in his sight.

3 He shall come down like showers
   Upon the fruitful earth:
Love, joy, and hope, like flowers,
   Spring in his path to birth:
Before him, on the mountains,
   Shall peace the herald go:
And righteousness in fountains,
   From hill to valley flow.

4 Arabia's desert ranger
   To him shall bow the knee;
The Ethiopian stranger
   His glory come to see:
With off-rings of devotion
   Ships from the isles shall meet,
To pour the wealth of ocean
   In tribute at his feet.

5 Kings shall fall down before him,
   And gold and incense bring;
All nations shall adore him,
   His praise all people sing:
For him shall prayer unceasing
   And daily vows ascend;
His kingdom still increasing,
   A kingdom without end.

6 O'er every foe victorious,
   He on his throne shall rest:
From age to age more glorious,
   All-blessing and all-blest.
The tide of time shall never
   His covenant remove;
His name shall stand for ever,
   His changeless name of Love.

587

7 6, 7 6, 7 6, 7 6.   Psalm lxxvii.

1 IN time of tribulation
   Hear, Lord, my feeble cries;
With humble supplication
   To thee my spirit flies;
My heart with grief is breaking,
   Scarce can my voice complain;
Mine eyes, with tears kept waking,
   Still watch and weep in vain.

2 The days of old, in vision,
   Bring banished bliss to view;
The years of lost fruition,
   Their joys, in pangs, renew;
Remembered songs of gladness,
   Through night's lone silence brought,
Strike notes of deeper sadness,
   And stir desponding thought.

3 Hath God cast off for ever?
   Can time his truth impair?
His tender mercy never
   Shall I presume to share?
Hath he his loving-kindness
   Shut up in endless wrath?
No; this is mine own blindness,
   That cannot see his path.

4 I call to recollection
   The years of his right hand;
And, strong in his protection,
   Again through faith I stand:
Thy deeds, O Lord, are wonder;
   Holy are all thy ways;
The secret place of thunder
   Shall utter forth thy praise.

5 Thee, with the tribes assembled,
   O God, the billows saw;

139

They saw thee, and they trembled,
  Turned, and stood still with awe;
The clouds shot hail, they lightened;
  The earth reeled to and fro;
Thy fiery pillar brightened
  The gulf of gloom below.

Thy way is in great waters,
  Thy footsteps are not known;
Let Adam's sons and daughters
  Confide in thee alone:
Through the wild sea thou leddest
  Thy chosen flock of yore;
Still on the waves thou treadest,
  And thy redeemed pass o'er.

588   Psalm lxxix.   L. M.

Prayer for Mercy on the Jews.

1 O LORD, how long shall heathens hold
    The heritage that once was thine?
  How long shall they invade thy fold,
    How long pollute thy holy shrine?

2 Behold the violence, the scorn,
    And all the wrongs thy people bear!
  Opprest, insulted, and forlorn,
    Shall they no more thy favour share?

3 O let their sins be washed away,
    For thy compassion, Lord, is great;
  For thy name's sake, forbear to slay,
    And lift them from their low estate.

4 Let Israel's captive sons be free;
    Restore them, and remove thy rod;
  That all the earth thy hand may see,
    And, wondering, own thee for their God.

589   Psalm lxxx.   L. M.

1 OF old, O God, thine own right hand
    A pleasant vine did plant and train;
  Above the hills, o'er all the land,
    It sought the sun, and drank the rain.

2 Its boughs like goodly cedars spread,
    Forth to the river went the root;
  Perennial verdure crowned its head,
    It bore in every season fruit.

3 That vine is desolate and torn,
    Its shoots low in the dust are laid;
  High o'er its branches springs the thorn,
    The wild boar revels in its shade.

4 Lord God of hosts, thine ear incline,
    Change into songs thy people's fears;
  Return, and visit this thy vine,
    Revive thy work amidst the years.

5 The plenteous and continual dew
    Of thy rich blessing here descend;
  So shall thy vine its leaf renew,
    Till o'er the earth its branches bend.

6 Then shall it flourish wide and fair,
    While realms beneath its shadow rest;
  The morning and the evening star
    Shall mark its bounds from east to west.

7 So shall thine enemies be dumb,
    Thy banished ones no more enslaved,
  The fulness of the Gentiles come,
    And Israel's youngest born be saved.

140

590   6 - 8 s.
Second Metre. Psalm lxxxiv.

1 HOW lovely are thy tents, O Lord!
    Where'er thou choosest to record
  Thy name, or place thy house of prayer,
  My soul outflies the angel-choir,
  And faints, o'erpowered with strong desire,
    To meet thy special presence there.

2 Happy the men to whom 'tis given
    To dwell within that gate of heaven,
  And in thy house record thy praise;
  Whose strength and confidence thou art,
  Who feel thee, Saviour, in their heart,
    The Way, the Truth, the Life of grace:

3 Who, passing through the mournful vale,
    Drink comfort from the living well,
  That flows replenished from above;
  From strength to strength advancing here,
  Till all before their God appear,
    And each receives the crown of love.

4 Better a day thy courts within
    Than thousands in the tents of sin;
  How base the noblest pleasures there!
  How great the weakest child of thine!
  His meanest task is all divine,
    And kings and priests thy servants are.

5 The Lord protects and cheers his own,
    Their light and strength, their shield and
       sun:
  He shall both grace and glory give:
  Unlimited his bounteous grant;
  No real good they e'er shall want:
    All, all is theirs, who righteous live.

6 O Lord of hosts, how blest is he
    Who steadfastly believes in thee!
  He all thy promises shall gain:
  The soul that on thy love is cast
  Thy perfect love on earth shall taste,
    And soon with thee in glory reign.

591   4 - 6 s & 2 - 8 s.   *Another.*

1 LORD of the worlds above!
    How pleasant and how fair
  The dwellings of thy love,
    Thy earthly temples, are!
  To thine abode My heart aspires,
  With warm desires To see my God.

2 O happy souls that pray
    Where God delights to hear!
  O happy men that pay
    Their constant service there!
  They praise thee still, And happy they
  Who love the way To Zion's hill!

3 They go from strength to strength,
    Through this dark vale of tears,
  Till each o'ercomes at length,
    Till each in heaven appears:
  O glorious seat! Thou God, our King,
  Shalt thither bring Our willing feet.

4 God is our sun and shield,
    Our light and our defence!
  With gifts his hands are filled,
    We draw our blessings thence:
  He shall bestow Upon our race
  His saving grace, And glory too.

5 The Lord his people loves;
    His hand no good withholds

From those his heart approves,
From holy, humble souls:
Thrice happy he, O Lord of hosts,
Whose spirit trusts Alone in thee!

592   *Another.*   L. M.

1 HOW pleasant, how divinely fair,
  O Lord of hosts, thy dwellings are!
With strong desire my spirit faints
To meet the assemblies of thy saints.

2 Blest are the saints that sit on high,
Around thy throne of majesty;
Thy brightest glories shine above,
And all their work is praise and love.

3 Blest are the souls that find a place
Within the temple of thy grace:
Here they behold thy gentler rays,
And seek thy face, and learn thy praise.

4 Blest are the men whose hearts are set
To find the way to Zion's gate;
God is their strength, and through the road
They lean upon their helper God.

5 Cheerful they walk with growing strength,
Till all shall meet in heaven at length;
Till all before thy face appear,
And join in nobler worship there.

593   *Another.*   8 - 7 s.

1 PLEASANT are thy courts above,
  In the land of light and love;
Pleasant are thy courts below,
In this land of sin and woe.
O! my spirit longs and faints
For the converse of thy saints,
For the brightness of thy face,
For thy fulness, God of grace!

2 Happy birds that sing and fly
Round thy altars, O most High!
Happier souls that find a rest
In a heavenly Father's breast!
Happy souls! their praises flow
Even in this vale of woe;
Waters in the desert rise,
Manna feeds them from the skies.

3 On they go from strength to strength,
Till they reach thy throne at length;
At thy feet adoring fall,
Who hast led them safe through all.
Sun and shield alike thou art,
Guide and guard my erring heart;
Grace and glory flow from thee:
Shower, O shower them, Lord, on me!

594   Psalm lxxxvii.   8 s & 7 s.

1 GLORIOUS things of thee are spoken,
  Zion, city of our God!
He, whose word cannot be broken,
Formed thee for his own abode.
On the Rock of ages founded,
What can shake thy sure repose?
With salvation's walls surrounded,
Thou may'st smile at all thy foes.

2 See, the streams of living waters,
Springing from eternal love,
Well supply thy sons and daughters,
And all fear of want remove:

Who can faint while such a river
Ever flows their thirst to assuage?
Grace which, like the Lord, the giver,
Never fails from age to age.

3 Saviour, if in Zion's city
Thou enrol my humble name,
Let the world deride or pity,
I will glory in the shame;
Fading is the sinner's pleasure,
All his boasted pomp and show:
Solid joys and lasting treasure
None but Zion's children know.

595   8 9 8, 8 9 8,   6 6, 4 4 4, 8.   *Another.*

1 BY the holy hills surrounded,
  On her firm base securely founded,
Stands fast the city of the Lord;
None shall rend her walls asunder;
On her men look with fear and wonder,
And mark who here keeps watch and
    ward.
  He slumbers not, nor sleeps,
  Who his loved Israel keeps.
    Hallelujah!
  Happy the race
  Who through God's grace
Shall have in her their dwelling-place!

2 Zion's gates Jehovah loveth,
And with especial grace approveth;
He maketh fast her bolts and bars;
Those who dwell in her he blesses,
And comforts them in their distresses
Who cast on him their griefs and cares.
  How wonderful the grace
  With which he doth embrace
    All his people!
  City of God,
  How sweet the abode
On which such blessings are bestowed!

3 Taught in thee is a salvation
Unknown to every other nation:
There great and holy things are heard,
In the midst of thee abiding,
Enlightening, comforting, and guiding,
Thou hast the Spirit, and the Word;
  There breathing peace around
  Is heard the joyful sound,
    Grace and mercy!
  How sweet that is,
  Which here speaks peace,
There crowns with everlasting bliss.

4 Nations that have never known thee,
From the world's end shall come to own
    thee,
And eagerly to Zion run;
Even to those in darkness sitting
The Lord shall show when he sees fitting,
What once for all the world was done,
  Where is the Son of God?
  Where is his blest abode?
    All enquiring.
  Till far and wide
  On every side,
The Lord is praised and magnified.

5 Dry your tears, ye hearts nigh broken,
Of Zion it shall yet be spoken,

"How do her citizens increase!"
Men shall see with fear and wonder
How God builds Zion up, and ponder
His love and truth who hath wrought
this.
Lift up your heads ; at last
The night of death has past
From the heathen ;
The day shall break
When they awake,
And Israel their joy partake.

6 Mother thou of every nation
Which here has sought and found salva-
tion,
O Zion, yet on earth shall be :
Hark ! what shouts the air are rending !
What cries to heaven's gates ascending !
All our fresh springs shall be in thee.
From thee the waters burst,
To slake our burning thirst.
Hallelujah !
From sin and death
God's own word saith
That he alone delivereth.

596 Psalm lxxxviiL. 10, 10, 10, 10.
10, 10, 10, 6.

1 HEAVY on me, O Lord, thy judgments
lie :
And curst I am, for God neglects my cry ;
O Lord, in darkness, in despair I groan ;
And every place is hell ; for God is gone !
O Lord, arise, and let thy beams control
These horrid clouds that press my frighted
soul,
O rise and save me from eternal night !
Thou art the God of light !

2 Downward I hasten to my destined place :
There none obtain thy aid, none sing thy
. praise :
Soon I shall lie in death's deep ocean
drowned ;
Is mercy there, is sweet forgiveness found ?
O save me yet, while on the brink I stand !
Rebuke   storms, and set me safe on
landthese
O make my longings and thy mercy sure !
Thou art the God of power !

3 Behold the weary prodigal is come,
To thee his hope, his harbour, and his
home.
No father can he find, no friend abroad ;
Deprived of joy, and destitute of God.
O let thy terrors and his anguish end !
Be thou his father, Lord, be thou his friend ;
Receive the son thou didst so long reprove !
Thou art the God of love !

(*For* Psalm xc., *see Hymn* 41.)

597 Psalm xcL. 8 s & 7 s.

1 CALL Jehovah thy salvation,
Rest beneath the Almighty's shade ;
In his secret habitation
Dwell, nor ever be dismayed ;
There no tumult can alarm thee,
Thou shalt dread no hidden snare :
Guile nor violence can harm thee,
In eternal safety there.
142

2 From the sword at noonday wasting,
From the noisome pestilence
In the depth of midnight blasting,
God shall be thy sure defence ;
Fear thou not the deadly quiver,
When a thousand feel the blow ;
Mercy shall thy soul deliver
Though ten thousand be laid low.

3 Since, with pure and firm affection,
Thou on God hast set thy love,
With the wings of his protection,
He will shield thee from above :
Thou shalt call on him in trouble,
He will hearken, he will save ;
Here for grief reward thee double,
Crown with life beyond the grave.

6 - 7 s. Psalm xcii. **598**

1 THOU who art enthroned above,
Thou in whom we live and move,
O how sweet with heart and tongue
To resound thy name in song,
When the morning paints the skies,
When the evening stars arise !

2 From thy works my joy proceeds :
How I triumph in thy deeds !
Who thy wonders can express ?
All thy thoughts are fathomless :
Lord, thou art most great, most high ;
God from all eternity.

3 All who in their sins delight
Shall be scattered by thy might ;
But, as palm-trees lift the head,
As the stately cedars spread,
So the righteous shall be seen,
Ever fruitful, ever green.

L. M. *Another.* **599**

1 SWEET is the work, my God, my King,
To praise thy name, give thanks, and
To show thy love by morning light, [sing ;
And talk of all thy truth at night.

2 Sweet is the day of sacred rest,
No mortal cares disturb my breast :
O may my heart in tune be found,
Like David's harp of solemn sound !

3 My heart shall triumph in the Lord,
And bless his works, and bless his word :
Thy works of grace, how bright they shine !
How deep thy counsels, how divine !

4 Fools never raise their thoughts so high ;
Like brutes they live, like brutes they die ;
Like grass they flourish, till thy breath
Dooms them to everlasting death.

5 But I shall share a glorious part,
When grace has well refined my heart ;
And fresh supplies of joy are shed,
Like holy oil to cheer my head.

6 Then shall I see, and hear, and know
All I desired and wished below ;
And every power find sweet employ
In that eternal world of joy.

L. M. Psalm xciii. **600**

1 WITH glory clad, with strength arrayed,
The Lord, that o'er all nature reigns,

The world's foundations strongly laid,
  And the vast fabric still sustains.
2 How sure established is thy throne,
  Which shall no change or period see !
For thou, O Lord, and thou alone,
  Art King from all eternity.
3 The floods, O Lord, lift up their voice,
  And toss their troubled waves on high ;
But God above can still their noise,
  And make the angry sea comply.
4 Thy promise, Lord, is ever sure :
  And they that in thy house would dwell,
That happy station to secure,
  Must still in holiness excel.

601

Another. 2 - 6 s & 4 - 7 s.

1 JEHOVAH reigns on high
  In peerless majesty ;
Boundless power his royal robe,
  Purest light his garment is ;
Rules his word the spacious globe,
  Stablished it in floating seas.

2 Ancient of days ! Thy name
  And essence is I AM ;
Thou, O Lord, and thou alone,
  Gav'st whatever is to be ;
Stood thine everlasting throne,
  Stands to all eternity.

3 The floods, with angry noise,
  Have lifted up their voice,
Lifted up their voice on high ;
  Fiends and men exclaim aloud ;
Rage the waves and dash the sky,
  Hell assails the throne of God.

4 Their fury cannot move
  The Lord who reigns above ;
Him the mighty waves obey,
  Sinking at his awful will,
Ocean owns his sovereign sway ;
  Hell at his command is still.

5 Thy statutes, Lord, are sure,
  And as thyself endure ;
Thine eternal house above
  Holy souls alone can see,
Fitted here by perfect love,
  There to reign enthroned with thee.

602

Psalm xciv. 4 - 6 s & 2 - 8 s.

1 O LORD, with vengeance clad,
  Most awful thou art seen !
Yet blessed when most sad
  Our chastened souls have been ;
For we have hope to rest in joy,
When all thy foes thou shalt destroy.

2 The Lord will not forsake
  Nor cast the souls away,
Who his salvation make
  Their refuge and their stay ;
But though they mourn awhile, his voice
Shall bid his faithful ones rejoice.

3 Had not thy help been nigh,
  O Lord, my soul had died ;
Thy mercy doth supply
  Strength when my footsteps slide :
With many a gloomy care oppressed,
I sought thy comforts, and found rest.

4 A sure defence in thee
  I never fail to find ;
The tower to which I flee
  When fears distract my mind :
Thy goodness, Lord, shall still defend,
And guide me to my journey's end.

603

S. M. Psalm xcv.

1 COME, sound his praise abroad,
  And hymns of glory sing !
Jehovah is the sovereign God,
  The universal King.

2 He formed the deeps unknown ;
  He gave the seas their bound :
The watery worlds are all his own,
  And all the solid ground.

3 Come, worship at his throne ;
  Come, bow before the Lord :
We are his works, and not our own ;
  He formed us by his word.

4 To-day attend his voice,
  Nor dare provoke his rod ;
Come, as the people of his choice,
  And own your gracious God.

604

8 s & 7 s. Psalm xcvi.

1 RAISE the psalm : let earth adoring,
  Through each kindred, tribe, and
To her God his praise restoring, [tongue,
  Raise the new accordant song.
Bless his name, each farthest nation ;
  Sing his praise, his truth display :
Tell anew his high salvation
  With each new return of day.

2 Tell it out beneath th' heaven,
  To each kindred, tribe, and tongue,
Tell it out from morn till even
  In your unexhausted song :
Tell that God for ever reigneth,
  He, who set the world so fast,
He, who still its state sustaineth
  Till the day of doom to last.

3 Tell them that the day is coming
  When that righteous doom shall be :
Then shall heaven new joys illumine,
  Gladness shine o'er earth and sea.
Yea, the far-resounding ocean
  Shall its thousand voices raise,
All its waves in glad commotion
  Chant the fulness of his praise.

4 And earth's fields, with herbs and flowers,
  Shall put on their choice array,
And in all their leafy bowers
  Shall the woods keep holyday :
When the Judge, to earth descending,
  Righteous judgment shall ordain,
Fraud and wrong shall then have ending,
  Truth, immortal truth, shall reign.

605

7 s & 6 s. Psalm xcviii.

1 SING we to our conquering Lord
  A new triumphant song ;
Joyfully his deeds record,
  And with a thankful tongue !
Wonders his right hand hath wrought ;
  Still his outstretched arm we see ;

He alone the fight hath fought,
And got the victory.

2 God, the almighty God, hath made
His great salvation known ;
Openly to all displayed
His glory in his Son :
Christ hath brought the life to light,
Bade the glorious gospel shine,
Showed in all the heathen's sight
His righteousness divine.

3 He to Israel's chosen race
His promise hath fulfilled :
Mindful of his word of grace
His saving health revealed :
He to all the sons of men
Hath his truth and mercy showed ;
Earth's remotest bounds have seen
The pardoning love of God.

4 Make a loud and cheerful noise
To him that reigns above ;
Earth, with all thy sons, rejoice
In the Redeemer's love :
Raise your songs of triumph high,
Bring him every tuneful strain,
Praise the Lord who stooped to die,
To ransom wretched man.

5 Him with lute and harp record,
With shawms and trumpets praise ;
Sing, rejoice, before the Lord,
And glory in his grace :
Hymn his grace, and truth, and power ;
Give him thanks, rejoice, and sing ;
Praise him, praise him evermore,
And triumph with your King.

6 Ocean, roar, with all thy waves,
In horrour of his name ;
He who all creation saves
Doth all their homage claim :
Clap your hands, ye floods ! Ye hills,
Joyful all his praise rehearse ;
Praise him till his glory fills
The vocal universe !

7 Lo ! he comes with clouds ! he comes
In dreadful pomp arrayed !
All his glorious power assumes,
To judge the world he made :
Righteous shall his sentence be :
Think of that tremendous bar !
Every eye the Judge shall see,
And thou shalt meet him there !

606   Psalm xcix.   8 7, 8 7, 4 7.

1 GOD the Lord is King ; before him
Earth with all thy nations wait !
Where the cherubim adore him,
Sitteth he in royal state ;
He is holy,
Blessed, only Potentate !

2 God the Lord is King of glory,
Zion, tell the world his fame :
Ancient Israel, the story
Of his faithfulness proclaim :
He is holy,
Holy is his awful name.

3 In old times when dangers darkened,
When, invoked by priest and seer,
144

To his people's cry he hearkened,
Answered them in all their fear ;
He is holy,
As they called, they found him near.

4 Laws divine to them were spoken
From the pillar of the cloud ;
Sacred precepts ! quickly broken,
Fiercely then his vengeance flowed ;
He is holy,
To the dust their hearts were bowed.

5 But their Father God forgave them,
When they sought his face once more ;
Ever ready was to save them,
Tenderly did he restore ;
He is holy,
We too will his grace implore.

6 God in Christ is all forgiving,
Waits his promise to fulfil ;
Come, exalt him all the living,
Come, ascend his holy hill ;
He is holy,
Worship at his holy hill.

607

L. M.   Psalm c.

1 ALL people that on earth do dwell,
Sing to the Lord with cheerful voice :
Him serve with fear, his praise forth tell,
Come ye before him and rejoice.

2 The Lord, ye know, is God indeed :
Without our aid he did us make ;
We are his flock, he doth us feed ;
And for his sheep he doth us take.

3 O enter then his gates with praise :
Approach with joy his courts unto ;
Praise, laud, and bless his name always,
For it is seemly so to do.

4 For why ? The Lord our God is good,
His mercy is for ever sure ;
His truth at all times firmly stood,
And shall from age to age endure.

608

L. M.   *Another.*

1 BEFORE Jehovah's awful throne,
Ye nations, bow with sacred joy ;
Know that the Lord is God alone ;
He can create, and he destroy.

2 His sovereign power, without our aid,
Made us of clay, and formed us men,
And when like wandering sheep we
strayed,
He brought us to his fold again.

3 We'll crowd thy gates with thankful songs;
High as the heavens our voices raise :
And earth, with her ten thousand tongues,
Shall fill thy courts with sounding praise.

4 Wide as the world is thy command ;
Vast as eternity thy love ;
Firm as a rock thy truth shall stand,
When rolling years shall cease to move.

609

C. M.   Psalm ci.

1 MERCY and judgment will I sing,
I sing, O Lord, to thee !
O when wilt thou descend and bring
Thy light and life to me ?

2 A perfect way in wisdom trod,
  A perfect heart at home,
A way, a heart, a house. O God,
  I seek, where thou wilt come.
3 I seek the faithful and the just;
  May I their help enjoy!
Be these the friends in whom I trust,
  The servants I employ!
4 From lies, from slander, and deceit,
  My dwelling shall be free;
May it be found a dwelling meet,
  O righteous Lord, for thee!

610   Psalm ciii.   S. M.

1 O BLESS the Lord, my soul!
  Let all within me join,
And aid my tongue to bless his name,
  Whose favours are divine.
2 O bless the Lord, my soul,
  Nor let his mercies lie
Forgotten in unthankfulness,
  And without praises die.
3 'Tis he forgives thy sins,
  'Tis he relieves thy pain,
'Tis he that heals thy sicknesses,
  And makes thee young again.
4 He fills the poor with good,
  He gives the sufferers rest;
The Lord hath judgments for the proud,
  And justice for the opprest.
5 His wondrous works and ways
  He made by Moses known;
But sent the world his truth and grace
  By his beloved Son.

SECOND PART.   S. M.

6 MY soul, repeat his praise,
  Whose mercies are so great,
Whose anger is so slow to rise,
  So ready to abate.
7 God will not always chide;
  And when his strokes are felt,
His strokes are fewer than our crimes,
  And lighter than our guilt.
8 High as the heavens are raised
  Above the ground we tread,
So far the riches of his grace
  Our highest thoughts exceed.
9 The pity of the Lord
  To those that fear his name
Is such as tender parents feel;
  He knows our feeble frame.
10 Our days are as the grass,
  Or like the morning flower;
If one sharp blast sweep o'er the field
  It withers in an hour.
11 But thy compassions, Lord,
  To endless years endure;
And children's children ever find
  Thy words of promise sure.

611   Psalm civ.   10 s & 11 s.

1 O WORSHIP the King, All glorious
  above;
O gratefully sing His power and his love:

Our shield and defender, The Ancient of
  days,   [praise.
Pavilioned in splendour, And girded with
2 O tell of his might, O sing of his grace,
  Whose robe is the light, Whose canopy
  space;
Whose chariots of wrath Deep thunder-
  clouds form;   [storm.
And dark is his path On the wings of the
3 The earth with its store Of wonders un-
  told,
Almighty! thy power Hath founded of old;
Hath stablished it fast By a changeless
  decree,   [sea.
And round it hath cast, Like a mantle, the
4 Thy bountiful care What tongue can recite?
It breathes in the air, It shines in the light,
It streams from the hills, It descends to
  the plain,   [rain.
And sweetly distils In the dew and the
5 Frail children of dust, And feeble as frail,
In thee do we trust, Nor find thee to fail;
Thy mercies how tender, How firm to the
  end,   [Friend!
Our Maker, Defender, Redeemer, and
6 O measureless Might! Ineffable Love!
While angels delight To hymn thee above,
The humbler creation, Though feeble their
  lays,
With true adoration Shall lisp to thy praise.

L. M.   Psalm cvi.   612

1 O RENDER thanks to God above,
  The fountain of eternal love,
Whose mercy firm through ages past
Hath stood, and shall for ever last.
2 Who can his mighty deeds express,
Not only vast but numberless?
What mortal eloquence can raise
His tribute of immortal praise?
3 Extend to me that favour, Lord,
Thou to thy chosen dost afford:
When thou return'st to set them free,
Let thy salvation visit me.
4 O may I worthy prove to see
Thy saints in full prosperity!
That I the joyful choir may join,
And count thy people's triumph mine.
5 Let Israel's God be ever blessed,
His name eternally confessed;
Let all his saints with full accord
In solemn hymns proclaim their Lord.

8 7, 8 7, 8 8 7.   Psalm cx.   613

1 THE Lord unto my Lord thus said,
  Rule thou of right enthroned,
Till, all thy foes thy footstool made,
  Thou by the earth art owned.
The Lord from Zion forth shall send
Thy sceptre, till to thee shall bend
  The foes that gather round thee.
2 Thy people in thy day of might
  Shall willingly confess thee:
They, numerous as at morning light
  The drops of dew, shall bless thee.

In holiness arrayed, shall they
With strength of youth their King obey;—
Their King a Priest for ever.

3 The Lord in his great wrath shall bring
On princes desolation :
He shall destroy each idol-king,
And visit every nation.
He shall, on his victorious way,
Drink of the brook, then rise to sway
The earth and heaven for ever.

(*For a Version of* Psalm cxiv., *see Hymn*
223.)

614   Psalm cxvi.   C. M.

1 O THOU who, when I did complain,
   Didst all my griefs remove,
O Saviour, do not now disdain
My humble praise and love.

2 Since thou a pitying ear didst give,
And hear me when I prayed,
I'll call upon thee while I live,
And never doubt thy aid.

3 Pale death, with all his ghastly train,
My soul encompassed round,
Anguish, and sin, and dread, and pain,
On every side I found.

4 To thee, O Lord of life, I prayed,
And did for succour flee :
O save (in my distress I said)
The soul that trusts in thee !

5 How good thou art ! how large thy grace !
How ready to forgive !
The helpless thou delight'st to raise :
And by thy love I live.

6 Then, O my soul, be never more
With anxious thoughts distrest !
God's bounteous love doth thee restore
To ease, and joy, and rest.

7 My eyes no longer drowned in tears,
My feet from falling free,
Redeemed from death and guilty fears,
O Lord, I'll live to thee.

SECOND PART.   C. M.

8 WHAT shall I render to my God
   For all his mercy's store ?
I'll take the gifts he hath bestowed,
And humbly ask for more.

9 The sacred cup of saving grace
I will with thanks receive,
And all his promises embrace,
And to his glory live.

10 My vows I will to his great name
Before his people pay,
And all I have, and all I am,
Upon his altar lay.

11 Thy lawful servant, Lord, I owe
To thee whate'er is mine,
Born in thy family below,
And by redemption thine.

12 Thy hands created me, thy hands
From sin have set me free,
The mercy that hath loosed my bands
Hath bound me fast to thee.

13 The God of all-redeeming grace
My God I will proclaim,

146

Offer the sacrifice of praise,
And call upon his name.

14 Praise him, ye saints, the God of love,
Who hath my sins forgiven,
Till, gathered to the church above,
We sing the songs of heaven.

L. M.   Psalm cxvii.   615

1 FROM all that dwell below the skies
   Let the Creator's praise arise :
Let the Redeemer's name be sung,
Through every land, by every tongue.

2 Eternal are thy mercies, Lord ;
Eternal truth attends thy word
Thy praise shall sound from shore to shore,
Till suns shall rise and set no more.

6 - 8 s.   616
Second Metre.   Psalm cxviii.

1 ALL glory to our gracious Lord !
   His love be by his church adored,
His love eternally the same !
His love let Aaron's sons confess,
His free and everlasting grace
Let all that fear the Lord proclaim.

2 The Lord I now can say is mine,
And, confident in strength divine,
Nor man, nor fiends, nor flesh I fear,
Jesus the Saviour takes my part,
And keeps the issues of my heart ;
My helper is for ever near.

3 Righteous I am in him, and strong,
He is become my joyful song,
My Saviour and salvation too :
I triumph through his mighty grace,
And pure in heart shall see his face,
And rise in Christ a creature new.

4 The voice of joy, and love, and praise,
And thanks for his redeeming grace
Among the justified is found :
With songs that rival those above,
With shouts proclaiming Jesu's love,
Both day and night their tents resound.

5 The Lord's right hand hath wonders
   wrought.
Above the reach of human thought,
The Lord's right hand exalted is ;
We see it still stretched out to save ;
The power of God in Christ we have,
And Jesus is the Prince of peace.

6 Open the gates of righteousness,
Receive me into Christ my peace,
That I his praises may record ;
He is the Truth, the Life, the Way,
The portal of eternal day,
The gate of heaven is Christ my Lord.

6 - 8 s.   2d Metre.   SECOND PART.
A Psalm for the Sabbath Day.

7 JESUS is lifted up on high,
   Whom man refused and doomed to
He is become the corner-stone ;   [die,
Head of the church he lives and reigns,
His kingdom over all maintains,
High on his everlasting throne.

8 The Lord the amazing work hath wrought,
Hath from the dead our Shepherd brought,
Revived on the third glorious day :

This is the day our God hath made,
The day for sinners to be glad
In him who bears their sins away.

9 Thee, Lord, with joyful lips we praise,
O send us now thy saving grace,
Make this the acceptable hour:
Our hearts would now receive thee in;
Enter, and make an end of sin,
And bless us with the perfect power.

10 Bless us, that we may call thee blest,
Sent down from heaven to give us rest,
Thy gracious Father to proclaim,
His sinless nature to impart,
In every new, believing heart,
To manifest his glorious name.

11 God is the Lord that shows us light,
Then let us render him his right,
The offerings of a thankful mind;
Present our living sacrifice,
And to his cross in closest ties
With cords of love our spirit bind.

12 Thou art my God, and thee I praise,
Thou art my God, I sing thy grace,
And call mankind to extol thy name:
All glory to our gracious Lord!
His name be praised, his love adored,
Through all eternity the same!

617

Psalm cxviii. 22, 23.   C. M.

1 BEHOLD the sure foundation-stone
Which God in Zion lays,
To build our heavenly hopes upon,
And his eternal praise.

2 Chosen of God, to sinners dear,
We now adore thy name;
We trust our whole salvation here,
Nor can we suffer shame.

3 The foolish builders, scribe and priest,
Reject it with disdain;
Yet on this rock the church shall rest,
And envy rage in vain.

4 What though the gates of hell withstood,
Yet must this building rise:
'Tis thine own work, almighty God,
And wondrous in our eyes.

618

Psalm cxxi.   7 s & 6 s.

1   the hills I lift mine eyes,
TO The everlasting hills;
Streaming thence in fresh supplies,
My soul the Spirit feels.
Will he not his help afford?
Help, while yet I ask, is given:
God comes down; the God and Lord
That made both earth and heaven.

2 Faithful soul, pray always; pray,
And still in God confide;
He thy feeble steps shall stay,
Nor suffer thee to slide:
Lean on thy Redeemer's breast:
He thy quiet spirit keeps;
Rest in him, securely rest;
Thy watchman never sleeps.

3 Neither sin, nor earth, nor hell
Thy Keeper can surprise;
Careless slumbers cannot steal
On his all-seeing eyes;

He is Israel's sure defence;
Israel all his care shall prove,
Kept by watchful providence,
And ever-waking love.

4 See the Lord, thy Keeper, stand
Omnipotently near!
Lo! he holds thee by thy hand,
And banishes thy fear;
Shadows with his wings thy head;
Guards from all impending harms:
Round thee and beneath are spread
The everlasting arms.

5 Christ shall bless thy going out,
Shall bless thy coming in;
Kindly compass thee about,
Till thou art saved from sin;
Like thy spotless Master, thou,
Filled with wisdom, love, and power,
Holy, pure, and perfect, now,
Henceforth, and evermore.

S. M.   Psalm cxxii.   **619**

1 GLAD was my heart to hear
My old companions say,
Come, in the house of God appear,
For 'tis an holy day.

2 Our willing feet shall stand
Within the temple door,
While young and old, in many a band,
Shall throng the sacred floor.

3 Thither the tribes repair,
Where all are wont to meet,
And joyful in the house of prayer
Bend at the mercy-seat.

4 Pray for Jerusalem,
The city of our God:
The Lord from heaven be kind to them
That love the dear abode!

5 Within these walls may peace
And harmony be found;
Zion, in all thy palaces
Prosperity abound!

6 For friends and brethren dear,
Our prayer shall never cease;
Oft as they meet for worship here,
God send his people peace!

7 s.   Psalm cxxiii.   **620**

1 UNTO thee I lift my eyes,
Thou that dwellest in the skies:
At thy throne I meekly bow,
Thou canst save, and only thou.

2 As a servant marks his lord,
As a maid her mistress' word,
So I watch and wait on thee,
Till thy mercy visit me.

3 Let thy face upon me shine,
Tell me, Lord, that thou art mine;
Poor and little though I be,
I have all in having thee.

8 7, 8 7, 4 7.   Psalm cxxiv.   **621**

1 IF our God had not befriended,
Now may grateful Israel say,

If the Lord had not defended,
  When with foes we stood at bay,
    Madly raging,
    Deeming our sad lives their prey:
2 Then the tide of vengeful slaughters
  O'er us had been seen to roll,
And their pride, like angry waters,
  Had engulfed our struggling soul,—
    The loud waters,
    Proud and spurning all control.
3 Praise to God, whose mercy-token
  Beamed to still that raging sea:
Lo, the snare is rent and broken,
  And our captive souls are free.
    Lord of glory,
    Help can come alone from thee!

622   Psalm cxxv.   S. M.

1 WHO in the Lord confide,
    And feel his sprinkled blood,
In storms and hurricanes abide,
  Firm as the mount of God:
Steadfast, and fixed, and sure,
  His Zion cannot move;
His faithful people stand secure
  In Jesu's guardian love.

2 As round Jerusalem
  The hilly bulwarks rise,
So God protects and covers them
  From all their enemies.
On every side he stands,
  And for his Israel cares;
And safe in his almighty hands
  Their souls for ever bears.

3 But let them still abide
  In thee, all-gracious Lord,
Till every soul is sanctified,
  And perfectly restored:
The men of heart sincere
  Continue to defend;
And do them good, and save them here,
  And love them to the end.

623   Psalm cxxvi.   2-6 s &
                          4-7 s.

1 WHEN our redeeming Lord
    Pronounced the pardoning word,
Turned our soul's captivity,
  O what sweet surprise we found!
Wonder asked, "And can it be!"
  Scarce believed the welcome sound.

2 And is it not a dream?
  And are we saved through him?
Yes, our bounding heart replied,
  Yes, broke out our joyful tongue,
Freely we are justified;
  This the new, the gospel-song!

3 The heathen too could see
  Our glorious liberty:
All our foes were forced to own
God for them hath wonders wrought;
Wonders he for us hath done,
  From the house of bondage brought.

4 To us our gracious God
  His pardoning love hath showed;
Now our joyful souls are free
  From the guilt and power of sin,
148

Greater things we soon shall see,
  We shall soon be pure within.
5 Who for thy coming wait,
  And wail their lost estate,
Poor, and sad, and empty still,
  Who for full redemption weep,
They shall thy appearing feel,
  Sow in tears, in joy to reap.
6 Who seed immortal bears,
  And wets his path with tears,
Doubtless he shall soon return,
  Bring his sheaves with vast increase,
Fully of the Spirit born,
  Perfected in holiness.

624
C. M.   Psalm cxxvii.

1 IN vain we build, unless the Lord
    The fabric still sustain;
Unless the Lord the city keep,
  The watchman wakes in vain.
In vain we rise before the day,
  And late to rest repair,
Allow no respite to our toil,
  And eat the bread of care.

2 But, if we trust our Father's love
  And in his ways delight,
He gives us needful food by day
  And quiet sleep by night.
Then children, relatives, and friends,
  Our real blessings prove;
And all the earthly joys he grants
  Are crowned with heavenly love.

625
C. M.   Psalm cxxx.

1 OUT of the depth of self-despair,
    To thee, O Lord, I cry;
My misery mark, attend my prayer,
  And bring salvation nigh.
2 If thou art rigorously severe,
  Who may the test abide?
Where shall the man of sin appear,
  Or how be justified?
3 But O forgiveness is with thee,
  That sinners may adore,
With filial fear thy goodness see,
  And never grieve thee more.
4 My soul, while still to him it flies,
  Prevents the morning ray:
O that his mercy's beams would rise,
  And bring the gospel day!
5 Ye faithful souls, confide in God,
  Mercy with him remains,
Plenteous redemption through his blood,
  To wash out all your stains.
6 His Israel himself shall clear,
  From all their sins redeem;
The Lord Our Righteousness is near,
  And we are just in him.

626
8 6, 8 6, 8 8, 7.   *Another.*

1 OUT of the depths I cry to thee,
    Lord God! O hear my prayer!
Incline a gracious ear to me,
  And bid me not despair:
If thou rememberest each misdeed,
If each should have its rightful meed,
  Lord, who shall stand before thee?

2 'Tis through thy love alone we gain
 The pardon of our sin;
 The strictest life is but in vain,
 Our works can nothing win;
That none should boast himself of aught,
But own in fear thy grace hath wrought
 What in him seemeth righteous.

3 Wherefore my hope is in the Lord,
 My works I count but dust,
I build not there, but on his word,
 And in his goodness trust.
Up to his care myself I yield,
He is my tower, my rock, my shield,
 And for his help I tarry.

4 And though it linger till the night,
 And round again till morn,
My heart shall ne'er mistrust thy might,
 Nor count itself forlorn.
Do thus, O ye of Israel's seed,
Ye of the Spirit born indeed,
 Wait for your God's appearing.

5 Though great our sins and sore our wounds,
 And deep and dark our fall,
His helping mercy hath no bounds,
 His love surpasseth all.
Our trusty loving Shepherd, he
Who shall at last set Israel free
 From all their sin and sorrow.

627

Psalm cxxxi.   6 6, 6 6.

1 THOU, Lord, my witness art
 I am not proud of heart;
Nor look with lofty eyes,
None envy nor despise:

2 Nor to vain pomp apply
My thoughts, nor soar too high;
But in behaviour mild,
And as a tender child

3 Weaned from his mother's breast,
On thee alone I rest;
O Israel, adore
The Lord for evermore.

4 Be thou the only scope
Of thy unfainting hope;
And in his saving grace
Thy constant comfort place.

628

Another.   7 s.

1 LORD, if thou the grace impart,
 Poor in spirit, meek in heart,
I shall as my Master be
Rooted in humility.

2 From the time that thee I know,
Nothing shall I seek below,
Aim at nothing great or high,
Lowly both my heart and eye.

3 Simple, teachable, and mild,
Awed into a little child,
Quiet now without my food,
Weaned from every creature-good.

4 O that all might seek and find
Every good in Jesus joined!
Him let Israel still adore,
Trust him, praise him evermore.

629

Psalm cxxxii.   L. M.

1 REMEMBER, Lord, the pious zeal
 Of every soul that cleaves to thee,

The troubles for thy sake they feel,
Their eager hopes thy house to see.

2 Arise, O Lord, into thy rest,
 Thou, and thy ark of perfect power;
God over all, for ever blessed,
 Thee, Jesus, let our hearts adore.

3 Thy priests be clothed with righteousness,
 Thy praise their happy lives employ,
The saints in thee their all possess,
 And shout the sons of God for joy.

4 O for thy love, thy Jesu's sake,
 Us, thine anointed ones receive,
In the Beloved accepted make,
 And bid us to thy glory live.

5 Zion, God saith, my rest shall be,
 The faithful shall my presence feel;
I long for all who long for me,
 And will in them for ever dwell.

6 I will increase their gracious store,
 My Zion every moment feed,
And satisfy the hungry poor,
 And fill their souls with living bread:

7 With garments of salvation deck
 Her priests, and clothe with robes of
  praise;
Her saints their joy aloud shall speak,
 And shout my all-sufficient grace.

8 There shall the horn of David bud;
 There I have set the lamp divine;
The wisdom and the power of God
 In mine anointed Son shall shine.

9 Messiah on my throne shall sit
 Supreme, till all his foes are slain,
Till death expires beneath his feet,
 The sinner's Advocate shall reign.

4 - 6 s &
2 - 8 s.   Psalm cxxxiii.   ## 630

1 BEHOLD, how good a thing
 It is to dwell in peace;
How pleasing to our King
 This fruit of righteousness;
When brethren all in one agree,
Who knows the joys of unity!

2 When all are sweetly joined,
 (True followers of the Lamb)
The same in heart and mind,
 And think and speak the same;
And all in love together dwell;
The comfort is unspeakable.

3 Where unity takes place,
 The joys of heaven we prove;
This is the gospel grace,
 The unction from above,
The Spirit on all believers shed,
Descending swift from Christ our Head.

4 Where unity is found,
 The sweet anointing grace
Extends to all around,
 And consecrates the place;
To every waiting soul it comes,
And fills it with divine perfumes.

5 Grace every morning new,
 And every night, we feel;
The soft, refreshing dew
 That falls on Hermon's hill i

On Zion it doth sweetly fall;
The grace of one descends on all.

6 Even now our Lord doth pour
 The blessing from above,
A kindly, gracious shower
 Of heart-reviving love,
The former and the latter rain,
The love of God and love of man.

7 In him when brethren join,
 And follow after peace,
The fellowship divine
 He promises to bless ;
His choicest graces to bestow,
Where two or three are met below.

8 The riches of his grace
 In fellowship are given
To Zion's chosen race,
 The citizens of heaven :
He fills them with his choicest store,
He gives them life for evermore.

631   Psalm cxxxvi.   7 s.

1 PRAISE, O praise our God and King !
 Hymns of adoration sing ;
 For his mercies still endure
 Ever faithful, ever sure.

2 Praise him that he made the sun
 Day by day his course to run ;
 For his mercies still endure
 Ever faithful, ever sure :

3 And the silver moon by night,
 Shining with her gentle light ;
 For his mercies still endure
 Ever faithful, ever sure.

4 Praise him that he gave the rain
 To mature the swelling grain ;
 For his mercies still endure
 Ever faithful, ever sure.

5 And hath bid the fruitful field
 Crops of precious increase yield ;
 For his mercies still endure
 Ever faithful, ever sure.

6 Praise him for our harvest-store,
 He hath filled the garner floor ;
 For his mercies still endure
 Ever faithful, ever sure :

7 And for richer food than this,
 Pledge of everlasting bliss ;
 For his mercies still endure
 Ever faithful, ever sure.

8 Glory to our bounteous King !
 Glory let creation sing !
 Glory to the Father, Son,
 And blest Spirit, Three in One.

632   Psalm cxxxix.   C. M.

1 IN all my vast concerns with thee,
 In vain my soul would try
To shun thy presence, Lord, or flee
 The notice of thine eye.

2 Thy all-surrounding sight surveys
 My rising and my rest,
My public walks, my private ways,
 The secrets of my breast.

150

3 My thoughts lie open to thee, Lord,
 Before they're formed within ;
And, ere my lips pronounce the word,
 Thou know'st the sense I mean.

4 O wondrous knowledge, deep and high !
 Where can a creature hide ?
Within thy circling arms I lie,
 Beset on every side.

5 So let thy grace surround me still,
 And like a bulwark prove,
To guard my soul from every ill,
 Secured by sovereign love.

633   8 - 7 s.   Another.

1 WHITHER shall a creature run,
 From Jehovah's Spirit fly ?
How Jehovah's presence shun,
 Screened from his all-seeing eye !
Holy Ghost, before thy face
 Where shall I myself conceal ?
Thou art God in every place,
 God incomprehensible.

2 If to heaven I take my flight ;
 With beatitude unknown
Filling all the realms of light,
 There thou sittest on thy throne !
If to hell I could retire,
 Gloomy pit of endless pains,
There is the consuming fire,
 There almighty vengeance reigns

3 If the morning's wings I gain,
 Fly to earth's remotest bound,
Could I hid from thee remain,
 In a world of waters drowned ?
Leaving lands and seas behind,
 Could I the Omniscient leave ?
There thy quicker hand would find,
 There arrest, the fugitive.

4 Covered by the darkest shade,
 Should I hope to lurk unknown,
By a sudden light bewrayed,
 By an uncreated sun,
Naked at the noon of night
 Should I not to thee appear ?
Forced to acknowledge in thy sight,
 God is light, and God is here !

634   S. M.   Psalm cxlii.

1 IN deep distress, to God
 I poured my care and grief ;
To him I raised my mournful cry,
 And sought from him relief.

2 I looked, but found no friend
 To aid me in distress ;
All refuge failed, and none vouchsafed
 To pity or redress.

3 To God at length I cried,
 "Thou, Lord, my refuge art ;
My portion in the land of life,
 Till life itself depart.

4 "Redeem my helpless soul,
 That I may praise thy name ;
So shall assembled saints with me
 Thy power and grace proclaim."

635

Psalm cxliii.   S. M.

1 HEAR thou my prayer, O Lord,
   And listen to my cry:
Remember now thy faithful word,
   And graciously reply.
Do not in judgment rise
   Thy servant's life to scan;
For righteous in thy spotless eyes
   Is found no living man.

2 I stretch my longing hands
   Towards thy holy place,
With soul athirst, like weary lands,
   For thy refreshing grace.
Haste thee, O Lord, I pray,
   My failing heart to save!
Hide not thy face: I droop as they
   That sink into the grave.

3 Thy mercy's early light
   My faith desires to see;
O let me walk before thy sight!
   I lift my soul to thee.
Let thy good Spirit lead
   My feet in righteous ways:
And for thy name's sake, Lord, my head
   Above my troubles raise.

636

Psalm cxlv.   6 - 8 s.

1 FAR as creation's bounds extend,
   Thy mercies, heavenly Lord, descend;
One chorus of perpetual praise
To thee thy various works shall raise;
Thy saints to thee in hymns impart
The transports of a grateful heart.

2 They chant the splendours of thy name,
Delighted with the wondrous theme;
And bid the world's wide realms admire
The glories of the Almighty Sire,
Whose throne all nature's wreck survives,
Whose power through endless ages lives.

3 From thee, great God, while every eye
Expectant waits the wished supply,
Their bread, proportioned to the day,
Thy opening hands to each convey;
In every sorrow of the heart
Eternal mercy bears a part.

4 Who ask thine aid with heart sincere
Shall find thy succours ever near;
To thee their prayer in each distress
Thy suffering servants, Lord, address;
And prove thee, verging on the grave,
Nor slow to hear, nor weak to save.

637

Another.   C. M.

1 SWEET is the memory of thy grace,
   My God, my heavenly King:
Let age to age thy righteousness
   In sounds of glory sing.

2 God reigns on high, but not confines
   His bounty to the skies:
Through the whole earth his goodness
     shines,
   And every want supplies.

3 With longing eyes the creatures wait
   On thee for daily food;
Thy liberal hand provides them meat,
   And fills their mouths with good.

4 How kind are thy compassions, Lord!
   How slow thine anger moves!
But soon he sends his pardoning word,
   To cheer the souls he loves.

5 Creatures, with all their endless race,
   Thy power and praise proclaim;
But we, who taste thy richer grace,
   Delight to bless thy name.

C. M.   SECOND PART.

6 LET every tongue thy goodness speak,
   Thou sovereign Lord of all:
Thy strengthening hands uphold the
     weak,
   And raise the poor that fall.

7 When sorrow bows the spirit down,
   Or virtue lies distressed,
Beneath the proud oppressor's frown,
   Thou giv'st the mourner rest.

8 The Lord supports our infant days,
   And guides our giddy youth;
Holy and just are all thy ways,
   And all thy words are truth.

9 Thou know'st the pains thy servants feel,
   Thou hear'st thy children cry;
And their best wishes to fulfil,
   Thy grace is ever nigh.

10 Thy mercy never shall remove
   From men of heart sincere:
Thou sav'st the souls whose humble love
   Is joined with holy fear.

11 My lips shall dwell upon thy praise,
   And spread thy fame abroad:
Let all the sons of Adam raise
   The honours of their God!

6 - 8 s.   Psalm cxlvi.   638

1 MY soul, inspired with sacred love,
   The Lord thy God delight to praise;
His gifts I will for him improve,
   To him devote my happy days:
To him my thanks and praises give,
And only for his glory live.

2 Long as my God shall lend me breath,
   My every pulse shall beat for him;
And when my voice is lost in death,
   My spirit shall resume the theme;
The gracious theme, for ever new,
Through all eternity pursue.

3 Soon as the breath of man expires,
   Again he to his earth shall turn;
Where then are all his vain desires,
   His love and hate, esteem and scorn?
All, all at that last gasp are o'er,
He falls to rise on earth no more.

4 He then is blest, and only he,
   Whose hope is in the Lord his God;
Who can to him for succour flee
   That spread the earth and heaven abroad;
That still the universe sustains,
And Lord of his creation reigns.

5 True to his everlasting word,
   He loves the injured to redress:
Poor helpless souls the bounteous Lord
   Relieves, and fills with plenteousness:
He sets the mournful prisoners free,
He bids the blind their Saviour see.

151

6 The Lord thy God, O Zion, reigns,
  · Supreme in mercy as in power,
The endless theme of heavenly strains,
  When time and death shall be no more :
And all eternity shall prove
Too short to utter all his love.
  (For another version see Hymn 224.)
  (For Psalm cxlvii. see Hymn 225.) .

639   Psalm cxlviii.   7 s.

1 YOU, who dwell above the skies,
  Free from human miseries ;
You, whom highest heaven embowers,
Praise the Lord with all your powers.

2 Angels, your clear voices raise ;
Him ye heavenly armies praise ;
Sun, and moon with borrowed light,
All ye sparkling eyes of night.

3 Waters hanging in the air,
Heaven of heavens, his praise declare ;
His deserved praise record ;
His, who made you by his word.

4 Let the earth his praise resound ;
Monstrous whales, and seas profound ;
Vapours, lightning, hail, and snow,
Storms which, when he bids you, blow.

5 Flowery hills, and mountains high ;
Cedars, neighbours to the sky :
Trees and cattle, creeping things ;
All that cut the air with wings :

6 You, who awful sceptres sway,
You, accustomed to obey,
Princes, judges of the earth,
All of high and humble birth :

7 Youths and virgins, flourishing
In the beauty of your spring ;
You, who were but born of late,
You, who bow with age's weight :

8 Praise his name with one consent :
O how great ! how excellent !
Than the earth profounder far ;
Higher than the highest star.

9 He will his to glory raise ;
You, his saints, resound his praise :
You, his sons, his chosen race,
Bless his love, and sovereign grace.

640   *Another.*   8 s & 7 s.

1 PRAISE the Lord! ye heavens, adore him,
  Praise him, angels in the height ;
Sun and moon, rejoice before him ;
  Praise him, all ye stars and light ;
Praise the Lord ! for he hath spoken ;
  Worlds his mighty voice obeyed ;
Laws, that never shall be broken,
  For their guidance he hath made.

2 Praise the Lord, for he is glorious ;
  Never shall his promise fail ;
God hath made his saints victorious ;
  Sin and death shall not prevail.
Praise the God of our salvation !
  Hosts on high his powers proclaim,
Heaven and earth, and all creation,
  Laud and magnify his name.
152

641   7 s & 6 s.   Psalm cl.

1 PRAISE the Lord, who reigns above,
  And keeps his court below,
Praise the holy God of love,
  And all his greatness show ;
Praise him for his noble deeds,
  Praise him for his matchless power :
Him from whom all good proceeds
  Let earth and heaven adore.

2 Publish, spread to all around
  The great Jehovah's name,
Let the trumpet's martial sound
  The Lord of hosts proclaim :
Praise him in the sacred dance,
  Harmony's full concert raise,
Let the virgin choir advance,
  And move but to his praise.

3 Celebrate the eternal God
  With harp and psaltery,
Timbrels soft and cymbals loud
  In his high praise agree :
Praise him every tuneful string ;
  All the reach of heavenly art,
All the powers of music bring,
  The music of the heart.

4 Him, in whom they move and live,
  Let every creature sing,
Glory to their Maker give,
  And homage to their King :
Hallowed be his name beneath,
  As in heaven on earth adored ;
Praise the Lord in every breath !
  Let all things praise the Lord !

SECTION II.

HYMNS OF ADORATION.

C. M.   *Hymn to God the Father.*   642

1 HAIL, Father, whose creating call
  Unnumbered worlds attend ;
Jehovah, comprehending all,
  Whom none can comprehend !

2 In light unsearchable enthroned,
  Whom angels dimly see,
The fountain of the Godhead owned,
  And foremost of the Three.

3 From thee, through an eternal now,
  The Son, thine offspring, flowed ;
An everlasting Father thou,
  An everlasting God.

4 Nor quite displayed to worlds above,
  Nor quite on earth concealed ;
By wondrous, unexhausted love,
  To mortal man revealed.

5 Supreme and all-sufficient God,
  When nature shall expire,
And worlds created by thy nod
  Shall perish by thy fire.

6 Thy name, Jehovah, be adored
  By creatures without end,
Whom none but thy essential Word
  And Spirit comprehend.

643

2 - 6 s & 4 - 7 s.

Hymn to the Trinity.

1 HAIL, co-essential Three,
    In mystic Unity!
Father, Son, and Spirit, hail!
God by heaven and earth adored,
God incomprehensible;
    One supreme, almighty Lord.

2 Thou sittest on the throne,
    Plurality in One:
Saints behold thine open face,
    Bright, insufferably bright;
Angels tremble as they gaze,
    Sink into a sea of light.

3 Ah! when shall we increase
    Their heavenly ecstasies?
Chant, like them, the Lord most High,
    Fall like them who dare not move;
"Holy, holy, holy," cry,
    Breathe the praise of silent love?

4 Come, Father, in the Son
    And in the Spirit down;
Glorious Triune Majesty,
God through endless ages blest,
Make us meet thy face to see,
    Then receive us to thy breast.

644

4 - 6 s & 2 - 8 s.

1 WE give immortal praise
    To God the Father's love,
For all our comforts here,
    And better hopes above;
He sent his own eternal Son,
To die for sins that man had done.

2 To God the Son belongs
    Immortal glory too,
Who bought us with his blood
    From everlasting woe:
And now he lives, and now he reigns,
And sees the fruit of all his pains.

3 To God the Spirit's name
    Immortal worship give,
Whose new-creating power
    Makes the dead sinner live:
His work completes the great design,
And fills the soul with joy divine.

4 Almighty God, to thee
    Be endless honours done,
The undivided Three,
    And the mysterious One:
Where reason fails, with all her powers,
There faith prevails, and love adores.

645

"*Gloria Patri.*"   7 s.

1 FATHER, live, by all things feared;
    Live the Son, alike revered;
Equally be thou adored,
Holy Ghost, Eternal Lord.

2 Three in person, one in power,
Thee we worship evermore:
Praise by all to thee be given,
Endless theme of earth and heaven.

646

1 HOLY, holy, holy, Lord God Almighty!
    Early in the morning our song shall
rise to thee.

Holy, holy, holy, merciful and mighty,
    God in Three Persons, blessed Trinity!

2 Holy, holy, holy! all the saints adore thee,
Casting down their golden crowns around
    the glassy sea;   [fore thee,
Cherubim and Seraphim falling down be-
Who wert, and art, and evermore shalt be.

3 Holy, holy, holy! though the darkness
    hide thee,   [may not see,
Though the eye of sinful man thy glory
Only thou art holy, there is none beside
    thee
Perfect in power, in love, and purity!

4 Holy, holy, holy, Lord God Almighty!
All thy works shall praise thy name, in
    earth and sky and sea:
Holy, holy, holy, merciful and mighty,
God in Three Persons, blessed Trinity!

647

6 - 8 s.   "*Te Deum laudamus.*"

1 INFINITE God, to thee we raise
    Our hearts in solemn songs of praise;
By all thy works on earth adored,
We worship thee, the common Lord;
The everlasting Father own,
And bow our souls before thy throne.

2 Thee all the choir of angels sings,
The Lord of hosts, the King of kings;
Cherubs proclaim thy praise aloud,
And seraphs shout the Triune God;
And, "Holy, holy, holy," cry,
"Thy glory fills both earth and sky!"

3 God of the patriarchal race,
The ancient seers record thy praise,
The goodly apostolic band
In highest joy and glory stand:
And all the saints and prophets join
To extol thy majesty divine.

4 Head of the martyrs' noble host,
Of thee they justly make their boast;
The church, to earth's remotest bounds,
Her heavenly Founder's praise resounds;
And strives, with those around the throne,
To hymn the mystic Three in One.

5 Father of endless majesty,
All might and love they render thee;
Thy true and only Son adore,
The same in dignity and power;
And God the Holy Ghost declare,
The saints' eternal Comforter.

648

6 - 8 s.   SECOND PART.

1 MESSIAH, joy of every heart,
Thou, thou the King of glory art!
The Father's everlasting Son!
Thee it delights thy church to own;
For all our hopes on thee depend,
Whose glorious mercies never end.

2 Bent to redeem a sinful race,
Thou, Lord, with unexampled grace,
Into our lower world didst come,
And stoop to a poor virgin's womb;
Whom all the heavens cannot contain,
Our God appeared a child of man!

3 When thou hadst rendered up thy breath,
And dying drawn the sting of death,

153

Thou didst from earth triumphant rise,
And ope the portals of the skies,
That all who trust in thee alone
Might follow, and partake thy throne.

4 Seated at God's right hand again,
Thou dost in all his glory reign ;
Thou dost, thy Father's image, shine
In all the attributes divine ;
And thou with judgment clad shalt come
To seal our everlasting doom.

5 Wherefore we now for mercy pray ;
O Saviour, take our sins away !
Before thou as our Judge appear,
In dreadful majesty severe,
Appear our Advocate with God,
And save the purchase of thy blood !

6 Hallow, and make thy servants meet,
And with thy saints in glory seat ;
Sustain and bless us by thy sway,
And keep to that tremendous day,
When all thy church shall chant above
The new eternal song of love.

649 THIRD PART. 6 - 8 s.

1 SAVIOUR, we now rejoice in hope,
That thou at last wilt take us up ;
With daily triumph we proclaim,
And bless and magnify thy name ;
And wait thy greatness to adore
When time and death shall be no more.

2 Till then with us vouchsafe to stay,
And keep us pure from sin to-day ;
Thy great confirming grace bestow,
And guard us all our days below ;
And ever mightily defend,
And save thy servants to the end.

3 Still let us, Lord, by thee be blest,
Who in thy guardian mercy rest :
Extend thy mercy's arms to me,
The weakest soul that trusts in thee ;
And never let me lose thy love,
Till I, even I, am crowned above.

650 4 - 6 s & 2 - 8 s.

1 THE Lord Jehovah reigns,
His throne is built on high ;
The garments he assumes
Are light and majesty :
His glories shine with beams so bright,
No mortal eye can bear the sight.

2 The thunders of his hand
Keep the wide world in awe ;
His wrath and justice stand
To guard his holy law ;
And where his love resolves to bless,
His truth confirms and seals the grace.

3 Through all his mighty works
Amazing wisdom shines,
Confounds the powers of hell,
And breaks their dark designs ;
Strong is his arm, and shall fulfil
His great decrees and sovereign will.

4 And will this sovereign King
Of glory condescend ?
And will he write his name,
My Father and my Friend ?
I love his name, I love his word,
Join all my powers to praise the Lord !
154

651 L. M.

1 GOD is a name my soul adores,
The almighty Three, the eternal One;
Nature and grace, with all their powers,
Confess the Infinite unknown.

2 Thy voice produced the sea and spheres,
Bade the waves roar, the planets shine :
But nothing like thyself appears [thine.
Through all these spacious works of

3 Still restless nature dies and grows,
From change to change the creatures
Thy being no succession knows, [run :
And all thy vast designs are one.

4 A glance of thine runs through the globe,
Rules the bright worlds, and moves
their frame ;
Of light thou form'st thy dazzling robe,
Thy ministers are living flame.

5 How shall polluted mortals dare
To sing thy glory or thy grace ?
Beneath thy feet we lie afar,
And see but shadows of thy face.

6 Who can behold the blazing light ?
Who can approach consuming flame ?
None but thy Wisdom knows thy might,
None but thy Word can speak thy name.

652 C. M.

O GOD, at thy command we rise
Thy glorious name to bless,
Thee the great Lord of earth and skies
We joyfully confess.
Our joy is now to sing of thee,
To triumph in thy love,
And this (transporting thought !) shall be
Our endless work above.

653 2 - 6 s & 4 - 7 s. *The Lord's Prayer.*

1 FATHER of earth and sky,
Thy name we magnify :
O that earth and heaven might join,
Thy perfections to proclaim ;
Praise the attributes divine,
Fear and love thy awful name !

2 When shall thy Spirit reign
In every heart of man ?
Father, bring the kingdom near,
Honour thy triumphant Son ;
God of heaven, on earth appear,
Fix with us thy glorious throne.

3 Thy good and holy will
Let all on earth fulfil ;
Men with minds angelic vie,
Saints below with saints above,
Thee to praise and glorify,
Thee to serve with perfect love.

4 This day with this day's bread,
Thy hungry children feed ;
Fountain of all blessings, grant
Now the manna from above ;
Now supply our bodies' want,
Now sustain our souls with love.

5 Our trespasses forgive :
And when absolved we live,
Thou our life of grace maintain ;
Lest we from our God depart,

Lose thy pardoning grace again,
Grant us a forgiving heart.

6 In every fiery hour
Display thy guardian power ;
Near in our temptation stay,
With sufficient strength defend ;
Bring us through the evil day,
Make us faithful to the end.

7 Father, by right divine
Assert the kingdom thine ;
Jesus, Power of God, subdue
Thy own universe to thee ;
Spirit of grace and glory too,
Reign through all eternity.

(*See also Hymns* 235, 236, 237.)

654
C. M.

1 BEING of beings, God of love !
To thee our hearts we raise ;
Thy all-sustaining power we prove,
And gladly sing thy praise.

2 Thine, only thine, we pant to be ;
Our sacrifice receive ;
Made, and preserved, and saved by thee,
To thee ourselves we give.

3 Heavenward our every wish aspires ;
For all thy mercies' store,
The sole return thy love requires
Is, that we ask for more.

4 For more we ask ; we open then
Our hearts to embrace thy will ;
Turn, and revive us, Lord, again,
With all thy fulness fill.

5 Come, Holy Ghost, the Saviour's love
Shed in our hearts abroad !
So shall we ever live, and move,
And be, with Christ in God.

655
L. M.

1 ETERNAL depth of love divine,
In Jesus, God with us, displayed ;
How bright thy beaming glories shine !
How wide thy healing streams are
spread !

2 With whom dost thou delight to dwell ?
Sinners, a vile and thankless race :
O God, what tongue aright can tell
How vast thy love, how great thy grace !

3 The dictates of thy sovereign will
With joy our grateful hearts receive :
All thy delight in us fulfil ;
Lo ! all we are to thee we give.

4 To thy sure love, thy tender care,
Our flesh, soul, spirit, we resign :
O fix thy sacred presence there,
And seal the abode for ever thine.

5 O King of glory, thy rich grace
Our feeble thought surpasses far ;
Yea, even our crimes, though numberless,
Less numerous than thy mercies are.

6 Still, Lord, thy saving health display,
And arm our souls with heavenly zeal ;
So fearless shall we urge our way
Through all the powers of earth and hell.
F

656
6-8 s.   Micah vii. 18.
A Pardoning God.

1 GREAT God of wonders ! all thy ways
Display the attributes divine ;
But countless acts of pardoning grace
Beyond thine other wonders shine :
Who is a pardoning God like thee ?
Or who has grace so rich and free ?

2 Crimes of such horror to forgive,
Such guilty, daring worms to spare ;
This is thy grand prerogative,
And none may in this honour share :
Who is a pardoning God like thee ?
Or who has grace so rich and free ?

3 In wonder lost, with trembling joy
We take the pardon of our God ;
Pardon for crimes of deepest dye,
A pardon bought with Jesu's blood :
Who is a pardoning God like thee ?
Or who has grace so rich and free ?

4 O may this strange, this matchless grace,
This God-like miracle of love,
Fill the wide earth with grateful praise,
As now it fills the choirs above !
Who is a pardoning God like thee !
Or who has grace so rich and free ?

657
C. M.   *An Act of Thanksgiving.*

1 WHEN all thy mercies, O my God,
My rising soul surveys,
Transported with the view, I'm lost
In wonder, love, and praise.

2 Thy Providence my life sustained,
And all my wants redressed,
While in the silent womb I lay,
And hung upon the breast.

3 To all my weak complaints and cries
Thy mercy lent an ear,
Ere yet my feeble thoughts had learned
To form themselves in prayer.

4 Unnumbered comforts on my soul
Thy tender care bestowed,
Before my infant heart conceived
From whom those comforts flowed.

5 When in the slippery paths of youth
With heedless steps I ran,
Thine arm, unseen, conveyed me safe,
And led me up to man.

6 Through hidden dangers, toils, and deaths,
It gently cleared my way ;
And through the pleasing snares of vice,
More to be feared than they.

7 When worn with sickness, oft hast thou
With health renewed my face,
And when in sins and sorrows sunk
Revived my soul with grace.

8 Ten thousand thousand precious gifts
My daily thanks employ ;
Nor is the least a thankful heart,
That takes those gifts with joy.

9 Through every period of my life
Thy goodness I'll pursue ;
And after death, in distant worlds
The pleasing theme renew.

10 Through all eternity, to thee
A grateful song I'll raise;
But O eternity's too short
To utter all thy praise!

658 L. M.

1 GOD of my life, through all my days
My grateful powers shall sound thy
praise;
My song shall wake with opening light,
And cheer the dark and silent night.

2 When anxious cares would break my rest,
And griefs would tear my throbbing breast,
Thy tuneful praises, raised on high,
Shall check the murmur and the sigh.

3 When death o'er nature shall prevail,
And all the powers of language fail,
Joy through my swimming eyes shall
break,
And mean the thanks I cannot speak.

4 But O when that last conflict's o'er,
And I am chained to earth no more,
With what glad accents shall I rise
To join the music of the skies!

5 Soon shall I learn the exalted strains
Which echo through the heavenly plains;
And emulate, with joy unknown,
The glowing seraphs round the throne.

6 The cheerful tribute will I give
Long as a deathless soul shall live:
A work so sweet, a theme so high,
Demands and crowns eternity.

659 *The faithfulness of God in His promises.* C. M.

1 BEGIN, my soul, some heavenly theme;
Awake, my voice, and sing
The mighty works, or mightier name,
Of our eternal King.

2 Tell of his wondrous faithfulness,
And sound his power abroad;
Sing the sweet promise of his grace,
And the performing God.

3 Proclaim salvation from the Lord,
For wretched, dying men:
His hand hath writ the sacred word
With an immortal pen.

4 Engraved as in eternal brass,
The mighty promise shines;
Nor can the powers of darkness rase
Those everlasting lines.

5 His every word of grace is strong
As that which built the skies;
The voice that rolls the stars along
Speaks all the promises.

6 Now shall my fainting heart rejoice
To know thy favour sure:
I trust the all-creating voice,
And faith desires no more.

660 *God our Trust.* 8 s.

THIS, this is the God we adore,
Our faithful, unchangeable Friend;
Whose love is as great as his power,
And neither knows measure nor end.
'Tis Jesus, the First and the Last,
Whose Spirit shall guide us safe home;
156

We'll praise him for all that is past,
And trust him for all that's to come.

661 *"In Him we live," &c.* 2-6 s & 4-7 s. Acts xvii. 27, 28.

1 FAR off we need not rove
To find the God of love;
In his providential care
Ever intimately near,
All his various works declare
God, the bounteous God is here!

2 We live, and move, and are,
Through his preserving care;
He doth still in life maintain
Every soul that moves and lives;
Give us back our breath again,
Being every moment gives.

3 Who live, O God, in thee
Entirely thine should be:
Thine we are, a heaven-born race,
Only to thy glory move, &
Thee with all our powers we praise,
Thee with all our being love.

662 C. M. Romans i. 20.

1 THERE is a book who runs may read,
Which heavenly truth imparts;
And all the lore its scholars need,
Pure eyes and Christian hearts.

2 The works of God, above, below,
Within us, and around,
Are pages in that book, to show
How God himself is found.

3 Two worlds are ours; 'tis only sin
Forbids us to descry
The mystic heaven and earth within,
Plain as the sea and sky.

4 Thou who hast given me eyes to see
And love this sight so fair,
Give me a heart to find out thee,
And read thee everywhere.

663 *"All Thy works praise Thee, O Lord."*

THE strain upraise of joy and praise,
To the glory of their King [Alleluia.
Shall the ransomed people sing Alleluia.

And the choirs that dwell on high
Shall re-echo through the sky Alleluia.

They in the rest of Paradise who dwell,
The blessed ones, with joy the chorus swell,
Alleluia.

The planets beaming on their heavenly way,
The shining constellations join; and say
Alleluia.

Ye clouds that onward sweep,
Ye winds on pinions light,
Ye thunders, echoing loud and deep,
Ye lightnings wildly bright,
In sweet consent unite your Alleluia.

Ye floods and ocean billows,
Ye storms and winter snow,
Ye days of cloudless beauty,
Hoar frost and summer glow,
Ye groves that wave in spring,
And glorious forests, sing Alleluia.

First let the birds, with painted plumage gay,
Exalt their great Creator's praise, and say
                    Alleluia.
Then let the beasts of earth, with varying
    strain,   [Alleluia.
Join in creation's hymn, and cry again
Here let the mountains thunder forth
    sonorous Alleluia.   [Alleluia.
There let the valleys sing in gentler chorus,
Thou jubilant abyss of ocean, cry Alleluia.
Ye tracts of earth and continents, reply
                    Alleluia.

To God, who all creation made,
The frequent hymn be duly paid : Alleluia.
This is the strain, the eternal strain, the
    Lord Almighty loves : Alleluia.
This is the song, the heavenly song, that
    Christ the King approves : Alleluia.
Wherefore we sing, both heart and voice
    awaking, Alleluia.   [Alleluia.
And children's voices echo, answer making,
Now from all men be out-poured
Alleluia to the Lord ;
With Alleluia evermore
The Son and Spirit we adore.
    Alleluia! Alleluia! Alleluia! Amen.

664   Genesis xxviii. 20—22.   C. M.

1 O GOD of Bethel, by whose hand
    Thy people still are fed ;
  Who through this weary pilgrimage
    Hast all our fathers led:

2 Our vows, our prayers, we now present
    Before thy throne of grace ;
  God of our fathers, be the God
    Of their succeeding race !

3 Through each perplexing path of life
    Our wandering footsteps guide ;
  Give us each day our daily bread,
    And raiment fit provide.

4 O spread thy covering wings around,
    Till all our wanderings cease,
  And at our Father's loved abode
    Our souls arrive in peace !

5 Such blessings from thy gracious hand
    Our humble prayers implore ;
  And thou shalt be our chosen God,
    And portion evermore.

SECTION III.

ON THE PERSON, OFFICES, AND WORK OF CHRIST.

665   Hymn to God the Son.   C. M.

1 HAIL, God the Son, in glory crowned,
    Ere time began to be ;   [round
  Throned with thy Sire, through half the
    Of vast eternity !

2 Let heaven and earth's stupendous frame
    Display their Author's power ;
  And each exalted seraph-flame,
    Creator, thee adore.

3 Thy wondrous love the Godhead showed
    Contracted to a span,—
  The co-eternal Son of God,
    The mortal Son of man.

4 To save us from our lost estate,
    Behold his life-blood stream :
  Hail, Lord, almighty to create,
    Almighty to redeem !

5 The Mediator's God-like sway
    His church below sustains:
  Till nature shall her Judge survey,
    The King Messiah reigns.

6 Hail, with essential glory crowned,
    When 'time shall cease to be ;
  Throned with thy Father, through the
    Of whole eternity !   [round

666   6 - 8 s.   Second Metre.
"God of God, Light of light."

1 O GOD of GOD, in whom combine
    The heights and depths of love divine,
  With thankful hearts to thee we sing !
  To thee our longing souls aspire,
  In fervent flames of strong desire ;
    Come, and thy sacred unction bring.

2 All things in earth, and air, and sea,
  Exist, and live, and move in thee ;
  All nature trembles at thy voice :
  With awe even we thy children prove
  Thy power : O let us taste thy love !
    So evermore shall we rejoice.

3 O powerful Love, to thee we bow ;
  Object of all our wishes thou,
  Our hearts are naked to thine eye,
  To thee, who from the eternal throne
  Cam'st emptied of thy glory down,
    For us to groan, to bleed, to die.

4 Grace we implore ; when billows roll,
  Grace is the anchor of the soul ;
  Grace every sickness knows to heal ;
  Grace can subdue each fond desire,
  And patience in all pain inspire,
    Howe'er rebellious nature swell.

5 O Love, our stubborn will subdue,
  Create our ruined frame anew,
  Dispel our darkness by thy light ;
  Into all truth our spirit guide,
  And from our eyes for ever hide
    All things displeasing in thy sight.

6 Be heaven, even now, our soul's abode,
  Hid he our life with Christ in God,
  Our spirit, Lord, be one with thine ;
  Let all our works in thee be wrought,
  And filled with thee be all our thought,
    Till in us thy full likeness shine.

667   7 6, 7 6, 7 6, 7 6.   Proverbs viii. 22—31.

1 ERE God had built the mountains,
    Or raised the fruitful hills ;
  Before he filled the fountains
    That feed the running rills ;
  In me, from everlasting,
    The wonderful I AM
  Found pleasures never wasting ;
    And Wisdom is my name.

2 When, like a tent to dwell in,
    He spread the skies abroad,
  And swathed about the swelling
    Of ocean's mighty flood,

He wrought by weight and measure;
And I was with him then:
Myself the Father's pleasure,
And mine, the sons of men.

3 Thus Wisdom's words discover
Thy glory and thy grace,
Thou everlasting lover
Of our unworthy race:
Thy gracious eye surveyed us
Ere stars were seen above:
In wisdom thou hast made us,
And died for us in love!

4 And couldst thou be delighted
With creatures such as we,
Who, when we saw thee, slighted
And nailed thee to a tree?
Unfathomable wonder,
And mystery divine!
The voice that speaks in thunder
Says, Sinner, I am thine!

668   Matthew xi. 27.   6-8s.

1 JESUS, the infinite I AM,
With God essentially the same,
With him enthroned above all height,
As God of God, and Light of Light,
Thou art by thy great Father known,
From all eternity his Son.

2 Thou only dost the Father know,
And wilt to all thy followers show,
Who cannot doubt thy gracious will
His glorious Godhead to reveal;
Reveal him now, if thou art he,
And live, eternal Life, in me.

669   Matthew xii. 21.   C. M.

1 HIS name is Jesus Christ the Just,
My Advocate with God;
In him alone I put my trust,
Who bought me with his blood:
A sinner of the Gentiles, I
My pardoning Lord embrace,
And on his only name rely
For all his depths of grace.

2 A sinner still, though saved, I am;
And this is all my boast,
I hang upon a God who came
To seek and save the lost:
The object of my love and fear,
Who hath my sins forgiven,
Shall sink me into nothing here,
And lift me up to heaven.

670   Luke ii. 34.   6-8s.

1 JEHOVAH'S Fellow, and his Son,
What numbers fall by thee and rise!
Precious, elect, and corner-stone,
Built on thy strength we reach the skies,
Or by thy cross ourselves o'erthrow,
And sink into eternal woe.

2 Thine anger casts the sinner down,
That lifted up by pardoning grace
He may his Prince and Saviour own,
Thy justice and thy mercy praise,
Raised from the dust to stand restored
In all the image of his Lord.

3 Jesus, thy killing, quickening power
On a poor abject worm exert,
158

Confound, abase me from this hour,
Humble, and break this stubborn heart,
And then my Resurrection be,
And live, my heavenly Life, in me.

671   *" I am the Way, the Truth, and*
C. M.   *the Life."*—John xiv. 6.

1 THOU art the Way; by thee alone
From sin and death we flee:
And he who would the Father seek
Must seek him, Lord, by thee.

2 Thou art the Truth; thy word alone
True wisdom can impart;
Thou only canst inform the mind,
And purify the heart.

3 Thou art the Life; the rending tomb
Proclaims thy conquering arm;
And those who put their trust in thee
Nor death nor hell shall harm.

4 Thou art the Way, the Truth, the Life;
Grant us that Way to know,
That Truth to keep, that Life to win,
Whose joys eternal flow.

672   Philippians i. 21.
7 s.

1 CHRIST, of all my hopes the ground,
Christ, the spring of all my joy,
Still in thee may I be found,
Still for thee my powers employ,

2 Let thy love my heart inflame,
Keep thy fear before my sight,
Be thy praise my highest aim,
Be thy smile my chief delight!

3 When affliction clouds my sky,
And the wintry tempests blow,
Let thy mercy-beaming eye
Sweetly cheer the night of woe.

4 When new triumphs of thy name
Swell the raptured songs above,
May I feel a kindred flame,
Full of zeal, and full of love!

5 Life's best joy, to see thy praise
Fly on wings of gospel light,
Leading on millennial days,
Scattering all the shades of night!

6 Fountain of o'erflowing grace,
Freely from thy fulness give;
Till I close my earthly race,
May I prove it "Christ to live!"

SECOND PART.
7 s.

7 WHEN, with wasting sickness worn,
Sinking to the grave I lie,
Or, by sudden anguish torn,
Startled nature dreads to die;

8 Jesus, my redeeming Lord,
Be thou then in mercy near!
Let thy smile of love afford
Full relief from all my fear.

9 Firmly trusting in thy blood,
Nothing shall my heart confound
Safely shall I pass the flood,
Safely reach Immanuel's ground.

10 When I touch the blessed shore,
Back the closing waves shall roll;
Death's dark stream shall never more
Part from thee my ravished soul.

11 Thus, O thus, an entrance give
To the land of cloudless sky;
Having known it "Christ to live,"
Let me find it "gain to die!"

673　　1 John v. 20.　　C. M.

1 WE know, by faith we surely know,
The Son of God is come;
Is manifested here below,
And makes our hearts his home:
To us he hath, in special love,
An understanding given,
To recognise him from above
The Lord of earth and heaven.

2 The true and faithful Witness, we
Jehovah's Son confess;
And in the face of Jesus see
Jehovah's smiling face;
In him we live, and move, and are,
United to our Head,
And, branches of the Vine, declare
That Christ is God indeed.

3 The self-existing God supreme,
Our Saviour we adore,
Fountain of life eternal, him
We worship evermore;
Out of his plenitude receive
Ineffable delight,
And shall through endless ages live,
Triumphant in his sight.

674　　*"I am Alpha and Omega, the first and the last."—Revelation i. 11.*　6-6, 6 6, 6 6.

1 JESUS, the first and last,
On thee my soul is cast:
Thou didst thy work begin
By blotting out my sin;
Thou wilt the root remove,
And perfect me in love.

2 Yet when the work is done,
The work is but begun:
Partaker of thy grace,
I long to see thy face;
The first I prove below,
The last I die to know.

675　　*The Offices of Christ.*　4-6 s & 2-8 s.

1 JOIN all the glorious names
Of wisdom, love, and power,
That ever mortals knew,
That angels ever bore;
All are too mean to speak his worth,
Too mean to set our Saviour forth.

2 But O what gentle means,
What condescending ways,
Doth our Redeemer use,
To teach his heavenly grace;
My soul, with joy and wonder see
What forms of love he bears for thee!

3 Arrayed in mortal flesh
The Covenant-Angel stands,
And holds the promises
And pardons in his hands;
Commissioned from his Father's throne
To make his grace to mortals known.

4 Great Prophet of my God,
My lips shall bless thy name;

By thee the joyful news
Of our salvation came;
The joyful news of sins forgiven,
Of hell subdued, and peace with heaven.

5 Be thou my Counsellor,
My Pattern, and my Guide;
And through this desert land
Still keep me near thy side:
O let my feet ne'er run astray,
Nor rove, nor seek the crooked way!

6 I love my Shepherd's voice;
His watchful eye shall keep
My wandering soul among
The thousands of his sheep:
He feeds his flock, he calls their names,
His bosom bears the tender lambs.

7 Jesus, my great High-priest,
Offered his blood and died;
My guilty conscience seeks
No sacrifice beside;
His powerful blood did once atone,
And now it pleads before the throne.

8 O thou almighty Lord,
My Conqueror and my King,
Thy sceptre and thy sword,
Thy reign of grace, I sing;
Thine is the power: behold, I sit
In willing bonds before thy feet.

9 Now let my soul arise,
And tread the tempter down;
My Captain leads me forth
To conquest and a crown:
March on, nor fear to win the day,
Though death and hell obstruct the way.

10 Should all the hosts of death,
And powers of hell unknown,
Put their most dreadful forms
Of rage and malice on,
I shall be safe; for Christ displays
Superior power, and guardian grace.

8-7 s.　　**676**

1 CHRIST, the true anointed seer,
Messenger from the most High,
Thy prophetic character
To my conscience signify:
Signify thy Father's will;
By that unction from above,
Mysteries of grace reveal,
Teach my heart that God is love.

2 Thou who didst for all atone,
Dost for all incessant pray;
Make thy priestly office known,
Take my cancelled sin away;
Let me peace with God regain,
Righteousness from thee receive;
Through thy meritorious pain,
Through thy intercession, live.

3 Sovereign, universal King,
Every faithful soul's desire,
Into me thy kingdom bring,
Into me thy Spirit inspire;
From mine inbred foes release;
Here set up thy gracious throne;
King of righteousness and peace,
Reign in every heart alone!

677   Canticles iii. 11.'   **L. M.**

1 JESUS, thou everlasting King,
    Accept the tribute which we bring;
Accept thy well-deserved renown,
And wear our praises as thy crown.

2 Let every act of worship be
    Like our espousals, Lord, to thee;
Like the glad hour when from above
We first received the pledge of love.

3 The gladness of that happy day,
    O may it ever with us stay!
Nor let our faith forsake its hold,
Our hope decline, our love grow cold.

4 Each following moment as it flies
    Increase thy praise, improve our joys,
Till we are raised to sing thy name
At the great supper of the Lamb.

678   Revelation v. 12, 13.   **C. M.**

1 COME, let us join our cheerful songs
    With angels round the throne;
Ten thousand thousand are their tongues,
    But all their joys are one.

2 " Worthy the Lamb that died," they cry,
    " To be exalted thus!"
" Worthy the Lamb!" our hearts reply;
    " For he was slain for us."

3 Jesus is worthy to receive
    Honour and power divine;
And blessings, more than we can give,
    Be, Lord, for ever thine!

4 The whole creation join in one
    To bless the sacred name
Of him that sits upon the throne,
    And to adore the Lamb.

679   *" Thou shalt call his name*   **C. M.**
          Jesus."—Matthew i. 21.

1 HOW sweet the name of Jesus sounds
    In a believer's ear!
It soothes his sorrows, heals his wounds,
    And drives away his fear.

2 It makes the wounded spirit whole,
    And calms the troubled breast;
'Tis manna to the hungry soul,
    And to the weary rest.

3 Dear name! the rock on which I build,
    My shield, and hiding-place,
My never-failing treasury, filled
    With boundless stores of grace!

4 Jesus, my Shepherd, Husband, Friend,
    My Prophet, Priest, and King;
My Lord, my Life, my Way, my End,
    Accept the praise I bring.

5 Weak is the effort of my heart,
    And cold my warmest thought;
But when I see thee as thou art,
    I'll praise thee as I ought.

6 Till then I would thy love proclaim
    With every fleeting breath;
And may the music of thy name
    Refresh my soul in death!

680   *The same subject.*   **C. M.**

1 JESU, the very thought of thee
    With sweetness fills my breast;

But sweeter far thy face to see,
    And in thy presence rest.

2 Nor voice can sing, nor heart can frame,
    Nor can the memory find
A sweeter sound than thy blest name,
    O Saviour of mankind!

3 O hope of every contrite heart,
    O joy of all the meek,
To those who fall how kind thou art!
    How good to those who seek!

4 But what to those who find? Ah! this
    Nor tongue nor pen can show;
The love of Jesus, what it is
    None but his loved ones know.

5 Jesu, our only joy be thou,
    As thou our prize wilt be;
Jesu, be thou our glory now,
    And through eternity.

" On his head were many crowns."   **681**
C. M.   Revelation xix. 12.

1 ALL hail the power of Jesu's name;
    Let angels prostrate fall;
Bring forth the royal diadem
    To crown him Lord of all.

2 Crown him, ye morning stars of light,
    Who launched this floating ball;
Now hail the Strength of Israel's might,
    And crown him Lord of all.

3 Crown him, ye martyrs of our God,
    Who from his altar call;
Of Jesse's stem extol the Rod,
    And crown him Lord of all.

4 Ye seed of Israel's chosen race,
    Ye ransomed from the fall,
Hail him who saves you by his grace,
    And crown him Lord of all.

5 Hail him, ye heirs of David's line,
    Whom David Lord did call,
The God incarnate, Man divine,
    And crown him Lord of all.

6 Ye Gentile sinners, ne'er forget
    The wormwood and the gall,
Go spread your trophies at his feet,
    And crown him Lord of all.

7 Let every tribe and every tongue
    Before him prostrate fall,
And shout in universal song
    The crowned Lord of all.

8 O that with yonder sacred throng
    We at his feet may fall,
Join in the everlasting song,
    And crown him Lord of all!

                           682
C. M.   Hebrews vi. 20.

1 THOU great Redeemer, dying Lamb,
    We love to hear of thee;
No music's like thy charming name,
    Nor half so sweet can be.

2 O may we ever hear thy voice
    In mercy to us speak!
And in our Priest we will rejoice,
    Thou great Melchizedek!

3 Our Jesus shall be still our theme,
    While in this world we stay:
We'll sing our Jesu's lovely name,
    When all things else decay.

4 When we appear in yonder cloud,
   With all that favoured throng,
Then will we sing more sweet, more loud,
   And Christ shall be our song.

(1.) ON THE BIRTH AND LIFE AND WORKS
OF CHRIST.

683
                          7 s.

1 HARK, the herald-angels sing
   "Glory to the new-born King,
Peace on earth, and mercy mild;
God and sinners reconciled."

2 Christ, by highest heaven adored,
Christ, the everlasting Lord,
Late in time behold him come,
Offspring of a virgin's womb!

3 Veiled in flesh the Godhead see;
Hail the incarnate Deity!
Pleased as man with men to appear,
Jesus our Immanuel here.

4 Hail the heaven-born Prince of peace!
Hail the Sun of righteousness!
Light and life to all he brings,
Risen with healing in his wings.

5 Mild he lays his glory by,
Born that man no more may die;
Born to raise the sons of earth,
Born to give them second birth.

6 Come, Desire of nations, come,
Fix in us thy humble home;
Rise, the woman's conquering Seed,
Bruise in us the serpent's head.

7 Adam's likeness now efface,
Stamp thine image in its place;
Second Adam from above,
Reinstate us in thy love.

684   *"Immanuel, God with us."*
       Matthew i. 23.   7 s & 6 s.

1 GLORY be to God on high,
   And peace on earth descend!
God comes down, he bows the sky,
   And shows himself our friend:
God the invisible appears!
   God, the blest, the great I AM,
Sojourns in this vale of tears,
   And Jesus is his name.

2 Him the angels all adored,
   Their Maker and their King;
Tidings of their humbled Lord
   They now to mortals bring.
Emptied of his majesty,
   Of his dazzling glories shorn,
Being's source begins to be,
   And God himself is born!

3 See the eternal Son of God
   A mortal Son of man;
Dwelling in an earthly clod,
   Whom heaven cannot contain!
Stand amazed, ye heavens, at this!
   See the Lord of earth and skies;
Humbled to the dust he is,
   And in a manger lies.

4 We, the sons of men, rejoice,
   The Prince of peace proclaim;
With heaven's host lift up our voice,
   And shout Immanuel's name:

Knees and hearts to him we bow;
Of our flesh and of our bone,
Jesus is our brother now,
And God is all our own.

685
4 - 6 s & 2 - 8 s.   *The same subject.*

1 LET earth and heaven combine,
   Angels and men agree,
To praise in songs divine
   The incarnate Deity,
Our God contracted to a span,
Incomprehensibly made man.

2 He laid his glory by,
   He wrapped him in our clay;
Unmarked by human eye,
   The latent Godhead lay;
Infant of days he here became,
And bore the mild Immanuel's name.

3 Unsearchable the love
   That hath the Saviour brought;
The grace is far above
   Or man or angel's thought;
Suffice for us that God, we know,
Our God, is manifest below.

4 He deigns in flesh to appear,
   Widest extremes to join;
To bring our vileness near,
   And make us all divine:
And we the life of God shall know,
For God is manifest below.

5 Made perfect first in love,
   And sanctified by grace,
We shall from earth remove,
   And see his glorious face:
Then shall his love be fully showed,
And man shall then be lost in God.

686
6 - 8 s.   Luke 1. 78.

1 STUPENDOUS height of heavenly love,
   Of pitying tenderness divine!
It brought the Saviour from above,
   It caused the springing day to shine;
The Sun of righteousness to appear,
And gild our gloomy hemisphere.

2 God did in Christ himself reveal,
   To chase our darkness by his light,
Our sin and ignorance dispel,
   Direct our wandering feet aright,
And bring our souls, with pardon blest,
To realms of everlasting rest.

3 Come then, O Lord, thy light impart,
   The faith that bids our terrors cease
Into thy love direct our heart,
   Into thy way of perfect peace;
And cheer the souls of death afraid,
And guide them through the dreadful
   shade.

4 Answer thy mercy's whole design,
   My God incarnated for me;
My spirit make thy radiant shrine,
   My light and full salvation be, [known
And through the shades of death un-
Conduct me to thy dazzling throne.

687
8 s & 7 s.   *The Light of the Gentiles.*
          Isaiah ix. 2.

1 LIGHT of those whose dreary dwelling
   Borders on the shades of death,

Come, and by thy love's revealing
Dissipate the clouds beneath:
The new heaven and earth's Creator,
In our deepest darkness rise,
Scattering all the night of nature,
Pouring eye-sight on our eyes.

2 Still we wait for thine appearing;
Life and joy thy beams impart,
Chasing all our fears, and cheering
Every poor benighted heart:
Come, and manifest the favour
God hath for our ransomed race;
Come, thou universal Saviour,
Come, and bring the gospel grace.

3 Save us in thy great compassion,
O thou mild, pacific Prince;
Give the knowledge of salvation,
Give the pardon of our sins:
By thy all-restoring merit,
Every burdened soul release;
Every weary, wandering spirit
Guide into thy perfect peace.

688 *"The Desire of all nations."*
Haggai ii. 7.   8 s & 7 s.

1 COME, thou long-expected Jesus,
Born to set thy people free,
From our fears and sins release us,
Let us find our rest in thee.
Israel's strength and consolation,
Hope of all the earth thou art;
Dear Desire of every nation,
Joy of every longing heart.

2 Born thy people to deliver,
Born a child and yet a king,
Born to reign in us for ever,
Now thy gracious kingdom bring:
By thine own eternal Spirit
Rule in all our hearts alone;
By thine all-sufficient merit
Raise us to thy glorious throne.

689   Luke ii. 11.   L. M.

1 TO us a child of royal birth,
Heir of the promises, is given;
The Invisible appears on earth,
The Son of man, the God of heaven.

2 A Saviour born, in love supreme
He comes our fallen souls to raise;
He comes his people to redeem
With all his plenitude of grace.

3 The Christ, by raptured seers foretold,
Filled with the eternal Spirit's power,
Prophet, and Priest, and King behold,
And Lord of all the worlds adore.

4 The Lord of hosts, the God most high,
Who quits his throne on earth to live,
With joy we welcome from the sky,
With faith into our hearts receive.

690 *"The Redeemer shall come to Zion."*—Isaiah lix. 20.   6 - 8 s.

1 O COME, O come, Immanuel,
And ransom captive Israel,
That mourns in lonely exile here,
Until the Son of God appear.
Rejoice! rejoice! Immanuel
Shall come to thee, O Israel!

2 O come, thou Rod of Jesse, free
Thine own from Satan's tyranny;

162

From depths of hell thy people save,
And give them victory o'er the grave.
Rejoice! rejoice! Immanuel
Shall come to thee, O Israel!

3 O come, thou **Dayspring**, come and cheer
Our spirits by thine advent here;
Disperse the gloomy clouds of night,
And death's dark shadows put to flight.
Rejoice! rejoice! Immanuel
Shall come to thee, O Israel!

4 O come, thou Key of David, come,
And open wide our heavenly home;
Make safe the way that leads on high,
And close the path to misery.
Rejoice! rejoice! Immanuel
Shall come to thee, O Israel!

5 O come, O come, thou Lord of might!
Who to thy tribes, on Sinai's height,
In ancient times didst give the law,
In cloud, and majesty, and awe.
Rejoice! rejoice! Immanuel
Shall come to thee, O Israel!

10 10, 10 10, 10 10.   Luke ii. 8-17.   **691**

1 CHRISTIANS, awake, salute the happy morn,
Whereon the Saviour of mankind was
Rise to adore the mystery of love, [born;
Which hosts of angels chanted from above;
With them the joyful tidings first begun
Of God incarnate and the Virgin's son.

2 Then to the watchful shepherds it was told,   ["Behold,
Who heard the angelic herald's voice:
I bring good tidings of a Saviour's birth
To you and all the nations upon earth;
This day hath God fulfilled his promised word,   [Lord."
This day is born a Saviour, Christ the

3 He spake; and straightway the celestial choir   [spire;
In hymns of joy, unknown before, con-
The praises of redeeming love they sang,
And heaven's whole orb with hallelujahs rang;
God's highest glory was their anthem still,
Peace upon earth, and unto men good-will.

4 To Bethlehem straight the enlightened shepherds ran,   [man:
To see the wonders God had wrought for
Then to their flocks, still praising God, return,   [burn;
And their glad hearts with holy rapture
Amazed, the wondrous tidings they proclaim,
The first apostles of his infant fame.

5 O! may we keep and ponder in our mind
God's wondrous love in saving lost mankind;   [loss,
Trace we the Babe, who hath retrieved our
From the poor manger to the bitter cross;
Tread in his steps, assisted by his grace,
Till man's first heavenly state again takes place.

6 Then may we hope, the angelic hosts among,   [throng;
To join, redeemed, a glad triumphant

He that was born upon this joyful day
Around us all his glory shall display;
Saved by his love, incessant we shall sing
Eternal praise to heaven's almighty King.

692 C. M.

1 O SAVIOUR, whom this holy morn
Gave to our world below;
To mortal want and labour born,
And more than mortal woe;

2 Incarnate Word! by every grief,
By each temptation tried,
Who lived to yield our ills relief,
And to redeem us died!

3 If gaily clothed and proudly fed
In dangerous wealth we dwell,
Remind us of thy manger bed
And lowly cottage cell.

4 If pressed by poverty severe
In anxious want we pine,
O may thy Spirit whisper near
How poor a lot was thine!

5 Through this life's ever-varying scene
From sin preserve us free;
Like us thou hast a mourner been,
May we rejoice with thee!

693 Matthew iv. 23. 7 s & 6 s †.

1 JESUS, thee thy works proclaim
Omnipotently good:
Moses thy forerunner came,
And mighty works he showed;
Minister of wrath divine,
His wonders plagued the sinful race;
Works of purest love are thine,
And miracles of grace.

2 All thy cures are mysteries,
And prove thy power to heal
Every sickness and disease
Which now our spirits feel;
Good Physician of mankind,
Thou wilt repeat thy sovereign word,
Chase the evils of our mind,
And speak our souls restored.

3 Who of other help despair,
And would thy word receive,
Us thou mak'st thy tenderest care,
And kindly dost relieve;
Every soul-infirmity,
And plague of heart, thou dost remove;
Heal'st whoe'er apply to thee,
With balm of bleeding love.

4 Still thou go'st about to teach,
And desperate souls to cure;
Still thou dost the kingdom preach
Which always shall endure;
Publishest the power of grace,
Which pardon and salvation brings,
Saves our fallen dying race,
And makes us priests and kings.

694 Luke xviii. 35—42. 7 7, 7 8, 8 8

1 LORD! we sit and cry to thee,
Like the blind beside the way;
Make our darkened souls to see
The glory of thy perfect day:
O Lord! rebuke our sullen night,
And give thyself unto our sight!
F 2

2 Lord! we do not ask to gaze
On our dim and earthly sun;
But on light that still shall blaze
When every star its course hath run;
The light that gilds thy blest abode,
The glory of the Lamb of God!

695 6 - 8 s. Matthew xxi. 10, 11.

1 WHAT means this eager, anxious
throng,
Which moves with busy haste along,
These wondrous gatherings day by day,
What means this strange commotion,
pray?
In accents hushed the throng reply,
"Jesus of Nazareth passeth by!"

2 Who is this Jesus? why should he
The city move so mightily?
A passing stranger, has he skill
To charm the multitude at will?
Again the stirring tones reply,
"Jesus of Nazareth passeth by!"

3 Jesus! 'tis he who once below
Man's pathway trod, 'mid pain and woe,
And burdened ones where'er he came
Brought out their sick and deaf and lame;
The blind rejoiced to hear the cry,
"Jesus of Nazareth passeth by!"

4 Again he comes! from place to place
His holy footsteps we can trace;
He pauses at our threshold, nay,
He enters, condescends to stay;
Shall we not gladly raise the cry?
"Jesus of Nazareth passeth by."

5 Ho! all ye heavy-laden, come;
Here's pardon, comfort, rest, and home;
Ye wanderers from a father's face,
Return, accept his proffered grace!
Ye tempted, there's a refuge nigh,
"Jesus of Nazareth passeth by."

6 But if you still his call refuse
And all his wondrous love abuse,
Soon will he sadly from you turn,
Your bitter prayer for pardon spurn;
"Too late, too late!" will be your cry,
Jesus of Nazareth *has passed by.*

696 "*Lord, help me!*" C. M. Matthew xv. 25.

1 O HELP us, Lord! each hour of need
Thy heavenly succour give;
Help us in thought, in word, and deed,
Each hour on earth we live.

2 O help us when our spirits bleed
With contrite anguish sore;
And when our hearts are cold and dead,
O help us, Lord, the more!

3 O help us, through the prayer of faith
More firmly to believe;
For still the more the servant hath,
The more shall he receive.

4 If, strangers to thy fold, we call,
Imploring at thy feet
The crumbs that from thy table fall,
'Tis all we dare intreat.

5 But be it, Lord of mercy, all,
So thou wilt grant but this,
The crumbs that from thy table fall
Are life, and light, and bliss.

6 O help us, Jesu, from on high !
  We know no help but thee !
O help us so to live and die,
  As thine in heaven to be !

697   Mark iv. 36—v. 19.   C. M.

1 THE winds were howling o'er the deep,
    Each wave a watery hill,
The Saviour wakened from his sleep,
  He spake, and all was still.

2 The madman in a tomb had made
    His mansion of despair ;
Woe to the traveller who strayed
  With heedless footsteps there !

3 He met that glance so thrilling sweet,
    He heard those accents mild,
And, melting at Messiah's feet,
  Wept like a weaned child.

4 O madder than the raving man !
    O deafer than the sea !
How long the time since Christ began
  To call in vain on *me ?*

5 He called me when my thoughtless prime
    Was early ripe to ill ;
I passed from folly on to crime,
  And yet he called me still.

6 He called me in the time of dread,
    When death was full in view,
I trembled on my feverish bed,
  And rose to sin anew.

7 Yet could I hear him once again,
    As I have heard of old,
Methinks he should not call in vain
  His wanderer to the fold.

8 O thou that every thought canst know,
    And answer every prayer ;
O give me sickness, want, or woe,
  But snatch me from despair !

9 My struggling will by grace control,
    Renew my broken vow !
What blessed light breaks on my soul ?
  O God ! I hear thee now.

698   Matthew xvii. 4.   L. M.

1 LORD ! it is good for us to be
    High on the mountain here with thee :
Here in an ampler, purer air,
Above the stir of toil and care,
Of hearts opprest with doubt and grief,
Believing in their unbelief,
Calling thy servants all in vain
To ease them of their bitter pain.

2 Lord ! it is good for us to be
Where rest the souls that dwell with thee ;
Where stand revealed to mortal gaze
The great old saints of other days,
Who once received on Horeb's height
The eternal laws of truth and right ;
Or caught the still small whisper higher
Than storm, than earthquake, or than fire.

3 Lord ! it is good for us to be
With thee, and with thy faithful three :
Here, where the apostle's heart of rock
Is nerved against temptation's shock ;
Here, where the son of thunder learns
The thought that breathes, the word that
  burns,
164

Here, where on eagles' wings we move
With him whose last, best word is love.

4 Lord ! it is good for us to be
Entranced, enwrapped, alone with thee,
Watching the glistening raiment glow
Whiter than Hermon's whitest snow,
The human lineaments which shine
Irradiant with a light divine,
Till we, too, change from grace to grace,
Gazing on that transfigured face.

5 Lord ! it is good for us to be
In life's worst anguish close to thee,
Within the overshadowing cloud
Which wraps us in its awful shroud ;
We wist not what to think or say,
Our spirits sink in sore dismay ;
They tell us of the dread "decease : "
But yet to linger here is peace.

6 Lord ! it is good for us to be
Here on the holy mount with thee,
When darkling in the depths of night,
When dazzled with excess of light, ;
We bow before the heavenly voice
Which bids bewildered souls rejoice ;
Though love wax cold, and faith grow dim,
This is my Son : O hear ye him !

(2.) ON THE SUFFERINGS AND DEATH, RESUR-
RECTION, AND ASCENSION OF CHRIST.

C. M.   **699**

1 PLUNGED in a gulf of dark despair
    We wretched sinners lay,
Without one cheerful beam of hope,
  Or spark of glimmering day.

2 With pitying eyes, the Prince of peace
    Beheld our helpless grief ;
He saw, and—O amazing love !
  He flew to our relief.

3 Down from the shining seats above
    With joyful haste he sped ;
Entered the grave in mortal flesh,
  And dwelt among the dead.

4 O for this love let rocks and hills
    Their lasting silence break,
And all harmonious human tongues
  The Saviour's praises speak !

5 Angels, assist our mighty joys,
    Strike all your harps of gold ;
But when you raise your highest notes,
  His love can ne'er be told.

L. M.   Galatians vi. 14.   **700**

1 WHEN I survey the wondrous cross
    On which the Prince of glory died,
My richest gain I count but loss,
    And pour contempt on all my pride.

2 Forbid it, Lord, that I should boast,
    Save in the death of Christ, my God :
All the vain things that charm me most,
  I sacrifice them to his blood.

3 See, from his head, his hands, his feet,
    Sorrow and love flow mingled down :
Did e'er such love and sorrow meet,
  Or thorns compose so rich a crown ?

4 Were the whole realm of nature mine,
    That were a present far too small ;

Love so amazing, so divine,
Demands my soul, my life, my all.

701   *Christ crucified.*   7 s & 6 s

1 GOD of unexampled grace,
    Redeemer of mankind,
Matter of eternal praise
We in thy passion find:
Still our choicest strains we bring,
Still the joyful theme pursue,
Thee the friend of sinners sing,
Whose love is ever new.

2 Endless scenes of wonder rise
From that mysterious tree,
Crucified before our eyes,
Where we our Maker see:
Jesus, Lord, what hast thou done?
Publish we the death divine,
Stop, and gaze, and fall, and own
Was never love like thine!

3 Never love nor sorrow was
Like that my Saviour showed:
See him stretched on yonder cross,
And crushed beneath our load!
Now discern the Deity,
Now his heavenly birth declare!
Faith cries out, "Tis He, 'tis He,
My God, that suffers there!"

702   *"A shadow of good things."*
     Hebrews x. 1.   L. M.

1 O THOU, whose offering on the tree
    The legal offerings all foreshowed,
Borrowed their whole effect from thee,
And drew their virtue from thy blood:

2 The blood of goats and bullocks slain
Could never for one sin atone:
To purge the guilty offerer's stain,
Thine was the work, and thine alone.

3 Vain in themselves their duties were,
Their services could never please,
Till joined with thine, and made to share
The merits of thy righteousness.

4 Forward they cast a faithful look
On thy approaching sacrifice;
And thence their pleasing savour took,
And rose accepted in the skies.

5 Those feeble types, and shadows old,
Are all in thee, the Truth, fulfilled:
We in thy sacrifice behold
The substance of those rites revealed.

6 Thy meritorious sufferings past,
We see by faith to us brought back;
And on thy grand oblation cast,
Its saving benefits partake.

703   *"It is not possible," &c.*
     Hebrews x. 4.   S. M.

1 NOT all the blood of beasts
    On Jewish altars slain,
Could give the guilty conscience peace,
Or wash away our stain.

2 But Christ, the heavenly Lamb,
Takes all our sins away;
A sacrifice of nobler name,
And richer blood, than they.

3 My faith would lay her hand
On that meek head of thine,

While as a penitent I stand,
And here confess my sin.

4 My soul looks back to see
The burden thou didst bear
When hanging on the accursed tree,
And knows her guilt was there.

5 Believing, we rejoice
To feel the curse remove;
We bless the Lamb with cheerful voice,
And trust his bleeding love.

S. M.   *"Our Passover."*
     1 Corinthians v. 7.   **704**

1 THOU very Paschal Lamb,
    Whose blood for us was shed,
Through whom we out of Egypt came,
Thy ransomed people lead.

2 Angel of gospel grace,
Fulfil thy character:
To guard and feed the chosen race,
In Israel's camp appear.

3 Throughout the desert way
Conduct us by thy light;
Be thou a cooling cloud by day,
A cheering fire by night.

4 Our fainting souls sustain
With blessings from above;
And ever on thy people rain
The manna of thy love.

S. M.   *"By water and blood."*
     I John v. 6.   **705**

1 THIS, this is he that came
    By water and by blood!
Jesus is our atoning Lamb,
Our sanctifying God.

2 See from his wounded side
The mingled current flow!
The water and the blood applied
Shall wash us white as snow.

3 The water cannot cleanse,
Before the blood we feel,
To purge the guilt of all our sins,
And our forgiveness seal.

4 But both in Jesus join,
Who speaks our sins forgiven,
And gives the purity divine
That makes us meet for heaven.

L. M.   *"It is finished."*—John xix. 30.   **706**

1 'TIS finished! the Messias dies,
    Cut off for sins, but not his own:
Accomplished is the sacrifice,
The great redeeming work is done.

2 'Tis finished! all the debt is paid;
Justice divine is satisfied;
The grand and full atonement made;
God for a guilty world hath died.

3 The veil is rent in Christ alone;
The living way to heaven is seen;
The middle wall is broken down,
And all mankind may enter in.

4 The types and figures are fulfilled;
Exacted is the legal pain;
The precious promises are sealed;
The spotless Lamb of God is slain.

5 The reign of sin and death is o'er,
And all may live from sin set free;

Satan hath lost his mortal power;
 'Tis swallowed up in victory.

6 Saved from the legal curse I am,
 My Saviour hangs on yonder tree;
See there the meek, expiring Lamb!
 'Tis finished! he expires for me.

7 Accepted in the Well-beloved,
 And clothed in righteousness divine,
I see the bar to heaven removed;
 And all thy merits, Lord, are mine.

8 Death, hell, and sin are now subdued;
 All grace is now to sinners given;
And, lo, I plead the atoning blood,
 And in thy right I claim thy heaven!

707   Lamentations i. 12.   5 5 12, 5 5 12.

1 ALL ye that pass by,
  To Jesus draw nigh:
To you is it nothing that Jesus should die?
 Your ransom and peace,
 Your surety he is:
Come, see if there ever was sorrow like his.

2 For what you have done
 His blood must atone: [Son.
The Father hath punished for you his dear
 The Lord, in the day
 Of his anger, did lay   [away.
Your sins on the Lamb, and he bore them

3 He answered for all:
 O come at his call,
And low at his cross with astonishment fall!
 But lift up your eyes
 At Jesus's cries:
Impassive, he suffers; immortal, he dies.

4 He dies to atone
 For sins not his own;   [hath done.
Your debt he hath paid, and your work he
 Ye all may receive
 The peace he did leave,   [give!"
Who made intercession, "My Father, for-

5 For you and for me
 He prayed on the tree:
The prayer is accepted, the sinner is free.
 That sinner am I,
 Who on Jesus rely,
And come for the pardon God cannot deny.

6 My pardon I claim;
 For a sinner I am,
A sinner believing in Jesus's name.
 He purchased the grace
 Which now I embrace: [place.
O Father, thou know'st he hath died in my

7 His death is my plea;
 My Advocate see,   [for me.
And hear the blood speak that hath answered
 My ransom he was
 When he bled on the cross; [cause.
And by losing his life he hath carried my

708   *"Nor yet that he should offer himself often."*—Heb. ix. 25.   6 - 8 s.

1 O THOU eternal Victim, slain
 A sacrifice for guilty man,
By the eternal Spirit made
An offering in the sinner's stead;
 Our everlasting Priest art thou,
 And plead'st thy death for sinners now.

2 Thy offering still continues new;
 Thy vesture keeps its bloody hue;
Thou stand'st the ever-slaughtered Lamb;
 Thy priesthood still remains the same;
Thy years, O God, can never fail;
 Thy goodness is unchangeable.

3 O that our faith may never move,
 But stand unshaken as thy love!
Sure evidence of things unseen,
 Now let it pass the years between,
And view thee bleeding on the tree,
 My God, who dies for me, for me!

6 - 7 s.   *Christ the Rock of ages.*   **709**
    Isaiah xxvi. 4.

1 ROCK of ages, cleft for me,
  Let me hide myself in thee;
Let the water and the blood,
From thy wounded side which flowed,
Be of sin the double cure,
Save from wrath and make me pure.

2 Could my tears for ever flow,
Could my zeal no languor know,
These for sin could not atone;
Thou must save and thou alone:
In my hand no price I bring,
Simply to thy cross I cling.

3 While I draw this fleeting breath,
When my eyes shall close in death,
When I rise to worlds unknown,
And behold thee on thy throne,
Rock of ages, cleft for me,
Let me hide myself in thee.

8 - 7 s.   **710**

1 SAVIOUR, when in dust to thee
 Low we bow the adoring knee;
When, repentant, to the skies,
Scarce we lift our weeping eyes,
O by all thy pains and woe
Suffered once for man below,
Bending from thy throne on high,
Hear our solemn litany!

2 By thy helpless infant years;
By thy life of want and tears;
By thy fasting and distress
In the savage wilderness;
By the dread mysterious hour
Of the subtle tempter's power;
Turn, O turn a favouring eye,
Hear our solemn litany!

3 By the sacred grief that wept
O'er the grave where Lazarus slept;
By the gracious tears that flowed
Over Salem's loved abode;
By the mournful word that told
Treachery lurked within thy fold;
From thy seat above the sky,
Hear our solemn litany!

4 By thine hour of whelming fear;
By thine agony of prayer;
By the purple robe of scorn;
By thy wounds, thy crown of thorn;
By the gloom that veiled the skies
O'er the dreadful sacrifice;
Listen to our humble cry,
Hear our solemn litany!

5 By thy deep expiring groan;
By the sealed sepulchral stone;

By the vault whose dark abode
Held in vain the rising God,
O from earth to heaven restored,
Mighty God, ascended Lord,
Listen, listen to the cry
Of our solemn litany !

711 *"Surely he hath borne our griefs,
and carried our sorrows."* **7 s.**
Isaiah liii. 4.

1 WHEN our heads are bowed with woe,
  When our bitter tears o'erflow,
When we mourn the lost, the dear,
Jesu, Son of David, hear.

2 When the heart is sad within
With the thought of all its sin,
When the spirit shrinks with fear,
Jesu, Son of David, hear.

3 Thou our throbbing flesh hast worn,
Thou our mortal griefs hast borne,
Thou hast shed the human tear ;
Jesu, Son of David, hear.

4 Thou hast bowed the dying head,
Thou the blood of life hast shed,
Thou hast filled a mortal bier ;
Jesu, Son of David, hear.

712 *On the Resurrection of Christ.* **L. M.**

1 HE dies ! the friend of sinners dies !
  Lo ! Salem's daughters weep around !
A solemn darkness veils the skies ;
A sudden trembling shakes the ground :
Come, saints, and with your tears bedew
The sufferer, bruised beneath your load,
He poured out cries and tears for you,
He shed for you his precious blood.

2 Here's love and grief beyond degree ;
The Lord of glory dies for man !
But lo ! what sudden joys I see !
Jesus, the dead, revives again !
The rising God forsakes the tomb :
The tomb in vain forbids his rise !
Cherubic legions guard him home,
And shout him welcome to the skies !

3 Break off your tears, ye saints, and tell
How high your great Deliverer reigns ;
Sing how he spoiled the hosts of hell,
And led the monster death in chains.
Say, "Live for ever, wondrous King !
Born to redeem, and strong to save !"
Then ask the monster, "Where's thy
  sting ?"   [grave ?"
And, "Where's thy victory, boasting

713
                              C. M.

1 YE humble souls, that seek the Lord,
  Chase all your fears away ;
And bow with rapture down to see
The place where Jesus lay.

2 Thus low the Lord of life was brought ;
Such wonders love can do :
Thus cold in death that bosom lay,
Which throbbed and bled for you.

3 But raise your eyes, and tune your songs,
The Saviour lives again :
Not all the bolts and bars of death
The Conqueror could detain.

4 High o'er the angelic bands he rears
His once dishonoured head ;
And through unnumbered years he reigns,
Who dwelt among the dead.

5 With joy like his shall every saint
His vacant tomb survey ;
Then rise with his ascending Lord
To realms of endless day.

714

6 - 7 s.   Irregular.

1 IN the bonds of death he lay,
  Who for our offence was slain,
But the Lord is risen to-day,
Christ hath brought us life again ;
Wherefore let us all rejoice,
Singing loud with cheerful voice
                    Hallelujah !

2 Jesus Christ, God's only Son,
Came at last our foe to smite,
All our sins away hath done,
Done away death's power and right ;
Only the form of death is left,
Of his sting he is bereft ;
                    Hallelujah !

3 'Twas a wondrous war I trow,
Life and death together fought,
But life hath triumphed o'er his foe,
Death is mocked, and set at nought ;
Yea, 'tis as the Scripture saith,
Christ through death hath conquered
                    death,
                    Hallelujah !

4 Now our Paschal Lamb is he,
And by him alone we live,
Who to death upon the tree
For our sake himself did give.
Faith his blood strikes on our door,
Death dares never harm us more,
                    Hallelujah !

5 On this day, most blest of days,
Let us keep high festival,
For our God hath showed his grace,
And his sun hath risen on all,
And our hearts rejoice to see
Sin and night before him flee.
                    Hallelujah !

6 To the supper of the Lord
Gladly will we come to-day ;
The word of peace is now restored,
The old leaven is put away ;
Christ will be our food alone,
Faith no life but his will own.
                    Hallelujah !

715

1 THE foe behind, the deep before, [sea :
  Our hosts have dared and passed the
And Pharaoh's warriors strew the shore,
And Israel's ransomed tribes are free.

2 Lift up, lift up your voices now !
The whole wide world rejoices now !
The Lord hath triumphed gloriously !
The Lord shall reign victoriously !

3   Happy morrow,
           Turning sorrow
       Into peace and mirth !
           Bondage ending,
           Love descending
           O'er the earth !

4   Seals assuring,
      Guards securing,
    Watch his earthly prison.
    Seals are shattered,
      Guards are scattered,
        Christ hath risen !

5 No longer must the mourners weep,
    Nor call departed Christians dead ;
    For death is hallowed into sleep, 1
    And every grave becomes a bed.

6   Now once more
      Eden's door
    Open stands to mortal eyes ;
For Christ hath risen, and man shall rise !

7   Now at last,
      Old things past,
    Hope, and joy, and peace begin ;
For Christ hath won, and man shall win !

8 It is not exile, rest on high :
    It is not sadness, peace from strife ;
    To fall asleep is not to die :
    To dwell with Christ is better life.

9   Where our banner leads us,
      We may safely go :
    Where our Chief precedes us,
      We may face the foe.

10   His right arm is o'er us,
      He our guide will be :
    Christ hath gone before us.
    Christians, follow ye !

716   7 s.

1 " CHRIST, the Lord, is risen to-day,"
      Sons of men and angels say !
Raise your joys and triumphs high :
Sing, ye heavens ; thou earth, reply.

2 Love's redeeming work is done ;
Fought the fight, the battle won ;
Lo ! the sun's eclipse is o'er,
Lo ! he sets in blood no more !

3 Vain the stone, the watch, the seal,
Christ hath burst the gates of hell ;
Death in vain forbids his rise,
Christ hath opened Paradise.

4 Lives again our glorious King !
Where, O death, is now thy sting ?
Once he died our souls to save ;
Where's thy victory, boasting grave ?

5 Soar we now where Christ hath led,
Following our exalted Head :
Made like him, like him we rise,
Ours the cross, the grave, the skies.

6 King of glory ! Soul of bliss !
Everlasting life is this,
Thee to know, thy power to prove,
Thus to sing, and thus to love.

717   7 s & 6 s.

1 FATHER, God, we glorify
      Thy love to Adam's seed ;
Love that gave thy Son to die,
    And raised him from the dead :
Him, for our offences slain,
    That we all might pardon find,
Thou hast brought to life again,
    The Saviour of mankind.
168

2 By thy own right hand of power
Thou hast exalted him,
Sent the mighty Conqueror
Thy people to redeem :
King of saints, and Prince of peace,
Him thou hast for sinners given,
Sinners from their sins to bless,
And lift them up to heaven.

3 Father, God, to us impart
The gift unspeakable ;
Now in every waiting heart
Thy glorious Son reveal :
Quickened with our living Lord,
Let us in thy Spirit rise,
Rise to all thy life restored,
And bless thee in the skies.

718   7 s   *On the Ascension of Christ.*

1 HAIL the day that sees him rise,
    Ravished from our wishful eyes !
Christ, awhile to mortals given,
Re-ascends his native heaven.

2 There the pompous triumph waits ;
" Lift your heads, eternal gates ;
Wide unfold the radiant scene ;
Take the King of glory in ! "

3 Circled round with angel powers,
Their triumphant Lord, and ours,
Conqueror over death and sin ;
" Take the King of glory in ! "

4 Him though highest heaven receives,
Still he loves the earth he leaves ;
Though returning to his throne,
Still he calls mankind his own.

5 See, he lifts his hands above !
See, he shows the prints of love !
Hark, his gracious lips bestow
Blessings on his church below !

6 Still for us his death he pleads ;
Prevalent he intercedes ;
Near himself prepares our place,
Harbinger of human race.

7 Master, (will we ever say)
Taken from our head to-day ;
See thy faithful servants, see,
Ever gazing up to thee.

8 Grant, though parted from our sight,
High above yon azure height,
Grant our hearts may thither rise,
Following thee beyond the skies.

9 Ever upward let us move,
Wafted on the wings of love ;
Looking when our Lord shall come,
Longing, gasping after home.

10 There we shall with thee remain,
Partners of thy endless reign ;
There thy face unclouded see,
Find our heaven of heavens in thee.

719

4 - 6 s & 2 - 8 s.

1 GOD is gone up on high,
    With a triumphant noise ;
The clarions of the sky
    Proclaim the angelic joys !
Join all on earth, rejoice and sing ;
Glory ascribe to glory's King.

2 God in the flesh below,
 For us he reigns above:
 Let all the nations know
 Our Jesu's conquering love!
Join all on earth, rejoice and sing;
Glory ascribe to glory's King.

3 All power to our great Lord
 Is by the Father given;
 By angel-hosts adored,
 He reigns supreme in heaven:
Join all on earth, rejoice and sing;
Glory ascribe to glory's King.

4 High on his holy seat,
 He bears the righteous sway;
 His foes beneath his feet
 Shall sink and die away:
Join all on earth, rejoice and sing;
Glory ascribe to glory's King.

5 His foes and ours are one,
 Satan, the world, and sin;
 But he shall tread them down,
 And bring his kingdom in:
Join all on earth, rejoice and sing;
Glory ascribe to glory's King.

6 Till all the earth, renewed
 In righteousness divine,
 With all the hosts of God
 In one great chorus join,
Join all on earth, rejoice and sing;
Glory ascribe to glory's King.

720
8 s & 7 s.

1 SEE the Conqueror mounts in triumph,
 See the King in royal state
Riding on the clouds his chariot
 To his heavenly palace gate;
Hark, the choirs of angel-voices
 Joyful Hallelujahs sing,
And the portals high are lifted
 To receive their heavenly King.

2 Who is this that comes in glory,
 With the trump of jubilee?
Lord of battles, God of armies,
 He has gained the victory;
He who on the cross did suffer,
 He who from the grave arose,
He has vanquished sin and Satan,
 He by death has spoiled his foes.

3 While he lifts his hands in blessing,
 He is parted from his friends;
While their eager eyes behold him,
 He upon the clouds ascends;
He who walked with God, and pleased him,
 Preaching truth and doom to come,
He, our Enoch, is translated
 To his everlasting home.

4 Now our heavenly Aaron enters,
 With his blood, within the veil;
Joshua now is come to Canaan,
 And the kings before him quail;
Now he plants the tribes of Israel
 In their promised resting-place;
Now our great Elijah offers
 Double portion of his grace.

5 He has raised our human nature
 In the clouds to God's right hand ·

There we sit in heavenly places,
 There with him in glory stand:
Jesus reigns, adored by angels;
 Man with God is on the throne;
Mighty Lord, in thine ascension
 We by faith behold our own.

8 s & 7 s. SECOND PART.

6 HOLY GHOST, Illuminator,
 Shed thy beams upon our eyes,
Help us to look up with Stephen,
 And to see, beyond the skies,
Where the Son of man in glory
 Standing is at God's right hand,
Beckoning on his martyr army,
 Succouring his faithful band;

7 See him, who is gone before us
 Heavenly mansions to prepare,
See him, who is ever pleading
 For us with prevailing prayer,
See him, who with sound of trumpet
 And with his angelic train,
Summoning the world to judgment,
 On the clouds will come again.

8 Raise us up from earth to heaven,
 Give us wings of faith and love,
Gales of holy aspirations
 Wafting us to realms above;
That, with hearts and minds uplifted,
 We with Christ our Lord may dwell,
Where he sits enthroned in glory
 In his heavenly citadel.

9 So at last, when he appeareth,
 We from out our graves may spring,
With our youth renewed like eagles,
 Flocking round our heavenly King,
Caught up on the clouds of heaven,
 And may meet him in the air,
Rise to realms where he is reigning,
 And may reign for ever there.

*The following Doxology may be sung at the
 end of either part.*

Glory be to God the Father;
 Glory be to God the Son,
Dying, risen, ascending for us,
 Who the heavenly realm has won;
Glory to the Holy Spirit;
 To one God in Persons Three
Glory both in earth and heaven,
 Glory, endless glory be. • Amen.

5 - 8 s. # 721

1 SINNERS, rejoice: your peace is made;
 Your Saviour on the cross hath bled:
Your God, in Jesus reconciled,
On all his works again hath smiled;
Hath grace through him and blessing given,
To all in earth and all in heaven.

2 Angels rejoice in Jesu's grace,
And vie with man's more favoured race;
The blood that did for us atone,
Conferred on them some gift unknown;
Their joy through Jesu's pains abounds,
They triumph by his glorious wounds.

3 Or, stablished and confirmed by him
Who did our lower world redeem,
Secure they keep their blest estate,
Firm on an everlasting seat;

Or, raised above themselves, aspire,
  In bliss improved, in glory higher.
4 Him they beheld our conquering God,
  Returned with garments rolled in blood !
  They saw, and kindled at the sight,
  And filled with shouts the realms of light ;
  With loudest hallelujahs met,
  And fell, and kissed his bleeding feet.
5 They saw him in the courts above,
  With all his recent prints of love ;
  The wounds, the blood! they heard its voice,
  That heightened all their highest joys ;
  They felt it sprinkled through the skies,
  And shared that better sacrifice.
6 Not angel-tongues can e   express
  The unutterable happiness ;
  Nor human hearts can e'er conceive
  The bliss wherein through Christ they live,
  But all your heaven, ye glorious powers,
  And all your God, is doubly ours !

722
             8 s & 7 s.
1 HAIL, thou once despised Jesus !
  Hail, thou Galilean King !
Thou didst suffer to release us ;
  Thou didst free salvation bring.
Hail, thou agonizing Saviour,
  Bearer of our sin and shame !
By thy merits we find favour ;
  Life is given through thy name.

2 Paschal Lamb, by God appointed,
  All our sins on thee were laid ;
By almighty love anointed,
  Thou hast full atonement made ;
All thy people are forgiven
· Through the virtue of thy blood ;
Opened is the gate of heaven,
  Peace is made 'twixt man and God.

3 Jesus, hail ! enthroned in glory,
  There for ever to abide ;
All the heavenly host adore thee,
  Seated at thy Father's side ;
There for sinners thou art pleading,
  There thou dost our place prepare,
Ever for us interceding,
  Till in glory we appear.

4 Worship, honour, power, and blessing,
  Thou art worthy to receive ;
Loudest praises without ceasing,
  Meet it is for us to give.
Help, ye bright, angelic spirits !
  Bring your sweetest, noblest lays,
Help to sing our Saviour's merits ;
  Help to chant Immanuel's praise.

723   *The Forerunner.*
      Hebrews vi. 20.   2 - 6 s & 4 - 7 s.
1 JESUS, to thee we fly,
  On thee for help rely ;
Thou our only refuge art,
  Thou dost all our fears control,
Rest of every troubled heart,
  Life of every dying soul.

2 We lift our joyful eyes,
  And see the dazzling prize,
See the purchase of thy blood,
  Freely now to sinners given ;
Thou the living way hast showed,
  Thou to us hast opened heaven.
170

3 We now, divinely bold,
  Of thy reward lay hold ;
All thy glorious joy is ours,
  All the treasures of thy love ;
Now we taste the heavenly powers,
  Now we reign with thee above.

4 Our anchor sure and fast
  Within the veil is cast ;
Stands our never-failing hope
  Grounded in the holy place ;
We shall after thee mount up,
  See the Godhead face to face.

5 By faith already there,
  In thee our Head, we are ;
With our great Forerunner we
  Now in heavenly places sit,
Banquet with the Deity,
  See the world beneath our feet.

6 Thou art our flesh and bone,
  Thou art to heaven gone ;
Gone, that we might all pursue,
  Closely in thy footsteps tread ;
Gone, that we might follow too,
  Reign triumphant with our Head.

7 s & 6 s †. *"Seeing . . . we have a* **724**
      great High-priest," &c.
      Hebrews iv. 14.
1 TRUSTING in our Lord alone,
  A great High-priest we have !
Jesus, God's eternal Son,
  Omnipotent to save,
With the virtue of his blood,
  Ascending to the holiest place,
Passed the heavenly courts, and stood
  Before his Father's face.

2 Separate now from sinful men,
  Our Advocate above
Doth his brethren's cause maintain
  Before the throne of love ;
Pleads for us on earth who dwell
  His one sufficient sacrifice ; ·
Us to save from sin and hell,
  He reigns above the skies.

3 Holy, like thyself, and pure
  Thou wilt thy brethren make,
From an evil world secure,
  And to thy bosom take ;
Us before thy Father's face
  Acknowledge for thy flesh and bone,
Higher than the angel's place,
  And nearest to thy throne.

C. M.   *The same subject.*   **725**
1 WITH joy we meditate the grace
  Of our High-priest above ;
His heart is made of tenderness,
  His bowels yearn with love.

2 Touched with a sympathy within,
  He knows our feeble frame ;
He knows what sore temptations mean,
  For he hath felt the same.

3 He in the days of feeble flesh
  Poured out his cries and tears ;
And, though exalted, feels afresh
  What every member bears.

4 He'll never quench the smoking flax,
  But raise it to a flame ;

The bruised reed he never breaks,
Nor seems the meanest name.
5 Then let our humble faith address
His mercy and his power :
We shall obtain delivering grace
In the distressing hour.

726   Hebrews ix. 24.   6 - 8 s.

1 ENTERED the holy place above,
Covered with meritorious scars,
The tokens of his dying love
Our great High-priest in glory bears ;
He pleads his passion on the tree,
He shows himself to God for me.

2 Before the throne my Saviour stands,
My Friend and Advocate appears ;
My name is graven on his hands,
And him the Father always hears ;
While low at Jesu's cross I bow,
He hears the blood of sprinkling now.

3 This instant now I may receive
The answer of his powerful prayer :
This instant now by him I live,
His prevalence with God declare ;
And soon my spirit, in his hands,
Shall stand where my Forerunner stands.
(*See also Hymn 557, Second Part.*)

(3.) THE KINGDOM OF CHRIST: ITS EXTEN-
SION AND TRIUMPHS.

727   2 - 6 s & 4 - 7 s.

1 JESU, my God and King,
Thy regal state I sing !
Thou, and only thou, art great,
High thine everlasting throne ;
Thou the sovereign Potentate,
Blessed, immortal, thou alone.

2 Essay your choicest strains,
The King Messiah reigns !
Tune your harps, celestial choir,
Joyful all your voices raise ;
Christ, than earth-born monarchs higher,
Sons of men and angels, praise !

3 Hail your dread Lord and ours,
Dominions, thrones, and powers !
Source of power, he rules alone :
Veil your eyes, and prostrate fail ;
Cast your crowns before his throne,
Hail the Cause, the Lord of all !

4 Let earth's remotest bound
With echoing joys resound ;
Christ to praise let all conspire ;
Praise doth all to Christ belong :
Shout, ye first-born sons of fire !
Earth, repeat the glorious song !

5 Worthy, O Lord, art thou,
That every knee shall bow.
Every tongue to thee confess,
Universal nature join,
Strong and mighty, thee to bless,
Gracious, merciful, benign !

6 Wisdom is due to thee,
And might, and majesty ;
Thee in mercy rich we prove ;
Glory, honour, praise, receive ;
Worthy thou of all our love,
More than all we pant to give.

7 Justice and truth maintain
Thine everlasting reign :
One with thine almighty Sire,
Partner of an equal throne,
King of saints, let all conspire
Gratefully thy sway to own !

7 s.   **728**

1 EARTH, rejoice, our Lord is King !
Sons of men, his praises sing ;
Sing ye in triumphant strains,
Jesus the Messiah reigns !

2 Power is all to Jesus given,
Lord of hell, and earth, and heaven,
Every knee to him shall bow ;
Satan, hear, and tremble now !

3 Angels and archangels join,
All triumphantly combine,
All in Jesu's praise agree,
Carrying on his victory.

4 Though the sons of night blaspheme,
More there are with us than them ;
God with us, we cannot fear :
Fear, ye fiends, for Christ is here !

5 Lo ! to faith's enlightened sight,
All the mountain flames with light,
Hell is nigh, but God is nigher,
Circling us with hosts of fire.

6 Christ the Saviour is come down,
Points us to the victor's crown,
Bids us take our seats above,
More than conquerors in his love.

4 - 6 s & 2 - 8 s.   **729**

1 REJOICE, the Lord is King !
Your Lord and King adore,
Mortals, give thanks, and sing,
And triumph evermore ;
Lift up your heart, lift up your voice,
Rejoice, again I say, rejoice.

2 Jesus the Saviour reigns,
The God of truth and love ;
When he had purged our stains,
He took his seat above :
Lift up your heart, lift up your voice,
Rejoice, again I say, rejoice.

3 His kingdom cannot fail,
He rules o'er earth and heaven ;
The keys of death and hell
Are to our Jesus given :
Lift up your heart, lift up your voice,
Rejoice, again I say, rejoice.

4 He sits at God's right hand,
Till all his foes submit,
And bow to his command,
And fall beneath his feet :
Lift up your heart, lift up your voice,
Rejoice, again I say, rejoice.

5 He all his foes shall quell,
Shall all our sins destroy,
And every bosom swell
With pure seraphic joy ;
Lift up your heart, lift up your voice,
Rejoice, again I say, rejoice.

6 Rejoice in glorious hope,
Jesus the Judge shall come,

171

And take his servants up
To their eternal home:
We soon shall hear the archangel's voice,
The trump of God shall sound, Rejoice!

730   7 s & 6 s.

1 SAVIOUR, whom our hearts adore,
  To bless our earth again,
Now assume thy royal power,
  And o'er the nations reign:
Christ, the world's desire and hope,
  Power complete to thee is given;
Set the last great empire up,
  Eternal Lord of heaven.

2 Where they all thy laws have spurned,
  Where they thy name profane,
Where the ruined world hath mourned
  With blood of millions slain,
Open there the ethereal scene,
  Claim the heathen tribes for thine;
There the endless reign begin
  With majesty divine.

3 Universal Saviour, thou
  Wilt all thy creatures bless;
Every knee to thee shall bow,
  And every tongue confess:
None shall in thy mount destroy;
  War shall then be learnt no more:
Saints shall their great King enjoy,
  And all mankind adore.

731   6 6 8, 6 6 8.

1 MY heart and voice I raise,
  To spread Messiah's praise;
Messiah's praise let all repeat;
  The universal Lord,
  By whose almighty word
Creation rose in form complete.

2 A servant's form he wore,
  And in his body bore.
Our dreadful curse on Calvary:
  He like a victim stood,
  And poured his sacred blood,
To set the guilty captives free.

3 But soon the Victor rose
  Triumphant o'er his foes,
And led the vanquished host in chains:
  He threw their empire down,
  His foes compelled to own,
O'er all the great Messiah reigns.

4 With mercy's mildest grace,
  He governs all our race
In wisdom, righteousness, and love:
  Who to Messiah fly
  Shall find redemption nigh,
And all his great salvation prove.

5 Hail, Saviour, Prince of peace!
  Thy kingdom shall increase,
Till all the world thy glory see;
  And righteousness abound,
  As the great deep profound,
And fill the earth with purity!

       SECOND PART.   6 6 8, 6 6 8.

6 JERUSALEM divine,
  When shall I call thee mine?

172

And to thy holy hill attain,
  Where weary pilgrims rest,
  And in thy glories blest,
With God Messiah ever reign?

7 There saints and angels join
  In fellowship divine,
And rapture swells the solemn lay:
  While all with one accord
  Adore their glorious Lord,
And shout his praise in endless day.

8 May I but find the grace
  To fill an humble place
In that inheritance above;
  My tuneful voice I'll raise
  In songs of loudest praise,
To spread thy fame, Redeeming Love!

9 Reign, true Messiah, reign!
  Thy kingdom shall remain
When stars and suns no more shall shine;
  Mysterious Deity,
  Who ne'er began to be,
To sound thy endless praise be mine!

732

4 - 6 s & 2 - 8 s.   Acts ii. 47.

1 SAVIOUR, we know thou art
  In every age the same:
Now, Lord, in ours exert
  The virtue of thy name:
And daily, through thy word, increase
Thy blood-besprinkled witnesses.

2 Thy people, saved below
  From every sinful stain,
Shall multiply and grow,
  If thy command ordain;
And one into a thousand rise,
And spread thy praise through earth and
  skies.

3 In many a soul, and mine,
  Thou hast displayed thy power:
But to thy people join
  Ten thousand thousand more,
Saved from the guilt and strength of sin,
In life and heart entirely clean.

733

7 s & 6 s †.   Acts iv. 24—33.

1 LORD of hosts, our God and Lord,
  To thee we lift our voice,
Praise thy name with one accord,
  And in thy strength rejoice;
Heaven is thine, and earth, and sea,
  The work of thine almighty hand
  Every creature made by thee
  Must bow to thy command.

2 Lord, the cause belongs to thee
  When truth's opposers rise,
Thou, who dost the evil see,
  Disperse it with thine eyes!
They and we are in thine hand,
Who sittest on thy righteous throne;
  Let thine awful counsel stand,
  Thy sovereign will be done.

3 Thou who once didst shake the place
  Where praying saints were met,
Spirit of faith and holiness,
  The miracle repeat;
Now exert thy power to heal,
Thy waiting servants, Lord, inspire,

Warm their hearts with heavenly zeal,
And touch their lips with fire.

4 Power to every messenger
And ready utterance give,
That we boldly may declare
The name through which we live,
Preach the reconciling Word,
Who did his peace to all bequeath,
Followers of our lamb-like Lord,
And faithful unto death.

734 *"The hand of the Lord was with
them."—Acts xi. 21.* S. M.

1 LORD, if at thy command
The word of life we sow,
Watered by thy almighty hand,
The seed shall surely grow:
The virtue of thy grace
A large increase shall give,
And multiply the faithful race
Who to thy glory live.

2 Now then the ceaseless shower
Of gospel blessings send,
And let the soul-converting power
Thy ministers attend.
On multitudes confer
The heart-renewing love,
And by the joy of grace prepare
For fuller joys above.

735 Acts xiv. 27. 2 - 6 s & 4 - 7 s.

1 THY messengers make known
What God by them hath done;
We who prayed for their success,
Thankful for their answered prayer,
Testify his faithfulness,
All his gracious works declare.

2 With joy we now approve
The truth of Jesu's love;
God, the universal God,
He the door hath opened wide,
Faith on heathens hath bestowed,
Washed them in his bleeding side.

3 Purged from the stains of sin,
By faith they enter in:
Purchased and redeemed of old,
Added to the chosen race,
Now received into the fold,
Heathens sing their Saviour's praise.

4 With them we lift our voice,
Partakers of their joys,
Conscious of the blood applied,
Freely all through faith forgiven:
Faith renews the justified
Faith unfolds the gates of heaven.

736 Acts xxi. 20. 7 7, 4 4, 7.
7 7, 4 4, 7.

1 OMNIPOTENT Redeemer,
Our ransomed souls adore thee,
Whate'er is done
Thy work we own,
And give thee all the glory;
With thankfulness acknowledge
Our time of visitation,
Thine hand confess,
And gladly bless
The God of our salvation.

2 Thou hast employed thy servants,
And blest their weak endeavours,

And lo! in thee
We myriads see
Of justified believers;
The church of pardoned sinners,
Exulting in their Saviour,
Sing all day long
The gospel song,
And triumph in thy favour.

3 Thy wonders wrought already
Require our ceaseless praises;
But show thy power,
And myriads more
Endue with heavenly graces.
But fill our earth with glory,
And, known by every nation,
God of all grace
Receive the praise
Of all thy new creation.

2 - 6 s &   *The Saviour glorified*   **737**
4 - 7 s.   *by all.*

1 THOU, Jesu, art our King,
Thy ceaseless praise we sing;
Praise shall our glad tongue employ,
Praise o'erflow our grateful soul,
While we vital breath enjoy,
While eternal ages roll.

2 Thou art the Eternal Light,
That shin'st in deepest night.
Wondering gazed the angelic train,
While thou bow'dst the heavens beneath,
God with God wast man with man,
Man to save from endless death.

3 Thou for our pain didst mourn,
Thou hast our sickness borne:
All our sins on thee were laid;
Thou with unexampled grace
All the mighty debt hast paid
Due from Adam's helpless race.

4 Thou hast o'erthrown the foe,
God's kingdom fixed below.
Conqueror of all adverse power,
Thou heaven's gates hast opened wide:
Thou thine own dost lead secure
In thy cross, and by thy side.

5 Enthroned above yon sky,
Thou reign'st with God most high,
Prostrate at thy feet we fall:
Power supreme to thee is given;
Thee, the righteous Judge of all,
Sons of earth and hosts of heaven.

6 Cherubs with seraphs join
And in thy praise combine;
All their choirs thy glories sing:
Who shall dare with thee to vie?
Mighty Lord, eternal King,
Sovereign both of earth and sky!

7 Hail, venerable train,
Patriarchs, first-born of men!
Hail, apostles of the Lamb
By whose strength ye faithful proved!
Join to extol his sacred name
Whom in life and death ye loved.

8 The church through all her bounds
With thy high praise resounds.
Confessors undaunted here
Unashamed proclaim their king;
Children's feebler voices there
To thy name Hosannas sing.

9 Midst danger's blackest frown
　　Thee hosts of martyrs own.
Pain and shame alike they dare,
　　Firmly, singularly good:
Glorying thy cross to bear
　　Till they seal their faith with blood.

10 Wide earth's remotest bound
　　Full of thy praise is found:
And all heaven's eternal day
　　With thy streaming glory flames:
All thy foes shall melt away
　　From the insufferable beams.

11 O Lord, O God of love,
　　Let us thy mercy prove!
King of all, with pitying eye
　　Mark the toil, the pains we feel;
Midst the snares of death we lie,
　　Midst the banded powers of hell.

12 Arise, stir up thy power,
　　Thou deathless Conqueror!
Help us to obtain the prize,
　　Help us well to close our race;
That with thee above the skies
　　Endless joys we may possess.

738 　　*The Year of Jubilee.*
　　　　　Leviticus xxv. 4 - 6 s & 2 - 8 s.

1 BLOW ye the trumpet, blow,
　　The gladly solemn sound,
Let all the nations know,
　　To earth's remotest bound;
The year of Jubilee is come!
Return, ye ransomed sinners, home.

2 Jesus, our great High-priest,
　　Hath full atonement made:
Ye weary spirits, rest,
　　Ye mournful souls, be glad;
The year of Jubilee is come!
Return, ye ransomed sinners, home.

3 Extol the Lamb of God,
　　The all-atoning Lamb,
Redemption in his blood
　　Throughout the world proclaim;
The year of Jubilee is come!
Return, ye ransomed sinners, home.

4 Ye slaves of sin and hell,
　　Your liberty receive,
And safe in Jesus dwell,
　　And blest in Jesus live;
The year of Jubilee is come!
Return, ye ransomed sinners, home.

5 Ye who have sold for nought
　　Your heritage above,
Receive it back unbought,
　　The gift of Jesu's love:
The year of Jubilee is come!
Return, ye ransomed sinners, home.

6 The gospel trumpet hear,
　　The news of heavenly grace,
And, saved from earth, appear
　　Before your Saviour's face:
The year of Jubilee is come!
Return, ye ransomed sinners, home.

739 　　Ecclesiastes xi. 6. 　　S. M.

1 SOW in the morn thy seed,
　　At eve hold not thine hand;
To doubt and fear give thou no heed,
　　Broadcast it o'er the land.
171

2 Beside all waters sow,
　　The highway furrows stock,
Drop it where thorns and thistles grow.
　　Scatter it on the rock.

3 The good, the fruitful ground,
　　Expect not here nor there,
O'er hill and dale, by plots 'tis found;
　　Go forth then everywhere.

4 And duly shall appear,
　　In verdure, beauty, strength,
The tender blade, the stalk, the ear,
　　And the full corn at length.

5 Thou canst not toil in vain;
　　Cold, heat, and moist, and dry,
Shall foster and mature the grain
　　For garners in the sky.

6 Thence, when the glorious end,
　　The day of God is come,
The angel-reapers shall descend,
　　And heaven cry "Harvest home!"

C. M. 　　　Isaiah ii. 1—5. 　　**740**

1 BEHOLD! the mountain of the Lord
　　In latter days shall rise
On mountain-tops above the hills,
　　And draw the wondering eyes.

2 To this the joyful nations round,
　　All tribes and tongues, shall flow;
Up to the hill of God, they'll say,
　　And to his house, we'll go.

3 The beam that shines from Zion's hill
　　Shall lighten every land;
The King who reigns in Salem's towers
　　Shall all the world command.

4 Among the nations he shall judge;
　　His judgments truth shall guide;
His sceptre shall protect the just,
　　And quell the sinner's pride.

5 No strife shall rage, nor hostile feuds
　　Disturb those peaceful years;
To ploughshares men shall beat their
　　To pruning-hooks their spears. [swords,

6 No longer hosts, encountering hosts,
　　Shall crowds of slain deplore;
They hang the trumpet in the hall,
　　And study war no more.

7 Come, then, O house of Jacob! come
　　To worship at his shrine;
And, walking in the light of God,
　　With holy beauties shine.

S. M. 　　　Isaiah lii. 7—10. 　　**741**

1 HOW beauteous are their feet,
　　Who stand on Zion's hill,
Who bring salvation in their tongues,
　　And words of peace reveal!

2 How cheering is their voice,
　　How sweet the tidings are!
"Zion, behold thy Saviour King;
　　He reigns and triumphs here."

3 How blessed are our ears,
　　That hear this joyful sound,
Which kings and prophets waited for,
　　And sought, but never found!

4 How blessed are our eyes,
　　That see this heavenly light!

Prophets and kings desired long,
 But died without the sight.
5 The watchmen join their voice,
 And tuneful notes employ ;
Jerusalem breaks forth in songs,
 And deserts learn the joy.
6 The Lord makes bare his arm
 Through all the earth abroad :
Let all the nations now behold
 Their Saviour and their God.

742   Isaiah lii. 10.   C. M.

1 SALVATION ! O the joyful sound !
 What pleasure to our ears !
A sovereign balm for every wound,
 A cordial for our fears.
Chorus—Glory, honour, praise, and power
 Be unto the Lamb for ever :
 Jesus Christ is our Redeemer :
 Hallelujah, Praise the Lord.

Salvation ! let the echo fly
 The spacious earth around ;
While all the armies of the sky
 Conspire to raise the sound !
 Glory, honour, praise, and power, &c.

3 Salvation ! O thou bleeding Lamb,
 To thee the praise belongs ;
Salvation shall inspire our hearts,
 And dwell upon our tongues.
 Glory, honour, praise, and power, &c.

743   *" So shall he sprinkle many*
 nations."—Isaiah lii. 15.   8 s & 7 s.

1 SAVIOUR, sprinkle many nations,
 Fruitful let thy sorrows be ;
By thy pains and consolations
 Draw the Gentiles unto thee :
Of thy cross the wondrous story,
 Be to all the nations told !
Let them see thee in thy glory,
 And thy mercy manifold.

2 Far and wide, though all unknowing,
 Pants for thee each mortal breast ;
Human tears for thee are flowing,
 Human hearts in thee would rest ;
Thirsting, as for dews of even,
 As the new-mown grass for rain,
Thee they seek, as God of heaven,
 Thee, as man for sinners slain.

3 Saviour, lo, the isles are waiting,
 Stretched the hand, and strained the
 sight,
For thy Spirit, new creating,
 Love's pure flame, and wisdom's light ;
Give the word, and of the preacher
 Speed the foot, and touch the tongue,
Till on earth by every creature
 Glory to the Lamb be sung.

744   Matthew ix. 36.   L. M.

1 JESU, thy wandering sheep behold ;
 See, Lord, with tenderest pity see
The sheep that cannot find the fold,
 Till sought and gathered in by thee.

2 Lost are they now, and scattered wide,
 In pain, and weariness, and want ;
With no kind shepherd near to guide
 The sick, and spiritless, and faint.

3 Thou, only thou, the kind and good
 And sheep-redeeming Shepherd art :
Collect thy flock, and give them food,
 And pastors after thine own heart.

4 Give the pure word of general grace,
 And great shall be the preachers' crowd ;
Preachers, who all the sinful race
 Point to the all-atoning blood.

5 Open their mouth, and utterance give ;
 Give them a trumpet-voice, to call
On all mankind to turn and live,
 Through faith in him who died for all.

6 Thy only glory let them seek ;
 O let their hearts with love o'erflow !
Let them believe, and therefore speak,
 And spread thy mercy's praise below.

S. M.   Matthew ix. 38.   **745**

1 LORD of the harvest, hear
 Thy needy servants cry ;
Answer our faith's effectual prayer,
 And all our wants supply.

2 On thee we humbly wait,
 Our wants are in thy view ;
The harvest truly, Lord, is great ;
 The labourers are few.

3 Convert, and send forth more
 Into thy church abroad ;
And let them speak thy word of power,
 As workers with their God.

4 Give the pure gospel word,
 The word of general grace ;
Thee let them preach, the common Lord,
 The Saviour of our race.

5 O let them spread thy name,
 Their mission fully prove,
Thy universal grace proclaim,
 Thy all-redeeming love.

L. M.   *Christian responsibility.*   **746**

1 THE heathen perish ; day by day,
 Thousands on thousands pass away !
O Christians, to their rescue fly ;
Preach Jesus to them ere they die.

2 Wealth, labour, talents, freely give,
Yea, life itself, that they may live ;
What hath your Saviour done for you !
And what for him will ye not do ?

3 Thou Spirit of the Lord, go forth,
Call in the south, wake up the north ;
In every clime, from sun to sun,
Gather God's children into one.

7 6, 7 6, 7 6, 7 6.   Acts xvi. 9.   **747**

1 FROM Greenland's icy mountains,
 From India's coral strand,
Where Afric's sunny fountains
 Roll down their golden sand,
From many an ancient river,
 From many a palmy plain,
They call us to deliver
 Their land from error's chain.

2 What though the spicy breezes
 Blow soft o'er Ceylon's isle,
Though every prospect pleases,
 And only man is vile !

In vain with lavish kindness
  The gifts of God are strewn;
The heathen in his blindness
  Bows down to wood and stone.

3 Can we, whose souls are lighted
  With wisdom from on high,
Can we to men benighted
  The lamp of life deny?
Salvation! O salvation!
  The joyful sound proclaim,
Till each remotest nation
  Has learnt Messiah's name.

4 Waft, waft, ye winds, his story,
  And you, ye waters, roll,
Till, like a sea of glory,
  It spreads from pole to pole;
Till o'er our ransomed nature,
  The Lamb for sinners slain,
Redeemer, King, Creator,
  In bliss returns to reign.

748   Revelation xix. 11, &c.   8 7, 8 7, 4 7.

1 COME, thou Conqueror of the nations,
  Now on thy white horse appear;
Earthquakes, dearths, and desolations
  Signify thy kingdom near:
    True and faithful!
  Stablish thy dominion here.

2 Thine the kingdom, power, and glory;
  Thine the ransomed nations are;
Let the heathen fall before thee,
  Let the isles thy power declare;
    Judge and conquer
  All mankind in righteous war.

3 Thee let all mankind admire,
  Object of our joy and dread!
Flame thine eyes with heavenly fire,
  Many crowns upon thy head;
    But thine essence
  None, except thyself, can read.

4 Yet we know our Mediator,
  By the Father's grace bestowed;
Meanly clothed in human nature,
  Thee we call the Word of God:
    Flesh thy vesture,
  Dipped in thy own sacred blood.

5 Captain, God of our salvation,
  Thou who hast the wine-press trod,
Borne the Almighty's indignation,
  Quenched the fiercest wrath of God,
    Take the kingdom,
  Claim the purchase of thy blood.

6 On thy thigh and vesture written,
  Show the world thy heavenly name,
That, with loving wonder smitten,
  All may glorify the Lamb;
    All adore thee,
  All the Lord of hosts proclaim.

7 Honour, glory, and salvation
  To the Lord our God we give;
Power, and endless adoration,
  Thou art worthy to receive;
    Reign triumphant,
  King of kings, for ever live!

749   " *The Spirit and the bride say, Come.*"—Rev. xxii. 17.   L. M.

1 HEAD of thy church, whose Spirit fills
  And flows through every faithful soul,

176

Unites in mystic love, and seals
  Them one, and sanctifies the whole;

2 "Come, Lord," thy glorious Spirit cries,
  And souls beneath the altar groan;
"Come, Lord," the bride on earth replies,
  "And perfect all our souls in one."

3 Pour out the promised gift on all,
  Answer the universal "Come!"
The fulness of the Gentiles call,
  And take thine ancient people home.

4 To thee let all the nations flow,
  Let all obey the gospel word;
Let all their bleeding Saviour know,
  Filled with the glory of the Lord.

5 O for thy truth and mercy's sake
  The purchase of thy passion claim!
Thine heritage the Gentiles take,
  And cause the world to know thy name.

SECTION IV.

ON THE HOLY SPIRIT.

C. M.   *Hymn to the Holy Spirit.*   **750**

1 HAIL, Holy Ghost, Jehovah, Third
  In order of the Three;
Sprung from the Father and the Word
  From all eternity!

2 Thy Godhead brooding o'er the abyss
  Of formless waters lay;
Spoke into order all that is,
  And darkness into day.

3 In deepest hell, or heaven's height,
  Thy presence who can fly?
Known is the Father to thy sight,
  The abyss of Deity.

4 Thy power through Jesu's life displayed,
  Quite from the virgin's womb,
Dying, his soul an offering made,
  And raised him from the tomb.

5 God's image, which our sins destroy,
  Thy grace restores below;
And truth, and holiness, and joy,
  From thee their fountain flow.

6 Hail, Holy Ghost, Jehovah, Third
  In order of the Three;
Sprung from the Father and the Word
  From all eternity!

6 - 8 s.   *Veni, Creator.*   **751.**

1 COME, Holy Ghost, our souls inspire,
  And lighten with celestial fire!
Thou the anointing Spirit art,
Who dost thy sevenfold gifts impart;
Thy blessed unction from above
Is comfort, life, and fire of love.

2 Enable with perpetual light
The dulness of our blinded sight;
Anoint and cheer our soiled face
With the abundance of thy grace;
Keep far our foes, give peace at home:
Where thou art guide no ill can come.

3 Teach us to know the Father, Son,
  And thee, of both, to be but One;

That through the ages all along
This, this may be our endless song,
All praise to thy eternal merit,
O Father, Son, and Holy Spirit!

752 *Another.* 6-8 s.

1 CREATOR Spirit, by whose aid
The world's foundations first were laid,
Come visit every waiting mind,
Come pour thy joys on human kind;
From sin and sorrow set us free,
And make thy temples worthy thee.

2 O source of uncreated heat,
The Father's promised Paraclete!
Thrice holy Fount, thrice holy Fire,
Our hearts with heavenly love inspire:
Come, and thy sacred unction bring,
To sanctify us while we sing.

3 Plenteous of grace, descend from high,
Rich in thy sevenfold energy!
Thou strength of his almighty hand
Whose power does heaven and earth command,
Refine and purge our earthly parts,
And stamp thine image on our hearts.

4 Create all new; our wills control,
Subdue the rebel in our soul:
Chase from our minds the infernal foe;
And peace, the fruit of faith, bestow:
And, lest again we go astray,
Protect and guide us in the way.

5 Immortal honours, endless fame,
Attend the Almighty Father's name;
The Saviour Son be glorified,
Who for lost man's redemption died;
And equal adoration be,
Eternal Comforter, to thee!

753 *Veni Sancte Spiritus.* 7 7 7.

1 HOLY Ghost! my Comforter!
Now from highest heaven appear,
Shed thy gracious radiance here.

2 Come to them who suffer dearth,
With thy gifts of priceless worth,
Lighten all who dwell on earth!

3 Thou the heart's most precious guest,
Thou of comforters the best,
Give to us, the o'er-laden, rest.

4 Come! in thee our toil is sweet,
Shelter from the noon-day heat,
From whom sorrow flieth fleet.

5 Blessed Sun of grace! o'er all
Faithful hearts who on thee call
Let thy light and solace fall.

6 What without thy aid is wrought,
Skilful deed or wisest thought,
God will count but vain and nought.

7 Cleanse us, Lord, from sinful stain,
O'er the parched heart O rain!
Heal the wounded of its pain.

8 Bend the stubborn will to thine,
Melt the cold with fire divine,
Erring hearts to right incline.

9 Grant us, Lord, who cry to thee,
Steadfast in the faith to be,
Give thy gift of charity.

10 May we live in holiness,
And in death find happiness,
And abide with thee in bliss!

754 L. M. John xv. 26, 27.

1 JESUS, we on the word depend,
Spoken by thee while present here,
"The Father in my name shall send
The Holy Ghost, the Comforter."

2 That promise made to Adam's race,
Now, Lord, in us, even us, fulfil;
And give the Spirit of thy grace,
To teach us all thy perfect will.

3 That heavenly Teacher of mankind,
That Guide infallible impart,
To bring thy sayings to our mind,
And write them on our faithful heart.

4 He only can the words apply
Through which we endless life possess,
And deal to each his legacy,
His Lord's unutterable peace.

5 That peace of God, that peace of thine,
O might he now to us bring in,
And fill our souls with power divine,
And make an end of fear and sin;

6 The length and breadth of love reveal,
The height and depth of Deity;
And all the sons of glory seal,
And change, and make us all like thee!

755 6-7 s. John xiv. 16, 17.

1 FATHER, glorify thy Son:
Answering his all-powerful prayer,
Send that Intercessor down,
Send that other Comforter,
Whom believingly we claim,
Whom we ask in Jesus's name.

2 Then by faith we know and feel
Him, the Spirit of truth and grace;
With us he vouchsafes to dwell,
With us while unseen he stays:
All our help and good, we own,
Freely flows from him alone.

3 Wilt thou not the promise seal,
Good and faithful as thou art,
Send the Comforter to dwell
Every moment in our heart?
Yes, thou must the grace bestow;
Christ hath said it shall be so.

756 7 s & 6 s †. Isaiah xi. 1—3.

1 BRANCH of Jesse's stem, arise,
And in our nature grow,
Turn our earth to paradise,
By flourishing below:
Bless us with the Spirit of grace,
Immeasurably shed on thee:
Give to all the faithful race
The promised Deity.

2 Let the Spirit of our Head
On all the members rest;
From thyself to us proceed,
And dwell in every breast;
Teach to judge and act aright,
Inspire with wisdom from above,
Holy faith, and heavenly might,
And reverential love.

3 Lord, of thee we fain would learn
  Thy heavenly Father's will ;
Give us quickness to discern,
  And boldness to fulfil:
All his mind to us explain,
And all his name on us impress ;
  Then our souls in thee attain
    The perfect righteousness.

757 *"He received gifts for men."*
    Ephesians iv. 8. 2 - 6 s & 4 - 7 s.

1 THOU art gone up on high
    Our Saviour in the sky,
Principalities and powers
  Thou hast spoiled, and captive led,
Conquered all thy foes and ours,
  More than conquered in our stead.

2 Mysterious gifts unseen
    Thou hast received for men,
Gifts for a rebellious race
  Streaming from thy throne above,
Contrite grief, and pardoning grace,
  Humble fear, and purest love.

3 The gift unspeakable,
    The witness, pledge, and seal,
Heavenly Comforter divine,
  Spirit of eternity,
Purchased by that blood of thine,
  Him thou hast received for me.

4 For me obtained he is,
    For all thine enemies ;
Jesus, thou the giver art !
  Now thy Father's name reveal,
Now the Holy Ghost impart,
  God in man for ever dwell !

758   7 s.

1 GRANTED is the Saviour's prayer,
    Sent the gracious Comforter ;
Promise of our parting Lord,
Jesus now to heaven restored :

2 Christ, who now gone up on high
Captive leads captivity ;
While his foes from him receive
Grace, that God with man may live.

3 God, the everlasting God,
Makes with mortals his abode :
Whom the heavens cannot contain,
He vouchsafes to dwell in man.

4 Never will he thence depart,
Inmate of an humble heart ;
Carrying on his work within,
Striving till he casts out sin.

5 There he helps our feeble moans,
Deepens our imperfect groans,
Intercedes in silence there,
Sighs the unutterable prayer.

6 Come, divine and peaceful Guest,
Enter our devoted breast ;
Life divine in us renew,
Thou the Gift, and Giver too !

759   *The day of Pentecost.*
             Acts ii.   L. M.

1 OUR Jesus is gone up on high,
    For us the blessing to receive :
It now comes streaming from the sky,
  The Spirit comes, and sinners live.
178

2 To every one whom God shall call
  The promise is securely made ;
To you far off ; he calls you all :
  Believe the word which Christ hath said :

3 "The Holy Ghost, if I depart,
    The Comforter shall surely come,
Shall make the contrite sinner's heart
    His loved, his everlasting home."

4 Lord, we believe to us and ours
    The apostolic promise given ;
We wait the Pentecostal powers,
    The Holy Ghost sent down from heaven.

5 Ah ! leave us not to mourn below,
    Or long for thy return to pine ;
Now, Lord, the Comforter bestow,
    And fix in us the guest divine.

6 Assembled here with one accord,
    Calmly we wait the promised grace,
The purchase of our dying Lord :
    Come, Holy Ghost, and fill the place.

7 If every one that asks may find,
    If still thou dost on sinners fall,
Come as a mighty rushing wind ;
    Great grace be now upon us all.

8 Behold, to thee our souls aspire,
    And languish thy descent to meet :
Kindle in each the living fire,
    And fix in every heart thy seat.

760

55 5 11, 55 5 11.

1 AWAY with our fears,
    Our troubles and tears !
The Spirit is come,
The witness of Jesus returned to his home ;
    The pledge of our Lord
    To his heaven restored
Is sent from the sky,
And tells us our Head is exalted on high.

2 Our Advocate there
    By his blood and his prayer
    The gift hath obtained,
For us he hath prayed, and the Comforter
    Our glorified Head   [gained ;
    His Spirit hath shed,
    With his people to stay,
And never again will he take him away.

3 Our heavenly guide
    With us shall abide,
    His comforts impart,
And set up his kingdom of love in the heart.
    The heart that believes
    His kingdom receives,
    His power and his peace,
His life, and his joy's everlasting increase.

4 The presence divine
    Doth inwardly shine,
    The Shechinah shall rest
On all our assemblies, and glow in our
    By day and by night   [breast ;
    The pillar of light
    Our steps shall attend,
And convoy us safe to our prosperous end.

5 Then let us rejoice
    In heart and in voice,
    Our leader pursue,   [through ;
And shout as we travel the wilderness

With the Spirit remove
To Zion above,
Triumphant arise,   [skies.
And walk with our God, till we fly to the

761
4 - 6 s & 2 - 8 s.
1 SINNERS, lift up your hearts,
    The promise to receive!
Jesus himself imparts,
    He comes in man to live ;
The Holy Ghost to man is given ;
Rejoice in God sent down from heaven.

2 Jesus is glorified,
    And gives the Comforter,
His Spirit, to reside
    In all his members here ;
The Holy Ghost to man is given ;
Rejoice in God sent down from heaven.

3 To make an end of sin,
    And Satan's works destroy,
He brings his kingdom in,
    Peace, righteousness, and joy ;
The Holy Ghost to man is given ;
Rejoice in God sent down from heaven.

4 The cleansing blood to apply,
    The heavenly life display,
And wholly sanctify,
    And seal us to that day,
The Holy Ghost to man is given ;
Rejoice in God sent down from heaven.

5 Sent down to make us meet
    To see his glorious face,
And grant us each a seat
    In that thrice happy place,
The Holy Ghost to man is given ;
Rejoice in God sent down from heaven.

6 From heaven he shall once more
    Triumphantly descend,
And all his saints restore
    To joys that never end ;
Then, then, when all our joys are given,
Rejoice in God, rejoice in heaven.

762
2 - 6 s & 4 - 7 s.
1 ETERNAL Spirit, come
    Into thy meanest home ;
From thy high and holy place,
Where thou dost in glory reign,
Stoop, in condescending grace,
Stoop to the poor heart of man.

2 For thee our hearts we lift,
    And wait the heavenly gift :
Giver, Lord of life divine,
To our dying souls appear,
Grant the grace for which we pine,
Give thyself, the Comforter.

763
C. M.
1 COME, Holy Spirit, heavenly Dove,
    With all thy quickening powers ;
Kindle a flame of sacred love
In these cold hearts of ours.

2 In vain we tune our formal songs,
In vain we strive to rise ;
Hosannas languish on our tongues,
And our devotion dies.

3 And shall we then for ever live
At this poor dying rate?

Our love so faint, so cold to thee,
And thine to us so great!

4 Come, Holy Spirit, heavenly Dove,
With all thy quickening powers ;
Come, shed abroad the Saviour's love
And that shall kindle ours.

C. M.   *The Spirit of Adoption.*   **764**
Romans viii. 15, 16.
1 SOVEREIGN of all the worlds on high,
    Allow my humble claim ;
Nor, while unworthy I draw nigh,
Disdain a Father's name.

2 " My Father God ! " that gracious sound
Dispels my guilty fear ;
Not all the harmony of heaven
Could so delight my ear.

3 Come, Holy Spirit, seal the grace
On my expanding heart ;
And show that in the Father's love
I share a filial part.

4 Cheered by a witness so divine,
Unwavering I believe ;
And, " Abba, Father," humbly cry ;
Nor can the sign deceive.

C. M.   **765**
1 WHY should the children of a king
    Go mourning all their days ?
Great Comforter, descend, and bring
The tokens of thy grace !

2 Dost thou not dwell in all thy saints,
And seal the heirs of heaven ?
When wilt thou banish my complaints,
And show my sins forgiven ?

3 Assure my conscience of its part
In the Redeemer's blood ;
And bear thy witness with my heart,
That I am born of God.

8 - 7 s.   Matthew iii. 11.   **766**
1 PURE baptismal Fire divine,
    All thy heavenly powers exert,
In my deepest darkness shine,   [heart :
    Spread thy warmth throughout my
Come, thou Spirit of burning, come,
Comforter through Jesus given ;
All my earthly dross consume,
Fill my soul with love from heaven.

2 Love in me intensely burn,
    Love mine inmost essence seize,
All into thy nature turn,
    All into thy holiness !
Spark of thy celestial flame,
Then my soul shall upward move,
Trembling on with steady aim,
Seek and join its Source above.

C. M.   **767**
1 SPIRIT of Truth ! on this thy day
    To thee for help we cry,
To guide us through the dreary way
Of dark mortality.

2 We ask not, Lord, thy cloven flame,
Or tongues of various tone ;
But long thy praises to proclaim
With fervour in our own.

3 We mourn not that prophetic skill
Is found on earth no more ;

179

Enough for us to trace thy will
In Scripture's sacred lore.

4 No heavenly harpings soothe our ear,
No mystic dreams we share ;
Yet hope to feel thy comfort near,
And bless thee in our prayer.

5 When tongues shall cease, and power de-
And knowledge empty prove.   [cay,
Do thou thy trembling servants stay,
With faith, with hope, with love.

768   7 s.

1 HOLY Spirit ! pity me,
Pierced with grief for grieving thee ;
Present, though I mourn apart,
Listen to a wailing heart.

2 Sins unnumbered I confess,
Of exceeding sinfulness,
Sins against thyself alone,
Only to Omniscience known ;

3 Deafness to thy whispered calls,
Rashness midst remembered falls,
Transient fears beneath the rod,
Treacherous trifling with my God ;

4 Tasting that the Lord is good,
Pining then for poisoned food ;
At the fountains of the skies
Craving creaturely supplies !

5 Worldly cares at worship-time :
Grovelling aims in works sublime ;
Pride, when God is passing by !
Sloth, when souls in darkness die !

6 Chilled devotions, changed desires,
Quenched corruption's earlier fires :
Sins like these my heart deceive,
Thee, who only know'st them, grieve.

7 O how lightly have I slept,
With thy daily wrongs unwept !
Sought thy chidings to defer,
Shunned the wounded Comforter.

8 Woke to holy labours fresh,
With the plague-spot in my flesh ;
Angel seemed to human sight,
Stood a leper in thy light !

9 Still thy comforts do not fail,
Still thy healing aids avail ;
Patient inmate of my breast,
Thou art grieved, yet I am blest.

10 O be merciful to me,
Now in bitterness for thee !
Father, pardon through thy Son
Sins against thy Spirit done !

769   6 - 7 s.

1 GRACIOUS Spirit, dwell with me !
I myself would gracious be,
And with words that help and heal
Would thy life in mine reveal ;
And with actions bold and meek
Would for Christ my Saviour speak.

2 Truthful Spirit, dwell with me !
I myself would truthful be,
And with wisdom kind and clear
Let thy life in mine appear ;
And with actions brotherly
Speak my Lord's sincerity.
180

3 Tender Spirit, dwell with me !
I myself would tender be ;
Shut my heart up like a flower
At temptation's darksome hour,
Open it when shines the sun,
And his love by fragrance own.

4 Mighty Spirit, dwell with me !
I myself would mighty be,
Mighty so as to prevail
Where unaided man must fail,
Ever by a mighty hope
Pressing on, and bearing up.

5 Holy Spirit, dwell with me !
I myself would holy be,
Separate from sin, I would
Choose, and cherish all things good
And whatever I can be
Give to him who gave me thee.

770   6 - 8 s.

1 BLEST Spirit ! from the eternal Sire
And Son proceeding ; promised, sent !
'Tis thine the first good thought to in-
By thee the reprobate repent,   [spire,
The penitent by thee believe,
The saints thy sanctity receive.

2 Thy Deity the saints adore,
Thy offices of mercy bless,
Thy help in utmost need implore,
Thy all-sufficiency confess ;
Without thee, wretched, poor, and blind,
Health, wisdom, joy in thee they find.

3 If e'er to forms of truth I gave
The homage due, great Lord, to thee,
E'er deemed the cross could, spell-like,
save,
While yet thou dwelledst not in me,
Reprove my folly, but forgive,
And make me understand and live.

4 Thou gav'st the word, and must apply ;
Thou know'st the Son, and must make
In vain he died, and rose on high, [known ;
And stoops beseeching from his throne,
Till thou this alien heart prepare,
And gain for Christ an entrance there.

5 O could I always know thee near,
Midst means and ministries of grace !
Thy footsteps in my closet hear,
Thy finger on my Bible trace !
My God ! here find, here grant thy rest,
Pleased inmate of my peaceful breast !

6 Nor me alone instruct, rejoice ;
All souls are thine, teach, comfort all !
Let each soon recognise thy voice
In every evangelic call,
Then feel thy halcyon rest within
Calming the storms of dread and sin.

7 Thus, searching the deep things of God,
And witnessing his mind to us,
Where'er peace dwells, or truth hath trod,
Reveal thy glorious person thus !
And, with all majesty divine,
All praise, Blest Spirit, shall be thine.

771   C. M.

1 SPIRIT Divine, attend our prayers,
And make this house thy home ;

Descend with all thy gracious powers,
O come, great Spirit, come !

2 Come as the light ! to us reveal
Our emptiness and woe ;
And lead us in those paths of life
Where all the righteous go.

3 Come as the fire ! and purge our hearts
Like sacrificial flame ;
Let our whole soul an offering be
To our Redeemer's name.

4 Come as the dew ! and sweetly bless
This consecrated hour ;
May barrenness rejoice to own
Thy fertilizing power.

5 Come as the dove ! and spread thy wings,
The wings of peaceful love ;
And let thy church on earth become
Blest as the church above.

6 Come as the wind, with rushing sound
And Pentecostal grace !
That all of woman born may see
The glory of thy face.

7 Spirit divine ! attend our prayers,
Make a lost world thy home ;
Descend with all thy gracious powers,
O come, great Spirit, come !

(*See also Hymns* 85, 86, 161, 165, 351,
374, 376, 377, 506.)

SECTION V.

PENITENTIAL HYMNS.

772 *The Love of Christ the
Sinner's Plea.* 8 s & 6 s.

1 O THOU who hast redeemed of old,
And bidd'st me of thy strength lay
And be at peace with thee, [hold,
Help me thy benefits to own,
And hear me tell what thou hast done,
O dying Lamb, for me !

2 Out of myself for help I go,
Thy only love resolved to know,
Thy love my plea I make ;
Give me thy love, 'tis all I claim ;
Give. for the honour of thy name,
Give, for thy mercy's sake.

3 Canst thou deny that love to me?
Say, thou Incarnate Deity,
Thou Man of sorrows, say ;
Thy glory why didst thou enshrine
In such a clod of earth as mine,
And wrap thee in my clay?

4 Ancient of days, why didst thou come,
And stoop to a poor virgin's womb,
Contracted to a span?
Flesh of our flesh why wast thou made,
And humbly in a manger laid,
The new-born Son of man?

5 Love, only love, thy heart inclined,
And brought thee, Saviour of mankind,
Down from thy throne above ;
Love made my God a man of grief,
Distressed thee sore for my relief :
O mystery of love !

6 Because thou lov'dst, and diedst for me,
Cause me, my Saviour, to love thee,
And gladly to resign
Whate'er I have, whate'er I am ;
My life be all with thine the same,
And all thy death be mine.

6 -8 s. } *Pleading with Christ for
Salvation.* **773**

1 REGARDLESS now of things below,
Jesus, to thee my heart aspires,
Determined thee alone to know,
Author and end of my desires ;
Fill me with righteousness divine:
To end, as to begin, is thine.

2 What is a worthless worm to thee?
What is in man thy grace to move?
That still thou seekest those who flee
The arms of thy pursuing love ?
That still thine inmost bowels cry,
" Why, sinner, wilt thou perish, why ? "

3 Ah, show me, Lord, my depth of sin !
Ah, Lord, thy depth of mercy show !
End, Jesus, end this war within !
No rest my spirit e'er shall know,
Till thou thy quickening influence give :
Breathe, Lord, and these dry bones shall
live.

4 There, there before the throne thou art,
The Lamb ere earth's foundation slain !
Take thou, O take this guilty heart !
Thy blood will wash out every stain :
No cross, no sufferings I decline ;
Only let all my heart be thine.

L. M. *For Condemned Malefactors.* **774**
Psalm lxxix. 11.

1 O THOU that hangedst on the tree,
Our curse and sufferings to remove,
Pity the souls that look to thee,
And save us by thy dying love.

2 We have no outward righteousness,
No merits or good works, to plead :
We only can be saved by grace :
Thy grace will here be free indeed.

3 Save us by grace, through faith alone,
A faith thou must thyself impart ;
A faith that *would* by works be shown,
A faith that purifies the heart.

4 A faith that doth the mountains move,
A faith that shows our sins forgiven,
A faith that sweetly works by love,
And ascertains our claim to heaven.

5 This is the faith we humbly seek,
The faith in thine all-cleansing blood,
That blood which doth for sinners speak ;
O let it speak us up to God !

L. M. SECOND PART.

6 CANST thou reject our dying prayer,
Or cast us out who come to thee?
Our sins, ah ! wherefore didst thou bear?
Jesus, remember Calvary !

7 Numbered with the transgressors thou,
Between the felons crucified,
Speak to our hearts, and tell us now,
Wherefore hast thou for sinners died ?

181

8 For us wast thou not lifted up?
    For us a bleeding victim made?
That we, the abjects we, might hope,
    Thou hast for all a ransom paid.

9 O might we with believing eyes,
    Thee in thy bloody vesture see,
And cast us on thy sacrifice !
    Jesus, my Lord, remember me !

775   *Thou triest me every*   8 s & 6 s.
     moment.—Job vii. 17, 18.

1 BY secret influence from above,
    Me thou dost every moment prove,
    And labour to convert ;
Ready to save I feel thee nigh,
And still I hear thy Spirit cry,
    "My son, give me thy heart."

2 Why do I not the call obey,
    Cast my besetting sin away,
    With every useless load ?
Why cannot I this moment give
The heart thou waitest to receive,
    And love my loving God ?

3 My loving God, the hindrance show,
    Which nature dreads, alas ! to know,
    And lingers to remove;
Stronger than sin, thy grace exert,
And seize, and change, and fill my heart
    With all the powers of love.

4 Then shall I answer thy design,
    No longer, Lord, my own, but thine ;
    Till all thy will be done,
Humbly I pass my trial here,
And ripe in holiness appear
    With boldness at thy throne.

776   Jeremiah viii. 20.   6 - 8 s.

1 THE harvest of my joys is past,
    The summer of my comforts fled,
Yet am I unredeemed at last,
    And sink unsaved among the dead,
If on the margin of the grave
Thou canst not in a moment save.

2 Destroy me not by thy delay ;
    Delay is endless death to me !
But the last moment of my day
    Is as a thousand years to thee :
Come, Jesus, while my head I bow,
And show me thy salvation now !

777   Jeremiah xv. 18.   8 s.

1 AH ! why am I left to complain
    In gloomy despair of relief ?
No end of oppression and pain,
    No respite, or ease of my grief !
To soothe my incurable wound
    No friendly physician I see ;
No balm is in Gilead found,
    No promise of mercy for me.

2 In vain for redemption I look ;
    My hope in a Saviour unknown,
It passes away like a brook
    Dried up in a moment and gone !
But God cannot finally fail ;
    The Fountain of life from above
Shall rise in the depth of the vale,
    Shall flow with a current of love.
182

778   C. M.   *"Ask, and it shall be given*   *you."—Matthew vii. 7.*

1 THOU bidd'st me ask, and with the word
    Dost give the power to pray ;
I ask the mercy of my Lord
    To take my sins away ;
The sins with which I cannot part
    I pray thee to remove,
And calm, and purify my heart
    By thy forgiving love.

2 If my obduracy impede
    The current of thy grace,
If unlamented crimes forbid,
    And will not let thee bless ;
The contrite sense, the grief divine,
    Thou only canst bestow ;
Strike this hard rocky heart of mine,
    And let the waters flow.

3 Repentance, permanent and deep,
    To thy poor suppliant give,
Indulge me at thy feet to weep,
    When thou hast bid me live ;
When thou record'st my sins no more
    O may I still lament,
A sinner, saved by grace, adore,
    A pardoned penitent.

4 I ask not aught whereof to boast,
    But let me feel applied
The blood that ransomed sinners lost,
    And by thy cross abide :
Myself the chief of sinners know,
    Till all my griefs are past ;
And of my gracious acts below,
    Repentance be the last.

779   6 - 8 s.   Matthew ix. 20—22.

1 UNCLEAN, of life and heart unclean,
    How shall I in his sight appear ?
Conscious of my inveterate sin,
    I blush and tremble to draw near ;
Yet, through the garment of his word,
I humbly seek to touch my Lord.

2 Turn then, thou good Physician, turn,
    Thou source of unexhausted love,
Sole Comforter of souls forlorn,
    Who only canst my plague remove,
O cast a pitying look on me
Who dare not lift mine eyes to thee !

3 Yet will I in my God confide,
    Who mildly comes to meet my soul ;
I wait to feel thy blood applied,
    Thy blood applied shall make me whole ,
And lo ! I trust thy gracious power
To touch, to heal me—in this hour.

780   6 - 8 s.   Mark ix. 24.

1 LORD, I believe thou *wilt* forgive,
    But help me to believe thou *dost ;*
The answer of thy promise give,
    Wherein thou causest me to trust ;
The gospel-faith divine impart,
Which seals my pardon on my heart.

2 I do believe thy blood was spilt
    To make my heart and nature clean,
But help me to believe thou wilt
    This moment cleanse me from my sin ;
Preserve me every moment thine,
A vessel pure of love divine.

781

Mark v. 24—34. 8 s & 6 s.

1 LONG have I lived in grief and pain,
 And suffered many things in vain,
  And all physicians tried;
Nor men nor means my soul can heal,
The plague is still incurable,
  The fountain is undried.

2 No help can I from these receive:
Nor men nor means can e'er relieve,
  Or give my spirit ease ;
Still worse and worse my case I find;
Here then I cast them all behind,
  From all my works I cease.

3 I find brought in a better hope,
Succour there is for me laid up,
  For every helpless soul ;
Salvation is in Jesu's name,
Could I but touch his garment's hem,
  Even I should be made whole.

4 'Tis here, in hope my God to find,
With humble awe I come behind
  And wait his grace to prove
Before his face I dare not stand,
But faith puts forth a trembling hand,
  To apprehend his love.

5 Surely his healing power is nigh:
I touch him now I by faith even I,
  My Lord, lay hold on thee :
Thy power is present now to heal,
I feel, through all my soul I feel
  That Jesus died for me.

6 I glory in redemption found ;
Jesus, my Lord and God, look round,
  The conscious sinner see ;
Yes, I have touched thy clothes, and own
The miracle thy grace hath done
  On such a worm as me.

7 With lowly reverential fear
I testify that thou art near,
  To all who seek thy love ;
Saviour of *all* I thee proclaim ;
The world may know thy saving name
  And all its wonders prove.

782 *"Now is the day of salvation."*
2 Corinthians vi. 2. L. M.

1 WHY should I till to-morrow stay
 For what thou wouldst bestow to-day,
What thou more willing art to give
Than I to ask, or to receive?

2 This moment, Lord, thou ready art
To break, and to bind up my heart,
To pour the balm of Gilead in,
Forgive, and take away my sin.

3 This is the time : I surely may
Salvation find on this glad day,
And knowing thee my Saviour prove
That thou art God, and God is love.

4 Give then the bliss for which I pray
To-day, while it is called to-day,
The nature pure, the life divine,
And make thy gracious fulness mine !

783 *"To-day if ye will hear his voice."*
Hebrews iii. 15. C. M.

1 TO-DAY, while it is called to-day,
 My willing heart I bow ;

I harden it no more, but pray
 And look for mercy now :
I look—till thou my peace create,
 My promised pardon seal,
And every solemn moment wait,
 Thy sprinkled blood to feel.

2 To-day, before to-morrow come,
 I yield to be renewed,
My Saviour's mean, but constant home,
 A temple filled with God.
Now, Saviour, now thy servant bless,
 Who always ready art,
And fully from this hour possess
 My unopposing heart.

C. M. *A prayer for Faith.* **784**

1 FATHER, I stretch my hands to thee,
 No other help I know ;
If thou withdraw thyself from me,
 Ah ! whither shall I go?

2 What did thy only Son endure
 Before I drew my breath :
What pain, what labour, to secure
 My soul from endless death !

3 O Jesus, could I this believe,
 I now should feel thy power ;
Now all my wants thou wouldst relieve
 In this, the accepted hour.

4 Author of faith, to thee I lift
 My weary, longing eyes :
O let me now receive that gift !
 My soul without it dies.

5 Surely thou canst not let me die :
 O speak, and I shall live !
For here I will unwearied lie,
 Till thou thy Spirit give.

6 How would my fainting soul rejoice,
 Could I but see thy face !
Now let me hear thy quickening voice,
 And taste thy pardoning grace !

C. M. *A prayer for the Light of Life.* **785**

1 O SUN of righteousness, arise,
 With healing in thy wing !
To my diseased, my fainting soul,
 Life and salvation bring.

2 These clouds of pride and sin dispel,
 By thy all-piercing beam ;
Lighten my eyes with faith, my heart
 With holy hope inflame.

3 My mind, by thy all-quickening power,
 From low desires set free ;
Unite my scattered thoughts, and fix
 My love entire on thee.

4 Father, thy long-lost son receive ;
 Saviour, thy purchase own ;
Blest Comforter, with peace and joy
 Thy new-made creature crown.

5 Eternal, undivided Lord,
 Co-equal One and Three,
On thee, all faith, all hope be placed ;
 All love be paid to thee !

C. M. *"Help thou mine unbelief."* **786**
Mark ix. 24.

1 HOW sad our state by nature is !
 Our sin, how deep it stains !

183

And Satan binds our captive souls
Fast in his slavish chains.

2 But hark! a voice of sovereign grace
Sounds from the sacred word;
" Ho, ye despairing sinners, come,
And trust upon the Lord!"

3 My soul obeys the Almighty's call,
And runs to this relief;
I would believe thy promise, Lord;
O help my unbelief!

4 To the blest fountain of thy blood,
Incarnate God, I fly;
Here let me wash my spotted soul
From sins of deepest dye.

5 A guilty, weak, and helpless worm,
Into thy hands I fall;
Be thou my strength and righteousness,
My Saviour, and my all.

787 *Unfaithfulness acknow-*
ledged. **C. M.**

1 O FOR a closer walk with God,
A calm and heavenly frame;
A light to shine upon the road
That leads me to the Lamb!

2 Where is the blessedness I knew
When first I saw the Lord?
Where is that soul-refreshing view
Of Jesus and his word?

3 What peaceful hours I then enjoyed!
How sweet their memory still!
But now I find an aching void,
The world can never fill.

4 Return, O holy Dove, return,
Sweet messenger of rest!
I hate the sins that made thee mourn,
That drove thee from my breast.

5 The dearest idol I have known,
Whate'er that idol be,
Help me to tear it from thy throne,
And worship only thee.

6 So shall my walk be close with God,
Calm and serene my frame;
So purer light shall mark the road
That leads me to the Lamb.

788 *Wanderings from God*
lamented. **C. M.**

1 INFINITE Power, eternal Lord,
How sovereign is thy hand!
All nature rose to obey thy word,
And moves at thy command.

2 With steady course the shining sun
Keeps his appointed way;
And all the hours obedient run
The circle of the day.

3 But, ah! how wide my spirit flies,
And wanders from her God!
My soul forgets the heavenly prize,
And treads the downward road.

4 The raging fire and stormy sea
Perform thy awful will;
And every beast and every tree
Thy great design fulfil.

5 Shall creatures of a meaner frame
Pay all their dues to thee?
Creatures that never knew thy name,
That ne'er were loved like me?

184

6 G at God! create my soul anew,
Conform my heart to thine;
Melt down my will, and let it flow,
And take the mould divine.

7 Then shall my feet no more depart,
Nor my affections rove;
Devotion shall be all my heart,
And all my passions, love.

C. M. *Prayer for Quickening* **789**
Grace.

1 LONG have I sat beneath the sound
Of thy salvation, Lord;
But still how weak my faith is found,
And knowledge of thy word!

2 How cold and feeble is my love!
How negligent my fear!
How low my hope of joys above!
How few affections there!

3 Great God! thy sovereign aid impart
To give thy word success;
Write thy salvation on my heart,
And make me learn thy grace.

4 Show my forgetful feet the way
That leads to joys on high,
Where knowledge grows without decay,
And love shall never die.

790

8 s & 7 s.
1 LORD, I hear of showers of blessing
Thou art scattering, full and free—
Showers, the thirsty land refreshing;
Let some drops now fall on me.
Even me.

2 Pass me not, O God, our Father,
Sinful though my heart may be!
Thou might'st leave me, but the rather
Let thy mercy light on me. Even me.

3 Pass me not, O gracious Saviour,
Let me live and cling to thee!
I am longing for thy favour;
Whilst thou'rt calling, O call me!
Even me.

4 Pass me not, O mighty Spirit!
Thou canst make the blind to see:
Witnesser of Jesu's merit!
Speak some word of power to me.
Even me.

5 Love of God so pure and changeless,
Blood of Christ so rich, so free,
Grace of God so strong and boundless,
Magnify it all in me! Even me.

791

8 7, 8 7, 4 7.
1 COME, ye sinners, poor and wretched,
Weak and wounded, sick and sore;
Jesus ready stands to save you,
Full of pity joined with power;
He is able,
He is willing; doubt no more.

2 Come, ye needy, come, and welcome,
God's free bounty glorify;
True belief, and true repentance,
Every grace that brings us nigh,
Without money,
Come to Jesus Christ and buy.

3 Let not conscience make you linger,
Nor of fitness fondly dream;

All the fitness he requireth,
Is to feel your need of him :
This he gives you ;
'Tis the Spirit's rising beam.

4 Come, ye weary, heavy-laden,
Bruised and mangled by the fall ;
If you tarry till you're better,
You will never come at all :
Not the righteous,
Sinners Jesus came to call.

5 Lo ! the incarnate God, ascended,
Pleads the merit of his blood :
Venture on him, venture wholly,
Let no other trust intrude ;
None but Jesus
Can do helpless sinners good.

792
C. M.

1 RETURN, O wanderer, to thy home !
Thy Father calls for thee ;
No longer now an exile roam
In guilt and misery.

2 Return, O wanderer, to thy home !
'Tis Jesus calls for thee ;
The Spirit and the Bride say, " Come ;"
O now for refuge flee !

3 Return, O wanderer, to thy home !
'Tis madness to delay ;
There are no pardons in the tomb,
And brief is mercy's day !

793
* Come unto me, all ye that labour and are
heavy laden, and I will give
you rest."—Matt. xi. 28. 8 5, 8 3.

1 ART thou weary, art thou languid,
Art thou sore distrest
" Come to me," saith One, " and coming
Be at rest ! "

2 Hath he marks to lead me to him,
If he be my guide ?
" In his feet and hands are wound-prints,
And his side."

3 Hath he diadem as monarch
That his brow adorns ?
" Yea, a crown, in very surety,
But of thorns ! "

4 If I find him, if I follow,
What his guerdon here ?
" Many a sorrow, many a labour,
Many a tear."

5 If I still hold closely to him,
What hath he at last ?
" Sorrow vanquished, labour ended,
Jordan past."

6 If I ask him to receive me,
Will he say me nay ?
" Not till earth, and not till heaven
Pass away."

794
1 0 10, 1 0 1 0.

1 WEARY of earth and laden with my sin,
I look at heaven and long to enter in,
But there no evil thing may find a home :
And yet I hear a voice that bids me
" Come."

2 So vile I am, how dare I hope to stand
In the pure glory of that holy land ?

Before the whiteness of that throne appear ?   [me near.
Yet there are hands stretched out to draw

3 The while I fain would tread the heavenly
Evil is ever with me day by day ;   [way,
Yet on mine ears the gracious tidings fall,
" Repent, believe, thou shalt be loosed
from all."

4 It is the voice of Jesus that I hear,
His are the hands stretched out to draw
me near,
And his the blood that can for all atone,
And set me faultless there before the
throne.

5 'Twas he who found me on the deathly
wild,   [child,
And made me heir of heaven, the Father's
And day by day, whereby my soul may
live,   [give.
Gives me his grace of pardon, and will

6 O great Absolver, grant my soul may
wear
The lowliest garb of penitence and prayer,
That in the Father's courts my glorious
dress
May be the garment of thy righteousness.

7 Yea, thou wilt answer for me, righteous
Lord :   [ward :
Thine all the merits, mine the great re-
Thine the sharp thorns, and mine the
golden crown,   [down.
Mine the life won, and thine the life laid

8 Nought can I bring thee, Lord, for all I
owe,
Yet let my full heart what it can bestow ;
Like Mary's gift, let my devotion prove,
Forgiven greatly, how I greatly love.

L. M.   Luke xviii. 13.   ## 795

1 WITH broken heart and contrite sigh,
A trembling sinner, Lord, I cry ;
Thy pardoning grace is rich and free ;
O God ! be merciful to me.

2 I smite upon my troubled breast,
With deep and conscious guilt oppressed ;
Christ and his cross my only plea ;
O God ! be merciful to me.

3 Far off I stand with tearful eyes,
Nor dare uplift them to the skies
But thou dost all my anguish see
O God ! be merciful to me.

4 Nor alms, nor deeds that I have done,
Can for a single sin atone ;
To Calvary alone I flee ;
O God ! be merciful to me.

5 And when, redeemed from sin and hell,
With all the ransomed throng I dwell,
My raptured song shall ever be,
God has been merciful to me.

8 8, 8 6.   " Just as I am."   ## 796

1 JUST as I am, without one plea,
But that thy blood was shed for me,
And that thou bidd'st me come to thee,
O Lamb of God, I come !

2 Just as I am, and waiting not
To rid my soul of one dark blot,

185

To thee, whose blood can cleanse each
   O Lamb of God, I come!   [spot,
3 Just as I am, though tossed about
With many a conflict, many a doubt,
Fighting and fears, within, without,
   O Lamb of God, I come !

4 Just as I am, poor, wretched, blind ;
Sight, riches, healing of the mind,
Yea, all I need, in thee to find,
   O Lamb of God, I come !

5 Just as I am, thou wilt receive,
Wilt welcome, pardon, cleanse, relieve !
Because thy promise I believe,
   O Lamb of God, I come !

6 Just as I am, (thy love unknown
Has broken every barrier down)
Now to be thine, yea, thine alone,
   O Lamb of God, I come !

7 Just as I am, of that free love
The breadth, length, depth, and height to
Here for a season, then above,   [prove,
   O Lamb of God, I come !

797   C. M.

1 O LORD, turn not thy face away
   From them that lowly lie,
Lamenting sore their sinful life
   With tears and bitter cry ;
Thy mercy's gates are open wide
   To them that mourn their sin ;
O shut them not against us, Lord !
   But let us enter in.

2 We need not to confess our fault,
   'For surely thou canst tell ;
What we have done, and what we are,
   Thou knowest very well :
Wherefore to beg and to intreat,
   With tears we come to thee,
As children that have done amiss
   Fall at their father's knee.

3 And need we, then, O Lord, repeat
   The blessing which we crave,
When thou dost know before we speak
   The thing that we would have ?
Mercy, O Lord ! mercy we ask,
   This is the total sum :
For mercy, Lord, is all our prayer ;
   O let thy mercy come !

798   *The Fountain opened.*   C. M.

1 THERE is a fountain filled with blood
   Drawn from Immanuel's veins ;
And sinners, plunged beneath that flood,
   Lose all their guilty stains.

2 The dying thief rejoiced to see
   That fountain in his day ;
And there may I, though vile as he,
   Wash all my sins away.

3 O dying Lamb, thy precious blood
   Shall never lose its power,
Till all the ransomed church of God
   Be saved to sin no more.

4 E'er since, by faith, I saw the stream
   Thy flowing wounds supply,
Redeeming love has been my theme,
   And shall be till I die.
186

5 Then in a nobler, sweeter song,
   I'll sing thy power to save ;
When this poor lisping, stammering tongue
   Lies silent in the grave.

6 Lord, I believe thou hast prepared,
   Unworthy though I be,
For me a blood- bought free reward,
   A golden harp for me !

7 'Tis strung and tuned for endless years,
   And formed by power divine,
To sound in God the Father's ears
   No other name but thine.

C.M.   *Hymn after Sermon on*   **799**
         Sunday Evening.

1 O BLESSED, blessed sounds of grace
   Still echoing in my ear,
Glad is the hour, and loved the place—
   But whence my sudden fear ?

2 What if a sternly righteous doom
   Have sealed this call my last !
Before me sickness, death, the tomb :
   Behind, the unpardoned past?

3 My Sabbath suns may all have set,
   My Sabbath scenes be o'er,
The place, at least, where we are met,
   May know my steps no more ;

4 The prophet of the cross no more,
   Again preach peace to me ;
The voice of interceding prayer
   A farewell voice may be.

5 While yet the life-proclaiming word
   Doth through my conscience thrill,
Breathe life ; and lo ! divinely stirred,
   I can repent ; I will.

6 Thou that a will in me hast wrought,
   Haste, work in me to do,
And lest the purpose leave my thought,
   Now my whole heart renew.

7 Dying Redeemer, to thy breast,
   A dying wretch I flee,
Bid me be reconciled and blest,
   And born of God, through thee.

SECTION VI.

THE EXPERIENCE AND PRIVILEGES OF BELIEVERS.

" I am thy shield, and thy
exceeding great reward."   **800**
6 6 8 4, 6 6 8 4.   *Genesis* xv. 1.

1 THE God of Abraham praise,
   Who reigns enthroned above,
Ancient of everlasting days,
   And God of love :
Jehovah, Great I AM,
   By earth and heaven confest ;
I bow and bless the sacred name,
   For ever blest.

2 The God of Abraham praise,
   At whose supreme command
From earth I rise, and seek the joys
   At his right hand :
I all on earth forsake,
   Its wisdom, fame, and power ;
And him my only Portion make,
   My Shield and Tower.

3 The God of Abraham praise,
  Whose all-sufficient grace
Shall guide me all my happy days,
  In all my ways.
    He calls a worm his friend,
    He calls himself my God ;
And he shall save me to the end,
    Through Jesu's blood.

4 He by himself hath sworn,
  I on his oath depend :
I shall, on eagles' wings upborne,
  To heaven ascend :
    I shall behold his face,
    I shall his power adore,
And sing the wonders of his grace
    For evermore.

6 6 8 4, 6 6 8 4.   SECOND PART.

5 THOUGH nature's strength decay,
      And earth and hell withstand,
To Canaan's bounds I urge my way,
    At his command.
    The watery deep I pass,
    With Jesus in my view ;
And through the howling wilderness
    My way pursue.

6 The goodly land I see,
  With peace and plenty blest ;
A land of sacred liberty,
    And endless rest :
    There milk and honey flow,
    And oil and wine abound,
And trees of life for ever grow,
    With mercy crowned.

7 There dwells the Lord our King,
  The Lord our righteousness,
Triumphant o'er the world and sin,
    The Prince of peace ;
    On Zion's sacred height
    His kingdom still maintains,
And glorious with his saints in light
    For ever reigns.

8 He keeps his own secure,
  He guards them by his side,
Arrays in garments white and pure'
    His spotless bride :
    With streams of sacred bliss,
    With groves of living joys,
With all the fruits of Paradise,
    He still supplies.

6 6 8 4, 6 6 8 4.   THIRD PART.

9 BEFORE the great Three-One
      They all exulting stand,
And tell the wonders he hath done,
    Through all their land :
    The listening spheres attend,
    And swell the growing fame ;
And sing, in songs which never end,
    The wondrous name.

10 The God who reigns on high
   The great archangels sing ;
And, "Holy, holy, holy," cry,
    "Almighty King !
    Who was and is the same,
    And evermore shall be ;
Jehovah, Father, Great I AM,
    We worship thee."

11 Before the Saviour's face
   The ransomed nations bow ;

O'erwhelmed at his almighty grace,
    For ever new :
    He shows his prints of love,—
    They kindle to a flame !
And sound through all the worlds above
    The slaughtered Lamb.

12 The whole triumphant host
   Give thanks to God on high :
" Hail, Father, Son, and Holy Ghost,"
    They ever cry :
    Hail, Abraham's God and mine !
    (I join the heavenly lays)
All might and majesty are thine,
    And endless praise.

" All his saints are in thy hand." **801**
C. M.   Deuteronomy xxxiii. 3.

1 WHOM Jesu's blood doth sanctify
    Need neither sin nor fear ;
Hid in our Saviour's hand we lie,
    And laugh at danger near :
His guardian hand doth hold, protect,
    And save, by ways unknown,
The little flock, the saints elect,
    Who trust in him alone.

2 Our Prophet, Priest, and King, to thee
    We joyfully submit ;
And learn, in meek humility,
    Our lesson at thy feet :
Spirit and life thy words impart,
    And blessings from above ;
And drop in every listening heart
    The manna of thy love.

" They that wait upon the Lord shall
L. M.   *renew their strength."* **802**
         Isaiah xl. 31.

1 AWAKE, our souls ! away, our fears !
    Let every trembling thought be gone!
Awake, and run the heavenly race,
    And put a cheerful courage on.

2 True, 'tis a strait and thorny road,
    And mortal spirits tire and faint ;
But they forget the mighty God,
    That feeds the strength of every saint.

3 O mighty God, thy matchless power
    Is ever new, and ever young ;
And firm endures, while endless years
    Their everlasting circles run.

4 From thee, the ever-flowing spring,
    Our souls shall drink a fresh supply ;
While such as trust their native strength
    Shall melt away, and droop, and die.

5 Swift as the eagle cuts the air,
    We'll mount aloft to thine abode ; !
On wings of love our souls shall fly,
    Nor tire along the heavenly road.

L. M.   Habakkuk iii. 17, 18. **803**

1 AWAY, my unbelieving fear !
    Fear shall in me no more have place ;
My Saviour doth not yet appear,
    He hides the brightness of his face ;
But shall I therefore let him go,
    And basely to the tempter yield?
No, in the strength of Jesus, no !
    I never will give up my shield.

2 Although the vine its fruit deny,
    Although the olive yield no oil,

The withering fig-tree droop and die,
The field illude the tiller's toil,
The empty stall no herd afford,
The flocks be cut off from their place,
Yet will I triumph in the Lord,
The God of my salvation praise.

3 Barren although my soul remain,
And no one bud of grace appear,
No fruit of all my toil and pain,
But desperate wickedness is here ;
Although, my gifts and comforts lost,
My blooming hopes cut off I see ;
Yet will I in my Saviour trust,
And glory that he died for me.

4 In hope, believing against hope,
Jesus my Lord and God I claim ;
Jesus my strength shall lift me up,
Salvation is in Jesu's name ;
To me he soon shall bring it nigh ;
My soul shall then outstrip the wind,
On wings of love mount up on high,
And leave the world and sin behind.

804 *The same subject.* 7 6, 7 6, 7 6, 7 6.

1 SOMETIMES a light surprises
The Christian while he sings ;
It is the Lord who rises
With healing in his wings.
When comforts are declining,
He grants the soul again
A season of clear shining,
To cheer it after rain.

2 In holy contemplation,
We sweetly then pursue
The theme of God's salvation,
And find it ever new.
Set free from present sorrow
We cheerfully can say,
E'en let the unknown to-morrow
Bring with it what it may :

3 It can bring with it nothing
But he will bear us through :
Who gives the lilies clothing
Will clothe his people too :
Beneath the spreading heavens
No creature but is fed ;
And he who feeds the ravens
Will give his children bread.

4 Though vine nor fig-tree neither
Their wonted fruit should bear,
Though all the field should wither,
Nor flocks, nor herds be there,
Yet, God the same abiding,
His praise shall tune my voice ;
For, while in him confiding,
I cannot but rejoice.

805 Matthew xvii. 20. C. M.

1 AUTHOR of faith, on me confer,
The all-obtaining grace,
Which wrestles and receives in prayer
Thy largest promises ;
The faith unfeigned and unreproved
Which can the test abide,
From false humility removed,
And self-deluding pride.

2 A perfect confidence inspire
From all presumption free,
183

A holy boldness to desire
The thing prepared for me ;
A wisdom to discern and know
The time by God designed,
A strength that will not let thee go
Till I the blessing find.

S. M. *" Whosoever hath not," &c.* **806**
Luke viii. 18.

1 THOUGH God in Christ reveal
Our sins through faith removed,
We lose the talent we conceal,
The blessing unimproved ;
Not labouring after more
Abundant righteousness,
Stripped of our former peace and power,
We forfeit all our grace.

2 Lord, if thy grace I have,
I plead thy word for more :
Whom thou hast saved, persist to save,
And all thy life restore :
If with a faithful heart
I simply follow thee,
Whate'er thou hast, whate'er thou art,
Thou art, and hast for me.

807
5 5 9, 5 5 9.

1 HOW happy are they
Who the Saviour obey,
And have laid up their treasure above !
Tongue cannot express
The sweet comfort and peace
Of a soul in its earliest love.

2 That comfort was mine,
When the favour divine
I first found in the blood of the Lamb ;
When my heart it believed,
What a joy it received,
What a heaven in Jesus's name !

3 Jesus all the day long
Was my joy and my song ;
O that all his salvation may see !
He hath loved me, I cried,
He hath suffered, and died,
To redeem such a rebel as me.

4 O the rapturous height
Of the holy delight,
Which I felt in the life-giving blood !
Of my Saviour possessed
I was perfectly blest,
As if filled with the fulness of God.

5 5 12. *" We joy in God through our Lord Jesus Christ," &c.* **808**
Romans v. 11.

1 O GOD of all grace,
Thy goodness we praise ;
Thy Son thou hast given to die in our place.

2 He came from above
Our curse to remove, [would love.
He hath loved, he hath loved us, because he

3 Love moved him to die,
And on this we rely, [tell why.
He hath loved, he hath loved us, we cannot

4 But this we can tell,
He hath loved us so well, [bell.
As to lay down his life to redeem us from

5 He hath ransomed our race,
O how shall we praise
Or worthily sing thy unspeakable grace ?

6 Nothing else will we know
   In our journey below,
But singing thy grace to thy paradise go.

7 Nay, and when we remove
   To the mansions above,
Our heaven shall be still to sing of thy love.

8 Thrice happy employ!
   We there shall enjoy
A fulness of pleasure that never can cloy.

9 The heavenly choir
   With us shall aspire,
And gladly our loving Redeemer admire.

10 We all shall commend
   The love of our Friend,
For ever beginning what never shall end.

11 When time is no more,
   We still shall adore
That ocean of love without bottom or shore.

809

7 s & 6 s †.

1 VAIN, delusive world, adieu,
   With all of creature-good!
Only Jesus I pursue,
   Who bought me with his blood:
All thy pleasures I forego,
   I trample on thy wealth and pride:
Only Jesus will I know,
   And Jesus crucified.

2 Other knowledge I disdain,
   'Tis all but vanity:
Christ, the Lamb of God, was slain,
   He tasted death for me.
Me to save from endless woe,
   The sin-atoning Victim died:
Only Jesus I know,
   And Jesus crucified.

3 Turning to my rest again,
   The Saviour I adore;
He relieves my grief and pain,
   And bids me weep no more.
Rivers of salvation flow
   From out his head, his hands, his side:
Only Jesus will I know,
   And Jesus crucified.

4 Here will I set up my rest;
   My fluctuating heart
From the haven of his breast
   Shall never more depart.
Whither should a sinner go?
   His wounds for me stand open wide:
Only Jesus will I know,
   And Jesus crucified.

810
" I know whom I have believed,
and am," &c.—2 Tim. i. 12. L. M.

1 I KNOW in whom I have believed,
   Who, when this precious faith he gave,
My soul into his hands received,
   And bade me trust his power to save:
His Spirit doth my heart assure,
   That what I still to him commend
His constant love shall keep secure,
   Till faith filled up in sight shall end.

811
The same subject. C. M.

1 I'm not ashamed to own my Lord,
   Nor to defend his cause,
Maintain the honour of his word,
   The glory of his cross,

2 Jesus, my God! I know his name,
   His name is all my trust;
Nor will he put my soul to shame,
   Nor let my hope be lost.

3 Firm as his throne his promise stands,
   And he can well secure
What I've committed to his hands,
   Till the decisive hour.

4 Then will he own my worthless name
   Before his Father's face;
And in the new Jerusalem
   Appoint my soul a place.

" The truth . . . shall be with
8 s & 6 s. *us for ever."*—2 John 2. **812**

JESUS, we steadfastly believe
   The grace thou dost this moment give
Thou wilt the next bestow;
Wilt keep us every moment here,
And show thyself the Finisher,
   And never let us go.

" Able to keep you from falling."
C. M. Jude 24. **813**

LORD, I believe thy mercy's power,
   Which hath my refuge been,
Will still in every future hour
   Preserve my soul from sin:
The help for which on thee I call
   Shall my protection prove;
And into sin I cannot fall,
   While hanging on thy love.

S. M. *The same subject.* **814**

1 TO God the only wise,
   Our Saviour and our King,
Let all the saints below the skies
   Their humble praises bring.

2 'Tis his almighty love,
   His counsels and his care,
Preserve us safe from sin and death,
   And every hurtful snare.

3 He will present our souls
   Unblemished and complete,
Before the glory of his face,
   With joys divinely great.

4 Then all the chosen seed
   Shall meet around the throne,
Shall bless the conduct of his grace,
   And make his wonders known.

L. M. *Trust in Christ.* **815**

1 O JESUS, full of truth and grace,
   O all-atoning Lamb of God,
I wait to see thy glorious face,
   I seek redemption through thy blood.

2 Now in thy strength I strive with thee,
   My Friend and Advocate with God;
Give me the glorious liberty,
   Grant me the purchase of thy blood.

3 Thou art the anchor of my hope,
   The faithful saying I receive;
Surely thy death shall raise me up,
   For thou hast died that I may live.

4 Satan, with all his arts, no more
   Me from the gospel hope shall move;
I shall receive the gracious power,
   And find the pearl of perfect love.

5 Though nature gives my God the lie,
    I all his truth and grace shall know ;
I shall, the helpless creature I,
    Shall perfect holiness below.

6 My flesh, which cries, "It cannot be,"
    Shall silence keep before the Lord ;
And earth, and hell, and sin shall flee
    At Jesu's everlasting word.

816 *"Heal me, O Lord," &c.* L. M.
        Jeremiah xvii. 14.

1 THAT health of soul I gasp to know
    Which only Jesus can bestow,
Jesus, thy sovereign skill display,
And take this seed of sin away ;
The original infirmity,
O were it now expelled by thee,
Who didst my every pain endure,
And die thyself to effect my cure !

2 The world with feeble saints agree
In vain to urge "It cannot be !
Sin must remain ; howe'er expelled
And healed ; ye never can be healed."
I trust my great Physician's skill,
And, saved according to thy will,
Shall live, a saint in love complete,
Shall die, a sinner at thy feet.

817 Matthew v. 8. 7s.

1 BLESSED are the pure in heart,
    They have learned the angel-art,
While on earth in heaven to be,
God, by sense unseen, to see.

2 Cleansed from sin's offensive stain,
Fellowship with him they gain ;
Nearness, likeness to their Lord,
Their exceeding great reward.

3 Worshipping in spirit now,
In his inner court they bow,
Bow before the brightening vail,
God's own radiance through it hail.

4 Serious, simple of intent,
Teachably intelligent,
Rapt, they search the written word,
Till his very voice is heard.

5 In creation him they own,
Meet him in its haunts, alone ;
Most amidst its Sabbath calm,
Morning light and evening balm.

6 Him they still through busier life,
Trust in pain and care and strife ;
These like clouds o'er noontide blaze,
Temper, not conceal his rays.

7 Hallowed thus their every breath,
Dying they shall not " see death ; "
With the Lord in Paradise,
Till, like his, their bodies rise.

8 Nearer than the seraphim
In their flesh shall saints see him,
With the Father, in the Son,
Through the Spirit, ever one !

818 Matthew vi. 13. 7 6, 7 6, 7 6, 7 6.

1 FROM trials unexempted
    Thy dearest children are ;
But let us not be tempted
    Above what we can bear ;
190

Exposed to no temptation
    That may our souls o'erpower,
Be thou our strong salvation
    Through every fiery hour.

2 Ah ! leave us not to venture
    Within the verge of sin ;
Or if the snare we enter,
    Thy timely help bring in ;
And if thy wisdom try us
    Till pain and woe are past,
Almighty Love, stand by us,
    And save from first to last !

3 Fain would we cease from sinning
    In thought and word and deed,
From sin in its beginning
    We languish to be freed ;
From every base desire,
    Our fallen nature's shame,
Jesus, we dare require
    Deliverance in thy name.

4 For every sinful action
    Thou hast atonement made,
The rigid satisfaction
    Thy precious blood has paid :
But take entire possession ;
    To make an end of sin,
To finish the transgression,
    Most holy God, come in !

8 s & 7 s. *The same subject.* **819**

1 LEAD me not into temptation,
    Father, leave me not alone,
Thou to whom my every passion,
    Every secret thought is known ;
If thy providence forsake me
    In the dark unguarded hour,
Sin is sure to overtake me,
    Hell is ready to devour.

2 In the feebleness of nature,
    Never from thy charge depart,
Infinitely good, and greater
    Than the evil of my heart ;
Watch, and hold me back from sinning,
    Self-inclined from thee to stray,
Stop me at the first beginning,
    Turn my tempted heart away.

3 With mine enemies surrounded,
    Sin, the world, and Satan's snare,
Let me never be confounded,
    Tempted more than I can bear ;
Rather from the dread occasion
    Thy poor helpless creature hide,
Bind the sinful inclination,
    Turn my stronger foe aside.

4 Conflicts I cannot require,
    Who myself can nothing do ;
If thou bring into the fire,
    Surely thou shalt bring me through ;
Shalt from every ill deliver,
    That I may thy glory see,
Magnify thy name for ever,
    Saved through all eternity.

C. M. *"Deliver us from evil."* **820**
        Matthew vi. 13.

1 VOUCHSAFE to keep me, Lord, this day
    Without committing sin,
And with me let thy Spirit stay,
    And ever dwell within.

2 Thou canst from every sin secure :
. And is it not thy will
Still to preserve thy servant pure
From every touch of ill ?

3 Thou canst, thou wilt for one short day
Preserve me spotless here,
And why not then (let Satan say)
A week, a month, a year ?

4 Why wilt thou not for all my life
My helpless soul defend,
And bear me through the doubtful strife,
And keep me to the end ?

5 Behold, with humble faith I bow
· My soul before thy throne ;
Deliver me from evil now,
For thou canst save thine own.

6 My soul on thee, O Lord, relies,
Thine arms are my defence,
My soul, hell, earth, and sin defies
To come and pluck me thence.

821   1 Corinthians ix. 24.   C. M.

O GOD, who dost thy sovereign might
And high prerogative
Most chiefly show in thy delight
To pity and forgive :
Vouchsafe the aid thy grace supplies,
So in thy ways to run,
That we may win the heavenly prize,
Through Jesus Christ, thy Son.

822   *Prayer for Charity.*
   1 Corinthians xiii.   C. M.

1 LORD, who hast taught to us on earth
This lesson from above,
That all our works are nothing worth,
Unless they spring from love ;
Send down thy Spirit from on high,
And pour in all our hearts
That precious gift of charity,
Which peace and joy imparts ;

2 The healing balm, the holy oil
Which calms the waves of strife,
The drop which sweetens every toil,
The breath of our new life,
Without this blessed bond of peace
God counts the living dead :
O heavenly Father, grant us this,
Through Christ, the living Head.

3 Let all who love the Lord join hands
To aid the common good,
And knit more close the sacred bands
Of Christian brotherhood.
Make all thy pastors one, O Lord,
In heart, in mind, in speech,
That they may set forth thy pure word,
And live the life they preach.

4 Let all hold fast the truths whereby
A church must stand or fall ;
In doubtful things grant liberty,
Show charity in all.
Thus shall we to our sacred name
Our title clearly prove,
While even our enemies exclaim,
" See how these Christians love."

823   *Prayer described.*   C. M.

1 PRAYER is the soul's sincere desire,
Uttered or unexpressed :

The motion of a hidden fire,
That trembles in the breast.

2 Prayer is the burden of a sigh,
The falling of a tear ;
The upward glancing of an eye,
When none but God is near.

3 Prayer is the simplest form of speech
That infant lips can try ;
Prayer the sublimest strains that reach
The Majesty on high.

4 Prayer is the contrite sinner's voice
Returning from his ways ;
While angels in their songs rejoice,
And cry, " Behold he prays ! "

5 Prayer is the Christian's vital breath,
The Christian's native air ;
His watchword at the gates of death ;
He enters heaven with prayer.

6 The saints in prayer appear as one,
In word, and deed, and mind ;
While with the Father and the Son
Sweet fellowship they find.

7 Nor prayer is made on earth alone ;
The Holy Spirit pleads :
And Jesus, on the eternal throne,
For sinners intercedes.

8 O Thou by whom we come to God,
The Life, the Truth, the Way !
The path of prayer thyself hast trod :
Lord ! teach us how to pray.

7 s.   **824**

1 COME, my soul, thy suit prepare,
Jesus loves to answer prayer ;
He himself has bid thee pray,
Therefore will not say thee nay.

2 Thou art coming to a King,
Large petitions with thee bring ;
For his grace and power are such,
None can ever ask too much.

3 With my burden I begin,
Lord, remove this load of sin !
Let thy blood for sinners spilt
Set my conscience free from guilt.

4 Lord, I come to thee for rest,
Take possession of my breast ;
There thy blood-bought right maintain,
And without a rival reign.

5 As the image in the glass
Answers the beholder's face :
Thus unto my heart appear,
Print thine own resemblance there.

6 While I am a pilgrim here,
Let thy love my spirit cheer :
As my guide, my guard, my friend,
Lead me to my journey's end.

L. M.   *The Mercy-seat.*   **825**

1 FROM every stormy wind that blows,
From every swelling tide of woes,
There is a calm, a sure retreat ;
'Tis found beneath the mercy-seat.

2 There is a place where Jesus sheds
The oil of gladness on our heads,
A place than all beside more sweet :
It is the blood-stained mercy-seat.

3 There is a spot where spirits blend,
  And friend holds fellowship with friend;
  Though sundered far, by faith they meet
  Around one common mercy-seat.

4 There, there on eagle-wing we soar,
  And time and sense seem all no more;
  And heaven comes down our souls to greet,
  And glory crowns the mercy-seat.

826   8 - 7 s.

GRANT, O Saviour, to our prayers,
  That this changeful world's affairs,
Ordered by thy governance,
May so peaceably advance,
That thy Church with ardour due.
May her proper work pursue,
In all godly quietness,
Through the name we ever bless.

827 *"And shall not God avenge*   L. M.
      his own elect?"
      Luke xviii. 7.

1 A WIDOW, poor, forlorn, oppressed,
    Importunate her suit could gain;
  And shall not we our joint request
  By persevering prayer obtain?

2 A stranger to the judge she was,
    But we God's chosen people are;
  And, wishing us to gain our cause,
    Himself doth all our burdens bear.

3 To an unrighteous judge she came,
    But to a righteous Father we,
  Who bids us confidently claim
    His grace for needy sinners free:

4 The widow's and the orphan's Friend
    Kindly commands us to draw nigh:
  And lo, our hearts to heaven ascend,
    And boldly Abba, Father, cry!

5 She had no promise to succeed,
    And but at times could find access;
  Encouraged we, and sure to speed,
    Both day and night our suit may press.

6 Her vehemence did the judge provoke;
    But God our earnestness approves,
  Watches our every sigh and look,
    And most the boldest suitor loves.

7 She had no friend or patron kind,
    To enforce and make her suit his own;
  But we a powerful spokesman find
    Before us at the Father's throne.

8 Our Advocate for ever lives
    For us in heaven to intercede,
  For us the Comforter receives,
    And sends him in our hearts to plead.

828 *"I say unto all, Watch."*   8 s & 6 s.
      Mark xiii. 37.

1 MASTER, thy grace vouchsafe to me,
    The loving firm fidelity.
      That mindful of thy word
  I may, with all my skill and might,
  Perform my every work aright,
      And please my heavenly Lord.

2 My heart, thy meanest house, I keep,
  If thou whose eyelids never sleep
      The watchful power bestow;
  I mark the thoughts that thence proceed,
  Not one shall pass into a deed
      Before thy mind I know.

192

3 Cautious the door of sense I close,
  And keep it shut against my foes,
      Who press to enter in;
  All commerce with the world preclude,
  Nor let the tempting fiend intrude,
      Or the besetting sin.

4 No unexamined thought or word
  Shall pass, but such as serve my Lord,
      And execute his will;
  I only live to watch and pray,
  And for thy second coming stay,
      And all thy mind fulfil.

5 Happy, if, watching to the end,
  I see thee gloriously descend,
      The man thou dost approve;
  Enter into my Master's joy,
  And all eternity employ
      In ecstasies of love.

      "Watch and pray."   **829**
7 7 7 3.   Mark xiii. 33.

1 CHRISTIAN! seek not yet repose,
    Cast thy dreams of ease away;
  Thou art in the midst of foes;
      Watch and pray.

2 Principalities and powers,
  Mustering their unseen array,
  Wait for thy unguarded hours;
      Watch and pray

3 Gird thy heavenly armour on,
  Wear it ever night and day;
  Ambushed lies the evil one;
      Watch and pray.

4 Hear the victors who o'ercame;
  Still they mark each warrior's way;
  All with one sweet voice exclaim.
      Watch and pray.

5 Hear, above all, hear thy Lord,
  Him thou lovest to obey;
  Hide within thy heart his word,
      Watch and pray.

6 Watch, as if on that alone
  Hung the issue of the day;
  Pray that help may be sent down;
      Watch and pray.

      "Forgive, and ye shall be for-   **830**
6 - 8 s.   *given."*—Luke vi. 37.

1 FORGIVE my foes? it cannot be:
    My foes with cordial love embrace?
  Fast bound in sin and misery,
    Unsaved, unchanged by hallowing grace.
  Throughout my fallen soul I feel
  With man this is impossible.

2 Great Searcher of the mazy heart,
    A thought from thee I would not hide;
  I cannot draw the envenomed dart,
    Or quench this hell of wrath and pride:
  Jesus, till I thy Spirit receive,
  Thou know'st, I never can forgive.

3 Root out the wrath thou dost restrain;
    And when I have my Saviour's mind,
  I cannot render pain for pain,
    I cannot speak a word unkind,
  An angry thought I cannot know,
  Or count mine injurer my foe.

S. M.   *Trust in Providence.*   **831**

1 COMMIT thou all thy griefs
    And ways into his hands,

To his sure truth and tender care,
Who heaven and earth commands.

2 Who points the clouds their course,
Whom winds and seas obey,
He shall direct thy wandering feet,
He shall prepare thy way.

3 Thou on the Lord rely,
So safe shalt thou go on;
Fix on his work thy steadfast eye,
So shall thy work be done.

4 No profit canst thou gain
By self-consuming care;
To him commend thy cause, his ear
Attends the softest prayer.

5 Thy everlasting truth,
Father, thy ceaseless love,
Sees all thy children's wants, and knows
What best for each will prove.

6 Thou everywhere hast sway,
And all things serve thy might;
Thy every act pure blessing is,
Thy path unsullied light.

7 When thou arisest, Lord,
What shall thy work withstand?
Whate'er thy children want, thou giv'st;
And who shall stay thy hand?

SECOND PART.   S. M.

8 GIVE to the winds thy fears,
Hope, and be undismayed:
God hears thy sighs, and counts thy tears,
God shall lift up thy head.

9 Through waves, and clouds, and storms,
He gently clears thy way:
Wait thou his time, so shall this night
Soon end in joyous day.

10 Still heavy is thy heart?
Still sink thy spirits down?
Cast off the weight, let fear depart,
Bid every care be gone.

11 What though thou rulest not?
Yet heaven, and earth, and hell
Proclaim, God sitteth on the throne,
And ruleth all things well!

12 Leave to his sovereign sway
To choose and to command;
So shalt thou wondering own his way,
How wise, how strong his hand.

13 Far, far above thy thought
His counsel shall appear,
When fully he the work hath wrought
That caused thy needless fear!

14 Thou seest our weakness, Lord;
Our hearts are known to thee;
O lift thou up the sinking hand,
Confirm the feeble knee!

15 Let us in life, in death,
Thy steadfast truth declare,
And publish with our latest breath
Thy love and guardian care.

832   *The same subject.*   S. M.

1 AWAY, my needless fears,
And doubts no longer mine;
A ray of heavenly light appears,
A messenger divine.

2 Thrice comfortable hope,
That calms my troubled breast;
My Father's hand prepares the cup,
And what he wills is best.

3 If what I wish is good,
And suits the will divine;
By earth and hell in vain withstood,
I know it shall be mine.

4 Still let them counsel take
To frustrate his decree,
They cannot keep a blessing back
By heaven designed for me.

5 Here then I doubt no more,
But in his pleasure rest,
Whose wisdom, love, and truth, and power
Engage to make me blest.

6 To accomplish his design
The creatures all agree;
And all the attributes divine
Are now at work for me.

L. M.   Matthew vi. 27.   **833**

1 UNPROFITABLE all and vain,
Away this soul-distracting care!
I cannot lengthen out my span,
I cannot change a single hair;

2 Then let me hang upon his word
Who keeps his saints in perfect peace,
My burden cast upon the Lord,
And only care my God to please.

3 Who stoops to clothe a fading flower
Will every needful blessing give,
And fit the creature of an hour
An endless life with him to live.

4 My Father knows the things I need,
My Father knows, let that suffice,
I trust him now to clothe and feed
His child who on his care relies.

5 The cause of my misgiving fear,
Lord, I my unbelief confess;
Author of faith in me appear,
And bid my doubts and terrors cease!

S. M.   Matthew vi. 33.   **834**

1 I SEEK the kingdom first,
The gracious joy and peace;
Thou know'st I hunger, Lord, and thirst
After thy righteousness;
My chief and sole desire
Thine image to regain,
And then to join the heavenly choir,
And with thine ancients reign.

2 My God will add the rest,
Will outward good provide;
But with thy kingdom in my breast
I nothing want beside;
Glory begun in grace
Delightfully I prove,
And earth and heaven at once possess
In thy sufficient love.

6-8s.   Matthew vi. 34.   **835**

1 THE past no longer in my power;
The future, who shall live to see?
Mine only is the present hour,
Lent to be all laid out for thee.

Now, Saviour, with thy grace endowed,
Now let me serve and praise my God.

2 Why should I ask the future load
    To aggravate my present care?
Strong in the grace to-day bestowed
    The evil of to-day I bear;
And if to-morrow's care I see,
Fresh grace shall still suffice for me.

836   *In Uncertainty.*   L. M.

1 FEEBLE in body, and in mind,
    Saviour, I cast them both on thee,
With humble confidence to find
    Thy perfect strength displayed in me.

2 Entangled in the worldly snare,
    With sore perplexity distrest,
O'erwhelmed with mountain-loads of care,
    Beneath thy mercy's wings I rest.

3 Thou seest I know not what to do,
    But fix mine eyes on thee alone,
Till thou thy secret counsel show,
    And bring the blind by ways unknown.

4 If thou direct my path aright,
    If thou before thy servant go,
The darkness shall be turned to light,
    The mountains at thy presence flow.

5 The crooked things shall at thy word
    Be straight, the rugged places plain,
The creatures all obey their Lord,
    And be whate'er thy will ordain:

6 My soul, escaped the fowler's net,
    Above all earthly things shall soar,
Or fall at my deliverer's feet,
    And love, and wonder, and adore.

837   6 6, 6 6, 6 6, 6 6.

1 THY way, not mine, O Lord,
    However dark it be!
Lead me by thine own hand,
    Choose out the path for me,
Smooth let it be or rough,
    It will be still the best,
Winding or straight, it leads
    Right onward to thy rest.

2 I dare not choose my lot;
    I would not, if I might:
Choose thou for me, my God,
    So shall I walk aright.
The kingdom that I seek
    Is thine; so let the way
That leads to it be thine,
    Else I must surely stray.

3 Take thou my cup, and it
    With joy or sorrow fill,
As best to thee may seem;
    Choose thou my good and ill.
Not mine, not mine the choice,
    In things or great or small;
Be thou my guide, my strength,
    My wisdom, and my all.

838   S. M.

1 THOU doest all things well,
    God only wise and true I
My days and nights alternate tell
    Of mercies always new.

194

2 With daily toil oppressed,
    I sink in welcome sleep;
Or wake in darkness and unrest,
    Yet patient vigil keep.

3 Soon finds each fevered day,
    And each chill night, its bourn;
Nor zeal need droop, nor hope decay,
    Ere rest, or light return.

4 But be the night-watch long,
    And sore the chastening rod,—
Thou art my health, my sun, my song,
    My glory, and my God!

5 Thy smiling face lights mine;
    If veiled it makes me sad;
Even tears in darkness, starlike, shine,
    And morning finds me glad.

6 For weeping, wakeful eyes
    Instinctive look above
And catch, through openings in the skies,
    Thy beams, unslumbering Love I

7 Hours spent with pain—and thee
    Lost hours have never seemed;
No! those are lost, which but might be
    From earth for heaven redeemed.

8 Its limit, its relief,
    Its hallowed issues, tell,
That, though thou cause thy servant grief,
    Thou doest all things well!

839

87, 87, 47.

1 GUIDE me, O thou great Jehovah,
    Pilgrim through this barren land;
I am weak, but thou art mighty,
    Hold me with thy powerful hand;
        Bread of heaven!
    Feed me now and evermore.

2 Open thou the crystal fountain
    Whence the healing stream shall flow;
Let the fiery, cloudy pillar,
    Lead me all my journey through;
        Strong Deliverer!
    Be thou still my help and shield.

3 When I tread the verge of Jordan,
    Bid my anxious fears subside;
Death of death, and hell's destruction,
    Land me safe on Canaan's side;
        Songs of praises
    I will ever give to thee.

840

" Get thee out of thy country."
Genesis xii. 1.
S. M.

1 IN every time and place
    Who serve the Lord most high,
Are called his sovereign will to embrace,
    And still their own deny;
To follow his command,
    On earth as pilgrims rove,
And seek an undiscovered land,
    And house, and friends above.

2 Father, the narrow path
    To that far country show;
And in the steps of Abraham's faith
    Enable me to go,
A cheerful sojourner
    Where'er thou bidd'st me roam,
Till, guided by thy Spirit here,
    I reach my heavenly home.

841   *"Thy will be done."*   8 8 8 4.
Matthew vi. 10.

1 MY God, and Father ! while I stray
   Far from my home, in life's rough
O teach me from my heart to say,   [way,
   Thy will be done !

2 Though dark my path, and sad my lot,
Let me be still and murmur not,
Or breathe the prayer divinely taught,
   Thy will be done.

3 If thou shouldst call me to resign
What most I prize—it ne'er was mine ;
I only yield thee what was thine ;
   Thy will be done.

4 Should pining sickness waste away
My life in premature decay,
My Father, still I strive to say,
   Thy will be done.

5 If but my fainting heart be blest
With thy sweet Spirit for its guest,
My God, to thee I leave the rest ;
   Thy will be done.

6 Renew my will from day to day,
Blend it with thine, and take away
All that now makes it hard to say,
   Thy will be done.

7 Then when on earth I breathe no more
The prayer oft mixed with tears before,
I'll sing upon a happier shore,
   Thy will be done.

842   *The Life of Love.*   8 6, 8 6, 8 6.
Irregular.

1 FATHER, I know that all my life
   Is portioned out for me,
And the changes that are sure to come
   I do not fear to see ;
But I ask thee for a present mind,
   Intent on pleasing thee.

2 I ask thee for a thoughtful love,
   Through constant watching wise,
To meet the glad with joyful smiles,
   And wipe the weeping eyes ;
And a heart at leisure from itself,
   To soothe and sympathise.

3 I would not have the restless will
   That hurries to and fro,
Seeking for some great thing to do
   Or secret thing to know ;
I would be treated as a child,
   And guided where I go.

4 Wherever in the world I am,
   In whatsoe'er estate,
I have a fellowship with hearts
   To keep and cultivate ;
And a work of lowly love to do
   For the Lord on whom I wait.

5 So I ask thee for the daily strength,
   To none that ask denied,
And a mind to blend with outward life,
   Still keeping at thy side ;
Content to fill a little space
   If thou be glorified.

6 And if some things I do not ask
   In my cup of blessing be ;
I would have my spirit filled the more
   With grateful love to thee,

G 2

And careful less to serve thee much
   Than to please thee perfectly.

7 There are briers besetting every path,
   That call for patient care ;
There is a cross in every lot,
   And a constant need for prayer ;
Yet a lowly heart, that leans on thee,
   Is happy anywhere.

8 In a service which thy will appoints
   There are no bonds for me ;
For my inmost soul is taught the truth
   That makes thy children free ;
And a life of self-renouncing love
   Is a life of liberty.

C. M.   *The Request.*   **843**

1 FATHER, whate'er of earthly bliss
   Thy sovereign will denies,
Accepted at thy throne of grace
   Let this petition rise :

2 "Give me a calm, a thankful heart,
   From every murmur free ;
The blessings of thy grace impart,
   And make me live to thee.

3 "Let the sweet hope that thou art mine
   My life and death attend :
Thy presence through my journey shine,
   And crown my journey's end."

C. M.   *"It is the Lord."*   **844**
1 Samuel iii. 18.

1 IT is the Lord ! enthroned in light,
   Whose works are all divine,
Who hath an everlasting right
   To govern me and mine.

2 It is the Lord ! should I distrust
   Or contradict his will,
Who cannot do what is unjust,
   Who must be righteous still ?

3 It is the Lord ! who gives me all,
   My wealth, my friends, my ease,
And of his bounties may recall
   Whatever part he please.

4 It is the Lord ! who can sustain
   Beneath the heaviest load ;
From whom I may assistance gain,
   To tread the thorny road.

5 It is the Lord ! whose wondrous skill
   Can, from afflictions, raise
Matter eternity to fill
   With ever-growing praise.

6 And can my soul with hopes like these
   Be sullen, or repine ?
No, gracious God, take what thou please,
   To thee I all resign.

C. M.   **845**

1 GOD moves in a mysterious way,
   His wonders to perform ;
He plants his footsteps in the sea,
   And rides upon the storm.
Deep in unfathomable mines
   Of never-failing skill,
He treasures up his bright designs,
   And works his sovereign will.

2 Ye fearful saints, fresh courage take !
   The clouds ye so much dread

Are big with mercy, and shall break
  In blessings on your head.
Judge not the Lord by feeble sense,
  But trust him for his grace:
Behind a frowning providence
  He hides a smiling face.

3 His purposes will ripen fast,
  Unfolding every hour;
The bud may have a bitter taste,
  But sweet will be the flower.
Blind unbelief is sure to err,
  And scan his work in vain:
God is his own interpreter,
  And he will make it plain.

846   C. M.

1 SINCE all the downward tracks of time
  God's watchful eye surveys,
O who so wise to choose our lot,
  And regulate our ways?

2 Good, when he gives, supremely good!
  Nor less when he denies:
Even crosses from his sovereign hand
  Are blessings in disguise.

3 Why should we doubt his equal love,
  Immeasurably kind?
To his unerring, gracious will
  Be every wish resigned.

847 *"A good Soldier of Jesus Christ."*
  2 Timothy ii. 3.   7 s.

1 OFT in danger, oft in woe,
  Onward, Christians, onward go;
Fight the fight, maintain the strife,
Strengthened with the bread of life.

2 Let your drooping hearts be glad;
March in heavenly armour clad;
Fight, nor think the battle long,
Soon shall victory tune your song.

3 Let not sorrow dim your eye,
Soon shall every tear be dry;
Let not fears your course impede,
Great your strength if great your need.

4 Onward, then, to glory move,
More than conquerors ye shall prove;
Though opposed by many a foe,
Christian soldiers, onward go.

848   6 4, 6 4, 6 6 4.

1 NEARER, my God, to thee!
  Nearer to thee!
E'en though it be a cross
  That raiseth me;
Still all my song shall be,
Nearer, my God, to thee!
  Nearer to thee!

2 Though like the wanderer,
  The sun gone down,
Darkness be over me,
  My rest a stone;
Yet in my dreams I'd be
Nearer, my God, to thee!
  Nearer to thee!

3 There let the way appear
  Steps unto heaven;
All that thou send'st to me
  In mercy given;

196

Angels to beckon me.
Nearer, my God, to thee!
  Nearer to thee!

4 Then, with my waking thoughts
  Bright with thy praise,
Out of my stony griefs
  Bethel I'll raise;
So by my woes to be
Nearer, my God, to thee!
  Nearer to thee!

5 Or if on joyful wing
  Cleaving the sky,
Sun, moon, and stars forgot,
  Upwards I fly,
Still all my song shall be,
Nearer, my God, to thee!
  Nearer to thee!

6 - 8 s.   **849**

1 WHEN gathering clouds around I view,
  And days are dark, and friends are
On him I lean, who not in vain [few,
Experienced every human pain;
He knows my wants, allays my fears,
And counts and treasures up my tears.

2 If aught should tempt my soul to stray
From heavenly wisdom's narrow way,
To fly the good I would pursue,
Or do the thing I would not do;
Still he, who felt temptation's power,
Shall guard me in that dangerous hour.

3 If wounded love my bosom swell,
Deceived by those I prized too well,
He shall his pitying aid bestow,
Who felt on earth severer woe,
At once betrayed, denied, or fled,
By those who shared his daily bread.

4 When sorrowing o'er some stone I bend,
Which covers what was once a friend;
And from his hand, his voice, his smile,
Divides me for a little while,
My Saviour marks the tears I shed;
For Jesus wept o'er Lazarus dead.

5 And O when I have safely passed
Through every conflict but the last,
Still, still unchanging, watch beside
My dying bed—for thou hast died!
Then point to realms of cloudless day,
And wipe the latest tear away.

"Lord, thou knowest all things."
  John xxi. 17.   **850**

11 10, 11 10, 10 10.

1 THOU knowest, Lord, the weariness and
  sorrow   [rest;
Of the sad heart that comes to thee for
Cares of to-day, and burdens for to-mor-
  row,   [fessed;
Blessings implored, and sins to be con-
We come before thee at thy gracious word,
And lay them at thy feet: Thou knowest,
  Lord.

2 Thou knowest all the past; how long and
  blindly   derer strayed;
On the dark mountains the lost wan-
How the good Shepherd followed, and how
  kindly   laid:
He bore it home, upon his shoulders

And healed the bleeding wounds, and
    soothed the pain, [strength again.
And brought back life, and hope, and
2 Thou knowest all the present, each temp-
    tation, . [fear ;
    Each toilsome duty, each foreboding
All to each one assigned of tribulation,
    Or to beloved ones than self more dear ;
All pensive memories, as we journey on,
Longings for vanished smiles, and voices
    gone. .

4 Thou knowest all the future ; gleams of
    gladness
    By stormy clouds too quickly overcast ;
Hours of sweet fellowship and parting
    sadness,
    And the dark river to be crossed at last.
O ! what could hope and confidence afford
To tread that path, but this, Thou know-
    est, Lord ?

5 Thou knowest, not alone as God, all
    knowing ; [proved ;
As man, our mortal weakness thou hast
On earth with purest sympathies o'erflow-
    ing, [hast loved ;
O Saviour, thou hast wept, and thou
And love and sorrow still to thee may
    come,
And find a hiding-place, a rest, a home.

6 Therefore we come, thy gentle call obey-
    ing, [feet ;
    And lay our sins and sorrows at thy
On everlasting strength our weakness
    staying, complete ;
Clothed in thy robe of righteousness
Then rising and refreshed we leave thy
    throne,
And follow on to know as we are known.

851

12, 4 4, 10, 6 6, 10, 6.

1 I WILL not let thee go, thou Help in
    time of need !
        Heap ill on ill,
        I trust thee still,
    Even when it seems that thou wouldst slay
        Do as thou wilt with me, [indeed !
        I yet will cling to thee,
    Hide thou thy face, yet, Help in time of
        I will not let thee go ! [need ;

2 I will not let thee go. Should I forsake my
        No, thou art mine, [bliss ?
        And I am thine,
    Thee will I hold when all things else I miss !
        Though dark and sad the night,
        Joy cometh with thy light,
    O thou my Sun ; should I forsake my
        I will not let thee go ! [bliss ?

3 I will not let thee go, my God, my Life, my
        Not death can tear [Lord !
        Me from his care,
    Who for my sake his soul in death out-
        Thou diedst for love to me, [poured.
        I say in love to thee,
    Even when my heart shall break, my God,
        my Life, my Lord,
        I will not let thee go !

"Looking unto Jesus." **852**
2 - 6 s & 4 - 7 s. Hebrews xii. 2.

1 AUTHOR of faith, appear !
    Be thou its finisher ;
Upward still for this we gaze,
Till we feel the stamp divine,
Thee behold with open face,
Bright in all thy glory shine.

2 Leave not thy work undone,
    But ever love thine own ;
Let us all thy goodness prove,
    Let us to the end believe ;
Show thine everlasting love,
    Save us, to the utmost save.

3 O that our life might be
    One looking up to thee !
Ever hasting to the day
    When our eyes shall see thee near ;
Come, Redeemer, come away,
    Glorious in thy saints appear.

7 7, 4 4, 7.
7 7, 4 4, 7. *For Times of Trouble.* **853**

1 HEAD of thy church triumphant,
    We joyfully adore thee ;
    Till thou appear,
    Thy members here
Shall sing like those in glory.
We lift our hearts and voices
With blest anticipation,
    And cry aloud,
    And give to God
The praise of our salvation.

2 While in affliction's furnace,
    And passing through the fire,
    Thy love we praise,
    Which knows our days,
And ever brings us nigher.
We clap our hands exulting
In thine almighty favour ;
    The love divine
    Which made us thine
Shall keep us thine for ever.

3 Thou dost conduct thy people
    Through torrents of temptation,
    Nor will we fear,
    While thou art near,
The fire of tribulation.
The world with sin and Satan
In vain our march opposes,
    Through thee we shall
    Break through them all,
And sing the song of Moses.

4 By faith we see the glory
    To which thou shalt restore us,
    The cross despise
    For that high prize
Which thou hast set before us.
And if thou count us worthy,
We each, as dying Stephen,
    Shall see thee stand
    At God's right hand,
To take us up to heaven.

7 7, 4 4, 7. 7 7, 4 4, 7. **854**

1 THE name we still acknowledge
    That burst our bonds in sunder,

And loudly sing
Our conquering King,
In songs of joy and wonder.
In every day's deliverance
Our Jesus we discover;
'Tis he! 'tis he!
That smote the sea,
And led us safely over.

2 In sin and Satan's onsets
He still our souls secures,
Our guardian God
Looks through the cloud,
And baffles our pursuers:
He fights his peoples' battles,
Omnipotently glorious,
He fights alone,
And makes his own
O'er earth and hell victorious.

3 Partakers of his triumph,
In vehement expectation
We now stand still,
To prove his will,
And see his great salvation;
With violent faith and patience
To seize the kingdom given,
The purchased rest
In Jesu's breast,
The inheritance of heaven.

855
7 7, 4 4, 7. 7 7, 4 4, 7.

1 SAFE in the fiery furnace,
Joyful in tribulation,
My soul adores
With all its powers
The God of my salvation.
Kept by the strength of Jesus,
Almighty to deliver,
I find his name
Is still the same,
A tower that stands for ever.

2 I see stretched out to save me
The arm of my Redeemer;
That arm shall quell
The powers of hell,
And silence the blasphemer.
I render thee the glory,
I know thou wilt deliver;
But let me rise
Above the skies,
And praise thy love for ever.

856
8 7, 8 7, 6 6, 6 6 7.

1 A SAFE stronghold our God is still,
A trusty shield and weapon;
He'll help us clear from all the ill
That hath us now o'ertaken.
The ancient prince of hell
Hath risen with purpose fell;
Strong mail of craft and power
He weareth in this hour,
On earth is not his fellow.

2 With force of arms we nothing can,
Full soon were we down-ridden;
But for us fights the proper Man,
Whom God himself hath bidden.
Ask ye, Who is this same?
Christ Jesus is his name,

198

The Lord Sabaoth's Son;
He, and no other one,
Shall conquer in the battle.

3 And were this world all devils o'er,
And watching to devour us,
We lay it not to heart so sore;
Not they can overpower us.
And let the prince of ill
Look grim as e'er he will,
He harms us not a whit:
For why? His doom is writ;
A word shall quickly slay him.

4 God's word, for all their craft and force,
One moment will not linger,
But, spite of hell, shall have its course;
'Tis written by his finger.
And though they take our life,
Goods, honour, children, wife,
Yet is their profit small;
These things shall vanish all.
The city of God remaineth.

L. M.
857

1 GO labour on; spend, and be spent,
Thy joy to do the Father's will;
'Tis the way the Master went,
Should not the servant tread it still?

2 Go labour on; 'tis not for nought,
Thy earthly loss is heavenly gain;
Men heed thee, love thee, praise thee not;
The Master praises; what are men?

3 Go labour on, while it is day,
The world's dark night is hastening on;
Speed, speed thy work, cast sloth away;
It is not thus that souls are won.

4 Men die in darkness at your side
Without a hope to cheer the tomb;
Take up the torch, and wave it wide,
The torch that lights time's thickest
gloom.

5 Toil on, faint not, keep watch, and pray;
Be wise, the erring soul to win;
Go forth into the world's highway,
Compel the wanderer to come in.

6 Toil on, and in thy toil rejoice;
For toil comes rest, for exile home;
Soon shalt thou hear the Bridegroom's
voice,
The midnight peal, Behold I come!

6 - 8 s.
"Not slothful in business; fervent in spirit," &c.
858
Romans xii. 11.

1 THEIR earthly task who fail to do,
Neglect their heavenly business too;
Nor know what faith and duty mean,
Who use religion as a screen,
Asunder put what God hath joined,
A diligent and pious mind.

2 Full well the labour of our hands
With fervency of spirit stands;
For God, who all our days hath given,
From toil excepts but one in seven:
And labouring while we time redeem,
We please the Lord, and work for him.

3 Happy we live, when God doth fill
Our hands with work, our hearts with zeal:

For every toil, if he enjoin,
Becomes a sacrifice divine,
And like the blessed spirits above,
The more we serve, the more we love.

SECTION VII.

CHRISTIAN ORDINANCES AND INSTITUTIONS.

859 10 s & 11 s.

1 YE servants of God, Your Master pro-
    claim,
And publish abroad His wonderful name;
The name all-victorious Of Jesus extol;
His kingdom is glorious, And rules over all.

2 The waves of the sea Have lift up their
    voice,
Sore troubled that we In Jesus rejoice;
The floods they are roaring, But Jesus is
    here;
While we are adoring, He always is near.

3 God ruleth on high, Almighty to save;
And still he is nigh, His presence we have;
The great congregation His triumph shall
    sing,
Ascribing salvation To Jesus our King.

4 "Salvation to God Who sits on the throne,"
Let all cry aloud, And honour the Son;
Our Jesus's praises The angels proclaim,
Fall down on their faces, And worship the
    Lamb.

5 Then let us adore, And give him his right,
All glory and power, All wisdom and might,
All honour and blessing, With angels
    above,   [love.
And thanks never-ceasing, And infinite

860 *"Peter and John went up into the temple at the hour of prayer."—Acts iii. 1.* 6 - 8 s.

1 WHO Jesus our example know,
    And his Apostles' footsteps trace,
We gladly to the temple go,
Frequent the consecrated place
At every solemn hour of prayer,
And meet the God of mercy there.

2 His offering pure we call to mind,
There on the golden altar laid,
Whose Godhead with the manhood joined,
For every soul atonement made;
And have whate'er we ask of God,
Through faith in that all-saving blood.

861 *"Again His disciples were within, and Thomas," &c.* 6 - 8 s.
John xx. 26.

1 IF but one faithless soul be here,
    Jesus assembled with thine own,
Wilt thou not in the midst appear,
Thy resurrection's power make known,
Sprinkle the sinner with thy blood,
And show thyself his Lord and God!
Slower of heart than Thomas, I
With thy sincere disciples meet;
A conscious unbeliever sigh
For faith and pardon at thy feet:

Thy feet, alas, I cannot see,
Or feel the blood that flows for me.

3 But nothing can obstruct thy way,
Thou omnipresent God of love:
Come, Saviour, come, thy wounds display,
My stubborn unbelief remove,
And me among thy people bless,
And fill our hearts with heavenly peace.

4 Occasion from my slowness take
Thy faithful followers to cheer,
For a poor abject sinner's sake,
Jesus, the second time appear,
Increase thy saints' felicity,
And bless them all by blessing me.

7 s & 6 s †. *An open-air service.* **862**

"And we kneeled down on the shore, and prayed."—Acts xxi. 5.

1 TWO or three in Jesu's name,
    According to his word
Humbly met, may boldly claim
The presence of their Lord;
He himself prepares the fane
With azure canopy o'erspread,
Ample dome to entertain
The members and their Head.

2 How august the hallowed place
To faith's discerning eye!
Hallowed by the present grace
Of him who fills the sky!
While the Spirit of love and prayer
Into their simple hearts is given,
Christ with all his church is there,
And turns their earth to heaven.

C. M.   *For a week-day service.* **863**

1 BEHOLD us, Lord, a little space
    From daily tasks set free,
And met within thy holy place
To rest awhile with thee.
Around us rolls the ceaseless tide
Of business, toil, and care,
And scarcely can we turn aside
For one brief hour of prayer.

2 Yet these are not the only walls
Wherein thou may'st be sought:
On homeliest work thy blessing falls
In truth and patience wrought.
Thine is the loom, the forge, the mart,
The wealth of land and sea;
The worlds of science and of art,
Revealed and ruled by thee.

3 Then let us prove our heavenly birth
In all we do and know;
And claim the kingdom of the earth
For thee, and not thy foe.
Work shall be prayer, if all be wrought
As thou wouldst have it done;
And prayer, by thee inspired and taught,
Itself with work be one.

L. M.   **864**

1 JESUS, where'er thy people meet,
    There they behold thy mercy-seat;
Where'er they seek thee thou art found,
And every place is hallowed ground.

2 For thou, within no walls confined,
Inhabitest the humble mind;

199

Such ever bring thee where they come,
And going take thee to their home.

3 Great Shepherd of thy chosen few,
Thy former mercies here renew ;
Here to our waiting hearts proclaim
The sweetness of thy saving name.

4 Here may we prove the power of prayer,
To strengthen faith and sweeten care,
To teach our faint desires to rise,
And bring all heaven before our eyes.

5 Lord, we are few, but thou art near ;
Nor short thine arm, nor deaf thine ear :
O rend the heavens, come quickly down,
And make a thousand hearts thine own !

865 *" The preparations of the heart."*
Proverbs xvi. 1.   C. M.

1 LORD, teach us how to pray aright,
With reverence and with fear ;
Though dust and ashes in thy sight,
We may, we must draw near.

2 We perish if we cease from prayer,
O grant us power to pray !
And when to meet thee we prepare,
Lord, meet us by the way.

3 Give deep humility ; the sense
Of godly sorrow give ;
A strong desiring confidence
To hear thy voice and live ;

4 Faith in the only sacrifice
That can for sin atone ;
To build our hopes, to fix our eyes,
On Christ, on Christ alone ;

5 Patience to watch, and wait, and weep,
Though mercy long delay;
Courage, our fainting souls to keep,
And trust thee though thou slay.

6 Give these, and then thy will be done ;
Thus strengthened with all might,
We through thy Spirit and thy Son,
Shall pray, and pray aright.

866   8 s & 7 s.

1 COME, thou fount of every blessing ;
Tune my heart to sing thy grace,
Streams of mercy, never ceasing,
Call for songs of loudest praise.
Teach me some celestial measure,
Sung by ransomed hosts above ;
O the vast, the boundless treasure
Of my Lord's unchanging love !

2 Here I raise my Ebenezer ;
Hither by thine help I'm come ;
And I hope, by thy good pleasure,
Safely to arrive at home.
Jesus sought me when a stranger,
Wandering from the fold of God.
He, to rescue me from danger,
Interposed his precious blood.

3 O to grace how great a debtor
Daily I'm constrained to be !
Let that grace, Lord, like a fetter,
Bind my wandering heart to thee ;
Prone to wander, Lord, I feel it,
Prone to leave the God I love ;
Take my heart, O take and seal it,
Seal it from thy courts above !
200

L.   *Joy in heaven."*—Luke xv. 7.   **867**

1 WHO can describe the joys that rise
Through all the courts of Paradise,
To see a prodigal return,
To see an heir of glory born ?

2 With joy the Father doth approve
The fruit of his eternal love :
The Son with joy looks down, and sees
The purchase of his agonies !

3 The Spirit takes delight to view
The contrite soul he formed anew ;
And saints and angels join to sing
The growing empire of their King.

L. M.   *The Institution of a Gospel Ministry from Christ.*   **868**
Ephesians iv. 7—12.

1 THE Saviour, when to heaven he rose,
In splendid triumph o'er his foes,
Scattered his gifts on men below,
And wide his royal bounties flow.

2 Hence sprung the Apostles' honoured
Sacred beyond heroic fame :   [name ;
In lowlier forms before our eyes,
Pastors from hence, and teachers rise.

3 From Christ their varied gifts derive,
And fed by Christ their graces live :
While guarded by his mighty hand,
'Midst all the rage of hell they stand. ;

4 So shall the bright succession run
Through the last courses of the sun ;
While unborn churches by their care
Shall rise and flourish large and fair.

5 Jesus, now teach our hearts to know
The spring whence all these blessings flow ;
Pastors and people shout thy praise
Through the long round of endless days.

10 s & 11 s.   **869**

1 DISPOSER Supreme, And Judge of the
earth,   [poor ;
Who choosest for thine The weak and the
To frail earthen vessels And things of no
worth   [dure ;
Entrusting thy riches, Which always en-

2 Those vessels soon fail, Though full of thy
light,
And at thy decree Are broken and gone ;
Then brightly appeareth The arm of thy
might,   [have shone.
As through the clouds riven The lightnings

3 Like clouds are they borne To do thy great
will,
And swift as the winds About the world go;
The fire of thy presence Their spirits doth
fill,   [o'erflow.
They thunder, they lighten, The waters

4 Their sound goeth forth, "Christ Jesus is
Lord : "
Then Satan doth fear, His citadels fall :
As when the dread trumpets Went forth
at thy word,   [ite's wall.
And one long blast shattered The Canaan-

5 Then loud be their trump, And stirring
their sound,
To rouse us, O Lord, From slumber of sin ;

The lights thou hast kindled In darkness around,
O may they illumine Our spirits within!
6 All honour and praise, Dominion and might,
To God Three in One Eternally be;
Who round us hath shed His marvellous light,   [see.
And called us from darkness His glory to

870   *" Let there be light ! "* 6 64, 6 6 6 4.

1 THOU whose Almighty word
    Chaos and darkness heard,
      And took their flight;
Hear us, we humbly pray,
And where the gospel-day
Sheds not its glorious ray,
      Let there be light !

2 Thou, who didst come to bring
On thy redeeming wing
      Healing and sight;
Health to the sick in mind,
Sight to the inly blind,
O now to all mankind
      Let there be light !

3 Spirit of truth and love,
Life-giving, holy Dove,
      Speed forth thy flight;
Move on the waters' face,
Spreading the beams of grace,
And in earth's darkest place
      Let there be light !

4 Blessed and holy Three,
Glorious Trinity,
      Grace, love, and might,
Boundless as ocean's tide,
Rolling in fullest pride,
Through the world far and wide,
      Let there be light !

871   *Show whom thou hast chosen, &c.*
      Acts i. 24, 25.   C. M.

1 TEACHER of hearts, 'tis thine alone
    Thine officers to ordain,
Point out thy instruments, unknown
  To undiscerning men;
The pastors of thy church apprise
Of thine unseen decree,
And stir them up to recognise
  The men designed by thee.

2 The men whom thou hast inly moved
Their charge to undertake,
And toil for precious souls, beloved
  For their Redeemer's sake;
Thy chosen ministers reveal,
  With whom thou always art,
And then their saving gospel seal
On every listening heart.

"Preaching the kingdom of God, and teaching
872 *those things which concern the Lord*
Jesus Christ."—Acts xxviii. 31. S. M.

1 JESUS, thy servants bless,
    Who, sent by thee, proclaim
The peace, and joy, and righteousness
Experienced in thy name:
The kingdom of our God,
Which thy great Spirit imparts,

The power of thy victorious blood,
  Which reigns in faithful hearts.
2 Their souls with faith supply,
  With life and liberty;
And then they preach and testify
The things concerning thee:
And live for this alone,
  Thy grace to minister,
And all thou hast for sinners done
In life and death declare.

" The Lord gave testimony unto the **873**
7 s & 6 s †.   *word."*—Acts xiv. 3.

1 BOLD in our Almighty Lord,
    While thee we testify,
Present to confirm the word
  We on thyself rely;
Thou thy confessors confess,
The truth in sinners' hearts reveal,
Welcome news of saving grace
  By thy own Spirit seal.

2 More than outward wonder show
On those that humbly hear,
Let their souls the witness know,
  The indwelling Comforter;
Let their lives resemble thine,
And preach the kingdom from above,
Holy joy and peace divine,
  And pure unbounded love.

3 Thus thy testimony give
To all who speak for thee,
Thus let thousands turn and live
  In faith's sincerity;
Through our ministerial hands
Ten thousand more with grace supply,
Power to practise thy commands,
  And live for God and die.

C. M.   Matthew xiv. 16—18.   **874**

1 NOT from a stock of ours but thine,
    Jesus, thy flock we feed,
Thy unexhausted grace divine
  Supplies their every need;
But if we trust thy providence,
  Thy power and will to save,
We have the treasure to dispense,
  And shall for ever have.

2 Jesus, if we aright confess
  Our heart-felt poverty,
We own the conscious want of grace
  Itself a gift from thee;
And who our poverty retain,
  More gifts we shall receive,
Multiplied grace and blessings gain,
  And all a God can give.

3 Our scanty stock as soon as known,
  Our insufficiency
For feeding famished souls we own,
  And bring it, Lord, to thee;
Our want received into thy hand
  Shall rich abundance prove,
Answer the multitude's demand,
  And fill them with thy love.

C. M.   Matthew xiv. 19.   **875**

1 JESUS, the needy sinner's friend,
    Command the crowd to sit,
Who hungry still on thee attend,
  And nothing have to eat;

They hear the word thy lips have said,
  Low at thy feet they bow.
Distribute now the heavenly bread,
  And feed their spirits now.

2 O'erwhelmed with blessings from above,
    Father, before we taste
  These freshest tokens of thy love,
    We thank thee for the past;
  Our eyes and hearts to heaven we lift,
    And, taught by Jesus, own
  That every grace and every gift
    Descends from thee alone.

3 The gospel by our Saviour blessed
    Doth efficacious prove,
  The loaves a thousand-fold increased
    Communicate his love;
  We banquet on the heavenly bread,
    When Christ himself imparts,
  By his disciples' hands conveyed
    To all believing hearts.

876 *"Then Philip opened his mouth, and
     began," &c.—Acts viii. 35.   6 - 7 s.*

1 WHEN thou hast disposed a heart
      Saving truth with joy to hear,
  Utterance, Lord, thou dost impart
    To thy chosen messenger;
  Then he finds the scripture key,
  Then he speaks, and preaches thee.

2 Jesus, in the sacred book
    Thou art everywhere concealed;
  There for thee alone we look,
    By thy Spirit's light revealed,
  Thee set forth before our eyes
  Faith in every page descries.

3 Thee we preach to sinful men,
    Urging them their Lord to embrace,
  Pardon in thy blood to gain,
    Hope for all the promised grace;
  None but Christ on earth we know,
  None but Christ to others show.

877 *"None of these things move 2 - 6 s &
     me," &c.—Acts xx. 24.   4 - 7 s.*

1 THE holy unconcern
    That I, even I may learn,
  Show me, Lord, the dazzling prize,
  Thou thyself my teacher be;
    Then I shall my life despise,
    Only wish to live for thee.

2 When I my Saviour love,
    Nor life nor death can move;
  Partner of thy weal or woe,
  For that blissful sight I sigh,
    Crucified to all below,
    Only wish for thee to die.

3 Thy gospel-minister,
    I see my business here,
  Witness of thy saving will,
  Of thy free unbounded grace,
    First mine office to fulfil,
    Then to win and close my race

4 I ask not how or when,
    But be my Saviour then;
  Grant in death my sole desire,
  Bid me lay this body down,
    Joyful in thine arms expire,
    Share thine everlasting crown.
202

878 *87, 87, 47. A Prayer for Missionaries.*

1 SPEED thy servants, Saviour, speed
      them,
  Thou art Lord of winds and waves;
  They were bound, but thou hast freed
      them,
  Now they go to free the slaves;
    Be thou with them:
  'Tis thine arm alone that saves.

2 Friends, and home, and all forsaking,
    Lord, they go at thy command;
  As their stay thy promise taking,
    While they traverse sea and land;
    O be with them!
  Lead them safely by the hand.

3 Speed them through the mighty ocean,
    In the dark and stormy day;
  When the waves in wild commotion
    Fill all others with dismay,
    Be thou with them,
  Drive their terrors far away.

4 When they reach the land of strangers,
    And the prospect dark appears,
  Nothing seen but toils and dangers,
    Nothing felt but doubts and fears,
    Be thou with them:
  Hear their sighs, and count their tears.

5 When they think of home, now dearer
    Than it ever seemed before,
  Bring the promised glory nearer;
    Let them see that peaceful shore,
    Where thy people
  Rest from toil, and weep no more.

6 Where no fruit appears to cheer them,
    And they seem to toil in vain,
  Then in mercy, Lord, draw near them,
    Then their sinking hopes sustain;
    Thus supported,
  Let their zeal revive again.

7 In the midst of opposition,
    Let them trust, O Lord, in thee;
  When success attends their mission,
    Let thy servants humbler be;
    Never leave them,
  Till thy face in heaven they see:

8 There to reap in joy for ever
    Fruit that grows from seed here sown,
  There to be with him who never
    Ceases to preserve his own,
    And with gladness
  Give the praise to him alone.

879 L. M.   *The Excellency of Christ's
     Religion.*

1 LET everlasting glories crown
    Thy head, my Saviour and my Lord;
  Thy hands have brought salvation down,
  And writ the blessing in thy word.

2 In vain our trembling conscience seeks
  Some solid ground to rest upon;
  With long despair our spirit breaks,
  Till we apply to thee alone.

3 How well thy blessed truths agree!
  How wise and holy thy commands!
  Thy promises, how firm they be!
  How firm our hope and comfort stands!

4 Should all the forms that men devise
Assault my faith with treacherous art,
I'd call them vanity and hes,
And bind thy gospel to my heart.

880   *The Scriptures.*   C. M.

1 FATHER of mercies, in thy word
What endless glory shines !
For ever be thy name adored
For these celestial lines.

2 Here may the wretched sons of want
Exhaustless riches find ;
Riches, above what earth can grant,
And lasting as the mind.

3 Here the fair tree of knowledge grows,
And yields a free repast ;
Sublimer sweets than nature knows
Invite the longing taste.

4 Here the Redeemer's welcome voice
Spreads heavenly peace around ;
And life and everlasting joys
Attend the blissful sound.

5 Divine Instructer, gracious Lord,
Be thou for ever near ;
Teach me to love thy sacred word,
And view my Saviour there.

881 *"The words that I speak unto you, they*
are spirit,"&c.—John vi. 63.   L. M.

1 JESUS, descended from the sky,
The power of God in man thou art ;
Thyself, to whom I now apply,
Speak thy own words into my heart :
Thy words are more than empty sound,
Inseparably one with thee ;
Spirit in them, and life is found,
And all the depths of Deity.

2 While, feebly gasping at thy feet,
A sinner in my sins I bow,
O might I now my Saviour meet,
And hear and feel thy sayings now !
Speak, and thy word the dead shall raise,
Shall me with spirit and life inspire ;
Speak on, and fill my soul with grace,
And add me to thy deathless choir.

882 *" Thou hast the words,"* &c.
John vi. 68.   87, 87.

1 O HOW blest the hour, Lord Jesus,
When we can to thee draw near,
Promises so sweet and precious
From thy gracious lips to hear !

2 Be with us this day to bless us,
That we may not hear in vain,
With the saving truths impress us,
Which the words of life contain.

3 See us eager for salvation
Sit, great Master, at thy feet,
And with breathless expectation
Hang upon thine accents sweet.

4 Open thou our minds, and lead us
Safely on our heavenward way ;
With the lamp of truth precede us,
That we may not go astray.

5 Make us gentle, meek, and humble,
And yet bold in doing right ;
Scatter darkness, lest we stumble ;
Men walk safely in the light.

6 Lord, endue thy word from heaven
With such light, and love, and power,
That in us its silent leaven
May work on from hour to hour.

7 Give us grace to bear our witness
To the truths we have embraced,
And let others both their sweetness
And their quickening virtue taste.

883 *" Of whom speaketh the prophet*
4 - 6 s & 2 - 8 s. *this ?"*—Acts viii. 34.

1 JESUS I humbly seek,
And of himself enquire,
Did not the prophet speak
Of thee, the world's Desire?
Thou poor, despised, afflicted Man,
His meaning to my heart explain.

2 Art thou the Lamb of God
Who didst from heaven come,
Led by the multitude,
Before thy shearers dumb.
The patient, speechless Man of woe,
By sinners crucified below?

3 Swept from the face of earth
Didst thou our sorrows bear,
Whose everlasting birth
God only can declare,
Whose countless seed shall soon arise,
And shine as stars beyond the skies?

4 Adopt me by thy grace
Into thy family,
My heart shall then confess
The prophet spake of thee.
Then, to mine inmost soul made known,
I feel he spake of thee alone.

884 *" Whose heart the Lord opened."*
L. M.   Acts xvi. 14.

1 TO me, almighty Saviour, give
Thy servant's sayings to receive,
The true simplicity impart,
The nobleness of Lydia's heart :
Of every heart thou hast the key,
Command that mine may yield to thee,
May hear thy whisper in thy word,
And opening now admit its Lord.

885 *" Blessed is he that readeth, and*
6 - 7 s. *they that hear,'* &c.—Rev. i. 3.

1 COME, divine Interpreter,
Bring me eyes thy book to read,
Ears the mystic words to hear,
Words which did from thee proceed,
Words that endless bliss impart,
Kept in an obedient heart.

2 All who read, or hear, are blessed,
If thy plain commands we do ;
Of thy kingdom here possessed,
Thee we shall in glory view ;
When thou com'st on earth to abide
Reign triumphant at thy side.

886 7 s & 6 s †.   *The same subject.*

LORD, with open heart and ear,
We would thy law receive,
All thy gracious sayings hear,
And savingly believe ;
All thy kind commands obey,
The pattern trace which thou hast given,
Walk in thee, the Truth, the Way,
The Life, and heaven of heaven.

887   *The same subject.*   C. M.

SAVIOUR, I still to thee apply,
  Before I read or hear,
Creator of the seeing eye,
  And of the hearing ear:
The understanding heart bestow,
  The wisdom from above,
So shall I all thy doctrines know,
  And all thy sayings love.

888   *At the Administration of Infant Baptism.*   C. M.

1 HOW large the promise, how divine,
  To Abraham and his seed!
"I am a God to thee and thine,
  Supplying all their need."

2 The words of his unbounded love
  From age to age endure;
The Angel of the Covenant proves
  And seals the blessings sure.

3 Jesus the ancient faith confirms,
  To our great father given;
He takes our children to his arms,
  And calls them heirs of heaven.

4 O God, how faithful are thy ways!
  Thy love endures the same;
Nor from the promise of thy grace
  Blots out our children's name.

889   C. M.

1 SEE Israel's gentle Shepherd stand
  With all-engaging charms:
Hark how he calls the tender lambs,
  And folds them in his arms!

2 "Permit them to approach," he cries,
  "Nor scorn their humble name:
For 'twas to bless such souls as these,
  The Lord of angels came."

3 We bring them, Lord, in thankful hands,
  And yield them up to thee:
Joyful that we ourselves are thine,
  Thine let our offspring be.

890   6 - 7 s.

1 LORD of all, with pure intent,
  From their tenderest infancy
In thy temple we present
  Whom we first received from thee;
Through thy well-beloved Son,
Ours acknowledge for thine own.

2 Sealed with the baptismal seal,
  Purchased by the atoning blood,
Jesus, in our children dwell,
  Make their heart the house of God:
Fill thy consecrated shrine,
Father, Son, and Spirit divine.

891   L. M.

1 O CRUCIFIED, triumphant Lord!
  Thy sceptre and thy cross we own;
And, taught by thine apostle's word,
  Repose our faith on thee alone.

2 The sign of faith ordained by thee
  We thy confessors scorn to shun;
All men our fellowship shall see,
  Our Lord, our faith, our symbol, one.

294

3 Not only for ourselves we claim
  The blessings of thy brotherhood;
The promise to our children came,
  Theirs is the water and the blood.

4 Who hath these little ones despised?
  Or those that brought them dare con-
Or who, in Jcsu's name baptized, [demn?
  Would blush to put that name on them?

5 Let sprinkled water seal them now
  The heirs of all-redeeming grace;
The truth thus symboled on the brow
  Thy Spirit on the heart shall trace!

6 Lord, spare them till their lives and tongues
  The heart-taught truth have well con-
That who to us, to thee belongs, [fessed,
  Early believing, ever blessed.

S. M.   *For Parents on the Baptism of a child.*   **892**

1 FATHER, our child we place
  Where we thy children kneel;
For thou hast made the sign of grace
  To *him*, to us, the seal.

2 Thine own a moment claim,
  Then lend *him* to our love,
Marked as thine own,—and bid the name
  Be registered above.

3 Rites cannot change the heart,
  Undo the evil done,
Or with the uttered name impart
  The nature of thy Son.

4 To meet our desperate want,
  There gushed a crimson flood:
O from his heart's o'erflowing font
  Baptize this soul with blood!

5 Be grace from Christ our Lord,
  And love from God supreme,
By the communing Spirit poured
  In a perpetual stream!

6 So cleanse our offering:
  Then will we, at thy call,
This pledge accepted, daily bring
  Ourselves, our house, our all.

C. M.   *" There were brought unto him little children."*   **893**
        Matthew xix. 13.

1 JESUS, in earth and heaven the same,
  Accept a parent's vow,
To thee, baptized into thy name,
  I bring my children now;
Thy love permits, invites, commands,
  My offspring to be blessed;
Lay on them, Lord, thy gracious hands,
  And hide them in thy breast.

2 To each the hallowing Spirit give
  Even from their infancy;
Into thy holy church receive
  Whom I devote to thee:
Committed to thy faithful care,
  Protected by thy blood,
Preserve by thine unceasing prayer,
  And bring them all to God.

C. M.   Genesis xlviii. 16.   **894**

1 THE great redeeming Angel, thee,
  O Jesus, I confess;
Who hast through life delivered me,
  Thou wilt my offspring bless;

Thou that hast borne my sins away,
My children's sins remove,
And bring them through their evil day,
To sing thy praise above.

2 My name be on the children? no!
But mark them, Lord, with thine,
Let all the heavenly offspring know
By characters divine;
Partakers of thy nature make,
Partakers of thy Son,
And then the heirs of glory take
To thine eternal throne.

895

7 8, 7 8, 8 8.

1 JESUS, Lord, thy servants see,
Offering here obedience willing;
Lo! this infant comes to thee,
Thus thy blest command fulfilling;
Tis for such, thyself declarest,
That the kingdom thou preparest.

2 Take the pledge we offer now,
To the font baptismal hastening;
Make *him*, Lord, thy child below,
Let *him* feel thy tender chastening,
That *he* here may love and fear thee,
And in heaven dwell ever near thee.

3 Prince of peace, thy peace bestow,
Shepherd, to thy sheep-fold take *him*,
Way of life, *his* pathway show,
Head, thy living member make *him*,
Vine, abundant fruit providing,
Keep this branch in thee abiding.

4 Lord of Grace! to thee we cry,
Filled our hearts to overflowing;
Heavenward take the burdened sigh,
Blessings on the babe bestowing;
Write the name we now have given,
Write it in the book of heaven.

896

1 Samuel i. 28.   L. M.

1 GOD of that glorious gift of grace
By which thy people seek thy face,
When in thy presence we appear,
Vouchsafe us faith to venture near.

2 Confiding in thy truth alone,
Here, on the steps of Jesu's throne,
We lay the treasure thou hast given
To be received and reared for heaven.

3 Lent to us for a season, we
Lend *him* for ever, Lord, to thee;
Assured that if to thee *he* live,
We gain in what we seem to give.

4 Large and abundant blessings shed
Warm as these prayers upon *his* head;
And on *his* soul the dews of grace,
Fresh as these drops upon *his* face.

5 Make *him* and keep *him* thine own child,
Meek follower of the Undefiled;
Possessor here of grace and love,
Inheritor of heaven above.

897

For the Lord's Supper.   S. M.

1 COME, all who truly bear
The name of Christ your Lord,
His last mysterious supper share,
And keep his kindest word.

Hereby your faith approve
In Jesus crucified:
"In memory of my dying love,
Do this," he said,—and died.

2 The badge and token this,
The sure confirming seal,
That he is ours, and we are his,
The servants of his will:
His dear peculiar ones,
The purchase of his blood,
His blood which once for all atones,
And brings us new to God.

3 Then let us still profess
Our Master's honoured name;
Stand forth his faithful witnesses,
True followers of the Lamb.
In proof that such we are,
His saying we receive,
And thus to all mankind declare
We do in Christ believe.

4 Part of his church below,
We thus our right maintain:
Our living membership we show,
And in the fold remain,
The sheep of Israel's fold,
In England's pastures fed;
And fellowship with all we hold,
Who hold it with our Head.

S. M.   ## 898

1 LET all who truly bear
The bleeding Saviour's name
Their faithful hearts with us prepare,
And eat the Paschal Lamb.

2 This eucharistic feast
Our every want supplies;
And still we by his death are blessed,
And share his sacrifice.

3 Who thus our faith employ,
His sufferings to record,
Even now we mournfully enjoy
Communion with our Lord.

4 We too with him are dead,
And shall with him arise:
The cross on which he bows his head
Shall lift us to the skies.

8 s & 7 s.   ## 899

1 COME, thou everlasting Spirit,
Bring to every thankful mind
All the Saviour's dying merit,
All his sufferings for mankind!
True Recorder of his passion,
Now the living faith impart;
Now reveal his great salvation;
Preach his gospel to our heart.

2 Come, thou Witness of his dying;
Come, Remembrancer Divine!
Let us feel thy power, applying
Christ to every soul,—and mine!
Let us groan thine inward groaning;
Look on him we pierced, and grieve;
All receive the grace atoning,
All the sprinkled blood receive.

7 s & 6 s †.   ## 900

1 LAMB of God, whose bleeding love
We now recall to mind,

Send the answer from above,
And let us mercy find;
Think on us, who think on thee;
And every struggling soul release;
O remember Calvary,
And bid us go in peace!

2 By thine agonising pain
And bloody sweat, we pray,
By thy dying love to man,
Take all our sins away:
Burst our bonds, and set us free;
From all iniquity release;
O remember Calvary,
And bid us go in peace!

3 Let thy blood, by faith applied,
The sinner's pardon seal;
Speak us freely justified,
And all our sickness heal;
By thy passion on the tree,
Let all our griefs and troubles cease;
O remember Calvary,
And bid us go in peace!

4 Never will we hence depart,
Till thou our wants relieve,
Write forgiveness on our heart,
And all thine image give!
Still our souls shall cry to thee,
Till perfected in holiness;
O remember Calvary,
And bid us go in peace!

901

C. M.

1 JESU, at whose supreme command
We now approach to God,
Before us in thy vesture stand,
Thy vesture dipped in blood!
Obedient to thy gracious word,
We break the hallowed bread,
Commemorate thee, our dying Lord,
And trust on thee to feed.

2 Now, Saviour, now thyself reveal,
And make thy nature known;
Affix thy blessed Spirit's seal,
And stamp us for thine own:
The tokens of thy dying love
O let us all receive;
And feel the quickening Spirit move,
And sensibly believe!

3 The cup of blessing, blessed by thee,
Let it thy blood impart;
The bread thy mystic body be,
And cheer each languid heart.
The grace which sure salvation brings
Let us herewith receive;
Satiate the hungry with good things,
The hidden manna give.

4 The living bread, sent down from heaven,
In us vouchsafe to be:
Thy flesh for all the world is given,
And all may live by thee.
Now, Lord, on us thy flesh bestow,
And let us drink thy blood,
Till all our souls are filled below
With all the life of God.
206

902

6 - 8 s.

1 VICTIM Divine, thy grace we claim,
While thus thy precious death we
Once offered up, a spotless Lamb, [show:
In thy great temple here below,
Thou didst for all mankind atone,
And standest now before the throne.

2 Thou standest in the holy place,
As now for guilty sinners slain;
The blood of sprinkling speaks, and prays,
All prevalent for helpless man;
Thy blood is still our ransom found,
And speaks salvation all around.

3 The smoke of thy atonement here
Darkened the sun, and rent the veil,
Made the new way to heaven appear,
And showed the great Invisible:
Well pleased in thee, our God looked down,
And called his rebels to a crown.

4 He still respects thy sacrifice;
Its savour sweet doth always please;
The offering smokes through earth and
skies,
Diffusing life, and joy, and peace:
To these, thy lower courts, it comes,
And fills them with divine perfumes.

5 We need not now go up to heaven,
To bring the long-sought Saviour down:
Thou art to all already given,
Thou dost even now thy banquet crown:
To every faithful soul appear,
And show thy real presence here!

903

C. M.

1 "THE promise of my Father's love
Shall stand for ever good,"
He said; and gave his soul to death,
And sealed the grace with blood.

2 To this sure covenant of thy word
I set my worthless name;
I seal the engagement to my Lord,
And make my humble claim.

3 Thy light, and strength, and pardoning
And glory shall be mine: [grace
My life and soul, my heart and flesh,
And all my powers are thine.

4 I call that legacy my own
Which Jesus did bequeath;
'Twas purchased with a dying groan,
And ratified in death.

5 Sweet is the memory of his name,
Who blest us in his will,
And to his testament of love
Made his own life the seal.

904

6 - 7 s.

1 BREAD of heaven! on thee I feed,
For thy flesh is meat indeed.
Ever may my soul be fed
With this true and living bread:
Day by day with strength supplied
Through the life of him who died.

2 Vine of heaven! thy blood supplies
This blest cup of sacrifice;

'Tis thy wounds my healing give;
To thy cross I look and live.
Thou my life! O let me be
Rooted, grafted, built on thee!

905
7 s & 6 s †.

1 JESUS, Master of the feast,
The feast itself thou art,
Now receive thy meanest guest,
And comfort every heart:
Give us living bread to eat,
Manna that from heaven comes down;
Fill us with immortal meat,
And make thy nature known.

2 In this barren wilderness
Thou hast a table spread,
Furnished out with richest grace,
Whate'er our souls can need;
Still sustain us by thy love,
Still thy servants' strength repair,
Till we reach the courts above,
And feast for ever there.

906
9 8, 9 8.

1 BREAD of the world, in mercy broken!
Wine of the soul, in mercy shed!
By whom the words of life were spoken,
And in whose death our sins are dead!

2 Look on the heart by sorrow broken,
Look on the tears by sinners shed,
And be thy feast to us the token
That by thy grace our souls are fed!

907
C. M.

1 IN memory of the Saviour's love,
We keep the sacred feast,
Where every humble, contrite heart
Is made a welcome guest.

2 By faith we take the bread of life
With which our souls are fed,
The cup in token of his blood
That was for sinners shed.

3 Under his banner thus we sing
The wonders of his love,
And thus anticipate by faith
The heavenly feast above.

908
C. M.

1 BE known to us in breaking bread,
But do not then depart;
Saviour, abide with us, and spread
Thy table in our heart.

2 There sup with us in love divine;
Thy body and thy blood,
That living bread, that heavenly wine,
Be our immortal food.

909
Renewing the Covenant.   6 - 8 s.

1 O GOD! how often hath thine ear
To me in willing mercy bowed!
While worshipping thine altar near,
Lowly I wept, and strongly vowed:
But ah! the feebleness of man!
Have I not vowed and wept in vain?

2 Return, O Lord of hosts, return!
Behold thy servant in distress;

My faithlessness again I mourn;
Again forgive my faithlessness;
And to thine arms my spirit take,
And bless me for the Saviour's sake.

3 In pity of the soul thou lov'st,
Now bid the sin thou bat'st expire;
Let me desire what thou approv'st,
Thou dost approve what I desire;
And thou wilt deign to call me thine,
And I will dare to call thee mine.

4 This day the covenant I sign,
The bond of sure and promised peace;
Nor can I doubt its power divine,
Since sealed with Jesu's blood it is:
That blood I trust, that blood alone,
And make the covenant peace mine own.

5 But, that my faith no more may know
Or change, or interval, or end,
Help me in all thy paths to go,
And now, as e'er, my voice attend,
And gladden me with answers mild,
And commune, Father, with thy child!

910
7 s.

1 GOD of truth and power and grace,
Drawn by thee to seek thy face,
Lo! I in thy courts appear,
Humbly come to meet thee here;

2 Trembling at thine altar stand,
Lift to heaven my heart and hand,
Of thy promised strength secure,
All my sins I now abjure.

3 All my promises renew,
All my wickedness eschew,
Chiefly that I called my own,
Now I hate, renounce, disown.

4 Never more will I commit,
Follow, or be led by it;
Only grant the grace I claim,
Arm my soul with Jesu's name.

5 Sure I am it is thy will,
I should never yield to ill,
Never lose thy gracious power,
Never sin or grieve thee more.

6 What doth then my hopes prevent?
Lord, thou stay'st for my consent;
My consent through grace I give,
Promise in thy fear to live.

7 Father, Son, and Holy Ghost,
Present with thy angel host,
While I at thy altar bow,
Witness to the solemn vow.

8 Now admit my bold appeal,
Now affix thy Spirit's seal,
Now the power from high be given,
Register the oath in heaven.

911
8 s.   *After the Renewal of the Covenant.*

1 O HOW shall a sinner perform
The vows he hath vowed to the Lord?
A sinful and impotent worm,
How can I be true to my word?
I tremble at what I have done:
O send me thy help from above;
The power of thy Spirit make known,
The virtue of Jesus's love!

2 My solemn engagements are vain,
  My promises empty as air;
My vows, I shall break them again,
  And plunge in eternal despair;
Unless my omnipotent God
  The sense of his goodness impart,
And shed by his Spirit abroad
  The love of himself in my heart.

3 O Lover of sinners, extend
  To me thy compassionate grace;
Appear my affliction to end,
  Afford me a glimpse of thy face!
That light shall enkindle in me
  A flame of reciprocal love;
And then I shall cleave unto thee,
  And then I shall never remove.

4 O come to a mourner in pain,
  Thy peace in my conscience reveal!
And then I shall love thee again,
  And sing of the goodness I feel:
Constrained by the grace of my Lord,
  My soul shall in all things obey,
And wait to be fully restored,
  And long to be summoned away.

912 *Renewal of Self-Dedication.* L. M.

1 O HAPPY day that fixed my choice
  On thee, my Saviour and my God!
Well may this glowing heart rejoice,
  And tell its raptures all abroad.

2 O happy bond that seals my vows
  To him who merits all my love!
Let cheerful anthems fill his house,
  While to that sacred shrine I move.

3 'Tis done, the great transaction's done,
  I am my Lord's, and he is mine;
He drew me, and I followed on,
  Charmed to confess the voice divine.

4 Now rest, my long-divided heart;
  Fixed on this blissful centre, rest:
Nor ever from my Lord depart,
  With him of every good possest.

5 High heaven, that heard the solemn vow,
  That vow renewed shall daily hear,
Till in life's latest hour I bow,
  And bless in death a bond so dear.

SECTION VIII.

DEATH AND THE FUTURE LIFE.

" *It is appointed unto men
  once to die.*"
Hebrews ix. 27.

913 L. M.

1 TREMENDOUS God, with humble fear,
  Prostrate before thy awful throne,
The irrevocable word we hear,
  The sovereign righteousness we own.

2 'Tis fit we should to dust return,
  Since such the will of the most High;
In sin conceived, to trouble born,
  Born only to lament and die.

3 Submissive to thy just decree,
  We all shall soon from earth remove;
But when thou sendest, Lord, for me,
  O let the messenger be love!
208

4 Whispering thy love into my heart,
  Warn me of my approaching end;
And then I joyfully depart,
  And then I to thy arms ascend.

7 s. *Prayer for a Dying Child.* **914**

1 FATHER, Lord of earth and heaven,
  Spare, or take what thou hast given;
Sole disposer of thine own,
Let thy sovereign will be done.

2 When thou didst our Isaac give,
  Him we trembled to receive,
Him we called not ours, but thine,
  Him we promised to resign.

3 Lo! we to our promise stand,
  Lo! we answer thy demand,
Will not murmur or complain,
  If thou claim thine own again.

4 Life or death depend on thee,
  Just and good is thy decree,
Safe in thy decree we rest,
  Sure whatever is, is best.

5 Meekly we our vow repeat,
  Nature shall to grace submit,
Let him on the altar lie,
  Let the victim live, or die.

6 Yet thou know'st what pangs of love
  In a father's bosom move,
What the agony to part,
  Struggling in a mother's heart.

7 Sorely tempted and distressed,
  Can we ask the fond request?
Dare we pray for a reprieve?
  Need we ask that he may live?

8 God we absolutely trust,
  Wise and merciful and just,
All thy works to thee are known,
  All thy blessed will be done.

9 If his life a snare would prove,
  Rob us of thy heavenly love,
Steal our hearts from God away;
  Mercy will not let him stay.

10 If his life would matter raise
  Of thine everlasting praise,
More his Saviour glorify,
  Mercy will not let him die.

6 - 7 s. *The Dying Father's Prayer.*
  Jeremiah xlix. 11. **915**

1 O THOU faithful God of love,
  Gladly I thy promise plead,
Waiting for my last remove,
  Hastening to the happy dead,
Lo, I cast on thee my care,
  Breathe my latest breath in prayer.

2 Trusting in thy word alone,
  I to thee my children leave;
Call my little ones thine own,
  Give them, all thy blessings give,
Keep them while on earth they breathe,
  Save their souls from endless death.

3 Whom I to thy grace commend
  Into thy protection take,
Be her sure immortal friend,
  Save her for my Saviour's sake;
Free from sin, from sorrow free,
  Let my widow trust in thee.

4 Father of the fatherless,
    Husband of the widow prove ;
Me and mine persist to bless,
    Tell me we shall meet above,
Seal the promise on my heart,
    Bid me then in peace depart.

916   For an Aged Christian.
        Isaiah xlvi. 4.   6 - 8 s.

1 JESU, thou hast to hoary hairs
    My manners and my burdens borne,
Carried me through ten thousand snares,
    And, when I would to sin return,
With a high hand and outstretched arm
Redeemed me from the mortal harm.

2 O let me still the promise plead,
    Thy kind continued aid engage !
Thy aid I every moment need,
    In childhood, youth, and trembling age ;
A sinner I, on mercy cast,
By mercy saved from first to last.

3 Still, O thou patient God of love,
    My soul's infirmity sustain,
Bear me on eagles' wings above
    The world of ill, the vale of pain,
The flesh that weighs my spirit down,
The fiend who strives to take my crown.

4 While, hanging on thy faithful word,
    My utter helplessness I feel,
Carry me in thy bosom, Lord,
    Beyond the reach of earth or hell,
Till on the margin of the grave
I prove thine utmost power to save.

5 Thou know'st the trials yet behind,
    The strength of sin, the tempter's power;
Support my feebleness of mind
    In every dark unguarded hour ;
Thy servant mightily defend,
And love and save me to the end.

6 Walk with me through the lions' den,
    Walk with me through the floods and
In form of God distinctly seen ;   [fires,
    And O I to crown my last desires,
In death my guide and Saviour be,
My God through all eternity !

917
                   6 - 8 s.

1 JUSTLY thou might'st, in helpless age,
    Thy most unworthy servant leave,
Leave me to faint in life's last stage,
    And never more my sins forgive,
Leave me to breathe my slighted prayer,
And perish in extreme despair.

2 But lo ! I from thy justice, Lord,
    To thy redeeming grace appeal !
Justice awakes its flaming sword
    Against the Man thou lov'st so well ;
He paid my ransom with his blood,
And God hath quenched the wrath of God.

3 Whate'er I have of evil done,
    Or said, or thought, on him was laid ;
My trust is in thy bleeding Son,
    My fainting soul on Christ is stayed :
Father, regard his sacrifice,
And bid me live, for Jesus dies.

4 With humble faith his death I plead,
    And, covered with the atoning blood,

Calmly I sink among the dead,
    The dead who ever live to God,
Secure in that great day to rise,
And share thy kingdom in the skies.

6 - 8 s.   A Last Wish.   ## 918

1 IN age and feebleness extreme,
    Who shall a helpless worm redeem ?
Jesus ! my only hope thou art,
    Strength of my failing flesh and heart ;
O could I catch one smile from thee,
And drop into eternity !

L. M.   Prayer for grace to die   ## 919
                 well.

1 WARNED of my dissolution near,
    As on the margin of the grave,
Jesus, with humble faith and fear,
    I now bespeak thy power to save ;
Thou who hast tasted death for me,
    Indulge me in my fond request,
And let a worm prescribe to thee
    The manner of my final rest.

2 My feeble heart's extreme desire '
    If now thine-eye with pity sees,
Whene'er thou dost my soul require,
    O let me then be found in peace !
In active faith and humble prayer,
    Resigned, yet longing to depart,
To rise, redeemed from earthly care,
    And see thee, Saviour, as thou art.

3 Walk with me through the dreadful shade,
    And, certified that thou art mine,
My spirit, calm and undismayed,
    I shall into thy hands resign ;
No anxious doubt, no guilty gloom,
    Shall damp whom Jesus presence
        cheers ;
My light, my life, my God, is come,
    And glory in his face appears !

C. M.   ## 920

1 LORD, it belongs not to my care
    Whether I die or live ;
To love and serve thee is my share,
    And this thy grace must give.

2 If life be long, I will be glad
    That I may long obey ;
If short, yet why should I be sad
    To soar to endless day ?

3 Christ leads me through no darker rooms
    Than he went through before ;
He that into God's kingdom comes
    Must enter by this door.

4 Come, Lord, when grace has made me
    Thy blessed face to see ;   [meet
For if thy work on earth be sweet,
    What will thy glory be ?

5 Then shall I end my sad complaints,
    And weary, sinful days,
And join with the triumphant saints
    That sing Jehovah's praise.

6 My knowledge of that life is small,
    The eye of faith is dim ;
But 'tis enough that Christ knows all,
    And I shall be with him.

921 *The dying Christian* 8-7s.
encouraged.

1 DEATHLESS principle, arise!
Soar, thou native of the skies;
Pearl of price by Jesus bought,
To his glorious likeness wrought,
Go to shine before his throne;
Deck his mediatorial crown;
Go, his triumph to adorn;
Made for God, to God return!

2 Lo, he beckons from on high!
Fearless to his presence fly;
Thine the merit of his blood.
Thine the righteousness of God.
Angels, joyful to attend,
Hovering round thy pillows bend,
Wait to catch the signal given,
And escort thee quick to heaven.

3 Is thy earthly house distressed,
Willing to retain her guest?
'Tis not thou, but she must die;
Fly, celestial inmate, fly!
Burst thy shackles, drop thy clay,
Sweetly breathe thyself away,
Singing to thy crown remove,
Mounting high on wings of love.

4 Shudder not to pass the stream;
Venture all thy care on him,
Him whose dying love and power
Stilled its tossing, hushed its roar;
Safe is the expanded wave,
Gentle as the summer's eve,
No one object of his care
Ever suffered shipwreck there.

5 Saints in glory perfect made
Wait thy passage through the shade;
See, they throng the blissful shore,
Ardent for thy coming o'er.
Mount, their transports to improve,
Join the longing choir above,
Swiftly to their wish be given,
Kindle higher joy in heaven!

922
8s & 7s.

1 HAPPY soul, thy days are ended,
All thy mourning days below:
Go, by angel guards attended,
To the sight of Jesus, go!

2 Waiting to receive thy spirit,
Lo! the Saviour stands above;
Shows the purchase of his merit,
Reaches out the crown of love.

3 Struggle through thy latest passion
To thy dear Redeemer's breast,
To his uttermost salvation,
To his everlasting rest.

4 For the joy he sets before thee,
Bear a momentary pain;
Die, to live the life of glory,
Suffer, with thy Lord to reign.

923 *The dying Christian.* 87, 87, 887.

1 MINE hour appointed is at hand,
Lord Jesu Christ, attend me;
Beside my bed, my Saviour, stand,
To comfort, help, defend me.
Into thy hands I will commend
My trembling soul at my last end,
How safe in thy sweet keeping!
210

2 Countless as sands upon the shore,
My sins are thronging round me;
But though they grieve and wound me
They never shall confound me [sore,
My sins are numberless, I know,
But o'er them all thy blood doth flow;
Thy wounds and death uphold me.

3 Lord, thou hast joined my soul to thine
In bonds no power can sever;
Grafted in thee, the living Vine,
I shall be thine for ever.
Lord, when I die, I die to thee,
Thy precious death hath won for me
A life that never endeth.

4 Since thou hast risen from the grave,
The grave cannot detain me:
Christ died; Christ "rose again," to save
These words shall still sustain me.
For where thou art, there I shall be,
That I may ever live with thee;
This is my joy in dying.

" Now lettest thou thy servant depart **924**
L. M. *in peace."—Luke ii. 29.*

1 THE hour of my departure's come,
I hear the voice that calls me home;
At last, O Lord, let trouble cease,
Now let thy servant die in peace!

2 Not in mine innocence I trust;
I bow before thee in the dust,
And through my Saviour's blood alone
I look for mercy at thy throne.

3 I leave the world without a tear,
Save for the friends I held so dear;
To heal their sorrows, Lord, descend,
And to the friendless prove a friend!

4 I come, I come at thy command,
I yield my spirit to thy hand!
Stretch forth thy everlasting arms,
And shield me in the last alarms.

5 The hour of my departure's come,
I hear the voice that calls me home:
Now, O my God, let trouble cease,
Now let thy servant die in peace!

" I am in a strait betwixt two." **925**
7 s & 6 s. *Philippians i. 23.*

1 HAPPY who in Jesus live;
But happier still are they
Who to God their spirits give,
And 'scape from earth away:
Lord, thou read'st the panting heart;
Lord, thou hear'st the praying sigh;
O 'tis better to depart,
'Tis better far to die!

2 Yet, if so thy will ordain,
For our companions' good,
Let us in the flesh remain,
And meekly bear the load:
When we have our grief filled up,
When we all our work have done,
Late partakers of our hope,
And sharers of thy throne.

3 To thy wise and gracious will
We quietly submit,
Waiting for redemption still,
But waiting at thy feet:

When thou wilt the blessing give,
  Call us up thy face to see ;
Only let thy servants live,
  And let us die, to thee.

" They . . . rest from their labours, and
926 *their works do follow them."* L. M.
  Revelation xiv. 13.

1 THE saints who die of Christ possest
    Enter into immediate rest;
For them no further test remains,
Of purging fires, and torturing pains.

2 Who trusting in the Lord depart,
Cleansed from all sin, and pure in heart,
The bliss unmixed, the glorious prize,
They find with Christ in paradise.

3 Close followed by their works they go,
Their Master's purchased joy to know ;
Their works enhance the bliss prepared,
And each hath its distinct reward.

4 Yet, glorified by grace alone,
They cast their crowns before the throne ;
And fill the echoing courts above
With praises of redeeming love.

927 *' I know that my Redeemer* 6 - 8 s.
  liveth." —Job xix. 25.

1 I CALL the world's Redeemer mine ;
    He lives who died for me, I know ;
Who bought my soul with blood divine,
Jesus, shall re-appear below,
Stand in that dreadful day unknown,
And fix on earth his heavenly throne.

2 Then the last judgment-day shall come ;
    And though the worms this skin devour,
The Judge shall call me from the tomb,
    Shall bid the greedy grave restore,
And raise this individual me,
God in the flesh, my God, to see.

3 In this identic body I,
    With eyes of flesh refined, restored,
Shall see that self-same Saviour nigh,
    See for myself my smiling Lord,
See with ineffable delight ;
Nor faint to bear the glorious sight.

4 Then let the worms demand their prey,
    The greedy grave my reins consume ;
With joy I drop my mouldering clay,
    And rest till my Redeemer come ;
On Christ, my Life, in death rely,
Secure that I can never die.

928 *" Whom I shall see for myself."* L. M.
  Job xix. 27.

1 I KNOW that my Redeemer lives,
    He lives, and on the earth shall stand;
And though to worms my flesh he gives,
    My dust lies numbered in his hand.

2 In this re-animated clay
    I surely shall behold him near ;
Shall see him in the latter day
    In all his majesty appear.

3 I feel what then shall raise me up,
    The eternal Spirit lives in me ;
This is my confidence of hope,
    That God I face to face shall see.

4 Mine own and not another's eyes
    The King shall in his beauty view ;
I shall from him receive the prize,
    The starry crown to victors due,

C. M.   **929**

1 WHY do we mourn departing friends,
    Or shake at death's alarms ?
'Tis but the voice that Jesus sends,
    To call them to his arms.

2 The graves of all his saints he blessed,
    And softened every bed :
Where should the dying members rest,
    But with their dying Head ?

3 Thence he arose, ascending high,
    And showed our feet the way :
Up to the Lord our flesh shall fly,
    At the great rising-day.

4 Then let the last loud trumpet sound,
    And bid our kindred rise ;
Awake, ye nations under ground ;
    Ye saints, ascend the skies.

S. M.   *Triumph over Death.*   **930**

1 AND must this body die ?
    This well-wrought frame decay ?
And must these active limbs of mine
Lie mouldering in the clay ?

2 Corruption, earth, and worms
    Shall but refine this flesh ;
Till my triumphant spirit comes
To put it on afresh.

3 God, my Redeemer, lives,
    And ever from the skies
Looks down, and watches all my dust,
Till he shall bid it rise.

4 Arrayed in glorious grace
    Shall these vile bodies shine ;
And every shape and every face
Be heavenly and divine.

5 These lively hopes we owe,
    Lord, to thy dying love :
O may we bless thy grace below,
And sing thy power above !

4 - 6 s & 2 - 8 s.   Job xix. 26.   **931**

1 MY life's a shade, my days
    Apace to death decline :
My Lord is life, he'll raise
    My dust again, even mine :
Sweet truth to me ! I shall arise
And with these eyes My Saviour see.

2 My peaceful grave shall keep
    My bones till that sweet day
I wake from my long sleep
    And leave my bed of clay ;
Sweet truth to me ! I shall arise
And with these eyes My Saviour see.

3 My Lord his angels shall
    Their golden trumpets sound,
At whose most welcome call
    My grave shall be unbound.
Sweet truth to me ! I shall arise
And with these eyes My Saviour see.

4 I said sometimes with tears,
    Ah me! I'm loth to die,
Lord, silence thou those fears ;
    My life's with thee on high.
Sweet truth to me ! I shall arise
And with these eyes My Saviour see.

5 What means my trembling heart
  To be thus shy of death?
With life I shall not part,
  Though I resign my breath.
Sweet truth to me! I shall arise
And with these eyes My Saviour see.

6 Then welcome, harmless grave;
  By thee to heaven I'll go,
My Lord his death shall save
  Me from the flames below.
Sweet truth to me! I shall arise
And with these eyes My Saviour see.

932   *The last Judgment.*   8 7, 8 7, 8 8 7.

1 GREAT God! what do I see and hear!
    The end of things created!
The Judge of mankind doth appear,
  On clouds of glory seated.
The trumpet sounds! the graves restore
The dead which they contained before!
  Prepare, my soul, to meet him.

2 The dead in Christ shall first arise,
  At the last trumpet's sounding.
Caught up to meet him in the skies,
  With joy their Lord surrounding:
No gloomy fears their souls dismay;
His presence sheds eternal day
  On those prepared to meet him.

3 The ungodly, filled with guilty fears,
  Behold his wrath prevailing;
In woe they rise, but all their tears
  And sighs are unavailing:
The day of grace is past and gone:
Trembling they stand before his throne,
  All unprepared to meet him.

4 Great God! what do I see and hear!
  The end of things created!
The Judge of mankind doth appear,
  On clouds of glory seated;
Beneath his cross I view the day
When heaven and earth shall pass away,
  And thus prepare to meet him.

933   8 8 8.

1 DAY of wrath! O day of mourning!
    See fulfilled the prophet's warning!
Heaven and earth to ashes burning!

2 O what fear man's bosom rendeth!
When from heaven the Judge descendeth,
On whose sentence all dependeth!

3 Wondrous sound the trumpet flingeth,
Through earth's sepulchres it ringeth,
All before the throne it bringeth.

4 Death is struck, and nature quaking,
All creation is awaking,
To its Judge an answer making.

5 Lo, the Book, exactly worded,
Wherein all hath been recorded!
Thence shall judgment be awarded.

6 When the Judge his seat attaineth,
And each hidden deed arraigneth,
Nothing unavenged remaineth.

7 What shall I, frail man, be pleading,
Who for me be interceding,
When the just are mercy needing?

212

8 King of majesty tremendous,
Who dost free salvation send us,
Fount of pity, then befriend us!

9 Think, good Jesu, my salvation
Caused thy wondrous incarnation;
Leave me not to reprobation.

10 Faint and weary thou hast sought me,
On the cross of suffering bought me:
Shall such grace be vainly brought me?

11 Righteous Judge! for sin's pollution
Grant thy gift of absolution,
Ere that day of retribution.

12 Guilty now I pour my moaning,
All my shame with anguish owning;
Spare, O God, thy suppliant groaning!

13 Thou the sinful woman savedst;
Thou the dying thief forgavest;
And to me a hope vouchsafest.

14 Worthless are my prayers and sighing,
Yet, good Lord, in grace complying,
Rescue me from fires undying.

15 With thy favoured sheep O place me,
Nor among the goats abase me;
But to thy right hand upraise me!

16 While the wicked are confounded,
Doomed to flames of woe unbounded,
Call me, with thy saints surrounded.

17 Low I kneel, with heart-submission;
See, like ashes, my contrition;
Help me in my last condition.

18 Ah, that day of tears and mourning!
From the dust of earth returning,
Man for judgment must prepare him;

19 Spare, O God, in mercy spare him!
Lord, all-pitying, Jesu blest,
Grant us thine eternal rest!

L. M.   *"The heaven departed," &c.*   934
Revelation vi. 14.

1 THE day of wrath, that dreadful day,
    When heaven and earth shall pass
    away;
What power shall be the sinner's stay?
How shall he meet that dreadful day?

2 When, shrivelling like a parched scroll,
The flaming heavens together roll,
And louder yet, and yet more dread,
Swells the high trump that wakes the
    dead;

3 O! on that day, that awful day,
When man to judgment wakes from clay,
Be thou, O Christ! the sinner's stay,
Though heaven and earth shall pass away.

6 - 8 s.   Matthew xiii. 37—43.   935

1 THIS is the field, the world below,
    In which the sowers came to sow,
Jesus the wheat, Satan the tares,
For so the word of truth declares:
And soon the reaping time will come,
And angels shout the harvest home.

2 Most awful truth! and is it so?
Must all the world that harvest know?
Is every man or wheat or tare?
Then for that harvest O prepare!

For soon the reaping time will come,
And angels shout the harvest home.

3 To love my sins.—a saint to appear,
To grow with wheat—yet be a tare,
May serve me while I live
Where tares and wheat together grow :
But soon the reaping time will come,
And angels shout the harvest home.

4 But all who truly righteous be
Their Father's kingdom then shall see ;
And shine like suns for ever there :
He that hath ears, now let him hear ;
For soon the reaping time will come,
And angels shout the harvest home.

936 *The last Judgment.* 8 7, 8 7, 4 7

1 LIFT your heads, ye friends of Jesus,
Partners in his sufferings here ;
Christ, to all believers precious,
Lord of lords, shall soon appear :
Mark the tokens
Of his heavenly kingdom near !

2 Close behind the tribulation
Of the last tremendous days,
See the flaming revelation,
See the universal blaze !
Earth and heaven
Melt before the Judge's face !

3 Sun and moon are both confounded,
Darkened into endless night,
When, with angel-hosts surrounded,
In his Father's glory bright,
Christ the Saviour
Shines, the everlasting Light.

4 See the stars from heaven falling,
Hark on earth the doleful cry,
Men on rocks and mountains calling,
While the glorious Judge draws nigh,
" Hide us, hide us,
Rocks and mountains, from his eye ! "

5 With what different exclamation
Shall the saints his banner see !
By the tokens of his passion,
By the marks received for me,
All discern him,
All with shouts cry out, " 'Tis he ! "

6 Lo ! 'tis he ! our hearts' desire,
Come for his espoused below ;
Come to join us to his choir,
Come to make our joys o'erflow,
Palms of victory,
Crowns of glory to bestow.

7 Yes, the prize shall now be given,
We his open face shall see ;
Love, the earnest of our heaven,
Love, our full reward shall be ;
Love shall crown us
Kings through all eternity !

937 *The Second Coming of Christ.* 7 s.

1 COME, Desire of nations, come !
Hasten, Lord, the general doom !
Hear the Spirit and the bride ;
Come, and take us to thy side.

2 Thou, who hast our place prepared,
Make us meet for our reward ;

Then with all thy saints descend ;
Then our earthly trials end.

3 Mindful of thy chosen race,
Shorten these vindictive days ;
Who for full redemption groan,
Hear us now, and save thine own.

4 Now destroy the man of sin ;
Now thine ancient flock bring in !
Filled with righteousness divine,
Claim a ransomed world for thine.

5 Plant thy heavenly kingdom here,
Glorious in thy saints appear ;
Speak the sacred number sealed ;
Speak the mystery revealed.

6 Take to thee thy royal power ;
Reign, when sin shall be no more,
Reign, when death no more shall be ;
Reign, to all eternity.

(See also Hymns 54 to 66.)

C. M. *The Heavenly Canaan.* **938**

1 THERE is a land of pure delight,
Where saints immortal reign,
Infinite day excludes the night,
And pleasures banish pain.

2 There everlasting spring abides,
And never-withering flowers :
Death, like a narrow sea, divides
This heavenly land from ours.

3 Sweet fields beyond the swelling flood
Stand dressed in living green :
So to the Jews old Canaan stood,
While Jordan rolled between.

4 But timorous mortals start and shrink
To cross this narrow sea ;
And linger, shivering on the brink,
And fear to launch away.

5 O could we make our doubts remove,
Those gloomy thoughts that rise,
And see the Canaan that we love
With unbeclouded eyes !

6 Could we but climb where Moses stood,
And view the landscape o'er,
Not Jordan's stream, nor death's cold flood,
Should fright us from the shore.

C. M. *The Heavenly Jerusalem.* **939**

1 JERUSALEM, my happy home !
Name ever dear to me ;
When shall my labours have an end,
In joy, and peace, and thee ?

2 When shall these eyes thy heaven-built
And pearly gates behold ?   [walls
Thy bulwarks, with salvation strong,
And streets of shining gold ?

3 There happier bowers than Eden's bloom,
Nor sin nor sorrow know :
Blest seats, through rude and stormy
I onward press to you.   [scenes,

4 Why should I shrink at pain and woe ?
Or feel at death dismay ?
I've Canaan's goodly land in view,
And realms of endless day.

5 Apostles, martyrs, prophets there
Around my Saviour stand ;

213

And soon my friends in Christ below
Will join the glorious band.

6 Jerusalem, my happy home!
My soul still pants for thee;
Then shall my labours have an end,
When I thy joys shall see.

940   *The Saints glorified.*   C. M.

1 GIVE me the wings of faith to rise
Within the veil, and see
The saints above, how great their joys,
How bright their glories be.

2 Once they were mourners here below,
And poured out cries and tears:
They wrestled hard, as we do now,
With sins, and doubts, and fears.

3 I ask them whence their victory came:
They, with united breath,
Ascribe their conquest to the Lamb,
Their triumph to his death.

4 They marked the footsteps that he trod,
His zeal inspired their breast;
And following their incarnate God,
Possess the promised rest.

5 Our glorious Leader claims our praise
For his own pattern given;
While the long cloud of witnesses
Show the same path to heaven.

941   7s & 6s †.

1 WHERE shall true believers go,
When from the flesh they fly?
Glorious joys ordained to know,
They mount above the sky,
To that bright celestial place;
There they shall in raptures live,
More than tongue can e'er express,
Or heart can e'er conceive.

2 When they once are entered there,
Their mourning days are o'er;
Pain, and sin, and want, and care,
And sighing are no more;
Subject then to no decay,
Heavenly bodies they put on,
Swifter than the lightning's ray,
And brighter than the sun.

3 But their greatest happiness,
Their highest joy, shall be,
God their Saviour, to possess,
To know, and love, and see:
With that beatific sight
Glorious ecstasy is given;
This is their supreme delight,
And makes a heaven of heaven.

4 Him beholding face to face,
To him they glory give,
Bless his name and sing his praise,
As long as God shall live.
While eternal ages roll,
Thus employed in heaven they are:
Lord, receive my happy soul
With all thy servants there!

942   *"When shall I come and appear before God?"*   4-6s & 2-8s.
      Psalm xlii. 2.

1 SWEET place; sweet place alone!
The court of God most high,
214

The heaven of heavens, the throne
Of spotless majesty!
O happy place! When shall I be,
My God, with thee, To see thy face?

2 The stranger homeward bends,
And sigheth for his rest:
Heaven is my home, my friends
Lodge there in Abraham's breast.
O happy place! When shall I be,
My God, with thee, To see thy face?

3 Earth's but a sorry tent,
Pitched but a few frail days,
A short-leased tenement;
Heaven's still my song, my praise.
O happy place! When shall I be,
My God, with thee, To see thy face?

4 No tears from any eyes
Drop in that holy choir:
But death itself there dies,
And sighs themselves expire.
O happy place! When shall I be,
My God, with thee, To see thy face?

5 There should temptations cease,
My frailties there should end,
There should I rest in peace
In the arms of my best friend.
O happy place! When shall I be,
My God, with thee, To see thy face?

4-6s & 2-8s.   SECOND PART.

6 JERUSALEM on high
My song and city is,
My home whene'er I die,
The centre of my bliss.
O happy place! When shall I be,
My God, with thee, To see thy face?

7 Thy walls, sweet city! thine
With pearls are garnished,
Thy gates with praises shine,
Thy streets with gold are spread.
O happy place! When shall I be,
My God, with thee, To see thy face?

8 No sun by day shines there,
No moon by silent night.
O no! these needless are;
The Lamb's the city's light.
O happy place! When shall I be,
My God, with thee, To see thy face?

9 There dwells my Lord, my King,
Judged here unfit to live;
There angels to him sing,
And lowly homage give.
O happy place! When shall I be,
My God, with thee, To see thy face?

10 The patriarchs of old
There from their travels cease:
The prophets there behold
Their longed-for Prince of Peace.
O happy place! When shall I be,
My God, with thee, To see thy face?

11 The Lamb's apostles there
I might with joy behold:
The harpers I might hear
Harping on harps of gold.
O happy place! When shall I be,
My God, with thee, To see thy face?

12 The bleeding martyrs, they
Within those courts are found;

All clothed in pure array,
  Their scars with glory crowned.
O happy place ! When shall I be,
My God, with thee, To see thy face?

13 Ah me ! ah me ! that I
  In Kedar's tents here stay ;
No place like this on high ;
  Thither, Lord ! guide my way.
O happy place ! When shall I be,
My God, with thee, To see thy face ?

" Here have we no continuing city,
943 *but we seek one to come."* 7 6, 7 6,
    Hebrews xiii. 14.   7 6, 7 6.

1 BRIEF life is here our portion,
  Brief sorrow, short-lived care ;
The life that knows no ending,
  The tearless life, is there.
O happy retribution !
  Short toil, eternal rest :
For mortals and for sinners,
  A mansion with the blest.

2 That we should look, poor wanderers,
  To have our home on high !
That worms should seek for dwellings
  Beyond the starry sky !
And now we fight the battle,
  But then shall wear the crown
Of full and everlasting
  And passionless renown.

3 And now we watch and struggle,
  And now we live in hope,
And Zion in her anguish
  With Babylon must cope ;
But he whom now we trust in
  Shall then be seen and known,
And they that know and see him
  Shall have him for their own.

SECOND PART.   7 6, 7 6, 7 6, 7 6.

4 FOR thee, O dear, dear country,
  Mine eyes their vigils keep ;
For very love, beholding
  Thy happy name, they weep :
The mention of thy glory
  Is unction to the breast,
And medicine in sickness,
  And love, and life, and rest.

5 O one, O only mansion !
  O paradise of joy !
Where tears are ever banished,
  And smiles have no alloy ;
The cross is all thy splendour,
  The Crucified thy praise,
His laud and benediction
  Thy ransomed people raise.

6 Jerusalem the glorious !
  Glory of the elect !
O dear and future vision
  That eager hearts expect !
Even now by faith I see thee,
  Even here thy walls discern ;
To thee my thoughts are kindled,
  And strive, and pant, and yearn.

7 Jerusalem, the only,
  That look'st from heaven below,
In thee is all my glory,
  In me is all my woe !
And though my body may not,
  My spirit seeks thee fain,

Till flesh and earth return me
  To earth and flesh again.

7 6, 7 6, 7 6, 7 6. THIRD PART.

8 JERUSALEM the golden,
  With milk and honey blest
Beneath thy contemplation
  Sink heart and voice oppressed.
I know not, O I know not,
  What social joys are there !
What radiancy of glory,
  What bliss beyond compare !

9 They stand, those halls of Zion,
  All jubilant with song,
And bright with many an angel
  And all the martyr throng ;
The Prince is ever in them ;
  The daylight is serene :
The pastures of the blessed
  Are decked in glorious sheen.

10 There is the throne of David,
  And there, from care released,
The song of them that triumph,
  The shout of them that feast ;
And they who with their Leader
  Have conquered in the fight,
For ever and for ever
  Are clad in robes of white.

7 6, 7 6, 7 6, 7 6. FOURTH PART.

11 JERUSALEM, exulting
  On that securest shore,
I hope thee, wish thee, sing thee,
  And love thee evermore !
I ask not for my merit :
  I seek not to deny
My merit is destruction,
  A child of wrath am I :

12 But yet with faith I venture
  And hope upon the way,
For those perennial guerdons
  I labour night and day.
The best and dearest Father
  Who made me, and who saved,
Bore with me in defilement,
  And from defilement laved ;

13 When in his strength I struggle,
  For very joy I leap ;
When in my sin I totter,
  I weep, or try to weep :
And grace, sweet grace celestial,
  Shall all its love display,
And David's royal fountain
  Purge every stain away.

14 O sweet and blessed country,
  Shall I ever see thy face ?
O sweet and blessed country,
  Shall I ever win thy grace ?
I have the hope within me
  To comfort and to bless !
Shall I ever win the prize itself ?
  O tell me, tell me, Yes !

15 Strive, man, to win that glory ;
  Toil, man, to gain that light ;
Send hope before to grasp it,
  Till hope be lost in sight.
Exult, O dust and ashes,
  The Lord shall be thy part :
His only, his for ever
  Thou shalt be, and thou art !

944 *For ever with the Lord.*   S. M.
1 Thessalonians iv. 17.

1 " FOR ever with the Lord ! "
    Amen ! so let it be !
Life from the dead is in that word,
    'Tis immortality !

2 Here in the body pent,
    Absent from him I roam,
Yet nightly pitch my moving tent
    A day's march nearer home.

3 My Father's house on high,
    Home of my soul ! how near,
At times, to faith's foreseeing eye,
    Thy golden gates appear !

4 Ah ! then my spirit faints
    To reach the land I love,
The bright inheritance of saints
    Jerusalem above !

5 " For ever with the Lord ! "
    Father, if 'tis thy will,
The promise of that faithful word
    Even here to me fulfil.

6 Be thou at my right hand,
    Then can I never fail ;
Uphold thou me, and I shall stand,
    Fight, and I must prevail.

7 So when my latest breath
    Shall rend the veil in twain,
By death I shall escape from death,
    And life eternal gain.

8 Knowing as I am known,
    How shall I love that word,
And oft repeat before the throne,
    " For ever with the Lord ! "

945 *" Whose faith follow."*   8 s & 6 s.
Hebrews xiii. 7.

1 O GOD, to whom the faithful dead
    Still live, united to their Head,
      Their Lord and ours the same :
For all thy saints, to memory dear,
Departed in thy faith and fear,
    We bless thy holy name.

2 By the same grace upheld, may we
So follow those who followed thee,
      As with them to partake
The full reward of heavenly bliss:
Merciful Father ! grant us this
    For our Redeemer's sake.

946   8 s.

1 O WHEN shall we sweetly remove,
    O when shall we enter our rest,
Return to the Zion above,
    The mother of spirits distrest !
That city of God the great King,
    Where sorrow and death are no more ;
But saints our Immanuel sing,
    And cherub and seraph adore.

2 Not all the archangels can tell
    The joys of that holiest place,
Where Jesus is pleased to reveal
    The light of his heavenly face ;
When caught in the rapturous flame,
    The sight beatific they prove,
And walk in the light of the Lamb,
    Enjoying the beams of his love.

3 Thou know'st, in the spirit of prayer,
    We long thy appearing to see,
Resigned to the burden we bear,
    But longing to triumph with thee :
'Tis good at thy word to be here,
    'Tis better in thee to be gone,
And see thee in glory appear,
    And rise to a share in thy throne.

4 To mourn for thy coming is sweet,
    To weep at thy longer delay ;
But thou, whom we hasten to meet,
    Shalt chase all our sorrows away.
The tears shall be wiped from our eyes,
    When thee we behold in the cloud,
And echo the joys of the skies,
    And shout to the trumpet of God.

C. M.   *The Hope of Heaven.*   **947**

1 HOW happy every child of grace,
    Who knows his sins forgiven !
This earth, he cries, is not my place,
    I seek my place in heaven !
A country far from mortal sight ;
    Yet O ! by faith I see
The land of rest, the saints' delight,
    The heaven prepared for me.

2 A stranger in the world below,
    I calmly sojourn here ;
Nor can its happiness or woe
    Provoke my hope or fear :
Its evils in a moment end,
    Its joys as soon are past ;
But O ! the bliss to which I tend
    Eternally shall last.

3 To that Jerusalem above
    With singing I repair ;
While in the flesh, my hope and love,
    My heart and soul, are there :
There my exalted Saviour stands,
    My merciful High-priest,
And still extends his wounded hands
    To take me to his breast.

4 What is there here to court my stay,
    Or hold me back from home,
While angels beckon me away,
    And Jesus bids me come ?
Shall I regret my parted friends,
    Still in the vale confined?
Nay, but whene'er my soul ascends,
    They will not stay behind.

5 The race we all are running now ;
    And if I first attain,
They too their willing head shall bow,
    They too the prize shall gain.
Now on the brink of death we stand ;
    And if I pass before,
They all shall soon escape to land,
    And hail me on the shore.

6 Then let me suddenly remove,
    That hidden life to share ;
I shall not lose my friends above,
    But more enjoy them there.
There we in Jesu's praise shall join,
    His boundless love proclaim,
And solemnize in songs divine
    The marriage of the Lamb.

7 O what a blessed hope is ours !
    While here on earth we stay,

We more than taste the heavenly powers,
And antedate that day :
We feel the resurrection near,
Our life in Christ concealed,.
And with his glorious presence here
Our earthen vessels filled.

8 O would he more of heaven bestow,
And let the vessel break,
And let our ransomed spirits go
To grasp the God we seek ;
In rapturous awe on him to gaze
Who bought the sight for me ;
And shout, and wonder at his grace,
Through all eternity !

*"The sufferings of this present time are not
worthy to be compared with the glory
which shall be revealed in us."*
Romans viii. 18.

948 C. M.

1 AND let this feeble body fail,
And let it droop and die ;
My soul shall quit the mournful vale,
And soar to worlds on high ;
Shall join the disembodied saints,
And find its long-sought rest,
(That only bliss for which it pants)
In my Redeemer's breast.

2 In hope of that immortal crown,
I now the cross sustain,
And gladly wander up and down,
And smile at toil and pain :
I suffer out my threescore years,
Till my Deliverer come,
And wipe away his servant's tears,
And take his exile home.

3 Surely he will not long delay :
I hear his Spirit cry,
"Arise, my love, make haste away !
Go, get thee up, and die.
O'er death, who now has lost his sting,
I give thee victory ;
And with me my reward I bring,
I bring my heaven for thee."

4 O what hath Jesus bought for me !
Before my ravished eyes
Rivers of life divine I see,
And trees of paradise ;
They flourish in perpetual bloom,
Fruit every month they give ;
And to the healing leaves who come
Eternally shall live.

5 I see a world of spirits bright
Who reap the pleasures there ;
he all are robed in purest white,
T And conquering palms they bear :
Adorned by their Redeemer's grace,
They close pursue the Lamb ;
And every shining front displays
The unutterable name.

6 They drink the vivifying stream,
They pluck the ambrosial fruit,
And each records the praise of him
Who tuned his golden lute :
At once they strike the harmonious wire,
And hymn the great Three-One :
He hears ; he smiles ; and all the choir
Fall down before his throne.

7 O what are all my sufferings here,
If, Lord, thou count me meet

With that enraptured host to appear,
And worship at thy feet !
Give joy or grief, give ease or pain,
Take life or friends away :
I come, to find them all again
In that eternal day.

*" Of whom the whole family in
heaven and earth is named."*
C. M. Ephesians iii. 15.

949

1 COME, let us join our friends above
That have obtained the prize,
And on the eagle wings of love
To joys celestial rise :
Let all the saints terrestrial sing,
With those to glory gone ;
For all the servants of our King,
In earth and heaven, are one.

2 One family we dwell in him,
One church, above, beneath,
Though now divided by the stream,
The narrow stream of death :
One army of the living God,
To his command we bow ;
Part of his host have crossed the flood,
And part are crossing now.

3 Ten thousand to their endless home
This solemn moment fly ;
And we are to the margin come,
And we expect to die :
His militant embodied host,
With wishful looks we stand,
And long to see that happy coast,
And reach the heavenly land.

4 Our old companions in distress
We haste again to see,
And eager long for our release,
And full felicity :
Even now by faith we join our hands
With those that went before ;
And greet the blood-besprinkled bands
On the eternal shore.

5 Our spirits too shall quickly join,
Like theirs with glory crowned,
And shout to see our Captain's sign,
To hear his trumpet sound.
O that we now might grasp our guide !
O that the word were given !
Come, Lord of hosts, the waves divide,
And land us all in heaven !

SECTION IX.

FOR THE LORD'S DAY, AND FOR VARIOUS SEASONS AND OCCASIONS.

C. M. **950**

1 THE Lord of Sabbath let us praise
In concert with the blest,
Who, joyful, in harmonious lays
Employ an endless rest.
Thus, Lord, while we remember thee,
We blest and pious grow ;
By hymns of praise we learn to be
Triumphant here below.

2 On this glad day a brighter scene
Of glory was displayed,

By God, the eternal Word, than when
  This universe was made.
HE RISES, who mankind has bought
  With grief and pain extreme :
'Twas great to speak a world from nought ;
  'Twas greater to redeem !

951   *"Sabbaths . . . a sign."*   L. M.
          Exodus xxxi. 13.

1 DEAR is the day which God hath made,
    Signal of peace to earth displayed ;
Its light the rainbow of the seven,
Its atmosphere the air of heaven.

2 The gay who rest nor worship prize
Jehovah's changeless sign despise ;
Still stand it to our eyes alone
With claims and blessings all its own !

3 The suffering scarce, alas ! can know
This from the other days of woe,
May we the worth of Sabbaths learn
Before we suffer in our turn !

4 The blest no sun save Jesus see,
No Sabbath save eternity ;
May our brief Sabbaths melt away
In the clear light of endless day !

5 Lord of the Sabbath, 'tis thy will
These hours to hallow ; bless them still !
Send down thy Spirit's sevenfold powers,
And make thy rest and gladness ours.

952   *" The Son of Man is Lord even*   2 - 6 s &
      of the Sabbath-day."   4 - 7 s.
        Matthew xii. 8.

1 SAVIOUR, thy sacred day
    Is subject to thy sway,
Made thy pleasure to fulfil ;
  Thou, the Son of man, alone
Canst, according to thy will,
 · Abrogate or change thine own.

2 Thy love the day designed
    A blessing to mankind ;
But thy more abundant grace,
  Gospel grace unsearchable,
Bade the Jewish feast give place,
  Fixed the Christian festival.

3 Lord of the hallowed day,
    Once more thy power display ;
Now returning from above,
  Change it to that heavenly feast,
Sabbath of celestial love,
  Sabbath of eternal rest.

953   *For the Lord's Day.*   6 - 8 s.

1 COME, let us with our Lord arise,
    Our Lord, who made both earth and
  skies ;
Who died to save the world he made,
And rose triumphant from the dead ; ·
He rose, the Prince of life and peace,
And stamped the day for ever his.

2 This is the day the Lord hath made,
That all may see his love displayed,
May feel his resurrection's power,
And rise again to fall no more,
In perfect righteousness renewed,
And filled with all the life of God.

3 Then let us render him his own,
With solemn prayer approach the throne,
218

With meekness hear the gospel-word,
With thanks his dying love record ;
Our joyful hearts and voices raise,
And fill his courts with songs of praise.

4 Honour and praise to Jesus pay
Throughout his consecrated day ;
Be all in Jesu's praise employed,
Nor leave a single moment void ;
With utmost care the time improve,
And only breathe his praise and love.

954

C. M.

1 COME let us join with one accord
    In hymns around the throne ;
This is the day our rising Lord
  Hath made and called his own.

2 This is the day which God hath blessed,
    The brightest of the seven ;
Type of that everlasting rest
  The saints enjoy in heaven.

3 Then let us in his name sing on,
    And hasten to that day
When our Redeemer shall come down,
  And shadows pass away.

4 Not one, but all our days below,
    Let us in hymns employ ;
And in our Lord rejoicing go
  To his eternal joy.
(See also Hymn 616, SECOND PART.)

955

6 - 8 s.   *Sabbath Morning.*

1 GREAT God, this sacred day of thine
    Demands our souls' collected powers
We would employ in works divine
These solemn, these devoted hours :
Our willing hearts adoring own
The grace which calls us to thy throne !

2 We bid life's cares and trifles fly,
And where thou art appear no more :
Omniscient Lord, thy piercing eye
Doth every secret thought explore :
O may thy grace our hearts refine,
And fix our thoughts on things divine !

3 The word of life, dispensed to-day,
Invites us to a heavenly feast ;
May every ear the call obey,
Be every heart a humble guest :
O bid the wretched sons of need
On soul-reviving dainties feed !

4 Thy Spirit's gracious aid impart,
And let thy word, with power divine,
Engage the ear, and warm the heart,
And make the day entirely thine !
Thus may our souls adoring own
The grace which calls us to thy throne !

956

S. M.

1 WELCOME, sweet day of rest,
    That saw the Lord arise ;
Welcome to this reviving breast,
  And these rejoicing eyes !

2 The King himself comes near,
    And feasts his saints to-day ;
Here we may sit, and see him here,
  And love, and praise, and pray.

3 One day amidst the place
    Where thou, my Lord, hast been

Is sweeter than ten thousand days
  Of pleasurable sin.
4 My willing soul would stay
  In such a frame as this,
And sit and sing herself away
  To everlasting bliss.

957
L. M.

1 SWEET is the sunlight after rain,
  And sweet the sleep which follows pain,
And sweetly steals the Sabbath rest
Upon the world's work-wearied breast.

2 Of heaven the sign, of earth the calm !
  The poor man's birthright, and his balm !
God's witness of celestial things !
A sun with healing in its wings.

3 New rising in this gospel time,
  And in its sevenfold light sublime,
Blest day of God ! we hail its dawn,
To gratitude and worship drawn.

4 O nought of gloom and nought of pride
  Should with the sacred hours abide !
At work for God in loved employ,
We lose the duty in the joy.

5 Breathe on us, Lord ! our sins forgive,
  And make us strong in faith to live :
Our utmost, sorest need supply,
And make us strong in faith to die.

958
7 6, 7 6, 7 6, 7 6.

1 O DAY of rest and gladness,
  O day of joy and light,
O balm of care and sadness,
  Most beautiful, most bright ;
On thee the high and lowly
  Before the eternal throne
Sing Holy, Holy, Holy,
  To the great Three in One !

2 On thee, at the creation,
  The light first had its birth ;
On thee for our salvation
  Christ rose from depths of earth ;
On thee our Lord victorious
  The Spirit sent from heaven ;
And thus on thee most glorious
  A triple light was given.

3 Thou art a cooling fountain
  In life's dry dreary sand ;
From thee, like Pisgah's mountain,
  We view our promised land ;
A day of sweet refection,
  A day of holy love,
A day of resurrection
  From earth to things above.

4 To-day on weary nations
  The heavenly manna falls,
To holy convocations
  The silver trumpet calls,
Where gospel-light is glowing
  With pure and radiant beams,
And living water flowing
  With soul-refreshing streams.

5 New graces ever gaining
  From this our day of rest,
We reach the rest remaining
  To spirits of the blest ;
H

To Holy Ghost be praises,
  To Father, and to Son ;
The Church her voice upraises
  To thee, blest Three in One.

L. M.   *The earthly and the* **959**
      heavenly Sabbath.

1 LORD of the Sabbath, hear our vows,
  On this thy day, in this thy house :
And own, as grateful sacrifice,
The songs which from thy servants rise.

2 Thine earthly Sabbaths, Lord, we love ;
  But there's a nobler rest above ;
To that our labouring souls aspire,
With ardent pangs of strong desire.

3 No more fatigue, no more distress,
  Nor sin nor hell shall reach the place ;
No sighs shall mingle with the songs
Which warble from immortal tongues.

4 No rude alarms of raging foes ;
  No cares to break the long repose ;
No midnight shade, no clouded sun,
But sacred, high, eternal noon.

5 O long-expected day, begin ;
  Dawn on these realms of woe and sin :
Fain would we leave this weary road,
And sleep in death, to rest with God.

C. M. *"I was in the Spirit on the Lord's* **960**
     day."—Revelation i. 10.

MAY I throughout this day of thine
  Be in thy Spirit, Lord,
Spirit of humble fear divine
  That trembles at thy word,
Spirit of faith my heart to raise,
  And fix on things above,
Spirit of sacrifice and praise,
  Of holiness and love !

L. M.   *Sunday Evening.* **961**

1 WE rose to-day with anthems sweet,
  To sing before the mercy-seat,
And ere the darkness round us fell,
We bade the grateful vespers swell.

2 Whate'er has risen from heart sincere,
  Each upward glance of filial fear,
Each true resolve, each solemn vow,
Jesus our Lord ! accept them now.

3 Whate'er beneath thy searching eyes
  Has wrought to spoil our sacrifice,
'Mid this sweet stillness while we bow,
Jesus our Lord ! forgive us now.

4 And teach us erring souls to win,
  And hide their multitude of sin ;
To tread in Christ's long-suffering way,
And grow more like him day by day.

5 So as our Sabbaths hasten past,
  And rounding years bring nigh the last ;
When sinks the sun behind the hill,
When all the weary wheels stand still ;

6 When by our bed the loved ones weep,
  And death-dews o'er the forehead creep,
And vain is help or hope from men ;
Jesus our Lord ! receive us then.

10 10, 10 10. *At the end of Service.* **962**

1 SAVIOUR, again to thy dear name we
  raise   [praise ;
With one accord our parting hymn of

We stand to bless thee ere our worship
  cease.   [peace.
Then, lowly kneeling, wait thy word of

2 Grant us thy peace upon our homeward
  way;   [day;
With thee began, with thee shall end the
Guard thou the lips from sin, the hearts
  from shame,   [name.
That in this house have called upon thy

3 Grant us thy peace, Lord, through the
  coming night,
Turn thou for us its darkness into light;
From harm and danger keep thy children
  free,
For dark and light are both alike to thee.

4 Grant us thy peace throughout our earthly
  li e,
Our balm in sorrow, and our stay in strife;
Then, when thy voice shall bid our con-
  flict cease,
Call us, O Lord, to thine eternal peace.
       (See also Hymn 799.)

963   *A Morning Hymn.*   6 - 7s.

1 CHRIST, whose glory fills the skies,
    Christ, the true, the only Light,
Sun of righteousness, arise,
    Triumph o'er the shades of night;
Day-spring from on high, be near;
Day-star, in my heart appear!

2 Dark and cheerless is the morn,
    Unaccompanied by thee:
Joyless is the day's return,
    Till thy mercy's beams I see:
Till thou inward light impart,
Glad my eyes, and warm my heart.

3 Visit then this soul of mine,
    Pierce the gloom of sin and grief;
Fill me, Radiancy Divine!
    Scatter all my unbelief:
More and more thyself display,
Shining to the perfect day!

964   L. M.

1 AWAKE, my soul, and with the sun
    Thy daily stage of duty run;
Shake off dull sloth, and joyful rise,
To pay thy morning sacrifice.

2 Redeem thy mis-spent moments past,
And live this day as if thy last;
Thy talents to improve take care;
For the great day thyself prepare.

3 Let all thy converse be sincere,
Thy conscience as the noon-day clear;
For God's all-seeing eye surveys
Thy secret thoughts, thy words and ways.

4 Wake, and lift up thyself, my heart,
And with the angels take thy part;
Who all night long unwearied sing
High praise to the eternal King.

5 All praise to thee, who safe hast kept,
And hast refreshed me whilst I slept;
Grant, Lord, when I from death shall wake,
I may of endless life partake!

6 Lord, I my vows to thee renew;
Disperse my sins as morning dew;
Guard my first springs of thought and will,
And with thyself my spirit fill.

220

---

7 Direct, control, suggest, this day,
All I design, or do, or say;
That all my powers, with all their might,
In thy sole glory may unite.

8 Praise God, from whom all blessings flow;
Praise him, all creatures here below;
Praise him above, ye heavenly host;
Praise Father, Son, and Holy Ghost.

L. M.   **965**

1 O TIMELY happy, timely wise,
    Hearts that with rising morn arise!
Eyes that the beam celestial view,
Which evermore makes all things new!

2 New every morning is the love
Our wakening and uprising prove;
Through sleep and darkness safely brought,
Restored to life, and power, and thought.

3 New mercies each returning day
Hover around us while we pray;
New perils past, new sins forgiven,
New thoughts of God, new hopes of heaven.

4 If on our daily course our mind
Be set to hallow all we find,
New treasures still of countless price
God will provide for sacrifice.

5 Old friends, old scenes, will lovelier be,
As more of heaven in each we see:
Some softening gleam of love and prayer
Shall dawn on every cross and care.

6 The trivial round, the common task,
Will furnish all we ought to ask;
Room to deny ourselves; a road
To bring us, daily, nearer God.

7 Only, O Lord, in thy great love
Fit us for perfect rest above;
And help us, this and every day,
To live more nearly as we pray.

C. M.   **966**

1 ONCE more the sun is beaming bright,
    Once more to God we pray,
That his eternal light may guide
And cheer our souls this day.

2 O may no sin our hands defile,
Or cause our minds to rove,
Upon our lips be simple truth,
And in our hearts be love!

3 Throughout the day, O Christ, in thee
May ready help be found,
To save our souls from Satan's wiles,
Who still is hovering round.

4 Subservient to thy daily praise
Our daily toil shall be;
So may our works, in thee begun,
Be furthered, Lord, by thee.

5 And lest the flesh, profane and proud,
Subdue the yielding soul,
May self-constraining temperance
Carnal desires control.

6 To God the Father, God the Son,
And God the Holy Ghost,
Eternal glory be from man,
And from the angel host!

967 *An Evening Hymn.* 10 10, 10 10.

1 O LORD, who by thy presence hast made
    light .
    The heat and burden of the toilsome day,
Be with me also in the silent night,
Be with me when the daylight fades
    away.

2 O speak a word of blessing. gracious Lord!
    Thy blessing is endued with soothing
    power;   [word
On the poor heart worn out with toil, thy
Falls soft and gentle as the evening
    shower.

3 How sad and cold if thou be absent, Lord,
    The evening leaves me, and my heart
    how dead!   [board.
But if thy presence grace my humble
    seem with heavenly manna to be fed;

4 Fraught with rich blessing, breathing
    sweet repose,
    The calm of evening settles on my breast;
If thou be with me when my labours close,
No more is needed to complete my rest.

5 Come then, O Lord, and deign to be my
    guest,
    After the day's confusion, toil, and din,
O come to bring me peace, and joy, and
    rest,
To give salvation, and to pardon sin !

6 Bind up the wounds, assuage the aching
    smart   [past.
    Left in my bosom from the day just
And let me on a Father's loving heart
Forget my griefs, and find sweet rest at
    last.

968

7 6, 7 6, 8 8.

1 THE day is past and over;
    All thanks, O Lord, to thee !
We pray thee now that sinless
    The hours of dark may be;
O Jesu, keep us in thy sight,
And save us through the coming night !

2 The joys of day are over;
    We lift our hearts to thee,
And ask thee that offenceless
    The hours of dark may be;
O Jesu, make their darkness light,
And save us through the coming night !

3 The toils of day are over;
    We raise our hymn to thee;
And ask that free from peril
    The hours of dark may be;
O Jesu, keep us in thy sight,
And guard us through the coming night !

4 Be thou our soul's preserver,
    For thou, O God, dost know
How many are the perils
    Awaiting us below;
O leving Jesu, hear our call,
And guard and save us from them all !

969

L. M.

1 AT even, ere the sun was set,
    The sick, O Lord, around thee lay ;

O in what divers pains they met !
    O with what joy they went away !

2 Once more 'tis eventide, and we
    Oppressed with various ills draw near :
What if thy form we cannot see?
We know and feel that thou art here.

3 O Saviour Christ, our woes dispel !
    For some are sick, and some are sad,
And some have never loved thee well,
    And some have lost the love they had ;

4 And some have found the world is vain,
    Yet from the world they break not free ;
And some have friends who give them pain,
    Yet have not sought a friend in thee ;

5 And all, O Lord, crave perfect rest,
    And to be wholly free from sin ;
And they who fain would serve thee best
    Are conscious most of wrong within.

6 O Saviour Christ, thou too art man!
    Thou hast been troubled, tempted, tried ;
Thy kind but searching glance can scan
    The very wounds that shame would hide ;

7 Thy touch has still its ancient power ;
    No word from thee can fruitless fall ;
Hear in this solemn evening hour,
    And in thy mercy heal us all.

8 7, 8 7, 7 7.   970

1 THROUGH the day thy love hath spared
    Wearied we lie down to rest ;   [us ;
Through the silent watches guard us,
    Let no foe our peace molest ;
Jesus, thou our guardian be,
Sweet it is to trust in thee.

2 Pilgrims here on earth and strangers,
    Dwelling in the midst of foes,
Us and ours preserve from dangers,
    In thine arms may we repose ;
And when life's short day is past,
Rest with thee in heaven at last.

7 s.   *"Lighten our darkness, we*   971
beseech thee, O Lord."

1 GOD the Father ! be thou near,
    Save from every harm to-night ;
Make us all thy children dear,
In the darkness be our light.

2 God the Saviour ! be our peace,
    Put away our sins to-night ;
Speak the word of full release,
Turn our darkness into light.

3 Holy Spirit ! deign to come !
    Sanctify us all to-night ;
In our hearts prepare thy home,
Turn our darkness into light.

4 Holy Trinity ! be nigh !
    Mystery of love adored,
Help to live, and help to die,
Lighten all our darkness, Lord !

10 10, 10 10.   *Abide with me.*   972

1 ABIDE with me ! fast falls the eventide ;
    The darkness deepens ; Lord, with me
    abide !
When other helpers fail, and comforts flee,
Help of the helpless, O abide with me !

2 Swift to its close ebbs out life's little day ;
Earth's joys grow dim, its glories pass
   away ;
Change and decay in all around I see ;
O thou who changest not, abide with me !

3 I need thy presence every passing hour :
What but thy grace can foil the tempter's
   power?
Who like thyself my guide and stay can be?
Through cloud and sunshine, O abide with
   me !

4 I fear no foe, with thee at hand to bless :
Ills have no weight, and tears no bitterness:
Where is death's sting? where, grave, thy
   victory ?
I triumph still, if thou abide with me !

5 Reveal thyself before my closing eyes ;
Shine through the gloom, and point me to
   the skies.
Heaven's morning breaks, and earth's vain
   shadows flee :
In life and death, O Lord, abide with me !

973   *Evening.*   L. M.

1 SUN of my soul ! thou Saviour dear,
    It is not night if thou be near;
O may no earth-born cloud arise,
To hide thee from thy servant's eyes !

2 When the soft dews of kindly sleep
My wearied eyelids gently steep,
Be my last thought, how sweet to rest
For ever on my Saviour's breast !

3 Abide with me from morn till eve,
For without thee I cannot live ;
Abide with me when night is nigh,
For without thee I dare not die.

4 If some poor wandering child of thine
Have spurned to-day the voice divine,
Now, Lord, the gracious work begin ;
Let him no more lie down in sin.

5 Watch by the sick, enrich the poor
With blessings from thy boundless store ;
Be every mourner's sleep to-night,
Like infant's slumbers, pure and light.

6 Come near and bless us when we wake,
Ere through the world our way we take,
Till in the ocean of thy love
We lose ourselves in heaven above.

974   L. M.

1 GLORY to thee, my God, this night,
    For all the blessings of the light ;
Keep me, O keep me, King of kings,
Beneath thine own almighty wings !

2 Forgive me, Lord, for thy dear Son,
The ill that I this day have done ;
That with the world, myself, and thee,
I, ere I sleep, at peace may be.

3 Teach me to live, that I may dread
The grave as little as my bed ;
Teach me to die, that so I may
Rise glorious at the awful day.

4 O may my soul on thee repose !
And may sweet sleep mine eyelids close ;
Sleep that may me more vigorous make
To serve my God when I awake.

222

5 If in the night I sleepless lie,
My soul with heavenly thoughts supply ;
Let no ill dreams disturb my rest,
No powers of darkness me molest.

6 My soul, when I shake off this dust,
Lord, in thy arms I will entrust ;
O make me thy peculiar care,
Some mansion for my soul prepare !

7 O may I always ready stand,
With my lamp burning in my hand ;
May I in sight of heaven rejoice,
Whene'er I hear the Bridegroom's voice !

8 All praise to thee in light arrayed,
Who light thy dwelling-place hast made ;
A boundless ocean of bright beams
From thy all-glorious Godhead streams.

9 The sun in its meridian height
Is very darkness in thy sight ;
My soul O lighten and inflame,
With thought and love of thy great name!

10 Praise God, from whom all blessings flow ;
Praise him, all creatures here below ;
Praise him above, ye heavenly host ;
Praise Father, Son, and Holy Ghost.
   (See also Hymns 227 and 287.)

975   6 - 7 s.   *Saturday Evening.*

1 SAFELY through another week
    God hath brought us on our way ;
Let us now a blessing seek
   On the approaching Sabbath-day,
Day of all the week the best,
Emblem of eternal rest.

2 Mercies multiplied each hour
   Through the week our praise demand ;
Guarded by almighty power,
   Fed and guided by his hand ;
Though ungrateful we have been,
Often made returns of sin.

3 While we pray for pardoning grace,
   In the great Redeemer's name,
Show thy reconciled face,
   Shine away our sin and shame :
From our worldly cares set free,
May we rest this night with thee.

4 When the morn shall bid us rise,
   May we feel thy presence near :
May thy glory meet our eyes,
   When we in thy house appear :
There afford us, Lord, a taste
Of our everlasting feast.

5 May thy gospel's joyful sound
   Conquer sinners, comfort saints ;
Make the fruits of grace abound,
   Bring relief for all complaints :—
Such may all our Sabbaths prove,
Till we join the church above !

976   C. M.   *The Watch Night.*

1 JOIN, all ye ransomed sons of grace,
    The holy joy prolong,
And shout to the Redeemer's praise
A solemn midnight song.

2 Blessing, and thanks, and love, and might,
Be to our Jesus given,
Who turns our darkness into light,
Who turns our hell to heaven.

3 Thither our faithful souls he leads,
· Thither he bids us rise,
With crowns of joy upon our heads,
To meet him in the skies.

977
6 - 8 s.

1 HOW many pass the guilty night
In revellings and frantic mirth !
The creature is their sole delight,
Their happiness the things of earth :
For *us* suffice the season past ;
We choose the better part at last.

2 We will not close our wakeful eyes,
We will not let our eyelids sleep ;
But humbly lift them to the skies,
And all a solemn vigil keep ;
So many years on sin bestowed,
Can we not watch one night for God ?

3 We can, O Jesus, for thy sake,
Devote our every hour to thee :
Speak but the word, our souls shall wake,
And sing with cheerful melody ;
Thy praise shall our glad tongues employ,
And every heart shall dance for joy.

4 Shout in the midst of us, O King
Of saints, and make our joys abound ;
Let us exult, give thanks, and sing,
And triumph in redemption found :
We ask for every waiting soul,
O let our glorious joy be full !

5 O may we all triumphant rise,
With joy upon our heads return,
And far above those nether skies,
By thee on eagles' wings upborne,
Through all yon radiant circles move,
And gain the highest heaven of love !

978
For New-Year's Day.   L. M.

1 ETERNAL Source of every joy,
Well may thy praise our lips employ,
While in thy temple we appear,
Whose goodness crowns the circling year.

2 The flowery spring at thy command
Embalms the air, and paints the land ;
The summer rays with vigour shine
To raise the corn, and cheer the vine.

3 Thy hand in autumn richly pours
Through all our coasts redundant stores ;
And Winters softened by thy care
No more a face of horror wear.

4 Seasons, and months, and weeks, and days,
Demand successive songs of praise :
Still be the cheerful homage paid
With opening light, and evening shade.

5 Here in thy house shall incense rise,
As circling Sabbaths bless our eyes ;
Still will we make thy mercies known
Around thy board, and round our own.

6 O may our more harmonious tongue
In worlds unknown pursue the song ;
And in those brighter courts adore,
Where days and years revolve no more !

979
C. M.

1 SING to the great Jehovah's praise !
All praise to him belongs :

Who kindly lengthens out our days
Demands our choicest songs.

2 His providence hath brought us through
Another various year :
We all with vows and anthems new
Before our God appear.

3 Father, thy mercies past we own ;
Thy still continued care ;
To thee presenting, through thy Son,
Whate'er we have or are.

4 Our lips and lives shall gladly show;
The wonders of thy love,
While on in Jesu's steps we go
To see thy face above.

5 Our residue of days or hours
Thine, wholly thine, shall be ;
And all our consecrated powers
A sacrifice to thee :

6 Till Jesus in the clouds appear
To saints on earth forgiven,
And bring the grand sabbatic year,
The jubilee of heaven.

6 - 8 s.   ## 980

1 WISDOM ascribe, and might, and praise,
To God, who lengthens out our days;
Who spares us yet another year,
And makes us see his goodness here :
O may we all the time redeem,
And henceforth live and die to him !

2 How often, when his arm was bared,
Hath he our sinful Israel spared !
" Let them alone," his mercy cried,
And turned the vengeful bolt aside ;
Indulged another kind reprieve,
And strangely suffered us to live.

3 Merciful God, how shall we raise
Our hearts to pay thee all thy praise ?
Our hearts shall beat for thee alone ;
Our lives shall make thy goodness known;
Our souls and bodies shall be thine,
A living sacrifice divine.

4 - 6 s &   *" Let it alone this year*   ## 981
2 - 8 s.   *also."—Luke xiii. 8.*

1 THE Lord of earth and sky,
The God of ages, praise ;
Who reigns enthroned on high,
Ancient of endless days ;
Who lengthens out our trial here,
And spares us yet another year.

2 Barren and withered trees,
We cumbered long the ground ;
No fruits of holiness
On our dead souls were found :
Yet doth he us in mercy spare
Another and another year.

3 When justice bared the sword,
To cut the fig-tree down,
The pity of our Lord
Cried, " Let it still alone ; "
Our gracious God inclines his ear,
And spares us yet another year !

4 Jesus, thy speaking blood
From God obtained the grace,
Who therefore hath bestowed
On us a longer space :

Thou didst in our behalf appear,
And lo, we see another year !

5 Then dig about our root,
    Break up the fallow ground,
And let our gracious fruit
    To thy great praise abound :
O let us all thy praise declare,
And fruit unto perfection bear !

982
                        C. M.

1 LET me alone another year,
    In honour of thy Son,
Who doth my Advocate appear
    Before thy gracious throne : .
Thou hast vouchsafed a longer space,
    And spared the barren tree,
Because for me my Saviour prays,
    And pleads his death for me.

2 Time to repent thou dost bestow ;
    But O the power impart !
And let my eyes with tears o'erflow,
    Ard break my stubborn heart !
To-day, while it is called to-day,
    The hindering thing remove ;
And lo, I now begin to pray
    And wrestle for thy love !

3 I now from all my sins would turn
    To my atoning God ;
And look on him I pierced, and mourn,
    And feel the sprinkled blood ;
Would nail my passions to the cross,
    Where my Redeemer died ;
And all things count but dung and loss,
    For Jesus crucified.

4 Giver of penitential pain,
    Before thy cross I lie,
In grief determined to remain,
    Till thou thy blood apply.
Forgiveness on my conscience seal,
    Bestow thy promised rest ;
With purest love thy servant fill,
    And number with the blest.

983
                        S. M.

1 YE worms of earth arise,
    Ye creatures of a day,
Redeem the time, be bold, be wise,
    And cast your bonds away ; →

2 Shake off the chains of sin,
    Like us assembled here,
With hymns of praise to usher in
    The acceptable year.

3 The year of gospel-grace,
    Like us, rejoice to see,
And thankfully in Christ embrace
    Your proffered liberty.

4 Saviour and Lord of all,
    Thy proffer we receive,
Obedient to thy gospel-call,
    That bids us turn and live !

5 Our former years mis-spent,
    Though late, we deeply mourn,
And softened by thy grace, repent,
    And to thy arms return.

6 Thy patience lifts us up,
    Thy free, unbounded grace,
224

And all our fear is lost in hope,
And all our grief in praise.

7 To thee, by whom we live,
    Our praise and lives we pay,
Praise. ardent, cordial, constant, give,
    And shout to see thy day.

S. M.
                        ## 984

1 A FEW more years shall roll,
    A few more seasons come ;
And we shall be with those that rest,
    Asleep within the tomb.

2 Then, O my Lord, prepare
    My soul for that great day ;
O wash me in thy precious blood,
    And take my sins away !

3 A few more suns shall set
    O'er these dark hills of time ;
And we shall be where suns are not,
    A far serener clime.

4 A few more storms shall beat
    On this wild rocky shore ; .
And we shall be where tempests cease,
    And surges swell no more.

5 A few more struggles here,
    A few more partings o'er,
A few more toils, a few more tears,
    And we shall weep no more.

6 A few more Sabbaths here
    Shall cheer us on our way ;
And we shall reach the endless rest,
    The eternal Sabbath-day.

8 s & 6 s.   *For the King or Queen.* ## 985

1 LORD, thou hast bid thy people pray
    For all that bear the sovereign sway,
        And thy vicegerents reign,—
Rulers, and governors, and powers ;
Aud lo, in faith we pray for ours,
        Nor can we pray in vain !

2 Jesu, thy chosen servant guard,
    And every threatening danger ward
        From *his* anointed head ;
Bid all *his* griefs and troubles cease,
And through the paths of heavenly peace
        To life eternal lead.

3 Cover *his* enemies with shame,
Defeat their every hostile aim,
        Their baffled hopes destroy :
But shower on *him* thy blessings down,
Crown *him* with grace, with glory crown,
        And everlasting joy.

4 To hoary hairs be thou *his* God ;
Late may *he* reach that high abode,
        Late to *his* heaven remove ;
Of virtues full, and happy days,
Accounted worthy by thy grace
        To fill a throne above.

5 Secure us, of *his* royal race,
A man to stand before thy face,
        And exercise thy power :
With wealth, prosperity, and peace,
Our nation and our churches bless,
        Till time shall be no more.

(*See also Hymn* 465.)

986 *In time of Pestilence.* C. M.

1 IN grief and fear, to thee, O Lord,
   We now for succour fly,
Thine awful judgments are abroad,
   O shield us, lest we die!

2 The fell disease on every side
   Walks forth with tainted breath;
And pestilence, with rapid stride,
   Bestrews the land with death.

3 O look with pity on the scene
   Of sadness and of dread,
And let thine angel stand between
   The living and the dead!

4 With contrite hearts to thee, our King,
   We turn, who oft have strayed;
Accept the sacrifice we bring,
   And let the plague be stayed.

987 *Harvest-Home.* 8 - 7 s.

1 COME, ye thankful people, come,
   Raise the song of harvest-home:
All is safely gathered in,
Ere the winter storms begin:
God our Maker doth provide
For our wants to be supplied;
Come to God's own temple, come,
Raise the song of harvest-home!

2 We ourselves are God's own field,
Fruit unto his praise to yield;
Wheat and tares together sown,
Unto joy or sorrow grown:
First the blade, and then the ear,
Then the full corn shall appear:
Grant, O harvest Lord, that we
Wholesome grain and pure may be.

3 For the Lord our God shall come,
And shall take his harvest home;
From his field shall in that day
All offences purge away;
Give his angels charge at last
In the fire the tares to cast;
But the fruitful ears to store
In his garner evermore.

4 Then, thou Church triumphant, come,
Raise the song of harvest-home!
All are safely gathered in,
Free from sorrow, free from sin;
There for ever purified,
In God's garner to abide:
Come, ten thousand angels, come,
Raise the glorious harvest-home!

988 *"The eyes of all wait upon thee, O Lord; and thou givest them their meat in due season."—Psalm cxlv. 15.*

1 WE plough the fields, and scatter
   The good seed on the land,
But it is fed and watered
By God's almighty hand;
He sends the snow in winter,
   The warmth to swell the grain,
The breezes, and the sunshine,
   And soft refreshing rain.
   All good gifts around us
     Are sent from heaven above,
   Then thank the Lord, O thank the Lord,
     For all his love!

2 He only is the Maker
   Of all things, near and far;
He paints the wayside flower,
   He lights the evening star;
The winds and waves obey him,
   By him the birds are fed;
Much more to us, his children,
   He gives our daily bread.
   All good gifts around us
     Are sent from heaven above,
   Then thank the Lord, O thank the Lord,
     For all his love!

3 We thank thee then, O Father,
   For all things bright and good,
The seed-time and the harvest,
   Our life, our health, our food;
Accept the gifts we offer
   For all thy love imparts,
And, what thou most desirest,
   Our humble, thankful hearts.
   All good gifts around us
     Are sent from heaven above,
   Then thank the Lord, O thank the Lord,
     For all his love!

(See also Hymns 578, 579.)

989 7 s & 6 s t. *On laying the Foundation of a Chapel.*

1 THOU, who hast in Zion laid
   The true foundation-stone,
And with those a covenant made,
   Who build on that alone:
Hear us, architect divine,
Great builder of thy church below!
Now upon thy servants shine,
   Who seek thy praise to show.

2 Earth is thine; her thousand hills
   Thy mighty hand sustains;
Heaven thy awful presence fills;
   O'er all thy glory reigns:
Yet the place of old prepared
By regal David's favoured son
Thy peculiar blessing shared,
   And stood thy chosen throne.

3 We, like Jesse's son, would raise
   A temple to the Lord;
Sound throughout its courts his praise,
   His saving name record;
Dedicate a house to him,
Who, once in mortal weakness shrined,
Sorrowed, suffered, to redeem,
   To rescue all mankind.

4 Father, Son, and Spirit, send
   The consecrating flame;
Now in majesty descend,
   Inscribe the living name;
That great name by which we live
Now write on this accepted stone;
Us into thy hands receive,
   Our temple make thy throne.

990 8 s & 7 s.

1 IN the name which earth and heaven
   Ever worship, praise, and fear,—
Father, Son, and Holy Spirit,—
   Shall a house be builded here:
Here with prayer its deep foundations
   In the faith of Christ we lay,
Trusting by his help to crown it
   With the top-stone in its day.

2 Here as in their due succession
　Stone on stone the workmen place,
Thus, we pray, unseen but surely,
　Jesu, build us up in grace ;
Till, within these walls completed,
　We complete in thee are found ;
And to thee, the one Foundation,
　Strong and living stones, are bound.

3 Fair shall be thine earthly temple :
　Here the careless passer-by
Shall bethink him, in its beauty,
　Of the holier house on high ;
Weary hearts and troubled spirits
　Here shall find a still retreat ;
Sinful souls shall bring their burden
　Here to The Absolver's feet.

4 Yet with truer nobler beauty,
　Lord, we pray, this house adorn,
Where thy bride, thy church redeemed,
　Robes her for her marriage morn ;
Clothed in garments of salvation,
　Rich with gems of heavenly grace, '
Spouse of Christ, arrayed and waiting
　Till she may behold his face.

5 Here in due and solemn order
　May her ceaseless prayer arise ;
Here may strains of holy gladness
　Lift her heart above the skies ;
Here the word of life be spoken ;
　Here the child of God be sealed ;
Here the bread of heaven be broken,
　" Till he come " himself revealed.

6 Praise to thee, O Master-Builder,
　Maker of the earth and skies ;
Praise to thee, in whom thy temple
　Fitly framed together lies :
Praise to thee, eternal Spirit,
　Binding all that lives in one :
Till our earthly praise be ended,
　And the eternal song begun !

" That thine eyes may be open upon this
991　*house day and night."*　4-6 s &
　　2 Chronicles vi. 20.　2 - 8 s.

1 CHRIST is our corner-stone,
　On him alone we build ;
With his true saints alone
　The courts of heaven are filled :
On his great love Our hopes we place
Of present grace And joys above.

2 O! then with hymns of praise
　These hallowed courts shall ring :
Our voices we will raise
　The Three in One to sing ;
And thus proclaim In joyful song,
Both loud and long, That glorious Name.

3 Here, gracious God, do thou
　For evermore draw nigh ;
Accept each faithful vow,
　And mark each suppliant sigh ;
On copious shower On all who pray
Each holy day Thy blessings pour.

4 Here may we gain from heaven
　The grace which we implore :
And may that grace, once given,
　Be with us evermore ;
Until that day, When all the blest
To endless rest Are called away.
226

L. M.　　　　　　**992**

1 O LORD of hosts, whose glory fills
　　The bounds of the eternal hills,
And yet vouchsafes in Christian lands
To dwell in temples made with hands ;

2 Grant that all we, who here to-day
　Rejoicing this foundation lay,
May be in very deed thine own,
Built on the precious corner-stone.

3 Endue the creatures with thy grace,
　That shall adorn thy dwelling-place ;
The beauty of the oak and pine,
The gold and silver, make them thine.

4 To thee they all pertain ; to thee
　The treasures of the earth and sea ;
And when we bring them to thy throne
We but present thee with thine own.

5 The heads that guide endue with skill ;
　The hands that work preserve from ill ;
That we, who these foundations lay,
May raise the top-stone in its day.

6 Both now and ever, Lord, protect
　The temple of thine own elect ;
Be thou in them, and they in thee,
O ever-blessed Trinity !

L. M.　　　　　　**993**

1 THIS stone to thee in faith we lay ;
　To thee this temple, Lord, we build ;
Thy power and goodness here display,
And be it with thy presence filled.

2 Here, when thy people seek thy face,
　And dying sinners pray to live,
Hear thou in heaven, thy dwelling-place;
And when thou hearest, Lord, forgive !

3 Here, when thy messengers proclaim
　The blessed gospel of thy Son,
Still, by the power of his great name,
Be mighty signs and wonders done.

4 Hosanna ! to their heavenly King,
　When children's voices raise that song,
Hosanna ! let their angels sing,　　[long
　And heaven with earth the strain pro-

5 But will indeed Jehovah deign
　Here to abide, no transient guest ?
Here will the world's Redeemer reign ?
　And here the Holy Spirit rest?

6 Thy glory never hence depart ;
　Yet choose not, Lord, this house alone ;
Thy kingdom come to every heart ;
　In every bosom fix thy throne !

L. M.　*On opening a Place of*　**994**
　　　Worship.

1 GREAT God, thy watchful care we bless,
　Which guards these sacred courts in
Nor dare tumultuous foes invade, [peace;
To fill thy worshippers with dread.

2 These walls we to thy honour raise,
　Long may they echo to thy praise !
And thou, descending, fill the place
With choicest tokens of thy grace.

3 And in the great decisive day,
　When God the nations shall survey,
May it before the world appear,
That crowds were born to glory here.

995

For a Wedding.   **6·7s.**

1 SAVIOUR, let thy sanction rest
   On the union witnessed now ;
Be it with thy presence blessed,
   Ratify the nuptial vow :
Hallowed let this union be,
With each other, and with thee.

2 Thou in Cana didst appear
   At a marriage-feast like this ; '
Deign to meet us, Saviour, here,
   Fountain of unmingled bliss !
Crown with joy this festive board,
Joy that earth cannot afford.

3 We no miracle require,
   Turning water into wine ;
All our panting hearts desire
   Is to taste thy love divine :
Holy influence from above,
Consecrating earthly love.

4 Let the path our friends pursue,
   From this hour together trod,
Many though its days, or few,
   Be a pilgrimage to God ;
To the land where rest is given,
To thy house, O Lord, in heaven.

996

         7 6, 7 6.

1 THE voice that breathed o'er Eden,
   That earliest wedding-day,
The primal marriage blessing,
   It hath not passed away.

2 Still in the pure espousal
   Of Christian man and maid,
The Holy Three are with us,
   The threefold grace is said,

3 For dower of blessed children,
   For love and faith's sweet sake,
For high mysterious union,
   Which nought on earth may break.

4 Be present, awful Father,
   To give away this bride,
As Eve thou gav'st to Adam
   Out of his own pierced side.

5 Be present, gracious Saviour,
   To join their loving hands,
As thou didst bind two natures
   In thine eternal bands.

6 Be present, Holiest Spirit,
   To bless them as they kneel,
As thou for Christ the Bridegroom
   The heavenly spouse dost seal.

7 O spread thy pure wings o'er them !
   Let no ill power find place,
When onward to thine altar
   The hallowed path they trace,

8 To cast their crowns before thee,
   In perfect sacrifice,
Till to the home of gladness
   With Christ's own bride they rise !
(See also Hymns 510 and 514.)

997

  Family Religion.   **L. M.**

1 FATHER of all, thy care we bless,
   Which crowns our families with peace :
From thee they spring ; and by thy hand
They are, and shall be still sustained.
H 2

2 To God, most worthy to be praised,
   Be our domestic altars raised ;
Who, Lord of heaven, yet deigns to come,
And sanctify our humblest home.

3 To thee may each united house
   Morning and night present its vows ;
Our servants there, and rising race,
Be taught thy precepts, and thy grace.

4 So may each future age proclaim
   The honours of thy glorious name ;
And each succeeding race remove
To join the family above.

C. M.   *After a Journey.*   ## 998

1 THOU, Lord, hast blest my going out ;
   O bless my coming in !
Compass my weakness round about,
   And keep me safe from sin.

2 Still hide me in thy secret place,
   Thy tabernacle spread ;
Shelter me with preserving grace,
   And screen my naked head.

3 To thee for refuge may I run
   From sin's alluring snare ;
Ready its first approach to shun,
   And watching unto prayer.

4 O that I never, never more
   Might from thy ways depart !
Here let me give my wanderings o'er,
   By giving thee my heart.

5 Fix my new heart on things above,
   And then from earth release ;
I ask not life, but let me love,
   And lay me down in peace.

7 s.   *On going on Shipboard.*   ## 999

1 LORD, whom winds and seas obey,
   Guide us through the watery way ;
In the hollow of thy hand
Hide, and bring us safe to land.

2 Jesus, let our faithful mind
   Rest, on thee alone reclined ;
Every anxious thought repress,
Keep our souls in perfect peace.

3 Keep the souls whom now we leave,
   Bid them to each other cleave ;
Bid them walk on life's rough sea ;
Bid them come by faith to thee.

4 Save, till all these tempests end,
   All who on thy love depend ;
Waft our happy spirits o'er ;
Land us on the heavenly shore.

7 s & 6 s †.   ## 1000

1 LORD of earth, and air, and sea,
   Supreme in power and grace,
Under thy protection, we
   Our souls and bodies place.
Bold an unknown land to try,
We launch into the foaming deep :
Rocks, and storms, and deaths defy,
   With Jesus in the ship.

2 Who the calm can understand
   In a believer's breast ?
In the hollow of his hand
   Our souls securely rest :

Winds may rise, and seas may roar,
We on his love our spirits stay ;
Him with quiet joy adore,
Whom winds and seas obey.

1001
To be sung at Sea. L. M.

1 LORD of the wide, extensive main,
Whose power the wind, the sea, con-
trols, [tain,
Whose hand doth earth and heaven sus-
Whose Spirit leads believing souls :

2 For thee we leave our native shore,
(We whom thy love delights to keep)
In other climes thy works explore,
And see thy wonders in the deep.

3 'Tis here thine unknown paths we trace,
Which dark to human eyes appear ;
While through the mighty waves we pass,
Faith only sees that God is here.

4 Throughout the deep thy footsteps shine,
We own thy way is in the sea,
O'erawed by majesty divine,
And lost in thy immensity.

5 Thy wisdom here we learn to adore,
Thine everlasting truth we prove ;
Amazing heights of boundless power,
Unfathomable depths of love.

SECOND PART. L. M.

6 INFINITE God, thy greatness spanned
These heavens, and meted out the
Lo ! in the hollow of thy hand [skies ;
The measured waters sink and rise !

7 Thee to perfection who can tell !
Earth and her sons beneath thee lie,
Lighter than dust within thy scale,
And less than nothing in thine eye.

8 Yet, in thy Son, divinely great,
We claim thy providential care ;
Boldly we stand before thy seat,
Our Advocate hath placed us there.

9 With him we are gone up on high,
Since he is ours, and we are his ;
With him we reign above the sky,
We walk upon our subject seas.

10 We boast of our recovered powers,
Lords are we of the lands and floods ;
And earth, and heaven, and all is ours,
And we are Christ's, and Christ is
God's !

1002
The Traveller's Hymn. C. M.

HOW are thy servants blest, O Lord !
How sure is their defence !
Eternal Wisdom is their guide,
Their help Omnipotence.

2 In foreign realms, in lands remote,
Supported by thy care,
Through burning climes they pass unhurt,
And breathe in tainted air.

3 When by the dreadful tempest borne
High on the broken wave,
They know thou art not slow to hear,
Nor impotent to save.

4 The storm is laid, the winds retire,
Obedient to thy will ;
228

The sea, that roars at thy command,
At thy command is still.

5 In midst of dangers, fears, and deaths,
Thy goodness we'll adore ;
We'll praise thee for thy mercies past,
And humbly hope for more.

6 Our life, while thou preserv'st that life,
Thy sacrifice shall be ;
And death, when death shall be our lot,
Shall join our souls to thee.

1003
C. M.

1 WHILE lone upon the furious waves,
Where danger fiercely rides,
There is a hand, unseen, that saves,
And through the ocean guides.

2 Almighty Lord of land and sea,
Beneath thine eye we sail ;
And if our hope be fixed on thee,
Our hearts can never quail.

3 Though tempests shake the angry deep,
And thunder's voice appal ;
Serene we wake, and calmly sleep,
Our Father governs all.

4 Still prove thyself through all the way,
The guardian and the friend ;
Cheer with thy presence every day,
And every night defend.

1004
6-8 s. *Intercession for those at Sea.*

1 ETERNAL Father ! strong to save,
Whose arm doth bind the restless
wave,
Who bidd'st the mighty ocean deep
Its own appointed limits keep :
O hear us when we cry to thee
For those in peril on the sea !

2 O Saviour ! whose almighty word
The winds and waves submissive heard,
Who walkedst on the foaming deep,
And calm amid its rage didst sleep :
O hear us when we cry to thee
For those in peril on the sea !

3 O Sacred Spirit ! who didst brood
Upon the chaos dark and rude,
Who bad'st its angry tumults cease,
And gavest light and life and peace :
O hear us when we cry to thee
For those in peril on the sea !

4 O Trinity of love and power !
Our brethren shield in danger's hour ;
From rock and tempest, fire and foe,
Protect them wheresoe'er they go ;
And ever let there rise to thee
Glad hymns of praise from land and sea.

1005
C. M. *"The grace of the Lord Jesus Christ, and," &c.*
2 Corinthians xiii. 14.

1 THE grace of Jesus Christ the Son
Be on his church bestowed :
Jesus, through thy free grace alone
We have access to God :
To favour now through thee restored,
O may we still retain
The mercy of our pardoning Lord,
And never sin again !

2 Father, thy love in Christ reveal,
Which spake us justified,
And let the gift unspeakable
In all our hearts abide :
Humbly we trust thy faithful love
Thy children to defend,
And hide our life with Christ above,
And keep us to the end.

3 Come, Holy Ghost, supply the want
Of all thy saints and me,
In all thy gifts and graces grant
Us fellowship with thee :
The pledge, the witness, and the seal,
We look for thee again,
In us eternally to dwell,
Eternally to reign.

(*See also Hymns* 252, 258, 525.)

1006
The same subject. 8 s & 7 s.

MAY the grace of Christ our Saviour,
And the Father's boundless love,
With the Holy Spirit's favour,
Rest upon us from above !
Thus may we abide in union
With each other in the Lord ;
And possess, in sweet communion,
Joys which earth cannot afford.

1007
8 s & 7 s.

LORD, dismiss us with thy blessing,
Bid us now depart in peace ;
Still on heavenly manna feeding,
Let our faith and love increase :
Fill each breast with consolation ;
Up to thee our hearts we raise :
When we reach yon blissful station,
Then we'll give thee nobler praise !
Hallelujah !

1008
87, 87, 47.

1 LORD, dismiss us with thy blessing,
Fill our hearts with joy and peace ;
Let us each, thy love possessing,
Triumph in redeeming grace ;
O refresh us,
Travelling through this wilderness !

2 Thanks we give, and adoration,
For thy gospel's joyful sound :
May the fruits of thy salvation
In our hearts and lives abound ;
May thy presence
With us evermore be found.

3 So, whene'er the signal's given
Us from earth to call away,
Borne on angels' wings to heaven,
Glad the summons to obey,
May we ever
Reign with Christ in endless day.

GRACES BEFORE AND AFTER MEAT.

1009
C. M.

COME then, our heavenly Adam, come,
Thy healing influence give ;
Hallow our food, reverse our doom,
And bid us eat, and live !

1010
2 - 6 s & 4 - 7 s.

THIS day with this day's bread
Thy hungry children feed ;
Fountain of all blessings, grant
Now the manna from above ;
Now supply our bodies' want,
Now sustain our souls with love.

1011
S. M.

FATHER of earth and heaven,
Thy hungry children feed,
Thy grace be to our spirits given,
That true immortal bread !
Grant us and all our race
In Jesus Christ to prove
The sweetness of thy pardoning grace,
The manna of thy love.

1012
8 - 7 s.

LORD of all, thy creatures see
Waiting for their food on thee ;
That we may with thanks receive,
Give, herewith thy blessing give ;
Fill our mouths with food and praise ;
Taste we in the gifts the grace,
Take it as through Jesus given,
Eat on earth the bread of heaven !

1013
10 s & 11 s.

1 O FATHER of all, Who fillest with good
The ravens that call On thee for their
food ; [tain,
Them ready to perish Thou lov'st to sus-
And wilt thou not cherish The children of
men ?

2 On thee we depend Our wants to supply,
Whose goodness shall send Us bread from
the sky ; [love,
On earth thou shalt give us A taste of thy
And shortly receive us To banquet above.

1014
S. M.

LIFE of the world, come down
And stir within our breast,
And by thy sacred presence crown
The sober Christian feast :
Thou Bread of life, and Well,
Come at thy creatures' call,
And give our inmost souls to feel
That thou art all in all !

1015
8 s & 6 s.

JESUS, to whom alone we live,
Now let us from thyself receive
Our consecrated food,
In nature's acts thy will pursue,
And do with faith whate'er we do,
To glorify our God.

1016
C. M.

1 O'ERWHELMED with blessings from
Father, before we taste [above,
These freshest tokens of thy love,
We thank thee for the past ; 239

2 Our eyes and hearts to heaven we lift,
  And taught by Jesus own
That every grace, and every gift,
  Descends from thee alone.

1017 L. M.

1 FATHER, 'tis thine each day to yield
    Thy children's wants a fresh supply;
Thou cloth'st the lilies of the field,
    And hearest the young ravens cry.

2 On thee we cast our care, we live
    Through thee, who know'st our every
O feed us with thy grace, and give [need;
  Our souls this day the living bread!

1018 7 s & 6 s.

FOR my life, and clothes, and food,
    And every comfort here,
Thee, my most indulgent God,
    I thank with heart sincere;
For the blessings numberless
    Which thou hast already given,
For my smallest spark of grace,
    And for my hope of heaven.

1019 7 s.

1 MEET and right it is to praise
    God the giver of all grace,
God, whose mercies are bestowed
On the evil and the good.

2 He prevents his creatures' call,
Kind and merciful to all;
Makes his sun on sinners rise,
Showers his blessings from the skies.

3 Least of all thy creatures, we
Daily thy salvation see,
As by heavenly manna fed,
Through a world of dangers led.

1020 C. M.

BEING of beings, God of love!
    To thee our hearts we raise,
Thy all-sustaining power we prove,
And gladly sing thy praise.

1021 7 s.

1 GIVE Him then, and ever give,
    Thanks for all that we receive;
Man we for his kindness love,
How much more our God above!
230

2 Worthy thou, our heavenly Lord,
To be honoured and adored;
God of all-creating grace,
Take the everlasting praise!

1022 7 s & 6 s.

FATHER, through thy Son receive
    Our grateful sacrifice;
All the wants of all that live
    Thine open hand supplies,
Fills the world with plenteous food;
    For the riches of thy grace
Take, thou universal Good,
    The universal praise.

1023 6 - 8 s.

BLESSING to God, for ever blest,
    To God the Master of the feast,
Who hath for us a table spread,
And with his daily bounties fed;
May he with all his gifts impart
The crown of all—a thankful heart!

1024 C. M.

BE known to us in breaking bread,
    But do not then depart;
Saviour, abide with us, and spread
    Thy table in our heart.

1025 10 s & 11 s.

1 AND can we forbear, In tasting our food,
    The grace to declare And goodness of
                                    God?
Our Father in heaven, With joy we partake
The gifts thou hast given For Jesus's sake.

2 By thee do we live, Thy daily supplies
As manna receive Dropped down from the
    skies;   [store,
In thanks we endeavour Thy gifts to re-
And praise thee for ever, When time is no
    more.

1026 77, 447, 77, 447.

AWAY with all our trouble
    And caring for the morrow!
    The God of love
    Shall still remove
Our every want and sorrow.

Still, Lord, with joy we bless thee,
    Of all good gifts the giver,
    For Christ our Lord
    Hath spoke the word
Which seals thee ours for ever.

INDEX TO THE HYMNS.

NOTES.—1. Where no name follows the first line in the Index, the hymn may be taken as the production of Mr. Charles Wesley. The letter *W* is affixed to those hymns which first appeared in publications for which the Wesleys were jointly responsible; in this case it cannot be determined with certainty to which of the two brothers a hymn should be ascribed.

2. The mark † affixed to certain hymns denotes that the sixth line of each verse contains eight syllables.

234

INDEX TO TEXTS PREFIXED
TO THE SEVERAL HYMNS.

241

AN INDEX

TO THE FIRST LINE OF EVERY VERSE, EXCEPT THE FIRST IN
EACH OF THE HYMNS.

242

245

THE METHODIST

SUNDAY-SCHOOL

HYMN-BOOK.

A COLLECTION OF

HYMNS AND SPIRITUAL SONGS

FOR USE IN

SCHOOLS AND FAMILIES.

COMPILED BY DIRECTION OF

THE WESLEYAN METHODIST CONFERENCE.

WESLEYAN-METHODIST SUNDAY-SCHOOL UNION,
2, LUDGATE CIRCUS BUILDINGS, : 2, CASTLE STREET, CITY ROAD,
LONDON, E.C.
1886.

Novello, Ewer and Co., Printers, London.

PREFACE.

THE need of a new Hymn-Book for our Sunday-Schools has been felt for some time, and the preparation of one was committed to the Connexional Sunday-School Union by the Conference. Through several causes, it was not possible to issue the book earlier.

It has been the aim of the Compilers to insert a large number of hymns of adoration and praise suitable for use in acts of worship. They have also included many spiritual songs, which, though not directly addressed to the Most High, are well fitted to express various religious emotions. The former class they would strongly recommend for the opening and closing of the school.

Many hymns appropriate for Anniversaries will be found in all parts of the book; and it is hoped that this will render it unnecessary to continue the practice of seeking new hymns for such occasions from very many different sources. Scholars are likely to profit most by thoroughly learning and frequently using their own hymn-book.

The Compilers have great pleasure in acknowledging the extreme courtesy of writers and publishers with reference to the insertion of hymns in this collection. In several instances, the authors of some of the choicest verses hold opinions widely different from those of Methodists, yet in no case have they failed to respond to the request of the Compilers for permission to use their hymns, and always in the most kind and generous way. It is possible that, in a very few instances, the authors may not have been traced, and unwittingly use may have been made of hymns without consent; if that is so, the Compilers beg the writers to accord to them their forbearance, and to give in answer to this request the permission for use that would have been asked in private correspondence, had that been possible.

Especial thanks and acknowledgments are presented to the following authors and publishers for permission courteously given to insert the hymns of which they have the copyright. The Rev. Sabine Baring-Gould, for Nos. 350, 477; the Right Rev. the Bishop of Bedford (Dr. W. Walsham How), for Nos. 104, 170, 519, 524, 532, 533, 567; the Rev. E. H. Bickersteth, for Nos. 22, 75; the Rev. Dr. Bonar, for Nos. 1, 4, 7, 14, 85, 272, 318, 326, 328, 376, 395, 401, 429; Mr. W. H. Broom, for No. 89, by the late F. Whitfield; Mr. G. T. Congreve, for Nos. 209, 412, from *Gems of Sacred Song*; the Rev. John Curwen, for Nos. 231, 256, 589, from the *Child's own Hymn-Book*, by special permission; the Rev. John Ellerton, for Nos. 59, 486, 505; the Rev. C. W. Furse, for Nos. 109, 338, 410, 521, 527, 529, by the late Dr. Monsell; Mr. Josiah Gilbert, for Nos. 226, 280, 359, 430, 517, by the late Mrs. Gilbert; Mr. J. T. Hayes, for Nos. 176, 295, 352, 492, from Dr. Neale's *Hymns of the Eastern Church*, and for No. 432; Messrs. Hodder and Stoughton, for No. 76, by Mr. E. Hodder; the Rev. E. Paxton Hood, for Nos. 106, 140, 325; the Proprietors of *Hymns Ancient and Modern*, for Nos. 21, 103, 154, 204, 213, 526; Messrs. Isbister and Co., for Nos. 144, 530, from the late Dean Alford's *Year of Praise*; the Rev. Dr. Littledale, for No. 192; the Right Rev. the Bishop of Lincoln, for Nos. 387, 502, from the *Holy Year*; Messrs. Masters and Co., for No. 180, from Dr. Neale's *Mediæval Hymns and Sequences*; Messrs. Morgan and Scott, for Nos. 117, 285, by Dr. Bonar, from *Sacred Songs and Solos*; the Rev. G. Moultrie, for No. 531; Cardinal Newman, and Messrs. Rivingtons and Co., for No. 336; Messrs. Novello and Co., for Nos. 20, 83, by Dr. Neale, from the *Hymnal Noted*; Messrs. Oliphant and Co., for Nos. 427, 491; Messrs. Pickering and Co., and the late Rev. E. Caswall's Executors, for Nos. 94, 347, 428; the Rev. T. B. Pollock, for Nos. 159, 205; the Religious Tract Society, for Nos. 316, 384, by Miss Charlotte Elliott, and 57, 93, 243, 252, 263, 264, 286, 313, by Mr. John Burton; Messrs. Richardson and Co., for Nos. 27, 112, 356, 490, by the late Dr. Faber; the Rev. Dr. W. F. Stevenson, for No. 230; the Sunday-School Union, for Nos. 190, 220, 322, by the Rev. W. P. Balfern, from *Songs of Gladness*.

Also to Mr. Edward Bailey, for Nos. 271, 549; Mr. C. C. Bell, for Nos. 52, 236, 484; the Rev. Julius Brigg, for Nos. 66, 422; Mr. W. Aver Duncan, for No. 538; the Rev. J. Finnemore, for No. 383; the Rev. E. E. Jenkins, for No. 23; the Rev. Dr. Lyth, for Nos. 441, 507; the Rev. T. McCullagh, for No. 12; Miss S. L. Moore (through Mr. C. D. Hardcastle), for No. 539; the Rev. Mark Guy Pearse, for Nos. 88, 135, 137, 138; the Rev. Dr. Punshon, for No. 560; the Rev. G. Stringer Rowe, for Nos. 131, 145, 409, 537; the Rev. Thornley Smith, for No. 552; the Rev. T. B. Stephenson, B.A., for Nos. 314, 487, 504; Mr. J. E. Vanner, for Nos. 475, 476; the Rev. S. Wray, for No. 535.

The Compilers are indebted to the late Miss Frances Ridley Havergal for the use of Nos. 196, 301, 349, 398, 399, 411. The letter of permission is dated May 12th, 1879, and says: 'The Committee are most welcome to use any hymns they wish of mine,' etc.

Acknowledgment is also made to Mr. W. T. Brooke, of 157 Richmond Road, Hackney, for most valuable help in ascertaining the authorship and copyright of hymns in this collection; and for Hymns 178, 565.

Permission has been purchased for the insertion of the following hymns:—Nos. 39, 133, and 164, by Mrs. Alexander, and No. 470, by Mrs. Shepcote, from Messrs. Masters and Co.; Nos. 127, 172, by Miss Winkworth, from *Lyra Germanica*, from Messrs. Longmans and Co.; No. 448, by Mrs. Shepherd, from Mr. G. Morrish: Nos. 136, 275, 379, from Mr. W. C. Dix.

CONTENTS.

INDEXES.

SUNDAY-SCHOOL HYMN-BOOK.

GOD.

THE HOLY TRINITY.

1 *Give unto the* LORD *the glory due unto His name.*—Psalm xcvi. 8.   7 7.7 7.

1 TO the name of God on high,
  God of might and majesty,
God of heaven and earth and sea,
Blessing, praise, and glory be.

2 To the name of Christ the Lord,
Son of God, incarnate Word,
Christ, by whom all things were made,
Be all honour ever paid.

3 To the Holy Spirit be
Equal praise eternally,
With the Father and the Son,
One in name, in glory one.

4 This the song of ages past,
Song that shall for ever last ;
Let the ages yet to be
Join the cheerful melody.

5 Glorious is our God, the Lord !
Praises, then, with one accord
To His holy name be given,
By the sons of earth and heaven.

2 *Holy, holy, holy, is the* LORD *of hosts.*
Isaiah vi. 3.   C.M.

1 HAIL ! holy, holy, holy Lord !
  Whom One in Three we know :
By all Thy heavenly host adored,
By all Thy Church below.

2 One undivided Trinity
  With triumph we proclaim :
Thy universe is full of Thee,
And speaks Thy glorious name.

3 Thee, holy Father, we confess,
Thee, holy Son, adore,
Thee, Spirit of truth and holiness,
We worship evermore.

4 Hail ! holy, holy, holy Lord !
  (Our heavenly song shall be)
Supreme, essential One, adored
In co-eternal Three !

3 *Holy, holy, holy, Lord God Almighty.*—Rev. iv. 8.   11 12.12 10.

1 HOLY, holy, holy, Lord God Almighty !
  Early in the morning our song shall
  rise to Thee ;
Holy, holy, holy, merciful and mighty !
God in Three Persons, blessèd Trinity !

2 Holy, holy, holy ! all the saints adore Thee,
Casting down their golden crowns around
  the glassy sea ;
Cherubim and seraphim falling down before Thee,
Which wert, and art, and evermore shalt be.

3 Holy, holy, holy ! though the darkness hide
  Thee,   [may not see,
Though the eye of sinful man Thy glory
Only Thou art holy : there is none beside
  Thee
Perfect in power, in love, and purity !

4 Holy, holy, holy, Lord God Almighty !
All Thy works shall praise Thy name in
  earth and sky and sea,
Holy, holy, holy, merciful and mighty !
God in Three Persons, blessèd Trinity !

4 *For He spake, and it was done.*
Psalm xxxiii. 9.   6 6.6 6.8 8.

1 TO Him who spread the skies,
  Who formed the sea and earth,
Creating all so good,
  To Him who gave us birth,
To Him be glory, honour given
From sons of earth and hosts of heaven.

2 To God on high be praise,
  The everlasting One,
Glorious in power and love,
  Who spake, and it was done ;
Who with His gifts our world did fill ;
Who giveth all things freely still.

3 In Him for evermore,
  Ye sons of men, be glad ;
In God, your God, rejoice,
  He lifteth up your head ;
He toucheth, and the sickness flies ;
He speaketh, and the dead arise.

4 Him praise and magnify,
  Sun, moon, and every star ;
His name exalt on high,
  Creation near and far !
To Him, the God of earth and heaven,
All blessing and all praise be given.

5 Unto the Father sing
  The everlasting song ;
Unto the Son the praise
  Eternally prolong ;
Unto the Holy Spirit sing :
The one Jehovah, Lord and King.

1

THE HOLY TRINITY.

5 *For in Him we live, and move, and have our being.*—Acts xvii. 28. 7 7.7 7.

1 GLORY to the Father give,
  God, in whom we move and live !
Children's prayers He deigns to hear,
Children's songs delight His ear.

2 Glory to the Son we bring,
Christ, our Prophet, Priest, and King !
Children, raise your sweetest strain
To the Lamb, for He was slain.

3 Glory to the Holy Ghost !
Be this day a pentecost ;
Children's minds may He inspire,
Touch their tongues with holy fire.

4 Glory in the highest be
To the blessèd Trinity,
For the Gospel from above,
For the word that God is love !

6 *Hear Thou from Thy dwelling-place, even from heaven.*—2 Chronicles vi. 21. 7 7.7 7.7 7.7 7.

1 GOD of glory, God of grace,
  Hear from heaven, Thy dwelling-
While our feeble voices sing   [place,
Grateful praises to our King ;
While we meet at Thy command,
Asking blessings from Thy hand,
  God of glory, God of grace,
  Hear from heaven, Thy dwelling-place.

2 God, our Maker, Thee we praise,
Guardian of our helpless days ;
Thou hast made us by Thy power,
Thou hast kept us to this hour ;
Thou hast given Thy Son to die,
Sent Thy Spirit from on high.
  God of glory, God of grace,
  Hear from heaven, Thy dwelling-place.

3 God the Saviour, Thee we bless
For Thy life of righteousness ;
For Thy cross and death of shame,
Infant voices bless Thy name ;
Should our tongues no praises bring,
Stones would find a voice to sing.
  God of glory, God of grace,
  Hear from heaven, Thy dwelling-place.

4 God the Spirit, Thee we praise
For Thy sanctifying grace ;
For the new and tender heart
Thou hast promised to impart ;
For the Word, inspired by Thee,
That reveals eternity.
  God of glory, God of grace,
  Hear from heaven, Thy dwelling-place.

5 Great, eternal Three in One,
Hear, O hear us from Thy throne !
We are children of a day—
Like the flowers we pass away ;
Yet Thy power can bid us rise
To adorn Thy paradise.
  God of glory, God of grace,
  Hear from heaven, Thy dwelling-place.
2

7 *To God only wise, be glory through Jesus Christ for ever.*—Romans xvi. 27.
87.8 7.4 7.

1 GLORY be to God the Father,
  Glory be to God the Son,
Glory be to God the Spirit,
  Great Jehovah, Three in One ;
    Glory, glory
  While eternal ages run !

2 Glory be to Him who loved us,
  Washed us from each spot and stain ;
Glory be to Him who bought us,
  Made us kings with Him to reign ;
    Glory, glory
  To the Lamb that once was slain !

3 Glory to the King of angels,
  Glory to the Church's King,
Glory to the King of nations,
  Heaven and earth your praises bring ;
    Glory, glory
  To the King of glory bring !

4 Glory, blessing, praise eternal !
  Thus the choir of angels sings ;
Honour, riches, power, dominion !
  Thus its praise creation brings ;
    Glory, glory,
  Glory to the King of kings !

8 *And I will commune with thee from above the mercy-seat.*—Exodus xxv. 22.
7 7.7 7.7 7.7 7.

1 GOD the Father ! full of grace,
  Dwell within this holy place ;
Still, as in the days of old,
Thy great deep of love unfold ;
Shining from the mercy-seat,
Here Thy waiting children meet.
  God of glory, God of grace,
  Make our hearts Thy dwelling-place.

2 God the Son ! for ever be
With us when we worship Thee ;
By Thine agony and sweat,
By Thy cross uplifted yet,
Hear us, Jesus, when we cry ;
Lamb of God, draw nigh, draw nigh.
  God of glory, God of grace,
  Make our hearts Thy dwelling-place.

3 God the Spirit ! in Thy might
Speak, and kindle life and light ;
Quicken, save, and guide, and bless,
Fill our souls with righteousness ;
When the Gospel sound is heard,
Fall on those that hear the word.
  God of glory, God of grace,
  Make our hearts Thy dwelling-place.

4 Holy Trinity ! give ear
To the worship offered here ;
Triune God, this temple own,
Make our hearts Thy living throne ;
So shall daily incense rise
To Thy temple in the skies.
  God of glory, God of grace,
  Make our hearts Thy dwelling-place.

9 *My Father, Thou art the Guide of my youth.—Jeremiah iii. 4.* L.M.

1 MY Father, when I come to Thee,
I would not only bend the knee,
But with my spirit seek Thy face,
With my whole heart desire Thy grace.

2 I plead the name of Thy dear Son,
All He has said, all He has done ;
Oh, may I feel His love to me,
Who died, from sin to set me free !

3 My Saviour, guide me with Thine eye,
My sins forgive, my wants supply ;
With favour crown my youthful days,
And my whole life shall speak Thy praise.

4 Thy Holy Spirit, Lord, impart ;
Impress Thy likeness on my heart ;
May I obey Thy truth in love,
Till raised to dwell with Thee above.

10 *For God is my defence, and the God of my mercy.—Psalm lix. 17.* 87.87.447.

1 LEAD us, heavenly Father, lead us
O'er the world's tempestuous sea ;
Guard us, guide us, keep us, feed us,
For we have no help but Thee :
Yet possessing
Every blessing,
If our God our Father be.

2 Saviour, breathe forgiveness o'er us,
All our weakness Thou dost know ;
Thou didst tread this earth before us,
Thou didst feel its keenest woe ;
Lone and dreary,
Faint and weary,
Through the desert Thou didst go.

3 Spirit of our God, descending,
Fill our hearts with heavenly joy ;
Love with every passion blending,
Pleasure that can never cloy ;
Thus provided,
Pardoned, guided,
Nothing can our peace destroy.

11 *For the LORD God is a sun.* *Psalm lxxxiv. 11.* L.M.

1 FATHER of lights, we sing Thy name,
Who kindlest up the lamp of day ;
Wide as he spreads his golden flame,
His beams Thy power and love display.

2 Fountain of good ! from Thee proceeds
In copious drops the gentle rain, [meads,
Which, through the fields and through the
Revives the grass, and swells the grain.

3 Through the wide world Thy bounties
Yet millions of our guilty race, [spread,
Though by Thy daily mercy fed,
Affront Thy law, and scorn Thy grace.

4 Not so may our forgetful hearts
O'erlook the tokens of Thy care,
But what Thy liberal hand imparts
Still own in praise, still ask in prayer.

5 So shall our suns more grateful shine,
And showers in sweeter drops shall fall,
When all our hearts and lives are Thine,
And, Thou, our God, art known in all.

6 Jesus, our brighter Sun, arise !
In plenteous showers Thy Spirit send ;
Earth then shall grow a paradise,
And in the heavenly Eden end.

12 *Out of the mouth of babes and sucklings Thou hast perfected praise.* *Matthew xxi. 16.* 87.87.87.87.

1 SERAPHS laud Thee, God the Father,
In the sweetest, noblest lays ;
Can it be that Thou wouldst rather
Listen unto children's praise?
Yea ; Thou hearkenest to our voices,
Children's voices though they be ;
Take the glory each rejoices,
Lord of all, to render Thee.

2 Cherubs praise Thee, God the Saviour,
In sublimest strains above ;
Wilt Thou grant to us Thy favour,
And accept of children's love?
Yes ; Thou listenest to our singing,
Children's singing though it be ;
Take the hearts we all are bringing,
Sovereign Son, to Thee, to Thee.

3 Angels praise Thee, God the Spirit,
Source of life and light and truth ;
Wilt Thou, for the Saviour's merit,
Hear the simpler songs of youth?
Thou receiv'st our adoration,
Children's homage though it be ;
Make our hearts a new creation,
Holy Spirit, fit for Thee.

4 Triune God, the heavens hail Thee,
Harpers, choirs, and white-robed throng;
Nor shall children's voices fail Thee
In the universal song.
Now receive our highest praises,
Children's praises though they be ;
Then to bliss at last upraise us,
Triune God, to worship Thee.

13 *God is light, and in Him is no darkness at all.—1 John i. 5.* 77.75.

1 THREE in One, and One in Three,
Ruler of the earth and sea,
Hear us, while we lift to Thee
Holy chant and psalm.

2 Light of lights ! with morning shine ;
Lift on us Thy light divine,
And let charity benign
Breathe on us her balm.

3 Light of lights ! when falls the even,
Let it close on sin forgiven ;
Fold us in the peace of heaven,
Shed a holy calm.

4 Three in One, and One in Three,
Dimly here we worship Thee ;
With the saints hereafter we
Hope to bear the palm.

3

14 *Thou that dwellest between the cherubims, shine forth.*
Psalm lxxx. 1. 7 6.7 6.7 7.

1 HOLY Father, mighty God,
Fountain of all blessing,
Hear us when on Thee we call,
Thy great name confessing!
Wellspring of all peace and grace,
Grant us to behold Thy face.

2 Holy Saviour, Son of God,
Fulness of all blessing,
Save us when to Thee we come,
Thy great name confessing!
Grant us heavenly joy and rest ;
Bless us, and we shall be blest.

3 Holy Spirit, Light and Love,
Giver of all blessing,
Shine on us when thus we come,
Thy great name confessing.
Mighty Comforter, impart
Comfort to the troubled heart.

15 *He will beautify the meek with salvation.—Psalm cxlix. 4.* 11 10.11 10.

1 PRAISE ye Jehovah, praise the Lord
most holy, [strength the weak ;
Who cheers the contrite, girds with
Praise Him who will with glory crown the
lowly,
And with salvation beautify the meek.

2 Praise ye the Lord for all His lovingkindness,
. And all the tender mercy He hath shown;
Praise Him who pardons all our sin and
blindness, [own.
And calls us sons, and marks us for His

3 Praise ye Jehovah, source of all our blessing, [dim ;
Before His gifts earth's richest boons are
Resting in Him, His peace and joy possessing, [Him.
All things are ours, for we have all in

4 Praise ye the Father, God the Lord, who
gave us,
With full and perfect love, His only Son ;
Praise ye the Son, who died Himself to
save us ; [One.
Praise ye the Spirit : praise the Three in

16 *Praise ye the LORD.*
Psalm cl. 1. 8 7.6 7.6 6.6 6.

1 LET all men praise the Lord,
In worship lowly bending ;
On His most holy word,
Redeemed from woe, depending.
He gracious is and just ;
From childhood us doth lead ;
On Him we place our trust
And hope in time of need.

2 Glory and praise to God—
To Father, Son, be given,
And to the Holy Ghost,
On high enthroned in heaven !
Praise to the Triune God :
With powerful arm and strong,
He changeth night to day :
Praise Him with grateful song !

4

17 *And for Thy pleasure they are and were created.—Revelation iv. 11.*
7 7.7 7.7 7.

1 ALL things praise Thee—Lord most high,
Heaven and earth, and sea and sky,
All were for Thy glory made,
That Thy greatness, thus displayed,
Should all worship bring to Thee ;
All things praise Thee : Lord, may we.

2 All things praise Thee—night to night
Sings in silent hymns of light ;
All things praise Thee—day to day
Chants Thy power in burning ray ;
Time and space are praising Thee,
All things praise Thee : Lord, may we.

3 All things praise Thee—high and low,
Rain, and dew, and seven-hued bow,
Crimson sunset, fleecy cloud,
Rippling stream, and tempest loud,
Summer, winter,—all to Thee
Glory render : Lord, may we.

4 All things praise Thee — heaven's high
Rings with melody divine ; [shrine
Lowly bending at Thy feet,
Seraph and archangel meet ;
This their highest bliss—to be
Ever praising : Lord, may we.

5 All things praise Thee—gracious Lord,
Great Creator, powerful Word,
Omnipresent Spirit, now
At Thy feet we humbly bow ;
Lift our hearts in praise to Thee ;
All things praise Thee : Lord, may we.

18 *I am thy shield, and thy exceeding great reward.—Genesis xv. 1.*
6 6.8 4.6 6.8 4.

1 THE God of Abraham praise,
Who reigns enthroned above,
Ancient of everlasting days,
And God of love :
Jehovah, Great I AM,
By earth and heaven confessed ;
I bow and bless the sacred name,
For ever blest.

2 The God of Abraham praise,
Whose all-sufficient grace
Shall guide me all my happy days,
In all my ways.
He calls a worm His friend,
He calls Himself my God ;
And He shall save me to the end,
Through Jesu's blood.

3 The whole triumphant host
Give thanks to God on high :
'Hail, Father, Son, and Holy Ghost !'
They ever cry ;
· Hail, Abraham's God and mine !
(I join the heavenly lays)
All might and majesty are Thine,
And endless praise.

19 *I dwell in the high and holy place, with him also, etc.*
Isaiah lvii. 15. 5 5.8 8.5 5.

1 FATHER, throned on high ;
Thou to us art nigh ;

With the heavenly hosts before Thee,
We in spirit would adore Thee,
    And with rapture raise
    Hymns of love and praise.

2 O eternal Word,
    Our incarnate Lord,
We to Thee thanksgiving render—
Thee Thy people's strong Defender,
    And as Sovereign own
    None but Thee alone.

3 Spirit of all grace,
    Source of holiness,
Who the Saviour's sceptre wieldest,
And from Satan's vengeance shieldest;
    'Tis by Thee we live:
    Praise to Thee we give!

4 Had we angel tongues,
    With seraphic songs,
Bowing hearts and knees before Thee,
Triune God, we would adore Thee,
    In the highest strain,
    For the Lamb once slain.

20 *All Thy works shall praise Thee, O*
    LORD.—Psalm cxlv 10.

THE strain upraise of joy and praise,
               Alle | luia.
To the glory of their King
Shall the ransomed | people sing
          Alle | luia, Alle | luia.
And the choirs that | dwell on high
Shall re-echo | through the sky,
          Alle | luia, Alle | luia.
They in the rest of | Paradise who dwell,
The blessèd ones, with joy the | chorus swell,
          Alle | luia, Alle | luia.
The planets beaming on their | heavenly way,
The shining constellations | join, and say
          Alle | luia, Alle | luia.
Ye clouds that onward sweep, Ye winds on |
    pinions light,
Ye thunders, echoing loud and deep, Ye
    lightnings | wildly bright,
In sweet con | sent unite your Alle | luia.
Ye floods and ocean billows, Ye storms and |
    winter snow,
Ye days of cloudless beauty, Hoar frost and |
    summer glow,
Ye groves that wave in spring, And glori-
ous | forests sing, Alle | luia.
First let the birds, with painted | plumage
    gay,
Exalt their great Creator's | praise, and say,
          Alle | luia, Alle | luia.
Then let the beasts of earth, with | varying
    strain,
Join in creation's hymn, and | cry again
          Alle | luia, Alle | luia.
Here let the mountains thunder forth so |
    norous Alle | luia.
There let the valleys sing in gentler | chorus
          Alle | luia
Thou jubilant abyss of | ocean, cry Alle | luia.
Ye tracts of earth and conti | nents, reply
          Alle | luia.

A 2

To God, who all cre | ation made,
The frequent hymn be | duly paid:
          Alle | luia, Alle | luia.
This is the strain, the eternal strain, the
    Lord Al | mighty loves: Alle | luia.
This is the song, the heavenly song, that
    Christ the | King approves: Alle | luia.
Wherefore we sing, both heart and voice
    a | waking, Alle | luia.
And children's voices echo, answer | making,
          Alle | luia.
Now from all men | be out-poured
Alleluia | to the Lord;
With Alleluia | evermore
The Son and Spirit | we adore.
Praise be done to the | Three in One,
Alle | luia! Alle | luia! Alle | luia! Amen.

21 *Intercession for those at sea.*
    Psalm cvii. 23-31.   8 8.8 8.8 8.

1 ETERNAL Father! strong to save,
    Whose arm hath bound the restless
Who bidd'st the mighty ocean deep [wave.
Its own appointed limits keep;
    O hear us, when we cry to Thee
    For those in peril on the sea!

2 O Saviour, whose almighty word
    The winds and waves submissive heard,
Who walkedst on the foaming deep,
And calm amid its rage didst sleep:
    O hear us, when we cry to Thee
    For those in peril on the sea!

3 O Sacred Spirit! who didst brood
Upon the chaos dark and rude,
Who bad'st its angry tumult cease,
And gavest light and life and peace:
    O hear us, when we cry to Thee
    For those in peril on the sea!

4 O Trinity of love and power!
    Our brethren shield in danger's hour;
From rock and tempest, fire and foe,
Protect them wheresoe'er they go:
    And ever let there rise to Thee
    Glad hymns of praise from land and sea.

22 *Then He arose, and rebuked the winds*
    and the sea ; and there was a
    great calm.—Matt. viii. 26.   L.M.

1 ALMIGHTY Father, hear our cry,
    As o'er the trackless deep we roam ;
Be Thou our haven always nigh,
On homeless waters, Thou our home.

2 O Jesu, Saviour, at whose voice
    The tempest sank to perfect rest,
Bid Thou the mourner's heart rejoice,
And cleanse and calm the troubled breast.

3 O Holy Ghost, beneath whose power
    The ocean woke to life and light,
Command Thy blessing in this hour, [might.
Thy fostering warmth, Thy quickening

4 Great God, Triune Jehovah, Thee
    We love, we worship, we adore ;
Our refuge on time's changeful sea,
Our joy on heaven's eternal shore.

5

23 *My presence shall go with thee, and I will give thee rest.*
Exodus xxxiii. 14. C.M.

1 WHILE lone upon the furious waves,
Where danger fiercely rides.
.There is a Hand, unseen, that saves,
And through the ocean guides.

2 Almighty Lord of land and sea,
Beneath Thine eye we sail ; '
And if our hope be fixed on Thee,
Our hearts can never quail.

3 Though tempests shake the angry deep,
And thunder's voice appal,
Serene we wake, and calmly sleep ;
Our Father governs all.

4 Still prove Thyself through all the way
The guardian and the friend ;
Cheer with Thy presence every day,
And every night defend.

THE FATHER.

24 *Our Father, which art in heaven.*
Matthew vi. 9. L.M.

1 OUR Father, God, who art in heaven,
To Thy great name be reverence
Thy peaceful kingdom wide extend, [given ;
And reign, O Lord, till time shall end.

2 Thy sacred will on earth be done,
As by the angels round the throne ;
And let us every day be fed
With earthly and with heavenly bread.

3 Our sins forgive, and teach us thus
To pardon those who injure us ;
Our shield in all temptations prove,
And every evil far remove.

4 Thine is the kingdom to control,
And Thine the power to save the soul ;
Great be the glory of Thy reign :
Let every creature say—Amen.

25 *O come, let us sing unto the
LORD.*—Psalm xcv. 1. 5 5 8.6 6 8.

1 O SING to the Lord,
In joyous accord,
Ye dwellers on earth and in heaven ;
The God of creation,
The God of salvation,
To Him all the glory be given !

2 Earth, ocean, and air
Unite to declare
The unspeakable worth of His name ;
Creation He founded
In wisdom unbounded,
Such wonders His glory proclaim.

3 But O ! the rich grace
To our perishing race,
Salvation, the purchase of blood ;
Lost sinners believing,
Free pardon receiving,
Become the blessed children of God.

4 What wonders untold
Will redemption unfold
When heaven its myriads shall bring,
In body and spirit
Bright crowns to inherit
With Christ, the victorious King !

6

26 *Thou art clothed with honour and
majesty.*—Psalm civ. 1. 10 10.11 11.

1 O WORSHIP the King, All glorious
above ;
O gratefully sing His power and His love :
Our Shield and Defender, The Ancient of
days,
Pavilioned in splendour, And girded with
praise.

2 O tell of His might, O sing of His grace,
Whose robe is the light, Whose canopy
space ; [clouds form ;
Whose chariots of wrath Deep thunder-
And dark is His path On the wings of the
storm.

3 The earth with its store Of wonders untold,
Almighty ! Thy power Hath founded of old ;
Hath stablished it fast By a changeless
decree, [the sea.
And round it hath cast, Like a mantle,

4 Thy bountiful care What tongue can recite ?
It breathes in the air, It shines in the light,
It streams from the hills, It descends to
the plain, [rain.
And sweetly distils In the dew and the

5 Frail children of dust, And feeble as frail,
In Thee do we trust, Nor find Thee to fail :
Thy mercies how tender, How firm to the
end, [Friend !
Our Maker, Defender, Redeemer, and

6 O measureless Might ! Ineffable Love !
While angels delight To hymn Thee above,
The humbler creation, Though feeble their
lays,
With true adoration Shall lisp to Thy
praise.

27 *Glorious in holiness, fearful in
praises, doing wonders.*
Exodus xv. 11. C.M.

1 MY God, how wonderful Thou art !
Thy majesty, how bright !
How radiant Thy mercy-seat,
In depths of burning light !

2 How dread are Thine eternal years,
O everlasting Lord !
By prostrate spirits, day and night,
Incessantly adored ! '

3 How glorious, how beautiful
The sight of Thee must be :
Thine endless wisdom, boundless power,
And awful purity !

4 Oh ! how I fear Thee, living God,
With deepest, tenderest fears,
And worship Thee with humble hope
And penitential tears !

5 Yet may I love Thee too, O Lord,
Almighty as Thou art ;
For Thou hast stooped to ask of me
The love of my poor heart.

6 No earthly father loves like Thee,
No mother, e'er so mild,
Bears and forbears as Thou hast done
With me, Thy sinful child.

28 *The heavens declare the glory of God.*—Psalm xix. 1.   8 7.8 7.8 7.8 7.

1 PRAISE the Lord! ye heavens, adore Him,
    Praise Him, angels, in the height;
Sun and moon, rejoice before Him;
    Praise Him, all ye stars and light:
Praise the Lord! for He hath spoken;
    Worlds His mighty voice obeyed;
Laws, that never shall be broken,
    For their guidance He hath made.

2 Praise the Lord! for He is glorious;
    Never shall His promise fail;
God hath made His saints victorious;
    Sin and death shall not prevail.
Praise the God of our salvation!
    Hosts on high His powers proclaim;
Heaven and earth, and all creation,
    Laud and magnify His name!

29 *O* LORD *our Lord, how excellent is Thy name in all the earth!*
    Psalm viii. 1.   C.M.

1 O LORD, how good, how great art Thou,
    In heaven and earth the same!
There angels at Thy footstool bow,
    Here babes Thy grace proclaim.

2 When glorious in the nightly sky
    Thy moon and stars I see,
O what is man, I wondering cry,
    To be so loved by Thee!

3 To him Thou hourly deign'st to give
    New mercies from on high;
Didst quit Thy throne with him to live,
    For him in pain to die;

4 Close to Thine own bright seraphim
    His favoured path is trod;
And all beside are serving him,
    That he may serve his God.

5 O Lord, how good, how great art Thou,
    In heaven and earth the same!
There angels at Thy footstool bow,
    Here babes Thy grace proclaim.

30 *I will praise Thee, O* LORD, *with my whole heart.*—Ps. ix. 1.   4 4 6.4 4 6.

1 MY God, my King,
    Thy praise I sing,
My heart is all Thine own:
    My highest powers,
    My choicest hours,
I yield to Thee alone.

2 My voice, awake,
    Thy part to take;
My soul, the concert join;
    Till all around
    Shall catch the sound,
And blend their hymns with mine.

3 But man is weak
    Thy praise to speak;
Your God, ye angels, sing;
    'Tis yours to see,
    More near than we,
The glories of our King.

4 His truth and grace
    Fill time and space;
As large His honours be,
    Till all that live
    Their homage give,
And praise my God with me.

31 *When the morning stars sang together, and all the sons of God shouted for joy.*—Job xxxviii. 7.   7 7.7 7.

1 SONGS of praise the angels sang,
    Heaven with alleluias rang,
When Jehovah's work begun,
When He spake, and it was done.

2 Songs of praise awoke the morn
When the Prince of peace was born;
Songs of praise arose when He
Captive led captivity.

3 Heaven and earth must pass away:
Songs of praise shall crown that day;
God will make new heavens and earth:
Songs of praise shall hail their birth.

4 Saints below, with heart and voice,
Still in songs of praise rejoice;
Learning here, by faithful love,
Songs of praise to sing above:

5 Borne upon their latest breath,
Songs of praise shall conquer death;
Then amidst eternal joy
Songs of praise their powers employ.

32 *Sing ye to the* LORD, *for He hath triumphed gloriously.*
    Ex. xv. 21.   10 11.11 11.12 11.10 11.

1 SOUND the loud timbrel o'er Egypt's
    dark sea!   [free!
Jehovah hath triumphed! His people are
Sing! for the pride of the tyrant is broken;
    His chariots, his horsemen, all splendid
    and brave:
How vain was their boasting! the Lord
    hath but spoken,
    And chariots and horsemen are sunk in
    the wave!   [sea!
Sound the loud timbrel o'er Egypt's dark
Jehovah hath triumphed! His people are
    free!

2 Praise to the Conqueror   praise to the
    Lord!   [our sword.
His word was our arrow, His breath was
Who shall return, to tell Egypt the story
    Of those she sent forth in the hour of her
    pride?   [of glory,
The Lord hath looked out from His pillar
    And all her brave thousands are dashed
    in the tide.   [sea!
Sound the loud timbrel o'er Egypt's dark
Jehovah hath triumphed! His people are
    free!

33 *Do not I fill heaven and earth? saith the* LORD.—Jer. xxiii. 24.   6 5.6 5.

1 WHEN o'er earth is breaking
    Rosy light, and fair,
Morn afar proclaimeth
    Sweetly—God is there.

7

2 When the spring is wreathing
Flowers rich and rare,
On each leaf is written,—
Nature's God is there.

3 When the storm is howling
Through the midnight air,
Fearfully its thunder
Tells us,—God is there.

34 *The goodness of God endureth
continually.*—Psalm lii. 1.   6 5.6 5.

1 SEE the shining dewdrops
On the flowers strewed,
Proving, as they sparkle,
God is ever good.

2 See the morning sunbeams
Lighting up the wood,
Silently proclaiming
God is ever good.

3 Hear the mountain streamlet
In its solitude,
With its ripple saying
God is ever good.

4 In the leafy tree-tops,
Where no fears intrude,
Merry birds are singing
God is ever good.

5 Bring, my heart, thy tribute,
Songs of gratitude:
All things join to tell us
God is ever good.

35 *Stand still, and consider the wondrous
works of God.*—Job xxxvii. 14.   C.M.

1 I SING the almighty power of God,
That made the mountains rise,
That spread the flowing seas abroad,
And built the lofty skies.

2 I sing the wisdom that ordained
The sun to rule the day:
The moon shines full at His command,
And all the stars obey.

3 I sing the goodness of the Lord,
That filled the earth with food;
He formed the creatures with His word,
And then pronounced them good.

4 Lord, how Thy wonders are displayed
Where'er I turn mine eye:
If survey the ground I tread,
Or gaze upon the sky!

5 There's not a plant or flower below
But makes Thy glories known;
And clouds arise and tempests blow
By order from Thy throne.

6 God's hand is my perpetual guard,
He guides me with His eye;
Why should I then forget the Lord,
Who is for ever nigh?

36 *Glory to God in the highest!*
Luke ii. 14.   10 9.10 9.10 10 8.10 10 8.

1 GLORY, glory to God in the highest!
Angels in chorus joyfully cry;

Glory, glory to God in the highest!
Trembling and weak our voices reply;
Fain would we echo their anthem above,
Fain would we sing to the Fountain of love,
Glory to God in the highest!
What though but feebly our accents arise,
Deigning to hearken, He bends from the
Glory to God in the highest!   skies:

2 Glory, glory to God in the highest!
Bright beaming stars of midnight pro-
Glory, glory to God in the highest! [claim,
Nature peals forth in praise to His name;
Warbles the woodland, and whispers the
breeze,
Roar out the torrents and tempest-tossed
Glory to God in the highest!   [seas,
Loud His creation still ceaseless prolongs
Praise to her Maker in all her glad songs:
Glory to God in the highest!

3 Glory, glory to God in the highest!
Joining the choir, our tribute we bring;
Glory, glory to God in the highest!
Mortals, break silence, gratefully sing;
Reigning in majesty thronèd above,
Yours is the royalest gift of His love:
Glory to God in the highest!
Spread through creation, His grandeur we
Only in man He revealeth His grace: [trace,
Glory to God in the highest!

37 *God is light; . . . God is love.*
1 John i. 5, iv. 16.   8 7.8 7.

1 GOD is love! His mercy brightens
All the path in which we rove;
Joy He gives, and woe He lightens:
God is light, and God is love!

2 Time and change are busy ever,
Man decays, and ages move;
But His wisdom waneth never:
God is light, and God is love!

3 E'en the hour that darkest seemeth
Will His changeless goodness prove;
From the mist His brightness streameth:
God is light, and God is love!

4 He with earthly cares entwineth
Hope and comfort from above;
Everywhere His glory shineth:
God is light, and God is love!

38 *The earth is full of the goodness of the
LORD.*—Psalm xxxiii. 5.   7 7.7 7.7 7.

1 EARTH with her ten thousand flowers,
Air with all its beams and showers,
Ocean's infinite expanse,
Heaven's resplendent countenance:
All around and all above
Bear the record, 'God is love.'

2 Sounds among the vales and hills,
In the woods, and by the rills,
Of the breeze, and of the bird,
By the gentle summer stirred:
All these sounds, beneath, above,
Have one burden, 'God is love.'

3 All the hopes and fears that start
From the fountain of the heart:

8

All the quiet bliss that lies
In our human sympathies :
These are voices from above,
Sweetly whispering, 'God is love.

4 But the great Redeemer's birth,
All He did and said on earth,
All His agonies and woes,
All the gifts His hand bestows,
All His pleadings now above,
Loudly publish, 'God is love.'

39 *All things were made by Him.*
John i. 3.　　7 6.7 6.

1 ALL things bright and beautiful,
　　All creatures great and small,
All things wise and wonderful,
　The Lord God made them all.

2 Each little flower that opens,
　Each little bird that sings,
He made their glowing colours,
　He made their tiny wings.

3 The rich man in his castle,
　The poor man at the gate,
God made them, high or lowly,
　And ordered their estate.

4 The purple-headed mountain,
　The river running by,
The sunset, and the morning
　That brightens up the sky.

5 The cold wind in the winter,
　The pleasant summer sun,
The ripe fruits in the garden,
　He made them every one.

6 He gave us eyes to see them,
　And lips that we might tell
How great is God almighty,
　Who has made all things well.

40 *For the world is Mine, and the fulness thereof*—Psalm l. 12.　C.M.

1 THERE'S not a tint that paints the rose,
　Or decks the lily fair,
Or streaks the humblest flower that blows,
　But God has placed it there.

2 There's not of grass a single blade,
　Or leaf of loveliest green,
Where heavenly skill is not displayed,
　And heavenly wisdom seen.

3 There's not a star whose twinkling light
　Shines on the distant earth,
And cheers the silent gloom of night,
　But God has given it birth.

4 There's not a place on earth's vast round,
　In ocean deep, or air,
Where skill and wisdom are not found ;
　For God is everywhere.

6 Around, within, below, above,
　His providence extends ;
He everywhere displays His love,
　And power with mercy blends.

41 *A God ready to pardon, gracious and merciful.*—Nehemiah ix. 17.
7 6.7 6.7 7.7 6.

1 THOU, my God, art good and wise,
　　And infinite in power,
Thee let all in earth and skies
　Continually adore :
Give me Thy converting grace,
　That I may obedient prove,
Serve my Maker all my days,
　And my Redeemer love.

2 Gracious God, my sins forgive,
　And Thy good Spirit impart ;
Then I shall in Thee believe
　With all my loving heart ;
Always unto Jesus look,
　Him in heavenly glory see,
Who my cause hath undertook,
　And ever prays for me.

42 *Then hear Thou their prayer and supplication in heaven Thy dwelling-place.*—1 Kings viii. 49.　7 7 7 5.

1 GOD of pity, God of grace,
　When we humbly seek Thy face,
Bend from heaven, Thy dwelling-place :
　Hear, forgive, and save.

2 When we in Thy temple meet,
Spread our wants before Thy feet,
Pleading at Thy mercy-seat :
　Look from heaven, and save.

3 When Thy love our hearts shall fill,
And we long to do Thy will,
Turning to Thy holy hill :
　Lord, accept, and save.

4 Should we wander from Thy fold,
And our love to Thee grow cold,
With a pitying eye behold :
　Lord, forgive, and save.

5 Should the hand of sorrow press,
Earthly care and want distress,
May our souls Thy peace possess :
　Jesus, hear, and save.

6 And whate'er our cry may be,
When we lift our hearts to Thee
From our burden set us free :
　Hear, forgive, and save.

43 *To the praise of the glory of His grace.*—Ephesians i. 6.　L. M.

1 GIVE to our God immortal praise,
　Mercy and truth are all His ways :
Wonders of grace to God belong,
Repeat His mercies in your song.

2 Give to the Lord of lords renown ;
The King of kings with glory crown :
His mercies ever shall endure,
When lords and kings are known no more.

3 He built the earth, He spread the sky,
And fixed the starry lights on high :
Wonders of grace to God belong,
Repeat His mercies in your song.

4 He fills the sun with morning light,
He bids the moon direct the night :

9

His mercies ever shall endure,
When sun and moon shall shine no more.

5 He sent His Son with power to save
From guilt and darkness and the grave:
Wonders of grace to God belong,
Repeat His mercies in your song.

Blessed are the pure in heart:
for they shall see God.
44 Matthew v. 8. D.L.M.

1 WE thank Thee, Lord, for this fair earth,
The glittering sky, the silver sea ;
For all their beauty, all their worth,
Their light and glory, come from Thee.
Thanks for the flowers that clothe the ground,
The trees that wave their arms above,
The hills that gird our dwellings round,
As Thou dost gird Thine own with love.

2 Yet teach us still how far more fair,
More glorious, Father, in Thy sight
Is one pure deed, one holy prayer,
One heart that owns Thy Spirit's might !
So, while we gaze with thoughtful eye
On all the gifts Thy love has given,
Help us in Thee to live and die,
By Thee to rise from earth to heaven.

Who crowneth thee with lovingkind-
ness and tender mercies.
45 Psalm ciii. 4. 7 7.7 7.

1 PRAISE to God, immortal praise,
For the love that crowns our days ;
Bounteous Source of every joy,
Let Thy praise our tongues employ !

2 For the blessings of the field,
For the stores the gardens yield,
For the joys the harvests bring,
Grateful praises now we sing.

3 Flocks that whiten all the plain,
Yellow sheaves of ripened grain,
Clouds that drop refreshing dews,
Suns that genial heat diffuse ;

4 All that spring with bounteous hand
Scatters o'er the smiling land,
All that liberal autumn pours
From her rich, o'erflowing stores :

5 These to Thee, our God, we owe,
Source whence all our blessings flow ;
And for these our souls shall raise
Grateful vows and solemn praise.

The LORD shall preserve thy going
out and thy coming in.
46 Psalm cxxi. 8. C.M.

THE TRAVELLER'S HYMN.

1 HOW are Thy servants blest, O Lord !
How sure is their defence !
Eternal Wisdom is their guide,
Their help Omnipotence.

2 In foreign realms, in lands remote,
Supported by Thy care,
Through burning climes they pass unhurt,
And breathe in tainted air.

10

3 When by the dreadful tempest borne
High on the broken wave,
They know Thou art not slow to hear,
Nor impotent to save.

4 The storm is laid, the winds retire,
Obedient to Thy will ;
The sea that roars at Thy command,
At Thy command is still.

5 In midst of dangers, fears, and deaths,
Thy goodness we'll adore ;
We'll praise Thee for Thy mercies past,
And humbly hope for more.

6 Our life, while Thou preserv'st that life,
Thy sacrifice shall be ;
And death, when death shall be our lot,
Shall join our souls to Thee.

Make a joyful noise unto the LORD,
all ye lands.—Psalm c. 1.
47 L.M.

1 ALL people that on earth do dwell,
Sing to the Lord with cheerful voice :
Him serve with fear, His praise forth tell ;
Come ye before Him and rejoice.

2 The Lord, ye know, is God indeed ;
Without our aid He did us make ;
We are His flock, He doth us feed ;
And for His sheep He doth us take.

3 O enter then His gates with praise ;
Approach with joy His courts unto ;
Praise, laud, and bless His name always,
For it is seemly so to do.

4 For why ? the Lord our God is good,
His mercy is for ever sure ;
His truth at all times firmly stood,
And shall from age to age endure.

By Him all things consist.
48 Colossians i. 17. L.M.

1 LORD of all being ! throned afar,
Thy glory flames from sun and star ;
Centre and soul of every sphere,
Yet to each loving heart how near !

2 Sun of our life, Thy quickening ray
Sheds on our path the glow of day ;
Star of our hope, Thy softened light
Cheers the long watches of the night.

3 Our midnight is Thy smile withdrawn ;
Our noontide is Thy gracious dawn ;
Our rainbow arch Thy mercies' sign ;
All, save the clouds of sin, are Thine !

4 Lord of all life, below, above,
Who e light is truth, whose warmth is
Before Thy ever-blazing throne [love,
We have no glory of our own.

5 Grant us Thy truth, to make us free,
And kindling hearts that burn for Thee ;
Till all Thy living altars claim
One holy light, one heavenly flame !

Both young men, and maidens ; old
men, and children : let them praise
49 *the . . . LORD.*—Psalm cxlviii. 12, 13.
7 6.7 6.7 6.10.8 7.8 9.

1 THE valleys and the mountains,
The woodland and the plain,

The rivers and the fountains,
  The sunshine and the rain,
The stars that shine above me,
  The flowers that deck the sod,
Proclaim aloud the glory of my God.
  Praises, holy adoration,
    Praises to our God above ;
Praises through the wide creation,
  Sound aloud His greatness and His love.

2 And shall the voice of nature
    Thus glorify its King,
  And man, the noblest creature,
    No grateful tribute bring?
  Shall mercy strew his pathway,
    And all his senses please,
And man withhold the sacrifice of praise ?
  Praise Him, ye that live for ever ;
    Praise Him, every heart and voice ;
  Praise Him, He's the glorious Giver : [joys.
    Praise Him in your sorrows and your

SECOND PART.

3 The Word of life He gave us
    To guide us to the sky ;
  That He might justly save us
    He gave His Son to die,
    To die in shame and anguish,
    To die a sacrifice,
To save us from the death that never dies.
  Praise Him, praise Him for salvation ;
    Praise Him, praise Him for His Son ;
  Praise Him, every tribe and nation,
    Praise Him for the battle He has won.

4 Then train your youthful voices
    To hymn His praise above ;
  For he who here rejoices
    In Jesu's dying love
    Around His throne of glory
    Shall all His love proclaim,
And sing the song of Moses and the Lamb.
  Praise Him, praise the eternal Father ;
    Praise Him, praise the eternal Son ;
  Praise Him, let us praise together,
    Father, Son, and Spirit, Three in One.

*Bless the LORD, O my soul, and
forget not all His benefits.*
50   Psalm ciii. 2.   8 7.8 7 8 7.

1 PRAISE, my soul, the King of heaven ;
    To His feet thy tribute bring ;
  Ransomed, healed, restored, forgiven,
    Evermore His praises sing :
      Alleluia ! Alleluia !
    Praise the everlasting King.

2 Praise Him for His grace and favour
    To our fathers in distress ;
  Praise Him, still the same as ever,
    Slow to chide and swift to bless :
      Alleluia ! Alleluia !
    Glorious in His faithfulness.

3 Father-like, He tends and spares us,
    Well our feeble frame He knows ;
  In His hands He gently bears us,
    Rescues us from all our foes :
      Alleluia ! Alleluia !
    Widely yet His mercy flows.

4 Angels in the height, adore Him !
    Ye behold Him face to face ;
  Saints triumphant, bow before Him !
    Gathered in from every race :
      Alleluia ! Alleluia !
    Praise with us the God of grace.

*O give thanks unto the LORD : . . . for
His mercy endureth for ever.*
51   Psalm cxxxvi. 1.   7 7.7 7.

1 LET us with a gladsome mind
    Praise the Lord, for He is kind ;
  For His mercies shall endure,
    Ever faithful, ever sure.

2 He, with all-commanding might,
  Filled the new-made world with light :
  For His mercies shall endure,
    Ever faithful, ever sure.

3 All things living He doth feed,
  His full hand supplies their need :
  For His mercies shall endure,
    Ever faithful, ever sure.

4 All our wants He doth supply,
  Loves to hear our humble cry :
  For His mercies shall endure,
    Ever faithful, ever sure.

5 He hath, with a piteous eye,
  Looked upon our misery :
  For His mercies shall endure,
    Ever faithful, ever sure.

6 His own Son He sent to die,
  Us to raise to joys on high :
  For His mercies shall endure,
    Ever faithful, ever sure.

7 Let us then with gladsome mind
  Praise the Lord, for He is kind :
  For His mercies shall endure,
    Ever faithful, ever sure.

*I will sing of the mercies of the
LORD for ever.—Ps. lxxxix. 1.*   C.M.
52

1 IN thankful songs our hearts we lift,
    Father divine, to Thee :
  Giver of every perfect gift,
    Pure let our praises be.

2 May Thine own Spirit, gracious Lord,
    Inspire our filial song,
  Lest selfish thought or empty word
    Should do Thy greatness wrong.

3 We thank Thee for the constant care
    That every want supplies,
  The goodness that prevents our prayer,
    The wisdom that denies ;

4 For helping hand and guiding eye,
    Pillar of fire and cloud,
  The angel of Thy presence nigh
    When storms grow dark and loud.

5 We thank Thee for the flowers that blow
    Around the path we tread,
  Green beauty of the earth below,
    Bright sunshine overhead ;

6 For every voice that breathes Thy name,
    For all things pure and clean,
  Each noble deed, each upward aim,
    For aught where Christ is seen.

11

7 We thank Thee, Lord, for dearer joys,
  For hearts more strong and true,
For love that feeds, and never cloys,
  On mercy ever new ;

8 For hope that lives on words divine,
  Nor fails with mortal breath ;
Of life immortal, one with Thine,
  Through Him who conquered death.

9 O Thou, to whom all hearts are known,
  Our hearts inspire and raise
To love Thee for Thyself alone,
  And live but for Thy praise.

Who daily loadeth us with benefits,
even the God of our salvation.
53   Psalm lxviii. 19.   C.M.

1 LORD, I would own Thy tender care,
  And all Thy love to me ;
The food I eat, the clothes I wear,
  Are all bestowed by Thee.

2 'Tis Thou preservest me from death
  And dangers every hour ;
I cannot draw another breath
  Unless Thou give me power.

3 My health and friends and parents dear,
  To me by God are given ;
I have not any blessing here
  But what is sent from heaven.

4 Such goodness, Lord, and constant care,
  A child can ne'er repay ;
But may it be my daily prayer
  To love Thee, and obey.

Blessed be the name of God for ever and
ever : for wisdom and might
54   *are His.*—Dan. ii. 20.   8 5.8 5.8 4 3.

1 ANGEL voices, ever singing
  Round Thy throne of light,
Angel harps for ever ringing,
  Rest not day nor night ;
Thousands only live to bless Thee,
  And confess Thee,
    Lord of might !

2 Thou, who art beyond the farthest
  Mortal eye can scan,
Can it be that Thou regardest
  Songs of sinful man ?
Can we feel that Thou art near us
  And wilt hear us ?
    Yea, we can.

3 Yea, we know Thy love rejoices
  O'er each work of Thine ;
Thou didst ears and hands and voices
  For Thy praise combine ;
Craftsman's art and music's measure
  For Thy pleasure
    Didst design.

55 *The whole disposing thereof is of*
the LORD.—Proverbs xvi. 33. C.M.

1 I THANK the goodness and the grace
  Which on my birth have smiled,
And made me, in these Christian days,
  A happy English child.

2 I was not born, as thousands are,
  Where God was never known ;
12

And taught to pray a useless prayer
  To blocks of wood and stone.

3 I was not born a little slave,
  To labour in the sun ;
Wishing I were but in the grave,
  And all my labour done.

4 I was not born without a home,
  Nor in some broken shed ;
Like some poor children taught to roam,
  And beg their daily bread.

5 My God, I thank Thee, who hast planned
  A better lot for me ;
And placed me in this happy land,
  Where I can hear of Thee.

Now unto the King eternal . . . be
honour and glory for ever and ever.
56   *Amen.*—1 Timothy i. 17.   10 10.11 11.

1 O HEAVENLY King, look down from
  above !
Assist us to sing Thy mercy and love :
So sweetly o'erflowing, So plenteous the store,
Thou still art bestowing, And giving us more.

2 O God of our life, We hallow Thy name !
Our business and strife Is Thee to proclaim;
Accept our thanksgiving For creating grace ;   [Thy praise.
The living, the living Shall show forth

3 Our Father and Lord, Almighty art Thou ;
Preserved by Thy word, We worship Thee now ;
The bountiful donor Of all we enjoy,
Our tongues to Thine honour, And lives we employ.

4 But O ! above all, Thy kindness we praise,
From sin and from thrall Which saves the lost race ;   [redeem,
Thy Son Thou hast given The world to
And bring us to heaven Whose trust is in Him.

5 Wherefore of Thy love We sing and rejoice,
With angels above We lift up our voice ;
Thy love each believer Shall gladly adore,
For ever and ever, When time is no more.

57 *The LORD He is God ; there is none*
else beside Him.—Deut. iv. 35. C.M.

1 NONE is like God, who reigns above,
  So great, so pure, so high ;
None is like God, whose name is love,
  And who is always nigh.

2 In all the earth there is no spot
  Excluded from His care ;
We cannot go where God is not,
  For He is everywhere.

3 He sees us when we are alone,
  Though no one else can see ;
And all our thoughts to Him are known,
  Wherever we may be.

4 He is our best and kindest Friend,
  And guards us night and day ;
To all our wants He will attend,
  And answer when we pray.

5 O if we love Him as we ought,
And on His grace rely,
We shall be joyful at the thought
That God is always nigh.

*The voice of a great multitude . . .
saying, Alleluia.*

58 Rev. xix. 6.   6 6.6 6.4.4 4 4.

1 ABOVE the clear blue sky,
In heaven's bright abode,
The angel host on high
Sing praises to their God
Alleluia!
They love to sing
To God their King
Alleluia!

2 But God from infant tongues
On earth receiveth praise;
We then our cheerful songs
In sweet accord will raise:
Alleluia!
We too will sing
To God our King
Alleluia!

3 O blessèd Lord, Thy truth
To us, Thy babes, impart,
And teach us in our youth
To know Thee as Thou art.
Alleluia!
Then shall we sing
To God our King
Alleluia!

4 O may Thy holy word
Spread all the world around;
All then with one accord
Shall lift the joyful sound,
Alleluia!
All then shall sing
To God their King
Alleluia!

59 *O magnify the* LORD *with me.*
Psalm xxxiv. 3.   8 7.8 7.

1 DAY by day we magnify Thee,
when our hymns in school we raise;
Daily work begun and ended
With the daily voice of praise.

2 Day by day we magnify Thee,
When, as each new day is born,
On our knees at home we bless Thee
For the mercies of the morn.

3 Day by day we magnify Thee,
In our hymns before we sleep;
Angels hear them, watching by us,
Christ's dear lambs all night to keep.

4 Day by day we magnify Thee,
Not in words of praise alone;
Truthful lips, and meek obedience,
Show Thy glory in Thine own.

5 Day by day we magnify Thee,
When for Jesu's sake we try
Every wrong to bear with patience,
Every sin to mortify.

6 Day by day we magnify Thee,
Till our days on earth shall cease,
Till we rest from these our labours,
Waiting for Thy day in peace.

60 *The God of love and peace shall be with
you.*—2 Corinthians xiii. 11.
8 3.8 3.8 8 8 3.

1 COME, let us all unite and sing,
God is love!
While heaven and earth their praises
God is love!   [bring:
Let every soul from sin awake,
Each in his heart sweet music make,
And sweetly sing for Jesu's sake:
God is love!

2 O tell to earth's remotest bound
God is love!
In Christ is full redemption found:
God is love!
His blood can cleanse our sins away;
His Spirit turns our night to day,
And leads our soul with joy to say,
God is love!

3 How happy is our portion here:
God is love!
His promises our spirits cheer:
God is love!
He is our Sun and Shield by day,
By night He near our tents will stay,
He will be with us all the way:
God is love!

4 What though our heart and flesh should
God is love!   [fail:
Through Christ we shall o'er death pre-
God is love!   [vail:
Through Jordan's swell we will not fear,
For Jesus will be with us there,
Our soul above the waves to bear:
God is love!

5 In Zion we shall sing again,
God is love!
Yes; this shall be our highest strain,
God is love!
Whilst endless ages roll along,
In concert with the heavenly throng,
This shall be still our sweetest song,
God is love!

61 *With favour wilt Thou compass him,
as with a shield.*
Psalm v. 12.   7 7.7 7.7 7.7 7.

1 HAPPY child whom God doth aid!
God our souls and bodies made;
God on us, in gracious showers,
Blessings every moment pours;
Compasses with angel-bands,
Bids them bear us in their hands:
Parents, friends, 'twas God bestowed,
Life, and all, descend from God.

2 He this flowery carpet spread,
Made the earth on which we tread;
God refreshes in the air,
Covers with the clothes we wear,
Feeds us with the food we eat,
Cheers us by His light and heat,
Makes His sun on us to shine;
All our blessings are divine!

3 Give Him, then, and ever give,
Thanks for all that we receive!
Man we for his kindness love,
How much more our God above?

13

Worthy Thou, our heavenly Lord,
To be honoured and adored ;
God of all-creating grace,
Take the everlasting praise !

One God and Father of all, who is
above all.—Ephesians iv. 6.

62 7 7 4. 7 7 4. 7 7.

1 LITTLE beam of rosy light,
 Who has made you shine so bright?
  ' 'Tis our Father.'
Little bird with golden wing,
Who has taught you how to sing?
  ' 'Tis our Father.'
' 'Tis our Father, God above ;
He has made us, He is love.'

2 Little blossom, sweet and rare,
Who has made you bloom so fair?
  ' 'Tis our Father.'
Little streamlet in the dell,
Who has made you, can you tell?
  ' 'Tis our Father.'
' 'Tis our Father, God above ;
He has made us, He is love.'

3 Little child, with face so bright,
Who has made your heart so light?
  ' 'Tis our Father.'
Who has taught you how to sing
Like the merry bird of spring?
  ' 'Tis our Father.'
' 'Tis our Father, God above ;
He has made us, He is love.'

Though the LORD *be high, yet hath He*
respect unto the lowly.

63 Psalm cxxxviii. 6. C. M.

1 FROM His high throne above the sky,
 The Lord can all things see :
I cannot see Him, but His eye
Looks kindly down on me.

2 He cared for me before I knew
That I had such a Friend :
When my first feeble breath I drew,
He did my life defend.

3 He keeps me still, by His great power,
From danger, night and day :
I could not live a single hour
If He were far away.

4 But He is always near and kind,
And loves to hear my prayer :
May I His tender mercy find,
And trust His love and care.

For He careth for you.

64 1 Peter v. 7. 5 5. 6 4.

1 GOD, who made the earth,
 The air, the sky, the sea,
Who gave the light its birth,
 Careth for me.

2 God, who made the grass,
 The flower, the fruit, the tree,
The day and night to pass,
 Careth for me.

3 God, who made the sun,
 The moon, and stars, is He

14

Who, when life's clouds come on,
 Careth for me.

4 God, who made all things
 On earth, in air, in sea,
Who changing seasons brings,
 Careth for me.

5 God, who gave me breath,
 Be this my prayer to Thee,
That when I sink in death
 Thou care for me.

6 God, who sent His Son
 To die on Calvary,
He, if I lean on Him,
 Will care for me.

7 When in heaven's bright land
 I all His loved ones see,
I'll sing with that blest band,
 God cared for me.

Thou shalt guide me with Thy
counsel.—Ps. lxxiii. 24.

65 8 7. 8 7. 4 7.

1 GUIDE me, O Thou great Jehovah,
 Pilgrim through this barren land ;
I am weak, but Thou art mighty,
Hold me with Thy powerful hand ;
 Bread of heaven !
Feed me now and evermore.

2 Open Thou the crystal fountain,
 Whence the healing waters flow ;
Let the fiery, cloudy pillar
Lead me all my journey through ;
 Strong Deliverer !
Be Thou still my help and shield.

3 When I tread the verge of Jordan,
 Bid my anxious fears subside ;
Death of death, and hell's destruction,
Land me safe on Canaan's side ;
 Songs of praises
I will ever give to Thee.]

Salvation belongeth unto the
LORD.—Psalm iii. 8.

66 8 7. 8 7. 8 7. 8 7.

1 LORD of angels pure and holy,
 Who in heaven Thy will obey,
Meek Thou art to those, and lowly,
 Who in earthly temples pray.
Listen to our supplication,
 Thou, who art the children's Friend,
Bless us with Thy great salvation
 While we at Thy footstool bend.

2 Give us now Thy Holy Spirit,
 Raise our thoughts to things on high,
Where the glorified inherit
 Pleasures that can never die.
We would pass the pearly portals,
 Gain the many mansions there,
And with all the bright immortals
 Heaven's unfading glory share.

3 From the guilt of sin deliver,
 From the power of sin set free ;
Thou of life the Lord and Giver,
 Make, O make us all like Thee.
Then, Thy blessèd will obeying,
 We shall gain that blissful shore,
Where, for ever safe from straying,
 We will praise Thee evermore.

67 *The place where God spake with him, Bethel.*—Gen. xxxv. 15.　C.M.

1 O GOD of Bethel, by whose hand
　　Thy people still are fed ;
Who through this weary pilgrimage
　　Hast all our fathers led :

2 Our vows, our prayers, we now present
　　Before Thy throne of grace ;
God of our fathers, be the God
　　Of their succeeding race.

3 Through each perplexing path of life
　　Our wandering footsteps guide ;
Give us each day our daily bread,
　　And raiment fit provide.

4 O spread Thy covering wings around,
　　Till all our wanderings cease,
And at our Father's loved abode
　　Our souls arrive in peace !

5 Such blessings from Thy gracious hand
　　Our humble prayers implore ;
And Thou shalt be our chosen God,
　　And portion evermore.

68 *For He hath said, I will never leave thee, nor forsake thee.*
　　Hebrews xiii. 5.　7 7.7 7.7 7.

1 POOR and needy though I be,
　　God Almighty cares for me ;
Gives me clothing, shelter, food,
Gives me all I have of good.
　　Poor and needy though I be,
　　God Almighty cares for me.

2 He will hear me when I pray ;
He is with me night and day ;
When I sleep and when I wake,
For the Lord my Saviour's sake.
　· Poor and needy though I be,
　　God Almighty cares for me.

3 He who reigns above the sky
Once became as poor as I ;
He whose blood for me was shed
Had not where to lay His head.
　　Poor and needy though I be,
　　God Almighty cares for me.

4 Though I labour here awhile,
He will bless me with His smile ;
And when this short life is past
I shall rest with Him at last.
　　Poor and needy though I be,
　　God Almighty cares for me.

69 *Thou, O LORD, art our Father.*
　　Isaiah lxiii. 16.　C.M.

1 OUR Father sits on yonder throne,
　　Amidst the hosts above ;
He reigns throughout the world alone—
He reigns the God of love.

2 He knew us when we knew Him not,
　　Was with us, though unseen :
His mercies came to us unsought,
　　His love has wondrous been.

3 O let us, while we dwell below,
　　Obey our Father's voice ;
To Him in meek submission bow,
　　And in His love rejoice :

4 That we may hear Him say, at last,
　· Ye blessèd children, come ;
The days of toil and sin are past,
And heaven is now your home.

70 *Thou art my Father, my God, and the rock of my salvation.*
　　Psalm lxxxix. 26.　L.M.

1 GREAT God, and wilt Thou condescend
　　To be my Father and my Friend ?
I a poor child, and Thou so high,
The Lord of earth and air and sky !

2 Art Thou my Father ? Canst Thou bear
To hear my poor, imperfect prayer ?
Or wilt Thou listen to the praise
That such a feeble one can raise ?

3 Art Thou my Father ? Let me be
A meek, obedient child to Thee :
And try in word and deed and thought
To serve and please Thee as I ought.

4 Art Thou my Father ? I'll depend
Upon the care of such a Friend,
And only wish to do and be
Whatever seemeth good to Thee.

5 Art Thou my Father ? Then, at last,
When all my days on earth are past,
Send down and take me, in Thy love,
To be Thy better child above.

71 *All we like sheep have gone astray.*—Isaiah liii. 6.　11 11.11 11.

1 OUR Father in heaven, Thou madest the
　　earth ;　　　　　　　[their birth ;
The sun, moon, and stars to Thy word owe
By Thee were they formed, by Thy counsel
　they stand,　　　　　　[hand.
And we are Thy children, the work of Thy

2 Thou gavest our life ; to Thy goodness we
　owe　　　　　　　[pathway below ;
All the blessings that bloom round our
In thousand endearments Thy love we
　may read,
Declaring that Thou art our Father indeed.

3 But we have all wandered, as sheep, from
　Thy fold ;　　　　　[have grown cold ;
The hearts of Thy children through sin
Though young, we have erred, and would
　humbly implore　　　　　[more.
The mercy we need, that we wander no

4 We own we are guilty, but Jesus has died ;
Nor shall we, when pleading His name, be
　denied ;　　　　　　　[wilt heed,
For hast Thou not promised that plea Thou
And through Thy free grace make us chil-
dren indeed ?

72 *Out of the mouth of babes and suck-lings hast Thou ordained strength.*—Psalm viii. 2.　C.M.

1 COME, let us join the hosts above,
　　Now in our youngest days,
Remember our Creator's love,
　　And sing our Father's praise.

15

2 His majesty will not despise
 The day of feeble things,
Grateful the songs of children rise,
 And please the King of kings.

3 He loves to be remembered thus,
 And honoured for His grace ;
Out of the mouths of babes like us
 His wisdom perfects praise.

4 Glory to God, and praise, and power,
 Honour and thanks be given ;
Children and cherubim adore
 The Lord of earth and heaven.

73 *The LORD is good.*—Nahum i. 7.
             L.M.

1 ALMIGHTY God, Thy works around
 In beauteous order speak Thy praise,
And years, with smiling mercy crowned,
 To Thee successive honours raise ;

2 Each changing season on our souls
 Its sweetest, kindest influence sheds ;
And every period, as it rolls,   [heads.
 Showers countless blessings on our

3 Yes ; God is good : in earth and sky,
 From ocean depths and spreading wood,
Ten thousand voices seem to cry,
 God made us all, and God is good !

4 The sun that keeps his trackless way,
 And downward pours his golden flood,
Night's sparkling hosts, all seem to say,
 In accents clear, that God is good.

5 The merry birds prolong the strain,
 Their song with every spring renewed ;
And balmy air and falling rain,
 Each softly whispers, God is good ;

6 We hear it in the rushing breeze ;
 The hills, that have for ages stood,
The echoing sky, and roaring seas,
 All swell the chorus, God is good.

7 Yes ; God is good, all nature says,
 By God's own hand with speech endued ;
And we, in louder notes of praise,
 Will sing for joy that God is good.

8 For all Thy gifts we bless Thee, Lord,
 But chiefly for our heavenly food ; [Word,
Thy pardoning grace, Thy quickening
 These prompt our song that God is good !

THE LORD JESUS CHRIST.

74 *A name which is above every
    name.*—Philippians ii. 9.   C.M.

1 O FOR a thousand tongues to sing
 My great Redeemer's praise,
The glories of my God and King,
 The triumphs of His grace !

2 My gracious Master and my God,
 Assist me to proclaim,
To spread through all the earth abroad
 The honours of Thy name.

3 Jesus ! the name that charms our fears,
 That bids our sorrows cease ;
'Tis music in the sinner's ears,
 'Tis life, and health, and peace.

16

4 He breaks the power of cancelled sin,
 He sets the prisoner free ;
His blood can make the foulest clean,
 His blood availed for me.

5 He speaks, and listening to His voice,
 New life the dead receive,
The mournful, broken hearts rejoice,
 The humble poor believe.

6 Hear Him, ye deaf ; His praise, ye dumb,
 Your loosened tongues employ ;
Ye blind, behold your Saviour come,
 And leap, ye lame, for joy.

7 Look unto Him, ye nations, own
 Your God, ye fallen race ;
Look, and be saved through faith alone,
 Be justified by grace.

75 *Thou wilt keep him in perfect peace, . . .
   because he trusteth in Thee.*
      Isaiah xxvi. 3.   10.10.

1 PEACE, perfect peace, in this dark world
 of sin ?—
The blood of Jesus whispers peace within.

2 Peace, perfect peace, by thronging duties
 pressed ?—
To do the will of Jesus, this is rest.

3 Peace, perfect peace, with sorrows surging
 round ?—
On Jesus' bosom nought but calm is found.

4 Peace, perfect peace, with loved ones far
 away ?—
In Jesus' keeping we are safe and they.

5 Peace, perfect peace, our future all unknown ?—
Jesus we know, and He is on the throne.

6 Peace, perfect peace, death shadowing us
 and ours ?—   [powers.
Jesus has vanquished death and all its

7 It is enough : earth's struggles soon shall
 cease,
And Jesus call us to heaven's perfect peace.

76 *And all thy children shall be taught
   of the LORD.*—Isa. liv. 13. 8 7.8 7.

1 JESUS, Saviour, wilt Thou hear us,
 Now we come to sing to Thee ?
Wilt Thou in Thy love draw near us,
 While our praise we bring to Thee ?

2 Thou dost hear the angels' praises
 Offered at Thy glorious throne ;
But the cry an infant raises
 Thou, dear Lord, wilt not disown.

3 We would thank Thee we are living,
 Thank Thee for Thy ceaseless love ;
Thou art daily, hourly giving
 Some new blessing from above.

4 All we have by Thee is given ;
 Food to eat and clothes to wear :
Friends, to make our home like heaven :
 Lord, we thank Thee for Thy care.

5 Now that Thou to-day hast brought us
 Here to meet and read and pray,
Bless, O Lord, the lessons taught us,
 Keep us near Thee all the day.

6 Teach us all to know and fear Thee,
  Lead us to the gate of heaven;
  May we all this day, Lord, hear Thee
  Say, 'Thy sins are all forgiven.'

77 *The Word was made flesh, and dwelt among us.*—John i. 14.   C.M.

1 O WISDOM, whose unfading power
  Beside the Eternal stood,
  To frame in nature's earliest hour
  The land, the sky, the flood:

2 Yet didst Thou not disdain awhile
  An infant's form to wear;
  To bless Thy mother with a smile,
  And lisp Thy faltering prayer.

3 But in Thy Father's own abode,
  With Israel's elders round,
  Conversing high with Israel's God,
  Thy greatest joy was found.

4 So may our youth adore Thy name!
  And, Saviour, deign to bless
  With fostering grace the timid flame
  Of early holiness!

78 *And let all the angels of God worship Him.*—Hebrews i. 6.
  6 6 4.6 6 6 4.

1 PRAISE God, ye seraphs bright,
  Praise Him, ye sons of light,
  Jesus adore!
  What earthly choirs can swell,
  What mortal tongue can tell
  Thy love, Immanuel?
  God evermore!

2 Come, saints, in God rejoice;
  Lift up a mighty voice;
  Sing to the Lamb!
  For us His blood was shed,
  For us He left the dead,
  His foes discomfited:
  Praise the I AM!

79 *Every good gift and every perfect gift is from above.*
  James i. 17.   7 7.7 7.7 7.

1 FOR the beauty of the earth,
  For the beauty of the skies,
  For the love which from our birth
  Over and around us lies:
  Christ, our God, to Thee we raise
  This our sacrifice of praise.

2 For the beauty of each hour
  Of the day and of the night,
  Hill and vale and tree and flower,
  Sun and moon and stars of light.
  Christ, our God, to Thee we raise
  This our sacrifice of praise.

3 For the joy of human love,
  Brother, sister, parent, child,
  Friends on earth and friends above;
  For all gentle thoughts and mild:
  Christ, our God, to Thee we raise
  This our sacrifice of praise.

4 For each perfect gift of Thine
  To our race so freely given,
  Graces, human and divine,
  Flowers of earth and buds of heaven:
  Christ, our God, to Thee we raise
  This our sacrifice of praise.

5 For Thy Church, that evermore
  Lifteth holy hands above,
  Offering up on every shore
  Its pure sacrifice of love:
  Christ, our God, to Thee we raise
  This our sacrifice of praise.

80 *Hosanna: Blessed is the King of Israel that cometh in the name of the Lord.*—John xii. 13.   C.M.

1 HOSANNA! be the children's song
  To Christ, the children's King;
  His praise to whom their souls belong
  Let all the children sing.

2 Hosanna! sound from hill to hill,
  And spread from plain to plain;
  While louder, sweeter, clearer still,
  Woods echo to the strain.

3 Hosanna! on the wings of light,
  O'er earth and ocean fly;
  Till morn to eve, and noon to night,
  And heaven to earth reply.

4 Hosanna! then, our song shall be,
  Hosanna! to our King;
  This is the children's jubilee,
  Let all the children sing.

81 *Who being the brightness of His glory.*—Hebrews i. 3.   8 7.8 7.6.

1 MIGHTY God, while angels bless Thee,
  May an infant lisp Thy name?
  Lord of men as well as angels,
  Every creature speaks Thy fame.
  Alleluia, Amen!

2 Lord of every land and nation,
  Ancient of eternal days,
  Sounded through the wide creation
  Be Thy just and rightful praise.
  Alleluia, Amen!

3 For the providence that governs
  Through Thine empire's wide domain,
  Sovereign Lord of earth and heaven,
  Blessèd be Thy gentle reign!
  Alleluia, Amen!

4 Brightness of the Father's glory,
  Shall Thy praise unuttered be?
  Shun, my soul, such guilty silence;
  Sing the Lord who died for me!
  Alleluia, Amen!

5 Come, return, immortal Saviour;
  Come, Lord Jesus, take Thy throne:
  Quickly come, and reign for ever;
  Be the kingdom all Thine own!
  Alleluia, Amen!

82 *Blessing, and honour, and glory, and power, be unto Him that sitteth upon the throne.*—Revelation v. 13.
  7 7.7 7.

1 LET us sing with one accord
  Praise to Jesus Christ our Lord;
  He is worthy whom we praise,
  Hearts and voices let us raise.

17

2 He hath made us by His power,
He hath kept us to this hour,
He redeems us from the grave,
He who died now lives to save.

3 What He bids us let us do;
Where He leads us let us go;
As He loves us let us love
All below and all above.

4 Angels praise Him, so will we,
Sinful children though we be;
Poor and weak, we'll sing the more,
Jesus helps the weak and poor.

5 Dear to Him is childhood's prayer;
Children's hearts to Him are dear;
Hearts and voices let us raise,
He is worthy whom we praise.

*Thou art worthy, O Lord, to receive
glory and honour and power.*
83 Revelation iv. 11.   7 6.7 6.

1 GLORY and praise and honour
To Thee, Redeemer, King!
To whom the lips of children
Made sweet hosannas ring!

2 Thou art the King of Israel;
Thou David's royal Son;
Who in the Lord's name camest,
The King and blessèd One.

3 The company of angels
Are praising Thee on high;
And mortal men, and all things
Created, make reply.

4 The people of the Hebrews
With psalms before Thee went;
· Our praise and prayer and anthems
To Thee we now present.

5 Thou didst accept their praises;
Accept the prayers we bring,
Who in all good delightest,
Thou good and gracious King.

*Christ came, who is over all, God
blessed for ever. Amen.*
84 Romans ix. 5.   L.M.

1 OUR Saviour is the sovereign Lord,
Who rules all nature by His word,
Supreme in power, in love supreme,
And heaven and earth depend on Him.

2 He is the true, eternal Word,
By all heaven's glorious hosts adored;
And He, the Son of man, made known
In a frail body, like our own.

3 He is the hope of all mankind,
A balm for every wounded mind;
The only name to sinners given,
Their title and their way to heaven.

4 The Son of God, the Son of man,
Who was before the world began,
Who is, and evermore shall be,
Our God to all eternity.

5 To Him be honour and renown
Who bore the cross, and wears the crown,
The King immortal, God supreme,
Let heaven and earth bow down to Him.
18

*But unto the Son He saith, Thy throne,
O God, is for ever and ever.*
85 Hebrews i. 8.   8 8 7.8 8 7.

1 LORD Jesus Christ, our God and King!
This sacrifice of song we bring;
And Thy name we magnify!
Son of the Blessèd, Thee we praise,
Ancient of everlasting days,
Thee, O Christ, we glorify!

2 Blessèd and only Potentate,
Thee in our hymns we celebrate;
Son of God and Son of man;
True speaker of the gracious words,
Yet King of kings and Lord of lords,
Faithful and unchanging One!

3 Great First and Last, the Christ of God,
Of Jesse's stem the regal Rod,
Prince of life, and Prince of peace!
Great King of saints and King of kings,
Still night and day Thy Church Thee sings,
Never shall Thy glories cease.

4 Thee, Thee we hail, now seen afar,
Herald of day, fair Morning Star,
Light of life, creation's Sun,
Bright Dayspring of our clouded sky,
Rising in gladness from on high,
Glorious and unsetting Sun.

5 Heir of all things, creation's Head,
And first-begotten of the dead;
Thou whose dying now is o'er:
We praise Thee, with the Spirit one,
The Father's co-eternal Son,
Praise we give Thee evermore!

*Out of the mouth of babes and
sucklings Thou hast perfected
praise.*—Matthew xxi. 16.   6 5.6 5.
86

1 JESUS, high in glory,
. Lend a listening ear;
When we bow before Thee,
Children's praises hear.

2 Though Thou art so holy,
Heaven's almighty King,
Thou wilt stoop to listen
When Thy praise we sing.

3 We are little children,
Weak and apt to stray;
Saviour, guide and keep us
In the heavenly way.

4 Save us, Lord, from sinning;
Watch us day by day:
Help us now to love Thee;
Take our sins away.

5 Then, when Jesus calls us
To our heavenly home,
We would gladly answer,
Saviour, Lord, we come.

*For His mercy endureth for
ever.*—Psalm cvi. 1.   8 7.8 7.4 7.
87

1 PRAISE the Lord! for still He reigneth
High o'er kingdoms, thrones, and
powers;

He the whole world's course ordaineth ;
We are His, yet He is ours.
    Alleluia !
For His mercy aye endures.

2 He of old creation founded,
    Earth below and heaven above,
Built in truth, and well surrounded
    With His boundless, changeless love.
    Alleluia !
For His mercy aye endures.

3 Bow we low in adoration :
    Us from endless woe to save,
He, the Lord of all creation,
    Chose the manger, cross, and grave.
    Alleluia !
For His mercy aye endures.

4 Lord of life, He lives for ever :
    Free to all His love extends ;
Us He shows His choicest favour,
    Calls us children, calls us friends.
    Alleluia !
For His mercy aye endures.

5 Wrath of man or rage of devil
    Shall not cause His work to fail ;
God is love, and o'er all evil
    He shall in the end prevail.
    Alleluia !
For His mercy aye endures.

6 Yield we Him our hearts' devotion ;
    Be His name alone adored ;
Sun and stars and earth and ocean,
    Men and angels, praise the Lord !
    Alleluia !
For His mercy aye endures.

For His great love wherewith He loved
88 *us.*—Ephesians ii. 4.
            8 7.8 7.7 7.3.

1 SAVIOUR, for Thy love we praise Thee,
    Love that brought Thee down to earth;
Like the angels we would praise Thee,
    Singing welcome at Thy birth ;
    Let Thy star, through all our gloom,
    Guide us to Thy manger home.
    Praise the Lord !

2 Saviour, for Thy life we praise Thee,
    Life that brings us from the dead :
Like the children we would praise Thee,
    Lay Thine hands upon our head.
    Call us, as Thou didst of old,
    Little lambs into Thy fold.
    Praise the Lord !

3 Saviour, for Thy death we praise Thee,
    Death that is our hope of life ;
Like the ransomed we would praise Thee,
    Who have passed beyond the strife.
    Wash us in Thy cleansing blood,
    Make us kings and priests to God.
    Praise the Lord !

4 Saviour, for Thy love we praise Thee.
    Love that lifts us up to Thee ;
With the angels let us praise Thee,
    Joining in their minstrelsy ;
    All our love for ever telling,
    And the mighty chorus swelling.
    Praise the Lord !

I will confess to Thee, . . . and sing
89 *unto Thy name.*—Romans xv. 9.
                     C.M.

1 THERE is a name I love to hear,
    I love to speak its worth ;
It sounds like music in my ear,
    The sweetest name on earth.

2 It tells me of a Saviour's love,
    Who died to set me free !
It tells me of His precious blood,
    The sinner's perfect plea.

3 It tells of One whose loving heart
    Can feel my deepest woe ;
Who in my sorrow bears a part
    That none can bear below.

4 It bids my trembling heart rejoice,
    It dries each rising tear ;
It tells me in a 'still small voice'
    To trust and never fear.

5 Jesus, the name I love so well,
    The name I love to hear !
No saint on earth its worth can tell,
    No heart conceive how dear !

And they sung a new song,
90 *saying, Thou art worthy.*
    Revelation v. 9.   6 6.6 6.8 8.

1 SHALL hymns of grateful love
    Through heaven's high arches ring,
And all the hosts above
    Their songs of triumph sing ;
And shall not we take up the strain,
And send the echo back again ?

2 Shall every ransomed tribe
    Of Adam's scattered race,
To Christ all power ascribe,
    Who saved them by His grace ;
And shall not we take up the strain,
And send the echo back again ?

3 Shall they adore the Lord,
    Who bought them with His blood,
And all the love record
    That led them home to God ;
And shall not we take up the strain,
And send the echo back again ?

4 O spread the joyful sound,
    The Saviour's love proclaim,
And publish all around
    Salvation through His name,
Till the whole world take up the strain,
And send the echo back again.

A multitude of the heavenly host,
91 *praising God.*—Luke ii. 13.
                6 6.7 7.7 7 6.

1 THERE was joy in heaven !
    There was joy in heaven !
When this goodly world to frame
God in might and mercy came ;
Shouts of joy were heard on high,
And the stars sang from the sky—
'Glory to God in heaven !'

2 There was joy in heaven !
    There was joy in heaven !
When the billows, heaving dark,
Sank around the stranded ark,

19

And the rainbow's watery span
Spake of mercy, hope to man,
  And peace with God in heaven ! .

3 There was joy in heaven !
There was joy in heaven !
When of love the midnight beam
Shone on towers of Bethlehem ;
And along the echoing hill
Angels sang—'On earth goodwill,
  And glory in the heaven l'

For unto you is born . . . a Saviour,
which is Christ the Lord.
92   Luke ii. 11.   7 6.7 6.7 6.7 6.

1 I LOVE to hear the story
  Which angel-voices tell,·
How once the King of glory
  Came down on earth to dwell.
I am both weak and sinful,
  But this I surely know,
The Lord came down to save me
  Because He loved me so.

2 I'm glad my blessèd Saviour
  Was once a child like me,
To show how pure and holy
  His little ones might be ;
And if I try to follow
  His footsteps here below,
He never will forget me,
  Because He loves me so.

3 To sing His love and mercy,
  My sweetest songs I'll raise ;
And though I cannot see Him,
  I know He hears my praise :
For He has kindly promised
  That even I may go
To sing among His angels,
  Because He loves me so.

I love them that love Me ; and those
that seek Me early shall find
93   *Me.*—Proverbs viii. 17.   7 7.7 7.7 7.

1 HARK ! a still small voice is heard
  Gently speaking from above :
'Tis the great Redeemer's word,
  'Tis the message of His love.
Hear the call to you addressed,
Ye who would be truly blessed.

2 'Those who with devoted mind
  Seek in early life My face,
Shall My lasting favour find,
  And enjoy My richest grace.
Early, then, while yet I wait,
Seek Me, ere it be too late.'

3 Lord, we come, without delay ;
  We would love and seek Thee thus :
Jesus, now Thy love display,
  Saving, guiding, blessing us l
May we dwell with Thee above,
Ever happy in Thy love l

I will praise Thee for ever . . . and
I will wait on Thy name.
94   Psalm lii. 9.   6 6 6.6 6 6.

1 WHEN morning gilds the skies,
  My heart awaking cries,
    May Jesus Christ be praised.

20

Alike at work and prayer
To Jesus I repair ;
  May Jesus Christ be praised·

2 To Thee, O God above,
I cry with glowing love,
  May Jesus Christ be praised.
This song of sacred joy,
It never seems to cloy :
  May Jesus Christ be praised.

3 When sleep her balm denies,
My silent spirit sighs,
  May Jesus Christ be praised.
When evil thoughts molest,
With this I shield my breast,
  May Jesus Christ be praised.

4 Does sadness fill my mind?
A solace here I find,
  May Jesus Christ be praised.
Or fades my earthly bliss?
My comfort still is this,
  May Jesus Christ be praised.

5 Be this, when day is past,
Of all my thoughts the last,
  May Jesus Christ be praised.
The night becomes as day,
When from the heart we say,
  May Jesus Christ be praised.

6 The powers of darkness fear,
When this sweet chant they hear,
  May Jesus Christ be praised.
Let earth and sea and sky
From depth to height reply,
  May Jesus Christ be praised.

7 Be this, while life is mine,
My canticle divine,
  May Jesus Christ be praised.
Be this the eternal song
Through all the ages long,
  May Jesus Christ be praised.

The praises of Him who hath called
you.—1 Peter ii. 9.
95   6 5.6 5.6 5.6 5

1 SAVIOUR, blessèd Saviour !
  Listen while we sing,
Hearts and voices raising
  Praises to our King.
All we have to offer,
  All we hope to be,
Body, soul, and spirit,
  May we yield to Thee.

2 Nearer, ever nearer,
  Christ, we draw to Thee.
Deep in adoration
  Bending low the knee.
Thou, for our redemption,
  Cam'st on earth to die ;
Thou, that we might follow,
  Hast gone up on high.

3 Great and ever greater
  Are Thy mercies here ;
True and everlasting
  Are the glories there.

Where no pain or sorrow,
Toil or care is known,
Where the angel legions
Circle round Thy throne.

SECOND PART.

4 Clearer still, and clearer,
Dawns the light from heaven,
In our sadness bringing
News of sin forgiven;
Life has lost its shadows,
Pure the light within:
Thou hast shed Thy radiance
On a world of sin.

5 Onward, ever onward,
Journeying o'er the road
Worn by saints before us,
Journeying on to God;
Leaving all behind us,
May we hasten on,
Backward never looking
Till the prize is won.

6 Higher, then, and higher
Bear the ransomed soul,
Earthly toils forgotten,
Saviour, to its goal;
Where, in joys unthought of,
Saints with angels sing,
Never weary, raising
Praises to their King.

96 *The children of God by faith in Christ Jesus.*—Gal. iii. 26.   7 7 7.3.

1 COME, ye children, sweetly sing
Praises to your Saviour King;
Hearts and voices gladly bring;
Praise His name.

2 Jesus is the children's Friend,
Loving, faithful to the end;
Richest gifts from Him descend,
Joy and peace.

3 Once from heaven to earth He came,
Suffered death, contempt, and blame,
Died upon a cross of shame
Crowned with thorns.

4 'Twas our sinful souls to save
Thus His precious blood He gave:
Ransomed now from sin's dark grave,
We may sing.

5 O. what boundless grace and love,
All our highest thoughts above!
Fear and unbelief remove
At the cross.

6 Blessèd Jesus, loving, kind,
We would early seek and find:
And our souls in covenant bind,
Thine to be.

7 For our sins we deeply grieve,
But Thy promise we believe,
'Him that cometh I receive:'
Lord, we come.

97 *Ye are My friends, if ye do whatsoever I command you.* John xv. 14.   C.M.

1 THOU Guardian of our earliest days,
To Thee our prayers ascend;

To Thee we'll tune our songs of praise;
Jesus, the children's Friend.

2 From Thee our daily mercies flow,
Our life and health descend;
O save our souls from sin and woe!
Thou art the children's Friend.

3 Teach us to prize Thy holy Word,
And to its truths attend:
Thus shall we learn to fear the Lord,
And love the children's Friend.

4 O! may we feel a Saviour's love,
To Him our souls commend,
Who left His glorious throne above
To be the children's Friend.

5 Lord, draw our youthful hearts to Thee;
And when this life shall end,
Raise us to live above the sky
With Thee, the children's Friend.

98 *And to know the love of Christ, which passeth knowledge.* Ephesians iii. 19.   8 7.8 7.8 7.8 7.

1 LOVE Divine, all loves excelling,
Joy of heaven, to earth come down!
Fix in us Thy humble dwelling,
All Thy faithful mercies crown;
Jesu, Thou art all compassion,
Pure, unbounded love Thou art;
Visit us with Thy salvation,
Enter every trembling heart.

2 Come, almighty to deliver,
Let us all Thy grace receive:
Suddenly return, and never,
Never more, Thy temples leave;
Thee we would be always blessing,
Serve Thee as Thy hosts above,
Pray, and praise Thee, without ceasing,
Glory in Thy perfect love.

3 Finish then Thy new creation,
Pure and spotless let us be;
Let us see Thy great salvation,
Perfectly restored in Thee;
Changed from glory into glory,
Till in heaven we take our place,
Till we cast our crowns before Thee,
Lost in wonder, love, and praise!

99 *And worshipped Him: and ... presented unto Him gifts,* etc. Matthew ii. 11.   7 6.7 6.7 6.7 6.

1 WE bring no glittering treasures,
No gems from earth's deep mine;
We come, with simple measures
To chant Thy love divine.
Children, Thy favours sharing,
Their voice of thanks would raise;
Father, accept our offering,
Our song of grateful praise.

2 The dearest gift of Heaven,
Love's written word of truth,
To us is early given,
To guide our steps in youth.
We hear the wondrous story,
The tale of Calvary,
We read of homes in glory,
From sin and sorrow free.

3 Redeemer, grant Thy blessing ;
 O teach us how to pray !
That each, Thy fear possessing,
 May tread life's onward way.
Then where the pure are dwelling,
 We hope to meet again ;
And, sweeter numbers swelling,
 For ever praise Thy name.

Hearest Thou what these say ? And
100 *Jesus saith unto them, Yea.*
 Matthew xxi. 16. 8 7.8 7.8 7.

1 JESUS, Lord of life and glory,
 Friend of children, hear our lays ;
Humbly would our souls adore Thee,
 Sing Thy name in hymns of praise.
Jesus, Lord of life and glory,
 Friend of children, hear our lays.

2 Lo, what debtors to Thy kindness
 Are we. God of boundless love !
Thousands wander on in blindness,
 Strangers to the light above.
Jesus, Lord of life and glory,
 Friend of children, hear our lays.

3 Jesus, on Thine arm relying,
 We would tread this earthly vale ;
Be our life when we are dying,
 Be our strength when strength shall fail.
Jesus, Lord of life and glory,
 Friend of children, hear our lays.

4 Let us climb the hills of glory,
 Far from sins and woes and pains,
There in perfect songs adore Thee,
 And in everlasting strains.
Jesus, Lord of life and glory,
 Friend of children, hear our lays.

That at the name of Jesus every
101 *knee should bow, etc.*
 Philippians ii. 10. 6 5.6 5.6 5.6 5.

1 AT the name of Jesus
 Every knee shall bow,
Every tongue confess Him
 King of glory now.
'Tis the Father's pleasure
 We should call Him Lord,
Who from the beginning
 Was the mighty Word.

2 At His voice creation
 Sprang at once to sight,
All the angel faces,
 All the hosts of light,
Thrones and dominations,
 Stars upon their way,
All the heavenly orders
 In their great array.

3 Humbled for a season,
 To receive a name
From the lips of sinners
 Unto whom He came ;
Faithfully He bore it,
 Spotless to the last,
Brought it back victorious
 When from death He passed.

SECOND PART.

4 Name Him, brothers, name Him,
 With love strong as death,

But with awe and wonder,
 And with bated breath ;
He is God the Saviour,
 He is Christ the Lord,
Ever to be worshipped,
 Trusted, and adored.

5 In your hearts enthrone Him ;
 There let Him subdue
All that is not holy,
 All that is not true :
Crown Him as your Captain
 In temptation's hour ;
Let His will enfold you
 In its light and power.

6 Brothers, this Lord Jesus
 Shall return again,
With His Father's glory,
 With His angel train.
For all wreaths of empire
 Meet upon His brow,
And our hearts confess Him
 King of glory now.

The man Christ Jesus ; who gave
102 *Himself a ransom for all.*
 1 Timothy ii. 5, 6. 5 5.5 5.6 5.6 5.

1 LET children proclaim
 Their Saviour and King ;
To Jesu's great name
 Hosannas we sing :
Our best adoration
 To Jesus we give,
Who purchased salvation
 For us to receive.

2 The meek Lamb of God
 From heaven came down,
To ransom with blood,
 And make us His own :
And Him without ceasing
 We all shall proclaim,
And ever be blessing
 Our Jesu's great name.

3 To Him will we give
 Our earliest days,
And thankfully live
 To publish His praise :
Our lives shall confess Him
 Who came from above :
Our tongues ever bless Him,
 And tell of His love.

Alleluia : for the Lord God omni-
103 *potent reigneth.*
 Revelation xix. 6. 7 6.7 6.7 6.7 6.

1 COME, sing with holy gladness !
 High alleluias sing,
Uplift your loud hosannas
 To Jesus, Lord and King !
Sing, boys, in joyful chorus
 Your hymn of praise to-day,
And sing, ye gentle maidens,
 Your sweet responsive lay.

2 'Tis good for boys and maidens
 Sweet hymns to Christ to sing,
'Tis meet that children's voices
 Should praise the children's King :

For Jesus is salvation,
    And glory, grace, and rest ;
To babe and boy and maiden
    The one Redeemer blest.

3 O boys, be strong in Jesus !
    To toil for Him is gain,
And Jesus wrought with Joseph,
    With chisel, saw, and plane ;
O maidens, live for Jesus !
    Who was a maiden's Son ;
Be patient, pure, and gentle,
    And perfect grace begun.

*He took them up in His arms, put
His hands upon them, and blessed
them.—Mark x. 16.*

104
7 6.7 6.7 6.7 6.

1 COME, praise your Lord and Saviour
    In strains of holy mirth :
Give thanks to Him, O children,
    Who lived a Child on earth.
He loved the little children,
    And called them to His side,
His loving arms embraced them,
    And for their sake He died.

(Boys only.)

2 O Jesu, we would praise Thee
    With songs of holy joy,
For Thou on earth didst sojourn,
    A pure and spotless boy.
Make us, like Thee, obedient,
    Like Thee, from sin-stains free,
Like Thee in God's own temple,
    In lowly home like Thee.

(Girls only.)

3 O Jesu, we too praise Thee,
    The lowly maiden's Son :
In Thee all gentlest graces
    Are gathered into one ;
O ! give that best adornment
    That Christian maid can wear,
The meek and quiet spirit
    Which shone in Thee so fair.

(All.)

4 O Lord, with voices blended
    We sing our songs of praise :
Be Thou the light and pattern
    Of all our childhood's days :
And lead us ever onward.
    That, while we stay below,
We may like Thee, O Jesu,
    In grace and wisdom grow.

*For Thou, LORD, hast made me glad.
. . . I will triumph in the works
of Thy hands.—Psalm xcii. 4.*

105
8 6.8 6.8 6.8 6.6 6 6.8 8.

1 WE love to sing our Saviour's praise,
    To sing the wondrous love
Of Him who guards us all our days,
    And leads to heaven above.
For He is good ; the Lord is good,
    And kind are all His ways :
With songs and anthems sounding
    The Lord Jehovah praise.   [loud,

While the rocks and the rills,
    While the vales and the hills,
    A glorious anthem raise,
Let all prolong their grateful song,
    And the God of our fathers praise.

2 We love to sing of mercies given
    Through every passing year ;
We love to sing to Him in heaven
    With voices loud and clear :
For He is good ; the Lord is good, etc.

3 We love to think of Sabbath days,
    While in this sacred place
Our youthful hearts, in songs of praise,
    Have magnified God's grace :
For He is good ; the Lord is good, etc.

*Suffer the little children to come
unto Me.—Mark x. 14.*

106
7 6.7 6.7 6.7 6.

1 GOD who hath made the daisies,
    And every lovely thing,
He will accept our praises,
    And hearken while we sing.
He says though we are simple,
    Though ignorant we be,
Suffer the little children,
    And let them come to Me.

2 Though we are young and simple,
    In praise we may be bold,
The children in the temple
    He heard in days of old.
And if our hearts be humble,
    He says of you and me,
Suffer the little children,
    And let them come to Me.

3 He sees the bird that wingeth
    Its way o'er earth and sky,
He hears the lark that singeth
    Up in the heaven so high ;
Yet sees the heart's low breathing,
    And says, well pleased to see,
Suffer the little children,
    And let them come to Me.

4 Therefore we will come near Him,
    And solemnly we'll sing,
No cause to shrink or fear Him,
    We'll make our voices ring :
For in His temple speaking,
    He says of you and me,
Suffer the little children,
    And let them come to Me.

*And to know the love of Christ, which
passeth knowledge.
Ephesians iii. 19.*

107
8 4.8 4.8 8 8 4.

1 ONE there is above all others :
    O, how He loves !
His is love beyond a brother's :
    O, how He loves !
Earthly friends may fail or leave us,
One day soothe, the next day grieve us,
But this Friend will ne'er deceive us :
    O, how He loves !

2 'Tis eternal life to know Him :
    O, how He loves !
Think, O think how much we owe Him :
    O, how He loves !

With His precious blood He bought us,
In the wilderness He sought us,
To His fold He safely brought us :
  O, how He loves !

3 We have found a friend in Jesus :
  O, how He loves !
'Tis His great delight to bless us :
  O, how He loves !
How our hearts delight to hear Him
Bid us dwell in safety near Him !
Why should we distrust or fear Him ?
  O, how He loves !

4 Through His name we are forgiven :
  O, how He loves !
Backward shall our foes be driven :
  O, how He loves !
Best of blessings He'll provide us,
Nought but good shall e'er betide us,
Safe to glory He will guide us :
  O, how He loves !

*I have loved Thee with an everlasting
love.*—Jeremiah xxxi. 3.

108
                     87.87.77.

1 ONE there is above all others
    Well deserves the name of Friend ;
His is love beyond a brother's,
  Costly, free, and knows no end :
They who will His kindness prove
Find it everlasting love.

2 Which of all our friends to save us
  Could or would have shed his blood ?
Christ, the Saviour, died to have us
  Reconciled in Him to God :
This was boundless love, indeed !
Jesus is a Friend in need.

3 When He lived on earth abased,
  Friend of sinners was His name ;
Now above all glory raised,
  He rejoices in the same.
Still He calls them brethren, friends,
And to all their wants attends.

4 O for grace our hearts to soften !
  Teach us, Lord, at length to love ;
We, alas ! forget too often
  What a Friend we have above ;
But when home our souls are brought,
We will love Thee as we ought.

*My Refuge, my Saviour ; . . .
worthy to be praised.*
2 Samuel xxii. 3, 4.

109
                     9 9.9 9.

1 REST of the weary, joy of the sad ;
  Hope of the dreary, light of the glad ;
Home of the stranger, strength to the end ;
Refuge from danger, Saviour and Friend.

2 Pillow where lying, love rests its head ;
Peace of the dying, life of the dead ;
Path of the lowly, prize at the end ;
Bliss of the holy, Saviour and Friend.

3 When my feet stumble, to Thee I'll cry,
Crown of the humble, cross of the high ;
When my steps wander, over me bend,
Truer and fonder, Saviour and Friend.
24

4 Thee still confessing, ever I'll raise
Unto Thee blessing, glory, and praise ;
All my endeavour, world without end,
Thine to be ever, Saviour and Friend.

*He shall feed His flock like a
shepherd.*—Isaiah xl. 11.

110
                     8 7.8 7.4 7.

1 SAVIOUR, like a shepherd, lead us ;
    Much we need Thy tenderest care ;
In Thy pleasant pastures feed us,
  For our use Thy fold prepare :
    Blessèd Jesus,
Thou hast bought us, Thine we are !

2 Thou hast promised to receive us,
  Poor and sinful though we be :
Thou hast mercy to relieve us,
  Grace to cleanse, and power to free :
    Blessèd Jesus,
Early let us turn to Thee !

3 Early let us seek Thy favour,
  Early let us do Thy will ;
Blessèd Lord and only Saviour,
  With Thy joy our bosoms fill :
    Blessèd Jesus,
Thou hast loved us ; love us still !

*He shall gather the lambs with His
arm, and carry them in His
bosom.*—Isaiah xl. 11.

111
                     C.M.

1 SEE Israel's gentle Shepherd stand
    With all-engaging charms :
Hark ! how He calls the tender lambs !
And folds them in His arms.

2 ' Permit them to approach,' He cries,
  ' Nor scorn their humble name :'
For 'twas to bless such souls as these
The Lord of angels came.

3 He'll lead us to the heavenly streams,
  Where living waters flow ;
And guide us to the fruitful fields,
Where trees of knowledge grow.

4 The feeblest lamb amidst the flock
  Shall be its Shepherd's care ;
While folded in the Saviour's arms
We're safe from every snare.

*I am the good Shepherd : the good
Shepherd giveth His life for
the sheep.*—John x. 11.

112
                     8 7.8 7.

1 WAS there ever kindest shepherd
    Half so gentle, half so sweet
As the Saviour, who would have us
Come and gather round His feet ?

2 There is welcome for the sinner ;
  There are graces for the good ;
There is mercy with the Saviour ;
  There is healing in His blood ;

3 There is plentiful redemption
  In the blood that has been shed ;
There is joy for all the members
  In the sorrows of the Head.

4 For the love of God is broader
  Than the measures of man's mind,
And the heart of the Eternal
  Is most wonderfully kind.

5 If our love were but more simple,
We should take Him at His word,
And our lives would be all sunshine
In the sweetness of our Lord.

He maketh me to lie down in green
113 *pastures.*—Psalm xxiii. 2.
87.87.

1 SAVIOUR, who Thy flock art feeding
With the Shepherd's kindest care,
All the feeble gently leading,
While the lambs Thy bosom share,

2 Now these little ones receiving,
Fold them in Thy gracious arm,
There we know, Thy word believing,
They are all secure from harm !

3 Never from Thy pasture roving,
Let them be the lion's prey;
Let Thy tenderness so loving
Keep them all life's dangerous way.

4 Then within Thy fold eternal
Let them find a resting-place,
Feed in pastures ever vernal,
Drink the rivers of Thy grace !

He . . . shall lead them, even by the
114 *springs of water shall He guide*
them.—Isaiah xlix. 10. C.M.

1 SHEPHERD of Israel, from above
Thy feeble flock behold ;
And let us never lose Thy love,
Nor wander from Thy fold.

2 Thou wilt not cast Thy lambs away ;
Thy hand is ever near,
To guide them lest they go astray,
And keep them safe from fear.

3 Thy tender care supports the weak,
And will not let them fall ;
Then teach us, Lord, Thy praise to speak,
And on Thy name to call !

4 We want Thy help, for we are frail ;
Thy light, for we are blind ;
Let grace o'er all our doubts prevail,
To prove that Thou art kind.

5 Teach us the things we ought to know ;
And may we find them true ;
And still in stature as we grow
Increase in wisdom too.

6 Guide us through life ; and when at last
We enter into rest,
Thy tender arms around us cast,
And fold us to Thy breast !

115 *The LORD is my Shepherd.*
Psalm xxiii. 1. 87.87.87.

1 GRACIOUS Saviour, gentle Shepherd,
Little ones are dear to Thee :
Gathered with Thine arms, and carried
In Thy bosom may we be;
Sweetly, fondly, safely tended,
From all want and danger free.

2 Tender Shepherd, never leave us,
From Thy fold to go astray ;
By Thy look of love directed,
May we walk the narrow way ;
Thus direct us, and protect us,
Lest we fall an easy prey.

3 Let Thy holy word instruct us ;
Fill our minds with heavenly light ;
Let Thy love and grace constrain us
To approve whate'er is right ;
Let us feel Thy yoke is easy ;
Let us prove Thy burden light.

4 Taught to lisp the holy praises
Which on earth Thy children sing,
Both with lips and hearts unfeigned
Glad thank-offerings may we bring ;
Then with all the saints in glory
Join to praise our Lord and King.

116 *He restoreth my soul.*
Psalm xxiii. 3. 77.77.77.77.

1 HAPPY soul that free from harms
Rests within his Shepherd's arms;
Who his quiet shall molest ?
Who shall violate his rest ?
Jesus doth his spirit bear,
Jesus takes his every care ;
He who found the wandering sheep,
Jesus still delights to keep.

2 O that I might so believe,
Stedfastly to Jesus cleave,
On His only love rely,
Smile at the destroyer nigh ;
Free from sin and servile fear,
Have my Jesus ever near,
All His care rejoice to prove,
All His paradise of love !

3 Jesus, seek Thy wandering sh
Bring me back, and lead, and keep ;
Take on Thee my every care,
Bear me, on Thy bosom bear :
Let me know my Shepherd's voice,
More and more in Thee rejoice,
More and more of Thee receive,
Ever in Thy Spirit live !

4 Live till all Thy life I know,
Perfect through my Lord below,
Gladly then from earth remove,
Gathered to the fold above.
O that I at last may stand
With the sheep at Thy right hand,
Take the crown so freely given,
Enter in by Thee to heaven !

117 *And rejoice in Christ Jesus.*
Philippians iii. 3. 11 11.13 13.

1 REJOICE and be glad ! the Redeemer
has come !
Go look on His cradle, His cross, and His
tomb !
Sound His praises, tell the story of Him
who was slain :
Sound His praises, tell with gladness He
liveth again.

2 Rejoice and be glad ! it is sunshine at last,
The clouds have departed, the shadows are
Sound His praises, etc. [past.

3 Rejoice and be glad! for the blood hath
been shed ;
Redemption is finished, the price hath
Sound His praises, etc. [been paid.

4 Rejoice and be glad! now the pardon is free!
The Just for the unjust has died on the tree.
Sound His praises, etc.

25

5 Rejoice and be glad! for the Lamb that
was slain
O'er death is triumphant, and liveth again.
Sound His praises, etc.

6 Rejoice and be glad! for our King is on high,
He pleadeth for us on His throne in the sky.
Sound His praises, etc.

7 Rejoice and be glad! for He cometh again:
He cometh in glory, the Lamb that was
Sound His praises, etc.   [slain.

For unto you is born this day in the
118 *city of David a Saviour.*
Luke ii. 11.   C.M.

1 HARK the glad sound! the Saviour
The Saviour promised long: [comes!
Let every heart prepare a throne,
And every voice a song.

2 He comes the prisoners to release
In Satan's bondage held;
The gates of brass before Him burst,
The iron fetters yield.

3 He comes the broken heart to bind,
The bleeding soul to cure,
And with the treasures of His grace
To enrich the humble poor.

4 Our glad hosannas, Prince of peace,
Thy welcome shall proclaim,
And heaven's eternal arches ring
With Thy belovèd name.

INCARNATION.

Behold, I bring you good tidings of
119 *great joy.—Luke ii. 10.*
10 10.10 10.10 10.

1 CHRISTIANS, awake, salute the happy
morn
Whereon the Saviour of mankind was
Rise to adore the mystery of love, [born;
Which hosts of angels chanted from above;
With them the joyful tidings first begun
Of God incarnate and the virgin's Son.

2 Then to the watchful shepherds it was told,
Who heard the angelic herald's voice: 'Be-
hold,
I bring good tidings of a Saviour's birth
To you and all the nations upon earth;
This day hath God fulfilled His promised
word,
This day is born a Saviour, Christ the Lord.'

3 He spake; and straightway the celestial
choir
In hymns of joy, unknown before, conspire;
The praises of redeeming love they sang,
And heaven's whole orb with alleluias rang;
God's highest glory was their anthem still,
Peace upon earth, and unto men goodwill.

4 To Bethlehem straight the enlightened
shepherds ran,   [man:
To see the wonders God had wrought for
Then to their flocks, still praising God,
return,
And their glad hearts with holy rapture
burn;
26

Amazed, the wondrous tidings they proclaim,
The first apostles of His infant fame.

5 O! may we keep and ponder in our mind
God's wondrous love in saving lost man-
kind;
Trace we the Babe, who hath retrieved
our loss,
From the poor manger to the bitter cross;
Tread in His steps, assisted by His grace,
Till man's first heavenly state again takes
place.

6 Then may we hope, the angelic hosts
among,
To join, redeemed, a glad, triumphant
throng;
He that was born upon this joyful day
Around us all His glory shall display;
Saved by His love, incessant we shall sing
Eternal praise to heaven's almighty King.

Glory to God in the highest, and on
120 *earth peace, goodwill toward*
men.—Luke ii. 14.   7 7.7 7.

1 HARK! the herald angels sing,
'Glory to the new-born King!
Peace on earth and mercy mild,
God and sinners reconciled!'

2 Christ, by highest heaven adored,
Christ, the everlasting Lord,
Late in time behold Him come,
Offspring of a virgin's womb!

3 Veiled in flesh the Godhead see;
Hail the incarnate Deity!
Pleased as man with men to appear,
Jesus our Immanuel here.

4 Hail the heaven-born Prince of peace!
Hail! the Sun of righteousness!
Light and life to all He brings,
Risen with healing in His wings.

5 Mild He lays His glory by,
Born that man no more may die,
Born to raise the sons of earth,
Born to give them second birth.

6 Come, Desire of nations, come,
Fix in us Thy humble home;
Rise, the woman's conquering Seed,
Bruise in us the serpent's head.

7 Adam's likeness now efface,
Stamp Thine image in its place:
Second Adam from above,
Reinstate us in Thy love.

There were ... shepherds ... keeping
121 *watch over their flock by night.*
Luke ii. 8.   D.C.M.

1 WHILE shepherds watched their flocks
All seated on the ground, [by night,
The angel of the Lord came down,
And glory shone around.
'Fear not!' said he, for mighty dread
Had seized their troubled mind;
'Glad tidings of great joy I bring
To you and all mankind.

2 'To you, in David's town, this day
Is born, of David's line,
The Saviour, who is Christ the Lord;
And this shall be the sign:

The heavenly Babe you there shall find
To human view displayed,
All meanly wrapped in swaddling bands,
And in a manger laid.'

3 Thus spake the seraph ; and forthwith
Appeared a shining throng
Of angels praising God, and thus
Addressed their joyful song :
' All glory be to God on high,
And to the earth be peace ;
Goodwill henceforth from heaven to men
Begin and never cease.'

122 *A Saviour, which is Christ the Lord.*—Luke ii. 11.　D.C.M.

1 HARK, hark ! the merry Christmas bells
Are chiming sweet and clear ;
O welcome, welcome, festive day,
The brightest of the year.
Chime on, for Christ the Lord has come;
Ring out o'er hills and dells ;
Chime on a glad and grateful peal,
Ye merry Christmas bells.

2 Let every living creature wake,
And hail His glorious birth,
Who came from heaven, the Prince of
To bring glad news to earth.　[peace,
Chime on, etc.

3 All glory be to God on high,
Let every soul proclaim ;
Goodwill and peace to man below,
Through Christ our Saviour's name !
Chime on, etc.

123 *And suddenly there was with the angel a multitude of the heavenly host.*—Luke ii. 13.　87.87.

1 HARK ! what mean those holy voices
Sweetly sounding through the skies?
Lo ! the angelic host rejoices :
Heavenly alleluias rise.

2 Listen to the wondrous story
Which they chant in hymns of joy ;
Glory, in the highest, glory !
Glory be to God most high !

3 Christ is born, the great Anointed ;
Heaven and earth His praises sing ;
Him receive whom God appointed
For your Prophet, Priest, and King !

4 Hasten, mortals, to adore Him,
Learn His name and taste His joy,
Till in heaven ye sing before Him,
' Glory be to God most high !'

124 *For unto us a Child is born, unto us a Son is given.*—Isaiah ix. 6.
D.C.M. WITH CHORUS.

1 RING, ring the bells, the joyful bells.
This merry Christmas morn !
Their sweet, melodious music tells
The day that Christ was born.
Sweetly they sound o'er vale and glen ;
Hark ! how their music swells
With ' Peace on earth, goodwill to men !'
O merry Christmas bells !　[bells,
Ring, ring the bells, the Christmas
The bells, the merry, merry Christmas
bells ;
Ring, ring the merry Christmas bells !

2 Ring, ring the bells, the Christmas bells !
For in their joyous chime
Once more on earth the chorus swells
Of angel song sublime.
The sweet old story, ever new,
Falls on the heart again,
Refreshing as the early dew
Or the soft summer rain.
Ring, ring, etc.

3 Ring, ring the bells, the Christmas bells !
Prophetic of the day
When He of whom their music tells
Shall all the nations sway ;
Shall bless and fill and rule each heart,
Shall bid all sorrows cease,
And give His own the better part
Of everlasting peace.
Ring, ring, etc.

125 *And there were in the same country shepherds abiding in the field,* etc.—Luke ii. 8.　86.887.9.7.888.

1 BY night on wild Judæa's plain,
Two thousand years ago,
Shepherds their wakeful vigils kept
O'er gathered flocks that round them slept,
As the stars were fading slow.
And the angels sang a Christmas lay
At the great Redeemer's birth :
' Glad tidings to the earth we bring,
Glad tidings from the Saviour-king,
Of peace and goodwill on the earth

2 Silence around them threw its spell,
And peace fell on the hour ;
When sudden light that filled the plain
Fell from the clouds like silver rain,
Or a sunset's golden shower.　[etc.
And the angels sang a Christmas lay.

3 To their bewildered sight appeared
A vision wondrous fair,
Of angel forms from out the clouds,
And angel voices hymning loud
Till their music filled the air.　[etc.
And the angels sang a Christmas lay.

4 ' In manger rude, His form enwrapped
In guise of lowliest birth,
You'll find Messiah, Christ the Lord,
Lo ! 'tis foretold in prophet-word ;
He shall bring sweet peace on earth.'
And the angels sang a Christmas lay,
etc.

126 *Let us now go even unto Bethlehem, and see this thing which is come to pass.*—Luke ii. 15.　IRREGULAR.

1 O COME, all ye faithful,
Joyful and triumphant ;
O come ye, O come ye to Bethlehem ;
Come, and behold Him
Born, the King of angels ;
O come, let us adore Him, Christ the Lord.

2 God of God,
Light of light ;
Lo ! He abhors not the virgin's womb ;
Very God,
Begotten, not created ;
O come, let us adore Him, Christ the Lord.

3 Sing, choirs of angels,
　Sing in exultation,
Sing, all ye citizens of heaven above,
　‘Glory to God
　　In the highest:’
O come, let us adore Him, Christ the Lord.

4 Yea, Lord, we greet Thee,
　Born this happy morning;
Jesu, to Thee be glory given:
　Word of the Father,
　　Now in flesh appearing;
O come, let us adore Him, Christ the Lord.

And she brought forth her firstborn
127 *Son, . . . and laid Him in a*
manger.—Luke ii. 7.　　8 6 6.8 6 6.

1 ALL my heart this night rejoices
　As I hear, far and near,
　　Sweetest angel voices;
‘Christ is born!’ their choirs are singing,
　Till the air, everywhere,
　　Now with joy is ringing.

2 Hark! a voice from yonder manger,
　Soft and sweet, doth entreat:
　　‘Flee from woe and danger;
Brethren, come: from all doth grieve you
　You are freed; all you need
　　I will surely give you.’

3 Come then, let us hasten yonder;
　Here let all, great and small,
　　Kneel in awe and wonder.
Love Him who with love is yearning;
　Hail the Star that from far
　　Bright with hope is burning.

4 Ye who pine in weary sadness,
　Weep no more, for the door
　　Now is found of gladness.
Cling to Him, for He will guide you
　Where no cross, pain, or loss
　　Can again betide you.

5 Thee, O Lord, with heed I'll cherish,
　Live to Thee, and with Thee
　　Dying, shall not perish,
But shall dwell with Thee for ever,
　Far on high, in the joy
　　That can alter never.

And let all the angels of God wor-
128 *ship Him.*—Hebrews i. 6.
8 7.8 7.4 7.

1 ANGELS from the realms of glory,
　Wing your flight o'er all the earth;
Ye who sang creation's story,
　Now proclaim Messiah's birth:
　　Come, and worship,
　Worship Christ, the new-born King.

2 Shepherds in the fields abiding,
　Watching o'er your flock by night,
God with man is now residing;
　Yonder shines the infant Light:
　　Come, and worship,
　Worship Christ, the new-born King.

3 Children, now your praises bringing,
　Lift your gladsome voices high;
Round the manger join in singing,
　‘Christ was born for us to die:’
　　Come, and worship,
　Worship Christ, the new-born King.

28

For unto you is born this day a
Saviour, which is Christ the
129 *Lord.*—Luke ii. 11.
7 5.7 7 7 5.7 7.8 5.

1 BLOW, ye golden trumpets, blow!
　Let the sleeping nations know
　　Christ the Lord is born.
Yonder see the Bethlehem star,
Guiding mortals from afar;
Peace shall reign for evermore,
　　Christ the Lord is born.
　　Alleluia! praise the Lord!
　　'Tis the blessèd Christmas morn;
　　Alleluia! alleluia!
　　　Christ the Lord is born!

2 Ring, O ring, ye silvery bells!
Far and near your cadence swells,
　　Christ the Lord is born.
Ring, and banish doubt and fear,
Ring, till all with joy shall hear
Sin is vanquished, victory's near,
　Christ the Lord is born. Alleluia! etc.

And, lo, the star, which they saw in
130 *the East, went before them.*
Matthew ii. 9.　11 10.11 10.

1 BRIGHTEST and best of the sons of the
　　morning,
　Dawn on our darkness, and lend us thine
Star of the East, the horizon adorning, [aid:
　Guide where our infant Redeemer is laid!

2 Cold on His cradle the dewdrops are
　　shining;　　　　　　　[stall;
　Low lies His head with the beasts of the
Angels adore Him in slumber reclining,
　Maker and Monarch and Saviour of all.

3 Say, shall we yield Him in costly devotion
　Odours of Edom and offerings divine,
Gems of the mountain, and pearls of the
　　ocean,
　Myrrh from the forest, or gold from the
　　mine?

4 Vainly we offer each ample oblation, [cure;
　Vainly with gifts would His favour se-
Richer by far is the heart's adoration,
　Dearer to God are the prayers of the poor.

5 Brightest and best of the sons of the morn-
　　ing,　　　　　　　　　[aid:
　Dawn on our darkness, and lend us thine
Star of the East, the horizon adorning,
　Guide where our infant Redeemer is laid!

And they . . . found . . . the Babe
131 *lying in a manger.*
Luke ii. 16.　8 7.8 7.8 7.

1 CRADLED in a manger, meanly
　Laid the Son of man His head;
Sleeping His first earthly slumber
　Where the oxen had been fed.
Happy were those shepherds listening
　To the holy angel's word!
Happy they, within that stable,
　Worshipping their infant Lord!

2 Happy all who hear the message
　Of His coming from above!
Happier still who hail His coming,
　And with praises greet His love!

Blessèd Saviour, Christ most holy !
  In a manger Thou didst rest :
Canst Thou stoop again, yet lower,
  And abide within my breast?

3 Evil things are there before Thee :
  In the heart, where they have fed,
Wilt Thou pitifully enter, .
  Son of man, and lay Thy head?
Enter then, O Christ most holy ;
  Make a Christmas in my heart ;
Make a heaven of my manger :
  It is heaven where Thou art.

4 And to those who never listened
  To the message of Thy birth,
Who have winter, but no Christmas
  Bringing them Thy 'peace on earth,'
Send to these the joyful tidings :
  By all people, in each home,
Be there heard the Christmas anthem,
  'Praise to God, the Christ has come !'

For we have seen His star in the East,
132 *and are come to worship Him.*
    Matthew ii. 2.   6 5.6 5.6 5.6 5.

1 IN the wintry heaven
  Shines a wondrous star ;
In the East the wise men
  Watched it from afar ;
Asking, 'What this lustre,
  So unearthly bright?'
Answering, 'Christ in glory
  Comes to earth to-night !'

2 O'er the dusty highway,
  O'er the deserts drear,
From the East, the wise men
  Watch it shining clear ;
Asking, 'Shall we follow
  In this starlit way?'
Answering, 'Yes ; 'twill lead us
  To the perfect day.'

3 In a lowly manger
  Lies an Infant weak ;
Is it He whom wise men
  Come so far to seek?
Asking, 'Where the Monarch? '
  Where Judæa's King?'
Saying, 'Gifts and worship
  To His throne we bring'?

4 In our hearts we children
  See this star once more :
Not as wise men saw it,
  In the days of yore ;
Asking, 'May we bring Him
  Childhood's love to-day?'
Answering, 'Come, dear children ;
  Jesus says we may.'

And laid Him in a manger : because
133 *there was no room for them in*
    the inn.—Luke ii. 7. 8 7.8 7.7 7.

1 ONCE in royal David's city
  Stood a lowly cattle shed,
Where a mother laid her Baby,
  In a manger for His bed.
Mary was that mother mild,
Jesus Christ her little Child.
B

2 He came down to earth from heaven,
  Who is God and Lord of all,
And His shelter was a stable,
  And His cradle was a stall :
With the poor and mean and lowly
Lived on earth our Saviour holy.

3 And through all His wondrous childhood
  He would honour, and obey,
Love, and watch the lowly maiden
  In whose gentle arms He lay.
Christian children all must be
Mild, obedient, good as He.

4 For He is our childhood's pattern ;
  Day by day like us He grew ;
He was little, weak, and helpless,
Tears and smiles like us He knew :
  And He feeleth for our sadness,
  And He shareth in our gladness.

5 And our eyes at last shall see Him,
  Through His own redeeming love,
For that Child, so dear and gentle,
  Is our Lord in heaven above ;
  And He leads His children on
  To the place where He is gone.

They made known abroad the saying
which was told them concerning
134 *this Child.*—Luke ii. 17.
    IRREGULAR.

1 THERE came a little Child to earth
  Long ago ;
And the angels of God proclaimed His birth
  High and low.

2 Out in the night, so calm and still,
  Their song was heard ;
For they knew that the Child on Bethlehem's
  Was Christ the Lord.   [hill

3 Far away in a goodly land,
  Fair and bright,
Children with crowns of glory stand,
  Robed in white.

4 They sing, the Lord of heaven so fair
  A Child was born ;
And that they might His crown of glory
  Wore crown of thorn.   [share.

5 In mortal weakness, want, and pain,
  He came to die,
That the children of earth might in glory
  With Him on high.   [reign

6 And evermore in robes so fair
  And undefiled,
Those ransomed children His praise declare
  Who was a Child.

Then took he Him up in his arms,
135 *and blessed God.*—Luke ii. 28.
    D.L.M.

1 HUSHED is the raging winter wild,
  And earth's ten thousand voices sing
As if to greet the holy Child,
  Whom to the temple courts they bring.
The flowers breathe their incense sweet,
  And spread themselves along His way ;
The birds pour forth their raptures meet,
  The gentle winds their homage pay.

2 Still lingering at the temple gates,
  With patient hope that cannot die,
The hoary Simeon daily waits,—
  He to the lowly group draws nigh.
With awe he finds the infant Lord,
  With trembling joy folds to his heart :
'Be it according to Thy word,
  And now in peace let me depart.'

3 Help us, O Lord, that we may seek,
  And to Thy temple Thou wilt come ;
The heart made lowly, pure, and meek
  Is that which Thou wilt make Thy home.
For arms that brought us to the Lord
  For ever let our thanks be given ;
But most for Him, the holy Child,
  Through whom we enter into heaven.

When they saw the star, they rejoiced
136 *with exceeding great joy.*
  Matthew ii. 10.   7.7.7.7.7.7.

1.   with gladness men of old
As Did the guiding star behold ;
As with joy they hailed its light,
Leading onward, beaming bright :
So, most gracious God, may we
Evermore be led to Thee.

2 As with joyful steps they sped
To that lowly manger-bed,
There to bend the knee before
Him whom heaven and earth adore :
So may we, with willing feet,
Ever seek Thy mercy-seat.

3 As they offered gifts most rare
At that manger, rude and bare,
So may we with holy joy,
Pure and free from sin's alloy,
All our costliest treasures bring,
Christ, to Thee, our heavenly King.

4 Holy Jesus, every day
Keep us in the narrow way,
And, when earthly things are past,
Bring our ransomed souls at last
Where they need no star to guide,
Where no clouds Thy glory hide.

They saw the young Child, . . . and
137 *fell down and worshipped Him.*
  Matthew ii. 11.   8 6.8 6.8 8.

1 O'ER Bethlehem's hill, in time of old,
  Came wise men from afar,
Bringing their costly gifts of gold,
  For they had seen His star.
In princely pomp, with presents meet,
  They came to worship at His feet.

2 The silvery lamp through all the night
  Led on their eager way,
Until upon His lowly home
  Was shed its gentle ray ;
And there they found the infant King,
  And on the ground fell worshipping.

3 So, gracious Spirit, by Thy light
  Shine Thou upon our way,
To guide our feet to Christ the Lord,
  We would our homage pay ;
For He who is the children's King
  Will not disdain what children bring.

4 Not as wise men, in princely robes,
  With offerings rich and rare :
We come with empty hands, O Lord,
  Burdened with sin and care,
With hands that wrought Thy misery :
  And yet Thou bidd'st us come to Thee.

5 For gifts : we give ourselves to Thee,
  Our hearts shall be Thy throne ;
For gold : we give Thee all our love,
  Oh, make it all Thine own !
As incense sweet Thy praise we sing,
  And bless Thy name, our Saviour-king.

He took the young Child and His
  mother by night, and departed
138 *into Egypt.*—Matthew ii. 14.
      D.L.M.

1 THE fierce wind howls about the hills,
  Most angrily, most drearily ;
The stars shine out with brilliant light,
  All tremblingly, all frostily ;
The bird lies sheltered in its nest,
The fox creeps to his crafty rest,
And angels watch by children blest,
  All tenderly, all tenderly.

2 But who are these that through the night
  Move wearily, all drearily ?
'Tis Joseph, forth from Bethlehem,
  All hastily, all eagerly ;
For Herod seeks the Child to slay,
And death will come if they delay,
And forth ere ever break of day
  They thus must flee, to Egypt flee.

3 The mother screens Him at her breast,
  All carefully, all prayerfully :
She feels Him shivering in the blast,
  All fearfully, all tearfully ;
And so along their way they go,
Now numbed by night winds as they blow,
Now starting, fearful of the foe,
  All helplessly, all homelessly.

4 Had we been there, O gracious Lord,
  Most tenderly, most lovingly,
Our hands, our home, our all were given,
  To comfort Thee, to shelter Thee.
And we may still : for Thou hast said
When hungry little ones are fed,
And outcast ones find home and bed,
  'Tis done to Thee, as unto Thee.

And the Desire of all nations shall
139 *come.*—Haggai ii. 7.
      8 7.8 7.8 7.8 7.

1 COME, Thou long-expected Jesus,
  Born to set Thy people free,
From our fears and sins release us,
  Let us find our rest in Thee.
Israel's strength and consolation,
  Hope of all the earth Thou art ;
Dear Desire of every nation,
  Joy of every longing heart.

2 Born Thy people to deliver ;
  Born a child and yet a king,
Born to reign in us for ever,
  Now Thy gracious kingdom bring :
By Thine own eternal Spirit
  Rule in all our hearts alone ;
By Thine all-sufficient merit
  Raise us to Thy glorious throne.

LIFE.

140
*And He went down with them, and came
to Nazareth, and was subject
unto them.*—Luke ii. 51. C.M.

1 I LOVE to think, though I am young,
My Saviour was a child ;
That Jesus walked this earth along
With feet all undefiled.

2 He kept His Father's word of truth,
As I am taught to do ;
And while He walked the paths of youth
He walked in wisdom too.

3 I love to think that He who spake,
And made the blind to see,
And called the sleeping dead to wake,
Was once a child like me ;

4 That He who wore the thorny crown,
And tasted death's despair,
Had a kind mother like my own,
And knew her love and care.

5 I know 'twas all for love of me
That He became a child,
And left the heavens, so fair to see,
And trod earth's pathway wild.

6 Then, Saviour, who wast once a child,
A child may come to Thee ;
And O ! in all Thy mercy mild,
Dear Saviour, come to me.

141
*And Jesus increased in wisdom and
stature, and in favour with God
and man.*—Luke ii. 52. 6 5.6 5.

1 GENTLE, holy Jesus,
Saviour meek and mild,
Thou who once wast fashioned
Like a little child ;

2 And in grace and meekness
Up to manhood grew ;
Sharing human weakness,
Human sorrow too :

3 In Thy word so holy,
Saviour, we can see,
That of us Thou sayest,
'Let them come to Me.'

4 Glad we come ! and render
All we have to give :
While our hearts are tender,
Help us, Lord, to live

5 Like Thy young disciples,
That the world may see
We are taught by Jesus,
And have learned of Thee.

6 May we copy closely
Him we so much love,
Till we bear His likeness,
Perfected above.

142
*He took them up in His arms, put
His hands upon them, and blessed
them.*—Mark x. 16. C.M.

1 SING to the Lord the children's hymn,
His gentle love declare,
Who bends amid the seraphim
To hear the children's prayer.

2 He held us to His mighty breast,
The children of the earth ;
He lifted up His hands, and blessed
The babes of human birth.

3 So shall He be to us our God,
Our gracious Saviour too ;
The ways we tread His footsteps trod,
The paths of youth He knew.

4 Lo ! from the stars His face will turn
On us with glances mild,
The angels of His presence yearn
To bless the little child.

5 Keep us, O Jesu Lord, for Thee,
That so by Thy great grace,
We children of Thy Church may see
Our heavenly Father's face.

143
*The Son of man hath not where to
lay His head.*—Matthew viii. 20.
7 7.7 7.

1 CHRIST is merciful and mild ;
He was once a little child ;
He whom heavenly hosts adore
Lived on earth among the poor.

2 Thus He laid His glory by
When for us He stooped to die ;
How I wonder when I see
His unbounded love to me !

3 He the sick to health restored,
To the poor He preached the word ;
Even children had a share
Of His love and tender care.

4 Every bird can build its nest,
Foxes have their place of rest ;
He by whom the world was made
Had not where to lay His head.

5 He who is the Lord most high
Then was poorer far than I,
That I might hereafter be
Rich to all eternity.

144
*Being found in fashion as a man, He
humbled Himself, and became
obedient unto death.*
Philippians ii. 8. C.M.

1 AS to His earthly parents' home
Went down the holy child,
And found His Father's business there,
Subjection meek and mild ;

2 And as obedience all those years
In lowly Nazareth
Forsook Him not, but bore Him on,
Obedient unto death :

3 So by Thy mercies teach us, Lord,
Our sacrifice to bring,
Our treasure, heart, and life, and love,
To spread before our King.

4 Thy presence is our guiding star,
We seek Thy holy hill ;
Transform us, Lord, renew our minds,
To prove Thy perfect will.

145
He first loved us.—1 John iv. 19.
7 6.8 6.7 6.8 6.

1 WHEN they brought little children
To Jesus to be blessed,

He would not have them sent away,
But took them to His breast,
And with such love looked on them,
That every tender child,
Having no fear of that sweet face,
Held out its arms and smiled.

2 For Jesus loved the children,
And said they were to come,
And in His love find happiness,
And in His arms a home :
And then He, looking heavenwards,
Prayed for each little one,
That each the Father's grace might know
In answer to the Son.

3 Still Jesus loves the children,
And kindly calls them still
To Him, who suffered that He might
Redeem them from all ill.
And into His bright kingdom
He would the children bring,
To serve Him in the kingdom's work,
The kingdom's joy to sing.

4 Then surely all the children
Should bring their blithest songs,
And warmest love, their Lord to praise,
To whom all praise belongs.
For, see, the hands He stretches
To take the children in
Were nailed upon the dreadful cross,
The children's life to win.

5 Come, let us sing our worship
To Him who loves us thus,
And let us give our hearts to Him
Who gave Himself for us :
And then, if we are faithful,
His love, when death is past,
Will suffer us to come to Him,
And share His heaven at last.

*Suffer little children, and forbid them
not, to come unto Me.*
146 Matthew xix. 14.   7 7 7 5.

1 JESUS, when He left the sky
And for sinners came to die,
In His mercy passed not by
Little ones like me.

2 Mothers then the Saviour sought
In the places where He taught,
And to Him their children brought :
Little ones like me.

3 Did the Saviour say them nay?
No, He kindly bade them stay :
Suffered none to turn away
Little ones like me.

4 Children then should love Him too,
Strive His holy will to do,
Pray to Him, and praise Him too
Little ones like me.

*And Jesus called a little child unto
Him.*—Matthew xviii. 2.
147   11 8.11 9.11 9.11 9.

1 I THINK, when I read that sweet story of
When Jesus was here among men, [old,
How He called little children, as lambs to
His fold,
I should like to have been with them then.
32

I wish that His hands had been placed on
my head,
That His arm had been thrown around
me ;
And that I might have seen His kind look
when He said,
Let the little ones come unto **Me.**

2 Yet still to His footstool in prayer I may go,
And ask for a share in His love ;
And if I now earnestly seek Him below,
I shall see Him and hear Him above,
In that beautiful place He is gone to pre-
pare
For all that are washed and forgiven :
And many dear children are gathering
there,
For of such is the kingdom of heaven.

3 But thousands and thousands, who wander
and fall,
Never heard of that heavenly home ;
I should like them to know there is room
for them all,
And that Jesus has bid them to come.
I long for the joy of that glorious time,
The sweetest, the brightest, and best,
When the dear little children of every clime
Shall crowd to His arms and be blest.

Who went about doing good.
148 Acts x. 38.   S.M

1 BY Jacob's ancient well
Sat Jesus long ago ;
The water-bearer heard Him tell
Where living waters flow.

2 The beggar day by day
Sat in a hopeless night,
Until the Master passed that way,
And said, 'Receive thy sight.'

3 The Gentile mother craved
A crumb of healing power ;
The child for whom she prayed was saved
And healed that selfsame hour.

4 Beside Bethesda's pool
He to the palsied said,
Before he prayed to be made whole
'Rise, and take up thy bed.'

5 'O Lord, remember me,'
The dying robber cries ;
'This day,' saith Jesus, 'thou shalt be
With Me in paradise.'

*And they brought young children to
Him, that He should touch them:*
149 Mark x. 13.   6 7.8 6.8 8 11.*

1 WHEN mothers of Salem
Their children brought to Jesus,
The stern disciples drove them back,
And bade them to depart ;
But Jesus saw them ere they fled,
And sweetly smiled and kindly said,
'Suffer little children to come unto Me.

2 'For I will receive them,
And fold them in My bosom ;
I'll be a shepherd to these lambs,
O drive them not away ;
For if their hearts to Me they give,
They shall with Me in glory live :
Suffer little children to come unto Me.

3 How kind was our Saviour
  To bid those children welcome !
But there are many thousands who
  Have never heard His name ;
The Bible they have never read,
They know not that the Saviour said.
  'Suffer little children to come unto Me.'

4 O soon may the heathen
  Of every tribe and nation
Fulfil Thy blessèd word, and cast
  Their idols all away ;
O shine upon them from above,
And show Thyself a God of love,   [Thee.
  Teach the little children to come unto

150 *Even the winds and the sea obey*
      Him.—Matthew viii. 27   C.M.

1 A LITTLE ship was on the sea,
    It was a pretty sight ;
It sailed along so pleasantly,
  And all was calm and bright.

2 When, lo ! a storm began to rise,
  The wind grew loud and strong ;
It blew the clouds across the skies,
  It blew the waves along.

3 And all but One were sore afraid
  Of sinking in the deep ,
His head was on a pillow laid,
  And He was fast asleep

4 'Master, we perish ! Master, save !'
  They cried.   Their Master heard :
He rose, rebuked the wind and wave,
  And stilled them with a word.

5 He to the storm says, 'Peace : be still !'
  The raging billows cease ;
The mighty winds obey His will.
  And all are hushed to peace.

6 O ! well we know it was the Lord.
  Our Saviour and our friend ;
Whose care of those who trust His word
  Will never, never end.

151 *Hosanna to the Son of David !*
      Matthew xxi. 9.   7 6.7 6.7 6.7 6.

1 HOSANNA ! loud hosanna !
  The little children sang :
Through pillared court and temple
  The glorious anthem rang ; .
To Jesus who had blessed them,
  Close folded to His breast,
The children sang their praises,
  The simplest and the best.

2 From Olivet they followed,
  'Midst an exultant crowd,
Waving the victor palm branch,
  And shouting clear and loud ;
Bright angels joined the chorus
  Beyond the cloudless sky,
'Hosanna in the highest !
  Glory to God on high !'

3 Fair leaves of silvery olive
  They strewed upon the ground,
Whilst Salem's circling mountains
  Echoed the joyful sound :

The Lord of men and angels
  Rode on in lowly state,
Nor scorned that little children
  Should on His bidding wait.

4 'Hosanna in the highest !'
  That ancient song *we* sing :
For Christ is our Redeemer,
  The Lord of heaven our King.
O ! may we ever praise Him
  With heart and life and voice,
And in His blissful presence
  Eternally rejoice !

152 *Hosanna in the highest !*
      Matthew xxi. 9.   7 6.7 6.7 6.7 6.

1 WHEN, His salvation bringing,
    To Zion Jesus came,
The children all stood singing
  Hosanna to His name.
Nor did their zeal offend Him,
  But, as He rode along,
He let them still attend Him,
  Well pleased to hear their song.

2 And since the Lord retaineth
  His love for children still,
Though now as King He reigneth
  On Zion's heavenly hill,
We'll prostrate fall before Him,
  Who sits upon the throne,
And joyfully adore Him,
  David's triumphant Son.

3 For should we fail proclaiming
  Our great Redeemer's praise,
The stones, our silence shaming,
  Would their hosannas raise
Nor will we only render
  The tribute of our words,
But while our hearts are tender,
  They, too, shall be the Lord's.

153 *Out of the mouth of babes and sucklings*
      hast Thou ordained strength.
      Psalm viii. 2.   7 7.7 7.7 7.

1 CHILDREN of Jerusalem
    Sang the praise of Jesus' name ;
Children, too, of later days
Join to sing the Saviour's praise.
  Hark ! while youthful voices sing
  Loud hosannas to our King.

2 We have often heard and read
What the royal Psalmist said,
Babes and sucklings' artless lays
Shall proclaim the Saviour's praise.
  Hark ! while youthful voices sing
  Loud hosannas to our King.

3 We are taught to love the Lord ;
We are taught to read His word :
We are taught the way to heaven :
Praise for all to God be given !
  Hark ! while youthful voices sing
  Loud hosannas to our King

4 Parents, teachers, old and young,
All unite to swell the song :
Higher and yet higher rise,
Till hosannas reach the skies.
  Hark ! while youthful voices sing
  Loud hosannas to our King.

33

O give thanks unto the LORD, for He is good.—Psalm cxviii. 1.

154 11 11.11 11.*

1 HOSANNA we sing, like the children dear,
In the olden days when the Lord lived here;
He blessed little children, and smiled on them,
While they chanted His praise in Jerusalem.

2 Alleluia we sing, like the children bright,
With their harps of gold and their raiment white,
As they follow their Shepherd with loving eyes
Through the beautiful valleys of Paradise.

3 Hosanna we sing, for He bends His ear,
And rejoices the hymns of His own to hear;
We know that His heart will never wax cold
To the lambs that He feeds in His earthly fold.

4 Alleluia we sing in the Church we love,
Alleluia resounds in the Church above;
To Thy little ones, Lord, may such grace be given,
That we lose not our part in the song of heaven.

And Jesus increased in wisdom and ture, and in favour with ᴗ and man.—Luke ii. 52.   C.M.

155

1 WHEN Jesus left the throne of God,
He chose a humble birth ;
A man of grief, like us He trod
A lowly path on earth.

2 Like Him, may we be found below
In wisdom's paths of peace ;
Like Him, in grace and knowledge grow
As years and strength increase.

3 When Jesus into Salem rode,
The children sang around,
For joy they plucked the palms, and strewed
Their garments on the ground.

4 Hosanna ! our glad voices raise,
Hosanna to our King !
Could we forget our Saviour's praise,
The stones themselves would sing.

5 For we have learned to love His name,
That name, divinely sweet,
May every pulse through life proclaim,
And our last breath repeat.

The Son of man came not to be ministered unto, but to minister, and to give His life, etc.—Matt. xx. 28.   L.M.

156

1 JESUS, who lived above the sky,
Came down to be a man and die :
And in the Bible we may see
How very good He used to be.

2 He went about—He was so kind—
To cure poor people who were blind ;
And many who were sick and lame,
He pitied them, and did the same.

3 And more than that, He told them, too,
The things that God would have them do ;
And was so gentle and so mild,
He would have listened to a child.
34

4 But such a cruel death He died :
By wicked men was crucified !
And those kind hands that did such good,
They nailed them to a cross of wood !

5 And so He died : and this is why
He came to be a man and die ;
The Bible says He came from heaven,
That w· might have our sins forgiven.

6 He knew how wicked men had been,
He knew that God must punish sin ;
So out pity Jesus said
He'd bear the punishment instead.

Jesus wept.—John xi. 35.

157 8 7.8 7.7 7.

1 JESUS wept ! Those tears are over,
But His heart is still the same :
Kinsman, Friend, and elder Brother,
Is His everlasting name.
Saviour, who can love like Thee,
Gracious One of Bethany !

2 When the pangs of trial seize us,
When the waves of sorrow roll,
We will cast our griefs on Jesus,
Helper of the troubled soul.
Surely none can mourn like Thee,
Weeping One of Bethany.

3 Jesus wept ! And now, in glory,
He still marks each mourner's tear;
Loving to retrace the story
Of the hearts He strengthened here.
Jesus ! while Thou callest me,
Let me think of Bethany.

4 Jesus wept ! That tear of sorrow
Is a legacy of love ;
Yesterday, to-day, to-morrow
He the same doth ever prove.
Thou art all in all to me,
Loving One of Bethany.

Christ also suffered for us, leaving us an example.—1 Peter ii. 21.

158 11 11.11 11.

1 HOW kind is the Saviour ! how great is His love !
To bless little children He came from above;
He left holy angels and their bright abode,
To live here with children, and teach them the road.

2 He wept in the garden, and died on the tree,
To open a fountain for sinners like me ;
His blood is that fountain, which pardon bestows,
And cleanses the foulest wherever it flows.

3 He went back to glory, but left us His word,
Which oft from our teachers and pastors we've heard ;
He sends forth His Spirit our hearts to inflame
With joy in His service and love to His [name.

4 O, help us, blest Jesus, more sweetly to praise,
And walk in Thy footsteps the rest of our days ;
Then raise us, dear Saviour, to taste of Thy love,
And praise Thee for ever with children above.

Hear me when I call, O God of my righteousness.
Psalm iv. 1.   7 7 7.6.

159

1 JESUS, from Thy throne on high,
  Far above the bright blue sky,
Look on us with loving eye:
  Hear us, holy Jesus.

2 Little children need not fear
When they know that Thou art near;
Thou dost love us, Saviour dear: Hear, etc.

3 Little lambs may come to Thee,
Thou wilt fold us tenderly,
And our careful Shepherd be: Hear, etc.

4 Little hearts may love Thee well,
Little lips Thy love may tell,
Little hymns Thy praises swell: Hear, etc.

5 Little lives may be divine,
Little deeds of love may shine,
Little ones be wholly Thine: Hear, etc.

SECOND PART.

6 Jesus, once an infant small,
Cradled in the oxen's stall,
Though the God and Lord of all: Hear, etc.

7 Once a Child, so good and fair,
Feeling want and toil and care,
All that we may have to bear: Hear, etc.

8 Jesus, Thou dost love us still,
And it is Thy holy will
That we should be safe from ill: Hear, etc.

9 Be Thou with us every day,
In our work and in our play,
When we learn and when we pray:
  Hear, etc.

10 When we lie asleep at night,
Ever may Thy angels bright
Keep us safe till morning light: Hear, etc.

11 Make us brave without a fear,
Make us happy, full of cheer,
Sure that Thou art always near: Hear, etc.

THIRD PART.

12 May we prize our Christian name,
May we guard it free from blame,
Fearing all that causes shame: Hear, etc.

13 May we grow from day to day,
Glad to learn each holy way,
Ever ready to obey: Hear, etc.

14 May we ever try to be
From all sinful tempers free,
Pure and gentle, Lord, like Thee: Hear, etc.

15 May our thoughts be undefiled,
May our words be true and mild,
Make us each a holy child: Hear, etc.

16 Jesus, Son of God most high,
Who didst in a manger lie,
Who upon the cross didst die: Hear, etc.

17 Jesus, from Thy heavenly throne
Watching o'er each little one,
Till our life on earth is done: Hear, etc.

18 Jesus, whom we hope to see
Calling us in heaven to be
Happy evermore with Thee: Hear, etc.

CRUCIFIXION.

Behold the Lamb of God!
John i. 36.   C.M.

160

1 BEHOLD the Saviour of mankind
  Nailed to the shameful tree!
How vast the love that Him inclined
  To bleed and die for thee!

2 Hark, how He groans! while nature shakes,
And earth's strong pillars bend;
The temple's veil in sunder breaks,
The solid marbles rend.

3 'Tis done! the precious ransom's paid.
'Receive My soul,' He cries!
See where He bows His sacred head!
He bows His head, and dies!

4 But soon He'll break death's envious chain,
And in full glory shine;
O Lamb of God! was ever pain,
Was ever love, like Thine?

Ye who . . . were far off are made nigh by the blood of Christ.
Ephesians ii. 13.   7 7.77.77.

161

1 LO! at noon 'tis sudden night;
  Darkness covers all the sky:
Rocks are rending at the sight!
Children, can you tell me why?
What can all these wonders be?—
Jesus dies on Calvary!

2 Nailed upon the cross, behold
How His tender limbs are torn;
For a royal crown of gold
They have made Him one of thorn!
Cruel hands that dare to bind
Thorns upon a brow so kind!

3 See, the blood is falling fast
From His forehead and His side!
Hark! He now has breathed His last;
With a mighty cry He died!
Children, shall I tell you why
Jesus condescends to die?

4 You were wretched, weak, and vile,
You deserved His holy frown;
But He saw you with a smile,
And to save you hastened down.
Listen, children: this is why
Jesus condescends to die.

But God forbid that I should glory, save in the cross of our Lord Jesus Christ.—Gal. vi. 14.   L.M.

162

1 WHEN I survey the wondrous cross
  On which the Prince of glory died,
My richest gain I count but loss,
  And pour contempt on all my pride.

2 Forbid it, Lord, that I should boast,
Save in the death of Christ, my God:
All the vain things that charm me most,
I sacrifice them to His blood.

3 See, from His head, His hands, His feet,
Sorrow and love flow mingled down:
Did e'er such love and sorrow meet,
Or thorns compose so rich a crown!

4 Were the whole realm of nature mine,
That were a present far too small;
Love so amazing, so divine,
Demands my soul, my life, my all.

35

163

Truly this was the Son of God.
Matthew xxvii. 54.

7 7.7 7.7 7.7 7.

1 BOUND upon the accursèd tree.
  Faint and bleeding, who is He?
By the eyes so pale and dim,
Streaming blood and writhing limb.
By the flesh with scourges torn,
By the crown of twisted thorn,
By the drooping, death-dewed brow;
Son of man, 'tis Thou! 'tis Thou!

2 Bound upon the accursèd tree,
  Dread and awful, who is He?
By the sun at noonday pale,
Shivering rocks and rending veil.
By Eden promised, ere He died,
To the felon at His side:
Crucified, we know Thee now;
Son of God, 'tis Thou! 'tis Thou!

3 Bound upon the accursèd tree,
  Sad and dying, who is He?
By the spoiled and empty grave,
By the souls He died to save,
By the conquest He hath won,
By the saints before His throne,
By the rainbow round His brow:
Son of God, 'tis Thou! 'tis Thou!

164

His great love wherewith He loved us.—Ephesians ii. 4.   C.M.

1 THERE is a green hill far away,
  Without a city wall,
Where the dear Lord was crucified,
  Who died to save us all.

2 We may not know, we cannot tell
  What pains He had to bear,
But we believe it was for us
  He hung and suffered there.

3 He died that we might be forgiven,
  He died to make us good,
That we might go at last to heaven,
  Saved by His precious blood.

4 There was no other good enough
  To pay the price of sin,
He only could unlock the gate
  Of heaven and let us in.

5 O, dearly, dearly has He loved:
  And we must love Him too,
And trust in His redeeming blood,
  And try His works to do.

165

Our Lord Jesus Christ, who died for us.—1 Thessalonians v. 9 10.   C.M.

1 I LOVE to sing of that great Power
  That made the earth and sea;
But better still I love the song
  Of 'Jesus died for me.'

2 I love to sing of shrub and flower,
  Of field and plant and tree;
My sweetest note for ever is,
  That 'Jesus died for me.'

3 I love to think of angels' songs,
  From sin and sorrow free;
But angels cannot strike their notes
  To 'Jesus died for me.'

36

4 I love to speak of God, of heaven.
  And all its purity;
God is my Father, heaven my home,
  For 'Jesus died for me.'

5 And when I reach that happy place,
  From all temptation free,
I'll tune my ever rapturous notes
  With 'Jesus died for me.'

6 There shall I, at His sacred feet,
  Adoring, bow the knee,
And swell the everlasting song,
  With 'Jesus died for me.'

166

Christ, the Rock of ages
Isaiah xxvi. 4.   7 7.7 7.7 7.

1 ROCK of ages, cleft for me,
  Let me hide myself in Thee;
Let the water and the blood,
From Thy wounded side which flowed,
Be of sin the double cure,
Save from wrath and make me pure.

2 Could my tears for ever flow,
  Could my zeal no languor know,
These for sin could not atone;
Thou must save and Thou alone;
In my hand no price I bring,
Simply to Thy cross I cling.

3 While I draw this fleeting breath,
  When my eyes shall close in death.
When I rise to worlds unknown,
And behold Thee on Thy throne.
Rock of ages, cleft for me,
Let me hide myself in Thee.

167

Worthy is the Lamb that was slain!
Revelation v. 12.   6 6 4.6 6 6 4

1 GLORY to God on high!
  Let earth to heaven reply;
Praise ye His name;
His love and grace adore,
Who all our sorrows bore,
And praise Him evermore;
Worthy the Lamb!

2 Jesus, our Lord and God.
  Bore sin's tremendous load:
Praise ye His name:
Tell what His arm hath done.
What spoils from death He won;
Sing His great name alone;
Worthy the Lamb!

3 Join, all the ransomed race,
  Our Lord and God to bless;
Praise ye His name:
In Him we will rejoice.
Making a joyful noise,
Shouting with heart and voice,
Worthy the Lamb!

4 Now let the hosts above,
  In realms of endless love.
Praise His great name:
To Him ascribèd be
Honour and majesty,
Through all eternity;
Worthy the Lamb!

And I heard the voice of many
168 *angels round about the throne.*
Revelation v. 11. C.M.

1 COME, let us join our cheerful songs
With angels round the throne ;
Ten thousand thousand are their tongues,
But all their joys are one.

2 'Worthy the Lamb that died,' they cry,
'To be exalted thus !'
'Worthy the Lamb !' our hearts reply,
'For He was slain for us.'

3 Jesus is worthy to receive
Honour and power divine ;
And blessings, more than we can give,
Be, Lord, for ever Thine !

4 The whole creation join in one
To bless the sacred name
Of Him that sits upon the throne,
And to adore the Lamb.

And Herod with his men of war
169 *... mocked Him.*—Luke xxiii 11.
8 7.8 7.8 7.8 7.

1 HAIL, Thou once despisèd Jesus !
Hail, Thou Galilean King !
Thou didst suffer to release us ;
Thou didst free salvation bring.
Hail, thou agonising Saviour,
Bearer of our sin and shame !
By Thy merits we find favour ;
Life is given through Thy name.

2 Paschal Lamb, by God appointed,
All our sins on Thee were laid ;
By almighty love anointed,
Thou hast full atonement made ;
All Thy people are forgiven
Through the virtue of Thy blood ;
Opened is the gate of heaven.
Peace is made 'twixt man and God.

For God so loved the world, that He
170 *gave His only begotten Son.*
John iii. 16. L.M.

1 IT is a thing most wonderful,
Almost too wonderful to be,
That God's own Son should come from [heaven
And die to save a child like me.

2 And yet I know that it is true :
He came to this poor world below,
And wept, and toiled, and mourned, and [died,
Only because He loved us so.

3 I cannot tell how He could love
A child so weak and full of sin ;
His love must be most wonderful,
If He could die my love to win.

4 I sometimes think about the cross,
And shut my eyes, and try to see
The cruel nails, and crown of thorns,
And Jesus crucified for me ;

5 But even could I see Him die,
I could but see a little part
Of that great love, which, like a fire,
Is always burning in His heart.
B 2

6 It is most wonderful to know
His love for me so free and sure ;
But 'tis more wonderful to see
My love for Him so faint and poor.

7 And yet I want to love Thee, Lord :
O, light the flame within my heart,
And I will love Thee more and more,
Until I see Thee as Thou art.

RESURRECTION.

He is not here : for He is risen, as
171 *He said.*—Matthew xxviii. 6.
7 7.7 7.

1 'CHRIST, the Lord, is risen to-day,'
Sons of men and angels say !
Raise your joys and triumphs high :
Sing, ye heavens ; thou earth, reply.

2 Love's redeeming work is done ;
Fought the fight, the battle won :
Lo ! the sun's eclipse is o'er ;
Lo ! he sets in blood no more !

3 Vain the stone, the watch, the seal,
Christ hath burst the gates of hell ;
Death in vain forbids His rise,
Christ hath opened Paradise.

4 Lives again our glorious King !
Where, O death, is now thy sting?
Once he died our souls to save ;
Where's thy victory, boasting grave?

5 Soar we now where Christ hath led,
Following our exalted Head :
Made like Him, like Him we rise,
Ours the cross, the grave, the skies.

6 King of glory ! Soul of bliss !
Everlasting life is this,
Thee to know, Thy power to prove,
Thus to sing, and thus to love.

When therefore He was risen from the
172 *dead, His disciples remembered.*
John ii. 22. 7 7.7 7 4.

1 CHRIST the Lord is risen again !
Christ hath broken every chain ;
Hark ! angelic voices cry,
Singing evermore on high, Alleluia !

2 He who gave for us His life,
Who for us endured the strife,
Is our paschal Lamb to-day ;
Now we sing our joyous lay. Alleluia !

3 He who bore all pain and loss,
Comfortless upon the cross,
Lives in glory now on high,
Pleads for us, and hears our cry : Alleluia !

4 He who slumbered in the grave
Is exalted now to save ;
Now through all the world it rings,
He, the Lamb, is King of kings ! Alleluia !

5 Now He bids us tell abroad
How the lost may be restored,
How the penitent forgiven,
How we, too, may enter heaven : Alleluia !

6 Thou, our paschal Lamb indeed,
Christ, Thy ransomed people feed :
Take our sins and guilt away,
Thee we sing by night and day, Alleluia !

173

The Lord is risen indeed, and hath appeared to Simon.
Luke xxiv. 34.   7 5.8 8.6 6.

1 CHRIST, the Lord, is risen to-day;
    He is risen indeed!
He captive led captivity,
He robbed the grave of victory,
    He broke the bars of death.
    Alleluia! Amen.

2 Christ, the Lord, is risen to-day!
    He is risen indeed!
Let every mourning soul rejoice,
All sing with one united voice;
    The Saviour rose to-day.
    Alleluia! Amen.

3 Christ, the Lord, is risen to-day!
    He is risen indeed!
The great and glorious work is done:
Free grace to all through Christ, the Son;
    Hosanna to His name!
    Alleluia! Amen.

4 Christ, the Lord, is risen to-day!
    He is risen indeed!
Let all that fill the earth and sea
Break forth in tuneful melody,
    And swell the mighty song.
    Alleluia! Amen.

174

Why seek ye the living among the dead?—Luke xxiv. 5.
6 5.6 4.7 9.11 11.6 7.

1 LOW in the grave He lay:
    Jesus, my Saviour;
Waiting the coming day:
    Jesus, my Lord.
    Up from the grave He arose,
    With a mighty triumph o'er His foes;
He arose a Victor from the dark domain,
And He lives for ever with His saints to
    He arose, He arose!   [reign;
    Alleluia! Christ arose!

2 Vainly they watch His bed:
    Jesus, my Saviour;
Vainly they seal the dead:
    Jesus, my Lord. Up from the grave, etc.

3 Death cannot keep his prey:
    Jesus, my Saviour;
He tore the bars away:
    Jesus, my Lord. Up from the grave, etc.

175

Whom God hath raised up, having loosed the pains of death,
etc.—Acts ii. 24.   8 8 8.4.

1 THE strife is o'er, the battle done;
    The victory of life is won;
The song of triumph has begun. Alleluia!

2 The powers of death have done their worst,
And Christ their legions hath dispersed:
Let shout of holy joy outburst. Alleluia!

3 The three sad days have quickly sped;
He rises glorious from the dead;
All glory to our risen Head! Alleluia!

4 Lord, by the stripes which wounded Thee,
From death's dread sting Thy servants free.
That we may live and sing to Thee. Alleluia!

176

Jesus met them, saying, All hail!
Matt. xxviii. 9.   7 6.7 6.7 6.7 6.

1 THE day of resurrection!
    Earth, tell it out abroad;
The passover of gladness,
    The passover of God!
From death to life eternal,
    From earth unto the sky,
Our Christ hath brought us over,
    With hymns of victory.

2 Our hearts be pure from evil,
    That we may see aright
The Lord in rays eternal
    Of resurrection light:
And, listening to His accents,
    May hear so calm and plain
His own 'All hail!' and hearing,
    May raise the victor strain.

3 Now let the heavens be joyful;
    Let earth her song begin;
Let the round world keep triumph,
    And all that is therein:
Invisible and visible,
    Their notes let all things blend:
For Christ the Lord hath risen,
    Our joy that hath no end.

ASCENSION.

177

While they beheld, He was taken up; and a cloud received Him.
Acts i. 9.   7 7.7 7.

1 HAIL the day that sees Him rise.
    Ravished from our wishful eyes;
Christ, awhile to mortals given,
Re-ascends His native heaven.

2 There the pompous triumph waits:
' Lift your heads, eternal gates;
Wide unfold the radiant scene;
Take the King of glory in!'

3 Circled round with angel powers,
Their triumphant Lord, and ours,
Conqueror over death and sin;
'Take the King of glory in!'

4 Him though highest heaven receives,
Still He loves the earth He leaves;
Though returning to His throne,
Still He calls mankind His own.

5 See, He lifts His hands above!
See, He shows the prints of love!
Hark. His gracious lips bestow
Blessings on His Church below!

6 Still for us His death He pleads;
Prevalent He intercedes;
Near Himself prepares our place.
Harbinger of human race.

SECOND PART.

7 Master, (will we ever say)
Taken from our head to-day;
See Thy faithful servants, see.
Ever gazing up to Thee.

8 Grant, though parted from our sight,
High above yon azure height.
Grant our hearts may thither rise,
Following Thee beyond the skies.

9 Ever upward let us move,
  Wafted on the wings of love ;
  Looking when our Lord shall come,
  Longing, gasping after home.
10 There we shall with Thee remain,
  Partners of Thy endless reign ;
  There Thy face unclouded see,
  Find our heaven of heavens in Thee.

I ascend unto My Father, and your
178 *Father.—John xx. 17.*
  7 6.7 6.7 6.7 6.

1 OUR God to heaven ascendeth,
    Let heaven and earth rejoice,
  With victor anthems blendeth
    The trumpet's pealing voice !
  Jesu, our hearts and voices
    Uplift in praise shall be,
  Thy holy Church rejoices
    Now it is well with Thee !

2 See yonder, shining faintly,
    The massy gates of light,
  The city of the saintly
    Is breaking on our sight :
  Lift, lift, each radiant portal ;
    Eternal doors give way ;
  The glorious King immortal
    In triumph comes to-day.

3 Hark, hark ! the hosts victorious
    Of angels make reply,
  'Who is this King so glorious,
    Ascending through the sky ?'
  O shout the wondrous story
    Through heaven's exulting coasts,
  He is the King of glory
    Who is the Lord of hosts !

SECOND PART.

4 Uplift, uplift, each portal ;
    Roll back, eternal gates ;
  For He, the King immortal,
    The King of glory waits !
  He, Judah's mighty Lion,
    Both death and hell His prey,
  In triumph comes to Sion,
    In joy returns to-day.

5 Angels fall low before Him,
    Our own Redeemer King ;
  Archangels all adore Him
    And alleluias sing !
  Each throne, each domination,
    Each princedom bends the knee,
  The God of our salvation
    In human form to see.

6 O Saviour, interceding
    Before the throne above,
  For sinners ever pleading
    Thy wounds of matchless love.
  We with the Father bless Thee,
    With Holy Ghost adore,
  And ever will confess Thee
    True God for evermore.

Worthy . . . to receive power, and
179 *riches, etc.—Revelation v. 12.*
  10 11.10 11.8 11.8 9.

1 O PRAISE ye the Lord with a trumpet
    sound,
  Let the anthem of joy through the earth
    resound ;

The veil of the temple is rent in twain,
Through Christ our Redeemer who liveth
    King of glory, Hail, mighty King! [again.
    Thou art exalted for ever, evermore.
    King of glory, Hail, mighty King !
    Thou our Deliverer, Thee we adore.

2 O praise ye the Lord, for the work is done ;
  Now the battle is fought, and the victory
    won ;
  The legions of hell and the boasting grave
  Are trophies of Him who is mighty to save.
    King of glory, etc.

3 O lift up your heads, all ye portals fair,
  For the King everlasting to enter there ;
  He comes with a shout to His throne on
    high,
  And loud alleluias now burst from the sky.
    King of glory, etc.

4 All honour to Him, our exalted King! [sing :
  Unto, Him all the praise let His children
  His truth and His mercy shall be our light,
  A pillar to lead us by day and by night.
    King of glory, etc.

Who is this King of glory ? The LORD
180 *of hosts, He is the King of*
  glory.—Psalm xxiv. 10. 8 4.8 4.

1 TO-DAY above the sky He soared.
    Alleluia !
  The King of glory, Christ the Lord.
    Alleluia !

2 He sitteth at the Father's hand, Alleluia !
  And rules the sky and sea and land.
    Alleluia !

3 Now all things have their end foretold,
    Alleluia !
  In holy David's song of old. Alleluia !

4 My Lord is seated with the LORD, Alleluia !
  Upon the throne of God adored. Alleluia !

5 In this great triumph of our King, Alleluia!
  To God on high all praise we bring.
    Alleluia !

6 To Him all thanks and praise give we,
    Alleluia !
  The ever blessèd Trinity. Alleluia !

The LORD *said unto my Lord, Sit*
181 *Thou at My right hand.*
  Psalm cx. 1. 6 6.6 6.8 8.

1 GOD is gone up on high,
    With a triumphant noise ;
  The clarions of the sky
    Proclaim the angelic joys !
  Join all on earth, rejoice and sing ;
  Glory ascribe to glory's King.

2 God in the flesh below,
    For us He reigns above ;
  Let all the nations know
    Our Jesu's conquering love ! Join, etc.

3 All power to our great Lord
    Is by the Father given ;
  By angel-hosts adored,
    He reigns supreme in heaven :
    Join, etc.
    39

4 High on His holy seat
  He bears the righteous sway;
His foes beneath His feet
    Shall sink and die away :   Join, etc.
5 Till all the earth, renewed
  In righteousness divine,
With all the hosts of God
    In one great chorus join.   Join, etc.

EXALTATION.

182 *Thy throne is established of old.*
       Psalm xciii. 2.   8 7.8 7.7 7.6.

1 HARK ! ten thousand harps and voices
  Sound the notes of praise above ;
Jesus reigns and heaven rejoices ;
Jesus reigns, the God of love.
  See ! He sits on yonder throne ;
  Jesus rules the world alone.
          Alleluia, Amen !

2 Jesus, hail ! whose glory brightens
  All above, and gives it worth ;
Lord of life, Thy smile enlightens,
  Cheers, and charms Thy saints on earth :
  When we think of love like Thine,
  Lord, we own it love divine !
          Alleluia, Amen !

3 King of glory, reign triumphant
  On Thine everlasting throne !
Nothing from Thy love can sever
  Those who trust in Thee alone.   [grace,
  More than conquerors through Thy
  They with joy shall see Thy face.
          Alleluia, Amen !

4 Saviour, hasten Thine appearing ;
  Bring, O bring the glorious day,
When, the awful summons hearing,
  Heaven and earth shall pass away :
  Then with golden harps we'll sing,
  Glory to our God and King.
          Alleluia, Amen !

183   *The LORD reigneth.*
       Psalm xciii. 1.   6 6.6 6.8 8.

1 REJOICE, the Lord is King !
  Your Lord and King adore ;
Mortals, give thanks, and sing,
  And triumph evermore :
Lift up your heart, lift up your voice,
Rejoice, again I say, rejoice.

2 Jesus the Saviour reigns,
  The God of truth and love ;
When He had purged our stains,
  He took His seat above : Lift up, etc.

3 His kingdom cannot fail ;
  He rules o'er earth and heaven ;
The keys of death and hell
  Are to our Jesus given : Lift up, etc.

4 He sits at God's right hand
  Till all His foes submit,
And bow to His command,
  And fall beneath His feet : Lift up, etc.

5 He all His foes shall quell.
  Shall all our sins destroy,
And every bosom swell
  With pure seraphic joy : Lift up, etc.
  40

6 Rejoice in glorious hope,
  Jesus the Judge shall come,
And take His servants up
  To their eternal home :
We soon shall hear the archangel's voice,
The trump of God shall sound, Rejoice !

184 *On His head were many crowns.*
       Revelation xix. 12.   C.M.

1 ALL hail the power of Jesu's name ;
  Let angels prostrate fall ;
Bring forth the royal diadem
  To crown Him Lord of all.

2 Crown Him, ye morning stars of light,
  Who launched this floating ball ;
Now hail the Strength of Israel's might,
  And crown Him Lord of all.

3 Crown Him, ye martyrs of our God,
  Who from His altar call ;
Of Jesse's stem extol the Rod,
  And crown Him Lord of all.

4 Ye seed of Israel's chosen race,
  Ye ransomed from the fall,
Hail Him who saves you by His grace,
  And crown Him Lord of all.

5 Let every tribe and every tongue
  Before Him prostrate fall,
And shout in universal song
  The crownèd Lord of all.

6 O that with yonder sacred throng
  We at His feet may fall,
Join in the everlasting song,
  And crown Him Lord of all !

185 *Thou art worthy, O Lord, to receive*
    glory and honour and power.
    Revelation iv. 11.   8 7.8 7.8 7.8 7

1 JESUS, hail ! enthroned in glory,
  There for ever to abide :
All the heavenly host adore Thee,
  Seated at Thy Father's side ;
There for sinners Thou art pleading,
  There Thou dost our place prepare,
Ever for us interceding,
  Till in glory we appear.

2 Worship, honour, power, and blessing,
  Thou art worthy to receive ;
Loudest praises without ceasing,
  Meet it is for us to give.
Help, ye bright, angelic spirits !
  Bring your sweetest, noblest lays ;
Help to sing our Saviour's merits ;
  Help to chant Immanuel's praise.

186 *Out of the mouth of babes and sucklings*
    Thou hast perfected praise.
    Matthew xxi. 16.   8 7.8 7.4 7.

1 LITTLE children, praise the Saviour ;
  He regards you from above :
Praise Him for His great salvation,
  Praise Him for His precious love !
    Sweet hosannas
  To the name of Jesus sing.

2 When He left His throne in glory,
  When He lived with mortals here,

Little children sang His praises,
  And it pleased His gracious ear.
    Sweet hosannas
    To the name of Jesus sing.

3 When the anxious mothers round Him,
  With their tender infants, pressed,
He with open arms received them,
  And the little ones He blessed.
    Sweet hosannas
    To the name of Jesus sing.

4 Up in yonder happy regions
  Angels sound the chorus high :
Twice ten thousand times ten thousand
  Sound His praises through the sky.
    Sweet hosannas
    To the name of Jesus sing.

5 Little children, praise the Saviour,
  Praise Him, your undying Friend ;
Praise Him till in heaven you meet Him,
  There to praise Him without end.
    Sweet hosannas
    To the name of Jesus sing.

*The sufferings of Christ, and the glory
that should follow.*

187 1 Peter i. 11. 6 6 8.6 6 8.

1 MY heart and voice I raise,
    To spread Messiah's praise ;
Messiah's praise let all repeat ;
  The universal Lord,
  By whose almighty word
Creation rose in form complete.

2 A servant's form He wore,
  And in His body bore
Our dreadful curse on Calvary :
  He like a victim stood,
  And poured His sacred blood,
To set the guilty captives free.

3 But soon the Victor rose
  Triumphant o'er His foes,
And led the vanquished host in chains ;
  He threw their empire down,
  His foes compelled to own,
O'er all the great Messiah reigns.

4 With mercy's mildest grace,
  He governs all our race
In wisdom, righteousness, and love :
  Who to Messiah fly
  Shall find redemption nigh,
And all His great salvation prove.

5 Hail, Saviour, Prince of peace !
  Thy kingdom shall increase,
Till all the world Thy glory see ;
  And righteousness abound,
  As the great deep profound,
And fill the earth with purity !

*Ten thousand times ten thousand,
and thousands of thousands.*

188 Revelation v. 11, 12. 8.4.8.4.8 8 8 4.

1 TIS the Church triumphant singing,
    Worthy the Lamb !
Heaven throughout with praises ringing :
    Worthy the Lamb !
Thrones and powers before Him bending,
Odours sweet with voice ascending,
Swell the chorus never ending,
    Worthy the Lamb !

2 Every kindred, tongue, and nation :
    Worthy the Lamb !
Join to sing the great salvation :
    Worthy the Lamb !
Loud as mighty thunder roaring,
Floods of mighty waters pouring,
Prostrate at His feet adoring :
    Worthy the Lamb !

3 Harps and songs for ever sounding
    Worthy the Lamb !
Mighty grace o'er sin abounding :
    Worthy the Lamb !
By His blood He dearly bought us,
Wandering from the fold He sought us,
And to glory safely brought us :
    Worthy the Lamb !

4 Sing with blest anticipation,
    Worthy the Lamb !
Through the vale of tribulation,
    Worthy the Lamb !
Sweetest notes, all notes excelling,
On the theme for ever dwelling,
Still untold, though ever telling,
    Worthy the Lamb !

189 *Hosanna to the Son of David !*
Matthew xxi. 9. C.M.

1 HOSANNA ! raise the pealing hymn
    To David's Son and Lord !
With cherubim and seraphim
    Exalt the incarnate Word.

2 Hosanna ! Lord, our feeble tongue
  No lofty strains can raise ;
But Thou wilt not despise the young,
  Who meekly chant Thy praise.

3 Hosanna ! Sovereign, Prophet, Priest,
  How vast Thy gifts ! how free !
Thy death, our life ; Thy word, our feast,
  Thy name, our only plea.

4 Hosanna ! Master, lo ! we bring
  Our offerings to Thy throne ;
Not gold nor myrrh nor earthly thing,
  But hearts to be Thine own.

5 Hosanna ! once Thy gracious ear
  Approved a lisping throng ;
Be gracious still, and deign to hear
  Our poor but grateful song.

6 O Saviour ! if, redeemed by Thee,
  Thy temple we behold,
Hosannas through eternity
  We'll sing to harps of gold.

190 *Behold the Lamb of God.*
John i. 29. 7 6.7 6.

1 O LAMB of God most holy,
    All free from spot and stain !
O help us now to seek Thee,
  And sing Thy praise again.

2 O Lamb of God most lowly,
  So great and yet so meek !
May we when pride allures us
  Thy lowly spirit seek.

3 O Lamb of God most gentle,
  And yet so good and true !
May we when passion tempts us
  Thy gentleness pursue.

41

4 O Lamb of God most lovely !
  To Thee our faith would flee ;
Reveal to us Thy beauty,
  And win our hearts to Thee.

191 *Lord, save me.*—Matthew xiv. 30.
                     7 7 7 5.

1 L ORD of mercy and of might,
   Of mankind the life and light,
Maker, Teacher infinite,
  Jesus, hear, and save !

2 Strong Creator, Saviour mild,
Humbled to a mortal Child,
Captive, beaten, bound, reviled ;
  Jesus, hear, and save !

3 Throned above celestial things,
Borne aloft on angels'' wings,
Lord of lords, and King of kings ;
  Jesus, hear, and save !

4 Soon to come to earth again,
Judge of angels and of men ;
Hear us now, and hear us then,
  Jesus, hear, and save !

192 *I am with you alway.*
    Matthew xxviii. 20.   7 7 7 6.

1 G OD the Father, God the Son,
   Holy Ghost the Comforter,
Ever blessèd Three in One :
  Spare us, holy Trinity.

2 Christ, whose mercy guideth still
Sinners from the paths of ill,
Rule our hearts, our spirits fill :
  Hear us, holy Jesus.

3 Thou who, at Thy prophet's prayer,
Didst the stiff-necked Hebrews spare,
Let us too Thy mercy share : Hear, etc.

4 Thou whose word, to David sent,
When his steps to evil bent,
Made the sinner penitent : Hear, etc.

5 Thou who bowedst down Thine ear
Nineveh in prayer to hear,
Faint with fasting, grief, and fear :
                     Hear, etc.

6 Thou who, leaving crown and throne,
Camest here, an outcast lone,
That Thou mightest save Thine own :
                     Hear, etc.

SECOND PART.

7 Thou with sinners wont to eat,
Who with loving words didst greet
Mary weeping at Thy feet : Hear, etc.

8 Thou whose saddened look did chide
Peter, when he thrice denied,
Till in grief he wept and sighed : Hear, etc.

9 Thou, despised, denied, refused,
And for man's transgressions bruised,
Sinless, yet of sin accused : Hear, etc.

10 Thou who, hanging on the tree,
To the thief saidst, ' Thou shalt be
To-day in Paradise with Me :' Hear, etc.

11 Thou who on the cross didst reign,
Dying there in bitter pain,
Cleansing with Thy blood our stain :
                     Hear, etc.

12 Thou whose will it is that we
Should from death return to Thee,
And should live eternally :   Hear, etc.

13 Shepherd of the straying sheep,
Comforter of them that weep,
Hear us crying from the deep : Hear, etc.

THIRD PART.

14 In our poverty and wealth,
In our sickness and in health,
Ever from the tempter's stealth
  Save us, holy Jesus.

15 From all lack of love and faith,
From a sudden evil death,
Thou whose arm delivereth,
  Save us, holy Jesus.

16 When our dying draweth near,
On the last great day of fear,
Master, King, Redeemer dear,
  Save us, holy Jesus.

17 That with lowly penitence
We may mourn o'er each offence,
Trembling, yet with confidence,
  We beseech Thee, Jesus.

18 That the blood for sinners shed
May be sprinkled on our head,
In Thy death our sins be dead,
  We beseech Thee, Jesus.

19 That we give to sin no place,
That we never quench Thy grace,
That we ever seek Thy face,
  We beseech Thee, Jesus.

20 That, denying evil lust,
Living godly, meek, and just,
In Thee only we may trust,
  We beseech Thee, Jesus.

21 That, to sin for ever dead,
We may live to Thee instead,
And the narrow pathway tread,
  We beseech Thee, Jesus.

THE HOLY SPIRIT.

193 *He shall give you another Com-*
     forter.—John xiv. 16.   8 6.8 4.

1 O UR blest Redeemer, ere He breathed
   His tender, last farewell,
A Guide, a Comforter bequeathed
  With us to dwell.

2 He came sweet influence to impart,
  A gracious, willing Guest,
While He can find one humble heart
  Wherein to rest.

3 And His that gentle voice we hear,
  Soft as the breath of even,
That checks each thought, that calms each
    And speaks of heaven.   [fear,

4 And every virtue we possess,
  And every conquest won,
And every thought of holiness,
  Are His alone.

5 Spirit of purity and grace,
  Our weakness, pitying, see :
O make our hearts Thy dwelling-place,
  And worthier Thee.

6 O praise the Father; praise the Son;
 Blest Spirit, praise to Thee;
All praise to God, the Three in One,
 The One in Three.

194 *I will pour out of My Spirit upon all flesh.*—Acts ii. 17. C.M.

1 SPIRIT divine! attend our prayers,
 And make this house Thy home;
Descend with all Thy gracious powers;
 O come, great Spirit, come!

2 Come as the light! to us reveal
 Our emptiness and woe;
And lead us in those paths of life
 Where all the righteous go.

3 Come as the fire! and purge our hearts
 Like sacrificial flame;
Let our whole soul an offering be
 To our Redeemer's name.

4 Come as the dew! and sweetly bless
 This consecrated hour;
May barrenness rejoice to own
 Thy fertilising power.

5 Come as the dove! and spread Thy wings,
 The wings of peaceful love;
And let Thy Church on earth become
 Blest as the Church above.

6 Come as the wind, with rushing sound
 And Pentecostal grace!
That all of woman born may see
 The glory of Thy face.

7 Spirit divine! attend our prayers,
 Make a lost world Thy home;
 Descend with all Thy gracious powers,
 O come, great Spirit, come!

195 *Open Thou mine eyes, that I may behold wondrous things out of Thy law.*—Psalm cxix. 18. C.M.

1 COME, Holy Ghost, our hearts inspire,
 Let us Thine influence prove,
Source of the old prophetic fire,
 Fountain of light and love.

2 Come, Holy Ghost (for moved by Thee
 The prophets wrote and spoke);
Unlock the truth, Thyself the key,
 Unseal the sacred book.

3 Expand Thy wings, celestial Dove,
 Brood o'er our nature's night;
On our disordered spirits move,
 And let there now be light.

4 God, through Himself, we then shall know,
 If Thou within us shine,
And sound, with all Thy saints below,
 The depths of love divine.

196 *The Comforter, which is the Holy Ghost.*—John xiv. 26. 8 8 6.

1 TO Thee, O Comforter divine,
 For all Thy grace and power benign,
 Sing we Alleluia!

2 To Thee, whose faithful love had place
In God's great covenant of grace,
 Sing we Alleluia!

3 To Thee, whose faithful voice doth win
The wandering from the ways of sin,
 Sing we Alleluia!

4 To Thee, whose faithful power doth heal,
Enlighten, sanctify, and seal,
 Sing we Alleluia!

5 To Thee, whose faithful truth is shown
 By every promise made our own,
 Sing we Alleluia!

6 To Thee, our Teacher and our Friend,
Our faithful Leader to the end,
 Sing we Alleluia!

7 To Thee, by Jesus Christ sent down,
Of all His gifts the sum and crown,
 Sing we Alleluia!

8 To Thee, who art with God the Son
And God the Father ever One,
 Sing we Alleluia!

197 *I will receive you, and will be a Father unto you.*—2 Corinthians vi. 17, 18. C.M.

1 SOVEREIGN of all the worlds on high,
 Allow my humble claim;
Nor, while unworthy I draw nigh,
 Disdain a Father's name.

2 'My Father God!' that gracious sound
 Dispels my guilty fear;
Not all the harmony of heaven
 Could so delight my ear.

3 Come, Holy Spirit, seal the grace
 On my expanding heart;
And show that in the Father's love
 I share a filial part.

4 heered by a witness so divine,
 Unwavering I believe;
And 'Abba, Father,' humbly cry;
 Nor can the sign deceive.

198 *As many as are led by the Spirit of God, they are the sons of God.* Romans viii. 14. L.M.

1 COME, gracious Spirit, heavenly Dove,
 With light and comfort from above;
Be Thou our Guardian, Thou our Guide,
O'er every thought and step preside.

2 The light of truth to us display,
And make us know and choose Thy way:
Plant holy fear in every heart,
That we from God may ne'er depart.

3 Lead us to holiness, the road
That we must take to dwell with God;
Lead us to Christ, the living Way,
Nor let us from His pastures stray.

4 Lead us to God, our final rest,
To be with Him for ever blest;
Lead us to heaven, that we may share
Fulness of joy for ever there.

199 *Be filled with the Spirit.* Ephesians v. 18. 7 7 7 5.

1 COME to our poor nature's night
 With Thy blessèd inward light,
Holy Ghost, the infinite
 Comforter divine!

43

2 We are sinful, cleanse us, Lord ;
  Sick and faint, Thy strength afford ;
  Lost, until by Thee restored,
    Comforter divine !

3 Friendless are our souls and poor ;
  Give us from Thy heavenly store
  Faith, love, joy for evermore,
    Comforter divine !

4 Like the dew Thy peace distil ;
  Guide, subdue our wayward will,
  Things of Christ unfolding still,
    Comforter divine !

5 Gentle, awful, holy Guest,
  Make Thy temple in each breast,
  There supreme to reign and rest,
    Comforter divine !

6 In us, for us intercede,
  And with voiceless groanings plead
  Our unutterable need,
    Comforter divine !

7 In us 'Abba, Father,' cry,
  Earnest of our bliss on high,
  Seal of immortality,
    Comforter divine !

8 Search for us the depths of God,
  Bear us up the starry road
  To the height of Thine abode,
    Comforter divine !

*The Comforter, . . . whom I will send
unto you from the Father.*
200   John xv. 26.   C.M.

1 COME, Holy Ghost, the Comforter,
  Whom Jesus sends from heaven,
O comfort us, Thy children, here,
  And show our sins forgiven.

2 O come, and in our hearts reside ;
  Let them Thy temples prove ;
Nor let our sinfulness and pride
  Provoke Thee to remove :

3 But with Thy gracious power descend,
  And all our sins subdue ;
O bid us to Thy sceptre bend,
  And form our souls anew.

4 Where God the Spirit is a guest,
  All graces there abound ;
Love, joy, and peace make calm the breast,
  And thanks and praise resound.

201 *I pray for them.*—John xvii. 9.
    7 6.7 6.7 7.7 6.

1 FATHER of our dying Lord,
  Remember us for good ;
O fulfil His faithful word,
  And hear His speaking blood !
Give us that for which He prays ;
  Father, glorify Thy Son !
Show His truth and power and grace,
  And send the Promise down.

2 True and faithful Witness, Thou,
  O Christ, Thy Spirit give !
Hast Thou not received Him now,
  That we might now receive ?
Art Thou not our living Head ?
  Life to all Thy limbs impart ;
Shed Thy love, Thy Spirit shed
  In every waiting heart.

44

3 Holy Ghost, the Comforter,
  The gift of Jesus, come ;
Glows our heart to find Thee near,
  And swells to make Thee room ;
Present with us Thee we feel,
  Come, O come, and in us be !
With us, in us, live and dwell,
  To all eternity.

*How much more shall your heavenly
Father give the Holy Spirit !*
202   Luke xi. 13.   S.M.

1 COME, Holy Spirit, come,
  Let Thy bright beams arise,
Dispel all sorrow from our minds,
  All darkness from our eyes

2 Cheer our desponding hearts,
  Thou heavenly Paraclete ;
Give us to lie, with humble hope,
  At our Redeemer's feet.

3 Revive our drooping faith,
  Our doubts and fears remove,
And kindle in our breasts the flame
  Of never-dying love.

4 Convince us of our sin,
  Then lead to Jesu's blood,
And to our wondering view reveal
  The secret love of God.

5 Dwell therefore in our hearts,
  Our minds from bondage free ;
Then we shall know, and praise, and love
  The Father, Son, and Thee !

*God, who hath also given unto us
His Holy Spirit.*
203 1 Thessalonians iv. 8.   7 7.7 7.7 7.

1 GRACIOUS Spirit, dwell with me !
  I myself would gracious be,
And with words that help and heal
Would Thy life in mine reveal ;
And with actions bold and meek
Would for Christ my Saviour speak.

2 Truthful Spirit, dwell with me !
  I myself would truthful be,
And with wisdom kind and clear
Let Thy life in mine appear ;
And with actions brotherly
Speak my Lord's sincerity.

3 Tender Spirit, dwell with me !
  I myself would tender be ;
Shut my heart up like a flower
At temptation's darksome hour,
Open it when shines the Sun,
And His love by fragrance own.

4 Mighty Spirit, dwell with me !
  I myself would mighty be,
Mighty so as to prevail
Where unaided man must fail,
Ever by a mighty hope
Pressing on and bearing up.

5 Holy Spirit, dwell with me !
  I myself would holy be,
Separate from sin, I would
Choose, and cherish all things good ;
And whatever I can be
Give to Him who gave me Thee.

Ye were sealed with that Holy Spirit of promise.—Ephesians i. 13.

204 C.M.

1 O HOLY Ghost, Thy people bless,
 Who long to feel Thy might,
And fain would grow in holiness
 As children of the light.

2 To Thee we bring, who art the Lord.
 Ourselves to be Thy throne;
Let every thought and deed and word
 Thy pure dominion own.

3 Life-giving Spirit, o'er us move,
 As on the formless deep;
Give life and order, light and love,
 Where now is death or sleep.

4 Great Gift of our ascended King,
 His saving truth reveal;
Our tongues inspire His praise to sing,
 Our hearts His love to feel.

5 True Wind of heaven, from south or north,
 For joy or chastening, blow;
The garden spices shall spring forth
 If Thou wilt bid them flow.

6 O Holy Ghost, of sevenfold might,
 All graces come from Thee;
Grant us to know and serve aright
 One God in Persons three.

And grieve not the Holy Spirit of God, whereby ye are sealed.
Ephesians iv. 30.

205 7 7 7 6.

1 SPIRIT blest, who art adored
 With the Father and the Word,
One eternal God and Lord:
 Hear us, Holy Spirit.

2 Source of strength and knowledge clear,
Wisdom, godliness sincere,
Understanding, counsel, fear: Hear, etc.

3 Thou, by whose indwelling taught,
Holy men of old have brought
Things of God to human thought: Hear, etc.

4 Thou by whom the virgin bore
Him whom heaven and earth adore,
Sent our nature to restore: Hear, etc.

5 Thou who camest like a dove
From the opened skies above,
With the Father's power and love: Hear, etc.

6 Thou whom Jesus, from His throne,
Gave to cheer and help His own,
That they might not be alone: Hear, etc.

SECOND PART.

7 Thou whose power inspiring came,
Falling down like tongues of flame,
Where they met in Jesus' name: Hear, etc.

8 Thou who yet the Church dost fill.
Making Jesus present still,
Showing us God's perfect will: Hear, etc.

9 Now Thy sevenfold gifts bestow;
Gifts of grace, our God to know,
Gifts of strength to quell our foe: Hear, etc.

10 Come to raise up those that fall.
Leading back with gentle call,
Those whose souls their sins enthrall:
 Hear, etc.

11 Come to rescue us from ill,
Bend aright our stubborn will,
Though we grieve Thee, patient still:
 Hear, etc.

12 Come to show us all Thy way,
Warn us when we go astray;
Plead within us when we pray: Hear, etc.

THIRD PART.

13 Come to bid our terrors cease;
Come to bid us go in peace;
Come to give our souls release: Hear, etc.

14 Come to help the hearts that yearn
More of truth divine to learn,
And with deeper love to burn: Hear, etc.

15 Come to strengthen all the weak,
Give Thy courage to the meek;
Teach our faltering tongues to speak:
 Hear, etc.

16 Come, Thou Fount of love and joy,
Bringing peace without alloy,
Hope that nothing can destroy: Hear, etc.

17 Holy, loving, as Thou art,
Come and dwell within our heart;
Never more from thence depart: Hear, etc.

18 May we soon, from sin set free,
Rise our Father's face to see,
Where Thy work shall perfect be:
 Hear, etc.

———

THE SCRIPTURES.

Thy word is very pure: therefore Thy servant loveth it.
Psalm cxix. 140.

206 7 7.7 7.

1 HOLY Bible, book divine,
 Precious treasure, thou art mine!
Mine, to tell me whence I came;
Mine, to teach me what I am;

2 Mine, to chide me when I rove;
Mine, to show a Saviour's love;
Mine art thou, to guide my feet;
Mine, to judge, condemn, acquit;

3 Mine, to comfort in distress,
If the Holy Spirit bless;
Mine, to show, by living faith,
Man can triumph over death;

4 Mine, to tell of joys to come,
And the rebel sinner's doom:
Holy Bible, book divine,
Precious treasure, thou art mine!

Thou shalt guide me with Thy counsel.—Psalm lxxiii. 24.

207 8 7. 8 7. 4 7

1 FATHER, in my life's young morning
 May Thy word direct my way;
Let me heed each gracious warning,
Lest my feet should go astray;
 And in sorrow
Let Thy promise be my stay.

2 Father, gentle is Thy teaching;
Be a docile spirit mine;
Fervently Thy grace beseeching,
Let Thy loving-kindness shine
 On my pathway,
And my heart be wholly Thine

3 Father, let me never covet
   Things of vanity and pride :
Teach me truth, and may I love
   More than all the world beside ;
     Blessèd Bible !
May it be my heavenward guide.

The word of God, which effectually
208 *worketh.*—1 Thessalonians ii. 13.
                                    C.M.

1 FATHER of mercies, in Thy word
   What endless glory shines !
For ever be Thy name adored
   For these celestial lines.

2 Here may the wretched sons of want
   Exhaustless riches find ;
Riches, above what earth can grant,
   And lasting as the mind.

3 Here the fair tree of knowledge grows,
   And yields a free repast ;
Sublimer sweets than nature knows
   Invite the longing taste.

4 Here th Redeemer's welcome voice
   Spreads heavenly peace around ;
And life and everlasting joys
   Attend the blissful sound.

5 Divine Instructor, gracious Lord,
   Be Thou for ever near ;
Teach me to love Thy sacred word,
   And view my Saviour there.

How precious also are Thy thoughts
209 *unto me, O God !*
       Psalm cxxxix. 17.   11 8.12 8.

1 HOW holy the Bible ! how pure is the light
   That streams from its pages divine !
'Tis a star that shines clear through the
   gloom of the night,
   Of jewels a wonderful mine.

2 'Tis bread for the hungry, 'tis food for the
   A balm for the wounded and sad ; [poor,
'Tis the gift of a Father : His likeness is there,
   And the hearts of His children are glad.

3 'Tis the voice of the Saviour ; how sweet
   in the storm
   It speaks to the sinner distressed !
The tempest is hushed, and the sea becomes
   The troubled and weary find rest. [calm,

4 'Tis a friend's loving counsel, the voice of
   a guide,
   How gentle and faithful and true !
No harm can the dear little pilgrim betide
   Whose feet its directious pursue.

5 No words like the words of the Saviour,
   nor can
   Their sweetness or value be told ;
They are words 'fitly spoken' to sorrowful
   Like beautiful 'apples of gold.'   [man,

6 O teach me, blest Jesus, to seek for Thy
   To me let Thy welcome be given ; [face,
Now speak to my heart some kind message
   of grace,
   Some words that shall guide me to
   heaven.

210 *His delight is in the law of the*
       LORD —Psalm i. 2.   C.M.

1 GREAT God, with wonder and with
   On all Thy works I look !   [praise
But still Thy wisdom, power, and grace
   Shine brightest in Thy book.

2 The stars that in their courses roll
   Have much instruction given ;
But Thy good word informs my soul
   How I may rise to heaven.

3 The fields provide me food, and show
   The goodness of the Lord ;
But fruits of life and glory grow
   In Thy most holy word.

4 Here are my choicest treasures hid,
   Here my best comfort lies ;
Here my desires are satisfied,
   And hence my hopes arise.

5 Lord, make me understand Thy law,
   Show what my faults have been ;
And from Thy gospel let me draw
   Pardon for all my sin.

6 Here would I learn how Christ hath died,
   To save my soul from hell ;
Not all the books on earth beside
   Such heavenly wonders tell.

7 Then may I love my Bible more,
   And take a fresh delight
By day to read these wonders o'er,
   And meditate by night !

211 *The law of the* LORD *is perfect, con-*
      verting the soul.—Psalm xix. 7.
                                   L.M.

1 THE heavens declare Thy glory, Lord,
   In every star Thy wisdom shines ;
But when our eyes behold Thy word,
   We read Thy name in fairer lines.

2 The rolling sun, the changing light,
   And night and day Thy power confess,
But the blest volume Thou hast writ
   Reveals Thy justice and Thy grace.

3 Sun, moon, and stars convey Thy praise
   Round the whole earth, and never stand :
So when Thy truth began its race,
   It touched and glanced on every land.

4 Nor shall Thy spreading gospel rest,
   Till through the world Thy truth has run,
Till Christ has all the nations blest
   That see the light or feel the sun.

5 Great Sun of Righteousness, arise,
   Bless the dark world with heavenly light ;
Thy gospel makes the simple wise ;
   Thy laws are pure, Thy judgments right.

212 *Thy word is a lamp unto my feet.*
       Psalm cxix. 105.   C.M.

1 HOW precious is the book divine,
   By inspiration given !
Bright as a lamp its doctrines shine,
   To guide our souls to heaven.

2 It sweetly cheers our drooping hearts
   In this dark vale of tears :
Life, light, and joy it still imparts,
   And quells our rising fears.

3 O'er all the strait and narrow way
   Its radiant beams are cast :
A light whose ever-cheering ray
   Grows brightest at the last.

4 This lamp through all the tedious night
   Of life shall guide our way,
Till we behold the clearer light
   Of an eternal day.

213 *The entrance of Thy words giveth*
      light.—Psalm cxix. 130.   6 o.6 6.

1 LORD, Thy word abideth,
   And our footsteps guideth ;
Who its truth believeth
Light and joy receiveth.

2 When our foes are near us,
   Then Thy word doth cheer us,
Word of consolation,
Message of salvation.

3 When the storms are o'er us,
   And dark clouds before us,
Then its light directeth,
And our way protecteth.

4 Who can tell the pleasure,
   Who recount the treasure,
By Thy word imparted
To the simple-hearted?

5 Word of mercy, giving
   Succour to the living ;
Word of life, supplying
Comfort to the dying

6 O ! that we discerning
   Its most holy learning,
Lord, may love and fear Thee,
Evermore be near Thee !

214 *The* LORD *called Samuel : and he*
      answered, Here am I.
      1 Samuel iii. 4.   6 6.6 6.8 8.

1 HUSHED was the evening hymn,
   The temple courts were dark,
The lamp was burning dim
   Before the sacred ark ;
When suddenly a voice divine
Rang through the silence of the shrine.

2 The old man meek and mild,
   The priest of Israel, slept ;
His watch the temple-child,
   The little Levite, kept ;
And what from Eli's sense was sealed
The Lord to Hannah's son revealed.

3 O ! give me Samuel's ear,
   The open ear, O Lord,
Alive and quick to hear
   Each whisper of Thy word ;
Like him to answer at Thy call,
And to obey Thee first of all.

4 O ! give me Samuel's heart,
   A lowly heart that waits
When in Thy house Thou art,
   Or watches at Thy gates
By day and night, a heart that still
Moves at the breathing of Thy will.

5 O ! give me Samuel's mind ;
   A sweet, unmurmuring faith,
Obedient and resigned
   To Thee in life and death ;
That I may read with childlike eyes
Truths that are hidden from the wise

215 *Speak,* LORD ; *for Thy servant*
      heareth.—1 Samuel iii. 9.
            6 6.6 6.8 8.

1 WHEN little Samuel woke,
   And heard his Maker's voice,
At every word He spoke
How much did he rejoice !
O blessed, happy child, to find
The God of heaven so near and kind !

2 If God would speak to me,
   And say He is my Friend,
How happy should I be !
O how would I attend !
The smallest sin I then should fear,
If God Almighty were so near.

3 And does He never speak?
   O yes ; for in His word
He bids me come and seek
The God that Samuel heard.
In almost every page I see
The God of Samuel calls to me.

4 And I beneath His care
   May safely rest my head ;
I know that God is there,
To guard my humble bed.
And every sin I well may fear,
Since God Almighty is so near.

5 Like Samuel let me say,
   Whene'er I read Thy word,
'Speak, Lord : I would obey
The voice that I have heard.'
And when I in Thy house appear,
'Speak, for Thy servant waits to hear.

216 *Both hearing them, and asking them*
      questions.—Luke ii. 46.
            C.M.

1 WHAT blest examples do I find
   Writ in the word of truth
Of children who began to mind
   Religion in their youth !

2 Samuel the child was weaned, and brought
   To wait upon the Lord ;
Young Timothy betimes was taught
   To know His holy word.

3 Jesus, who reigns above the sky,
   And keeps the world in awe,
Was once a child as young as I,
   And kept His Father's law.

4 At twelve years old He talked with men,
   The Jews all wondering stand ;
Yet He obeyed His mother then,
   And came at her command.

5 Then why should I so long delay
   What others learned so soon ?
I would not pass another day
   Without this work begun.

47

217
And that 'from a child thou hast known the holy Scriptures.
2 Timothy iii. 15.   7 7.7 7.7 7.

1 O THAT I, like Timothy,
    Might the holy Scriptures know
From mine earliest infancy,
    Till for God mature I grow;
Made unto salvation wise,
    Ready for the glorious prize!

2 Jesus, all-redeeming Lord,
    Full of truth and full of grace,
Make me understand Thy word:
    Teach me, in my youthful days,
Wonders in Thy word to see,
    Wise through faith which is in Thee.

3 Open now mine eyes of faith;
    Open now the book of God;
Show me here the secret path
    Leading to Thy blessed abode:
Wisdom from above impart,
    Speak the meaning to my heart.

218
Let the word of Christ dwell in you richly in all wisdom.
Colossians iii. 16.   S.M.

1 THE praises of my tongue
    I offer to the Lord,
That I was taught, and learned so young,
    To read His holy word.

2 Dear Lord, this book of Thine
    Informs me where to go
For grace to pardon all my sin,
    And make me holy too.

- 3 O may Thy Spirit teach,
    And make my heart receive,
Those truths which all Thy servants preach,
    And all Thy saints believe.

4 Then shall I praise the Lord
    In a more cheerful strain,
That I was taught to read His word,
    And have not learned in vain.

219
The sword of the Spirit, which is the word of God.—Ephesians vi. 17.
10 8.10 9.10 9.10 9.

1 GUARD the Bible well, All its foes repel,
    The sweet story tell Of the Lord:
Guard what God revealed, As our sun and
    shield;
    Never, never yield His holy word.
Rouse then, Christians! Rally for the Bible!
Work on, pray on, Spread the truth
    abroad;
Stand then like men, In the cause triumph-
For the Bible is the word of God.   [ant,

2 Book of love divine, Precious word of Thine,
    Let it ever shine All abroad!
In the Spirit's might We must win the fight
    For this gospel light, The truth of God.
Rouse then, Christians! etc.

3 Shout the Bible song, Swell the mighty
    throng!
    In the cause be strong Of the right;
Look to God in prayer, When the foe you
    dare,
    And for ever wear His armour bright.
Rouse then, Christians! etc.
48

4 O ye Christian band, For this Bible stand!
    By the Lord's command, Ne'er give o'er;
Lead the army on, Till the strife is done,
    And the cause is won For evermore!
Rouse then, Christians! etc.

220
And when He had opened the Book, etc.—Luke iv. 17.   C.M.

1 O GENTLE Teacher, ever near,
    Our hearts with knowledge feed,
Thou wilt not quench the smoking flax,
    Nor break the bruisèd reed.

2 Though now Thou art exalted high,
    Our frailty Thou hast known;
O teach us in Thy tender love,
    Thy wisdom make us own.

3 O stoop and take us in Thy arms,
    And hear us as of old;
So shall our faith its zeal maintain,
    Nor will our love grow cold.

4 O write Thy laws upon our hearts
    In lines of truth and love;
And we at last shall see Thy face,
    And hymn Thy praise above!

221
This is a faithful saying.
1 Tim. i. 15.   7 6.7 6.7 6.7 6.7 6.

1 TELL me the old, old story
    Of unseen things above,
Of Jesus and His glory,
    Of Jesus and His love.
Tell me the story simply,
    As to a little child,
For I am weak and weary,
    And helpless and defiled.
    Tell me the old, old story
    Of Jesus and His love.

2 Tell me the story slowly,
    That I may take it in,
That wonderful redemption,
    God's remedy for sin.
Tell me the story often,
    For I forget so soon!
The early dew of morning
    Has passed away at noon. Tell me, etc.

3 Tell me the story softly,
    With earnest tones and grave:
Remember! I'm the sinner
    Whom Jesus came to save.
Tell me the story always,
    If you would really be,
In any time of trouble,
    A comforter to me.   Tell me, etc.

4 Tell me the same old story,
    When you have cause to fear
That this world's empty glory
    Is costing me too dear.
Yes, and when that world's glory
    Is dawning on my soul,
Tell me the old, old story,
    'Christ Jesus makes thee whole.'
    Tell me, etc.

222
Give me now wisdom and know-ledge.—2 Chronicles i. 10.   L.M.

1 I ASK not wealth, nor pomp, nor power,
    Nor the vain pleasures of an hour;
My soul aspires to nobler things
Than all the pride and state of kings.

2 One thing I ask, O! wilt Thou hear,
And grant my soul a gift so dear;
Wisdom descending from above,
The choicest token of Thy love:

3 Wisdom, betimes to know the Lord,
To fear His name and keep His word;
To lead my feet in paths of truth,
And guide and guard my wandering youth.

4 Then, should'st Thou grant me length of
days,
My life shall still proclaim Thy praise;
Or early death, I'll soar away
To realms of everlasting day.

223 *Better unto me than thousands of
gold and silver.—Psalm cxix. 72.*
118.129.66.129.

1 THANK God for the Bible, 'tis there that
we find
The story of Christ and His love;
How He came down to earth from His
beautiful home
In the mansions of glory above;
Thanks to Him we will bring,
Praise to Him we will sing;
For He came down to earth from His beau-
tiful home
In the mansions of glory above.

2 While He lived on this earth, to the sick
and the blind,
And to mourners, His blessings were
given;
And He said, 'Let the little ones come unto
Me,
For of such is the kingdom of heaven.'
Jesus calls us to come,
He's prepared us a home;
And He said, 'Let the little ones come unto
Me,
For of such is the kingdom of heaven.'

3 In the Bible we read of a beautiful land,
Where sorrow and pain never come;
For Jesus is there with a heavenly band,
And there He prepares us a home.
Jesus calls, shall we stay?
No! we will gladly obey;
For Jesus is there with a heavenly band,
And 'tis there He prepares us a home.

4 Thank God for the Bible; its truths o'er the
We'll scatter with bountiful hand; [earth
But we never can tell what a Bible is worth
Till we go to that beautiful land.
There our thanks we will bring,
There with angels we'll sing.
And its worth we can tell, when with Jesus
we dwell,
In heaven, that beautiful land.

224 *Holding fast the faithful word.
Titus i. 9.* 76.86.76.86.

1 WE won't give up the Bible,
God's holy book of truth;
The blessèd staff of hoary age,
The guide of early youth:
The sun that sheds a glorious light
O'er every dreary road;
The voice that speaks a Saviour's love,
And calls us home to God.

2 We won't give up the Bible
For pleasure or for pain;
We'll buy the truth, and sell it not
For all that we might gain.
Though man should try to take our prize
By guile or cruel might,
We'd suffer all that man could do;
God would defend the right.

3 We won't give up the Bible,
But spread it far and wide,
Until its saving words be heard
Beyond the rolling tide;
Till all shall know its gracious power,
And with one voice and heart
Resolve, that from God's sacred word
They'll never, never part.

225 *Thou hast the words of eternal
life.—John vi. 68.* 87.87.

1 O HOW blest the hour, Lord Jesus,
When we can to Thee draw near,
Promises so sweet and precious
From Thy gracious lips to hear!

2 Be with us this day to bless us,
That we may not hear in vain,
With the saving truths impress us
Which the words of life contain.

3 See us eager for salvation
Sit, great Master, at Thy feet,
And with breathless expectation
Hang upon Thine accents sweet.

4 Open Thou our minds, and lead us
Safely on our heavenward way;
With the lamp of truth precede us,
That we may not go astray.

5 Make us gentle, meek, and humble,
And yet bold in doing right;
Scatter darkness, lest we stumble;
Men walk safely in the light.

6 Lord, endue Thy word from heaven
With such light and love and power
That in us its silent leaven
May work on from hour to hour.

7 Give us grace to bear our witness
To the truths we have embraced,
And let others both their sweetness
And their quickening virtue taste.

226 *Take heed therefore how ye
hear.—Luke viii. 18.* S.V

1 LORD, help us as we hear,
To treasure up Thy word;
And not to-morrow to appear
As if it were unheard.

2 Lord, help us as we sing,
To mean the words we use;
And not to mock our heavenly King,
And all His love abuse.

3 Lord, help us as we pray,
To come with heart sincere;
And as we run in wisdom's way,
To seek Thy blessing here.

4 Lord, help us while we live,
Thy servants to abide;
Our food and raiment kindly give,
And all we need provide.

49

5 Lord, help us when we die,
　To reach yon heavenly shore;
And, with Thy holy ones on high,
　To praise Thee evermore.

227 *I will instruct thee and teach thee.*—Psalm xxxii. 8.　L.M.

1 GREAT Saviour, who didst condescend
　Young children in Thine arms to take,
Still prove Thyself the children's Friend,
　And save us for Thy mercy's sake.

2 'Tis by the guidance of Thy hand
　That we within Thy house appear;
Now in Thine awful presence stand
　To hear Thy word and join in prayer.

3 Like precious seed in fruitful ground
　Let the instruction we receive
With fruits of righteousness abound,·
　And make us to Thy glory live.

4 Then, through the slippery paths of youth
　Be Thou our Guardian and our Guide,
That we, directed by Thy truth,
　May never from Thy precepts slide.

5 To read Thy word our hearts incline;
　To understand it, light impart;
Great Saviour, may we all be Thine,
　Take full possession of each heart.

THE CHRISTIAN LIFE.
EARLY PIETY.

228 *I thy servant fear the* LORD *from my youth.*—1 Kings xviii. 12.　　C.M.

1 HAPPY the child whose youngest years
　Receive instruction well,
Who hates the sinner's path, and fears
　The road that leads to hell.

2 When we devote our youth to God,
　'Tis pleasing in His eyes;
A flower, when offered in the bud,
　Is no vain sacrifice.

3 'Twill save us from a thousand snares
　To mind religion young;
Grace will preserve our following years,
　And make our virtues strong.

4 To Thee, Almighty God, to Thee
　Our childhood we resign;
'Twill please us to look back and see
　That our whole lives were Thine.

5 Let the sweet work of prayer and praise
　Employ my youngest breath:
Thus I'm prepared for longer days,
　Or fit for early death.

229 *Suffer the little children to come unto Me.*—Mark x. 14.　8 6.8 6.8 8 8 6.

1 'LET little children come to Me,'
　So said our blessèd Lord;
And I, a little child, must be
　Obedient to His word;
On all my days must sing His praise,
　And bow before Him, for He said,
'Let little children come to Me,
　Let little children come.'

50

2 'Let little children come to Me,'
　It is my Saviour's call;
He spake it not to two or three,
　But to the children all.
And so when they His law obey,
　It is as if they heard Him say,
'Let little children come to Me,
　Let little children come.

3 'Let little children come to Me:'
　O Saviour, Lord, I come;
Through life and death I'll go with Thee,
　Thine arms shall be my home:
I cannot fear when Thou art near,
　And Thy sweet words I seem to hear,
'Let little children come to Me,
　Let little children come.'

230 *The* LORD *is my Shepherd.* Psalm xxiii. 1.　7 7.8 8.7 7.

1 I AM Jesus' little lamb,
　Ever glad at heart I am;
Jesus loves me, Jesus knows me,
All things fair and good He shows me,
　Even calls me by my name:
　Every day He is the same.

2 Safely in and out I go,
　Jesus loves and keeps me so.
When I hunger, Jesus feeds me;
When I thirst, my Shepherd leads me
　Where the waters softly flow,
　Where the sweetest pastures grow.

3 Should I not be always glad?
　Jesus would not have me sad;
And when this short life is ended,
Those whom the Good Shepherd tended
　Will be taken to the skies,
　There to dwell in Paradise.

231 *But now they desire a better country.*—Heb. xi. 16.　6 5.6 5.

1 I'M a little pilgrim,
　And a stranger here;
Though this world is pleasant,
　Sin is always near.

2 Mine's a better country,
　Where there is no sin;
Where the tones of sorrow
　Never enter in.

3 But a little pilgrim
　Must have garments clean,
If he'd wear the white robes,
　And with Christ be seen.

4 Jesus, cleanse and save me;
　Teach me to obey;
Holy Spirit, guide me
　On my heavenly way.

5 I'm a little pilgrim,
　And a stranger here,
But my home in heaven
　Cometh ever near.

232 *Grow in grace, and in the knowledge of our Lord and Saviour Jesus Christ.*—2 Peter iii. 18.　7 7.7 7.

1 EVERY little step I take
　Forward in my heavenly way,
Every little effort make
　To grow Christ-like day by day,

2 Little sighs and little prayers,
  Even little tears which fall,
  Little hopes and fears and cares,
  Saviour, Thou dost know them all.

3 Thus my greatest joy is this,
  That my Saviour, loving, mild,
  Knows the children's weaknesses,
  And Himself was once a child.

Him that cometh to Me I will in no
233 *wise cast out.—John vi. 37.*
7 7. 7 7.

1 SAVIOUR, bless a little child,
    Teach my heart the way to Thee;
  Make it gentle, meek, and mild;
  Loving Saviour, care for me.

2 I am young, but Thou hast said
  All who will may come to Thee;
  Feed my soul with living bread;
  Loving Saviour, care for me.

3 Jesus, help me, I am weak;
  Let me put my trust in Thee;
  Teach me how and what to speak;
  Loving Saviour, care for me.

4 I would never go astray,
  Never turn aside from Thee;
  Keep me in the heavenly way;
  Loving Saviour, care for me.

234 *Lord, teach us to pray.*
Luke xi. 1. C.M.

1 LORD, teach a little child to pray,
    Thy grace betimes impart,
  And grant Thy Holy Spirit may
  Renew my youthful heart.

2 A sinful creature I was born,
  And from my birth have strayed;
  I must be wretched and forlorn
  Without Thy mercy's aid.

3 But Christ can all my sins forgive,
  And wash away their stain;
  Can fit my soul with Him to live,
  And in His kingdom reign.

4 To Him let little children come,
  For He has said they may;
  His bosom then shall be their home,
  Their tears He'll wipe away.

5 All those who early seek His face
  Shall surely taste His love.
  Jesus shall guide them by His grace,
  To dwell with Him above.

235 *God be merciful to me a sinner.*
Luke xviii. 13. L.M.

1 LORD, look upon a little child,
    By nature sinful, rude, and wild;
  O, lay Thy gracious hand on me,
  And make me all I ought to be!

2 Make me Thy child, a child of God,
  Washed in my Saviour's precious blood;
  And my whole heart, from sin set free,
  A little vessel full of Thee.

3 O Jesus, take me to Thy breast,
  And bless me,—then I shall be blest;
  Both when I wake, and when I sleep,
  Thy little lamb in safety keep.

236 *My soul trusteth in Thee.*
Psalm lvii. 1. 10 4.10 4.10 10.

1 JESUS, who calledst little ones to Thee,
    To Thee I come;
  O take my hand in Thine, and speak to me,
      And lead me home; [stray,
  Lest from the path of life my feet should
  And Satan prowling make Thy lamb his
      prey.

2 I love to think that Thou with holy feet
      My path hast trod,
  Along life's common lane and dusty street
  Hast walked with God,
  On Mary's bosom drawn a baby's breath,
  And served Thy parents dear at Nazareth.

3 O gentle Jesus, make this heart of mine
      (So full of sin)
  As holy, harmless, undefiled, as Thine,
      And dwell therein: [know,
  Then, God my Father, I like Thee shall
  And grow in wisdom as in strength I grow.

4 To Thee, my Saviour, then, with morning
      Glad songs I'll raise, [light
  My saddest hours and darkest shall be
      With silent praise; [bright
  And should my work or play my thoughts
      employ,
  Thy will shall be my law, Thy love my joy.

237 *And they followed Jesus.*
John i. 37. L.M.

1 I WOULD a youthful pilgrim be,
    Resolved alone to follow Thee,
  Thou Lamb of God, who now art gone
  Up to Thine everlasting throne.

2 I would my heart to Thee resign;
  O come, and make it wholly Thine!
  Set up Thy kingdom, Lord, within,
  And cast out every thought of sin.

3 Be it my chief desire to prove
  How much I owe, how much I love;
  Contentedly my cross to take,
  And meekly bear it for Thy sake.

4 Then, when my pilgrimage is o'er,
  And I can serve Thee here no more,
  Within Thy temple, God of love,
  I'll serve Thee day and night above.

238 *Thou art my trust from my youth.*
Psalm lxxi. 5. S.M.

1 I'M not too young to sin,
    I'm not too young to die;
  I'm not too little to begin
    A life of faith and joy.

2 Jesus, I love Thy name;
    From evil set me free;
  And ever keep Thy feeble lamb,
    Who puts his trust in Thee.

Learn of Me; for I am meek and
239 *lowly in heart.—Matthew xi. 29.*
7 7.7 7.

1 GENTLE Jesus, meek and mild,
    Look upon a little child;
  Pity my simplicity,
  Suffer me to come to Thee.

51

2 Fain I would to Thee be brought;
  Gracious God, forbid it not;
  Give me, O my God! a place
  In the kingdom of Thy grace.

3 Fain I would be as Thou art;
  Give me Thy obedient heart:
  Thou art pitiful and kind;
  Let me have Thy loving mind.

4 Meek and lowly may I be;
  Thou art all humility:
  Let me to my betters bow;
  Subject to Thy parents Thou.

5 Let me above all fulfil
  God my heavenly Father's will;
  Never His good Spirit grieve,
  Only to His glory live.

240 *A new heart and a new spirit.*
    Ezekiel xviii. 31.   C.M.

1 BLEST Saviour, let me be a child,
   A little child of Thine;
  Thou hast on infant spirits smiled,
  O kindly smile on mine.

2 Make me a child in simple ways,
  In heart more simple still;
  Believing all the Father says,
  And doing all His will.

3 Give me a nature pure and true,
  My evil heart control;
  And day by day may grace renew
  The childhood of my soul.

4 May this sweet spirit ne'er depart,
  Midst all my joys and cares;
  And may I be a child in heart,
  Through all my following years.

241 *These little ones that believe in*
    Me.—Mark ix. 42.   8 8 6.8 8 6.

1 AND is it true, as I am told,
   That there are lambs within the fold
  Of God's belovèd Son?
  That Jesus Christ, with tender care,
  Will in His arms most gently bear
  The helpless little one?

2 And I, a little straying lamb,
  May come to Jesus as I am,
  Though goodness I have none;
  May now be folded on His breast,
  As birds within the parent-nest,
  And be His little one?

3 Others there are who love me too;
  But who, with all their love, could do
  What Jesus Christ has done?
  Then if He teaches me to pray,
  I'll surely go to Him., and say,
  Lord, keep Thy little one.

4 Then by this gracious Shepherd fed,
  And by His mercy gently led
   Where living waters run,
  My greatest pleasure will be this:
  That I'm a little lamb of His,
   His own dear little one

242 *While the evil days come not.*
    Ecclesiastes xii. 1. 7 6.7 6.

1 COME, while from joy's bright fountain
   The streams of pleasure flow;
  Come, ere thy buoyant spirits
  Have felt the blight of woe.

2 Remember thy Creator
  Now, in thy youthful days,
  And He will guide thy footsteps
  Through life's uncertain ways.

3 Remember thy Creator,
  He calls in tones of love;
  And offers endless blessing
  In brighter worlds above.

4 And in the hour of sadness,
  When earthly joys depart,
  His love shall be thy solace,
  And cheer thy drooping heart.

5 And when life's storms are over,
  And thou from earth art free,
  Thy God will be thy portion
  Throughout eternity.

243 *Remember now thy Creator in*
    the days of thy youth.
    Ecclesiastes xii. 1. C.M.

1 REMEMBER thy Creator now,
   In these thy youthful days;
  He will accept thine early vow,
  And listen to thy praise.

2 Remember thy Creator now,
  And seek Him while He's near;
  For evil days will come, when thou
  Shalt find no comfort near.

3 Remember thy Creator now;
  His willing servant be;
  Then, when thy head in death shall bow,
  He will remember thee.

4 Almighty God! our hearts incline
  Thy heavenly voice to hear;
  Let all our future days be Thine,
  Devoted to Thy fear.

244 *Whoso trusteth in the LORD, happy*
    is he.—Proverbs xvi. 20.
    L.M.

1 HOW sweet it is in early youth
   To tread the sacred paths of truth,
  From sin's deceitful snares to run,
  And find a heaven on earth begun!

2 How happy is the soul that knows
  What perfect peace and calm repose
  A gracious Father deigns to give
  To them who by His precepts live!

3 Forbid it, Lord, that we should stray
  Far distant from Thy holy way,
  Or so deceived and thoughtless be
  As to love pleasure more than Thee.

4 Though fools may make a mock of sin,
  O teach us wisely to begin
  To seek the safe and narrow road
  That leads to happiness and God.

245
Those that seek Me early shall find Me.—Proverbs viii. 17.

8 7.8 7.7 7.

1 THEY are blest, and blest for ever,
　　Who in childhood's early day
Seek the care of Him who never
　　Turns the seeking soul away.
Jesus, lest their feet should slide,
Condescends to be their guide.

2 Who the world's temptations scorning,
　　Keep in view the great reward,
And in youth's delightful morning
　　Yield themselves unto the Lord;
Jesus will their portion be
Now and through eternity.

3 He, their Shepherd and their Saviour,
　　Will with eyes of love behold,
And regard with kindest favour,
　　Every lamb within His fold.
He will guide them by His love
To His blessèd fold above.

246
Follow Me.—Matthew iv. 19.

8 7.8 7.

1 CHILDHOOD'S years are passing o'er us,
　　Youthful days will soon be gone;
Cares and sorrows lie before us,
　　Hidden dangers, snares unknown.

2 O may He who, meek and lowly,
　　Trod Himself this vale of woe,
Make us His, and make us holy,
　　Guard and guide us while we go.

3 Hark! it is the Saviour calling,
　　'Children, come, and follow Me!'
Jesus, keep our feet from falling;
　　Teach us all to follow Thee.

4 Soon we part; it may be never,
　　Never here to meet again;
O to meet in heaven for ever!
　　O the crown of life to gain!

247
Her ways are ways of pleasantness, and all her paths are peace.
Proverbs iii. 17.　8 8 6.8 8 6.

1 HAPPY beyond description he
　　Who in the paths of piety
Loves from his youth to run:
Its ways are ways of pleasantness,
And all its paths are joy and peace,
And heaven on earth begun.

2 If this felicity were mine,
I every other would resign,
　　With just and holy scorn;
Cheerful and blithe my way pursue,
And with the promised land in view,
　　Singing to God return.

248
Narrow is the way, which leadeth unto life.—Matthew vii. 14.
C.M.

1 THERE is a path that leads to God,
　　All others lead astray;
Narrow but pleasant is the road,
And Christians love the way

2 It leads straight through this world of sin,
　　And dangers must be passed;
But those who boldly walk therein
　　Will come to heaven at last.

3 How shall a little pilgrim dare
　　This dangerous path to tread?
For on the way is many a snare,
　　For youthful travellers spread.

4 While the broad road, where thousands go,
　　Lies near, and opens fair;
And many turn aside, I know,
　　And walk with sinners there.

5 But lest my feeble steps should slide,
　　Or wander from Thy way,
Lord, condescend to be my Guide,
　　And I shall never stray.

6 Thus I may safely venture through,
　　Beneath my Shepherd's care,
And keep the gate of heaven in view
　　Till I shall enter there.

249
Jesus beholding him loved him.
Mark x. 21.　C.M.

1 BY cool Siloam's shady rill
　　How sweet the lily grows!
How sweet the breath beneath the hill
Of Sharon's dewy rose!

2 Lo! such the child whose early feet
　　The paths of peace have trod.
Whose secret heart with influence sweet
　　Is upward drawn to God.

3 By cool Siloam's shady rill
　　The lily must decay;
The rose that blooms beneath the hill
　　Must shortly fade away.

4 And soon, too soon, the wintry hour
　　Of man's maturer age
Will shake the soul with sorrow's power
And stormy passion's rage.

5 O Thou, whose infant feet were found
　　Within Thy father's shrine!
Whose years, with changeless virtu
Were all alike divine:　[crowned.

6 Dependent on Thy bounteous breath,
　　We seek Thy grace alone,
In childhood, manhood, age, and death,
　　To keep us still Thine own!

250
The fear of the Lord, that is wisdom.
Job xxviii. 28
8 8 6.8 8 6.

1 BE it my only wisdom here
　　To serve the Lord with filial fear,
With loving gratitude;
Superior sense may I display,
By shunning every evil way,
　　And walking in the good.

2 O may I still from sin depart!
A wise and understanding heart,
　　Jesus, to me be given!
An let me through Thy Spirit know
To lorify my God below,
　　And find my way to heaven.

53

251 *Redeeming the time.*
Ephesians v. 16.　　C.M.

1 SWIFT as the wingèd arrow flies
　My time is hastening on;
Quick as the lightning from the skies
　My wasting moments run.

2 My follies past, O God, forgive,
　And every sin subdue;
And teach me henceforth how to live,
　With glory in my view.

3 'Twere better I had not been born,
　Than live without Thy fear!
For they are wretched and forlorn
　Who have their portion here.

4 But thanks to Thy great love and grace
　That in my early youth
I have been taught to seek Thy face,
　And know the way of truth.

5 O let Thy Spirit lead me still
　Along the happy road;
Conform me to Thy holy will,
　My Father and my God.

252 *Happy is the man that findeth
wisdom.*—Proverbs iii. 13.
C.M.

1 WHY should we spend our youthful days
　In folly and in sin,
When wisdom shows her pleasant ways
　And bids us walk therein?

2 Folly and sin our peace destroy;
　They glitter, and are past;
They yield us but a moment's joy,
　And end in death at last.

3 But if true wisdom we possess,
　Our joys shall never cease;
Her ways are ways of pleasantness,
　And all her paths are peace.

4 O may we in our youthful days
　Attend to wisdom's voice;
And make these holy, happy ways
　Our own delightful choice!

253 *Chosen that good part.*
Luke x. 42.　　77.77.

1 'IS religion that can give
　Sweetest pleasures while we live;
'Tis religion must supply
Solid comfort when we die.

2 After death, its joys will be
Lasting as eternity:
Be the living God my Friend,
Then my bliss shall never end.

254 *Early will I seek Thee.*
Psalm lxiii. 1.　　C.M.

1 LORD, now my journey's just begun,
　My course so little trod,
O, help me, ere I further run,
　To give my heart to God.

2 What sorrows may my steps attend
　I cannot now foretell;
But if the Lord will be my friend,
　I know that all is well.

3 If I am poor, He can supply
　Who has my table spread,
Who feeds the ravens when they cry,
　And fills His poor with bread.

4 And, Lord, whatever grief or ill
　For me may be in store,
Make me submissive to Thy will,
　And I would ask no more.

5 Attend me through my youthful way,
　Whatever be my lot;
And when I'm feeble, old, and grey,
　O Lord, forsake me not.

255 *The Son of man is come to save
that which was lost.*
Matthew xviii. 11.　　87.87.47.

1 YOUTHFUL, weak, and unprotected,
　Prone in folly's path to stray;
By no friendly hand directed,
We shall surely lose our way.
　Who shall guide us
To the realms of endless day?

2 Christian teachers may instruct us,
　Friends their generous aid bestow;
Will no powerful arm conduct us
Safely all the journey through?
　Who shall keep us,
Wanderers in a world of woe?

3 Christ, our Shepherd, waits to gather
　Every wanderer to His fold;
And with love our heavenly Father
Will each humble child behold.
　Lord, receive us;
'Tis Thy kindness makes us bold.

4 Thankful for the love that bought us,
　Now our feeble songs we raise;
Hither hath Thy mercy brought us,
Here with joy we sound Thy praise.
　To Thine honour
We would yield our future days.

256 *O come, let us worship and bow
down.*—Psalm xcv. 6.　　87.87.

1 LORD, a little band and lowly,
　We are come to worship Thee;
Thou art great and high and holy,
　Meek and humble let us be!

2 Fill our hearts with thoughts of Jesus,
　And of heaven, where He is gone;
And let nothing ever please us
　He would grieve to look upon.

3 For we know the Lord of glory
　Always sees what children do,
And is writing now the story
　Of our thoughts and actions too.

4 Let our sins be all forgiven;
　Make us fear whate'er is wrong;
Lead us on our way to heaven,
　There to sing a nobler song.

257 *Create in me a clean heart, O
God.*—Psalm li. 10.　　C.M.

1 O FOR a heart to praise my God,
　A heart from sin set free!
A heart that always feels Thy blood,
　So freely spilt for me!

2 A heart resigned, submissive, meek,
  My great Redeemer's throne,
  Where only Christ is heard to speak,
  Where Jesus reigns alone;

3 A humble, lowly, contrite heart,
  Believing, true, and clean;
  Which neither life nor death can part
  From Him that dwells within;

4 A heart in every thought renewed,
  And full of love divine;
  Perfect, and right, and pure, and good,
  A copy, Lord, of Thine!

5 Thy nature, gracious Lord, impart
  Come quickly from above,
  Write Thy new name upon my heart,
  Thy new, best name of love.

PRAYER.

258 *Pray without ceasing.*
1 Thessalonians v. 17.　　C.M.

1 PRAYER is the soul's sincere desire,
  Uttered or unexpressed;
  The motion of a hidden fire
  That trembles in the breast.

2 Prayer is the burden of a sigh,
  The falling of a tear;
  The upward glancing of an eye,
  When none but God is near.

3 Prayer is the simplest form of speech
  That infant lips can try;
  Prayer the sublimest strains that reach
  The Majesty on high.

4 Prayer is the Christian's vital breath,
  The Christian's native air,
  His watchword at the gates of death;
  He enters heaven with prayer.

5 O Thou by whom we come to God,
  The Life, the Truth, the Way!
  The path of prayer Thyself hast trod:
  Lord! teach us how to pray.

259 *Ask, and ye shall receive.*
John xvi. 24.　　7 7.77.

1 COME, my soul, thy suit prepare,
  Jesus loves to answer prayer;
  He Himself has bid thee pray,
  Therefore will not say thee nay.

2 Thou art coming to a King,
  Large petitions with thee bring;
  For His grace and power are such,
  None can ever ask too much.

3 With my burden I begin,
  Lord, remove this load of sin!
  Let Thy blood for sinners spilt
  Set my conscience free from guilt.

4 Lord, I come to Thee for rest,
  Take possession of my breast;
  There Thy blood-bought right maintain,
  And without a rival reign.

5 As the image in the glass
  Answers the beholder's face,
  Thus unto my heart appear,
  Print Thine own resemblance there.

260 *My voice shalt Thou hear in the morning, O LORD.*—Psalm v. 3.
7 6.7 6.7 6.7 6.

1 GO when the morning shineth,
  Go when the noon is bright,
  Go when the eve declineth,
  Go in the hush of night;
  Go with pure mind and feeling,
  Cast every fear away,
  And in thy chamber kneeling,
  Do thou in secret pray.

2 Remember all who love thee,
  All who are loved by thee;
  Pray, too, for those who hate thee,
  If any such there be.
  Then, for thyself, in meekness,
  A blessing humbly claim,
  And link with each petition
  Thy great Redeemer's name.

3 Or if 'tis e'er denied thee
  In solitude to pray,
  Should holy thoughts come o'er thee,
  When friends are round thy way;
  E'en then thy silent breathing
  Of spirit raised above
  May reach His throne of glory,
  Of mercy, truth, and love.

4 Whene'er thou pinest in sadness,
  Before His footstool fall;
  Remember, in thy gladness,
  His grace who gave thee all:
  O, not a joy or blessing
  With this can we compare,
  The power that He has given us
  To pour our souls in prayer.

261 *Let us draw near with a true heart.*—Hebrews x. 22.
7 7.7 7.7 7.

1 HOLY Lord, our hearts prepare
  For the solemn hour of prayer;
  Grant that while we bend the knee,
  All our thoughts may turn to Thee;
  Let Thy presence here be found,
  Breathing peace and joy around.

2 Lord, when we approach Thy throne,
  Make Thy power and glory known;
  As Thy children, may we call
  On our Father, Lord of all,
  And with holy love and fear
  At Thy footstool now appear.

3 Teach us, while we breathe our woes,
  On Thy promise to repose,
  All Thy tender love to trace
  In the Saviour's work of grace;
  Let us all in faith depend
  On our gracious God and Friend.

262 *Worship at His footstool.*
Psalm xcix. 5.　　8 7.8 7.4 7.

1 SAVIOUR, round Thy footstool bending,
  See our youthful band appear;

55

Let Thy Spirit, now descending,
  Our petitions deign to hear:
    Thou art willing,
  For Thy grace is always near.

2 Once on earth, to share Thy blessing
  Children sought to meet Thine eye,
While the anxious parents, pressing,
Brought their helpless infants nigh;
    For Thy favour
All their wants could well supply.

3 No harsh word of indignation
  Drove those tender lambs from Thee
Gentle was the invitation,
  Suffer them to come to Me:
    Holy children
Shall My heavenly kingdom see.

4 Gracious Saviour, Thou hast taught us
  That Thy words unchanged remain;
To Thy feet our friends have brought us,
  Heavenly blessings to obtain;
    O receive us,
Thou wilt not our prayer disdain.

5 Take us, then, Thou kind Protector,
  Fold us 'neath Thy watchful care,
Be our Shepherd, Friend, Director,
  In Thine arms of mercy bear:
    Guide to glory,
We shall dwell in safety there.

Ye ask, and receive not, because ye
263 *ask amiss.—James iv. 3.*
        S.M.

1 I OFTEN say my prayers;
    But do I ever pray?
And do the wishes of my heart
  Go with the words I say?

2 I may as well kneel down
  And worship gods of stone,
As offer to the living God
  A prayer of words alone.

3 For words without the heart
  The Lord will never hear;
Nor will He to those lips attend
  Whose prayers are not sincere.

4 Lord, teach me what I want,
  And teach me how to pray;
Nor let me ask Thee for Thy grace,
  Not feeling what I say.

If we ask anything according to His
264 *will, He heareth us.*
      1 John v. 14.   C.M.

1 THE Lord attends when children pray,
    A whisper He can hear;
He knows, not only what we say,
  But what we wish or fear.

2 He sees us when we are alone,
  Though no one else can see;
And all our thoughts to Him are known,
  Wherever we may be.

3 'Tis not enough to bend the knee,
  And words of prayer to say:
The heart must with the lips agree,
  Or else we do not pray.

56

4 Teach us, O Lord, to pray aright,
  Thy grace to us impart;
That we in prayer may take delight,
  And serve Thee with the heart.

5 Then, heavenly Father, at Thy throne,
  Thy praise we will proclaim,
And daily our requests make known
  In our Redeemer's name.

O LORD, . . . remember me, and
265 *visit me.—Jeremiah xv. 15. C.M.*

1 SOON as my youthful lips can speak
    Their feeble prayer to Thee,
O let my heart Thy favour seek;
  Good Lord, remember me.

2 In childhood's following years, my tongue
  Tuned to Thy praise shall be,
And this the heartfelt, humble song,
  Good Lord, remember me.

3 From every sin that wounds the heart
  May I be taught to flee;
O bid them all from me depart,
  Good Lord, remember me.

4 When, with life's heavy load oppressed,
  I bend the trembling knee,
Then give my suffering spirit rest,
  Good Lord, remember me.

5 O let me, on the bed of death,
  Thy great salvation see:
And cry with my expiring breath,
  Good Lord, remember me.

He shall call upon Me, and I will
266 *answer him.—Psalm xci. 15.*
        C.M.

1 THERE is an eye that never sleeps
    Beneath the wing of night;
There is an ear that never shuts
  When sink the beams of light.

2 There is an arm that never tires
  When human strength gives way;
There is a love that never fails
  When earthly loves decay.

3 That eye is fixed on seraph throngs;
  That arm upholds the sky;
That ear is filled with angel songs;
  That love is throned on high.

4 But there's a power which man can wield,
  When mortal aid is vain,
That eye, that arm, that love to reach,
  That listening ear to gain.

5 That power is prayer; which soars on high
  Through Jesus to the throne,
And moves the hand which moves the
  To bring salvation down.   [world,

That we may obtain mercy, and
267 *find grace to help.*
      Hebrews iv. 16.   C.M.

1 O FATHER, we are very weak,
    And need Thy constant care;
And therefore we have come to speak
  To Thee in humble prayer.

2 Now teach us Thy most holy will,
  And lead us in Thy way;
Protect our souls from every ill,
  And cleanse our hearts, we pray.

3 Preserve our childhood from the snares
  That Satan lays for youth;
In mercy hear our simple prayers,
  And guard us by Thy truth.

4 And as we grow in years, bestow
  Yet more and more of grace;
And ever to Thy children show
  A loving Father's face.

5 Be Thou our Guide through all our days;
  Conduct us to the end;
And then a heavenly song we'll raise
  To Thee, the children's Friend.

268 *And I will commune with thee from
above the mercy-seat.*
Exodus xxv. 22.   L.M.

1 FROM every stormy wind that blows,
From every swelling tide of woes,
There is a calm, a safe retreat;
'Tis found beneath the mercy-seat.

2 There is a place where Jesus sheds
The oil of gladness on our heads,
A place than all beside more sweet;
It is the blood-stained mercy-seat.

3 There is a spot where spirits blend,
And friend holds fellowship with friend;
Though sundered far, by faith they meet
Around one common mercy-seat.

4 There, there on eagles' wings we soar,
And time and sense appear no more;
There heavenly joys our spirits greet,
And glory crowns the mercy-seat.

269 *Give me now wisdom.*
2 Chronicles i. 10.   C.M.

1 ALMIGHTY God! in humble prayer
  To Thee our souls we lift;
Do Thou our waiting minds prepare
  For Thy most needful gift.

2 We ask not golden streams of wealth
  Along our path to flow;
We ask not undecaying health,
  Nor length of years below;

3 We ask not honours, which an hour
  May bring and take away;
We ask not pleasure, pomp, and power,
  Lest we should go astray.

4 We ask for wisdom: Lord, impart
  The knowledge how to live;
A wise and understanding heart
  To all before Thee give.

270 *Teach me to do Thy will.*
Psalm cxliii. 10.   7.7.7.7.

1 JESUS, Saviour, Son of God,
Who for me life's pathway trod,
Who for me became a Child,
Make me humble, meek, and mild.

2 I Thy little lamb would be,
Jesus, I would follow Thee;
Samuel was Thy child of old,
Take me, too, within Thy fold.

3 Teach me how to pray to Thee,
Make me holy, heavenly;
Let me love what Thou dost love,
Let me live with Thee above.

271 *He will guide you into all truth.*
John xvi. 13.   7.7.7.7.7.7.

1 WHEN our hearts are glad and light,
  When the path is fair and bright,
When from care and sorrow free,
Help us, Lord, to cling to Thee;
  Be our Comforter and Friend,
  Guide and keep us to the end.

2 When the way is dark and drear,
When no loving friend is near;
When we suffer pain or loss,
When we bow beneath the cross,
  Be our Comforter and Friend,
  Guide and keep us to the end.

3 When we strive to do the right,
When we follow, serve, or fight,
When we seek to do Thy will,
When we hear Thee say, 'Stand still,'
  Be our Comforter and Friend,
  Guide and keep us to the end.

4 When we near our endless home,
When the closing hour shall come,
When we cross death's chilling tide,
Lead us to the other side;
  Be our Comforter and Friend,
  Guide and keep us to the end.

5 When we reach that other land,
When before the Judge we stand,
When the books shall opened be,
Saviour, we would cling to Thee.
  Living, dying, be our Friend;
  Bless us, keep us to the end.

272 *Hear Thou from heaven Thy dwelling-place, and forgive.*
2 Chron. vi. 30.   7.5.7.5.7.5.8.8.

1 WHEN the weary, seeking rest,
  To Thy goodness flee;
When the heavy-laden cast
  All their load on Thee;
When the troubled, seeking peace,
  On Thy name shall call;
When the sinner, seeking life,
  At Thy feet shall fall:
Hear, then, in love, O Lord, the cry
In heaven, Thy dwelling-place on high.

2 When the worldling, sick at heart,
  Lifts his soul above;
When the prodigal looks back
  To his Father's love;
When the proud man from his pride
  Stoops to seek Thy face;
When the burdened brings his guilt
  To Thy throne of grace: Hear, then, etc.

3 When the stranger asks a home,
  All his toils to end;
When the hungry craveth food,
  And the poor a friend;
When the sailor on the wave
  Bows the suppliant knee;
When the soldier on the field
  Lifts his heart to Thee: Hear, then, etc.

57

4 When the man of toil and care
    In the city crowd,
  When the shepherd on the moor
    names the name of God ;
  When the learnèd and the high,
    Tired of earthly fame,
  Upon nobler joys intent,
  Name the blessèd name : Hear, then, etc.

REPENTANCE.

273 *God be merciful to me a sinner.*
        Luke xviii. 13.   C.M.

1 A SINNER, Lord, behold, I stand,
    In thought and word and deed ;
  But Jesus sits at Thy right hand
    For such to intercede.

2 Thou, Lord, canst change this evil heart,
    Canst give a holy mind,
  And Thine own heavenly grace impart,
    Which those who seek shall find.

3 To heaven can reach the softest word,
    A child's repentant prayer ;
  For tears are seen, and sighs are heard,
    And thoughts regarded there.

4 Then let me all my sins confess,
    And pardoning grace implore,
  That I may love my follies less,
    And love my Saviour more.

274 *Let the wicked forsake his way.*
        Isaiah lv. 7.   L.M.

1 BESET with snares on every hand,
    In life's uncertain path I stand ;
  Saviour divine, diffuse Thy light,
  To guide my youthful steps aright.

2 Incline this roving, treacherous heart,
  Great God! to choose the better part,
  To scorn the trifles of a day
  For joy that none can take away.

3 Then let the wildest storms arise,
  Let tempests rage through earth and skies :
  No fatal shipwreck shall I fear,
  But all my treasures with me bear.

4 If Thou, my Saviour, still be nigh,
  Cheerful I live, and joyful die ;
  Secure, when mortal comforts flee,
  To find ten thousand worlds in Thee.

275 *Come unto me. . . . and I will give*
        you rest.—Matthew xi. 28.
                    7 6.7 6.7 6.7 6.

1 'COME unto Me, ye weary,
    And I will give you rest.'
  O blessèd voice of Jesus,
    Which comes to hearts oppressed!
  It tells of benediction,
    Of pardon, grace, and peace,
  Of joy that hath no ending,
    Of love which cannot cease.

2 'Come unto me, dear children,
    And I will give you light.'
  O loving voice of Jesus,
    Which comes to cheer the night!
  Our hearts were filled with sadness,
    And we had lost our way ;
  But morning brings us gladness,
    And songs the break of day.

58

---

3 'Come unto me, ye fainting,
    And I will give you life.'
  O peaceful voice of Jesus,
    Which comes to end our strife!
  The foe is stern and eager,
    The fight is fierce and long ;
  But Thou hast made us mighty,
    And stronger than the strong.

4 'And whosoever cometh
    I will not cast him out.'
  O patient love of Jesus,
    Which drives away our doubt ;
  Which calls us, very sinners,
    Unworthy though we be
  Of love so free and boundless,
    To come, O Lord, to Thee!

276 *And make you a new heart and a*
        new spirit.—Ezekiel xviii. 31.
                            7 7.7 7.

1 GOD of mercy, God of love!
    Hear me from Thy throne above ;
  Teach me how in truth to pray :
  Take my sinful heart away.

2 Oft I disobedient grow,
  And unlovely tempers show ;
  Evil things I do and say :
  Take my wicked heart away.

3 Mould my nature all afresh,
  Give to me the heart of flesh ;
  For I know that grace divine
  Changes even hearts like mine.

277 *Haste thee, escape thither!*
        Genesis xix. 22.   8 8.8 8.4.

1 HASTE, traveller, haste! the night
    comes on,
  And many a shining hour is gone ;
  The storm is gathering in the west,
  And thou art far from home and rest :
      Haste, traveller, haste!

2 O, far from home thy footsteps stray ;
  Christ is the life, and Christ the way,
  And Christ the light : thy setting sun
  Sinks ere the morn is scarce begun :
      Haste, traveller, haste!

3 Then linger not in all the plain ;
  Flee for thy life, the mountain gain ;
  Look not behind, make no delay ;
  O, speed thee, speed thee on thy way!
      Haste, traveller, haste!

4 Poor, lost, benighted soul! art thou
  Willing to find salvation now?
  There yet is hope ; hear mercy's call ;
  Truth, life, light, way,—in Christ is all!
      Haste to Him, haste!

278 *Seek ye My face. . . . Thy face,*
        LORD, *will I seek.*
        Psalm xxvii. 8.   7 7.7.7.7.7.

1 JESUS bids me seek His face ;
    Lord, I come to ask Thy grace ;
  Send Thy Spirit from above,
  Teach me to obey and love.
  Unto Thee I fain would go ;
  All I want Thou canst bestow.

2 Wilt Thou, Lord, a child receive?
  Wilt Thou all my sins forgive?
  O, dissolve this heart of stone!
  Make me Thine, and Thine alone.
  Sin is present with me still;
  Disobedient is my will.

3 Sinful thoughts too oft prevail,
  Vain desires my heart assail;
  O my Saviour, make me whole,
  Form anew my inmost soul;
  Kindly guide me every day;
  Be my everlasting stay.

That we may rejoice and be glad all
279 *our days.—Psalm xc. 14.*
          5 5 11.5 5 11.

1 COME, let us embrace,
    In our earliest days,
The offers of life and salvation by grace;
  Let us gladly believe,
    And the pardon receive, [doth give.
Which the Father of mercies through Jesus

2 His kingdom below
    He hath called us to know,
And in stature and heavenly wisdom to grow:
  In His work to remain,
    Till His image we gain,
And the fulness of Christ in perfection attain.

3 Then let us begin
    By renouncing all sin, [clean,
And by faith in the blood that washes us
  With endeavour sincere
    To Jesus draw near, [appear,
And be instant in prayer till our Saviour

4 If now Thou art nigh,
    Appear at our cry,
Thy love to reveal, and Thy blood to apply;
  Thy little ones own,
    And perfect in one,
And admit us at last to a share of Thy throne.

I thought on my ways, and turned
280 *my feet unto Thy testimonies.*
    Psalm cxix. 59.   S.M.

1 IF Jesus Christ was sent
    To save us from our sin,
And kindly teach us to repent,
    We should at once begin.

2 'Tis not enough to *say*,
  'We're sorry and repent,'
Yet still go on from day to day
  Just as we always went.

3 Repentance is to leave
    The sins we loved before,
And show that we in earnest grieve
    By doing so no more.

4 Lord, make us thus sincere,
    To watch as well as pray;
However small, however dear,
    Take all our sins away.

And I . . . . will draw all men unto
281 *Me.—John xii. 32.*
          6 6.6 6.6 6.6 6.3.

1 COME to the Saviour now!
    He gently calleth thee;
In true repentance bow,
    Before Him bend the knee.

He waiteth to bestow
  Salvation, peace, and love,
True joy on earth below,
  A home in heaven above.
    Come, come, come.

2 Come to the Saviour now!
    Gaze on that mystic tide,
Water and blood that flow
    Forth from His wounded side.
  Hark to that suffering One!
  ''Tis finished!' now He cries;
  Redemption's work is done,
    Then bows His head and dies.
    Come, come, come.

3 Come to the Saviour now!
    He suffered all for thee,
And in His merits thou
    Hast an unfailing plea.
  No vain excuses frame,
    For feelings do not stay;
  one who to Jesus came
    Were ever sent away.
    Come, come, come.

4 Come to the Saviour now!
    Ye who have wandered far,
Renew your solemn vow,
    For His by right you are.
  Come, like poor, wandering sheep
    Returning to His fold,
  His arm will safely keep,
    His love will ne'er grow cold.
    Come, come, come.

5 Come to the Saviour, all!
    Whate'er your burdens be;
Hear now His loving call,
    'Cast all your care on Me.'
  Come, and for every grief
    In Jesus you will find
  A sure and safe relief,
    A loving Friend and kind.
    Come, come, come.

282 *There shall be showers of blessing.*
    Ezekiel xxxiv. 26.   8 7.8 7.3.

1 LORD, I hear of showers of blessing
    Thou art scattering full and free,
Showers, the thirsty land refreshing;
    Let some drops now fall on me.
          Even me.

2 Pass me not, O God, my Father,
    Sinful though my heart may be!
Thou might'st leave me, but the rather
    Let Thy mercy light on me.   Even me.

3 Pass me not, O gracious Saviour,
    Let me live and cling to Thee!
I am longing for Thy favour:
    Whilst Thou'rt calling, O call me!
          Even me.

4 Pass me not, O mighty Spirit!
    Thou canst make the blind to see:
Witnesser of Jesu's merit!
    Speak some word of power to me.
          Even me.

5 Love of God so pure and changeless,
    Blood of Christ so rich, so free,
Grace of God so strong and boundless,
    Magnify it all in me!   Even me.

283 *Strive to enter in at the strait gate.*
Luke xiii. 24.   11 11.11 11.11 11.

1 ONWARD, children ! onward ! leave the
    paths of sin ;
Hasten to the strait gate, strive to enter in :
None can knock unheeded, none can strive
    in vain,
For the Saviour's welcome, all that seek
    obtain.
  Onward, children ! onward ! is the call
    to-day ;
  Come with ready footsteps, and that call
    obey.

2 Onward, children ! onward ! in the narrow
    way,
Christ your Lord shall lead you safely day
    by day,
And with such a Leader what have you to
    fear?
Satan may oppose you, but your King is
    near.
  Onward, children ! etc.

3 Onward, children ! onward ! seek no cross
    to shun ;
Mind when night approaches, that your
    work is done ;
That you may with gladness, as life closes
    here,
Enter death's dark valley, having nought
    to fear.
  Onward, children ! etc.

4 Onward, children ! onward ! guardian
    angels sing :
Hasten to the palace of your God and King;
Clad in heavenly armour, to the end endure;
You with Christ shall triumph, victory is
    sure.
  Onward, children ! etc.

5 Onward, ever onward ! till you join the
    throng
Who in dazzling raiment sing the triumph-
    song;
And to heavenly music cry with one accord,
'Holy ! holy ! holy ! is our sovereign Lord.'
  Onward, children ! etc.

284 *The Holy Ghost saith, To-day, if ye
    will hear His voice.*
Hebrews iii. 7.   S.M.

1 THERE is a precious day,
    In youth that day is ours,
When we should dedicate to God
  Our life with all its powers.

2 There is a gracious day,
    When conscience speaks within ;
Tis now, for now the Spirit strives,
  Convincing us of sin.

3 There is a holy day,
    Of faith and hope and love :
It reaches through our Christian life
  On earth to heaven above.

4 There is a solemn day,
    When we must yield our breath :
And live to die no more, or die
  An everlasting death.

5 There is an awful day
    Of judgment and decree :
Lord ! be we all through Christ prepared
  That last of days to see.

60

6 There is a glorious day
    Of sweet Sabbatic rest :
O, may we its eternal length
  Enjoy with all the blest !

285 *Yet there is room.*
Luke xiv. 22.   10 10.4 6.

1 YET there is room ! the Lamb's bright
    hall of song,
With its fair glory, beckons thee along.
    Room, room, still room !
    O, enter, enter now !

2 Day is declining, and the sun is low ;
The shadows lengthen, light makes haste
    Room, room, etc.   [to go.

3 The bridal hall is filling for the feast,
Pass in, pass in, and be the Bridegroom's
    Room, room, etc.   [guest.

4 It fills, it fills, that hall of jubilee !
Make haste, make haste : 'tis not too full
    Room, room, etc.   [for thee.

5 Yet there is room ! Still open stands the
    gate,
The gate of love ; it is not yet too late.
    Room, room, etc.

6 Pass in, pass in ! That banquet is for thee ;
That cup of everlasting love is free.
    Room, room, etc.

7 All heaven is there : all joy ! Go in, go in ;
The angels beckon thee the prize to win.
    Room, room, etc.

8 Louder and sweeter sounds the loving call ;
Come, lingerer, come ; enter that festal
    Room, room, etc.   [hall.

9 Ere night that gate may close, and seal thy
    doom :
Then the last low long cry : 'No room, no
    No room, no room !   [room !'
    O, woeful cry, 'No room !'

286 *O* LORD, *forgive.*—Daniel ix. 19.
C.M

1 WE do not love Thee as we ought
    For blessings we receive ;
We sin in word, in deed, and thought :
  Our sins, O Lord, forgive.

2 Oft to bad tempers we give way,
    And ill designs conceive ;
And often we neglect to pray :
  These youthful sins forgive.

3 The Saviour died our guilt to bear,
    That we to Him might live ;
Hence we with hope present this prayer
  Our youthful sins forgive.

287 *All we like sheep have gone
    astray.*—Isaiah liii. 6.   C.M

1 ALMIGHTY Father, God of grace,
    We all, like sheep astray,
In folly from Thy paths have turned
  Each to his sinful way.

2 Sins of omission and of act
    Through all our lives abound ;
Alas ! in thought and word and deed
  No health in us is found.

3 O spare us, Lord, in mercy spare:
Our contrite souls restore;
Through Him who suffered on the cross,
And man's transgression bore.

4 And grant, O Father, for His sake,
That we through all our days
A just and godly life may lead,
To Thine eternal praise.

288

Behold, I stand at the door, and knock.—Revelation iii. 20,
7 7.8 7.8 7.

1 KNOCKING, knocking, who is there?
Waiting, waiting, O, how fair!
'Tis a Pilgrim, strange and kingly,
Never such was seen before.
Ah! my soul, for such a wonder
Wilt thou not undo the door?

2 Knocking, knocking, still He's there,
Waiting, waiting, wondrous fair;
But the door is hard to open,
For the weeds and ivy-vine,
With their dark and clinging tendrils,
Ever round the hinges twine.

3 Knocking, knocking—what, still there!
Waiting, waiting, grand and fair;
Yes, the piercèd hand still knocketh,
And beneath the crownèd hair
Beam the patient eyes, so tender,
Of thy Saviour, waiting there.

289

If any man . . . open the door, I will come in to him, etc.
Revelation iii. 20.   L.M

1 BEHOLD! a Stranger at the door;
He gently knocks, has knocked before,
Has waited long, is waiting still:
You use no other friend so ill.

2 But will He prove a friend indeed?
He will, the very friend you need;
Jesus of Nazareth, 'tis He,
With garments dyed at Calvary.

3 O, wondrous attitude! He stands
With loving heart and outstretched hands;
O, matchless kindness! and He shows
This matchless kindness to His foes!

4 Admit Him, for the human breast
Ne'er entertained so kind a guest;
No mortal tongue their joys can tell
With whom He condescends to dwell.

5 Yet know—nor of the terms complain—
Where Jesus comes, He comes to reign,
To reign with universal sway;
E'en thoughts must die that disobey.

6 Sovereign of souls! Thou Prince of peace!
O may Thy gentle reign increase!
Throw wide the door, each willing mind;
And be His empire all mankind!

290

He calleth thee.
Mark x. 49.   7 5.7 5.

1 COME to Jesus, little one,
Come to Jesus now;
Humbly at His gracious throne
In submission bow.
C

2 At His feet confess your sin;
Seek forgiveness there:
For His blood can make you clean;
He will hear your prayer.

3 Seek His face without delay;
Give Him now your heart;
Tarry not, but, while you may,
Choose the better part.

4 Come to Jesus, little one,
Come to Jesus now;
Humbly at His gracious throne
In submission bow.

291

Ho, every one that thirsteth, come ye to the waters!—Isaiah lv. 1.
7 7.8 7.7 7.8 7.

1 HO, every one that thirsteth,
Hear Jesu's invitation:
O come, and welcome all to take
The waters of salvation!
All ye that have no money,
Come to the flowing river,
For milk and wine and bread divine,
And eat and live for ever.

2 Come to your loving Saviour,
Who gives this gracious token,
To contrite hearts His love imparts,
And gently heals the broken!
Abundant pardon waits thee,
Heaven's bliss lies straight before thee,
Good angels yearn for thy return,
To strike their harps in glory.

3 O seek for pardoning mercy,
While mercy still is proffered,
While God is near, in humble fear
Accept the pardon offered!
O cry for true repentance,
The Spirit's mighty working,
And turn to God through Jesu's blood,
Thy every sin forsaking.

4 Come then, O trembling sinner,
Hear Jesu's invitation;
Accept His love, and sweetly prove
His promise of salvation!
Bid doubt and sorrow vanish,
From sin and Satan sever,
In Jesu's strength cry out at length,
I am the Lord's for ever.

292

To-day, if ye will hear His voice.
Hebrews iv. 7.   6 4.0 4.

1 TO-DAY the Saviour calls;
Ye wanderers, come.
O ye misguided souls,
Why longer roam?

2 To-day the Saviour calls;
O listen now;
Within these sacred walls
To Jesus bow.

3 To-day the Saviour calls;
For refuge fly;
The storm of vengeance falls,
Ruin is nigh.

4 The Spirit calls to-day;
Yield to His power;
O grieve Him not away,
'Tis mercy's hour.

293 *Jesus of Nazareth passeth by.*
Luke xviii. 37. C.M.

1 JESU, if still Thou art to-day
As yesterday the same,
Present to heal, in me display
The virtue of Thy name.

2 If still Thou goest about to do
Thy needy creatures good,
On me, that I Thy praise may show,
Be all Thy wonders showed.

3 Blind from my birth to guilt and Thee,
And dark I am within;
The love of God I cannot see,
The sinfulness of sin.

4 But Thou, they say, art passing by;
O let me find Thee near !
Jesu, in mercy hear my cry,
Thou Son of David, hear !

5 Behold me waiting in the way
For Thee, the heavenly light :
Command me to be brought, and say,
' Sinner, receive Thy sight !'

294 *Lord, what wilt Thou have me
to do ?*—Acts ix. 6. C.M.

1 WHAT is there, Lord, a child can do
That feels with guilt oppressed?
There's evil that I never knew
Before, within my breast.

2 My thoughts are vain ; my heart is hard,
My temper quick to rise ;
And when I seem upon my guard
Sin takes me by surprise.

3 Ashamed, to Thy commands I turn,
For I have broken them ;
And in Thy holy Scriptures learn
The laws that sin condemn.

4 With pity to my prayer attend,
My humble voice regard ;
And Thine own Holy Spirit send,
To melt a heart so hard.

5 I feel there is no strength in me
To love my God alone ;
But, Lord, I come and look to Thee
To break this heart of stone.

295 *Come unto Me, all ye that labour and
are heavy laden,* etc.
Matthew xi. 28. 85.83.

1 ART thou weary, art thou languid,
Art thou sore distressed?
' Come to Me,' saith One, ' and coming
Be at rest !'

2 Hath He marks to lead me to Him,
If He be my guide?
In His feet and hands are wound-prints,
And His side

3 Hath He diadem as monarch
That His brow adorns?
Yea, a crown, in very surety,
But of thorns !

4 If I find Him, if I follow,
What His guerdon here?
Many a sorrow, many a labour,
Many a tear.

62

5 If I still hold closely to Him,
What hath He at last?
Sorrow vanquished, labour ended,
Jordan past,

6 If I ask Him to receive me,
Will He say me nay ?
— Not till earth, and not till heaven
Pass away.

296 *Ye will not come to Me, that ye might
have life.*—John v. 40.
9 10.9 6.9 9 9.6.

1 COME to the Saviour, make no delay ;
Here in His word He has shown us the
Here in our midst He standeth to-day, [way;
Tenderly saying, ' Come !'
Joyful, joyful will the meeting be,
When from sin our hearts are pure and
free,
And we shall gather, Saviour, with Thee,
In our eternal home.

2 ' Suffer the children !' O, hear His voice !
Let every heart leap forth and rejoice !
And let us freely make Him our choice !
Do not delay, but come.
Joyful, joyful will the meeting be, etc.

3 Think once again, He's with us to-day ;
Heed now His blessèd command, and obey ;
Hear now His accents tenderly say,
' Will you, My children, come ?'
Joyful, joyful will the meeting be, etc.

297 *Our Father which art in heaven.*
Matthew vi. 9. C.M.

1 TO God, who reigns above the sky,
Our Father and our Friend,
Him let all our vows be paid,
And all our prayers ascend.

2 'Tis He who claims our youthful hearts,
He loves to hear us pray ;
By night we'll think upon His love,
And praise Him every day.

3 When we offend against our God,
We'll ask His pardoning love ;
'Twas for our sins the Saviour died,
And pleads for us above.

4 With all the love a father feels,
He pities and forgives ;
And though our earthly parents die,
Our heavenly Father lives.

298 *The darkness and the light are
both alike to Thee.*
Psalm cxxxix. 12. C.M.

1 ALMIGHTY God, Thy piercing eye
Strikes through the shades of night,
And our most secret actions lie
All open to Thy sight.

2 There's not a sin that we commit,
Nor wicked word we say,
But in Thy dreadful book 'tis writ,
Against the judgment day.

3 And must the crimes that I have done
Be read and published there,
Be all exposed before the sun,
While men and angels hear ?

4 Lord, at Thy foot ashamed I lie,
Upward I dare not look ;
Pardon my sins before I die,
And blot them from Thy book

5 Remember all the dying pains
That my Redeemer felt ;
And let His blood wash out my stains,
And answer for my guilt.

6 O may I now for ever fear
To indulge a sinful thought ;
Since the great God can see and hear,
And writes down every fault.

299 *Able also to save them to the utter-*
most.—Heb. vii. 25.   8 7.8 7.4 7.

1 COME, ye sinners, poor and wretched
Weak and wounded, sick and sore :
Jesus ready stands to save you,
Full of pity joined with power ;
He is able,
He is willing ; doubt no more.

2 Come, ye needy, come, and welcome,
God's free bounty glorify ;
True belief, and true repentance,
Every grace that brings us nigh,
Without money,
Come to Jesus Christ and buy.

3 Let not conscience make you linger,
Nor of fitness fondly dream ;
All the fitness He requireth
Is to feel your need of Him :
This He gives you ;
'Tis the Spirit's rising beam.

4 Come, ye weary, heavy laden,
Bruised and mangled by the fall ;
If you tarry till you're better,
You will never come at all :
Not the righteous,
Sinners Jesus came to call.

5 Lo ! the incarnate God ascended,
Pleads the merit of His blood :
Venture on Him, venture wholly,
Let no other trust intrude ;
None but Jesus
Can do helpless sinners good.

FAITH.

300 *Seeing He ever liveth to make*
intercession for them.
Hebrews vii. 25.   6 6.6 6.8 8.

1 ARISE, my soul, arise,
Shake off thy guilty fears ;
The bleeding Sacrifice
In my behalf appears ;
Before the throne my Surety stands ;
My name is written on His hands.

2 He ever lives above,
For me to intercede,
His all-redeeming love,
His precious blood, to plead ;
His blood atoned for all our race,
And sprinkles now the throne of grace.

3 Five bleeding wounds He bears,
Received on Calvary ;
They pour effectual prayers,
They strongly speak for me :
'Forgive him, O forgive,' they cry,
'Nor let that ransomed sinner die !'

4 The Father hears Him pray,
His dear Anointed One ;
He cannot turn away
The presence of His Son :
His Spirit answers to the blood,
And tells me I am born of God.

5 My God is reconciled,
His pardoning voice I hear,
He owns me for His child,
I can no longer fear,
With confidence I now draw nigh,
And, Father, Abba, Father, cry !

301 *Trusting in the* LORD.
Psalm cxii. 7.   8 5.8 3.

1 I AM trusting Thee, Lord Jesus,
Trusting only Thee !
Trusting Thee for full salvation,
Great and free.

2 I am trusting Thee for pardon,
At Thy feet I bow ;
For Thy grace and tender mercy,
Trusting now.

3 I am trusting Thee for cleansing
In the crimson flood ;
Trusting Thee to make me holy
By Thy blood.

4 I am trusting Thee to guide me ;
Thou alone shalt lead,
Every day and hour supplying
All my need.

5 I am trusting Thee for power,
Thine can never fail ;
Words which Thou Thyself shalt give me
Must prevail.

6 I am trusting Thee, Lord Jesus ;
Never let me fall ;
I am trusting Thee for ever,
And for all.

302 *As an hiding-place from the wind,*
and a covert from the tempest.
Isaiah xxxii. 2.   7 7.7 7.7 7.7 7.

1 JESU, Lover of my soul,
Let me to Thy bosom fly,
While the nearer waters roll,
While the tempest still is high :
Hide me, O my Saviour, hide.
Till the storm of life be past !
Safe into the haven guide,
O receive my soul at last !

2 Other refuge have I none,
Hangs my helpless soul on Thee ;
Leave, ah ! leave me not alone,
Still support and comfort me :
All my trust on Thee is stayed,
All my help from Thee I bring ;
Cover my defenceless head
With the shadow of Thy wing.

63

3 Thou, O Christ, art all I want,
  More than all in Thee I find!
Raise the fallen, cheer the faint,
  Heal the sick, and lead the blind;
Just and holy is Thy name,
  I am all unrighteousness;
False and full of sin I am,
  Thou art full of truth and grace.

4 Plenteous grace with Thee is found,
  Grace to cover all my sin,
Let the healing streams abound;
  Make and keep me pure within:
Thou of life the fountain art,
  Freely let me take of Thee,
Spring Thou up within my heart,
  Rise to all eternity.

303 *Once, when He offered up Himself.*
Hebrews vii. 27.   6 5.6 5.

1 LET me learn of Jesus:
    He is kind to me;
  Once He died to save me,
    Nailed upon the tree.

2 If I go to Jesus,
    He will hear me pray,
  Make me good and holy,
    Take my sins away.

3 Let me think of Jesus:
    He is full of love,
  Looking down upon me
    From His throne above.

4 If I trust in Jesus,
    If I do His will,
  Then I shall be happy,
    Safe from every ill.

5 O how good is Jesus!
    May He hold my hand,
  And at last receive me
    To a better land.

304 *Looking unto Jesus.*
Hebrews xii. 2.   6 6 4.6 6 6 4.

1 MY faith looks up to Thee,
    Thou Lamb of Calvary:
  Saviour divine!
Now hear me while I pray,
Take all my guilt away;
O, let me from this day
    Be wholly Thine.

2 May Thy rich grace impart
Strength to my fainting heart,
  My zeal inspire:
As Thou hast died for me,
O, may my love to Thee
Pure, warm, and changeless be,
    A living fire.

3 When life's dark maze I tread,
And griefs around me spread,
  Be Thou my guide.
Bid darkness turn to day,
Wipe sorrow's tears away,
Nor let me ever stray
    From Thee aside.

4 When ends life's transient dream,
When death's cold, sullen stream
    Shall o'er me roll;

Blest Saviour! then in love,
  Fear and distrust remove,
O, bear me safe above,
    A ransomed soul.

305 *Having made peace through the blood of His cross.*
Colossians i. 20.   C.M.

1 O JESUS, to Thy cross we fly,
    For shelter from distress;
Through Thee for pardon we apply,
  For peace and holiness.

2 Thou art the true, eternal Rock,
    On which our faith is built:
Thou art the Shepherd of the flock,
  Whose blood for us was spilt.

3 From Thee the streams of blessing flow;
    By Thee the grace is given:
Thy blood can wash us white as snow,
  And make us meet for heaven.

4 Thou hast atoned for all our race,
    Thy sacrifice we plead;
Since Thou, before Thy Father's face,
  For us dost intercede.

5 O Lamb of God, for sinners slain!
    Look from Thy lofty throne;
Wash Thou away our guilty stain,
  And claim us for Thine own.

306 *Shew us Thy mercy, O LORD, and grant us Thy salvation.*
Psalm lxxxv. 7.   8 7.87.4 7.

1 SHOWERS of blessings fall on many,
    May not we receive them too?
Lord, we need as much as any,
    And may love as others do;
      May Thy Spirit
Fall on us like morning dew.

2 Though we are but life beginning,
    We have hearts with sin defiled,
Yet we may, like others sinning,
    Like them, too, be reconciled;
      God of mercy,
Save and bless each little child.

3 Save us through our Saviour's merit,
    Making us on Him depend;
Save us by Thy Holy Spirit,
    And preserve us to the end;
      Trusting, loving
Thee, our best and truest Friend.

307 *A man shall be as an hiding-place, . . . a covert, . . . the shadow of a great rock.*—Isaiah xxxii. 2.
7 6.7 6.7 8.7 6.

1 TO the haven of Thy breast,
    O Son of man, I fly!
Be my refuge and my rest,
    For O the storm is high!
Save me from the furious blast,
    A covert from the tempest be!
Hide me, Jesus, till o'erpast
    The storm of sin I see.

2 Welcome as the water-sprin
To a dry, barren place,
O descend on me, and bring
Thy sweet refreshing grace ;
O'er a parched and weary land
As a great rock extends its shade,
Hide me, Saviour, with Thine hand,
And screen my naked head.

For by grace are ye saved through
faith.—Ephesians ii. 8.

308
6 7.7 7 6.7 7 7 6.

WEEPING will not save me !
Though my face were bathed in
That could not allay my fears. [tears,
Could not wash the sin of years ;
Weeping will not save me.
Jesus wept and died for me ;
Jesus suffered on the tree ;
Jesus waits to make me free ;
He alone can save me !

2 Working will not save me :
Purest deeds that I can do,
Holiest thoughts and feelings too,
Cannot form my soul anew ;
Working will not save me. Jesus wept. etc.

3 Waiting will not save me :
Helpless, guilty, lost I lie,
In my ears is mercy's cry,
If I wait I can but die ;
Waiting will not save me. Jesus wept. etc.

4 Faith in Christ *will* save me :
Let me trust Thy weeping Son,
Trust the work that He has done.
To His arms help me to run ;
Faith in Christ *will* save me.
Jesus wept. etc.

He is able also to save them . . . that
come unto God by Him.

309
Hebrews vii. 25. 6 5.6 5.6 5.6 5.

1 IF I come to Jesus,
He will make me glad ;
He will give me pleasure
When my heart is sad.
If I come to Jesus,
Happy I shall be ;
He is gently calling
Little ones like me.

2 If I come to Jesus,
He will hear my prayer,
He will love me dearly,
He my sins did bear.
If I come to Jesus, etc.

3 If I come to Jesus,
He will take my hand,
He will kindly lead me
To a better land.
If I come to Jesus, etc.

4 There with happy children
Robed in snowy white,
I shall see my Saviour
In that world so bright.
If I come to Jesus, etc.

We would see Jesus.

310
John xii. 21. 10 9.10 9.

1 LEAD me to Jesus, lead me to Jesus,
Teach me to love Him, teach me to
pray ;
He is my Saviour, I would believe Him,
I would be like Him, show me the way.

2 Lead me to Jesus, He will protect me,
He is so loving, gentle, and mild ;
Calling the children, bidding them wel-
Surely He calls me—I am a child. [come ;

3 Lord, I am coming ! Jesus, my Saviour,
Pity my weakness, make me Thy child ;
I would receive Thee, trust, and believe
Thee,
I would be like Thee, gentle and mild.

Thou shalt guide me with Thy counsel,
and afterward receive me to

311
glory.—Psalm lxxiii. 24. D.S.M.

1 JESUS, we come to Thee,
That we may be forgiven ;
O ! let us all Thy children be,
And make us fit for heaven.
O ! be our Guide, we pray,
While through this world we roam,
And lead us so that every day
May find us nearer home.

2 Though we are taught the road,
We cannot go alone ;
Unless Thou lead us, O our God,
We ne'er shall reach Thy throne.
O ! be our Guide, we pray, etc.

3 Give us from Thy rich store
Of wisdom from above ;
That we may love and serve Thee more,
And better learn Thy love.
O ! be our Guide, we pray, etc.

4 Then shall we walk aright,
While keeping close to Thee ;
When Satan tempts have strength to fight,
And make the tempter flee.
A little pilgrim-band,
While through this world we roam,
O ! guide us with Thy loving hand,
Till Thou shalt take us home.

I will call on the LORD ; . . . so shall
I be saved.—2 Samuel xxii. 4.

312
6 5.6 5.7 7.6 5.

1 O MY Saviour, hear me,
Draw me close to Thee ;
Thou hast paid my ransom,
Thou hast died for me ;
Now by simple faith I claim
Pardon through Thy gracious name ;
Thou, my Ark of safety,
Let me fly to Thee.

2 O my Saviour, bless me !
Bless me while I pray ;
Grant Thy grace to help me,
Take my sins away :
I believe Thy promise, Lord,
I will trust Thy holy word ;
Thou my soul's Redeemer,
Bless me while I pray.

3 O my Saviour, love me !
Make me all Thine own ;
Leave me not to wander
In this world alone :
Bless my way with light divine,
Let Thy glory round me shine ;
Thou, my Rock, my Refuge,
Make me all Thine own.

4 O my Saviour, guard me !
Keep me evermore ;
Bless me, love me, guide me,
Till my work is o'er :
May I then, with glad surprise,
Chant Thy praise beyond the skies ;
There with Thee, my Saviour,
Dwell for evermore.

313 *I am Thine, save me.*
Psalm cxix. 94.   8 7.8 7.8 7.8 7

1 SAVIOUR, while my heart is tender
I would yield that heart to Thee ;
All my powers to Thee surrender,
Thine, and only Thine, to be.
Take me now, Lord Jesus, take me ;
Let my youthful heart be Thine ;
Thy devoted servant make me ;
Fill my soul with love divine.

2 Send me, Lord, where Thou wilt send me,
Only do Thou guide my way ;
May Thy grace through life attend me,
Gladly then shall I obey.
Let me do Thy will, or bear it,
I would know no will but Thine ;
Shouldst Thou take my life, or spare it,
I that life to Thee resign.

3 May this solemn consecration
Never once forgotten be ;
Let it know no revocation,
Registered, confirmed by Thee.
Thine I am, O Lord, for ever
. To Thy service set apart :
Suffer me to leave Thee, never ;
Stamp Thine image on my heart.

314 *He shall save His people from their sins.*—Matthew i. 21.
8 6.8 5.5 5.8 5.

1 THIS is the glorious Gospel word,
Our God His heavens doth bow,
And cry to each believing heart,
Jesus saves thee now !
Jesus saves thee now !
Jesus saves thee now !
Yes, Jesus saves thee all the time,
Jesus saves thee now !

2 God speaks, who cannot lie ; why then
One doubt should I allow ?
I doubt Him not, but take His word,
Jesus saves me now ! Jesus saves, etc.

3 I trust not self, 'twould throw me back
Into despond's deep slough ;
From self I look to Christ, and find
Jesus saves me now ! Jesus saves, etc.

4 Whate'er my future may require,
His grace will sure allow ;
I live a moment at a time,
66   Jesus saves me now ! Jesus saves, etc.

5 Why doubt Him ? He who died now lives,
The crown is on His brow ;
The Son of man hath power on earth,
Jesus saves me now ! Jesus saves, etc.

315 *The blood of Jesus Christ His Son cleanseth us from all sin.*
1 John i 7   S.M. WITH CHORUS.

1 I HEAR Thy welcome voice
That calls me, Lord, to Thee,
For cleansing in Thy precious blood
That flowed on Calvary.   [Thee !
I am coming, Lord ! Coming now to
Wash me, cleanse me, in the blood
That flowed on Calvary

2 Though coming weak and vile,
Thou dost my strength assure ;
Thou dost my vileness fully cleanse,
Till spotless all and pure.
I am coming, Lord ! etc.

3 'Tis Jesus calls me on
To perfect faith and love,
To perfect hope and peace and trust,
For earth and heaven above.
I am coming, Lord ! etc.

4 'Tis Jesus who confirms
The blessèd work within,
By adding grace to welcomed grace,
Where reigned the power of sin.
I am coming, Lord ! etc.

5 And He the witness gives
To loyal hearts and free,
That every promise is fulfilled,
If faith but bring the plea.
I am coming, Lord ! etc.

316 *My blood, which is shed for you.*
Luke xxii. 20.   8 8 8 6.

1 JUST as I am, without one plea,
But that Thy blood was shed for me,
And that Thou bidd'st me come to Thee,
O Lamb of God, I come !

2 Just as I am, and waiting not
To rid my soul of one dark blot,
To Thee, whose blood can cleanse each spot,
O Lamb of God, I come !

3 Just as I am, though tossed about
With many a conflict, many a doubt,
Fighting and fears, within, without,
O Lamb of God, I come !

4 Just as I am, poor, wretched, blind ;
Sight, riches, healing of the mind,
Yea, all I need, in Thee to find,
O Lamb of God, I come !

5 Just as I am, Thou wilt receive,
Wilt welcome, pardon, cleanse, relieve ;
Because Thy promise I believe,
O Lamb of God, I come !

6 Just as I am (Thy love unknown
Has broken every barrier down)
Now to be Thine, yea, Thine alone,
O Lamb of God, I come !

7 Just as I am, of that free love
The breadth, length, depth, and height to
Here for a season, then above,   [prove
O Lamb of God, I come !

317 *Suffer the little children to come unto me.*—Mark x. 14. 87.87.

1 THOU who art so high and holy,
    Dwelling in eternity,
Once an infant meek and lowly,
    Suffer us to come to Thee.

2 Saviour, who in accents tender
    Saidst, Let children come to Me,
We our hearts would now surrender;
    Suffer us to come to Thee.

3 In the hour of dark temptation,
    When we can no succour see,
Be our strength and our salvation,
    Suffer us to come to Thee.

4 When our spirits, worn and weary,
    Toil on life's tumultuous sea,
And our path is rough and dreary,
    Suffer us to come to Thee.

5 When we pass through death's cold river
    Let Thy love our solace be;
From all fear our souls deliver,
    Suffer us to come to Thee.

318 *The LORD hath laid on Him the iniquity of us all.*—Isaiah liii. 6. 76.76.76.76.

1 I LAY my sins on Jesus,
    The spotless Lamb of God;
He bears them all, and frees us
    From the accursèd load:
I bring my guilt to Jesus,
    To wash my crimson stains
White in His blood most precious,
    Till not a spot remains!

2 I lay my wants on Jesus,
    All fulness dwells in Him;
He heals all my diseases,
    He doth my soul redeem:
I lay my griefs on Jesus,
    My burdens and my cares;
He from them all releases,
    He all my sorrows shares.

3 I rest my soul on Jesus,
    This weary soul of mine;
His right hand me embraces,
    I on His breast recline:
I love the name of Jesus,
    Immanuel, Christ, the Lord;
Like fragrance on the breezes,
    His name abroad is poured.

4 I long to be like Jesus,
    Meek, loving, lowly, mild;
I long to be like Jesus,
    The Father's holy Child!
I long to be with Jesus,
    Amid the heavenly throng,
To sing with saints His praises,
    To learn the angels' song.

319 *A fountain opened . . . for sin and for uncleanness.*
Zechariah xiii. 1. C.M.

1 THERE is a fountain filled with blood
    Drawn from Immanuel's veins;
And sinners, plunged beneath that flood,
    Lose all their guilty stains.

2 The dying thief rejoiced to see
    That fountain in his day;
And there may I, though vile as he,
    Wash all my sins away.

3 O dying Lamb, Thy precious blood
    Shall never lose its power,
Till all the ransomed church of God
    Be saved to sin no more.

4 E'er since, by faith, I saw the stream
    Thy flowing wounds supply,
Redeeming love has been my theme,
    And shall be till I die.

5 Then in a nobler, sweeter song,
    I'll sing Thy power to save;
When this poor lisping, stammering tongue
    Lies silent in the grave.

320 *I count all things but loss . . . that I may win Christ.*
Philippians iii. 8. 77.77.77.77.

1 I AM coming to the cross;
    I am poor and weak and blind;
I am counting all but dross;
    I shall full salvation find.
I am trusting, Lord, in Thee,
    Blessèd Lamb of Calvary;
Humbly at Thy cross I bow;
    Save me, Jesus, save me now.

2 Long my heart has sighed for Thee,
    Long has evil reigned within;
Jesus, sweetly speak to me,
    'I will cleanse thee from all sin.'
I am trusting, Lord, in Thee, etc.

3 Here I give my all to Thee,
    Friends and time and earthly store,
Soul and body, Thine to be,
    Wholly Thine for evermore.
I am trusting, Lord, in Thee, etc.

321 *Save me, and I shall be saved.*
Jeremiah xvii. 14. C.M.

1 JESUS, before Thy feet I fall,
    Since Thou dost bid me pray;
To Thee, in guilt and fear, I call,
    Save me this very day.

2 To Thee my humble prayer I lift,
    Because Thy grace is free;
Salvation is Thy sovereign gift,
    O! give it then to me!

3 All who love Thee Thy kindness prove,
    All who believe Thee live:
And I can both believe and love,
    If Thou Thy Spirit give.

4 With gladness may I do Thy will;
    May praise my tongue employ;
And may Thy Holy Spirit fill
    My heart with love and joy.

5 O! draw me, Jesus, by Thy grace,
    As I before Thee bow:
I wish to love Thee all my days,
    I wish to love Thee now.

322 *Come unto Me.*—Matthew xi. 28. C.M.

(Teachers.)

1 'COME unto Me!' The Saviour speaks,
    He calls you to His rest;
O children, hear His loving voice,
    And nestle on His breast.

(*Children.*)

2 We hear the voice of truth and love
  When Jesus bids us come,
And in His tender heart would find
  Our everlasting home.

(*Teachers.*)

3 'Come unto Me!' Again Christ calls;
  O hear His gentle voice;
O children, give your hearts to Him,
  And make His love your choice.

(*Children.*)

4 We hear the voice of truth and love
  When Jesus bids us come;
And in His tender heart would find
  Our everlasting home.

(*Teachers.*)

5 'Come unto Me!' Dear children, hear
  The loving, gentle call;
For Him who gave His life for you
  Will you not give up all?

(*Children.*)

6 We hear the voice of truth and love
  When Jesus bids us come;
And in His tender heart would find
  Our everlasting home.

CONFIDENCE AND JOY.

323 *Ye are not your own.*
1 Cor. vi. 19. 6 5.6 5.6 5.6 5.

1 I BELONG to Jesus;
    'Twas a happy day
  When His blood most precious
  Washed my sins away;
  When His Holy Spirit
  Changed my heart of stone,
  Set His mark upon me,
  Sealed me for His own.

2 I belong to Jesus;
    So I'll try to spend
  All my life in pleasing
  My almighty Friend.
  Since He is so holy,
  I must watch and pray,
  That I may grow like Him
  More and more each day.

3 I belong to Jesus;
    Therefore I can sing,
  For I'm safe and happy
  Underneath His wing;
  But so many round me
  Are all dark and cold,
  I must try to bring them
  Into Jesu's fold.

4 I belong to Jesus;
    Soon He will be here;
  If I love and trust Him,
  What have I to fear?
  Round about Him gathered
  Will His people be!
  And I'm sure that Jesus
  Will remember me.

324 *I have set the LORD always before
me.*—Psalm xvi. 8. 7 7.8 8.7 7.

1 I AM Jesu's little friend;
    On His mercy I depend;

If I try to please Him ever,
If I grieve His Spirit never.
  O how very good to me
  Will my Saviour always be!

2 Very young and weak am I,
  Yet He guides me with His eye;
In a pleasant path He leads me,
With a gentle hand He feeds me,
  Chides me when I'm doing wrong,
  Listens to my happy song.

3 He is with me all the day,
  With me in my busy play;
O'er my waking and my sleeping
Jesus still a watch is keeping:
  I can lay me down and rest,
  Sweetly pillowed on His breast.

4 I am Jesu's little friend;
  On His mercy I depend;
Jesus will forsake me never;
He will keep me safe for ever;
  How I wish my heart could be,
  Loving Saviour, more like Thee!

325 *Fear not, for I am with thee.*
Genesis xxvi. 24. 8 3.8 3.8 8 3 8.

1 I HEAR a sweet voice ringing clear,
    All is well!
  It is my Father's voice I hear;
    All is well!
  Where'er I walk that voice is heard:
  It is my God, my Father's word,
  'Fear not, but trust: I am the Lord:'
    All is well!

2 Clouds cannot long obscure my sight;
    All is well!
  I know there is a land of light;
    All is well!
  From strength to strength, from day to day,
  I tread along the world's highway;
  Or often stop to sing or say,
    All is well!

3 In morning hours, serene and bright,
    All is well!
  In evening hours or darkening night
    All is well!
  And when to Jordan's side I come,
  'Midst chilling waves and raging foam,
  O! let me sing as I go home,
    All is well!

326 *Come unto Me: . . . I will give
you rest.*—Matt. xi. 28. D.C.M.

1 I HEARD the voice of Jesus say,
    'Come unto Me, and rest;
  Lay down, thou weary one, lay down
    Thy head upon My breast:'
  I came to Jesus as I was,
    Weary and worn and sad;
  I found in Him a resting-place,
    And He has made me glad.

2 I heard the voice of Jesus say,
    'Behold, I freely give
  The living water; thirsty one,
    Stoop down, and drink, and live:'
  I came to Jesus, and I drank
    Of that life-giving stream;
  My thirst was quenched, my soul revived,
    And now I live in Him.

68

3 I heard the voice of Jesus say,
'I am this dark world's Light;
Look unto Me, thy morn shall rise,
And all thy day be bright:'
I looked to Jesus, and I found
In Him my Star, my Sun!
And in that Light of life I'll walk
Till travelling days are done.

327 *My foot hath held His steps, His way have I kept.*—Job xxiii. 11.
7 6.8 6.8 6.7 6.10 4.

1 I KNOW not what awaits me,
God kindly veils my eyes,
And o'er each step of my onward way
He makes new scenes to rise;
And every joy He sends me comes
A sweet and glad surprise.
Where He may lead I'll follow,
My trust in Him repose;
And every hour in perfect peace I'll sing,
He knows, He knows.

2 One step I see before me,
'Tis all I need to see,
The light of heaven more brightly shines
When earth's illusions flee;
And sweetly through the silence comes,
His loving, 'Follow Me!' Where, etc.

3 O, blissful lack of wisdom!
'Tis blessèd not to know;
He holds me with His own right hand,
And will not let me go,
And lulls my troubled soul to rest
In Him who loves me so. Where, etc.

4 So on I go, not knowing;
I would not if I might;
I'd rather walk in the dark with God
Than go alone in the light,
I'd rather walk by faith with Him
Than go alone by sight. Where, etc.

328 *Whereas I was blind, now I see.*
John ix. 25. D.S.M.

1 I WAS a wandering sheep,
I did not love the fold,
I did not love my Shepherd's voice,
I would not be controlled.
I was a wayward child,
I did not love my home,
I did not love my Father's voice,
I loved afar to roam.

2 The Shepherd sought His sheep,
The Father sought His child;
He followed me o'er vale and hill,
O'er deserts waste and wild;
He found me nigh to death,
Famished and faint and lone:
He bound me with the bands of love,
He saved the wandering one.

3 Jesus my Shepherd is:
'Twas He that loved my soul;
'Twas He that washed me in His blood;
'Twas He that made me whole;
'Twas He that sought the lost,
That found the wandering sheep;
'Twas He that brought me to the fold;
'Tis He that still doth keep.

c 2

4 I was a wandering sheep,
I would not be controlled;
But now I love my Shepherd's voice,
I love, I love the fold.
I was a wayward child,
I once preferred to roam;
But now I love my Father's voice,
I love, I love His home.

329 *The very hairs of your head are all numbered.*—Matt. x. 30. L.M.

1 MY Father, who in heaven reigns,
Though King of all the angels, deigns
To watch o'er me by day and night,
And ever keep my footsteps right.

2 The sparrow on the roof He feeds,
And gives the raven all it needs;
He early calls the birds to raise,
In sweetest notes, their songs of praise.

3 My name stood written on His hand,
Long ere I learned to understand;
And I to Jesus am so dear,
And He is God! what need I fear?

4 When from my head doth fall a hair,
He knows it, knows my every care;
From Him I nothing may conceal,
My very thoughts He can reveal.

5 My Father God, how good Thou art!
Let me in evil ne'er take part,
Make me as angels are above,
And lead me to the realms of love.

330 *The LORD is my Shepherd.*
Psalm xxiii. 1. 6 5.6 5.6 5.6 5.

1 JESUS is our Shepherd,
Wiping every tear;
Folded in His bosom,
What have we to fear?
Only let us follow
Whither He doth lead,
To the thirsty desert
Or the dewy mead.

2 Jesus is our Shepherd;
Well we know His voice;
How its gentle whisper
Makes our heart rejoice!
Even when He chideth,
Tender is His tone;
None but He shall guide us,
We are His alone.

3 Jesus is our Shepherd;
For the sheep He bled;
Every lamb is sprinkled
With the blood He shed.
Then on each He setteth
His own secret sign,
'They that have My Spirit,
These,' saith He, 'are Mine.'

4 Jesus is our Shepherd;
Guarded by His arm,
Though the wolves may raven,
None can do us harm;
When we tread death's valley,
Dark with fearful gloom,
We will fear no evil,
Victors o'er the tomb.

69

*Let us run with patience the race
that is set before us.*—Heb. xii. 1.

331
10 8. 10 8. 10 8. 10 8.

1 IN the march of life, through the toil and
strife
Of the winding path before us,
We have nought to fear with a Saviour
near,
And His banner waving o'er us.
If the tempest rise in the darkening skies,
We will yield to no repining;
Though the storm roar loud, through the
rifted cloud
There's a golden sunbeam shining.

2 In the Christian race, if we take our place,
We may run and weary never;
Daily pressing on till the goal be won,
Unto Jesus looking ever.
Casting all our care on the Lord by prayer,
He will keep our feet from falling;
We'll the crown obtain, nor have run in
vain
For the prize of God's high calling.

332
Unto God my exceeding joy.
Psalm xliii. 4.   C.M.

1 MY God, the spring of all my joys,
The life of my delights,
The glory of my brighest days,
And comfort of my nights!

2 In darkest shades, if Thou appear,
My dawning is begun;
Thou art my soul's bright morning star,
And thou my rising sun.

3 The opening heavens around me shine
With beams of sacred bliss,
If Jesus shows His mercy mine,
And whispers I am His.

4 My soul would leave this heavy clay
At that transporting word:
Run up with joy the shining way,
To see and praise my Lord.

5 Fearless of hell and ghastly death,
I'd break through every foe,
The wings of love and arms of faith
Would bear me conqueror through.

*Unto you therefore which believe He
is precious.*—1 Peter ii. 7.

333
9 9. 9 9. 9 9.

1 JESUS, I love Thee! Thou art to me
Dearer than ever mortal can be;
Jesus, I trust Thee, Saviour divine;
Sinning I sorrow, mercy is Thine!'
Graciously pardoned, safe on Thy breast,
There be my refuge, there let me rest!

2 Full of compassion, plenteous in grace,
Give me Thy blessing, show me Thy face;
Give me Thy Spirit, rid me of sin,
Make my life godly, cleanse me within:
Blessèd Redeemer, precious to me,
Draw me still closer, closer to Thee!

3 Jesus, I trust Thee! reign in my heart;
Thence let Thy Spirit never depart.
Jesus, I love Thee! Thou wilt be mine,
Living or dying, I would be Thine:
Tenderly folded safe on Thy breast,
'T ere be my refuge, there be my rest!

*Let the children of Zion be joyful in
their King.*—Psalm cxlix. 2.

334
C.M.

1 O GOD of Israel, deign to smile
With pitying love on me;
And bless my hours of lonely toil,
And raise my heart to Thee.

2 Then, happy in my lowly state,
I never can repine;
I envy not the rich or great,
If Thou confess me Thine.

3 Let others mourn their humble lot,
But I will work and sing;
For, though the world regard me not,
My Father is a King.

4 From His bright palace in the skies
He sees me where I roam;
And soon He'll call me to arise,
And bid me welcome home.

*Yea, happy is that people, whose God
is the LORD.*—Psalm cxliv. 15.

335
L.M.

1 O HAPPY day that fixed my choice
On Thee, my Saviour and my God!
Well may this glowing heart rejoice,
And tell its raptures all abroad.

2 O happy bond that seals my vows
To Him who merits all my love!
Let cheerful anthems fill His house,
While to that sacred shrine I move.

3 'Tis done, the great transaction's done,
am my Lord's, and He is mine;
He drew me, and I followed on,
Charmed to confess the voice divine.

4 Now rest, my long-divided heart;
Fixed on this blissful centre, rest;
Nor ever from Thy Lord depart,
With Him of every good possest.

5 High heaven, that heard the solemn vow,
That vow renewed shall daily hear,
Till in life's latest hour I bow,
And bless in death a bond so dear.

336
I am the Light of the world.
John viii. 12.   10 4. 10 4. 10 10.

1 LEAD, kindly Light! amid the encircling
Lead Thou me on;   [gloom,
The night is dark, and I am far from home:
Lead Thou me on.
Keep Thou my feet; I do not ask to see
The distant scene, one step's enough for me.

2 I was not ever thus, nor prayed that Thou
Shouldst lead me on.
I loved to choose and see my path; but now
Lead Thou me on.
I loved the garish day, and, spite of fears,
Pride ruled my will: remember not past
years.

3 So long Thy power hath blessed me, sure
Will lead me on   [it still
O'er moor and fen, o'er crag and torrent,
The night is gone;   [till
And with the morn those angel faces smile
Which I have loved long since, and lost
awhile.

337

He calleth His own sheep by name, and leadeth them out.
John x. 3.   C.M.

1 SEE ! the kind Shepherd, Jesus, stands,
  And calls His sheep by name ;
Gathers the feeble in His arms,
  And feeds the tender lambs.

2 He'll lead us to the heavenly streams,
  Where living waters flow,
And guide us to the fruitful fields
  Where trees of knowledge grow.

3 If, wandering from the fold, we leave
  The strait and narrow way,
Our faithful Shepherd still is near,
  To guide us when we stray.

4 The feeblest lamb amidst the flock
  Shall be its Shepherd's care ;
While folded in our Saviour's arms
  We're safe from every snare.

338

Rejoicing in hope.
Romans xii. 12.   6 5.6 5.6 5.6 5.

1 ON our way rejoicing
    As we homeward move,
  Hearken to our praises,
    O Thou God of love.
  Thou, who givest seed-time,
    Wilt give large increase,
  Crown the head with blessings,
    Fill the heart with peace.
  On our way rejoicing,
    As we homeward move,
  Hearken to our praises,
    O Thou God of love.

2 On our way rejoicing
    Gladly let us go,
  Jesus is our Leader,
    Vanquished is the foe.
  Christ without, our safety,
    Christ within, our joy ;
  Who, if we be faithful,
    Can our hope destroy? On our, etc.

3 Unto God the Father
    Joyful songs we sing ;
  Unto God the Saviour
    Thankful hearts we bring ;
  Unto God the Spirit
    Bow we and adore,
  On our way rejoicing
    Ever, evermore.   On our, etc.

339

My Beloved is mine, and I am His.
Canticles ii. 16.   6 4.6 4.6 6 6 4.

1 NOW I have found a Friend,
    Jesus is mine ;
His love shall never end,
    Jesus is mine.
Though earthly joys decrease,
Though earthly friendships cease,
Now I have lasting peace,
    Jesus is mine.

2 Though I grow poor and old,
    Jesus is mine ;
Though I grow faint and cold,
    Jesus is mine.

He shall my wants supply,
His precious blood is nigh,
Nought can my hope destroy,
    Jesus is mine.

3 When death is sent to me,
    Jesus is mine ;
Welcome eternity,
    Jesus is mine.
He my redemption is,
Wisdom and righteousness,
Life, light, and holiness,
    Jesus is mine.

4 When earth shall pass away,
    Jesus is mine ;
In the great judgment day
    Jesus is mine ;
O what a glorious thing
Then to behold my King,
With tuneful harp to sing,
    Jesus is mine !

5 Father, Thy name I bless,
    Jesus is mine ;
Thine was the sovereign grace,
    Praise shall be Thine.
Spirit of holiness,
Sealing the Father's grace,
By Thee I still embrace
    Jesus as mine.

340

I am Thine, save me.
Psalm cxix. 94.   7 7.7 7.

1 THINE for ever ! God of love,
    Hear us from Thy throne above ;
Thine for ever may we be,
Here and in eternity.

2 Thine for ever ! Lord of life,
Shield us through our earthly strife ;
Thou the Life, the Truth, the Way,
Guide us to the realms of day.

3 Thine for ever ! O, how blest
They who find in Thee their rest !
Saviour, Guardian, heavenly Friend,
O defend us to the end.

4 Thine for ever ! Saviour, keep
Us Thy frail and trembling sheep ;
Safe alone beneath Thy care,
Let us all Thy goodness share.

5 Thine for ever ! Thou our Guide,
All our wants by Thee supplied,
All our sins by Thee forgiven,
Lead us, Lord, from earth to heaven.

341

Let us walk in the light of the
LORD.—Isa. ii. 5.   IRREGULAR.

1 NEVER be faint or weary,
    Children of light Beaming so bright ;
How can the way be dreary ?
    Jesus our friend is near ;
Trusting His love to guide us,
Doing His will Cheerfully still,
Jesus will walk beside us ;
    What has the heart to fear ?
Yes, happy are we ; yes, happy are
Ever we sing, Jesus our King,   [we ;
Honour and glory to Thee ;
Ever in hope rejoicing,
Loving our blessèd Redeemer,
Happy are we, happy are we,
Yes, happy are we.

2 Never repine in sorrow;
  Think of the care Others may bear;
    Tell them a golden morrow,
      Smiling, their path will cheer;
  Comfort the sad and lonely;
  Walk in the light Beaming so bright;
    Trusting in Jesus only,
      He will be always near.
      Yes, happy are we, etc.

342 *They are more than can be*
numbered.—Psalm xl. 5. C.M.

1 WHEN all Thy mercies, O my God,
  My rising soul surveys,
Transported with the view, I'm lost
  In wonder, love, and praise.

2 To all my weak complaints and cries
  Thy mercy lent an ear,
Ere yet my feeble thoughts had learned
  To form themselves in prayer.

3 Unnumbered comforts on my soul
  Thy tender care bestowed,
Before my infant heart conceived
  From whom those comforts flowed.

4 Through every period of my life,
  Thy goodness I'll pursue;
And after death, in distant worlds,
  The pleasing theme renew.

5 Through all eternity, to Thee
  A grateful song I'll raise:
But O eternity's too short
  To utter all Thy praise!

343 *Underneath are the everlasting*
arms.—Deuteronomy xxxiii. 27.
7 6.7 6.7 6.7 6.

1 SAFE in the arms of Jesus,
  Safe on His gentle breast,
There, by His love o'ershaded,
  Sweetly my soul shall rest.
Hark! 'tis the voice of angels,
  Borne in a song to me,
Over the fields of glory,
  Over the jasper sea.
    Safe in the arms of Jesus,
      Safe on His gentle breast,
    There, by His love o'ershaded,
      Sweetly my soul shall rest.

2 Safe in the arms of Jesus,
  Safe from corroding care,
Safe from the world's temptations,
  Sin cannot harm me there.
Free from the blight of sorrow,
  Free from my doubts and fears:
Only a few more trials,
  Only a few more tears · Safe in, etc.

3 Jesus, my heart's dear refuge,
  Jesus has died for me;
Firm on the Rock of ages
  Ever my trust shall be.
Here let me wait with patience,
  Wait till the night is o'er;
Wait till I see the morning
  Break on the golden shore Safe in. etc
79

344 *I will follow Thee whithersoever Thou*
goest.—Matthew viii. 19.
7 6.7 6.7 6.7 3

1 THE world looks very beautiful,
  And full of joy to me;
The sun shines out in glory
  On everything I see;
I know I shall be happy
  While in the world I stay,
For I will follow Jesus
    All the way.

2 I'm but a youthful pilgrim;
  My journey's just begun;
They say I shall meet sorrow
  Before my journey's done.
The world is full of trouble,
  And trials too, they say;
But I will follow Jesus
    All the way.

3 Then like a youthful pilgrim,
  Whatever I may meet,
I'll take it—joy or sorrow—
  And lay it at His feet.
He'll comfort me in trouble,
  He'll wipe my tears away;
With joy I'll follow Jesus
    All the way.

4 Then trials shall not vex me,
  And pain I need not fear,
For when I'm close to Jesus,
  Grief will not come too near.
Not even death can harm me,
  When death I meet one day;
To heaven I'll follow Jesus
    All the way.

345 *And thou shalt call His name*
JESUS.—Matthew i. 21. C.M.

1 HOW sweet the name of Jesus sounds
  In a believer's ear!
It soothes his sorrows, heals his wounds,
  And drives away his fear.

2 It makes the wounded spirit whole,
  And calms the troubled breast;
'Tis manna to the hungry soul,
  And to the weary rest.

3 Dear name! the Rock on which I build,
  My shield, and hiding-place,
My never-failing treasury, filled
  With boundless stores of grace!

4 Jesus, my Shepherd, Husband, Friend,
  My Prophet, Priest, and King;
My Lord, my Life, my Way, my End,
  Accept the praise I bring.

5 Weak is the effort of my heart,
  And cold my warmest thought;
But when I see Thee as Thou art
  I'll praise Thee as I ought.

6 Till then I would Thy love proclaim
  With every fleeting breath;
And may the music of Thy name
  Refresh my soul in death!

346 *I press toward the mark for the prize*
of the high calling.—Phil. iii. 14.
6 5.6 5.6 5.6 5.6 5.6 5.

1 FORWARD! be our watchword;
  Steps and voices joined;

Seek the things before us,
　　Not a look behind ;
Burns the fiery pillar
　　At our army's head ;
Who shall dream of shrinking,
　　By our Captain led?
Forward, through the desert,
　　Through the toil and fight ;
Canaan lies before us,
　　Sion beams with light.

2 Forward, flock of Jesus,
　　Salt of all the earth,
Till each yearning purpose
　　Spring to glorious birth ;
Sick, they ask for healing,
　　Blind, they grope for day,
Pour upon the nations
　　Wisdom's loving ray :
Forward, out of error,
　　Leave behind the night ,
Forward, through the darkness,
　　Forward into light.

SECOND PART.

3 Glories upon glories
　　Hath our God prepared,
By the souls that love Him
　　One day to be shared ;
Eye hath not beheld them,
　　Ear hath never heard ;
Nor of these hath uttered
　　Thought or speech a word.
Forward, ever forward,
　　Clad in armour bright,
Till the veil be lifted,
　　Till our faith be sight.

4 Far o'er yon horizon
　　Rise the city towers,
Where our God abideth,
　　That fair home is ours ;
Flash the gates with jasper,
　　Shine the streets with gold ;
Flows the gladdening river,
　　Shedding joys untold.
Thither, onward thither,
　　In the Spirit's might :
Pilgrims to your country,
　　Forward into light !

347 *Our consolation also aboundeth by Christ.*—2 Cor. i. 5.　C.M.

1 JESU, the very thought of Thee
　　With sweetness fills my breast ;
But sweeter far Thy face to see,
　　And in Thy presence rest.

2 Nor voice can sing, nor heart can frame,
　　Nor can the memory find
A sweeter sound than Thy blest name,
　　O Saviour of mankind !

3 O hope of every contrite heart,
　　O joy of all the meek,
To those who fall how kind Thou art !
　　How good to those who seek !

4 But what to those who find ? Ah ! this
　　Nor tongue nor pen can show ;
The love of Jesus, what it is
　　None but His loved ones know.

5 Jesu, our only joy be Thou,
　　As Thou our prize wilt be ;
Jesu, be Thou our glory now,
　　And through eternity.

348 *A people near unto Him.* Psalm cxlviii. 14.　6 4.6 4.6 6 4

1 NEARER, my God, to Thee !
　　Nearer to Thee !
E'en though it be a cross
　　That raiseth me ;
Still all my song shall be,
Nearer, my God, to Thee !
　　Nearer to Thee !

2 Though like the wanderer,
　　The sun gone down,
Darkness be over me,
　　My rest a stone ;
Yet in my dreams I'd be
Nearer, my God, to Thee !
　　Nearer to Thee !

3 There let the way appear
　　Steps unto heaven :
All that Thou send'st to me
　　In mercy given ;
Angels to beckon me
Nearer, my God, to Thee !
　　Nearer to Thee !

4 Then, with my waking thoughts
　　Bright with Thy praise,
Out of my stony griefs
　　Bethel I'll raise ;
So by my woes to be
Nearer, my God, to Thee !
　　Nearer to Thee !

5 Or if on joyful wing
　　Cleaving the sky,
Sun, moon, and stars forgot,
　　Upwards I fly,
Still all my song shall be,
Nearer, my God, to Thee !
　　Nearer to Thee !

349 *For my strength is made perfect in weakness.*—2 Corinthians xii. 9.　7 6.7 6.7 6.7 6

1 I COULD not do without Thee,
　　O Saviour of the lost,
Whose precious blood redeemed me
　　At such tremendous cost ;
Thy righteousness, Thy pardon,
　　Thy precious blood must be
My only hope and comfort,
　　My glory and my plea.

2 I could not do without Thee,
　　I cannot stand alone,
I have no strength or goodness,
　　No wisdom of my own ;
But Thou, beloved Saviour,
　　Art all in all to me,
And weakness will be power
　　If leaning hard on Thee.

3 I could not do without Thee,
　　For, O, the way is long,
And I am often weary,
　　And sigh replaces song ;

How could I do without Thee?
I do not know the way;
Thou knowest, and Thou leadest,
And wilt not let me stray.

SECOND PART.

4 I could not do without Thee,
O Jesus, Saviour dear;
E'en when my eyes are holden,
I know that Thou art near;
How dreary and how lonely
This changeful life would be
Without the sweet communion,
The secret rest with Thee!

5 I could not do without Thee;
No other friend can read
The spirit's strange, deep longings,
Interpreting its need;
No human heart could enter
Each dim recess of mine,
And soothe, and hush, and calm it,
O blessèd Lord, but Thine.

6 I could not do without Thee,
For years are fleeting fast,
And soon in solemn loneliness
The river must be passed;
But Thou wilt never leave me,
And though the waves roll high,
I know Thou wilt be near me,
And whisper, 'It is I.'

350 *Be strong in the Lord, and in the power of His might.*
Ephesians vi. 10.   6 5.6 5.6 5.6 5.

1 ONWARD, Christian soldiers,
Marching as to war,
With the cross of Jesus
Going on before;
Christ, the royal Master,
Leads against the foe;
Forward, into battle,
See His banners go!
Onward, Christian soldiers,
Marching as to war;
With the cross of Jesus
Going on before.

2 At the sign of triumph
Satan's host doth flee;
On then, Christian soldiers,
On to victory!
Hell's foundations quiver
At the shout of praise;
Brothers, lift your voices,
Loud your anthems raise!
Onward, etc.

3 Like a mighty army
Moves the Church of God;
Brothers, we are treading
Where the saints have trod;
We are not divided,
All one body we,
One in hope and doctrine,
One in charity.   Onward, etc.

4 Crowns and thrones may perish,
Kingdoms rise and wane,
But the Church of Jesus
Constant will remain;

Gates of hell can never
'Gainst that Church prevail;
We have Christ's own promise,
Which can never fail. Onward, etc.

5 Onward, then, ye people,
Join our happy throng,
Blend with ours your voices
In the triumph song;
Glory, laud, and honour
Unto Christ the King;
This through countless ages
Saints and angels sing.
Onward, etc.

351 *Hold fast till I come.*
Rev. ii. 25.   8 5.8 5.8 5.8 5.

1 HO, my comrades! see the signal
Waving in the sky!
Reinforcements now appearing,
Victory is nigh!
'Hold the fort, for I am coming,'
Jesus signals still;
Wave the answer back to heaven,
'By Thy grace we will.'

2 See the mighty host advancing,
Satan leading on:
Mighty men around us falling,
Courage almost gone! 'Hold,' etc.

3 See the glorious banner waving!
Hear the trumpet blow!
In our Leader's name we'll triumph
Over every foe!   'Hold,' etc.

4 Fierce and long the battle rages,
But our help is near:
Onward comes our great Commander;
Cheer, my comrades, cheer!
'Hold,' etc.

352 *Strangers and pilgrims on the earth.*—Hebrews xi. 13.   7 6.7 6.

1 O HAPPY band of pilgrims,
If onward ye will tread,
With Jesus as your Leader,
To Jesus as your Head!

2 O happy, if ye labour
As Jesus did for men:
O happy if ye hunger
As Jesus hungered then!

3 The faith by which ye see Him,
The hope in which ye yearn,
The love that through all troubles
To Him alone will turn,

4 The trials that beset you,
The sorrows ye endure,
The manifold temptations
That death alone can cure,

5 What are they but His jewels,
Of right celestial worth!
What are they but the ladder
Set up to heaven on earth!

6 O happy band of pilgrims,
Look upward to the skies,
Where such a light affliction
Shall win you such a prize.

353

Let the children of Zion be joyful in their King.—Psalm cxlix. 2.

7 7.7 7.

1 CHILDREN of the heavenly King,
   As we journey, sweetly sing:
Sing our Saviour's worthy praise,
Glorious in His works and ways!

2 We are travelling home to God
In the way our fathers trod ;
They are happy now, and we
Soon their happiness shall see.

3 Fear not, then, but joyful stand
On the borders of our land ;
Jesus Christ, our Father's Son,
Bids us undismayed go on.

4 Lord, obediently we go,
Gladly leaving all below ;
Only Thou our leader be,
And we still will follow Thee.

5 Hymns of glory and of praise,
Father, unto Thee we raise ;
Praise to Thee, O Christ our King,
And the Holy Ghost, we sing.

354

It is a good thing to give thanks unto the LORD.—Psalm xcii. 1.

D.S.M.

1 COME, ye that love the Lord,
   And let your joys be known ;
Join in a song with sweet accord
While ye surround His throne :
Let those refuse to sing
Who never knew our God ;
But servants of the heavenly King
May speak their joys abroad.

2 The God that rules on high,
That all the earth surveys,
That rides upon the stormy sky,
And calms the roaring seas ;
This awful God is ours,
Our Father and our love ;
He will send down His heavenly powers,
To carry us above.

3 There we shall see His face,
And never, never sin ;
There, from the rivers of His grace,
Drink endless pleasures in :
Yea, and before we rise
To that immortal state,
The thoughts of such amazing bliss
Should constant joys create.

4 The men of grace have found
Glory begun below ;
Celestial fruit on earthly ground
From faith and hope may grow :
Then let our songs abound,
And every tear be dry ;
We are marching through Immanuel's
To fairer worlds on high.   [ground

355

Now they desire a better country, that is, an heavenly.
Hebrews xi. 16.   5 5.6 5.6 5.6

1 BRIGHTLY gleams our banner,
   Pointing to the sky,
Waving wanderers onward
To their home on high.

Journeying o'er the desert
Gladly thus we pray,
And with hearts united
Take our heavenward way.
   Brightly gleams our banner,
   Pointing to the sky,
   Waving wanderers onward
   To their home on high.

2 Jesu, Lord and Master,
At Thy sacred feet,
Here, with hearts rejoicing,
See Thy children meet.
Often have we left Thee,
Often gone astray ;
Keep us, mighty Saviour,
In the narrow way.   Brightly, etc.

SECOND PART.

3 Pattern of our childhood,
Once Thyself a child,
Make our childhood holy,
Pure, and meek, and mild.
In the hour of danger
Whither can we flee
But to Thee, O Saviour ?
Only unto Thee.   Brightly, etc.

4 All our days direct us
In the way we go ;
Lead us on victorious
Over every foe ;
Bid Thine angels shield us
When the storm-clouds lour,
Pardon, Lord, and save us
In the last dread hour. Brightly, etc.

356

Lo, I am with you alway.
Matthew xxviii. 20.   C.M.

1 DEAR Jesus, ever at my side,
   How loving must Thou be,
To leave Thy home in heaven to guard
A little child like me !

2 Thy beautiful and shining face
I see not, though so near ;
The sweetness of Thy soft, low voice
I am too deaf to hear ;

3 I cannot feel Thee touch my hand,
With pressure light and mild,
To check me, as my mother did
When I was but a child :

4 But I have felt Thee in my thought,
Fighting with sin for me ;
And when my heart loves God, I know
The sweetness is from Thee.

5 And when, dear Saviour, I kneel down,
Morning and night, to prayer,
Something there is within my heart
Which tells me Thou art there.

6 Yes ; when I pray Thou prayest too,
The prayer is all for me ;
But when I sleep Thou sleepest not,
But watchest patiently.

357

His ears are open unto their prayers.—1 Peter iii. 12   8 7.8 7.

1 GOD Almighty heareth ever
   When His little children pray :
He is faint and weary never,
And He turneth none away.   75

2 More than we deserve He sends us,
    More than we can ask bestows ;
Every moment He befriends us,
    And supports us in our woes.

3 Let us then, in Him confiding,
    Tell Him all we think and feel,
Never one dark secret hiding,
    Seeking nothing to conceal.

4 Through His Son, our precious Saviour,
    God will pardon all our sin,
Will forgive our past behaviour,
    Open heaven and take us in.

The LORD is my Shepherd ; I shall
not want.—Psalm xxiii. 1.

358   10 10.11 11.10 11.

1 THOUGH troubles assail And dangers
    affright,
Though friends should all fail, And foes
  all unite,
Yet one thing secures us Whatever betide,
The Scripture assures us The Lord will
  provide.
    So happy am I ; yes, happy am I,
    The Lord is my Shepherd, and He will
    provide.

2 The birds without barn Or storehouse are
  fed ;
From them let us learn To trust for our
  bread ;
His saints what is fitting Shall ne'er be
  denied,
So long as 'tis written, The Lord will pro-
    So happy am I, etc.   [vide.

3 His call we obey Like Abram of old, [bold;
Not knowing our way, But faith makes us
For though we are strangers We have a
  sure Guide,
And trust in all dangers The Lord will pro-
    So happy am I, etc.   [vide.

4 No strength of our own Or goodness we
  claim ;
Yet since we have known The Saviour's
  great name,
In this our strong tower For safety we hide,
Almighty His power: The Lord will provide.
    So happy am I, etc.

CONDUCT.

359   *Thou God seest me.*
    Genesis xvi. 13.   C.M.

1 GOD is in heaven ! Can He hear
    A little prayer like mine?
Yes, that He can ; I need not fear :
    He'll listen unto mine.

2 God is in heaven ! Can He see
    When I am doing wrong?
Yes, that He can ; He looks at me
    All day and all night long.

3 God is in heaven ! Would He know
    If I should tell a lie?
Yes ; though I said it very low,
    He'd hear it in the sky.

4 God is in heaven ! Does He care,
    Or is He good to me?
Yes ; all I have to eat or wear,
    'Tis God that gives it me,

5 God is in heaven ! May I pray
    To go there when I die?
Yes ; love Him, seek Him, and one day
    He'll call me to the sky.

360   *And be ye kind one to another.*
    Eph. iv. 32.   64.64.6664.64.

1 KIND words can never die,
    Cherished and blest,
God knows how deep they lie,
    Stored in the breast :
Like childhood's simple rhymes,
Said o'er a thousand times,
Ay, in all years and climes
    Distant and near.
      Kind words can never die,
        No, never die.

2 Sweet thoughts can never die,
    Though, like the flowers,
Their brightest hues may fly
    In wintry hours.
But when the gentle dew
Gives them their charms anew,
With many an added hue
    They bloom again.
      Sweet thoughts can never die,
        No, never die.

3 Our souls can never die,
    Though in the tomb
We may all have to lie,
    Wrapped in its gloom.
What though the flesh decay,
Souls pass in peace away,
Live through eternal day
    With Christ above.
      Our souls can never die,
        No, never die.

361   *The servant of the Lord must . . . be*
    gentle unto all men.—2 Tim. ii. 24.
    D.C.M. WITH CHORUS.

1 THE sun may raise the grass to life,
    The dew the drooping flower ;
And eyes grow bright, and watch the light
    Of autumn's opening hour ;
But words that breathe of tenderness
    And smiles we know are true,
Are warmer than the summer-time
    And brighter than the dew.
      Gentle words ! Loving smiles !
How beautiful are gentle words and loving
  smiles !

2 It is not much the world can give,
    With all its subtle art ;
And gold and gems are not the things
    To satisfy the heart ;
But O ! if those who cluster round
    The altar and the hearth
Have gentle words and loving smiles,
    How beautiful is earth !
      Gentle words ! Loving smiles !
How beautiful are gentle words and loving
  smiles !

362 LORD, *who shall abide . . . ? He that . . . speaketh the truth in his heart.*—Psalm xv. 1, 2.   L.M.

1 HAPPY the well-instructed youth,
   Who, in his earliest infancy,
Loves from his heart to speak the truth,
   And, like his God, abhors a lie.

2 He that hath practised no deceit
   With false, equivocating tongue ;
Nor ever durst o'erreach or cheat,
   Or slanderously his neighbour wrong :

3 He in the house of God shall dwell,
   He on His holy hill shall rest,
The comforts of religion feel,
   And then be numbered with the blest :

4 But who or guile or falsehood use,
   Or take God's name in vain, or swear,
Or ever lie, themselves to excuse,
   They shall their dreadful sentence bear.

5 The Lord, the true and faithful Lord,
   Himself hath said that every liar
Shall surely meet his just reward
   Assigned him in eternal fire.

363 *This is my commandment,* etc. John xv. 12.   11 11.11 11.*

THIS is My commandment, That ye love
   one another,
That ye love one another, As I have lovèd
   you.

1 Blessèd words of Jesus we have heard
   to-day,
Saviour, by Thy Spirit, help us to obey :
May Thy love unite us to the living Vine !
May our hearts, enlightened, glow with
   love divine !

2 May we seek Thy glory, strife and envy flee ;
By our love to others prove our love to
   Thee.
Evermore as brethren in sweet union live ;
As we wish forgiveness, may we each
   forgive.

3 Grant us Thy salvation, fill us with Thy
   love ;
Give us each a foretaste of the joys above :
Ever meek and lowly, ever kind and true,
Ever pure and holy, paths of peace pursue.

364 *Let all . . . anger . . . be put away from you, with all malice.* Ephesians iv. 31.   7 7.7 7.

1 JESUS, Lord, we look to Thee ;
   Meek and humble may we be ·
Pride and anger put away,
Love Thee better day by day.

2 May we hate a lying tongue ;
Never seek another's wrong ;
From all paths of sin abstain,
Paths that lead to endless pain.

3 Teach us for our friends to pray,
And our parents to obey ;
Richest blessings from above
Give them for their tender love.

4 May we find the times of prayer
Sweeter than our pastimes are ;
Love the Sabbath and the place
Where we learn to seek Thy face.

5 Thou didst once our nature take,
Born a child for sinners' sake ;
May we, while we live below,
In Thy holy likeness grow !

365 *Honour thy father and mother.* Ephesians vi. 2.   8 7.8 7.

1 TO thy father and thy mother
   Honour, love, and reverence pay ;
This command, before all other,
   Must a Christian child obey.

2 Help me, Lord, in this sweet duty ;
   Guide me in Thy steps divine ;
Show me all the joy and beauty
   Of obedience such as Thine.

3 Teach me how to please and gladden
   Those who toil and care for me ;
Many a grief their heart must sadden,
   Let me still their comfort be !

4 Then when years are gathering o'er them,
   When they're sleeping in the grave,
Sweet will seem the love I bore them,
   Right the reverence I gave.

366 *Learn of Me ; for I am meek and lowly in heart.*—Matthew xi. 29.   7 7.7 7.

1 LAMB of God, I look to Thee,
   Thou shalt my example be ;
Thou art gentle, meek, and mild ;
Thou wast once a little child.

2 Fain I would be as Thou art,
Give me Thy obedient heart ;
Thou art pitiful and kind ;
Let me have Thy loving mind.

3 Let me above all fulfil'
God my heavenly Father's will ;
Never His good Spirit grieve,
Only to His glory live.

4 Loving Jesus, gentle Lamb,
In Thy gracious hands I am :
Make me, Saviour, what Thou art ;
Live Thyself within my heart.

5 I shall then show forth Thy praise,
Serve Thee all my happy days ;
Then the world shall always see
Christ, the holy Child, in me.

367 *Set a watch, O LORD, before my mouth : keep the door of my lips.* Psalm cxli. 3.   7 7.7 7.7 7.

1 WORDS are things of little cost,
   Quickly spoken, quickly lost ;
We forget them, but they stand
Witnesses at God's right hand,
And a testimony bear
For us, or against us, there.

2 O how often ours have been
Idle words and words of sin ;
Words of anger, scorn, or pride,
Or deceit, our faults to hide ;
Envious tales, or strife unkind,
Leaving bitter thoughts behind !

3 Grant us, Lord, from day to day
Strength to watch and grace to pray;
May our lips, from sin set free,
Love to speak and sing of Thee;
Till in heaven we learn to raise
Hymns of everlasting praise.

368 *Because thou hast been faithful in a very little, have thou authority.*
Luke xix. 17.   6 5. 6 5.

1 LITTLE drops of water,
Little grains of sand,
Make the mighty ocean
And the beauteous land.

2 And the little moments,
Humble though they be,
Make the mighty ages
Of eternity.

3 And our little errors
Lead the soul away
From the paths of virtue,
Far in sin to stray.

4 Little deeds of mercy
Sown by youthful hands
Grow to bless the nations,
Far in heathen lands.

5 Little deeds of kindness,
Little words of love,
Make our earth an Eden,
Like the heaven above.

369 *I will put My laws into their mind, and write them in their hearts.*
Hebrews viii. 10.   C.M.

1 O THAT the Lord would guide my ways
To keep His statutes still!
O that my God would grant me grace
To know and do His will!

2 O send Thy Spirit down to write
Thy law upon my heart;
Nor let my tongue indulge deceit,
Nor act the liar's part.

3 Order my footsteps by Thy word,
And make my heart sincere;
Let sin have no dominion, Lord,
But keep my conscience clear.

370 *Thou shalt not steal.*
Exodus xx. 15.   8 7. 8 7.

1 WHY should I deprive my neighbour
Of his goods against his will?
Hands were made for honest labour,
Not to plunder or to steal.

2 'Tis a foolish self-deceiving
By such tricks to hope for gain:
All that's ever got by thieving
Turns to sorrow, shame, and pain.

3 Theft will not be always hidden!
Though we fancy none can spy,
When we take a thing forbidden,
God beholds it with His eye.

4 Guard my heart, O God of heaven!
Lest I covet what's not mine;
Lest I steal what is not given,
Guard my heart and hands from sin.

371 *Even a child is known by his doings.*—Proverbs xx. 11.   **L.M.**

1 WE are but little children weak,
Nor born in any high estate;
What can we do for Jesu's sake,
Who is so high and good and great?

2 O, day by day, each Christian child
Has much to do, without, within;
A death to die for Jesu's sake,
A weary war to wage with sin.

3 When deep within our swelling hearts
The thoughts of pride and anger rise,
When bitter words are on our tongues,
And tears of passion in our eyes;

4 Then we may stay the angry blow,
Then we may check the hasty word,
Give gentle answers back again,
And fight a battle for our Lord.

5 With smiles of peace and looks of love
Light in our dwellings we may make,
Bid kind good humour brighten there,
And still do all for Jesu's sake.

6 There's not a child so small and weak
But has his little cross to take,
His little work of love and praise
That he may do for Jesu's sake.

372 *Thine ears shall hear a word behind thee, saying, This is the way.*
Isaiah xxx. 21.   C.M.

1 THERE is a still, small, holy voice,
The voice of God most high,
That whispers always in our heart,
And says that He is nigh.

2 This voice will blame us when we're wrong,
And praise us when we're right;
We hear it in the light of day,
And in the quiet night.

3 And even they whose ears are deaf
To every other sound,
When they have listened, in their hearts
The still small voice have found.

4 And they have felt that God is good,
And thanked Him for the voice
That told them what was right and true,
And made their hearts rejoice.

373 *In all thy ways acknowledge Him, and He shall direct thy paths.*
Proverbs iii. 6.   L.M.

1 LET children to their God draw near,
With reverence and holy fear;
Let every knee before Him bend,
Our Judge, our Saviour, and our Friend.

2 Lord, may Thy mercies, great and free,
Fill us with gratitude to Thee;
And still as through the world we go,
More of these mercies may we know.

3 Far from our hearts, O Lord, remove
The evil thoughts that sinners love;
And give us wisdom, day by day,
To choose the strait and narrow way.

4 In times of sickness or of health,
In times of poverty or wealth,
And in our last and dying hour,
Save us by Thine almighty power.

5 Then may we join the happy band,
　That in Thy heavenly temple stand ;
And as Thy goodness we adore,
　Sing glory, glory, evermore.

374 *Let this mind be in you, which was also in Christ Jesus.*
Philippians ii. 5.　　7 6.8 6.

1 I WANT to be like Jesus,
　So lowly and so meek :
For no one marked an angry word
That ever heard Him speak.

2 I want to be like Jesus,
　So frequently in prayer ;
Alone upon the mountain top,
　He met His Father there.

3 I want to be like Jesus ;
　I never, never find
That He, though persecuted, was
　To any one unkind.

4 I want to be like Jesus,
　Engaged in doing good :
So that of me it may be said,
　'She hath done what she could.'

5 Alas ! I'm not like Jesus,
　As any one may see :
O gentle Saviour, send Thy grace,
　And make me like to Thee !

375 *But one thing is needful.*
Luke x. 42.　　C.M.

1 LORD, grant us at Thy feet to sit,
　Like Mary, day by day ;
And teach us that good part to choose
Which none shall take away :

2 In quietness and lowliness
　To listen to Thy voice,
To know that all Thy will is love,
　To have no selfish choice.

3 We cannot do great things for Thee ;
　Thou dost not such require :
To walk in wisdom's holy ways,
　Be this our chief desire.

4 The one thing needful is to have
　Our souls prepared for heaven :
Such grace e'en little ones may crave,
　Such grace to us be given.

376 *Behold, Thou desirest truth in the inward parts.*—Psalm li. 6.
S.M.

1 HELP me, my God, to speak
　True words to Thee each day,
True let my heart be when I praise,
　And truthful when I pray.

2 Thy words are true to me,
　Let mine to Thee be true,
The words of my whole heart and soul,
　However low and few :

3 True words of grief for sin,
　Of longing to be free,
Of groaning for deliverance,
　And likeness, Lord, to Thee ;

4 True words of faith and hope,
　Of godly joy and grief,
Lord, I believe, O hear my cry ;
　Help Thou mine unbelief.

377 *And all thy children shall be taught of the LORD.*—Isaiah liv. 13.
6 4.6 4.6 6 4.

1 I'M but a little child,
　Foolish and frail,
Yet with the Saviour mild
　My prayers avail ;
He deigns to hear me speak,
And though my words be weak,
　They will prevail.

2 O Thou benignant Lord,
　Loving and true !
Write on my heart Thy word,
　Help me to do
All Thou ordainest me,
While Thou sustainest me,
　All my life through.

3 Jesus, Thy Spirit give,
　In me to dwell :
That I to Thee may live
　Wisely and well ;
As the years gather, still
Working Thy gentle will,
　Nor e'er rebel.

4 If to maturer age
　I should e'er grow,
'Mid all life's pilgrimage
　Help me to show
Still the child-spirit, free,
True, pure, and good like Thee
　When here below.

5 So, as Thine own dear child,
　When years shall end,
Where saints dwell undefiled,
　I shall ascend ;
There near Thy throne to be,
There Thy loved face to see,
　Saviour and Friend !

378 *But let us watch and be sober.*
1 Thessalonians v. 6.　　D.C.M.

1 I WANT a principle within
　Of jealous, godly fear,
A sensibility of sin,
　A pain to feel it near :
I want the first approach to feel
　Of pride or fond desire,
To catch the wandering of my will,
　And quench the kindling fire.

2 That I from Thee no more may part,
　No more Thy goodness grieve,
The filial awe, the fleshly heart,
　The tender conscience, give.
Quick as the apple of an eye,
　O God, my conscience make !
Awake my soul when sin is nigh,
　And keep it still awake.

3 If to the right or left I stray,
　That moment, Lord, reprove ;
And let me weep my life away,
　For having grieved Thy love :
O may the least omission pain
　My well-instructed soul,
And drive me to the blood again
　Which makes the wounded whole !

379 *I will guide thee with Mine eye.*
Psalm xxxii. 8.   7 7.7 7.

1 IN our work and in our play,
  Jesus, be Thou ever near,
Guarding, guiding all the day,
  Keeping in Thy holy fear.

2 Thou didst toil, a lowly child,
  In the far-off Holy Land,
Blessing labour undefiled,
  Pure and honest, of the hand.

3 Thou wilt bless our playtime too,
  If we ask Thy succour strong;
Watch o'er all we say and do,
  Hold us back from guilt and wrong.

4 O! how happy thus to spend
  Work and playtime in His sight,
Till the rest which shall not end,
  Till the day which knows not night!

380 *We love Him, because He first loved us.*—1 John iv. 19.   7 7.7 7.

1 SAVIOUR! teach me, day by day,
  Love's sweet lesson to obey;
Sweeter lesson cannot be,
  Loving Him who first loved me.

2 With a childlike heart of love,
  At Thy bidding may I move;
Prompt to serve and follow Thee,
  Loving Him who first loved me.

3 Teach me all Thy steps to trace,
  Strong to follow in Thy grace;
Learning how to love from Thee,
  Loving Him who first loved me.

4 Love in loving finds employ,
  In obedience all her joy;
Ever new that joy will be,
  Loving Him who first loved me.

5 Thus may I rejoice to show
  That I feel the love I owe;
Singing, till Thy face I see,
  Of His love who first loved me.

381 *Thou . . . art acquainted with all my ways.*—Ps. cxxxix. 3.   S.M.

1 STILL with Thee, O my God,
  I would desire to be,
By day, by night, at home, abroad,
  I would be still with Thee:

2 With Thee when dawn comes in,
  And calls me back to care,
Each day returning, to begin
  With Thee, my God, in prayer:

3 With Thee amid the crowd
  That throngs the busy mart:
To hear Thy voice 'mid clamour loud
  Speak softly to my heart:

4 With Thee when day is done,
  And evening calms the mind,
The setting as the rising sun,
  With Thee my heart would find:

5 With Thee when darkness brings
  The signal of repose;
Calm, in the shadow of Thy wings,
  Mine eyelids I would close:

80

6 With Thee, in Thee, by faith
  Abiding I would be:
By day, by night, in life, in death,
  I would be still with Thee.

382 *For I am not ashamed of the gospel of Christ.*—Romans i. 16.   L.M.

1 JESUS! and shall it ever be,
  A mortal man ashamed of Thee?
Ashamed of Thee, whom angels praise,
Whose glories shine through endless days?

2 Ashamed of Jesus! sooner far
Let evening blush to own a star;
He sheds the beams of light divine
O'er this benighted soul of mine.

3 Ashamed of Jesus! just as soon
Let midnight be ashamed of noon:
'Tis midnight with my soul, till He,
Bright Morning Star! bid darkness flee.

4 Ashamed of Jesus! that dear Friend
On whom my hopes of heaven depend;
No; when I blush be this my shame,
That I no more revere His name.

5 Ashamed of Jesus! yes, I may,
When I've no guilt to wash away,
No tear to wipe, no good to crave,
No fears to quell, no soul to save.

6 Till then—nor is my boasting vain,
Till then I boast a Saviour slain!
And O, may this my glory be,
That Christ is not ashamed of me.

383 *Nevertheless, not My will, but Thine, be done.*—Luke xxii. 42.   6 6.6 6.4 6.

1 IN sorrow, care, and strife
  I would not, Lord, repine;
But say, through all my life,
  Not my will, Lord, but Thine.
    Not mine, but Thine,
  Not my will, Lord, but Thine.

2 My life I would this day
  To Thee alone resign,
And with my heart would say,
  Not my will, Lord, but Thine. Not, etc.

3 Choose Thou my lot, I pray,
  And give my heart the sign,
And teach me now to say,
  Not my will, Lord, but Thine. Not, etc.

4 And choose my place for me,
  Where light for Thee may shine,
My word still ever be,
  Not my will, Lord, but Thine. Not, etc.

5 My times are in Thy hand,
  Let life or death be mine!
I'll say, if Thou command,
  Not my will, Lord, but Thine. Not, etc.

6 Thy way is always best,
  O let that way be mine!
In this my soul shall rest,
  Not my will, Lord, but Thine. Not, etc.

384
Thy will be done.
Matthew vi. 10.　　　8 8 8 4.

1 MY God, and Father! while I stray
　　Far from my home, in life's rough
　O teach me from my heart to say,　[way,
　　　Thy will be done!

2 Though dark my path, and sad my lot,
　Let me be still and murmur not,
　Or breathe the prayer divinely taught,
　　Thy will be done.

3 If Thou shouldst call me to resign
　What most I prize—it ne'er was mine;
　I only yield Thee what was Thine;
　　Thy will be done.

4 Should pining sickness waste away
　My life in premature decay,
　My Father, still I strive to say,
　　Thy will be done.

5 If but my fainting heart be blest
　With Thy sweet Spirit for its guest,
　My God, to Thee I leave the rest;
　　Thy will be done.

6 Renew my will from day to day,
　Blend it with Thine, and take away
　All that now makes it hard to say,
　　Thy will be done.

7 Then when on earth I breathe no more
　The prayer oft mixed with tears before,
　I'll sing upon a happier shore,
　　Thy will be done.

385
*My Father, Thou art the guide
of my youth.*—Jer. iii. 4.　7 7.7 7.

1 GOD of mercy, throned on high,
　　Listen from Thy lofty seat;
　Hear, O hear our feeble cry;
　　Guide, O guide our wandering feet.

2 Young and erring travellers, we
　All our dangers do not know;
　Scarcely fear the stormy sea,
　Hardly feel the tempest blow.

3 Jesu, Lover of the young,
　Cleanse us with Thy blood divine;
　Ere the tide of sin grow strong,
　Save us, Lord, and keep us Thine.

4 When perplexed in danger's snare,
　Thou alone our Guide canst be:
　When oppressed with woe and care,
　Whom have we to trust but Thee?

5 Let us ever hear Thy voice,
　Ask Thy counsel every day;
　Saints and angels will rejoice,
　If we walk in wisdom's way.

6 Saviour, give us faith, and pour
　Hope and love on every soul!
　Hope, till time shall be no more!
　Love, while endless ages roll!

386
*Who through faith . . . wrought
righteousness.*—Hebrews xi. 33.
　　　7 7 7 5.7 7 7 5.

1 CHILDREN of the pious dead,
　　Who for conscience nobly bled,
　By the blood those martyrs shed
　　Guard their holy cause:

Theirs the cause of truth and right,
Theirs the fight of faith to fight,
Theirs the souls of earnest might,
　And the great applause.

2 Thorny was their path below,
　Path of torture, fire, and foe;
　Sighs of grief and tears of woe
　　Were their common lot:
　Yet undaunted on they went,
　Up to heaven their prayer was sent,
　They, on crowns of glory bent,
　　All their pains forgot.

3 Shall the fathers stand alone?
　Is their noble spirit gone?
　Is their mantle fallen on none?
　　Are such men no more?
　No! the truth shall yet prevail,
　Strong in souls that never quail;
　Sons, arise! you will not fail
　　In the trying hour.

4 From the lofty courts above
　Sires are bending eyes of love,
　They your fight of faith approve,
　　And on you look down.
　See the martyrs, prophets there,
　There apostles, angels are,
　See the King of kings prepare
　　Your immortal crown.

387
*He shall gather the lambs with His
arm, and carry them in His bosom.*
Isaiah xl. 11.　8 7.8 7.8 7.8 7.

1 HEAVENLY Father, send Thy blessing
　　On Thy children gathered here;
　May they all, Thy name confessing,
　　Be to Thee for ever dear;
　May they be, like Joseph, loving,
　　Dutiful, and chaste, and pure;
　And their faith, like David, proving,
　　Stedfast unto death endure.

2 Holy Saviour, who in meekness
　　Didst vouchsafe a child to be,
　Guide their steps, and help their weakness,
　　Bless, and make them like to Thee;
　Bear Thy lambs, when they are weary,
　　In Thine arms and at Thy breast;
　Through life's desert, dry and dreary,
　　Bring them to Thy heavenly rest.

3 Spread Thy golden pinions o'er them,
　　Holy Spirit, from above;
　Guide them, lead them, go before them,
　　Give them peace and joy and love;
　Thy true temples, Holy Spirit,
　　May they with Thy glory shine,
　And immortal bliss inherit,
　　And for evermore be Thine.

388
*If any man serve Me, let him follow
Me.*—John xii. 26.　8 8 8 6.

1 ACCEPTING, Lord, Thy gracious call,
　　Low at Thy feet I humbly fall;
　Now set me free from Satan's thrall,
　　And let me follow Thee.

2 My Teacher, Ruler, Pattern, Guide,
　Ne'er let me wander from Thy side,
　Nor from the narrow pathway slide,
　　But closely follow Thee.

3 By meekness, patience, kindness, prayer,
By works of love and friendly care,
By holy conduct everywhere,
Help me to follow Thee.

4 When fears and foes beset my way,
When darkest clouds obscure my day,
And easier paths tempt me to stray,
Help me to follow Thee.

And to godliness brotherly kind-
ness, and to brotherly kindness
389 *charity.*—2 Peter i. 7.
7 6.8 6.7 6.8 6.

1 BE kind to one another:
This is a world of care,
And there's enough of needful woe
For every one to bear;
But if you ease the burden
That weighs another down,
That work of Christian charity
Will lighten half your own.

2 Be kind to one another:
Scatter the seeds of love
Wide o'er the field of hearts, and rich
The harvest wealth will prove:
A wealth more truly precious
Than aught beneath the sun,
Which India's diamonds could not buy;
And yet how lightly won!

3 Be kind to one another:
Not to the good alone;
E'en to the cold and selfish heart
Let deeds of love be shown;
So shall ye be His children
Who rains His gifts on all,
And even on the thankless ones
Bids His bright sunbeams fall.

Children, obey your parents in the
390 *Lord.*—Ephesians vi. 1.
L.M.

1 CHILDREN, your parents' will obey:
The Lord commands it to be done;
And those that from the precept stray
To misery and ruin run.

2 Your parents honour and revere,
Be tender, generous, and kind;
Let filial love wipe every tear,
And chase the sorrows from their mind.

3 The disobedient children meet
The vengeance of the Lord most high;
His curse pursues their wandering feet;
Oft ere they reach their prime they die.

4 But those who pay the honour due,
Serve with respect and filial fear,
In all their doings just and true,
And in obedience persevere:

5 With length of days and mercies crowned,
Their peaceful hours shall glide away;
In blessings multiplied abound,
Which never wither nor decay!

Forbearing one another, and
391 *forgiving one another.*
Colossians iii. 13.   7 3.7 3.7 7 7 3.

1 BE not swift to take offence,
Let it pass!

Anger is a foe to sense,
Let it pass!
Brood not darkly o'er a wrong,
Which will disappear ere long;
Rather sing this cheery song,
Let it pass!

2 Echo not an angry word,
Let it pass!
Think how often you have erred,
Let it pass!
Since our joys must pass away,
Like the dewdrops on the spray,
Wherefore should our sorrow stay?
Let it pass!

3 If for good you suffer ill,
Let it pass!
O, be kind and gentle still,
Let it pass!
Time at last makes all things straight;
Let us not resent but wait,
And our triumph shall be great:
Let it pass!

Lead me in the way everlasting.
392 Psalm cxxxix. 24.   7 7.7 7.

1 FATHER, lead me day by day
Ever in Thine own sweet way;
Teach me to be pure and true,
Show me what I ought to do.

2 When in danger, make me brave;
Make me know that Thou canst save;
Keep me safe by Thy dear side;
Let me in Thy love abide.

3 When I'm tempted to do wrong,
Make me stedfast, wise, and strong;
And when all alone I stand
Shield me with Thy mighty hand.

4 When my heart is full of glee,
Help me to remember Thee,
Happy most of all to know
That my Father loves me so.

5 When my work seems hard and dry,
May I press on cheerily;
Help me patiently to bear
Pain and hardship, toil and care.

6 May I see the good and bright
When they pass before my sight;
May I hear the heavenly voice
When the pure and wise rejoice.

7 May I do the good I know,
Be Thy loving child below,
Then at last go home to Thee,
Evermore Thy child to be.

Beloved, if God so loved us, we ought
393 *also to love one another.*
1 John iv. 11.   D.C.M.

1 DEAR Saviour, to Thy little lambs
A lamb-like temper give,
And daily, hourly grace bestow,
In joy and peace to live.
It was Thine own command that we
Should one another love,
And ever give Thee thanks, as do
Thine holy ones above.

2 Our hearts, by nature full of sin,
   Do Thou, O Lord, renew;
And take each evil thought away,
   And all self-will subdue:
Thine own meek, lowly mind impart,
   The spirit like a dove;
   And daily may we learn of Thee
   To love as Thou dost love.

3 As Thou forgivest all our sins,
   So teach us to forgive;
As freely we receive from Thee,
   So may we freely give.
O teach us to forbear like Thee,
   Not answering again,
Remembering how our Saviour bore
   The scoffs of wicked men.

4 When we are for our faults reproved
   May we the fault confess,
And humbly seek Thy grace, that we
   May not again transgress:
Make us affectionate and kind,
   Gentle and meek and good,
Mindful how dearly we were bought
   With Thy most precious blood.

SERVICE.

Go ye into all the world, and preach
the Gospel.—Mark xvi. 15.

394
6 5.6 5.6 5.6 5.

1 LIFT the Gospel banner,
      Wave it far and wide,
Through the crowded city,
   Over ocean's tide:
Sound the proclamation,
   Peace to all mankind,
Jesus and salvation
   All the world may find.

2 Let us raise the fallen,
   Lend the oppressed a hand,
Teach the Christly lesson
   All may understand;
Go, where hardening vices
   Have their strongest hold,
Like a sweet dove, gentle,
   Like a lion, bold.

3 Lift the Gospel standard,
   Spread the Gospel light,
Let the blessèd radiance
   Flame o'er heathen night;
Love is God's own sunshine,
   Such as angels prove:
Conquer men by kindness,
   God Himself is love.

4 Let us rise to action,
   Work with one design,
Work with Christ, and triumph
   In the work divine;
Victory's palm awaits us,
   Let us then work on
Till we hear the welcome,
   'Faithful ones, well done!'

395 *Go ye also into the vineyard.*
      Matthew xx. 4.   L.M.

1 GO labour on; spend, and be spent,
   Thy joy to do the Father's will;
It is the way the Master went,
   Should not the servant tread it still?

2 Go labour on; 'tis not for nought;
   Thy earthly loss is heavenly gain;
Men heed thee, love thee, praise thee not;
   The Master praises; what are men?

3 Go labour on while it is day,
   The world's dark night is hastening on;
Speed, speed thy work, cast sloth away;
   It is not thus that souls are won.

4 Men die in darkness at your side
   Without a hope to cheer the tomb;
Take up the torch, and wave it wide,
   The torch that lights time's thickest
      gloom.

5 Toil on, faint not, keep watch, and pray;
   Be wise the erring soul to win;
Go forth into the world's highway,
   Compel the wanderer to come in.

6 Toil on, and in thy toil rejoice;
   For toil comes rest, for exile home;
Soon shalt thou hear the Bridegroom's
      voice,
   The midnight peal, Behold, I come.

396 *And unto one he gave five talents, to*
      another two, and to another one.
      Matthew xxv. 15.   5 6.5 6.5 6.5 6.

1 GOD entrusts to all
      Talents few or many;
None so young or small
      That they have not any.
Though the great and wise
   Have a greater number,
Yet my one I prize,
   And it must not slumber.

2 Little drops of rain
      Bring the springing flowers;
And I may attain
      Much by little powers.
Every little mite,
   Every little measure
Helps to spread the light,
   Helps to swell the treasure.

3 God will surely ask,
      Ere I enter heaven,
Have I done the task
      Which to me was given.
God entrusts to all
   Talents few or many;
None so young or small
   That they have not any.

397 *Keep that which is committed to*
      thy trust.—1 Tim. vi. 20.   S.M.

1 A CHARGE to keep I have,
      A God to glorify,
A never-dying soul to save,
   And fit it for the sky;
To serve the present age,
   My calling to fulfil:
O may it all my powers engage
   To do my Master's will!

2 Arm me with jealous care,
      As in Thy sight to live;
And O Thy servant, Lord, prepare
   A strict account to give!
Help me to watch and pray,
   And on Thyself rely,
Assured, if I my trust betray,
   I shall for ever die.

398

Speak, LORD ; for Thy servant heareth.—1 Samuel iii. 9.

87.87.77.

1 MASTER, speak ! Thy servant heareth,
   Waiting for Thy gracious word,
Longing for Thy voice that cheereth;
   Master ! let it now be heard.
   I am listening, Lord, for Thee ;
   What hast Thou to say to me?

2 Speak to me by name, O Master,
   Let me know it is to me ;
Speak, that I may follow faster,
   With a step more firm and free,
   Where the Shepherd leads the flock,
   In the shadow of the Rock.

3 Master, speak ! though least and lowest,
   Let me not unheard depart ;
Master, speak ! for O, Thou knowest
   All the yearning of my heart ;
   Knowest all its truest need ;
   Speak ! and make me blest indeed.

4 Master, speak ! and make me ready,
   When Thy voice is truly heard,
With obedience glad and steady
   Still to follow every word.
   I am listening, Lord, for Thee ;
   Master, speak, O, speak to me !

399

Present your bodies a living sacrifice.—Romans xii. 1.   7 7.7 7.

1 TAKE my life, and let it be
   Consecrated, Lord, to Thee ;
Take my moments and my days,
Let them flow in ceaseless praise.

2 Take my hands, and let them move
At the impulse of Thy love ;
Take my feet, and let them be
Swift and beautiful for Thee.

3 Take my voice, and let me sing
Always, only for my King ;
Take my lips, and let them be
Filled with messages from Thee.

4 Take my silver and my gold,
Not a mite would I withhold ;
Take my intellect, and use
Every power as Thou shalt choose.

5 Take my will, and make it Thine ;
It shall be no longer mine :
Take my heart, it is Thine own ;
It shall be Thy royal throne.

6 Take my love ; my Lord, I pour
At Thy feet its treasure-store :
Take myself, and I will be
Ever, only, all for Thee.

400

My times are in Thy hand.
Psalm xxxi. 15.   IRREGULAR.

THE LIFE OF LOVE.

1 FATHER, I know that all my life
   Is portioned out for me,
And the changes that are sure to come
   I do not fear to see ;
But I ask Thee for a present mind,
   Intent on pleasing Thee.

84

2 I ask Thee for a thoughtful love,
   Through constant watching wise,
To meet the glad with joyful smiles,
   And wipe the weeping eyes ;
And a heart at leisure from itself,
   To soothe and sympathise.

3 I would not have the restless will
   That hurries to and fro,
Seeking for some great thing to do
   Or secret thing to know ;
I would be treated as a child,
   And guided where I go.

4 Wherever in the world I am,
   In whatsoe'er estate,
I have a fellowship with hearts
   To keep and cultivate ;
And a work of lowly love to do
   For the Lord on whom I wait.

SECOND PART.

5 So I ask Thee for the daily strength,
   To none that ask denied,
And a mind to blend with outward life,
   Still keeping at Thy side ;
Content to fill a little space
   If Thou be glorified.

6 And if some things I do not ask
   In my cup of blessing be :
I would have my spirit filled the more
   With grateful love to Thee,
And careful less to serve Thee much
   Than to please Thee perfectly.

7 There are briars besetting every path,
   That call for patient care ;
There is a cross in every lot,
   And a constant need for prayer ;
Yet a lowly heart, that leans on Thee,
   Is happy anywhere.

8 In a service which Thy will appoints
   There are no bonds for me ;
For my inmost soul is taught the truth
   That makes Thy children free ;
And a life of self-renouncing love
   Is a life of liberty.

401

All Thy works shall praise Thee, O LORD.—Psalm cxlv. 10.   S.M.

1 MAKE use of me, my God,
   Let me not be forgot ;
A broken vessel cast aside,
   One whom Thou needest not.

2 Thou usest all Thy works,
   The weakest things that be ;
Each has a service of its own,
   For all things wait on Thee.

3 Thou usest the high stars,
   The tiny drops of dew,
The giant peak, the little hill ;
   My God, O use me too.

4 All things do serve Thee here ;
   All creatures, great and small ;
Make use of me, of me, my God,
   The weakest of them all.

402

She hath done what she could.
Mark xiv. 8.   87.87.87.87.

1 IF you cannot on the ocean
   Sail among the swiftest fleet,

Rocking on the highest billows,
  Laughing at the storms you meet:
You can stand among the sailors,
  Anchored yet within the bay,
You can lend a hand to help them,
  As they launch their boats away.

2 If you are too weak to journey
  Up the mountain steep and high,
You can stand within the valley,
  While the multitudes go by;
You can chant in happy measure,
  As they slowly pass along;
Though they may forget the singer,
  They will not forget the song.

3 If you cannot in the conflict
  Prove yourself a soldier true,
If where fire and smoke are thickest
  There's no work for you to do;
When the battle-field is silent,
  You can go with careful tread,
You can bear away the wounded,
  You can cover up the dead.

4 Do not, then, stand idly waiting
  For some greater work to do;
O! improve each passing moment,
  For these moments may be few.
Go, and toil in any vineyard,
  Do not fear to do or dare;
If you want a field of labour,
  You can find it anywhere.

We love Him, because He first loved
403 *us.*—1 John iv. 19.
      7 6.7 6.7 6.7 6.

1 I LOVE my precious Saviour
  Because He died for me;
And if I did not serve Him,
  How sinful I should be!
I know He makes me happy,
  And hears me when I pray:
I'll keep my hold on Jesus,
  The Bible says I may.

2 Though I can do but little,
  Yet I will always try
To tell some little children
  How Jesus came to die.
God help me to be useful
  In all I do or say!
I mean to work for Jesus,
  The Bible says I may.

3 And while I'm loving Jesus,
  I feel so glad to know
That making others happy
  Will make me happy too.
When others hear me singing,
  I'll not forget to say,
You too can be as happy,
  The Bible says you may.

4 And since I've found my Saviour,
  The first link in the chain,
I'll trust in Him for ever,
  Till heaven at last I gain.
I love that blessèd country
  Where tears are wiped away;
I want to live with Jesus,
  The Bible says I may.

Out of the mouth of babes and suck-
404 *lings Thou hast perfected praise.*
    Matthew xxi. 16.   7 6.8 8 6.

1 O! WHAT can little hands do
  To please the King of heaven?
The little hands some work may try
That will some simple want supply:
  Such grace to mine be given!

2 O! what can little lips do
  To please the King of heaven?
The little lips can praise and pray,
And gentle words of kindness say:
  Such grace to mine be given!

3 O! what can little eyes do
  To please the King of heaven?
The little eyes can upward look,
Can learn to read God's holy Book:
  Such grace to mine be given!

4 O! what can little hearts do
  To please the King of heaven?
Young hearts, if He His Spirit send,
Can love their Maker, Saviour, Friend:
  Such grace to mine be given!

Go, . . . tell how great things the Lord
405 *hath done for thee.*—Mark v. 19.
      7 6.7 6.7 6.7 6.7 7 7 6.

1 I LOVE to tell the story
  Of unseen things above,
Of Jesus and His glory,
  Of Jesus and His love.
I love to tell the story,
  Because I know it's true;
It satisfies my longings
  As nothing else could do.
    I love to tell the story,
      'Twill be my theme in glory
    To tell the old, old story
      Of Jesus and His love.

2 I love to tell the story:
  More wonderful it seems
Than all the golden fancies
  Of all our golden dreams.
I love to tell the story,
  It did so much for me:
And that is just the reason
  I tell it now to thee.
    I love to tell the story, etc.

3 I love to tell the story;
  'Tis pleasant to repeat
What seems each time I tell it
  More wonderfully sweet.
I love to tell the story,
  For some have never heard
The message of salvation
  From God's own holy word.
    I love to tell the story, etc.

4 I love to tell the story,
  For those who know it best
Seem hungering and thirsting
  To hear it, like the rest.
And when in scenes of glory,
  I sing the new, new song,
'Twill be the old, old story,
  That I have loved so long.
    I love to tell the story, etc.

85

406
The harvest truly is plenteous, but the labourers are few.
Matthew ix. 37.   5 6.6 5 9.

1 THE fields are all white,
    And the reapers are few;
We children are willing,
    But what can we do
To work for our Lord in His harvest?

2 Our hands are so small,
    And our words are so weak,
We cannot teach others;
    How then shall we seek
To work for our Lord in His harvest?

3 We'll work by our prayers,
    By the pennies we bring,
By small self-denials;
    The least little thing
May work for our Lord in His harvest.

4 Until, by-and-by,
    As the years pass at length,
We too may be reapers,
    And go forth in strength
To work for our Lord in His harvest.

407
In the name of our God we will set up our banners.—Psalm xx. 5.
10 8.10 9.10 9.10 9.

1 SOUND the battle-cry! See! the foe is nigh;
Raise the standard high for the Lord;
Gird your armour on; Stand firm, every one;
Rest your cause upon His holy word.
    Rouse, then, soldiers! rally round the banner!
    Ready! steady! pass the word along;
    Onward! forward! shout a loud hosanna!
    Christ is Captain of the mighty throng.

2 Strong to meet the foe, Marching on we go,
While our cause, we know, must prevail;
Shield and banner bright Gleaming in the light;
Battling for the right, we ne'er can fail.
    Rouse, then, soldiers! etc.

3 O Thou God of all! Hear us when we call;
Help us, one and all, by Thy grace; [won,
When the battle's done, And the victory
May we wear the crown before Thy face!
    Rouse, then, soldiers! etc.

408
Fear not: for they that be with us are more than they that be with them.
2 Kings vi. 16.   7 7 7 5.7 7 7 5.

1 LORD, before Thy throne we bow,
    And with one united vow
To Thy sacred service now
    All our lives resign.
Only, to each youthful heart,
Courage, patience, help impart;
Then, if Thou our Leader art,
    Glory shall be Thine.

2 But can such a feeble band
Satan's gathered host withstand,
And resist with dauntless hand
    All their mighty powers?

86

Saviour, in Thy name we go,
Thou hast conquered every foe;
And if Thou Thy strength bestow,
    Saving help is ours.

3 Far above our mortal sight,
Near Thy throne in shining light,
Happy spirits clothed in white
    Strike their harps and cry:
Jesus triumphed when He rose,
Jesus conquered all our foes;
Now His faithful hand bestows
    Palms of victory.

4 Saviour, if Thy cross we bear,
We are sure Thy joy to share,
And with ransomed hosts to wear
    Crowns of light on high:
Hear us, then, we humbly pray,
Take us in our early day;
Let us by Thy banner stay
    Faithful till we die.

409
If God be for us, who can be against us?—Romans viii. 31.
7 7.8 7.7.7.8 7.

1 BEHOLD Thy youthful army;
    At Thy command we gather,
And thankful stand, a sacred band,
    To serve our heavenly Father.
Our lives and powers are hallowed,
    To Thy high service given:
We bear that sign, and seal of Thine,
    Devoting us to heaven.

2 There stand arrayed against us
    The world, the flesh, the devil;
Great foes and strong to do us wrong,
    And drive us to all evil.
But though our foes be mighty,
    If Thou, O Lord, be o'er us,
Strong in Thy might, we'll boldly fight,
    And evil drive before us.

3 Out of the mouth of sucklings
    And babes, Thou strength ordainest:
In us, O Lord, fulfil this word,
    Thou who all victory gainest.
When the good fight is finished,
    Where sin can reach us never,
Crowned shall we stand, palms in our [hand,
    To sing Thy love for ever.

410
Go ye also into the vineyard.
Matthew xx. 4.   7 6.7 6.7 6.7 6.

1 LORD of the living harvest,
    That whitens o'er the plain,
Where angels soon shall gather
    Their sheaves of golden grain:
Accept these hands to labour,
    These hearts to trust and love,
And deign with them to hasten
    Thy kingdom from above.

2 As labourers in Thy vineyard,
    Send us out, Christ, to be
Content to bear the burden
    Of weary days for Thee;
We ask no other wages,
    When Thou shalt call us home,
But to have shared the travail
    Which makes Thy kingdom come.

3 Come down, O Holy Spirit,
  And fill our souls with light;
Clothe us in spotless raiment,
  In linen clean and white;
Within Thy sacred temple
  Be with us where we stand,
And sanctify Thy people
  Throughout this happy land.

4 Be with us, God the Father!
  Be with us, God the Son!
And God the Holy Spirit!
  O blessèd Three in One!
Make us a royal priesthood,
  Thee rightly to adore,
And fill us with Thy fulness,
  Now and for evermore.

411 *What shall I render unto the* LORD
for all His benefits toward me?
Psalm cxvi. 12.   6 6.6 6.6 6.

1 THY. life was given for me,
    Thy blood, O Lord, was shed,
That I might ransomed be,
  And quickened from the dead;
    Thy life was given for me;
    What have I given for Thee?

2 Long years were spent for me
    In weariness and woe,
That through eternity
  Thy glory I might know;
    Long years were spent for me;
    Have I spent one for Thee?

3 The Father's home of light,
    Thy rainbow-circled throne,
Were left for earthly night,
  For wanderings sad and lone;
    Yea, all was left for me;
    Have I left aught for Thee?

4 Thou, Lord, hast borne for me
    More than my tongue can tell
Of bitterest agony,
  To rescue me from hell;
    Thou sufferedst all for me;
    What have I borne for Thee?

5 And Thou hast brought to me
    Down from Thy home above
Salvation full and free,
  Thy pardon and Thy love;
    Great gifts Thou broughtest me;
    What have I brought to Thee?

6 O let my life be given,
    My years for Thee be spent;
World-fetters all be riven,
  And joy with suffering blent;
    Thou gav'st Thyself for me,
    I give myself to Thee.

412 *To serve the* LORD *thy God with all*
thy heart and with all thy soul.
Deut. x. 12.   7 6.8 6.7 6.8 6.

1 WHAT can I give to Jesus,
    Who gave Himself for me?
How can I show my love to Him
  Who died on Calvary?
    Myself I give to Jesus,
    Who gave Himself for me:
Thus will I show my love to Him
  Who died on Calvary.

2 I give my mind to Jesus,
    To think upon His word;
That I may learn His holy will,
  And truly love the Lord.
    This will I give to Jesus, etc.

3 I give my heart to Jesus,
    To love Him ever best;
And trusting in His dying love,
  Hope to be ever blest.
    This will I give to Jesus, etc.

4 I give my life to Jesus,
    My strength and health and all;
Assured He'll be my constant Friend,
  Whatever may befall.
    This will I give to Jesus, etc.

5 Thy Spirit give, Lord Jesus,
    To strengthen me for this;
That I may have Thy loving smile,
  And share Thine endless bliss.
    Then shall I give to Jesus
      A song more sweet, more free;
    And ever show my love to Him
      Who died on Calvary.

413 *And children: let them praise the*
name of the LORD.—Psalm cxlviii.
12, 13.   14 13.12 12.14 13.

1 TO and fro, to and fro, hear the tread of
    little children,
As they go, as they go; busy march of
    busy feet!
Here and there, everywhere, joyous song
    we're singing;
Loud and clear, full of cheer, happy tones
    are ringing.
    To and fro, to and fro, etc.

2 To and fro, to and fro, hear the tread of
    little children,
As they go, as they go; busy march of
    busy feet!
We will tell, we will tell of the wondrous
    story,
While we raise songs of praise to our Lord
    in glory.
    To and fro, to and fro, etc.

3 To and fro, to and fro, hear the tread of
    little children,
As they go, as they go; busy march of
    busy feet!
Through the world, through the world,
    doing angels' duty,
Bright and fair, bright and fair, clothed
    in angel beauty.
    To and fro, to and fro, etc.

414 *Son, go work to-day in my vine-*
yard.—Matthew xxi. 28.
11 11.11 11.11 11.

1 GO work in My vineyard, the Master
    saith, go!
The fruitage is ripening with rich, ruddy
    glow;
The sun of the morning is now in the west,
The day's early gleaners are fainting for
    rest;
With holy compassion and hearts all aglow,
Go work in My vineyard, the Master saith,
    go!

87

2 O, heed now the calling; up, while it is day;
　Perhaps in life's dawning thy strength may
　　　decay;
　Then give unto Jesus the dew of thy youth,
　And seek through His mercy the sunlight
　　　of truth;
　With holy compassion and hearts all aglow,
　Go work in My vineyard, the Master saith,
　　　go!　．

3 O, haste to the vineyard; the Master's own
　　　voice
　Has called you to duty; He'll bid you
　　　rejoice
　When, safe in His kingdom, on heaven's
　　　bright shore,
　The fruitage is gathered, and labour is o'er;
　With holy compassion, and hearts all
　　　aglow,
　O, haste to the vineyard, the Master saith,
　　　Go!

4 For ever in glory the faithful shall sing,
　'Our day's work was given to Jesus our
　　　King;
　And, through the rich fulness of faith in
　　　His love,
　The vintage is gathered, and garnered
　　　above;
　We entered the vineyard with hearts all
　　　aglow,
　And toiled for our Master, when Jesus said,
　　　Go!'

In the morning sow thy seed, and in the
evening withhold not thine hand.

415 Ecclesiastes xi. 6.
9 9.9 9.7 7.10 10.9 8.

1 SOWING the seed by the daylight fair,
　　Sowing the seed by the noonday glare,
　Sowing the seed by the fading light,
　Sowing the seed in the solemn night:
　　O, what shall the harvest be?
　．O, what shall the harvest be?
　Sown in the darkness or sown in the light,
　Sown in our weakness or sown in our might,
　Gathered in time or eternity,
　　Sure, ah, sure will the harvest be!

2 Sowing the seed by the wayside high,
　Sowing the seed on the rocks to die,
　Sowing the seed where the thorns will spoil,
　Sowing the seed in the fertile soil:
　　．O, what shall the harvest be?　[etc.
　Sown in the darkness or sown in the light,

3 Sowing the seed with an aching heart,
　Sowing the seed while the tear-drops start,
　Sowing the seed till the reapers come,
　Gladly to gather the harvest home:
　　O, what shall the harvest be?　[etc.
　Sown in the darkness or sown in the light,

The night cometh, when no man can
work.—John ix. 4.

416 7 6.7 5.7 6.7 5.

1 WORK, for the night is coming!
　　Work through the morning hours;
　Work while the dew is sparkling,
　．Work 'mid springing flowers;
88

Work when the day grows brighter,
　Work in the glowing sun;
Work, for the night is coming.
　When man's work is done.

2 Work, for the night is coming;
　Work through the sunny noon;
Fill brightest hours with labour,
　Rest comes sure and soon;
Give every flying minute
　Something to keep in store;
Work, for the night is coming,
　When man works no more.

3 Work, for the night is coming,
　Under the sunset skies;
While their bright tints are glowing,
　Work, for daylight flies.
Work, till the last beam fadeth,
　Fadeth, to shine no more;
Work, while the night is darkening,
　When man's work is o'er.

He that overcometh shall inherit all
things.—Revelation xxi. 7.

417 7 6.7 6.7 6.7 6.

1 STAND up! stand up for Jesus!
　　Ye soldiers of the cross;
Lift high His royal banner,
　It must not suffer loss:
From victory unto victory
　His army shall He lead,
Till every foe is vanquished,
　And Christ is Lord indeed.

2 Stand up! stand up for Jesus!
　The trumpet-call obey:
Forth to the mighty conflict,
　In this His glorious day:
Ye that are men now serve Him
　Against unnumbered foes;
Let courage rise with danger,
　And strength to strength oppose.

3 Stand up! stand up for Jesus!
　Stand in His strength alone;
The arm of flesh will fail you;
　Ye dare not trust your own:
Put on the Christian's armour,
　And watching unto prayer,
Where duty calls, or danger,
　Be never wanting there.

4 Stand up! stand up for Jesus!
　The strife will not be long;
This day the noise of battle,
　The next the victor's song:
To him that overcometh
　A crown of life shall be;
He with the King of glory
　Shall reign eternally.

And take the helmet of salvation,
and the sword of the Spirit.

418 Ephesians vi. 17.　8 7.8 7.8 7.8 7.

1 LO! the day of God is breaking;
　　See it gleaming from afar!
Sons of earth, from slumber waking,
　Hail the bright and morning Star!
Hear the call! Gird on your armour,
　Grasp the Spirit's mighty sword,
Take the helmet of salvation,
　Battling bravely for the Lord!

2 Trust in Him who is your Captain;
   Let no heart in terror quail;
Jesus leads the gathering legions,
   In His name we shall prevail.
      Hear the call! etc.

3 Onward marching, firm and steady,
   Faint not, fear not Satan's frown;
For the Lord is with you alway,
   Till you wear the victor's crown.
      Hear the call! etc.

4 Conquering hosts with banners waving,
   Sweeping on o'er hill and plain.
Ne'er shall halt till swells the anthem,
   Christ o'er all the world doth reign!
      Hear the call! etc.

Above all, taking the shield of
   faith.—Ephesians vi. 16.

419   11 11.11 11.8 8.8 8.

1 STRIKE! O strike for victory, Soldiers of
      the Lord,
Hoping in His mercy, Trusting in His word;
Lift the Gospel banner High above the
   world;
Let its folds of beauty Ever be unfurled.
   Strike! strike for victory, heroes bold;
   Strike! till the victory you behold.
   Strike! strike for victory, ne'er give o'er;
   Rest then in glory evermore!

2 What, though raging lions Meet us on the
      way,
Zionward we're marching, Toward the
   gates of day;
Ever pressing onward, Onward to the light,
Till we reach the Jordan With our home in
   sight.   Strike! strike for victory, etc.

3 Strike! O strike for victory, Heroes of the
      cross,
Sacrificing pleasure, Glorying in loss;
Bind the helmet stronger, Tighter grasp
   the sword;
Conquering and to conquer, Battle for the
   Lord.   Strike! strike for victory, etc.

4 Hand to hand united, Heart to heart as one,
Let us still keep marching Till our journey's
   done,
Till we see the angels Come in glory down,
With the shining garments And the victor's
   crown.   Strike! strike for victory, etc.

Be strong and of a good courage.

420   Joshua i. 6.   11 11 11 7.11 11 11 7,
                              AND CHORUS.

1 WE are marching on with shield and
      banner bright;
We will work for God and battle for the
   right;
We will praise His name, rejoicing in His
   might;
   And we'll work till Jesus calls.
In the Sunday-school our army we prepare,
As we rally round our blessèd standard
   there,
And the Saviour's cross we early learn to
   bear.
      While we work till Jesus calls.
      Then awake, then awake,
      Happy song, happy song;
      Shout for joy, shout for joy
      As we gladly march along.

We are marching onward, singing as we
   go,
To the promised land where living waters
   flow;
Come and join our ranks as pilgrims here
   below,
   Come and work till Jesus calls.

2 We are marching on; our Captain, ever
   near,
Will protect us still; His cheering voice
   we hear;
Let the foe advance, we'll never, never fear,
   For we'll work till Jesus calls.
Then awake, awake, our happy, happy
   song;
We will shout for joy, and gladly march
   along;
In the Lord of hosts let every heart be
   strong,
   While we work till Jesus calls.
                        Then, etc.

3 We are marching on the strait and narrow
   way,
That will lead to life and everlasting day,
To the smiling fields that never will decay:
   But we'll work till Jesus calls.
We are marching on and pressing toward
   the prize,
To a glorious crown beyond the glowing
   skies;
To the radiant fields where pleasure never
   dies,
   And we'll work till Jesus calls.
                        Then, etc

Wherefore take unto you the
   whole armour of God.

421   Ephesians vi. 13.   D.S.M.

1 SOLDIERS of Christ, arise,
      And put your armour on,
Strong in the strength which God supplies
   Through His eternal Son;
   Strong in the Lord of hosts,
   And in His mighty power,
Who in the strength of Jesus trusts
   Is more than conqueror.

2 Stand then in His great might,
   With all His strength endued;
But take, to arm you for the fight,
   The panoply of God:
   Leave no unguarded place,
   No weakness of the soul,
Take every virtue, every grace,
   And fortify the whole.

3 To keep your armour bright,
   Attend with constant care,
Still walking in your Captain's sight,
   And watching unto prayer.
   To God your every want
   In instant prayer display;
Pray always; pray, and never faint;
   Pray, without ceasing pray!

4 From strength to strength go on,
   Wrestle and fight and pray,
Tread all the powers of darkness down,
   And win the well-fought day;
   Still let the Spirit cry
   In all His soldiers, 'Come,'
Till Christ the Lord descend from high,
   And take the conquerors home.

89

They that sow in tears shall reap in joy.—Psalm cxxvi. 5.

422

8 7.8 7.8 7.8 7.

1 FATHER, from Thy throne in glory,
Where Thou reign'st the God of love,
See us worshipping before Thee,
Now our reverent act approve:
Joined in bonds of holy union,
Knit by living faith to Thee,
Sanctify our sweet communion,
Ever-blessèd Trinity.

2 By Thy hallowing inspiration
Every teacher's heart illume ;
By Thy brightest revelation
Scatter all our mental gloom :
Give to each the signs attesting
Work accepted of the Lord ;
Give the faith of spirits resting
On Thine own eternal word.

3 Often have we gone forth weeping,
Bearing precious gospel seed ;
Hasten, Lord, the time of reaping,
Days of plenteous gathering speed,
When, the fruits of labour sharing,
Joyfully again we come,
Sheaves of souls immortal bearing,
Sweetly singing, 'Harvest home !'

For by one Spirit are we all baptized into one body.

423

1 Corinthians xii. 13.   L.M.

FOR TEACHERS.

1 LOVE is the theme of saints above ;
Love be the theme of saints below ;
Love is of God, for God is love ;
With love let every bosom glow :

2 Love, stronger than the grasp of death ;
That love rejoices o'er the grave ;
Love to the Author of our breath ;
Love to the Son, who came to save ;

3 Love to the Spirit of all grace ;
Love to the Scriptures of all truth ;
Love to our whole apostate race,
Love to the agèd, love to youth ;

4 Love to each other : soul and mind,
And heart and hand, with full accord,
In one sweet covenant combined
To live and die unto the Lord.

5 Christ's little flock we then shall feed ;
The lambs we in our arms shall bear,
Reclaim the lost, the feeble lead,
And watch o'er all in faith and prayer.

6 Thus through our isle, on all our bands,
The beauty of the Lord shall be ;
And Britain, glory of all lands,
Plant Sabbath-schools from sea to sea.

The fire shall ever be burning upon the altar ; it shall never go out.

424

Leviticus vi. 13.   L.M.

1 O THOU who camest from above
The pure celestial fire to impart,
Kindle a flame of sacred love
On the mean altar of my heart !

90

2 There let it for Thy glory burn
With inextinguishable blaze ;
And trembling to its source return,
In humble prayer and fervent praise.

3 Jesus, confirm my heart's desire
To work, and speak, and think for Thee ;
Still let me guard the holy fire,
And still stir up Thy gift in me ;

4 Ready for all Thy perfect will,
My acts of faith and love repeat,
Till death Thine endless mercies seal,
And make the sacrifice complete.

And ye yourselves like unto men that wait for their lord.—Luke xii. 36.

425

6 5.6 5.6 5.6 5.

1 WHILE the sun is shining
Brightly in the sky,
Ere his rays declining
Tell that night is nigh ;
Ere the shadows falling
Lengthen on thy way,
Hark ! a voice is calling,
'Work while it is day.'

2 Work, but not in sadness,
For your Lord above ;
He will make it gladness
With His smile of love :
When that Lord returning
Knocketh at the gate,
Let your lights be burning,
Be like men who wait.

3 Happy then the meeting
When you see His face ;
Welcome then the greeting
From the throne of grace :
'Good and faithful servants,
Of My Father blest,
Now your work is ended,
Enter into rest.'

THE LIFE TO COME.

The grass withereth, and the flower thereof falleth away.

426

1 Peter i. 24.   L.M.

1 THE morning flowers display their
sweets.
And gay their silken leaves unfold,
As careless of the noontide heats,
As fearless of the evening cold.

2 Nipt by the wind's unkindly blast,
Parched by the sun's directer ray,
The momentary glories waste,
The short-lived beauties die away.

3 So blooms the human face divine,
When youth its pride of beauty shows ;
Fairer than spring the colours shine,
And sweeter than the virgin rose.

4 Or worn by slowly rolling years,
Or broke by sickness in a day,
The fading glory disappears,
The short-lived beauties die away.

5 Yet these, new rising from the tomb,
With lustre brighter far shall shine ;
Revive with ever-during bloom,
Safe from diseases and decline.

6 Let sickness blast, let death devour,
  If heaven must recompense our pains :
Perish the grass, and fade the flower,
  If firm the word of God remains.

Then shall I know even as also
I am known.
427 1 Corinthians xiii. 12. 7 7.7 7.7 7.

1 WHEN this passing world is done,
    When has sunk yon radiant sun,
When I stand with Christ on high,
Looking o'er life's history :
Then, Lord, shall I fully know,
Not till then, how much I owe.

2 When I stand before the throne,
  Clad in beauty not my own ;
When I see Thee as Thou art,
Love Thee with unsinning heart :
Then, Lord, shall I fully know,
Not till then, how much I owe.

3 When the praise of heaven I hear,
  Loud as thunder to the ear,
Loud as many waters' noise,
Sweet as harp's melodious voice :
Then, Lord, shall I fully know,
Not till then, how much I owe.

4 E'en on earth, as through a glass
  Darkly let Thy glory pass ;
Make forgiveness feel so sweet,
Make Thy Spirit's help so meet :
E'en on earth, Lord, let me know
Something of the debt I owe.

5 Chosen not for good in me,
  Wakened up from wrath to flee ;
Hidden in the Saviour's side,
By the Spirit sanctified ;
Teach me, Lord, on earth to show
By my love how much I owe.

e spend our years as a tale that
428 *is told.—Psalm xc. 9.* 8 7.8 7.

1 DAYS and moments quickly flying
    end the living with the dead ;
Soon will you and I be lying
  Each within his narrow bed.

2 Soon our souls to God, who gave them,
  Will have sped their rapid flight :
Able now by grace to save them,
  O, that while we can we might !

3 Jesu, infinite Redeemer,
  Maker of this wondrous frame,
Teach, O teach us to remember
  What we are and whence we came ;

4 Whence we came, and whither wending :
  Soon we must through darkness go,
To inherit bliss unending,
  Or eternity of woe.

Teach us to number our days.
429 *Psalm xc. 12.* D.S.M.

1 A FEW more years shall roll,
    A few more seasons come,
And we shall be with those that rest
  Asleep within the tomb.
    Then, O my Lord, prepare
    My soul for that great day :
O ! wash me in Thy precious blood,
  And take my sins away !

2 A few more suns shall set
  O'er these dark hills of time ;
And we shall be where suns are not,
  A far serener clime !
    Then, O my Lord, prepare, etc.

3 A few more storms shall beat
  On this wild, rocky shore ;
And we shall be where tempests cease,
  And surges swell no more.
    Then, O my Lord, prepare, etc.

4 A few more struggles here,
  A few more partings o'er,
A few more toils, a few more tears,
  And we shall weep no more.
    Then, O my Lord, prepare, etc.

5 A few more Sabbaths here
  Shall cheer us on our way ;
And we shall reach the endless rest,
  The eternal Sabbath-day.
    . Then, O my Lord, prepare, etc.

Prepare to meet thy God.
430 *Amos iv. 12.* C.M.

1 DEATH has been here, and borne away
    A scholar from our side !
Just in the morning of life's day,
  One young as we has died.

2 Perhaps our time may be as short,
  Our days may fly as fast ;
O Lord, impress the solemn thought,
  This day may be our last.

3 May we come up with willing feet
  To meet our Saviour here,
And wait around the mercy-seat
  With hope as well as fear.

4 All needful strength is Thine to give ;
  To Thee our souls apply
For grace to teach us how to live,
  And make us fit to die.

5 Lord, to Thy wisdom and Thy care
  May we resign our days ;
Content to live and serve Thee here,
  Or die, and sing Thy praise.

Our light affliction . . . is but for a
431 *moment.—2 Corinthians iv. 17.*
    7 7 6.6 6.6 7.

1 HERE we suffer grief and pain,
    Here we meet to part again,
In heaven we part no more.
  O ! that will be joyful,
  Joyful, joyful, joyful,
  O ! that will be joyful,
When we meet to part no more.

2 All who love the Lord below,
  When they die to heaven will go,
And sing with saints above.
  O ! that will be joyful, etc.

3 Little children will be there,
  Who have sought the Lord by prayer,
From every land below.
  O ! that will be joyful, etc.

4 Teachers, too, will meet above,
  Pastors, parents, whom we love,
Will meet to part no more.
  O ! that will be joyful, etc.

5 O! how happy we shall be,
    For our Saviour we shall see,
      Exalted on His throne!
        O! that will be joyful, etc.

6 There we all shall sing with joy,
    And eternity employ
      In praising Christ the Lord.
        O! that will be joyful, etc.

432 *The holy city, new Jerusalem.*
    Rev. xxi. 2.   7 6.7 6 7 6.7 6.

1 JERUSALEM the golden,
    With milk and honey blest,
Beneath thy contemplation
    Sink heart and voice oppressed.
I know not, O I know not
    What social joys are there,
What radiancy of glory,
    What bliss beyond compare!

2 They stand, those halls of Zion,
    All jubilant with song,
And bright with many an angel,
    And all the martyr throng;
The Prince is ever in them;
    The daylight is serene;
The pastures of the blessèd
    Are decked in glorious sheen.

3 There is the throne of David,
    And there, from care released,
The shout of them that triumph,
    The song of them that feast;
And they who with their Leader
    Have conquered in the fight,
For ever and for ever
    Are clad in robes of white.

433 *That where I am, there ye may be*
    also.—John xiv. 3.   L.M.

1 I SHALL be with Thee where Thou art,
    Jesus, my Saviour and my Lord;
For never wilt Thou say, Depart;
    To those who love and keep Thy word

2 I shall be with Thee where Thou art,
    To praise Thee for Thy love divine;
When Thou hast made my sinful heart
    Perfect and pure and good, like Thine.

3 I shall be with Thee where Thou art,
    To dwell within Thy blessed abode;
Where nothing shall Thy ransomed part
    From Thee, and from their Father, God.

4 I shall be with Thee where Thou art,
    My Father's house within the skies;
And with those dearest to my heart
    Walk in Thy promised paradise.

5 I shall be with Thee to behold
    The glory God to Thee hath given;
Not gems, not perishable gold,
    But the eternal throne of heaven.

6 I shall be with Thee to adore,
    Worship, and serve, like those above;
And with more knowledge love Thee more,
    Through an eternity of love.

434 *For the former things are passed*
    away.—Revelation xxi. 4.
    7 6.8 6.7 6.8 6.

1 TEN thousand times ten thousand,
    In shining raiment bright,
The armies of the ransomed saints
    Throng up the steeps of light:
'Tis finished! all is finished,
    Their fight with death and sin;
Lift up, lift up, ye golden gates,
    And let the victors in.

2 What rush of alleluias
    Fills all the earth and sky!
What harping of a thousand harps
    Bespeaks the triumph nigh!
O day, for which creation
    And all its tribes were made!
O joy, for all its former woes
    A thousandfold repaid!

3 O, then what rapturous greetings
    On Canaan's happy shore,
What knitting severed friendships up,
    Where partings are no more!
Then eyes with joy shall sparkle,
    That flowed with tears of late;
Orphans no longer fatherless,
    Nor widows desolate.

4 Bring near Thy great salvation,
    Thou Lamb for sinners slain,
Fill up the roll of Thine elect,
    Then take Thy power and reign:
Appear, Desire of nations,
    Thine exiles long for home;
Show in the heavens Thy promised sign;
    Thou Prince and Saviour, come!

435 *A city which hath foundations, whose*
    builder and maker is God.
    Hebrews xi. 10.   C.M.

1 JERUSALEM, my happy home!
    Name ever dear to me;
When shall my labours have an end,
    In joy, and peace, and thee?

2 When shall these eyes thy heaven-built
    And pearly gates behold,   [walls
Thy bulwarks, with salvation strong,
    And streets of shining gold?

3 There happier bowers than Eden's bloom,
    Nor sin nor sorrow know:
Blest seats, through rude and stormy
    I onward press to you.   [scenes,

4 Why should I shrink at pain and woe?
    Or feel at death dismay?
I've Canaan's goodly land in view,
    And realms of endless day.

5 Apostles, martyrs, prophets there
    Around my Saviour stand;
And soon my friends in Christ below
    Will join the glorious band.

6 Jerusalem, my happy home!
    My soul still pants for thee;
Then shall my labours have an end,
    When I thy joys shall see.

436
Lo, a great multitude, which no man could number.
Revelation vii. 9.   8 6.8 6.8 8 8.

1 TEN thousand times ten thousand sung
Their anthems round the throne,
When lo! one solitary tongue
Began a song unknown;
A song unknown to angels' ears,
A song that spoke of banished fears,
Of pardoned sins, of dried-up tears.

2 Not one of all that heavenly host
Could such high notes attain;
But spirits from a distant coast
United in the strain:
Till he who first began the song,
To sing alone not suffered long,
Was mingled in a countless throng.

3 And still, as hours are fleeting by,
The angels ever bear
Some newly-ransomed soul on high,
To join the chorus there.
And still the song will louder grow,
Till all the saved by Christ below
To that fair world of rapture go.

4 O give me, Lord, my golden harp,
And tune my broken voice,
That I may sing of troubles sharp
Exchanged for endless joys:
The song that ne'er was heard before
A sinner reached the heavenly shore,
Shall now be sung for evermore!

437
A better country, that is a heavenly.
Hebrews xi. 16.   C.M.

1 THERE is a land of pure delight,
Where saints immortal reign,
Infinite day excludes the night,
And pleasures banish pain.

2 There everlasting spring abides,
And never-withering flowers:
Death, like a narrow sea, divides
This heavenly land from ours.

3 Sweet fields beyond the swelling flood
Stand dressed in living green:
So to the Jews old Canaan stood,
While Jordan rolled between.

4 But timorous mortals start and shrink
To cross this narrow sea;
And linger, shivering on the brink,
And fear to launch away.

5 O could we make our doubts remove,
Those gloomy thoughts that rise,
And see the Canaan that we love
With unbeclouded eyes!

6 Could we but climb where Moses stood,
And view the landscape o'er,
Not Jordan's stream, nor death's cold [flood,
Should fright us from the shore.

438
The land that is very far off.
Isaiah xxxiii. 17.   6 4.6 4.6 7 6 4.

1 THERE is a happy land,
Far, far away,
Where saints in glory stand,
D   Bright, bright as day.

O! how they sweetly sing,
Worthy is our Saviour King,
Loud let His praises ring,
Praise, praise for aye!

2 Come to this happy land,
Come, come away!
Why will ye doubting stand?
Why still delay?
O! we shall happy be
When from sin and sorrow free,
Lord, we shall live with Thee,
Blest, blest for aye.

3 Bright in that happy land
Beams every eye,
Kept by a Father's hand,
Love cannot die.
On, then, to glory run,
Be a crown and kingdom won,
And bright above the sun
Reign, reign for aye.

439
God shall wipe away all tears from their eyes.—Revelation vii. 17.
6 6.6 6.5 5.7 6.

1 THERE is a land of love,
God's children know it well;
A holy place above,
Where saints and angels dwell.
Little children, come,
Come at God's command;
Find a sweeter, dearer home
In yonder happy land.

2 No vexing thoughts are there,
No sorrow and no pains;
Eternal blessings where
Your dear Redeemer reigns.
Little children, come, etc.

3 And hallowed songs are sung
By loving hearts and true;
And golden harps are strung
To strains for ever new.
Little children, come, etc.

4 In that divine abode
The Sabbath shines for aye,
The ransomed worship God
In everlasting day.
Little children, come, etc.

5 Your loving Saviour stands,
A welcome there to give;
And calls with outstretched hands,
'O, come to Me, and live.'
Little children, come, etc.

6 And striving now with you,
The Holy Spirit given,
Is waiting to renew
And fit you all for heaven.
Little children, come, etc.

440
Holy Jerusalem, ... having the glory of God.—Revelation xxi. 10, 11.
8 8.8 8.

1 WE sing of the realms of the blest,
That country so bright and so fair;
And oft are its glories confessed,
But what must it be to be there!

93

2 We sing of its pathways of gold,
  Its walls decked with jewels so rare,
  Its wonders and pleasures untold ;
  But what must it be to be there !

3 We sing of its freedom from sin,
  From sorrow, temptation, and care,
  From trials, without and within ;
  But what must it be to be there !

4 We sing of its service of love,
  Of robes which the glorified wear,
  The church of the firstborn above ;
  But what must it be to be there !

5 Do Thou, Lord, midst pleasure or woe,
  For heaven our spirits prepare ;
  And shortly we also shall know
  And feel what it is to be there.

There shall be no more death, . . .
441 *neither shall there be any more*
pain.—Rev. xxi. 4.   8 3.8 3.8 8 8 3.

1 THERE is a better world, they say,
    O, so bright !
Where sin and woe are done away,
    O, so bright !
And music fills the balmy air,
And angels bright and pure are there,
And harps of gold and mansions fair,
    O, so bright !

2 No clouds e'er pass along its sky,
    Happy land !
No tear-drops glisten in the eye,
    Happy land !
They drink the living streams of grace,
And gaze upon the Saviour's face,
Whose brightness fills the holy place ;
    Happy land !

3 And wicked things and beasts of prey
    Come not there ;
And ruthless death and fierce decay
    Come not there ;
There all are holy, all are good :
But hearts unwashed in Jesus' blood,
And guilty sinners unrenewed,
    Come not there.

4 But though we're sinners every one,
    Jesus died ;
And though our crown of peace is gone,
    Jesus died ;
We may be cleansed from every stain ;
We may be crowned with bliss again,
And in that land of pleasure reign :
    Jesus died.

5 Then, parents, brothers, sisters, come,
    Come away ;
We long to reach our Father's home,
    Come away ;
O come, the time is fleeting past,
And men and things are fading fast ;
Our turn will surely come at last,
    Come away.

They shall be Mine . . . in that day
442 *when I make up My jewels.*
Malachi iii. 17.   8 6.8 5.7 6.7 5.

1 WHEN He cometh, when He cometh,
    To make up His jewels,

All His jewels, precious jewels,
  His loved and His own.
    Like the stars of the morning,
    His bright crown adorning,
    They shall shine in their beauty,
    Bright gems for His crown.

2 He will gather, He will gather
  The gems for His kingdom ;
All the pure ones, all the bright ones,
  His loved and His own.
    Like the stars of the morning, etc.

3 Little children, little children,
  Who love their Redeemer,
Are His jewels, precious jewels,
  His loved and His own.
    Like the stars of the morning, etc.

Let both grow together until the
443 *harvest.*—Matthew xiii. 30.
8 6.8 6.8 6.10 7.9 6.8 7.

1 GROWING together, wheat and tares,
  Clustering thick and green,
Fanned by the gentle summer airs,
  Under the sky serene.
Over them both the sunlight falls,
  Over them both the rain,
Till the angels come when the Master calls,
  To gather the golden grain.
    Jesus, O grant when Thine angels come,
    To reap the fields for Thee,
    We may be gathered safely home,
    Where the precious wheat may be.

2 Growing together, side by side,
  Both shall the reaper meet,
Tares aloft in their scornful pride,
  Bowing their heads the wheat.
Swift and sure o'er the waving plain
  The sickle sharp shall fly,
And the pre ious wheat, the abundant grain,
  Shall becharvested in the sky.   [etc.
    Jesus, O grant when Thine angels come,

3 But for the tares, for them the word
  Of a terrible doom is cast ;
'Bind and burn,' said the blessèd Lord ;
  They shall leave the wheat at last.
Never again the summer rain,
  Never the sunshine sweet,
That were lavished freely, all in vain,
  On the tares among the wheat.   [etc.
    Jesus, O grant when Thine angels come,

4 Where shall the reapers look for us
  When that day of days shall come ?
Solemn the thought, with grandeur
    fraught,
  Of that wondrous harvest home.
None but the wheat shall be gathered in,
  By the Master's own command,
For the tares alone the doom of sin
  And the flame in the Judge's hand. [etc.
    Jesus, O grant when Thine angels come,

For the Lord God giveth them
444 *light.*—Rev. xxii. 5.   11 11.11 11.

1 THEY are perfectly blest, the redeemed
    and the free,
Who are resting in joy by the smooth glassy
    sea ;

They breathed here on earth all their sorrowful sighs,
And Jesus has wiped all the tears from
their eyes.

2 They are happy at home ! They have learnt
the new song,
And sing it so sweetly amid the glad throng:
No faltering voices, no discords are there,
The rapturous praises swell high through
the air.

3 There falls not on them the deep silence
of night,
They always are wakeful ; ne'er fadeth the
light ;
So throughout the long day new hosannas
they raise,
And never grow weary of singing His
praise.

4 And thus would we praise Thee, O Saviour
divine ;
We too would be with Thee, loved children
of Thine ;
O teach us, that we may sing happily there,
When we too are called to that city so fair.

And so shall we ever be with the
445 *Lord.*—1 Thessalonians iv. 17.
D.S.M.

1 'FOR ever with the Lord !'
Amen ! so let it be !
Life from the dead is in that word,
'Tis immortality !
Here in the body pent,
Absent from Him I roam :
Yet nightly pitch my moving tent
A day's march nearer home.

2 My Father's house on high,
Home of my soul ! how near,
At times to faith's foreseeing eye,
Thy golden gates appear ! Here, etc.

3 Ah ! then my spirit faints
To reach the land I love,
The bright inheritance of saints,
Jerusalem above ! Here, etc.

4 'For ever with the Lord !'
Father, if 'tis Thy will,
The promise of that faithful word
Even here to me fulfil. Here, etc.

5 Be Thou at my right hand,
Then can I never fail ;
Uphold Thou me, and I shall stand,
Fight, and I must prevail. Here, etc.

6 So when my latest breath
Shall rend the veil in twain,
By death I shall escape from death,
And life eternal gain. Here, etc.

7 Knowing as I am known,
How shall I love that word,
And oft repeat before the throne,
'For ever with the Lord ! ' Here, etc.

The whole family in heaven and
446 *earth.*—Ephesians iii. 15.
7 6.7 6.

1 CHILDREN above are singing,
With voices sweet and clear :
The saints with joy are bringing
Their heavenly music near.

2 Children who live in heaven
Are happy round the throne ;
Their sins are all forgiven,
Through Jesus Christ alone.

3 Children on earth are praying
That they may worthy be ;
Through Jesus Christ each saying,
' O ! save a child like me.'

4 Children on earth are praising
The Saviour for His love ;
Children on earth are raising
A song like those above.

5 Children who live in heaven
Are saved through Christ alone ;
Children on earth forgiven,
The same Redeemer own.

6 Soon we shall join the chorus
Of anthems sung above,
With children gone before us,
Around the throne of love.

Thy crown.—Revelation iii. 11.
447 6 4.6 4.

1 A CROWN of glory bright
By faith I see,
In yonder realms of light
Prepared for me.

2 O may I faithful prove,
Keep it in view,
And through the storms of life
My way pursue !

3 Jesus, be Thou my guide,
My steps attend :
O keep me near Thy side,
Be Thou my friend ;

4 Be Thou my shield and sun,
My guide and guard :
And when my work is done,
My great reward.

A great multitude . . . clothed with
448 *white robes.*—Revelation vii. 9.
C.M., WITH CHORUS.

1 AROUND the throne of God in heaven
Thousands of children stand ;
Children whose sins are all forgiven,
A holy, happy band,
Singing glory, glory, glory.

2 In flowing robes of spotless white
See every one arrayed ;
Dwelling in everlasting light,
And joys that never fade,
Singing glory, glory, glory.

3 Once they were little ones like you,
And lived on earth below,
And could not praise as now they do
The Lord who loved them so,
Singing glory, glory, glory.

4 What brought them to that world above,
That heaven so bright and fair,
Where all is peace and joy and love ?
How came those children there ?
Singing glory, glory, glory.

5 Because the Saviour shed His blood
To wash away their sin :
Bathed in that purple, precious flood,
Behold them white and clean,
Singing glory, glory, glory.

6 On earth they sought the Saviour's grace,
On earth they loved His name ;
So now they see His blessèd face,
And stand before the Lamb,
Singing glory, glory, glory.

*Be thou faithful unto death, and
I will give thee a crown of
life.*—Revelation ii. 10.

449 11 9.12 9.11.12 8.

1 I KNOW there's a crown for the saints of
renown,
And for saints whose good deeds are
unsung ;
But O, say is it true, if their days are but
few,
That a crown is laid up for the young?
Yes, yes, yes ; I know there's a crown
for the young ;
If their lives daily prove that the
Saviour they love,
I know there's a crown for the young.

2 The youthful shall stand in that beautiful
land,
While the song of salvation they sing,
And the infant of days strike its harp in
the praise
Of Emmanuel, its Saviour and King.
Yes, yes, yes ; I know there's a crown,
etc.

3 The noble of birth, and the poor of the earth,
Both the man and the youth and the child,
If in Jesus they trust, when they rise from
the dust,
Shall be crowned in the land undefiled.
Yes, yes, yes ; I know there's a crown,
e c.

*The redeemed of the Lord shall . . .
come with singing unto Zion.*
Isaiah li. 11.

450 10 10.10 10.*

1 JOYFULLY, joyfully onward we move,
Bound to the land of bright spirits
above ;
Jesus, our Saviour, in mercy says, ' Come !
Joyfully, joyfully haste to your home.'

2 Soon will our pilgrimage end here below,
Soon to the presence of God we shall go ;
Then, if to Jesus our hearts have been given,
Joyfully, joyfully rest we in heaven.

3 Teachers and kindred have passed on
before,
Waiting, they watch us approaching the
shore,
Singing to cheer us, and bidding us come,
Joyfully, joyfully haste to your home.

4 Sounds of sweet music there ravish the ear ;
Harps of the blessèd, your strains we shall
hear,
Filling with harmony heaven's high dome ;
Joyfully, joyfully, Jesus, we come.

5 Death with his arrow may soon lay us low,
Safe in our Saviour, we fear not the blow ;
Jesus hath broken the bars of the tomb ;
Joyfully, joyfully will we go home.

6 Bright will the morn of eternity dawn,
Death will be conquered, his sceptre be
gone ;
Over the plains of sweet Canaan we'll roam,
Joyfully, joyfully, safely at home.

Strangers and pilgrims on the earth.
Hebrews xi. 13.

451 6 4.6 4.6 6 6 4.

1 I'M but a stranger here,
Heaven is my home ;
Earth's joys will disappear,
Heaven is my home.
Danger and sorrow stand
Round me on every hand ;
Heaven is my fatherland,
Heaven is my home.

2 What though the tempest rage,
Heaven is my home ;
Short is my pilgrimage,
Heaven is my home.
And time's wild wintry blast
Soon will be overpast ;
I shall reach home at last :
Heaven is my home.

3 There at my Saviour's side,
Heaven is my home ;
I shall be glorified,
Heaven is my home.
There are the good and blest,
Those I love most and best ;
And there I too shall rest,
Heaven is my home.

4 Therefore I murmur not,
Heaven is my home :
Whate'er my earthly lot,
Heaven is my home.
And I shall surely stand
There at my Lord's right hand :
Heaven is my fatherland,
Heaven is my home.

*Thou shalt rest . . . at the end of
the days.*—Daniel xii. 13.

452 7 6.7 6.7 6.7 6, WITH CHORUS.

1 THOUGH often here we're weary,
There is sweet rest above ;
A rest that is eternal,
Where all is peace and love.
O let us then press forward,
That glorious rest to gain,
We'll soon be free from sorrow,
From toil and care and pain.
There is sweet rest in heaven.

2 Our Saviour will be with us
E'en to our journey's end,
In every sore affliction
His present help to lend.
H never will grow weary,
Though often we request ;
He'll give us grace to conquer,
And take us home to rest.
There is sweet rest in heaven.

3 All glory to the Father,
Who gives us every good ;
All glory be to Jesus,
Who bought us with His blood ;
And glory to the Spirit,
Who keeps us to the end ;
To the Triune God be glory,
The sinner's only Friend !
There is sweet rest in heaven.

453
These are they which came out of great tribulation.
Revelation vii. 14.　　C.M.

1 HOW bright those glorious spirits shine!
　　Whence all their bright array?
How came they to the blissful seats
　　Of everlasting day?

2 Lo! these are they from sufferings great
　　Who came to realms of light;
And in the blood of Christ have washed
　　Those robes that shine so bright.

3 Now with triumphal palms they stand
　　Before the throne on high,
And serve the God they love, amidst
　　The glories of the sky.

4 Hunger and thirst are felt no more,
　　Nor sun with scorching ray;
God is their Sun, whose cheering beams
　　Diffuse eternal day.

5 The Lamb, who dwells amidst the throne,
　　Shall o'er them still preside,
Feed them with nourishment divine,
　　And all their footsteps guide.

6 'Midst pastures green He'll lead His flock,
　　Where living streams appear;
And God the Lord from every eye
　　Shall wipe off every tear.

7 To Father, Son, and Holy Ghost,
　　The God whom we adore,
Be glory, as it was, is now,
　　And shall be evermore.

454
Thanks be to God, which giveth us the victory through our Lord Jesus Christ.—1 Cor. xv. 57.　　C.M.

1 GIVE me the wings of faith to rise
　　Within the veil, and see
The saints above, how great their joys,
　　How bright their glories be.

2 Once they were mourners here below,
　　And poured out cries and tears:
They wrestled hard, as we do now,
　　With sins, and doubts, and fears.

3 I ask them whence their victory came:
　　They, with united breath,
Ascribe their conquest to the Lamb,
　　Their triumph to His death.

4 They marked the footsteps that He trod,
　　His zeal inspired their breast;
And following their incarnate God,
　　Possess the promised rest.

5 Our glorious Leader claims our praise
　　For His own pattern given;
While the long cloud of witnesses
　　Show the same path to heaven.

455
One generation passeth away, and another generation cometh.
Ecclesiastes i. 4.　　8 7.8 7.4 7.

1 PASSING onward, quickly passing:
　　Yes, but whither, whither bound?
Is it to the many mansions
　　Where eternal rest is found?
　　　Passing onward:
Yes, but whither, whither bound?

2 Passing onward, quickly passing,
　　Nought the wheels of time can stay;
Sweet the thought, that some are going
　　To the realms of perfect day:
　　　Passing onward,
Christ their leader, Christ their way.

3 Passing onward, quickly passing,
　　Many in the downward road,
Careless of their souls immortal,
　　Heeding not the call of God;
　　　Passing onward,
Trampling on the Saviour's blood.

4 Passing onward, quickly passing,
　　Time its course will quickly run;
Still we hear the fond entreaty
　　Of the ever-gracious One,
　　　'Come, and welcome:
'Tis by Me that life is won.'

456
He bringeth them unto their desired haven.—Psalm cvii. 30.
8 7.8 7.8 7.8 7.8 7.8 7.

1 WE are sailing o'er an ocean
　　To a far and foreign shore,
And the waves are dashing round us,
　　And we hear the breakers roar;
But we look above the billows,
　　In the darkness of the night,
And we see the steady gleaming
　　Of our changeless beacon light.
　　　O the light is flashing brightly
　　　　From a calm and stormless shore,
　　Where we hope to cast our anchor
　　　When the voyage of life is o'er.

2 Though the skies are dark above us,
　　And the waves are dashing high,
Let us look towards the beacon;
　　We shall reach it by and by.
'Tis the light of God's great mercy,
　　And He holds it up in view,
As a guide-star to His children,
　　As a guide to me and you.
　　　O the light is flashing brightly, etc.

SECOND PART.

3 Rising high on mountain billow,
　　Sinking low beneath the wave;
Clouds may oft obscure our vision,
　　Fear extort the cry, Lord, save!
Let the tempest rage around us,
　　Lightning flash and thunder roar,
Firm as rock our beacon standeth,
　　Shining from yon heavenly shore.
　　　O the light is flashing brightly, etc.

4 He will keep it ever burning
　　From the lighthouse of His love;
And it always shines the brightest
　　When the skies are dark above.
If we keep our eyes upon it,
　　And we steer our course aright,
We shall reach the harbour safely,
　　By the blessèd beacon light.
　　　O the light is flashing brightly, etc.

457
That where I am, there ye may be also.—John xiv. 3.
8 6.7 6.7 6.7 6.

1 THERE'S a Friend for little children
　　Above the bright blue sky;
A Friend who never changeth,
　　Whose love can never die.

97

Unlike our friends by nature,
Who change with changing years,
This I riend is always worthy
The precious name He bears.

2 There's a rest for little children
Above the bright blue sky;
For those who love the Saviour,
And Abba, Father, cry.
A rest from every trouble,
From sin and danger free,
Where every little pilgrim
Shall rest eternally.

3 There's · home for little children
Above the bright blue sky;
Where Jt sus reigns in glory,
A home of peace and joy.
No home on earth is like it,
Nor can with it compare,
For every one is happy,
For evei happy there.

SECOND PART.

4 There's a crown for little children
Above the bright blue sky,
And all who look to Jesus
Shall wear it by and by.
A crown of brightest glory,
Which He will then bestow
On tho who've found His favour,
And ved Him here below.

5 There's a song for little children
Above the bright blue sky;
A song that will not weary,
Though sung continually;
A song which even angels
Can never, never sing;
They know not Christ as Saviour,
But worship Him as King.

6 There's a robe for little children
Above the bright blue sky,
And a harp of sweetest music,
And a palm of victory.
All, all above is treasured,
And found in Christ alone;
O come, dear little children,
That all may be your own.

458 *I press toward the mark for the prize.*—Philippians iii. 14.
8 7.8 7.8 8.6 8.

1 PRESS on! press on! a glorious throng
In heaven are watching o'er you;
Press on! press on! with courage bold
To run the race before you.
Press on to win the heavenly prize,
A crown of life beyond the skies!
Press on to win the prize—
A crown of life beyond the skies!

2 Press on! press on! though trials come,
No time for sad repining;
Press on! press on! let faith be strong
And hope still brightly shining.   [etc.
Press on to win the heavenly prize,

3 Press on! press on! through storm and
In Jesus trusting ever;   [clouds
Press on! press on! be not afraid,
There's light beyond the river.   [etc.
98   Press on to win the heavenly prize,

459 *Beautiful . . . is mount Zion, . . . the city of the great King.*
Psalm xlviii. 2.   8 8.8 8.8 8.*

1 BEAUTIFUL Sion built above;
Beautiful city that I love;
Beautiful gates of pearly white;
Beautiful temple, God its light:
He who was slain on Calvary
Opens those pearly gates to me!

2 Beautiful heaven, where all is light;
Beautiful angels, clothed in white;
Beautiful harps through all the choir;
Beautiful strains that never tire:
There shall I join the chorus sweet,
Worshipping at the Saviour's feet!

3 Beautiful crowns on every brow;
Beautiful palms the conquerors show;
Beautiful robes the ransomed wear;
Beautiful all who enter there:
Thither I press with eager feet;
There shall my rest be long and sweet.

4 Beautiful throne of Christ our King;
Beautiful songs the angels sing;
Beautiful rest, where wanderings cease;
Beautiful home of perfect peace:
There shall my eyes the Saviour see;
Haste to this heavenly home with me.

460 *Of such is the kingdom of God.*
Luke xviii. 16.   7 7.7 7.7 7.

1 CHILDREN'S voices, high in heaven,
Make sweet music round the throne;
Them the King of kings hath given
Glory, lasting as His own:
Lord, it was Thy mercy free
Suffered them to come to Thee.

2 We would think of them to-day,
And their everlasting song;
We would sing, as blest as they,
In that happy land ere long:
Lord, let us Thy children be,
Suffer us to come to Thee;

3 Now to come with loving mind,
Simple faith, and earnest prayer,
Clinging to Thy cross, to find
Full and free salvation there:
Lamb of God! our Saviour be,
Suffer us to come to Thee.

4 Lord, we come, be Thou our Guide
Through life's dark and troubled way;
And when trained and sanctified,
Raise us to the perfect day:
Then in heaven Thy words shall be,
'Suffer them to come to Me.'

461 *They serve Him day and night in His temple.*—Revelation vii. 15.
7 6.7 6.7 6.7 6.

1 WHILE we on earth are raising
Our tuneful voices high,
The heavenly hosts are praising
The Saviour in the sky.
We cannot sing so sweetly
As angels do above;
Yet we'll endeavour meekly
To celebrate His love.

2 O, when shall we triumphant
    Our Lord and King behold,
And walk, with hearts exultant,
    The streets of shining gold ;
And swell the blissful chorus
    Of happy saints above,
Who reached their home before us,
    And sing and praise and love?

3 Lord, fit us to inherit
    The glory and the throne ;
And, through the Saviour's merit,
    Receive us as Thine own :
May we possess that treasure
    Unfolded in Thy word,
And find seraphic pleasure
    For ever with the Lord !

462
*What are these which are arrayed in
white robes ?*—Revelation vii. 13.
    7 7.7 7.7 7.7 7.

1 WHAT are these arrayed in white,
    Brighter than the noon-day sun ?
Foremost of the sons of light,
    Nearest the eternal throne?
These are they that bore the cross,
    Nobly for their Master stood ;
Sufferers in His righteous cause,
    Followers of the dying God.

2 Out of great distress they came,
    Washed their robes by faith below
In the blood of yonder Lamb,
    Blood that washes white as snow :
Therefore are they next the throne,
    Serve their Maker day and night ;
God resides among His own,
    God doth in His saints delight.

3 More than conquerors at last,
    Here they find their trials o'er ;
They have all their sufferings past,
    Hunger now and thirst no more ;
No excessive heat they feel
    From the sun's directer ray,
In a milder clime they dwell,
    Region of eternal day.

4 He that on the throne doth reign,
    Them the Lamb shall always feed,
With the tree of life sustain,
    To the living fountains lead ;
He shall all their sorrows chase,
    All their wants at once remove,
Wipe the tears from every face,
    Fill up every soul with love.

463
*The streams whereof shall make glad
the city of God.*—Psalm xlvi. 4.
    11 7.11 7.7 7.10 7.

1 O HAVE you not heard of a beautiful
    stream
That flows through our Father's land?
Its waters gleam bright in the heavenly
    And ripple o'er golden sand. [light,
    O seek that beautiful stream,
       O seek that beautiful stream ;
    Its waters so free are flowing for thee,
       O seek that beautiful stream.

2 With murmuring sound doth it wander
    Through fields of eternal green, [along
Where songs of the blest in their haven of
    Float soft on the air serene. [rest
       O seek, etc.

3 Its fountains are deep, and its waters are
    And sweet to the weary soul ; [pure,
It flows from the throne of Jehovah alone:
    O come where its bright waves roll.
       O seek, etc.

4 This beautiful stream is the river of life,
    It flows for all nations free ;
A balm for each wound in its waters is
    O sinner, it flows for thee. [found,
       O seek, etc.

5 O will you not drink of the beautiful stream,
    And dwell on its peaceful shore ?
The Spirit says, ' Come, all ye weary ones,
    And wander in sin no more.' [home,
       O seek, etc.

464
*He showed me a pure river of water
of life.*—Revelation xxii. 1.
    8 7.8 7.8 9.9 7.

1 SHALL we gather at the river,
    Where bright angel feet have trod,
With its crystal tide for ever
    Flowing by the throne of God?
    Yes, we'll gather at the river ;
       The beautiful, the beautiful river ;
    Gather with the saints at the river,
       That flows by the throne of God.

2 On the margin of the river,
    Washing up its silver spray,
We will walk and worship ever,
    All the happy golden day.
       Yes, we'll gather at the river, etc.

3 Ere we reach the shining river,
    Lay we every burden down ;
Grace our spirits will deliver,
    And provide a robe and crown.
       Yes, we'll gather at the river, etc.

4 At the smiling of the river,
    Mirror of the Saviour's face,
Saints whom death will never sever
    Lift their songs of saving grace.
       Yes, we'll gather at the river, etc.

5 Soon we'll reach the shining river,
    Soon our pilgrimage will cease,
Soon our happy hearts will quiver
    With the melody of peace.
       Yes, we'll gather at the river, etc.

465
He shall go no more out.
Rev. iii. 12. C.M., WITH CHORUS.

1 WE'RE marching to the promised
    A land all fair and bright ; [land,
Come join our happy youthful band,
    And seek the plains of light.
We are marching through Immanuel's
    ground,
And soon shall hear the trumpet sound ;
And there we shall with Jesus reign,
    And never, never part again.
What never part again? No, never part again;
What never part again? No, never part again;
    And there we shall with Jesus reign,
    And never, never part again.

2 The Saviour feeds His little flock,
    His grace is freely given,
The living water from the rock,
    And daily bread from heaven.
We are marching through Immanuel's
    ground, etc.

99

3 In that bright land no sin is found,
But all are happy there,
And youthful voices sweetly blend
In the angelic choir.
We are marching through Immanuel's
ground, etc.

4 Our teachers kindly point the way
And guide our feet aright,
To the bright realms of endless day,
Where Jesus is the light.
We are marching through Immanuel's
ground, etc.

TIMES AND SEASONS.

MORNING.

*The Sun of righteousness arise, with
healing in His wings.*
466 Malachi iv. 2. 7.7.7.7.7.7.

1 CHRIST, whose glory fills the skies,
Christ, the true, the only Light,
Sun of righteousness, arise,
Triumph o'er the shades of night;
Day-spring from on high, be near:
Day-star, in my heart appear!

2 Dark and cheerless is the morn,
Unaccompanied by Thee;
Joyless is the day's return,
Till Thy mercy's beams I see;
Till Thou inward light impart,
Glad my eyes, and warm my heart.

3 Visit then this soul of mine,
Pierce the gloom of sin and grief;
Fill me, Radiancy divine!
Scatter all my unbelief;
More and more Thyself display,
Shining to the perfect day!

*My voice shalt Thou hear in the
morning, O LORD.*—Psalm v. 3.
467 L.M.

1 AWAKE, my soul, and with the sun
Thy daily stage of duty run;
Shake off dull sloth, and joyful rise,
To pay thy morning sacrifice.

2 Let all thy converse be sincere,
Thy conscience as the noon-day clear;
For God's all-seeing eye surveys
Thy secret thoughts, thy words, and ways.

3 Wake, and lift up thyself, my heart,
And with the angels take thy part;
Who all night long unwearied sing
High praise to the eternal King.

4 All praise to Thee, who safe hast kept
And hast refreshed me while I slept;
Grant, Lord, when I from death shall wake,
I may of endless light partake!

5 Lord, I my vows to Thee renew;
Disperse my sins as morning dew;
Guard my first springs of thought and [will,
And with Thyself my spirit fill.

6 Direct, control, suggest, this day,
All I design, or do, or say;
That all my powers, with all their might,
In Thy sole glory may unite.
100

7 Praise God, from whom all blessings flow;
Praise Him, all creatures here below;
Praise Him above, ye heavenly host;
Praise Father, Son, and Holy Ghost.

*In the morning will I direct my
prayer unto Thee.*
468 Psalm v. 3. C.M.

1 GOD of our life, our morning songs
To Thee we cheerful raise;
Thine acts of love 'tis good to sing,
And pleasant Thee to praise.

2 Sustained by Thee, our opening eyes
Salute the morning light;
Secure we stand, unhurt by all
The dangers of the night.

3 Our life renewed, our strength repaired,
To Thee, O God, are due:
Teach us Thy ways, and give us grace
Our duty to pursue.

4 From every enemy defend,
But guard us most from sin:
Direct our going out, O Lord,
And bless our coming in.

5 O may Thy holy fear command
Each action, thought, and word!
Then shall we sweetly close the day,
Approved of Thee, our Lord.

*Keep me, . . . hide me under the
shadow of Thy wings.*
469 Psalm xvii. 8. 4 4 6.4 4 6.

1 THE morning, bright
With rosy light,
Has waked me from my sleep;
Father, I own
Thy love alone
Thy little one doth keep.

2 All through the day,
I humbly pray,
Be Thou my guard and guide;
My sins forgive,
And let me live,
Blest Jesus, near Thy side.

3 O make Thy rest
Within my breast,
Great Spirit of all grace;
Make me like Thee,
Then shall I be
Prepared to see Thy face.

*The Day-spring from on high, . . . to
guide our feet into the way of
peace.*—Luke i. 78, 79.
470 7 7.7 7.

1 JESUS, holy, undefiled,
Listen to a little child:
Thou hast sent the glorious light,
Chasing far the silent night;

2 Thou hast sent the sun to shine
O'er this beauteous world of Thine,
Warmth to give, and pleasant glow,
On each tender flower below.

3 Now the little birds arise,
Chirping gaily in the skies:
Thee their warbling voices praise,
In the early songs they raise.

4 Thou, by whom the birds are fed,
Give to me my daily bread;
And Thy Holy Spirit give,
Without whom I cannot live.

5 Make me, Lord, obedient, mild,
As becomes a little child;
All day long, in every way,
Teach me what to do and say.

6 Help me never to forget
That in Thy great book is set
All that children think and say,
For the awful judgment-day.

7 Let me never say a word
That will make Thee angry, Lord;
Help me so to live in love,
As Thine angels do above.

8 Make me, Lord, in work and play,
Thine more truly, every day;
And when Thou at last shalt come,
Take me to Thy heavenly home.

It is a good thing . . . to show forth
Thy loving-kindness in the morning.

471 Psalm xcii. 1, 2.　　L.M.

1 MY God, how endless is Thy love!
Thy gifts are every evening new;
And morning mercies from above
Gently distil like early dew.

2 Thou spread'st the curtains of the night,
Great Guardian of my sleeping hours;
Thy sovereign word restores the light,
And quickens all my drooping powers.

3 I yield my powers to Thy command,
To Thee I consecrate my days;
Perpetual blessings from Thy hand
Demand perpetual songs of praise.

Not slothful in business, . . . serving
the Lord.—Romans xii. 11.

472　　C.M.

1 MY God, who makes the sun to know
His proper hour to rise,
And, to give light to all below,
Doth send him round the skies.

2 When, from the chambers of the east,
His morning race begins,
He never tires, nor stops to rest,
But round the world he shines.

3 So, like the sun, would I fulfil
The business of the day;
Begin my work betimes, and still
March on my heavenly way.

4 Give me, O Lord, Thy early grace,
Nor let my soul complain,
That the young morning of my days
Has all been spent in vain.

O God, Thou art my God; early will
I seek Thee.—Psalm lxiii. 1.

473　　L.M.

1 O TIMELY happy, timely wise,
Hearts that with rising morn arise!
Eyes that the beam celestial view,
Which evermore makes all things new!

2 New every morning is the love
Our wakening and uprising prove;
Through sleep and darkness safely brought,
Restored to life, and power, and thought.

D 2

3 New mercies each returning day
Hover around us while we pray;
New perils past, new sins forgiven,
New thoughts of God, new hopes of heaven.

4 If on our daily course our mind
Be set to hallow all we find,
New treasures still of countless price
God will provide for sacrifice.

5 Old friends, old scenes, will lovelier be,
As more of heaven in each we see:
Some softening gleam of love and prayer
Shall dawn on every cross and care.

6 The trivial round, the common task,
Will furnish all we ought to ask;
Room to deny ourselves; a road
To bring us, daily, nearer God.

7 Only, O Lord, in Thy great love
Fit us for perfect rest above;
And help us, this and every day,
To live more nearly as we pray.

Evening, and morning, and at noon,
. . . He shall hear my voice.

474 Psalm lv. 17.　　C.M.

1 THROUGH all the dangers of the night
Preserved, O Lord, by Thee,
Again we hail the cheerful light,
Again we bow the knee.

2 Preserve us, Lord, throughout the day,
And guide us by Thy arm;
For they are safe, and only they,
Whom Thou dost keep from harm.

3 Let all our words, and all our ways,
Show forth that we are Thine,
That so the light of truth and grace
Before the world may shine.

4 Let us ne'er turn away from Thee!
O Saviour, hold us fast,
Till, with immortal eyes, we see
Thy glorious face at last.

I will sing aloud of Thy mercy in
the morning.—Psalm lix. 16.

475　　8 7. 8 7. 7 7.

1 MORNING comes with light all-cheering,
Shades of night have fled apace;
Source of light by Thine appearing
From our minds all darkness chase:
Thou hast blest us in our sleep,
Through the day direct and keep.

2 Earth refreshed Thy praise is sounding;
All Thy works Thy glory sing;
May our hearts, with love abounding,
Gratefully their tribute bring:
Thou hast taught the birds their lays,
Teach our hearts to sing Thy praise.

3 All day long to praise Thee help us,
And to strive against all sin;
Finding all our help in Jesus,
Who for us the fight did win:
He was tempted here below,
And doth all our weakness know.

4 Man goes to his work till evening
Brings again the needed rest;
Grant that we, Thy grace receiving,
May in all we do be blest:
And wherever we may be
Find our joy in pleasing Thee.

EVENING.

*He that keepeth thee will not
slumber.*—Psalm cxxi. 3.

476 87.87.77.

1 PRAISE the Lord who hath divided
   Days of toil by nights for rest,
Home and friends for us provided,
   And for every bird its nest;
   Saviour, Thou wast homeless here,
   Nights for us didst spend in prayer.

2 Praise to Thee for all Thy blessing,
   Which hath made our joy to-day;
We draw nigh, our sin confessing,
   May Thy blood wash all away.
   Jesu, who for this hast come,
   Make our loving hearts Thy home.

3 Hear us, Lord, for those who suffer;
   Ease their pain, and give them sleep;
Some there are whom none can succour
   But the Lord, who here did weep:
   Thou who cam'st to bear our grief,
   Send to burdened hearts relief.

4 Keeping us Thou wilt not slumber,
   Grant us in Thy love to rest;
Thou our very hairs dost number,
   Sleeping, waking, make us blest;
   And as days shall come and go
   Make us in Thy love to grow.

477 *I will both lay me down in peace,
and sleep.*—Psalm iv. 8.   65.65.

1 NOW the day is over,
   Night is drawing nigh,
Shadows of the evening
   Steal across the sky.

2 Jesu, grant the weary
   Calm and sweet repose;
With Thy tenderest blessing
   May their eyelids close.

3 Grant to little children
   Visions bright of Thee;
Guard the sailors tossing
   On the angry sea;

4 Comfort every sufferer
   Watching late in pain;
Those who plan some evil
   From their sins restrain.

5 Through the long night-watches
   May Thine angels spread
Their bright wings above me,
   Standing round my bed.

6 When the morning wakens,
   Then may I arise,
Pure and fresh and sinless
   In Thy holy eyes.

7 Glory to the Father,
   Glory to the Son,
And to the blest Spirit,
   Whilst all ages run.

478 *For Thou, LORD, only makest me
dwell in safety.*—Psalm iv. 8.
84.84.8884.

1 GOD that madest earth and heaven,
   Darkness and light;
102

Who the day for toil hast given,
   For rest the night;
May Thine angel-guards defend us,
Slumber sweet Thy mercy send us,
Holy dreams and hopes attend us,
   This livelong night.

2 Guard us waking, guard us sleeping,
   And when we die,
May we in Thy mighty keeping
   All peaceful lie:
When the last dread call shall wake us,
Do not Thou our God forsake us;
But to reign in glory take us
   With Thee on high.

479 *Abide with us: for it is toward evening, and the day is far spent.*
Luke xxiv. 29.   10 10.10 10.

1 ABIDE with me! fast falls the eventide;
   The darkness deepens; Lord, with me
   abide!
When other helpers fail, and comforts flee,
Help of the helpless, O abide with me!

2 Swift to its close ebbs out life's little day;
Earth's joys grow dim, its glories pass away;
Change and decay in all around I see;
O Thou who changest not, abide with me!

3 I need Thy presence every passing hour:
   What but Thy grace can foil the tempter's
   power?
Who like Thyself my guide and stay can be?
Through cloud and sunshine, O abide with
   me!

4 I fear no foe, with Thee at hand to bless:
Ills have no weight, and tears no bitterness:
Where is death's sting? where, grave, thy
   victory?
I triumph still, if Thou abide with me!

5 Reveal Thyself before my closing eyes;
Shine through the gloom, and point me to
   the skies.
Heaven's morning breaks, and earth's vain
   shadows flee:
In life and death, O Lord, abide with me!

480 *And He went in to tarry with them.*
Luke xxiv. 29.   L.M.

1 SUN of my soul! Thou Saviour dear,
   It is not night if Thou be near;
O may no earth-born cloud arise,
To hide Thee from Thy servant's eyes!

2 When the soft dews of kindly sleep
My wearied eyelids gently steep,
Be my last thought, How sweet to rest
For ever on my Saviour's breast!

3 Abide with me from morn till eve,
For without Thee I cannot live;
Abide with me when night is nigh,
For without Thee I dare not die.

4 If some poor wandering child of Thine
Have spurned to-day the voice divine,
Now, Lord, the gracious work begin;
Let him no more lie down in sin.

5 Watch by the sick, enrich the poor
With blessings from Thy boundless store;
Be every mourner's sleep to-night,
Like infant's slumbers, pure and light.

6 Come near and bless us when we wake,
Ere through the world our way we take,
Till in the ocean of Thy love
We lose ourselves in heaven above.

At even, when the sun did set. . . . He
healed many that were sick.
481 Mark i. 32, 34.　　L.M.

1 AT even, ere the sun was set,
The sick, O Lord, around Thee lay ;
O, in what divers pains they met !
O, with what joy they went away !

2 Once more 'tis eventide, and we
Oppressed with various ills draw near :
What if Thy form we cannot see ?
We know and feel that Thou art here.

3 O Saviour Christ, our woes dispel !
For some are sick, and some are sad,
And some have never loved Thee well,
And some have lost the love they had ;

4 And some have found the world is vain,
Yet from the world they break not free ;
And some have friends who give them pain,
Yet have not sought a friend in Thee.

5 O Saviour Christ, Thou too art man !
Thou hast been troubled, tempted, tried ;
Thy kind but searching glance can scan
The very wounds that shame would hide ;

6 Thy touch has still its ancient power ;
No word from Thee can fruitless fall :
Hear in this solemn evening hour,
And in Thy mercy heal us all.

The angel of the LORD *encampeth*
round about them that fear Him.
482 Psalm xxxiv. 7.　　6 6 4.6 6 6 4.

1 FATHER of love and power,
Guard Thou our evening hour,
Shield with Thy might.
For all Thy care this day,
Our grateful thanks we pay,
And to our Father pray ;
Bless us to-night.

2 Jesus, Immanuel,
Come in Thy love to dwell
In hearts contrite ;
For all our sins we grieve,
But we Thy grace receive,
And in Thy word believe ;
Bless us to-night.

3 Spirit of truth and love,
Life-giving, holy Dove,
Shed forth Thy light ;
Heal every sinner's smart,
Still every throbbing heart,
And Thine own peace impart ;
Bless us to-night.

483 *The* LORD *shall preserve thee from*
all evil.—Psalm cxxi. 7.　　8 3 3 6.

1 ERE I sleep, for every favour
This day showed
By my God,
I will bless my Saviour.

2 O my Lord, what shall I render
To Thy name,
Still the same,
Merciful and tender ?

3 Leave me not, but ever love me :
Let Thy peace
Be my bliss,
Till Thou hence remove me.

4 Thou, my rock, my guard, my tower,
Safely keep,
While I sleep,
Me with sovereign power.

5 So whene'er in death I slumber,
Let me rise
With the wise,
Counted in their number.

Ye shall lie down, and none shall
make you afraid.
484 Leviticus xxvi. 6.　　L.M.

1 ETERNAL Father ! hear, we pray,
Thy children's hymn at close of day ;
Thou dost not with the sun decline,
For day and night alike are Thine.

2 Thou makest daylight dark with night,
The shades of death with morning bright ;
Yet wilt Thou to Thy children prove
Unclouded light, unchanging love.

3 O raise, O purge our earth-dimmed eyes,
And in Thy wisdom make us wise :
Our sin subdue, our darkness chase
With light of truth and strength of grace !

4 Great Father, grant that in Thy Son
We all with Thee may be but one :
Our light, our life, our all be He,
That light in Thy light we may see.

Thou hast been my help, therefore in
the shadow of Thy wings will I
485 *rejoice.*—Psalm lxiii. 7.　　L.M.

1 GLORY to Thee, my God, this night,
For all the blessings of the light,
Keep me, O keep me, King of kings,
Beneath Thine own almighty wings !

2 Forgive me, Lord, for Thy dear Son,
The ill that I this day have done ;
That with the world, myself, and Thee,
I, e'er I sleep, at peace may be.

3 Teach me to live, that I may dread
The grave as little as my bed ;
Teach me to die, that so I may
Rise glorious at the awful day.

4 O may my soul on Thee repose !
And may sweet sleep mine eyelids close ;
Sleep that may me more vigorous make
To serve my God when I awake.

5 If in the night I sleepless lie,
My soul with heavenly thoughts supply ;
Let no ill dreams disturb my rest,
No powers of darkness me molest.

SECOND PART.

6 My soul, when I shake off the dust,
Lord, in Thy arms I will entrust :
O make me Thy peculiar care,
Some mansion for my soul prepare !

7 O may I always ready stand,
With my lamp burning in my hand ;
May I in sight of heaven rejoice,
Whene'er I hear the Bridegroom's voice !

8 All praise to Thee in light arrayed,
Who light Thy dwelling-place hast made;
A boundless ocean of bright beams
From Thy all-glorious Godhead streams.

9 The sun in its meridian height
Is very darkness in Thy sight;
My soul O lighten and inflame,
With thought and love of Thy great name!

10 Praise God, from whom all blessings flow;
Praise Him, all creatures here below;
Praise Him above, ye heavenly host;
Praise Father, Son, and Holy Ghost.

My peace I give unto you: not as the world giveth, give I unto you.
486
John xiv. 27. 10 10.10 10.

1 SAVIOUR, again to Thy dear name we raise
With one accord our parting hymn of praise;
We stand to bless Thee ere our worship cease,
Then, lowly kneeling, wait Thy word of peace.

2 Grant us Thy peace upon our homeward way;
With Thee began, with Thee shall end the day:
Guard Thou the lips from sin, the hearts from shame,
That in this house have called upon Thy name.

3 Grant us Thy peace, Lord, through the coming night,
Turn Thou for us its darkness into light;
From harm and danger keep Thy children free,
For dark and light are both alike to Thee.

4 Grant us Thy peace throughout our earthly life,
Our balm in sorrow, and our stay in strife;
Then, when Thy voice shall bid our conflict cease,
Call us, O Lord, to Thine eternal peace.

Continue in prayer, and watch in the same.—Colossians iv. 2.
487
11 11.8 8 8 6.11 12.

1 FADING like a life-time ends another day;
Bend in mercy, Jesu, hear us as we pray.
The morning's glory's long since fled,
The noon's strong manhood too is dead,
And evening, like old age, is here,
And midnight's stroke is near.
Fading, surely fading, dies another day;
Its solemn voice to each doth say, Life glides away.

2 Just beyond the nightfall comes another day:
Thou in glory thronèd, hear us as we pray.
The grave is not the end of all,
Our souls shall hear the trumpet-call,
The summons to a higher state,
Where faith's reward is great.
From beyond death's nightfall shines another day;
'If ye would live,' faith hears it say, 'love, work, and pray.

104

Let them also that love Thy name be joyful in Thee.—Psalm v. 11.
488
7 7.7 7.7 7.

1 LORD of power, Lord of might,
God and Father of us all,
Lord of day and Lord of night,
Listen to our solemn call,
Listen whilst to Thee we raise
Songs of prayer and songs of praise.

2 Light and love and life are Thine;
Great Creator of all good,
Fill our souls with light divine;
Give us with our daily food
Blessings from Thy heavenly store,
Blessings rich for evermore.

3 Graft within our heart of hearts
Love undying for Thy name,
Bid us, ere the day departs,
Spread afar our Maker's fame:
Young and old together bless,
Clothe our souls with righteousness.

4 Full of years and full of peace,
May our life on earth be blest;
When our trials here shall cease,
And at last we sink to rest,
Fountain of eternal love,
Call us to our home above.

At evening time it shall be light.
489
Zechariah xiv. 7. 7 7 7 5.

1 HOLY Father, cheer our way
With Thy love's perpetual ray;
Grant us every closing day
Light at evening time.

2 Holy Saviour, calm our fears
When earth's brightness disappears;
Grant us in our latter years
Light at evening time.

3 Holy Spirit, be Thou nigh
When in mortal pains we lie;
Grant us, as we come to die,
Light at evening time.

4 Holy, blessèd Trinity,
Darkness is not dark with Thee;
Those Thou keepest always see
Light at evening time.

I am the Light of the world.
490
John viii. 12. 8 8.8 8.8 8.

1 SWEET Saviour, bless us ere we go,
Thy word into our minds instil,
And make our lukewarm hearts to glow
With lowly love and fervent will.
Through life's long day and death's dark night,
O gentle Jesus, be our light.

2 The day is gone, its hours have run,
And Thou hast taken count of all:
The scanty triumphs grace hath won,
The broken vow, the frequent fall.
Through life's long day and death's dark night,
O gentle Jesus, be our light.

3 Grant us, dear Lord, from evil ways
True absolution and release;
And bless us, more than in past days,
With purity and inward peace.
Through life's long day and death's dark night,
O gentle Jesus, be our light.

4 Do more than pardon ; give us joy,
  Sweet fear, and sober liberty,
And simple hearts without alloy,
  That only long to be like Thee.
Through life's long day and death's dark
O gentle Jesus, be our light.   [night,

5 Labour is sweet, for Thou hast toiled ;
  And care is light, for Thou hast cared ;
Ah ! never let our works be soiled
  With strife, or by deceit ensnared.
Through life's long day and death's dark
O gentle Jesus, be our light ;   [night,

6 For all we love, the poor, the sad,
  The sinful, unto Thee we call ;
O, let Thy mercy make us glad ;
  Thou art our Jesus and our All.
Through life's long day and death's dark
O gentle Jesus, be our light.   [night.

I . . . know my sheep, and am known
491 *   of mine.*—John x. 14.
                87.8 7.
1 JESUS, tender Shepherd, hear me !
  Bless Thy little lamb to-night ;
Through the darkness be Thou near me ;
Keep me safe till morning light.

2 Through this day Thy hand has led me,
  And I thank Thee for Thy care ;
Thou hast warmed and clothed and fed me :
Listen to my evening prayer.

3 Let my sins be all forgiven ;
  Bless the friends I love so well ;
Take me, when I die, to heaven,
Happy there with Thee to dwell.

When thou liest down, thou shalt not
492 * be afraid.*—Proverbs iii. 24.
               7 6.7 6.8 8.
1 THE day is past and over ;
  All thanks, O Lord, to Thee !
We pray Thee now that sinless
  The hours of dark may be ;
O Jesu, keep us in Thy sight,
And save us through the coming night !

2 The joys of day are over ;
  We lift our hearts to Thee,
And ask Thee that offenceless
  The hours of dark may be ;
O Jesu, make their darkness light,
And save us through the coming night !

3 The toils of day are over ;
  We raise our hymn to Thee ;
And ask that free from peril
  The hours of dark may be ;
O Jesu, keep us in Thy sight,
And guard us through the coming night !

4 Be Thou our soul's preserver,
  For Thou, O God, dost know
How many are the perils
  Awaiting us below ;
O loving Jesu, hear our call,
And guard and save us from them all !

Blessed is that man that maketh the
493 * LORD his trust.*—Psalm xl. 4
                4 4 6.4 4 6.
1 THE daylight fades,
  The evening shades
Are gathering round my head :

Father above,
  I praise the love
Which smooths and guards my bed.

2 While Thou art near,
  I need not fear
The gloom of midnight hour ;
  Blest Jesus, still
  From every ill
Defend me with Thy power.

3 Pardon my sin,
  And enter in,
And sanctify my heart ;
  Spirit divine,
  O make me Thine,
And ne'er from me depart.

Whoso hearkeneth unto Me, . . . shall
494 * be quiet from fear of evil.*
        Proverbs i. 33.   L.M.
1 O THOU, whose love throughout this day
  Hath cheered our hearts and fenced
    our way,
Now may Thy presence round us close,
And hush our souls in sweet repose.

2 Unrestful, eager, still we chafe
Against Thy bidding ; only safe
When quiet in Thy hand we lie,
Or walk directed by Thine eye.

3 So would we walk, so would we rest,
Both day and night of Thee possessed.
By nought endangered, nought dismayed,
With Thee for light, and Thee for shade.

4 All praise, O Lord, to Thee we give,
In whom we are, and move, and live !
Grant us Thy peace this eventide,
And with us evermore abide.

The LORD shall be unto Thee an
495 * everlasting light.*—Isaiah lx. 19.
             7 6.7 6.7 6.7 6.
1 THE radiant sun, declining,
  Will soon have passed away,
And silver stars out-shining
  Make but as transient stay :]
O Light, all light excelling,
  When sun or stars decline,
Shine forth, our gloom dispelling
  With light and joy divine.

2 Like sunbeams, quickly flying
  Before the dusky night,
Or stars' fair lustre, dying
  With morning's clearer light :
So swift beyond our measure
  Life's little day speeds on ;
A moment's fleeting pleasure,
  And light and life are gone.

3 Thou, who in human fashion
  Didst render up Thy breath,
And by Thy bitter passion
  Destroy the sting of death :
When life's brief day is over,
  Its toil, and care, and sin,
Open Thine arms of mercy,
  And take the weary in.

4 O Saviour, be Thou near us
  Till all our toil is o'er,
Till heavenly light shall cheer us
  And night return no more :

So, to the life immortal,
With joy we'll haste away,
And pass through death's dark portal
To never-ending day.

This is the promise that He hath pro-
mised us, even eternal life.
496 1 John ii. 25.   8 7.8 7.

1 SAVIOUR, breathe an evening blessing
  Ere repose our spirits seal;
Sin and want we come confessing;
Thou canst save, and Thou canst heal.

2 Though destruction walk around us,
  Though the arrows past us fly,
Angel-guards from Thee surround us;
We are safe, for Thou art nigh.

3 Though the night be dark and dreary,
  Darkness cannot hide from Thee,
Thou art He who, never weary,
Watchest where Thy people be.

4 Should swift death this night o'ertake us,
  And our couch become our tomb,
May the morn in heaven awake us,
Clad in light and deathless bloom.

He giveth you rest, . . . so that ye
dwell in safety.
497 Deuteronomy xii. 10.   8 7.8 7.7 7.

1 THROUGH the day Thy love hath spared
  Wearied we lie down to rest ;   [us ;
Through the silent watches guard us,
Let no foe our peace molest ;
Jesus, Thou our guardian be,
Sweet it is to trust in Thee.

2 Pilgrims here on earth and strangers,
  Dwelling in the midst of foes,
Us and ours preserve from dangers,
In Thine arms may we repose ;
And when life's short day is past,
Rest with Thee in heaven at last.

498 *The* LORD *is thy keeper.*
Psalm cxxi. 5.   88.8 4.8 4.
NURSERY HYMN.

1 O LITTLE child ! lie still and sleep ;
    Jesus is near, Thou need'st not fear,
No one need fear whom God doth keep
    By day or night ;
Then lay thee down in slumber deep
    Till morning light.

2 O little child ! be still and rest ;
He sweetly sleeps, Whom Jesus keeps ;
And in the morning wake so blest,
    His child to be ;
Love every one, but love Him best :
    He first loved thee.

3 O little child ! when thou must die,
Fear nothing then, But say 'Amen'
To God's commands, and quiet lie
    In His kind land,
Till He shall say, 'Dear child, come, fly
    To heaven's bright land.'

4 Then with thine angel-wings quick grown,
Thou shalt ascend To meet thy Friend ;
Jesus the little child will own,
    Safe at His side ;
And thou shalt live before the throne,
    Because He died.

THE LORD'S DAY AND SANCTUARY.

499 *The sabbath of the* LORD *thy God.*
Exodus xx. 10.   L.M.

1 AGAIN our weekly labours end,
    And we the Sabbath's call attend :
Improve, our souls, the sacred rest.
And seek to be for ever blest.

2 This day let our devotions rise
To heaven, a grateful sacrifice ;
May God that peace divine bestow,
Which none but they who feel it know.

3 This holy calm within the breast
Prepares for that eternal rest,
Which for the sons of God remains ;
The end of cares, the end of pains.

4 In holy duties let the day,
In holy pleasures, pass away :
How sweet the Sabbath thus to spend,
In hope of that which ne'er shall end !

The Son of man is Lord also of the
500 *sabbath.—*Mark ii. 28.
    ¡6 6.6 6.6 6.6 6.

1 JESUS, we love to meet
    On this Thy holy day ;
We worship round Thy seat,
    On this Thy holy day.
Thou tender, heavenly Friend,
To Thee our prayers ascend ;
O'er our young spirits bend
    On this Thy holy day.

2 We dare not trifle now,
    On this Thy holy day ;
In silent awe we bow
    On this Thy holy day.
Check every wandering thought,
And let us all be taught
To serve Thee as we ought
    On this Thy holy day.

3 We listen to Thy word
    On this Thy holy day ;
Bless all that we have heard
    On this Thy holy day ;
Go with us when we part,
And to each youthful heart
Thy saving grace impart
    On this Thy holy day.

Praise waiteth for Thee, O God, in
501 *Sion.—*Psalm lxv. 1.   C.M.

1 NOW condescend, almighty King,
    To bless this happy throng ;
And deign to listen while we sing
    Our humble, grateful song.

2 We come to own the power divine
    That watches o'er our days ;
For this our cheerful voices join
    In hymns of grateful praise.

3 We come to learn Thy holy word,
    And ask Thy tender care ;
Before Thy throne, almighty Lord,
    We bend in humble prayer.

4 May we in safety pass this day,
    From sin and danger free ;
And ever walk in that sure way
    That leads to heaven and Thee.

502

The LORD blessed the sabbath day, and hallowed it.—Exodus xx. 11.
7 6.7 6.7 6.7 6.

1 O DAY of rest and gladness,
  O day of joy and light,
O balm of care and sadness,
  Most beautiful, most bright;
On thee the high and lowly,
  Through ages joined in tune,
Sing Holy, Holy, Holy,
  To the great God Triune.

2 On thee, at the creation,
  The light first had its birth:
On thee for our salvation
  Christ rose from depths of earth
On thee our Lord victorious
  The Spirit sent from heaven;
And thus on thee most glorious
  A triple light was given.

3 Thou art a port protected
  From storms that round us rise;
A garden intersected
  With streams of Paradise;
Thou art a cooling fountain
  In life's dry, dreary sand:
From thee, like Pisgah's mountain,
  We view our promised land.

SECOND PART.

4 Thou art a holy ladder,
  Where angels go and come;
Each Sunday finds us gladder,
  Nearer to heaven our home;
A day of sweet refection,
  A day thou art of love,
A day of resurrection
  From earth to things above.

5 To-day on weary nations
  The heavenly manna falls,
To holy convocations
  The silver trumpet calls,
Where gospel light is glowing
  With pure and radiant beams,
And living water flowing
  With soul-refreshing streams.

6 New graces ever gaining
  From this our day of rest,
We reach the rest remaining
  To spirits of the blest;
To Holy Ghost be praises,
  To Father, and to Son:
The Church her voice upraises
  To Thee, blest Three in One.

503

Blessed is the man . . . that keepeth the sabbath.—Isa. lvi. 2.   C.M.

1 BLEST day of God, most calm, most bright,
  The first and best of days:
The labourer's rest, the saint's delight,
  A day of joy and praise.

2 My Saviour's face did make thee shine,
  His rising did thee raise;
This made thee heavenly and divine
  Beyond the common days.

3 The first-fruits do a blessing prove
  To all the sheaves behind;
And they that do a Sabbath love,
  A happy week shall find.

4 This day must I for God appear,
  For, Lord, the day is Thine;
O let me spend it in Thy fear,
  Then shall the day be mine!

5 Throughout the day, cease work and play,
  That I to God may rest;
Now let me talk with God, and walk
  With God, and I am blest.

504

Call the sabbath a delight, the holy of the LORD, honourable.
Isaiah lviii. 13.   8 7.8 7.8 8.4 8.

1 SWEETLY dawns the Sabbath morning
  On the world, so full of care;
Bidding man forget his labour,
  Calling to the house of prayer.
O, sweet and strong, His saints among,
We sing to God our Sabbath song,
  Our Sabbath song,
We raise to Christ our Sabbath song.

2 'Tis the day when man's Redeemer
  Rose triumphant o'er the grave;
Sealing thus His work completed,
  Telling thus His power to save.
Then loud and long, To Christ so strong
To save the lost, we raise our song,
  Our Sabbath song,
We raise to Christ our Sabbath song.

3 'Tis the day whose rest and gladness
  Show what all my life should be;
Yielding all by faith to Jesus,
  Finding Jesus all in me.
O, how I long, In Christ made strong,
To sing each day faith's Sabbath song,
  Faith's Sabbath song,
I'd sing each day faith's Sabbath song.

4 'Tis the day whose calm, so holy,
  Shadows forth the better rest,
Where the crownèd saints are singing
  With their Lord, supremely blest.
'Twill not be long Till 'mid that throng
We sing the eternal Sabbath song,
  Heaven's Sabbath song,
We'll sing the eternal Sabbath song.

505

The sabbath of rest, an holy convocation.—Lev. xxiii. 3.   S.M.

1 THIS is the day of light!
  Let there be light to-day;
O Dayspring, rise upon our night,
  And chase its gloom away.

2 This is the day of rest!
  Our failing strength renew;
On weary brain and troubled breast
  Shed Thou Thy freshening dew.

3 This is the day of peace!
  Thy peace our spirits fill;
Bid Thou the blasts of discord cease,
  The waves of strife be still.

4 This is the day of prayer!
  Let earth to heaven draw near:
Lift up our hearts to seek Thee there,
  Come down to meet us here.

5 This is the first of days!
  Send forth Thy quickening breath,
And wake dead souls to love and praise
  O Vanquisher of death.

*The day which the LORD hath made;
we will rejoice and be glad in it.*
506 Psalm cxviii. 24.　　　C.M.

1 THIS is the day the Lord hath made,
　　He calls the hours His own :
Let heaven rejoice, let earth be glad,
　　And praise surround the throne.

2 To-day He rose and left the dead,
　　And Satan's empire fell ;
To-day the saints His triumphs spread,
　　And all His wonders tell.

3 Hosanna to the anointed King,
　　To David's holy Son !
Help us, O Lord, descend, and bring
　　Salvation from Thy throne.

4 Blest be the Lord, who comes to men
　　With messages of grace ;
Who comes, in God His Father's name,
　　To save our sinful race.

5 Hosanna, in the highest strains,
　　The Church on earth can raise :
The highest heavens in which He reigns
　　Shall give Him nobler praise.

My sabbaths ye shall keep.
507 Exodus xxxi. 13.　　76.8 6.8 6.8 6.

1 WE won't give up the Sabbath,
　　The day which God hath blessed,
That all the weary sons of toil
　　Might taste of heavenly rest ;
The day of joy, and praise, and prayer,
　　The brightest of the seven,
When, loosed from every earthly care,
　　We think of God and heaven.

2 We won't give up the Sabbath
　　For pleasure or for gain,
Or waste its consecrated hours
　　In vanities profane ;
We'll crowd into the house of God
　　To see His wonders there ;
We'll tread the courts His saints have
　　In hope their joy to share.　[trod,

3 We won't give up the Sabbath,
　　The day which God hath blessed ;
The type, the promise, and the seal
　　Of everlasting rest ;
Sweet peace it brings to man below,
　　Sweet rest in Jesus' love,
And they who keep it holy now
　　Shall rest with Him above.

*Blessed are they that dwell in Thy
house: they will be still praising*
508 *Thee.*—Ps. lxxxiv. 4.　　6 6.6 6.8 8.

1 LORD of the worlds above !
　　How pleasant and how fair
The dwellings of Thy love,
　　Thy earthly temples, are !
To Thine abode My heart aspires,
With warm desires To see my God.

2 O happy souls that pray
　　Where God delights to hear !
O happy men that pay
　　Their constant service there !
They praise Thee still, And happy they
Who love the way To Zion's hill !

3 They go from strength to strength,
　　Through this dark vale of tears,

Till each o'ercomes at length,
　　Till each in heaven appears :
O glorious seat ! Thou God, our King,
Shall thither bring Our willing feet.

4 God is our sun and shield,
　　Our light and our defence !
With gifts His hands are filled,
　　We draw our blessings thence :
He shall bestow Upon our race
His saving grace, And glory too.

5 The Lord His people loves ;
　　His hand no good withholds
From those His heart approves,
　　From holy, humble souls :
Thrice happy he, O Lord of hosts,
Whose spirit trusts Alone in Thee !

*How amiable are Thy tabernacles, O
LORD of hosts !*—Psalm lxxxiv. 1.
509 7 7.7 7.7 7.7 7.

1 PLEASANT are Thy courts above,
　　In the land of light and love ;
Pleasant are Thy courts below,
In this land of sin and woe.
O ! my spirit longs and faints
For the converse of Thy saints,
For the brightness of Thy face,
For Thy fulness, God of grace !

2 Happy birds that sing and fly
Round Thy altars, O most High !
Happier souls that find a rest
In a heavenly Father's breast !
Happy souls ! their praises flow
Even in this vale of woe ;
Waters in the desert rise,
Manna feeds them from the skies.

3 On they go from strength to strength,
Till they reach Thy throne at length ;
At Thy feet adoring fall,
Who hast led them safe through all.
Sun and shield alike Thou art,
Guide and guard my erring heart ;
Grace and glory flow from Thee :
Shower, O shower them, Lord, on me !

*Christ also loved the church, and
gave Himself for it.*
510 Ephesians v. 25.　　S.M.

1 I LOVE Thy kingdom, Lord,
　　The house of Thine abode,
The church our blessed Redeemer saved
　　With His own precious blood.

2 I love Thy church, O God !
　　Her walls before Thee stand,
Dear as the apple of Thy eye,
　　And graven on Thy hand.

3 For her my tears shall fall, ·
　　For her my prayers ascend ;
To her my cares and toils be given
　　Till toils and cares shall end.

4 Beyond my highest joy
　　I prize her heavenly ways,
Her sweet communion, solemn vows,
　　Her hymns of love and praise.

5 Jesus, Thou Friend divine,
　　Our Saviour, and our King :
Thy hand from every snare and foe
　　Shall great deliverance bring.

6 Sure as Thy truth shall last,
    To Zion shall be given
The brightest glories earth can yield,
    And brighter bliss of heaven.

511 *I will dwell in the house of the* LORD
        for ever.—Psalm xxiii. 6.   5 5 5 11.
1 O JESUS! chold
    The lambs of Thy fold,
Who join in Thy praise,
And sing alleluia in rapturous lays.

2 Every Sabbath we meet
    In this hallowed retreat,
    We join with delight
In praises to Christ from morning till night.

3 In Thy word we are told
    How children of old
    By Jesus wer blest,
Taken up in His arms and kindly caressed.

4 Hosanna! they sang,
    And Jerusalem rang .
    With their beautiful songs: [tongues.
Hosanna to Christ! from thousands of

5 Like them we would join
    In worship divine,
    And Jesus adore   [more.
On earth and in heaven, when time is no

6 Weak children are we,
    But trusting in Thee,
    And pleading Thy blood,
Through Jesus we find a reconciled God.

7 So we hail the bright day,
    More welcome than May,
    The best of the seven ;   [heaven.
And in worshipping Christ we anticipate

8 When our Sabbaths are past,
    And we get there at last,
    We'll sing of Thy grace,
And evermore live in the smile of Thy face.

512 *An house for the name of the* LORD,
        and an house for His kingdom.
        2 Chronicles ii. 1.   L.M.
1 A CHILDREN'S temple here we build,
    And dedicate it, Lord, to Thee ;
In hope that with Thy presence filled
    These humble walls henceforth may be.

2 When Christ, Thy holy child, was born,
    He had not where to lay His head ;
Though King of kings, He did not scorn
    The meanness of a manger-bed. .

3 He, who the throne of glory shares, [love,
    Came down, that we, through sovereign
Might be God's children and God's heirs,
    Joint heirs with Him in bliss above.

4 And here, where simple souls are taught
    To know and do His Father's will,
Or infants to His arms are brought,
    He welcomes all, and blesses still.

5 Come, Holy Ghost, while we draw nigh,
    Such life and power to us afford,
That each may Abba, Father, cry, .
    And young and old call Jesus. Lord.

THE NEW YEAR.

513 *Like unto men that wait for their*
        Lord.—Luke xii. 36.   5 5 5 11.
1 C OME, let us anew
    Our journey pursue,

Roll round with the year,
And never stand still till the Master appear.

2 His adorable will
    Let us gladly fulfil,
    And our talents improve,   [love.
By the patience of hope, and the labour of

3 Our life is a dream ;
    Our time as a stream
    Glides swiftly away,
And the fugitive moment refuses to stay.

4 The arrow is flown,
    The moment is gone ;
    The millennial year
Rushes on to our view, and eternity's here.

5 O that each in the day
    Of His coming may say,
    'I have fought my way through,
I have finished the work Thou didst give me
to do!'

6 O that each from his Lord
    May receive the glad word,
    'Well and faithfully done!
Enter into My joy, and sit down on My throne.'

514 *Thou crownest the year with Thy*
        goodness.—Psalm lxv. 11.   C.M.
1 S ING to the great Jehovah's praise!
    All praise to Him belongs :
Who kindly lengthens out our days
    Demands our choicest songs.

2 His providence hath brought us through
    Another various year :
We all with vows and anthems new
    Before our God appear.

3 Father, Thy mercies past we own ;
    Thy still continued care ;
To Thee presenting, through Thy Son,
    Whate'er we have or are.

4 Our lips and lives shall gladly show
    The wonders of Thy love,
While on in Jesu's steps we go
    To see Thy face above.

5 Our residue of days or hours
    Thine, wholly Thine, shall be ;
And all our consecrated powers
    A sacrifice to Thee :

6 Till Jesus in the clouds appear
    To saints on earth forgiven,
And bring the grand sabbatic year,
    The jubilee of heaven.

515 *Thou carriest them away as*
        with a flood.—Psalm xc. 5.
                7 7.7 7.7 7.7 7.
1 W HILE with ceaseless course the sun
    Hasted round the former year,
Many souls their race have run,
    Never more to meet us here.
Fixed in an eternal state,
    They have done with all below ;
We a little longer wait,
    But how little none can know.

2 As the wingèd arrow flies
    Speedily the mark to find ;
As the lightning from the skies
    Darts, and leaves no trace behind :
Swiftly thus our fleeting days
    Bear us down life's rapid stream ;
Upward, Lord, our spirits raise ;
    All below is but a dream.

8 Thanks for mercies past receive,
Pardon of our sins renew,
Teach us henceforth how to live
With eternity in view.
Bless Thy word to young and old,
Fill us with the Saviour's love ;
And when life's short tale is told,
May we live with Thee above.

516 *I trust in the mercy of God for*
ever and ever.—Ps. lii. 8. L.M.

1 GREAT God, we sing that mighty hand
By which supported still we stand ;
The opening year Thy mercy shows,
That mercy crowns it till it close.

2 By day, by night, at home, abroad,
Still are we guarded by our God :
By His incessant bounty fed,
By His unerring counsel led.

3 With grateful hearts the past we own,
The future, all to us unknown,
We to Thy guardian care commit,
Content with what Thou deemest fit.

4 In scenes exalted or depressed
Thou art our joy, and Thou our rest ;
Thy goodness all our hopes shall raise,
Adored throughout our changing days.

5 When death shall interrupt these songs,
And seal in silence mortal tongues,
Our Helper, God. in whom we trust,
Shall keep our souls, and guard our dust.

SPRING AND SEED-TIME.

Make a joyful noise unto the LORD,
517 *all the earth.*—Psalm xcviii. 4.
S.M.

1 SPARED to another spring,
We raise our grateful songs :
'Tis pleasant, Lord, Thy praise to sing,
And praise to Thee belongs.

2 Ten thousand different flowers
To Thee sweet offerings bear ;
And cheerful birds in shady bowers
Sing forth Thy tender care.

3 The fields on every side,
The trees, and every hill,
The glorious sun, the rolling tide,
Proclaim Thy wondrous skill.

4 But trees and fields and skies
Still praise a God unknown,
For gratitude and love can rise
From living hearts alone.

5 These living hearts of ours
Thy holy name would bless ;
The blossom of ten thousand flowers
Would please Thee, Saviour, less.

6 Though earth itself decays,
Our souls can never die ;
O tune them all to sing Thy praise
In better songs on high.

All Thy works shall praise Thee,
518 *O LORD.*—Psalm cxlv. 10.
6 4.6 4.6 6.6 4.

1 COME, join the festive song,
Wake voices all ;
Chime with the vernal throng,
List to the call.

Hear we in every breeze,
From vale and mountain trees,
Glad notes of nature say,
Join ye my lay.

2 Lord of the rolling year,
Round and above,
Boundless Thy works appear,
Boundless Thy love.
All, all in earth and sky,
As glide the seasons by,
New glories of Thy name
Ever proclaim.

3 Joyous we swell the strain,
Thankful to Thee,
Watched by Thy care, again
Spring-tide we see.
Still in this gospel land
Throngs forth the Sabbath band,
To praise and worship Thee,
Happy and free.

4 Onward for ever flow,
Truth's mighty wave ;
Soon every tribe below
Conquer and save.
Sweet as the voice of spring,
Then every tongue shall sing,
Glory to God on high,
Glory for aye.

O LORD, how manifold are Thy
works ! . . . the earth is full of
519 *Thy riches.*—Psalm civ. 24.
IRREGULAR.

1 FOR all Thy love and goodness, so
bountiful and free,
Thy name, Lord, be adored !
On the wings of joyous praise our hearts
soar up to Thee :
Glory to the Lord !

2 The spring time breaks all round about,
waking from winter's night :
Thy name, Lord, be adored !
The sunshine, like God's love, pours down
in floods of golden light :
Glory to The Lord !

3 A voice of joy is in all the earth, a voice is
in all the air :
Thy name, Lord, be adored !
All nature singeth aloud to God ; there is
gladness everywhere :
Glory to the Lord !

4 The flowers are strewn in field and copse,
on the hill and on the plain :
Thy name, Lord, be adored !
The soft air stirs in the tender leaves that
clothe the trees again :
Glory to the Lord !

5 The works of Thy hands are very fair ;
and for all Thy bounteous love
Thy name, Lord, be adored !
But what, if this world is so fair, is the
better land above ?
Glory to the Lord !

6 O, to awake from death's short sleep, like
the flowers from their wintry grave !
Thy name, Lord, be adored !
And to rise all glorious in the day when
Christ shall come to save !
Glory to the Lord !

7 O, to dwell in that happy land, where the
   heart cannot choose but sing!
      Thy name, Lord, be adored!
And where the life of the blessèd ones is a
   beautiful endless spring!
      Glory to the Lord! Alleluia!

520 *Truly the light is sweet.*
      Ecclesiastes xi. 7.   S.M.
1 SWEET is the time of spring,
    When nature's charms appear;
The birds with ceaseless pleasure sing,
   And hail the opening year.

2 But sweeter far the spring
   Of wisdom and of grace,
When children bless and praise their King,
   Who loves their youthful race.

3 Sweet is the dawn of day,
   When light just streaks the sky:
When shades and darkness pass away,
   And morning beams are nigh.

4 But sweeter far the dawn
   Of piety in youth,
When shades of darkness are withdrawn
   Before the light of truth.

5 Sweet is the opening flower,
   Which just begins to bloom,
Which every day and every hour
   Fresh beauties will assume.

6 But sweeter that young heart,
   When faith and love and peace
Blossom and bloom in every part,
   With sweet and varied grace.

7 O may life's early spring,
   And morning, ere they flee,
Youth's flower, and its fair blossoming
   Be given, my God, to Thee!

521 *The earth is full of Thy riches.*
      Psalm civ. 24.   4 4 6.4 4 6.
1 THE spring-tide hour
    Brings leaf and flower,
With songs of life and love;
   And many a lay
   Wears out the day
In many a leafy grove.

2 Bird, flower, and tree
   Seem to agree
Their choicest gifts to bring;
   But this poor heart
   Bears not its part,
In it there is no spring.

3 Dews fall apace,
   The dews of grace,
Upon this soul of sin;
   And love divine
   Delights to shine
Upon the waste within.

4 Yet year by year
   Fruits, flowers appear,
And birds their praises sing;
   But this poor heart
   Bears not its part,
Its winter has no spring.

5 Lord, let Thy love,
   Fresh from above.
Soft as the south wind blow,
   Call forth its bloom,
   Wake its perfume,
And bid its spices flow.

6 And when Thy voice
   Makes earth rejoice,
And the hills laugh and sing,
   Lord, teach this heart
   To bear its part,
And join the praise of spring.

522 *The earth is satisfied with the fruit*
     of Thy works.—Psalm civ. 13.
      7 6.7 6.7 6.7 6.6 6.8 4.
1 WE plough the fields, and scatter
    The good seed on the land,
But it is fed and watered
   By God's almighty hand;
He sends the snow in winter,
   The warmth to swell the grain,
The breezes, and the sunshine,
   And soft refreshing rain.
     All good gifts around us
     Are sent from heaven above,
Then thank the Lord, O thank the Lord,
     For all His love!

2 He only is the Maker
   Of all things, near and far;
He paints the wayside flower,
   He lights the evening star;
The winds and waves obey Him,
   By Him the birds are fed;
Much more to us His children,
   He gives our daily bread.
     All good gifts around us, etc.

3 We thank Thee then, O Father,
   For all things bright and good,
The seed-time and the harvest,
   Our life, our health, our food;
Accept the gifts we offer
   For all Thy love imparts,
And, what Thou most desirest,
   Our humble, thankful hearts.
     All good gifts around us, etc.

523 *Man goeth forth unto his work.*
      Psalm civ. 23.
      7 6.7 6.7 6.7 6.6 6.8 6.
1 WE plough the fertile meadows,
    We sow the furrowed land;
But all the growth and increase
   Are in God's mighty hand.
He gives the showers and sunshine
   To swell the quickening grain,
The springing corn He blesses,
   He clothes the golden plain.
     Every bounteous blessing
      His faithful love bestows,
Then magnify His glorious name,
     From whom all goodness flows.

2 By Him all things were fashioned
   Around us and afar,
He formed the earth and ocean,
   He kindled every star,
His love ordained the seasons,
   By Him are all things fed,
He for the sparrow careth,
   He gives our daily bread.
     Every bounteous blessing, etc.

3 All praise to Thee, great Father,
   Thou Giver of all good,
Upon whose care dependeth
   Our life and health and food:
We bring our glad thanksgiving,
   Our gifts of love and praise;

Be Thine our grateful service,
The harvest of our days.
Every bounteous blessing, etc.

SUMMER.

524 *Lo, this is our God, . . . and He will save us.*—Isa. xxv. 9.   6 5.6 5.

1 SUMMER suns are glowing
Over land and sea,
Happy light is flowing,
Bountiful and free.

2 Everything rejoices
In the mellow rays,
All earth's thousand voices
Swell the psalm of praise.

3 God's free mercy streameth
Over all the world,
And His banner gleameth
Everywhere unfurled.

4 Broad and deep and glorious
As the heaven above,
Shines in might victorious
His eternal love.

5 Lord, upon our blindness
Thy pure radiance pour ;
For Thy loving-kindness
Make us love Thee more.

6 And when clouds are drifting
Dark across our sky,
Then, the veil uplifting,
Father, be Thou nigh.

7 We will never doubt Thee,
Though Thou veil Thy light ;
Life is dark without Thee ;
Death with Thee is bright.

8 Light of light ! shine o'er us
On our pilgrim way ;
Go Thou still before us
To the endless day.

AUTUMN AND HARVEST.

525 *The first-fruits of the land, which Thou, O LORD, hast given me.* Deuteronomy xxvi. 10.   S.M.

1 FAIR waved the golden corn
in Canaan's pleasant land,
When full of joy, some shining morn,
Went forth the reaper band.

2 To God, so good and great,
Their cheerful thanks they pour ;
Then carry to His temple gate
The choicest of their store.

3 Like Israel, Lord, we give
Our earliest fruits to Thee,
And pray that, long as we shall live,
We may Thy children be.

4 Thine is our youthful prime,
And life and all its powers ;
Be with us in our morning time,
And bless our evening hours.

5 In wisdom let us grow,
As years and strength are given,
That we may serve Thy Church below,
And join Thy saints in heaven.

6 To God, the Father, Son,
And Spirit, ever blest,
The One in Three, the Three in One,
Be endless praise addressed.

112

526 *For His mercy endureth for ever.* Psalm cxxxvi.   7 7.7 7.

1 PRAISE, O praise our God and King !
Hymns of adoration sing ;
For His mercies still endure,
Ever faithful, ever sure.

2 Praise Him that He made the sun
Day by day his course to run ;   For, etc.

3 And the silver moon by night,
Shining with her gentle light.   For, etc.

4 Praise Him that He gave the rain
To mature the swelling grain ;   For, etc.

5 And hath bid the fruitful field
Crops of precious increase yield.   For, etc.

6 Praise Him for our harvest-store,
He hath filled the garner floor ;   For, etc.

7 And for richer food than this,
Pledge of everlasting bliss.   For, etc.

8 Glory to our bounteous King !
Glory let creation sing !
Glory to the Father, Son,
And blest Spirit, Three in One.

527 *According to the joy in harvest.* Isaiah ix. 3.   6 5.6 5.6 5.6 5.6 5.6 5.

1 EARTH below is teeming,
Heaven is bright above,
Every brow is beaming
In the light of love ;
Every eye rejoices,
Every thought is praise ;
Happy hearts and voices
Gladden nights and days.
O almighty Giver !
Bountiful and free,
As the joy in harvest
Joy we before Thee.

2 Every youth and maiden
On the harvest plain,
Round the waggons laden
With their golden grain,
Swell the happy chorus,
On the evening air,
Unto Him who o'er us
Bends with constant care.
O almighty Giver, etc.

3 For the sun and showers,
For the rain and dew,
For the nurturing hours
Spring and summer knew ;
For the golden autumn,
And its precious stores,
For the love that brought them
Teeming at our doors.
O almighty Giver, etc.

4 Earth's broad harvest whitens
In a brighter sun :
Thou the orb that lightens
All we tread upon ;
Send out labourers, Father !
Where fields ripening wave ;
All the nations gather,
Gather in and save.
O almighty Giver !
Bountiful and free,
Then as joy in harvest
We shall joy in Thee.

528 *Thou crownest the year with Thy goodness.*—Ps. lxv. 11.   10 10 7.

1 GREAT Giver of all good, to Thee again
    We humbly now present, in joyous
        strain,
    Our harvest-tide thanksgiving.

2 To Thee, in whom we live and move, we
        come,
    To praise Thee for the sheaves brought
        safely home,
    With harvest-tide thanksgiving.

3 Thou dost prepare the corn, and year by
        year
    Within Thine house, O Lord, will we appear
    With harvest-tide thanksgiving.

4 Thine was the former and the latter rain,
    Enriching earth, and calling forth again
    The harvest-tide thanksgiving.

5 Thou openest wide once more Thy bounte-
        ous hand,
    And far and wide ascends from all the land
    Glad harvest-tide thanksgiving.

6 Thou fillest all that live with plenteousness,
    They in return Thy sacred name all bless,
    In harvest-tide thanksgiving.

7 Thy clouds drop fatness on the teeming
        earth,
    Accept these festal songs of reverent mirth,
    This harvest-tide thanksgiving.

8 The year is crowned with goodness, Lord,
        by Thee,
    Then meet it is that we should offer Thee
    The harvest-tide thanksgiving.

9 On every side, both hills and dales rejoice,
    On every side sounds forth the grateful
        voice
    Of harvest-tide thanksgiving.

10 For all Thy blessings, Lord, our thanks we
        sing,
    We all, who sow and reap, together bring
    Our harvest-tide thanksgiving.

529 *He giveth to all life, and breath, and all things.*—Acts xvii. 25.
    7 6.7 6.7 6.7 6.

1 SING to the Lord of harvest,
    Sing songs of love and praise;
    With joyful hearts and voices
        Your alleluias raise:
    By Him the rolling seasons
        In fruitful order move,
    Sing to the Lord of harvest
        A song of happy love.

2 By Him the clouds drop fatness,
    The deserts bloom and spring,
    The hills leap up in gladness,
        The valleys laugh and sing:
    He filleth with His fulness
        All things with large increase,
    He crowns the year with goodness,
        With plenty and with peace.

3 Bring to His sacred altar
    The gifts His goodness gave,
    The golden sheaves of harvest,
        The souls He died to save:
    Your hearts lay down before Him,
        When at His feet ye fall,
    And with your lives adore Him,
        Who gave His life for all.

4 To God the gracious Father,
    Who made us ' very good;'
    To Christ, who, when we wandered,
    Restored us with His blood;
    And to the Holy Spirit,
    Who doth upon us pour
    His blessèd dews and sunshine,
    Be praise for evermore.

530 *The field is the world.*
    Matthew xiii. 38.   7 7.7 7.7 7.7 7.

1 COME, ye thankful people, come,
    Raise the song of harvest-home!
    All is safely gathered in,
    Ere the winter storms begin;
    God, our Maker, doth provide
    For our wants to be supplied ·
    Come to God's own temple, come,
    Raise the song of harvest-home!

2 All this world is God's own field,
    Fruit unto His praise to yield;
    Wheat and tares together sown,
    Unto joy or sorrow grown,
    First the blade, and then the ear,
    Then the full corn shall appear:
    Lord of harvest, grant that we
    Wholesome grain and pure may be.

3 For the Lord our God shall come,
    And shall take His harvest home;
    From His field shall in that day
    All offences purge away;
    Give His angels charge at last
    In the fire the tares to cast;
    But the fruitful ears to store
    In His garner evermore.

4 Even so, Lord, quickly come,
    To Thy final harvest-home!
    Gather Thou Thy people in,
    Free from sorrow, free from sin;
    There for ever purified,
    In Thy presence to abide;
    Come with all Thine angels, come,
    Raise the glorious harvest-home.

531 *The harvest is the end of the world.*
    Matt. xiii. 39.   5 5 5 11.5 5 5 11.

1 OUR voices we raise
        Thy mercies to praise,
        O Giver of life,
    For the first-fruits of harvest with happiness
        Of ourselves we are nought,   [rife;
        But Thy mercy hath brought,
        Through the summer of grace,
    Our spirits in peace to a bountiful place.

2 The seed has been sown,
        The green blade hath grown,
        The full ear hath borne
    The crown of the summer, the beautiful corn;
        Another year sped
        Its sunlight hath shed
        On the spirit of man,   [scan.
    And the Lord of the harvest its ripeness may

3 In the turn of a day,
        Bright flowers pass away,
        Then the fruit cometh on:
    The sunlight matures when the blossom is
        Like the fall of the flower,   [gone.
        In a day, in an hour,
        Our hopes drop their bloom;
    But the sunlight of heaven draws life from
    the tomb.

113

4 When the full time is come
  For the great harvest-home,
  Then cometh the end;
The Lord of the harvest His reapers shall
  They gather the corn   [send
  In the dew of the morn,
  At the dawn of the day;
To the garner of heaven they bear it away.

5 O Master of life,
  From the toil and the strife
  When at last we are free,
In the harvest of souls be our portion with
  Where the day has no night, [Thee;
  Nor is mildew nor blight,
  Nor frail blossoms fall,
But God in His fulness shines forth all in all.

532 *But grow in grace.*
        2 Peter iii. 18.   7 6.7 6.

1 THE year is swiftly waning;
    The summer days are past;
  And life, brief life, is speeding;
    The end is nearing fast.

2 The ever-changing seasons
    In silence come and go;
  But Thou, eternal Father,
    No time or change canst know.

3 O pour Thy grace upon us,
    That we may worthier be,
  Each year that passes o'er us,
    To dwell in heaven with Thee.

4 Behold the bending orchards
    With bounteous fruit are crowned;
  Lord, in our hearts more richly
    Let heavenly fruit abound.

5 O! by each mercy sent us,
    And by each grief and pain,
  By blessings like the sunshine,
    And sorrows like the rain.

6 Our barren hearts make fruitful,
    With every goodly grace,
  That we Thy name may hallow,
    And see at last Thy face.

WINTER.

He giveth snow like wool: He scat-
533 *tereth the hoarfrost like ashes.*
        Psalm cxlvii. 16.   7 7.7 7.

1 WINTER reigneth o'er the land,
    Freezing with its icy breath,
  Dead and bare the tall trees stand;
    All is chill and drear as death.

2 Yet it seemeth but a day
    Since the summer flowers were here,
  Since they stacked the balmy hay,
    Since they reaped the golden ear.

3 Sunny days are past and gone;
    So the years go, speeding fast,
  Onward ever, each new one
    Swifter speeding than the last.

4 Life is waning; life is brief;
    Death, like winter, standeth nigh:
  Each one, like the falling leaf,
    Soon shall fade and fall and die.

5 But the sleeping earth shall wake,
    And the flowers shall burst in bloom,
  And all nature, rising, break
    Glorious from its wintry tomb.

114

6 So, Lord, after slumber blest
  Comes a bright awakening,
And our flesh in hope shall rest
  Of a never-fading spring.

ANNIVERSARIES.

        Thou hast granted me life and
534 *favour.*—Job x. 12.   8 6.8 6.7 6.

1 ANOTHER year has passed away,
    Time swiftly speeds along;
  We come again to praise and pray,
    And sing our joyous song.
  We come with song of greeting,
    We come with song again.

2 We come, the Saviour's name to praise,
    To sing the wondrous love
  Of Him who guards us all our days,
    And guides to heaven above. We, etc.

3 We'll sing of mercies daily given
    Through every passing year,
  We'll sing the promises of heaven
    With voices loud and clear. We, etc.

        Therefore shall the people praise Thee
535 *for ever and ever.*—Psalm xlv. 17.
                              9 8.9 8.12 8.11 8.

1 A YEAR since in concord assembling,
    Here sang we all jubilant then;
  And now with rejoicing and trembling
    We gather together again.   [youth
For the mercy and truth Of the Guide of our
    And all that to us He hath given
We sing and give praise, And still walk in the
                              ways
  That will end in the rest of heaven.

2 Rejoicing in blessings unnumbered,
    We follow our heavenly ways;
  Yet are we with weakness encumbered,
    And therefore we tremble to-day.
                    For the mercy, etc.

3 Youth passes, the seasons are fleeting,
    And time to eternity flies:
  O Jesus, come Thou to our meeting,
    And make us more fit for the skies.
                    For the mercy, etc.

4 Sweet blossoms, the orchards adorning,
    Have yielded sweet fruit in their place,
  And we in our life's early morning
    Would bear the bright blossoms of
      grace.   For the mercy, etc.

5 The gardens, and cornfields, and pastures,
    The flocks in the valleys that stray,
  Are bringing more wealth to their
      masters:
  Shall we be less fruitful than they?
                    For the mercy, etc.

6 O Thou whose omnipotence made us,
    O Thou who wast slain on the tree,
  Great Spirit, blest Comforter, aid us
    To live and to labour for Thee.
                    For the mercy, etc.

        According to the multitude of His
536 *loving-kindnesses.*—Isaiah lxiii. 7.
                                        S.M.

1 LET all assembled here,
    On this returning day,
  Review the mercies of the year,
    And grateful homage pay.

2 Yes, we adore Thee, Lord,
    Within this sacred place ;
Where oft we meet with sweet accord,
    To seek Thy gracious face.

3 To Thee our God and King,
    We glad hosannas raise ;
O deign to hear our voices sing
    With joyfulness Thy praise.

4 Command Thy blessing, Lord,
    On all assembled here :
And may we still Thy grace record
    Through every circling year.

*The LORD your God is gracious and
    merciful.—2 Chronicles xxx. 9.*

537
    6 6 8.6 6 8.

1 COME, children all, and praise,
    With childhood's happiest lays,
The loving God who brings us here ;
    Whose hand each one has led,
    And every one has fed,
And kept us through another year.

2 To Thee, O Lord, we sing,
    To Thee thanksgiving bring,
Glad to tell forth Thy bounteous love :
    Help us, while we have breath,
    To praise, and after death
To praise Thee evermore above.

3 We thank Thee for Thy care
    Who giv'st us clothes to wear,
And feedest us with daily bread ; .
    Who guardest all our ways,
    The light of all our days,
The rest and shelter of our bed.

4 But most we thank Thee, Lord,
    That we are taught Thy word,
That we are fed with heavenly food :
    We know the blessèd name ;
    We know that Jesus came
To give us everlasting good.

5 O may we daily feed
    Upon that heavenly bread,
So freely, bountifully given ;
    Live blest and holy here,
    While looking forward, there
To live for ever blest in heaven !

538 *And with my song will I praise
    Him.—Ps. xxviii. 7.* IRREGULAR.

1 JOYFUL our voices we raise
    In a glad anthem of praise
To the Father above, Whose infinite love
Thus lengthens the span of our days.
Blessings unnumbered and vast
Have crowned the year that is past ;
And this much we know, If we serve Him
He'll bring us to heaven at last.   [below,
    Glory to God ! our song shall be,
    For His boundless love, so rich and free ;
    Glory to God our song shall be
    Through all the years of eternity.

2 Tribute of praises we bring
Unto our Saviour and King,
Incarnated Word, Redeemer, and Lord,
Of life everlasting the Spring.
Himself He all-willingly gave,
That man He might succour and save ;
He died on the tree That we might be free,
For us He slew death and the grave.
    Glory to God ! our song shall be, etc.

3 Chanting our sweetest of lays,
    Praise we the Spirit of grace,
With the eternal Son, And the Father one,
The Guardian and Guide of our days,
Author of life and of light,
The Source of the pure and the right,
True Fountain of joy, Without stint or alloy,
And Giver of wisdom and might.
    Glory to God ! our song shall be, etc.

*Sing unto the LORD with thanksgiv-
    ing.—Psalm cxlvii. 7.*

539
    8 7.8 7.6 6.6 5.

1 FATHER, from Thy throne of glory
    Listen to our praise and prayer,
Thou hast spared us in Thy mercy,
    Here to meet another year.
        Crown, crown it, God of love,
        With blessings from above ;
        Fill our hearts, fill our hearts
        With Thy fear and love.

2 Blessings more than we can number
    Hitherto have marked our way ;
And Thine eye that knows no slumber,
    Hath watched o'er us every day.
        Praise, praise unto Thy name,
        Praise, praise we loud proclaim ;
        Heaven shall ring, heaven shall ring
        With the loud acclaim ;

3 Still vouchsafe to us Thy blessing,
    And direct our future course ;
Still surround our every dwelling,
    Thou who art of life the source. ,
        Shine, shine upon our way, .
        May we Thy laws obey ;
        Hear us now, hear us now,
        Bless our school, we pray.

4 Wilt Thou, O Almighty Father,
    Bless our meeting here to-day
Ere the night's dark shades shall gather,
    And our praises die away ?
        Come, Lord, and bless us now,
        Thy grace and mercy show ;
        Evermore, evermore
        May Thy blessings flow.

5 May we all, when life is over,
    Teachers, children, meet above, .
Joining in that song for ever
    Of our risen Saviour's love.
        Then shall we sweetly sing
        Praise to our Saviour King ;
        Heaven shall ring, heaven shall ring
        With the strain we sing.

*We thank Thee, and praise Thy glo-
    rious name.—1 Chronicles xxix. 13.*

540
    8 8.8 8.10 9.10.10.

1 WE sing our song of jubilee,
    Our voices rising loud and free ;
And with the notes of sweet accord
We praise our ever-blessèd Lord.
Singing together, singing together,
    Teachers and scholars glady unite ;
Singing together, singing together,
    Love fills our hearts, and our faces are
        bright.

2 We praise Him for the year now past,
    And at His feet our cares we cast ;
And O may He who guides our way
Forbid our youthful steps to stray !
    Singing together, etc.

115

3 Our Sabbath-school, O may He bless,
And guard its lambs with tenderness ;
And lead us gently when we die
To our Good Shepherd's fold on high !
Singing together, etc.

Blessed be the LORD *God of Israel for
ever and ever.*—1 Chronicles xvi. 36.

541 11 11.11 11.

1 BLEST Saviour, we gather, our tribute
to bring
Of joy and of love, like the blossoms of
spring ;
Our gracious Redeemer, we gratefully raise
Our hearts and our voices in hymning Thy
praise.

2 Our Saviour is loving, our Saviour is kind,
He came down from heaven, the lost ones
to find ;
He never refuseth or sendeth away [stray.
The soul which returneth, no longer to

3 His arms, which embraced the children of
old,
Still gently encircle the lambs of the fold ;
His grace, which inviteth the wandering
home,
Has never forbidden the youngest to come.

4 How many poor children have leaned on
His breast,
How many poor children His name have
confessed,
Believing and happy His goodness to prove,
Have lived to His glory, and died in His
love.

5 Hosanna, hosanna, blest Saviour, we raise
Our hearts and our voices in hymning Thy
praise,
For love so abounding to all the lost race,
For blessings of earth and glories of grace.

6 Blest Saviour, be with us throughout this
glad day,
O teach us Thy way with joy to pursue :
From sin and temptation may we ever
depart,
And let Thy salvation revive every heart.

Let the people praise Thee, O God.
Psalm lxvii. 3.

542 8 7.8 7.8 7.8 7.8 7.6 6.

1 WAKE the song of joy and gladness,
Hither bring your sweetest lays ;
Banish every thought of sadness,
Pouring forth your highest praise ;
Sing to Him whose care has brought us
Once again with friends to meet,
Who with loving hearts have taught us
Of the way to Jesus' feet.
Wake the song, wake the song,
The song of joy and gladness ;
Wake the song, wake the song,
The song of jubilee.

2 Some who came with songs and banners
On our last high festal day
Now are singing glad hosannas,
Where the angels homage pay :
In the presence of His glory.
Jesus' praise they chant above,
Telling still the old, old story,
Precious theme—redeeming love.
Wake the song, etc.

116

3 Thanks to Thee, O holy Father,
For the mercies of the year ;
May each heart, as here we gather,
Swell with gratitude sincere ;
Thanks to Thee, O loving Saviour,
For redemption through Thy blood :
Thanks to Thee, O Holy Spirit,
Sweetly drawing us to God.
Wake the song, etc.

*The voice of many angels round about
the throne.*—Revelation v. 11.

543 6 5.6 5.6 6 6 5.

1 HARK ! round the God of love
Angels are singing ;
Saints at His feet above
Their crowns are flinging.
And may poor children dare
Hope for acceptance there,
Their simple praise and prayer
To His throne bringing ?

2 Yes ; through adoring throngs
His pity sees us ;
'Midst their seraphic songs
Our offering pleases ;
And Thou who here didst prove
To babes so full of love,
Thou art the same above,
Merciful Jesus !

3 Not a poor sparrow falls
But Thou art near it ;
When the young raven calls,
Thou, Lord, dost hear it :
Flowers, worms, and insects share
Hourly Thy guardian care ;
Wilt Thou bid us despair ?
Lord, can we fear it ?

4 Lord, then Thy mercy send
On all before Thee ;
Children and children's friend,
Bless, we implore Thee :
Lead us from grace to grace
On through our earthly race,
Till all before Thy face
Meet to adore Thee.

Though the LORD *be high, yet hath
He respect unto the lowly.*
Psalm cxxxviii. 6.   C.M.

544

1 THY throne, O God, in righteousness
For ever shall endure ;
We bow before it ; deign to bless
The children of the poor.

2 Thy wisdom fixed our lowly birth,
Yet we Thy goodness share ;
Still make us, while we dwell on earth,
The children of Thy care.

3 Strangers to Thee, though Thine by name,
We heard Thy welcome voice,
And, gathered from the world, became
The children of Thy choice.

4 Thou art our Shepherd, glorious God !
Thy little flock behold :
And guide us by Thy staff and rod,
The children of Thy fold.

5 We praise Thy name that we were brought
To this delightful place,
Where we are watched and warned and
The children of Thy grace.   [taught.

6 O, may our friends, Thy servants here,
  Meet all our souls above;
And they and we in heaven appear,
  The children of Thy love.

MISSIONS.

*O praise the LORD, all ye nations:
praise Him, all ye people.*
  545 Psalm cxvii. 1.   L. M.

1 FROM all that dwell below the skies
  Let the Creator's praise arise:
Let the Redeemer's name be sung
Through every land, by every tongue.

2 Eternal are Thy mercies, Lord;
Eternal truth attends Thy word:
Thy praise shall sound from shore to shore,
Till suns shall rise and set no more.

3 Your lofty themes, ye mortals, bring;
In songs of praise divinely sing;
The great salvation loud proclaim,
And shout for joy the Saviour's name.

4 Praise God, from whom all blessings flow;
Praise Him, all creatures here below;
Praise Him above, ye heavenly host;
Praise Father, Son, and Holy Ghost!

546 *There stood a man, . . . saying, Come
  over . . . and help us.*
Acts xvi. 9.   7 6.7 6.7 6.7 6.

1 FROM Greenland's icy mountains,
    From India's coral strand,
  Where Afric's sunny fountains
    Roll down their golden sand,
  From many an ancient river,
    From many a palmy plain,
  They call us to deliver
    Their land from error's chain.

2 What though the spicy breezes
    Blow soft o'er Ceylon's isle,
  Though every prospect pleases,
    And only man is vile!
  In vain with lavish kindness
    The gifts of God are strewn;
  The heathen, in his blindness,
    Bows down to wood and stone.

3 Can we, whose souls are lighted
    With wisdom from on high,
  Can we to men benighted
    The lamp of life deny?
  Salvation! O, salvation!
    The joyful sound proclaim,
  Till each remotest nation
    Has learnt Messiah's name.

4 Waft, waft, ye winds, His story,
    And you, ye waters, roll,
  Till, like a sea of glory,
    It spreads from pole to pole;
  Till o'er our ransomed nature,
    The Lamb for sinners slain,
  Redeemer, King, Creator,
    In bliss returns to reign.

547 *The redeemed of the LORD shall return,
  and come with singing unto Zion.*
Isaiah li. 11.   11 10.11 10.

1 HAIL to the brightness of Zion's glad
    morning!
  Joy to the lands that in darkness have
    lain!

Hushed be the accents of sorrow and
    mourning!
  Zion in triumph begins her mild reign.

2 Hail to the brightness of Zion's glad morn-
    ing,
  Long by the prophets of Israel foretold!
Hail to the millions from bondage return-
    ing!
  Gentiles and Jews now the Saviour be-
    hold.

3 Lo! in the desert the rich flowers are
    springing,
  Rivers abundant are gliding along;
Loud from the mountains the echoes are
    ringing,
  Wastes break in verdure and mingle in
    song.

4 Hear from all lands, from the isles of the
    ocean,
  Praise to Jehovah ascending on high,
Hushed be the tumult of war and commo-
    tion,
  Shouts of salvation are rending the sky.

548 *His name shall endure for ever:
  all nations shall call Him blessed.*
Psalm lxxii. 17.   L. M.

1 JESUS shall reign where'er the sun
    Doth his successive journeys run;
His kingdom stretch from shore to shore,
Till suns shall rise and set no more.

2 For Him shall endless prayer be made,
And praises throng to crown His head;
His name like sweet perfume shall rise
With every morning sacrifice.

3 People and realms of every tongue
Dwell on His love with sweetest song;
And infant voices shall proclaim
Their young Hosannas to His name.

4 Blessings abound where'er He reigns;
The prisoner leaps to lose his chains;
The weary find eternal rest;
And all the sons of want are blest.

5 Let every creature rise, and bring
Its grateful honours to our King:
Angels descend with songs again,
And earth prolong the joyful strain.

549 *God our Saviour; who will have all
  men to be saved.*
1 Timothy ii. 3, 4.   8 7.8 7.4 7.

1 GRACIOUS God! almighty Father,
    Saviour! Prince of Israel's race,
Holy Spirit! source of comfort,
    Hear from heaven, Thy dwelling place,
      Hear and answer,
    As we humbly seek Thy face.

2 Breathe on us Thy benediction,
    Purge our hearts from every stain,
Grant us pardon through the merits
    Of the Lamb for sinners slain.
      Hear and answer,
    Speak the word of peace again.

3 Help us all to tell the story
    Of Thy great redeeming love;
Bless the seed of life we scatter,
    Let our friends Thy mercy prove.
      Hear and answer,
    From Thy glorious throne above.

4 Bless this highly favoured country,
　　Save the people, Lord! we pray,
Lead them from the paths of folly
　　To the strait and narrow way.
　　　　Hear and answer,
　　Bless and keep us day by day.

5 Break the bonds of superstition,
　　Let the senseless idols fall;
Speak, Redeemer of the nations,
　　Bid them crown Thee Lord of all;
　　　　Hear and answer,
　　As to Thee we humbly call.

6 Thus may every tribe and people,
　　Through the blood of Christ forgiven,
Sing the gladsome alleluia
　　To the God of earth and heaven.
　　　　All the glory
　　Shall unto Thy name be given.

Oh that the salvation of Israel were
come out of Zion!—Psalm xiv. 7.
550　　　　　　7 6.7 6.

1 O THAT the Lord's salvation
　　　Were out of Zion come,
To heal His ancient nation,
　　To lead His outcasts home!

2 How long the holy city
　　Shall heathen feet profane?
Return, O Lord, in pity;
　　Rebuild her walls again.

3 Let fall Thy rod of terror,
　　Thy saving grace impart;
Roll back the veil of error,
　　Release the fettered heart.

4 Let Israel, home returning,
　　Her lost Messiah see;
Give oil of joy for mourning,
　　And bind all hearts to Thee.

All kings shall fall down before Him:
551　　*all nations shall serve Him.*
　　　　Psalm lxxii. 11.　 7 6.7 6.7 6.7 6.

1 HAIL to the Lord's Anointed!
　　　Great David's greater Son!
Hail, in the time appointed,
　　His reign on earth begun!
He comes to break oppression,
　　To set the captive free,
To take away transgression,
　　And rule in equity.

2 He comes, with succour speedy,
　　To those who suffer wrong;
To help the poor and needy,
　　And bid the weak be strong:
To give them songs for sighing,
　　Their darkness turn to light,
Whose souls, condemned and dying,
　　Were precious in His sight.

3 He shall come down like showers
　　Upon the fruitful earth:
Love, joy, and hope, like flowers,
　　Spring in His path to birth:
Before Him, on the mountains,
　　Shall peace the herald go;
And righteousness in fountains,
　　From hill to valley flow.

　　　　SECOND PART.

4 Arabia's desert ranger
118　　To Him shall bow the knee;

The Ethiopian stranger
　　His glory come to see;
With offerings of devotion
　　Ships from the isles shall meet,
To pour the wealth of ocean
　　In tribute at His feet.

5 Kings shall fall down before Him,
　　And gold and incense bring;
All nations shall adore Him,
　　His praise all people sing;
For Him shall prayer unceasing
　　And daily vows ascend;
His kingdom still increasing,
　　A kingdom without end.

6 O'er every foe victorious,
　　He on His throne shall rest;
From age to age more glorious,
　　All-blessing and all-blest.
The tide of time shall never
　　His covenant remove;
His name shall stand for ever,
　　His changeless name of Love.

Then shalt thou cause the trumpet
552　*of the jubilee to sound.*
　　　　Leviticus xxv. 9.　 8 7.8 7.8 7.

1 HARK! the joyous sound is swelling,
　　　Hark! the song of jubilee;
Of the Saviour's triumphs telling,
　　Of His conquests yet to be:
　　　　Jubilate! Jubilate!
　　Christ shall reign from sea to sea.

2 Christian missions! they were founded
　　Heathen nations to release;
Faithful men went forth and sounded
　　The glad trump proclaiming peace:
　　　　Jubilate! Jubilate!
　　Never shall the tidings cease.

3 Rich has been the tide of blessing,
　　Loud the song of liberty,
Light has pierced the Indian's dwelling,
　　Afric's sons have been set free:
　　　　Jubilate! Jubilate!
　　Saviour, we rejoice in Thee.

4 See the Gospel banner waving
　　Where the Hindu's temple stood;
See the isles of Fiji craving
　　For the bread of life as food:
　　　　Jubilate! Jubilate!
　　They no longer thirst for blood.

5 Wider fields are still before us
　　Where to sow the precious seed; [house
And that seed from heaven's rich store-
　　Will supply the world's vast need:
　　　　Jubilate! Jubilate!
　　Onward let the work proceed.

6 Bring your offerings, Christians, bring
　　　them,
Bring your offerings, rich and poor;
Bring your sons and daughters, bring
　　Let them enter every door:　　　[them;
　　　　Jubilate! Jubilate!
　　Spread the tidings more and more.

All the ends of the earth shall see
　　the salvation of our God.
553　　　　Isaiah lii. 10.
　　　　　C.M., WITH CHORUS.

1 SALVATION! O the joyful sound!
　　　What pleasure to our ears!

A sovereign balm for every wound,
A cordial for our fears.
    Glory, honour, praise, and power,
    Be unto the Lamb for ever:
    Jesus Christ is our Redeemer:
    Alleluia, praise the Lord.

2 Salvation! let the echo fly
    The spacious earth around;
While all the armies of the sky
    Conspire to raise the sound!
    Glory, honour, etc.

3 Salvation! O Thou bleeding Lamb,
    To Thee the praise belongs;
Salvation shall inspire our hearts,
    And dwell upon our tongues.
    Glory, honour, etc.

It is the jubilee; it shall be holy unto
554 *you.*—Leviticus xxv. 12.
    7.7.7.7.7.7.

1 HARK! the song of jubilee,
    Loud as mighty thunders roar,
Or the fulness of the sea
    When it breaks upon the shore.
Alleluia! for the Lord
    God omnipotent shall reign;
Alleluia! let the word
    Echo round the earth and main.

2 Alleluia! Hark! the sound,
    From the centre to the skies,
Wakes above, beneath, around,
    All creation's harmonies.
See Jehovah's banner furled,
    Sheathed His sword; He speaks, 'tis
And the kingdoms of this world [done,
    Are the kingdoms of His Son.

3 He shall reign from pole to pole
    With illimitable sway;
He shall reign, when, like a scroll,
    Yonder heavens have passed away;
Then the end: beneath His rod
    Man's last enemy shall fall;
Alleluia! Christ in God,
    God in Christ, is all in all.

Quit you like men, be strong.
555 1 Corinthians xvi. 13.   D.L.M.

1 STAND up for Jesus, Christian, stand!
    Firm as a rock on ocean's strand,
Beat back the waves of sin that roll,
Like raging floods, around thy soul!
    Stand up for Jesus, nobly stand!
    Firm as a rock on ocean's strand;
    Stand up, His righteous cause defend;
    Stand up for Jesus, your best friend.

2 Stand up for Jesus, Christian, stand!
Sound forth His name o'er sea and land!
Spread ye His glorious name abroad,
Till all the world shall own Him Lord.
    Stand up for Jesus, nobly stand! etc.

3 Stand up for Jesus, Christian, stand!
Lift high the cross with stedfast hand;
Till heathen lands with wondering eye
Its rising glory shall descry.
    Stand up for Jesus, nobly stand! etc.

4 Stand up for Jesus, Christian, stand!
Soon with the blest, immortal band,
We'll dwell for aye, life's journey o'er,
In realms of light, on heaven's bright shore.
    Stand up for Jesus, nobly stand! etc.

God said, Let there be light: and
556 *there was light.*—Genesis i. 3.
    6 6 4.6 6 6 4.

1 THOU whose Almighty Word
    Chaos and darkness heard,
    And took their flight;
Hear us, we humbly pray,
And where the gospel-day
Sheds not its glorious ray,
    Let there be light!

2 Thou, who didst come to bring
On Thy redeeming wing
    Healing and sight;
Health to the sick in mind,
Sight to the inly blind,
O now to all mankind
    Let there be light!

3 Spirit of truth and love,
Life-giving, holy Dove,
    Speed forth Thy flight;
Move on the waters' face,
Spreading the beams of grace,
And in earth's darkest place
    Let there be light!

4 Blessèd and holy Three,
Glorious Trinity,
    Grace, love, and might,
Boundless as ocean's tide,
Rolling in fullest pride,
Through the world far and wide;
    Let there be light!

O Lord, revive Thy work.
557 Habakkuk iii. 2.   S.M.

1 REVIVE Thy work, O Lord;
    Thy mighty arm make bare;
Speak with the voice that wakes the dead,
    And make Thy people hear.

2 Revive Thy work, O Lord;
    Exalt Thy glorious name;
And by Thy Spirit, Lord, our love
    For Thee and Thine inflame.

3 Revive Thy work, O Lord;
    Give power unto Thy Word;
Grant that Thy blessèd gospel may
    In living faith be heard.

4 Revive Thy work, O Lord,
    Give Pentecostal showers;
The glory shall be all Thine own,
    The blessing, Lord, be ours.

They go astray as soon as they be
558 *born.*—Psalm lviii. 3.
    8 8.8 8.8 8.8 8.9 9.

1 THE streets of the city are full
    Of poor little perishing souls,
Who wander away from the light
    In places that Satan controls!
They see not the snare at their feet;
    They know not the danger they're in;
O Saviour, can these be Thy lambs,
    So changed and disfigured by sin?
Famishing, perishing every day;
    Lambs of the flock, how they go astray!

2 Then out of the desert of sin,
    And out of the darkness of night,
Go, bring the dear lambs to the flock,
    And lead them up into the light.
Their voices with tenderness train,
    Their wilfulness try to subdue;

110

Be patient and tender with them,
As Christ has been patient with you.
Famishing, perishing every day;
Lambs of the flock, how they go astray!

And they shall come . . . and shall
559 *sit down in the kingdom of God.*
Luke xiii. 29.   7 7.7 7.7 7.7 7.

1 LITTLE travellers Zionward,
  Each one entering into rest,
In the kingdom of your Lord,
  In the mansions of the blest:
There to welcome Jesus waits,
  Gives the crown His followers win ;
Lift your heads, ye golden gates,
  Let the little travellers in !

2 Who are they whose little feet,
  Pacing life's dark journey through,
Now have reached the heavenly seat
  They had ever kept in view?
'I from Greenland's frozen land,'
  'I from India's sultry plain,'
'I from Afric's barren sand.'
  'I from islands of the main ;'

3 'All our earthly journey past,
  Every tear and pain gone by,
Here together met at last,
  At the portal of the sky.'
Each the welcome, 'Come ! ' awaits,
  Conquerors over death and sin ;
Lift your heads, ye golden gates,
  Let the little travellers in !

Go work to-day in My vineyard.
560 Matthew xxi. 28.
8 7.9 8.8 7.9 8.12 12.11 12.

1 LISTEN ! the Master beseecheth,
  Calling each one by his name ;
His voice to each loving heart reacheth,
  Its cheerfulest service to claim.
Go where the vineyard demandeth
  Vinedressers' nurture and care ;
Or go where the white harvest standeth,
  The joy of the reaper to share.
Then work, brothers, work ! let us slumber
  no longer,
For God's call to labour grows stronger and
  stronger,
The light of this life shall be darkened full
  soon,
But the light of the better life resteth at noon.

2 Seek those of evil behaviour,
  Bid them their lives to amend ;
Go, point the lost world to the Saviour,
  And be to the friendless a friend.
Still be the lone heart of anguish
  Soothed by the pity of thine ;
By waysides, if wounded ones languish,
  Go, pour in the oil and the wine.
Then work, brothers, work ! etc.

SECOND PART.

3 Work for the good that is nighest ;
  Dream not of greatness afar,
That glory is ever the highest
  Which shines upon men as they c   ;
Work, though the world would defa 'vou ;
  Heed not its slander and scorn ;
Nor weary till angels shall greet you
  With smiles through the gates of the
Then work, brothers, work ! etc.   [morn.
120

4 Offer thy life on the altar ;
  In the high purpose be strong ;
And if the tired spirit should falter,
  Then sweeten thy labour with song.
What, if the poor heart complaineth,
  Soon shall its wailing be o'er,
For there in the rest which remaineth
  It shall grieve and be weary no more.
Then work, brothers, work ! etc.

In the morning sow thy seed, and in
561 *the evening withhold not thine*
hand.—Ecclesiastes xi. 6.   S.M.

1 SOW in the morn thy seed,
  At eve hold not thine hand ;
To doubt and fear give thou no heed,
  Broadcast it o'er the land.

2 Beside all waters sow,
  The highway furrows stock,
Drop it where thorns and thistles grow,
  Scatter it on the rock.

3 The good, the fruitful ground,
  Expect not here nor there,
O'er hill and dale, by plots 'tis found ;
  Go forth then everywhere.

4 Thou know'st not which may thrive,
  The late or early sown ;
Grace keeps the precious germs alive,
  When and wherever strewn.

5 And duly shall appear,
  In verdure, beauty, strength,
The tender blade, the stalk, the ear,
  And the full corn at length.

6 Thou canst not toil in vain ;
  Cold, heat, and moist, and dry,
Shall foster and mature the grain
  For garners in the sky.

7 Thence, when the glorious end,
  The day of God is come,
The angel-reapers shall descend,
  And heaven cry 'Harvest-home ! '

O magnify the LORD with me, and
562 *let us exalt His name together.*
Psalm xxxiv. 3.   5 5 5 11.

1 COME, children, and join
  With ardour divine,
  And help to do good,
By publishing peace through Jesus's blood.

2 The glorious news
  Let each one diffuse ;
  The gospel proclaim,
And world-wide salvation, in Jesus's name.

3 Come, children, and sing,
  To Jesus our King,
  Alleluias of joy,
Such as angels and glorified spirits employ.

4 Come, children, and pray,
  Lord, hasten the day
  When the earth shall be filled
With glory, and Christ in His kingdom
  revealed !

5 Come, children, and give,
  And Christ will receive
  Whatever is given ;
And your offerings arise, as incense, to
  heaven.

6 Come, children, and join,
  With ardour divine,
  With triumph and mirth ;
Proclaim the glad news to the end of the
earth !

563 *O* LORD, *I beseech Thee, send now
prosperity.*—Psalm cxviii. 25.
6 6 4.6 6 6 4.

1 FATHER of heaven, bless
  Missions with great success,
  We humbly pray !
Soon may the gospel sound
Through all the world around,
Till earth's remotest bound
  Shall own Thy sway.

2 From Greenland's frozen land
  To Afric's burning strand,
    May Christ be known !
Till on Him all shall call,
Till every idol fall,
Till He be loved by all,
  And served alone.

3 O'er every hill and plain
  Washed by the mighty main
    Echo the call !
Till gods of wood and stone
Shall all be overthrown,
And Jesus reigns alone,
  Supreme o'er all !

4 Then spread the gospel's light
  Till nations all unite
    Beneath His sway !
And let us, as we sing
Praise to our Saviour King,
Our grateful offerings bring,
  To haste the day !

NATIONAL.

564 *Our fathers trusted in Thee : they
trusted, and Thou didst deliver
them.*—Psalm xxii. 4.   S.M.

1 TO Thee, in ages past,
    Our pious fathers came ;
On Thee, O Lord, their cares they cast,
  Nor were they put to shame.

2 Thy holy day they loved ;
    They loved the means of grace ;
And oft Thy faithfulness they proved,
  When they had sought Thy face.

3 Their faith in Thee was strong ;
    Their godliness was pure :
And while Thou wast their strength and
  They all things could endure.   [song

4 Their steps may we pursue,
    As they obeyed their Lord ;
So may our hearts and lives be new,
  And with Thy will accord.

565 *Blessed is the nation whose God is
the* LORD.—Psalm xxxiii. 12.
7 6.7 6.7 6.7 6.

1 O GOD of our salvation,
    We thank Thee for the love,
The blessings, as a nation,
    Showered on us from above ;
And when the noble story
  Of England's life is told,
To Thee we give the glory,
  As in the days of old.

2 Our fathers, faithful-hearted,
    Kept foreign foes at bay,
Nor has their strength departed
    From us, their sons, to-day ;
Of old, Thou bad'st contention
  And civil discord cease :
Keep far from us dissension,
  And, in our time, give peace.

3 From superstitious error,
    From papal tyranny,
From persecution s terror,
    Thou didst Thy people free.
O, for the great salvation
  Thy mighty arm then wrought,
God of the Reformation,
  We praise Thee, as we ought.

4 O God of our salvation,
    Our fathers' God and ours,
May we, a righteous nation,
    Serve Thee with all our powers,
Until the sunrise glorious
  To longing eyes be given,
And Jesus reigns victorious
  King over earth and heaven.

566 *And seek the peace of the city . . .
and pray unto the* LORD *for it*
Jeremiah xxix. 7.   C.M.

1 LORD, while for all mankind we pray,
    Of every clime and coast,
O hear us for our native land,
  The land we love the most.

2 O guard our shores from every foe !
    With peace our borders bless,
With prosperous times our cities crown,
  Our fields with plenteousness.

3 Unite us in the sacred love
    Of knowledge, truth, and Thee :
Nor let our hills and valleys cease
  Their songs of liberty.

4 Strength for our days of labour give ;
    Upon our Sabbaths smile ;
Enrich our Queen with health and grace:
  God bless our native isle !

567 *Righteousness exalteth a nation.*
Proverbs xiv. 34.   6 6.6 6.8 8

1 TO Thee, our God. we fly
    For mercy and for grace ;
O ! hear our lowly cry,
    And hide not Thou Thy face.
O Lord, stretch forth Thy mighty hand,
And guard and bless our fatherland.

2 Arise, O Lord of hosts !
    Be jealous for Thy name,
And drive from out our coasts
    The sins that put to shame.
O Lord, stretch forth Thy mighty hand,
And guard and bless our fatherland.

3 Thy best gifts from on high
    In rich abundance pour,
That we may magnify
    And praise Thee more and more.
O Lord, stretch forth Thy mighty hand,
And guard and bless our fatherland.

4 The powers ordained by Thee
    With heavenly wisdom bless ;

May they Thy servants be,
And rule in righteousness.
O Lord, stretch forth Thy mighty hand,
And guard and bless our fatherland.

SECOND PART.

5 The Church of Thy dear Son
Inflame with love's pure fire,
Bind her once more in one,
And life and truth inspire.
O Lord, stretch forth Thy mighty hand,
And guard and bless our fatherland.

6 The pastors of Thy fold
With grace and power endue,
That faithful, pure, and bold,
They may be pastors true.
O Lord, stretch forth Thy mighty hand,
And guard and bless our fatherland.

7 O! let us love Thy house,
And sanctify Thy day,
Bring unto Thee our vows,
And loyal homage pay.
O Lord, stretch forth Thy mighty hand,
And guard and bless our fatherland.

8 Give peace, Lord, in our time;
O! let no foe draw nigh,
Nor lawless deed of crime
Insult Thy majesty.
O Lord, stretch forth Thy mighty hand,
And guard and bless our fatherland.

9 Though vile and worthless, still
Thy people, Lord, are we;
And for our God we will
None other have but Thee.
O Lord, stretch forth Thy mighty hand,
And guard and bless our fatherland.

That we may lead a quiet and peaceable
568 *life in all godliness and honesty.*
1 Timothy ii. 2.   6 6 4.6 6 6 4.

1 GOD bless our native land,
May Heaven's protecting hand
Still guard our shore;
May peace her power extend,
Foe be transformed to friend,
And Britain's rights depend
On war no more.

2 Through every changing scene,
O Lord, preserve our Queen,
Long may she reign;
Her heart inspire and move
With wisdom from above;
And in a nation's love
Her throne maintain.

3 May just and righteous laws
Uphold the public cause,
And bless our isle;
Home of the brave and free,
The land of liberty,
We pray that still on Thee
Kind Heaven may smile.

4 Not in this land alone;
But be Thy mercies known
From shore to shore:
Lord, make the nations see
That men should brothers be,
And form one family
The wide world o'er.

122

That . . prayers . . . be made for
569 *all men.*—1 Timothy ii. 1.
6 6 4.6 6 6 4.

1 GOD bless our native land:
Her strength and glory stand
Ever in Thee!
Her faith and laws be pure;
Her throne and hearths secure;
And let her name endure,
Home of the free.

2 God smile upon our land,
And countless as the sand
Her blessings be!
Arise, O Lord, Most High!
And call her children nigh,
Till heart and voice reply
Glory to Thee.

3 Through every changing scene,
O Lord, preserve our Queen;
Long may she reign!
Her heart inspire and move
With wisdom from above;
And in a nation's love
Her throne maintain!

For kings, and for all that are in
570 *authority.*—1 Timothy ii. 2.
6 6 4.6 6 6 4.

1 GOD save our gracious Queen,
Long live our noble Queen,
God save the Queen!
Send her victorious,
Happy and glorious,
Long to reign over us,
God save the Queen!

2 Crowned by a nation's love,
Guarded by Heaven above,
Long live the Queen!
Loud may each voice proclaim,
Wide as Britannia's fame,
Long live Victoria's name,
God save the Queen!

GRACES.

571 *He took bread, and blessed it.*
Luke xxiv. 30.   L.M.
BE present at our table, Lord,
Be here and everywhere adored:
These creatures bless, and grant that we
May feast in Paradise with Thee.

572 *And He took the cup, and gave*
thanks.—Matt. xxvi. 27.   L.M.
WE bless Thee, Lord, for this our food,
But more for Jesu's flesh and blood,
The manna to our spirits given,
The living bread sent down from heaven.

573 *I will sing of mercy.*
Psalm ci. 1.   L.M.
FOR mercies that we taste and see,
For love unmerited and free,
For every promise in Thy word,
We bless Thy holy name, O Lord.

Thou openest Thine hand, they are
574 *filled with good.*—Psalm civ. 28.
C.M.
TO God, who gives our daily bread,
A thankful song we'll raise;
And pray that He who sends us food
Will fill our hearts with praise.

575 *Unto Thee, O God, do we give thanks. 1.*—Psalm lxxv. 1. L.M.

GREAT God, Thou giver of all good,
  Accept our praise, and bless our food:
Grace, health, and strength to us afford,
Through Jesus Christ, our risen Lord.

576 *He was known of them in breaking of bread.*—Luke xxiv. 35. C.M.

BE known to us in breaking bread,
  And do not then depart;
Saviour, abide with us, and spread
Thy table in our heart.

577 *O Lord, Thou preservest man and beast.*—Psalm xxxvi. 6. L.M.

THY providence supplies my food,
  And 'tis Thy blessing makes it good;
My soul is nourished by Thy word;
Let soul and body praise the Lord.

578 *Bless the Lord, O my soul, and forget not all His benefits.* Psalm ciii. 2. 7 6.7 6.7 6.7 6.

FOR my life, and clothes, and food,
  And every comfort here,
Thee, my most indulgent God,
  I thank with heart sincere;
For the blessings numberless
  Which Thou hast already given,
For my smallest spark of grace,
  And for my hope of heaven.

579 *I will bless the Lord at all times.* Psalm xxxiv. 1. 7 7.7 7.

1 GIVE Him then, and ever give,
  Thanks for all that we receive;
Man we for his kindness love,
How   uch more our God above!

2 Worthy Thou, our heavenly Lord,
To be honoured and adored;
God of all-creating grace,
Take the everlasting praise!

580 *He took the five loaves and the two fishes, and looking up to heaven, He blessed them.*—Luke ix. 16. C.M.

PARENT of good, whose bounteous grace
  O'er all creation flows:
Humbly we ask Thy power to bless
The food Thy love bestows.

581 *Bless the Lord, . . . who satisfieth thy mouth with good things.* Psalm ciii. 2, 5. 4 4 4.4 4 4 4.

1 HOW kind and good,
  To give us food,
Art Thou, O Lord!
Our thanks receive,
Thy blessing give,
Help us to live
Upon Thy word.

2 O Thou, the guest
At Cana's feast,
With us abide;
Our faith increase,
From sin release,
Give us Thy peace,
And be our guide.

3 Spirit above,
Unite in love
This social band;
And grant that we,
Eternally,
May dwell with Thee
In Canaan's land.

BENEDICTIONS.

582 *He sent the multitudes away.* Matthew xiv. 22. 87.87.87.87.

LORD, dismiss us with Thy blessing,
  Bid us now depart in peace;
Still on heavenly manna feeding,
  Let our faith and love increase:
Fill each breast with consolation;
  Up to Thee our hearts we raise:
When we reach yon blissful station,
  Then we'll give Thee nobler praise!
    Alleluia!

583 *The grace of the Lord Jesus Christ, and the love of God, etc.* 2 Cor. xiii. 14. 87.87.87.87.

MAY the grace of Christ our Saviour,
  And the Father's boundless love,
With the Holy Spirit's favour,
  Rest upon us from above!
Thus may we abide in union,
  With each other in the Lord;
And possess, in sweet communion,
  Joys which earth can not afford.

584 *To guide our feet into the way of peace.*—Luke i. 79. 87.87.77.44.77.

OF Thy love some gracious token
  Grant us, Lord, before we go;
Bless Thy word which has been spoken;
  Life and peace on all bestow:
When we join the world again,
Let our hearts with Thee remain:
  O direct us,
  And protect us,
Till we gain the heavenly shore,
Where Thy people want no more.

585 *Commend you to God, and to the word of His grace.*—Acts xx. 32. 77.77.

1 FOR a season called to part,
  Let us now ourselves commend
To the gracious eye and heart
Of our ever-present Friend.

2 Jesus, hear our humble prayer,
Tender Shepherd of Thy sheep,
Let Thy mercy and Thy care
All our souls in safety keep.

3 What we each have now been taught,
Let our memories retain:
May we, if we live, be brought
Here to meet in peace again.

586 *God also hath highly exalted Him.* Phil. ii. 9. 6 6.6 6.6 6.6 6.

1 COME, children, ere we part,
  Bless the Redeemer's name,
Join every tongue and heart,
To celebrate His fame.

123

Jesus the children's Friend,
Him whom our souls adore,
His praises have no end;
Praise Him for evermore.

2 If here we meet no more,
May we in realms above,
With all the saints, adore
Redeeming grace and love.
Jesus, the children's Friend,
Him whom our souls adore,
His praises have no end;
Praise Him for evermore.

Peace be with you all that are in
587 *Christ Jesus.*—1 Peter v. 14.
6 6.6 6.8 8.

1 OUR Father, ere we part,
O let Thy grace descend,
And fill each youthful heart
With peace from Christ our Friend;
May plenteous blessings from above
Inspire our souls with grateful love.

2 We know that soon, on earth,
The fondest ties must end;
Our own most cherished hopes
To death's cold hand must bend;
The fairest flowers in all their bloom,
Must soon lie withered in the tomb.

3 Then, when our spirits leave
These tenements of clay,
May we, through grace, receive
A life of endless day;
And sing with parents, teachers, friends,
That anthem sweet which never ends.

The grace of our Lord Jesus Christ be
588 *with you all.*—2 Thess. iii. 18.
8 7.8 7.4 7.

1 LORD, dismiss us with Thy blessing,
Fill our hearts with joy and peace;
Let us each, Thy love possessing,
Triumph in redeeming grace;
O refresh us,
Travelling through this wilderness!

2 Thanks we give, and adoration,
For Thy gospel's joyful sound;
May the fruits of Thy salvation
In our hearts and lives abound;
May Thy presence
With us evermore be found.

3 So, whene'er the signal's given
Us from earth to call away,
Borne on angels' wings to heaven,
Glad the summons to obey,
May we ever
Reign with Christ in endless day.

Grace be with you all. Amen.
589 Titus iii. 15. 8 7.8 7.4 7.

1 FATHER, let Thy benediction,
Gently falling as the dew,
And Thy ever-gracious presence
Bless us all our journey through:
May we ever
Keep the end of life in view.

2 Young in years, we need the wisdom
Which can only come from Thee;
In the morn of our existence
Let us Thy salvation see:
Changed in spirit,
We shall then Thy children be.

3 When temptations shall assail us,
When we falter by the way,
Let Thine arm of strength defend us;
Saviour, hear us when we pray:
Thou art mighty,
Be Thou then our rock and stay.

4 Praise and blessing, power and glory,
Will we render, Lord, to Thee;
For the news of Thy salvation
Shall extend from sea to sea;
All the nations
Joyfully shall worship Thee.

INDEX TO THE HYMNS.

INDEX TO THE HYMNS.

123

INDEX OF HYMNS FOR INFANTS.

INDEX OF HYMNS FOR TEACHERS' MEETINGS.

INDEX TO TEXTS PREFIXED TO THE HYMNS.

INDEX TO THE SUBJECTS OF THE HYMNS.

INDEX TO THE SUBJECTS OF THE HYMNS.

INDEX TO THE SUBJECTS OF THE HYMNS.

WS - #0005 - 251120 - C0 - 229/152/22 [24] - CB - 9780331756043